Cracks in the Pavement

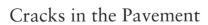

Cracks in the Pavement

*Social Change and Resilience
in Poor Neighborhoods*

Martín Sánchez-Jankowski

UNIVERSITY OF CALIFORNIA PRESS
Berkeley · Los Angeles · London

University of California Press, one of the most distinguished university presses in the United States, enriches
lives around the world by advancing scholarship in the
humanities, social sciences, and natural sciences. Its
activities are supported by the UC Press Foundation
and by philanthropic contributions from individuals
and institutions. For more information, visit
www.ucpress.edu.

University of California Press
Berkeley and Los Angeles, California

University of California Press, Ltd.
London, England

Library of Congress Cataloging-in-Publication Data

Sánchez-Jankowski, Martín.
    Cracks in the pavement : social change and resilience
in poor neighborhoods / Martín Sánchez-Jankowski.
        p.   cm.
    Includes bibliographical references and index.
    ISBN 978-0-520-25644-6 (cloth : alk. paper)
    ISBN 978-0-520-25675-0 (pbk. : alk. paper)
    1. Urban poor—United States—Case studies.
2. Inner cities—United States—Case studies.   3. Urban
poor—Social networks—New York (State)—New
York.   4. Urban poor—Social networks—California—
Los Angeles.   5. Social change—United States—New
York (State)—New York   6. Social change—United
States—California—Los Angeles   I. Title.

HV4045.J36   2008
362.50973'091732—dc22   2007046956

Manufactured in the United States of America

17   16   15   14   13   12   11   10   09   08
10   9   8   7   6   5   4   3   2   1

The paper used in this publication meets the minimum
requirements of ANSI/NISO Z39.48-1992 (R 1997)
(*Permanence of Paper*).

To the memory of my mother- and father-in-law,

Nilda and Francisco Carrasquillo,

and my parents,

Leo and Anna,

cuyas vidas parecieron a las mismas representadas en este libro

The good things of prosperity are to be wished;
but the good things that belong to adversity are to
be admired.

Seneca, Letters to Lucilius (28 CE)

Contents

Tables and Figures

Preface

Sir Isaac Newton was reported to have said, "If I have been able to see farther, it was only because I stood on the shoulders of giants." I would like to acknowledge the contributions of three giants in the study of poor American neighborhoods to the research in this book—William Foote Whyte, Herbert J. Gans, and Gerald D. Suttles. I had the privilege of briefly meeting William Foote Whyte and Gerald D. Suttles at two different annual meetings of the American Sociological Association, and I had the opportunity to meet, talk, and correspond with Herbert J. Gans a few years back. It is fair to say that the work of Gans has had the most influence on the present work, followed by that of Suttles, but I have had the pleasure of empirically and theoretically interacting with all three over the course of researching and writing this book.

Of course my gratitude to the three "giants" who conducted field research in poor neighborhoods is not meant to slight the significant work that other researchers have contributed, many of whom are cited in the text and notes of this book. Elijah Anderson, Robert Sampson, and William Julius Wilson are three such scholars, to mention a few. Some of the most important findings in the present book converse with their work and that of other researchers. It is hoped that this dialogue advances our sociological understanding of the human condition of those inhabiting neighborhoods where the majority of residents are poor and the resources available and used to affect their lives are scant.

Now, to thank those who directly helped this book come to fruition. My colleagues Michael Hout and Claude Fischer have been a constant source of support throughout. They also were kind enough to read drafts of the manuscript and provide detailed comments. It is an honor to have them as colleagues and a pleasure to have them as friends.

I would also like to thank Corey Abramson for reading the entire manuscript and providing important substantive comments as well as performing various other tasks that made this book better; Henry Brady, whose support at a particularly important point in the project was critical; Eileen Hout, who provided the art that dons the cover of this book; and UC Press's Naomi Schneider, who provided sage guidance throughout the process of bringing the project to print. I could not have worked with a more wonderful group.

My friend Mike Rogin tragically passed away from a disease he contracted in St. Petersburg, Russia, a few years ago. Mike had read every book manuscript that I wrote and provided me with invaluable insights. This is the first one where he is "missing," and it feels lonely to write this preface without acknowledging him, but he will never be forgotten.

Financial assistance was provided by the University of California at Berkeley's Committee on Research, the Spencer Foundation, and the John D. and Catherine T. MacArthur Foundation. I thank them all for the support required to complete this research.

On the personal front, my wife, Carmen, has been special. She has a full-time job as a social worker in a kidney dialysis clinic and is the mother of our three boys, all of whom were small during the time of the research. Her willingness to be a single parent for the periods of fieldwork over the nine years was nothing short of heroic. Simply stated, without her effort I could not have done this research; and although I have consistently expressed my appreciation over the years, it will never be enough.

This book is dedicated to the memory of my mother- and father-in-law and my parents, all of whom experienced the life this book is about. Their lives are a testament to the fact that the poor can just as easily be people we are proud of and inspirations to follow as people with material wealth.

I would also like to thank my brother Mike and his family; my brothers-in-law Frank and Luciano and their families; and my three sons, Javier, Julián, and Andrés, for their support and love during the writing of this book.

There is little question that special, special thanks must go to the people in the five neighborhoods who allowed me to become a part of their daily lives over the nine years of this project. Some even provided me with a place to stay and occasional meals. I will always remember their generosity and cherish the time I spent with them all.

I would like to remind every reader that all of the people and institutions I have thanked made this research project and book better. Whatever errors of commission and omission remain in this book are solely my responsibility.

A REFLECTION ON THE TITLE

Before ending this preface, I turn to a reflection on the book's title. As a young boy I once lay on the ground resting after a long stint of playing baseball. My friends had left, and I wanted to relax a few minutes more before I started home. Rolling over on my stomach and briefly looking down, I noticed three ants making their way along the terrain. They seemed solitary in their efforts, even nomadic in some romantic way. Then I moved a couple of feet and found a long crack in the earth running about three feet long and a half-centimeter wide. I saw another ant go into the crack and decided to have a look. Taking out my pocketknife, I stuck it into the crack and twisted it around to expand the crack and peer into it. What I saw was astonishing to me. There were thousands of ants frantically moving very quickly in what appeared to be total chaos. I remember feeling a little uneasy at this "alien activity." However, the longer I looked, the more patterns I could see to the movement. After an hour of total immersion in my continuous discovery of the ants' immense organization, I realized that my first observations had been mistaken. I was watching a sophisticated society with an organized division of labor and a communication system that allowed them to gather food and build a large shelter. Just as I was attempting to see how big the colony was, I tipped over my bottle of warm Vernor's Ginger Ale into the crack. This trauma first appeared to create a breakdown in their organized routine, but that was an inaccurate observation too. I was astonished—but happy since I felt guilty about splashing the soda into their house—that the ants engaged in organized behavior to fix the problem and reestablish both their routine and existing society.

When thinking about a title for this book that would capture what I had discovered about poor neighborhoods, I was reminded of this childhood experience. Cracks allow us to see things hidden from a casual view that is likely to lead to misunderstandings. Pavement appears as something solid, nondescript, and drab, much like the poor slum areas of a city. A crack in the pavement reminds us that nothing is permanent, that what appears to be solid actually experiences change; yet this change does not automatically compromise the entire pavement. Plus these cracks provide us an opportunity to view something heretofore unknown or unobservable. At the margins of socioeconomic life, cracks allow us to peek into a world and discover new aspects of the human condition.

Introduction

Poor there must be everywhere. Indigence will find its way and
set up its hideous state in the heart of a great and luxurious
city. Amid the thousand narrow lanes and by-streets of a
populous metropolis there must always, we fear, be much
suffering—much that offends the eye—much that lurks unseen.

Frederick Engels, *The Condition of the
Working Class in England* (1845)

It is about ten in the evening, and I have just arrived at Newark International Airport in New Jersey. I am to give a lecture the next day at a local
university about my research on poor neighborhoods. My host has been
kind enough to pick me up and take me to my hotel. He has brought his
wife and six-year-old daughter with him. On our way there, the car over-
heats and smoke begins pouring out of the hood. My host takes the next
exit off the toll road and pulls into a gas station. His wife urges, "Please
hurry. This is a bad neighborhood." Getting out of the car, he takes a hose
and adds water to the radiator. After checking the temperature gauge, which
now reads as normal, we start on our way again as his wife repeats, "Please
hurry. This is a bad neighborhood and I just want to get out of here." "What
do you mean, a bad neighborhood?" the little girl asks. Her mother replies,
"Well, dear, it's a place where people are poor and there's a lot of crime and
violence." My host remonstrates, "Dear, that's a little strong." "Well," she
retorts, "we have both lived in this area all our lives, and this neighborhood
has always been poor and run down. You always hear on the news about
something bad happening here. Am I wrong?" My host nods with a pained
expression suggesting that, although he would like it to be different, he must
agree with her. As we continue on our way, I cannot help but think how this
image of life in poor neighborhoods has also continued on its way.

THE PATH OF A DOMINANT PARADIGM

Poor neighborhoods have been a significant part of the American urban landscape for the greater part of two centuries. During the nineteenth century these neighborhoods developed as a result of racial and ethnic discrimination and inequality in both the labor and the housing markets. Much of this discrimination emerged from the remnants of slavery, industrial growth, and immigration. In essence, the economics of the plantation and factory produced economic, social, and ecological inequalities that persisted in American cities.

People who were poor during the nineteenth century were housed in separate sections and considered social pariahs, something that the Irish, Jews, Italians, and Africans had in common. The overwhelming majority of each group came to the United States poor. They were used for their labor, considered socially and genetically inferior by Anglo-Americans, and shunned.[1] It was not unusual for these groups to live in dilapidated housing geographically segregated from other, more affluent populations. Although whites and nonwhites were strictly segregated, Jews, Irish, and Italians, despite their light complexions, were not considered "white" and shared neighborhoods with African Americans because of both their impoverished condition and their ethnicity.[2]

Massive immigration from 1850 to 1928 brought people to U.S. cities who needed to find affordable housing while trying to secure employment and save for a better place in the future. The neighborhoods housing the immigrant poor were often dilapidated and overcrowded. Although many of these neighborhoods continued to house the poor, they also became identified with certain ethnic groups. The association between poverty and ethnicity and the question of their causal relationship preoccupied social science research on the American poor for much of the nineteenth and twentieth centuries. Many studies vividly described the horrific conditions experienced by those living in slums in an effort to motivate public action to improve the lives of the poor.[3]

Like many social reformers of the time, members of the Department of Sociology at the University of Chicago recognized that American modernity would be defined by the American urban condition. They viewed the city as a "social laboratory" and their university as perfectly situated to investigate this emerging urbanism.[4] Research generated by this department starting in the 1920s was impressive in its scope and its systematic investigation of the conditions distinguishing urban from rural life, the dynamics of urban growth, and the city's social structure.

This agenda demanded that researchers understand the role of industrialization and immigration in urban development and that they study poverty and poor neighborhoods as part of the general urbanization process.[5] In the early work of Robert Park and his students, such neighborhoods were seen as the natural physical consequence of immigration, industrialization, and urban growth.[6]

The work of the Chicago School highlighted the importance of structure and ecology in the making of the modern American city.[7] It found that poor neighborhoods, or slums, as they were known, could be either socially organized or socially disorganized and that these two conditions were part of the more general process of ethnic assimilation. The Chicago School viewed social organization as a community's ability to communicate mutual interests and work collectively to achieve them, as well as the ability to exercise social control to eliminate such problems as disease, crime, disorder, vice, insanity, and suicide.[8] Simplified, their findings suggested that new ethnic groups in the United States would encounter an alien cultural world. Their natural reaction was to create an environment like the one they had left, but the dynamics of the modern industrial city steadily intruded on their world, forcing them to relinquish the institutions, customs, and practices that had supported their ethnic enclave. As this process continued, there would be a period of "breakdown" and "disorganization" followed by assimilation, cultural disappearance, and a physical move to a new neighborhood.[9] Thus, in the Chicago School early analyses, living in poor neighborhoods was an integral phase of ethnic assimilation.[10]

Increasing restrictions on immigration to the United States in the 1920s and the coming of the Great Depression in the 1930s sharply curtailed both the number of new ethnic groups to be assimilated and opportunities for economic growth. During this period less research focused specifically on poor ethnic neighborhoods, since poverty was now experienced across most social strata in America. Wealthy and middle-class businessmen, industrial workers, and farmers and agricultural workers all lost their businesses, farms, or jobs.[11] The poor ethnic slums remained. Then, in 1936, William Foote Whyte initiated his classic study of Boston's Italian North End. He was one of the first to break with the older Chicago School's paradigm of disorganization in his description of how ethnicity and culture structured a slum neighborhood. Whyte pointed out that poor neighborhoods were structured not only by ethnic culture but also by a culture emanating from the condition of poverty itself. He reported that Italian ethnicity provided solidarity among the slum's residents but that poverty forced people to live in overcrowded quarters and thus encouraged men to spend most of their idle time on street corners. For Whyte, their interaction there organized life in this slum, and he titled his study *Street Corner Society*.[12]

Poverty in the war years was less of a social issue, but it did not disappear. During this period St. Clair Drake and Horace Cayton undertook what would become the classic study of Chicago's South Side "Black Belt."[13] A sociological examination of America's largest settlement of African Americans, the study indicated that social organization existed in the broader "Black Belt" but that some neighborhoods there, marked by high rates of unemployment, births out of wedlock, and crime, were more economically depressed and more disorganized than others. Drake and Cayton's study documented that African American areas were not synonymous with slums,[14] that an enormous amount of socioeconomic diversity existed within these segregated areas, and that only the poorest neighborhoods experienced social disorganization.[15] Later their work would influence analyses of African American poverty during the 1990s.[16]

With the conclusion of World War II, the return of the soldiers, and the transition from a wartime to a peacetime economy, research on poverty expanded again. Two studies significantly contributed to the general understanding of poverty. The first of these was an examination of the social life of the West End slum in Boston.[17] It may well be the most influential of such studies, for it challenged many of the theoretical foundations of the Chicago School. The researcher, Herbert J. Gans, advanced the position that urbanism was not so powerful as to disorganize the traditional culture of immigrants. Rather, immigrants could reproduce their lives, even their rural lives, in the modern industrial city, despite inhospitable conditions for traditional ethnic cultural survival. Most important, his study demonstrated that poor communities, with the aid of ethnicity, could maintain their existence without experiencing disorganization.[18]

Shortly after Gans's study, Gerald Suttles looked at an urban slum in Chicago.[19] Like Boston's West End, the Taylor Street area of Chicago was considered a traditional Italian slum neighborhood. Suttles's study integrated the theoretical contributions of Whyte and Gans with those of the old Chicago School. He found the interplay of ethnicity and class produced a socio-ecological niche (i.e., community) characterized by ethnic segmentation and a shared morality based on goals and ideals related to the "American dream" and the prevailing social norms that both the residents and the greater society believed desirable but that the residents knew they were unlikely to completely or consistently realize.[20] Like Whyte and Gans, Suttles documented that poor areas could have structure but argued that most of this structure was shaped by ethnicity rather than the material conditions of lower-class life. Gans's and Suttles's studies moved beyond many of the earlier understandings of poor neighborhoods, but they were not able to completely divorce their analyses from the early Chicago School's emphasis on the impact of urban development on the creation and dissolution of poor neighborhoods because each neighborhood they studied had succumbed to the pressures of urban redevelopment projects.[21]

The most radical paradigmatic departure in understanding poor neighborhoods came from Oscar Lewis's research on the Mexican and Puerto Rican poor. Lewis proposed that poverty could be sustained through a culture predicated on the material conditions of poverty alone. Contrary to the Chicago School's theoretical premise, it was not dependent on ethnicity, industrialization, or urban development. Rather, Lewis argued, this culture among the poor originated in macrostructural conditions of capitalist development that made material inequality produce long-term poverty for a segment of society. Once this "culture of poverty" was established, it could influence individual beliefs and behaviors and sustain them across generations even when there were more economic opportunities and people became more affluent.[22]

Lewis's theory had an important impact on social policy,[23] but it was quickly attacked by many social scientists and policy advocates as blaming the poor for their plight.[24] This was not an entirely accurate reading of Lewis, but the criticism stigmatized and delegitimized his "culture of poverty" theory and any studies that resembled his analysis, leading to the demise of his framework within sociology.[25]

After Lewis's study, there was a general decline in the study of poor neighborhoods. The question of the nature of poor neighborhoods did not die, but the focus began to include issues of racial exclusion,[26] the threat that poor nonwhite neighborhoods posed for urban economic development,[27] and local political reactions to the expansion of racialized poor neighborhoods.[28] During this period, the dominant conception of poor neighborhoods was of physically dirty areas with high crime rates and other social ills.

Ruth Horowitz's study of a poor Mexican American neighborhood in Chicago represented an important shift from the other analyses dominating the 1980s in that it brought culture to the forefront of the analysis.[29] Horowitz described how ethnic culture could compensate for the stresses of limited material resources in building community solidarity while competing with the materialistic culture of American society for the hearts and minds of the residents. Her findings supported the early findings of Suttles but did not break with the old Chicago School's understanding that the tension between ethnic cultures and the dominant culture was the most salient feature of poor neighborhoods of the United States.[30]

During the 1990s and the early twenty-first century, no person was more important in setting the research agenda on poor areas than William Julius Wilson. Wilson reinvigorated the use of a structural analysis for studying the African American poor, arguing that the African American working class was becoming more and more downwardly mobile. He maintained that industrial production jobs were being transported to places where workers received wages considerably below those paid in America's industrial heartland and that African Americans were the most vulnerable to changes in this sector because racial exclusionary policies in the past had made them the last to gain access to unionized production jobs.[31] Interestingly, his emphasis on how macrostructural conditions in the economy affected the plight of the African American poor was an extension of the early Chicago School paradigm. The early Chicago School had emphasized the dual processes of industrialization and urbanization in influencing the form that poverty assumed, while Wilson focused on the dual processes of deindustrialization and suburban relocation.[32]

Wilson's argument was challenged by a host of scholars. The most significant challenge came from Douglas Massey and his colleagues. In *American Apartheid*, Massey and Nancy Denton agreed with Wilson that poor African American neighborhoods suffered from social disorganization and that structural conditions were the cause of African American poverty but claimed that these conditions sprang less from the changes taking place in the new global economy than from racial exclusionary practices in the urban housing market.[33]

After the publication of Massey and Denton's book, Wilson returned to the question of poverty to clarify his position and reconcile his findings with theirs. His book *When Work Disappears* provided a more vivid portrait of the effects of macroeconomic structural changes on poor African American neighborhoods.[34] Wilson agreed with Massey and colleagues that the African American poor were more spatially concentrated than they had been before and that housing market segregation exacerbated this concentration, but he maintained that the lack of jobs caused by changes in the international economy was what hurt the African American poor the most. It increased their social isolation from whites, from the African American middle and working classes, and from the geographic areas where there were jobs, creating attitudinal and behavioral traits that made their socioeconomic mobility more difficult.[35] One of the most important contributions of Wilson's research was his demonstration that the poverty conditions within the African American community were substantively different from those in Mexican American neighborhoods. He found that the Mexican American poor were less isolated and tended to have more internal community support, and he reintroduced the notion of social disorganization to explain the differences between the two groups.[36] African American communities were socially more disorganized because macroeconomic conditions had dislodged their residents from the unionized production jobs they had been using to advance the entire group's socioeconomic condition, causing many of those who fell into poverty to be concentrated in particular neighborhoods with few resources to combat poverty-related social problems. This disorganization could not be endemic to the African American community, for in the past, particularly in the 1950s, the same community, though segregated, had not been socially disorganized. Rather, Wilson maintained, macroeconomic changes caused a loss of jobs, forcing the African American poor to concentrate in certain neighborhoods because they needed to find cheap housing. As more poor African Americans came to live in these areas, working- and middle-class African Americans moved to escape the social problems they associated with the poor.[37]

Wilson's thesis that poor communities, particularly African American ones, suffer from social disorganization has become the conventional wisdom in the considerable amount of research that has addressed the topic since.[38] In addition, some research suggests that urban renewal projects have caused poor neighborhoods to experience an increase in social problems, marginalization, and vulnerability to social extinction.[39]

In sum, a remarkable consistency exists in the most recent research on poor neighborhoods. Research utilizing both survey and ethnographic data has coalesced around two related observations regarding poor neighborhoods: (1) deteriorating social conditions and social disorganization dominate everyday life; and (2) social change continually makes conditions worse, further exacerbating social disorganization.[40] Thus the conclusions of this research are remarkably similar to the observations of my host's wife.

Yet is the "organized slum" described in some of the previous research of Gans, Suttles, and Whyte just a peculiar remnant of the social past, or, in light of the hegemony of social disorganization theory, the sociological equivalent of a UFO sighting? This very issue was taken up by Daniel Dohan's study of two poor Mexican American communities in California and Mario Small's study of a poor Puerto Rican neighborhood in Boston's South End.[41] These studies were designed to determine how living in a poor neighborhood influenced the ability to be actively involved in economic and civic affairs.[42] Both found that, despite the conditions that might lead us to expect residents to be apathetic, they were actively engaged in economic and voluntary civic organizations designed to help themselves, their families, and the neighborhood. Although both studies provided important new insights into the organization of poor neighborhoods, each study was for only a two-year period and each focused on a Latino population, leaving some nagging questions. Is there something unique about Latino, as opposed to African American or white Appalachian, ethnicity that influences behavioral capability to organize within poor neighborhoods?[43] What about social change in the vast majority of poor neighborhoods that have existed as such for a long time or even expanded over the years? Has there been no social change in these neighborhoods, other than an increase in suffering, as the studies using the social disorganization framework have reported? How could the residents of these neighborhoods, or the neighborhoods as social entities, survive for so long under conditions of both increased suffering and social disorganization? How should we understand their longevity?[44]

THIS BOOK IN CONTEXT

This book addresses these questions and provides a different picture of poor neighborhoods. Several important empirical findings from this study significantly diverge from those that dominate the current literature. The first of these is the concept of social disorganization. I argue that there is no way to understand the longevity of poor neighborhoods through disorganization theory. Poor neighborhoods are generally structured rather than disorganized, and they feature both social mechanisms through which social change is initiated and brought to fruition and social mechanisms that work to preserve the existing social order and structure. I found that the prevailing "disorganization" paradigm is the result of a mistaken understanding of the organization, functioning, and interactions within poor neighborhoods more generally. Researchers like William Julius Wilson and Robert Sampson have described social disorganization as the absence of extensive local friendship ties, low levels of participation in "formal and informal voluntary associations," low numbers of stable formal organizations, and a very limited ability to collectively control behavior and solve community problems—in essence, places with little, if any, social cohesion—and have argued that social disorganization results in high levels of crime and other social problems.[45] However, during my nine-year study of five poor neighborhoods, I only once experienced (and only briefly) social disorganization, even at times when the number of businesses had shriveled to two or three. They all had structure and a social order even on the most hectic of days. Further, the social conditions seen by many contemporary researchers as signs of social disorganization, like violence, crime, an inordinately high number of female-headed households, and illicit drug use, were used by the residents of these neighborhoods to build a functional social structure.[46]

My second divergence from the contemporary consensus on poor neighborhoods involves my approach to the nature of social change in these neighborhoods. Most recent research views such change as arising from macrosocietal agents that increase the misery in these neighborhoods linearly or from the process of physically relocating the poor of a particular area to other areas in the city.[47] However, I found that in most poor neighborhoods change agents from both inside and outside the neighborhood were present every day. In addition, agents within the community acted as conservators of the status quo with respect to both the social structure and its social order. It will be seen throughout this book that the internal agents of both change and preservation are involved in a constant struggle whereby each experiences gains and losses. Though this process does not lead to the disorganization or destruction of the neighborhood, I am not arguing that poor neighborhoods never experience social death. They do, as other kinds of neighborhoods do, but one should not jump to the conclusion that social death is inevitable from the observation that change agents are active within the neighborhood and have disrupted its social equilibrium.[48]

A third departure in this study involves culture in poor neighborhoods. The present study employs a notion of culture that combines "culture as worldview/values" with "culture as practices" and places it within the framework of Claude Fischer's subcultural theory of urbanism.[49] Thus my analysis draws on Fischer's work in finding that poor neighborhoods have developed a subculture related to their life situation and that its development has been facilitated, though not caused, by the processes of urbanism.[50] It will be seen that this subculture has many similarities to, as well as differences from, Oscar Lewis's "culture of poverty." While I agree with Lewis's argument that persistent poverty can create a culture, I also argue that there is important variation in this culture associated with poverty and that this culture, to remain vibrant, must have a structural and physical environment that nurtures it. Further, Lewis theorized that the "culture of poverty" produced a disorganizing effect on the communities where it was present, whereas the culture that I found in poor neighborhoods had a definite organizing effect on social life.[51]

Although some readers may regard my analysis as "blaming the poor" for their hardships in life or "praising the poor" for their heroic effort to endure hardships, both evaluations would be inaccurate. Rather, I have conscientiously tried to analyze the nature of poor neighborhoods as dispassionately as possible to provide reliable information that could aid policy makers who have the capacity to relieve the difficulties associated with living in such conditions.[52]

The analysis that follows presents poor neighborhoods through systematic observation over nine years without making any value judgments concerning the traits of the subculture I observed. In brief, my intent, though modest in comparison, is like that of Eugene Genovese's historical work on the life of slaves. His classic study of slave society in the southern United States described the life the slaves made for themselves in a condition of extreme bondage,[53] and my own investigation analyzes the life the urban poor have made for themselves under conditions of severe deprivation.

THE STUDY

In this section I will briefly sketch the questions the study addresses, the data used, and the method of data collection. Those interested in a more detailed discussion of the logic and mechanisms of the study may consult the Methodological Appendix.

This study is an effort to understand the social life that poor people make while experiencing hardships associated with economic deprivation. To effectively provide this understanding, I chose to look at social change and preservation through the window of five important institutions in poor neighborhoods—state-managed public housing projects, small grocery stores, barbershops and hair salons, gangs, and local high schools. These five establishments were chosen because previous research had failed to see their institutional character and functions in the social life of poor neighborhoods. All five establishments had physical buildings associated with them. It might seem that gangs would not, but they usually had a clubhouse where organizational meetings and entertainment gatherings occurred and/or a physical location outside where members regularly congregated that became known and respected by everyone in the neighborhood as if it were a building. Further, "disorganization theorists" have consistently characterized gangs as destabilizing a neighborhood or as evidence that the neighborhood was experiencing social disorganization, so it was important to study how they did this. As will be seen, the presence of gangs does not signal that a neighborhood is disorganized, nor do gangs automatically undermine the social structure of the neighborhood. Gangs, like the other establishments studied, can be either neighborhood institutions, however illegitimate they may appear in the eyes of the general public, or a force that undermines the social structure of a neighborhood, depending on their specific behavior. Other establishments could have been added to these five: local taverns, lotteries (i.e., numbers joints), and churches, for example. Yet while the establishments chosen are not the only ones that could have been included in a study of social change and preservation in a poor neighborhood, little social change or preservation could take place without their involvement. Thus they serve as barometers of socioeconomic and cultural conditions and as such are indispensable in any study of poor neighborhoods.

In selecting the establishments for this study, I wished to obtain a sample in which men and women would be equally distributed. With the exception of gangs, each of the establishments had nearly equal distributions of men and women interacting there, and even gangs usually had a women's auxiliary. In the case of hair shops, which included male barbershops, female beauty salons, and unisex shops for both, an effort was made to study each type. The sample included more barbershops than beauty salons because these neighborhoods contained more barbershops, but equal amounts of time were devoted to each type of establishment. A more complete description of the issues faced and strategies used to gain access to each establishment is provided in the Appendix.

The period of this study, from January 1991 through December 1999, addresses issues of social change and preservation in poor neighborhoods. Most observers would note that this was a period of sustained growth, high employment, and welfare reform. As such, it provided an excellent opportunity to assess some of the factors previously identified as having an impact on the poor. The neighborhoods chosen were social areas with a history of harboring poor people. In fact, all the neighborhoods had 50 percent of their residents listed as living below the official poverty level for more than twenty-five years. Yet this period of economic growth had little impact on such neighborhoods' socioeconomic composition or on residents' behavior (though welfare reform did have an impact on the residents, particularly single mothers, and is addressed in the chapters on grocery stores and beauty salons). Because most residents of such neighborhoods have limited human capital to take advantage of economic growth periods, they are rarely benefited by periods of high employment like the 1990s. The jobs most commonly held by the residents in the neighborhoods I studied during this period were either low-paying jobs in the secondary labor market or relatively higher-paying jobs for short periods like a couple of months. Given the persistence of these adverse conditions, exploring how poor people living together in neighborhoods with scarce resources manage to live their lives, confront difficulties, and create an existence that has rewards, happiness, contentment, and pride as well as difficulty, sadness, frustration, and resentment is of critical importance.

I set out, through a comparative study design, to identify what, where, when, and how agents were involved in both the change and preservation processes and to analyze how and why they behaved as they did. Five neighborhoods were chosen from two cities: three in New York City (two in the Bronx and one in Brooklyn) and two in Los Angeles (one in South Central L.A., and the other in East L.A.). Below I give a general description of what the neighborhoods looked like physically, ethnically, and architecturally; a more detailed description pertaining to the sample of neighborhoods, particularly its rationale and method of selection, as well as the process through which access was gained, can be found in the Methodological Appendix.

Each of these five neighborhoods had a minimum of 50 percent of its population at or below the official poverty line, and most of its remaining population had incomes only marginally over the poverty level.[54] The history of the neighborhoods' experience with poverty extended twenty-five years or longer. It was important to choose neighborhoods that had experienced long-term poverty because this was the only way to determine how poor neighborhoods functioned over time.

People of different ethnic groups inhabited the neighborhoods selected, and the length of time that each of these ethnic groups had resided in these neighborhoods also varied. In addition, the amount of time that individuals or their families had lived in the United States varied; some residents had recently immigrated, and some were fifth generation. Finally, in the sample of neighborhoods, some people had just moved to the area, and others came from families that had lived in these neighborhoods for two generations or longer.

The neighborhoods in New York and Los Angeles were specifically selected for their divergent ethnic demographics. The New York neighborhoods were inhabited by Irish, Italians, African Americans, Puerto Ricans, Dominicans, and African West Indians (mostly Jamaicans, Trinidadians, Barbadians, Haitians, and Guyanese). The Los Angeles neighborhoods were inhabited by first-, second-, third-, and fourth-generation Mexican Americans, recent Mexican immigrants, Salvadorans, Nicaraguans, Guatemalans, and African Americans. The presence of different ethnic configurations in each neighborhood provided an ideal context and comparative axis for analyzing the effect of ethnicity on neighborhood social life. In addition, for purposes of analysis one of the five neighborhoods was randomly selected as a "control group." This is discussed in the Appendix, but briefly, this neighborhood, which is in Brooklyn, had some of the conditions that existed in the other four but not all of them. Thus its inclusion allowed me to more accurately identify which factors were most salient and how and under what conditions they operated.

Although more information is available in the Methodological Appendix, I will briefly describe the process of data collection here. I studied processes of social change and preservation by investigating five establishments present in most, if not all, poor neighborhoods: public housing projects; small grocery stores; barbershops and hair salons; local gangs; and local high schools. During the nine years of study, I stayed in the housing projects with people with whom I had become friendly.[55] Since I was not eligible to occupy public housing, I had to wait until I met someone who lived in the housing project before I could gain access without suspicion and possible danger. Thus, through normal conversations, various people in the neighborhood invited me to stay with them overnight until I met people willing to let me stay in their public housing unit, which generally took about two weeks. After establishing friendships with as many people living in these projects as I could, I would be invited to stay overnight whenever I wanted. In this way, I was able to live in public housing without having to set up official residence. In three of the five neighborhoods some people had an extra bedroom in their unit, and I often arranged to stay with them when in their area. In the other two neighborhoods, I was able to make arrangements to stay with people living in apartment buildings. These buildings were in much need of repair and were regularly referred to as tenements by most of the people from the area. However, even while staying in these tenement apartments, I became friendly with people living in the local housing project who routinely invited me to stay with them.

To observe the small grocery stores, barbershops, beauty salons, gangs, and local high schools every day, I visited each for varying periods of time at different parts of the day. Sometimes I visited all the institutions within a single twenty-four-hour period, and at other times I visited two or three. The amount of time spent in each of the institutions during a particular day varied depending on what was occurring while I was there. However, over the nine-year period I was able to thoroughly observe each institution in each neighborhood.

The data gathered in this study consist of both direct observations of people's behavior and conversations in which they expressed their morality, values, attitudes, and opinions to others in their neighborhoods. I never conducted a formal in-depth interview, but I made it a point to listen carefully to all the "normal" conversation. I also tried to strategically place myself in a position to both observe people's behavior and overhear their conversations. I first recorded the raw data in a small three-by-five-inch notebook using a formal shorthand technique. Then at the end of the day, I transferred the data from the notepads to a computer file. At the end of each week I wrote weekly summaries, and at the end of each month I wrote monthly summaries, both of which were added to a computerized data set. This practice proved invaluable for placing the daily data in the broader context of the occurrences at each site.

To collect the data, I tried to observe people in the neighborhood as they went about their various activities each day. I hung around the housing projects and their common areas and visited the grocery stores, barbershops, hair salons, gang clubhouses and meeting spaces, local high schools, and other places in the neighborhood at different times of the day and night. While in each place I would talk to people, but with a conscious effort to observe behavior and listen to conversations wherever they occurred. In most places my presence was not unusual, except in the hair salons, where men were not ordinarily present. To gain access to the salons and create an atmosphere for my presence being taken for granted, I approached the owners and told them that I was going to live in their neighborhood for quite a while and would be writing a book about the community's activities. I went on to say that I wanted to include the activities in the hair salons and asked if they would let me come and observe their establishment. All of the salon owners were excited that I wanted to include hair salons and complained that barbershops always got more attention than they did. They all agreed to let me observe the interactions in their establishments, but because all the shops were quite small the owners asked that I sit in their back rooms so that I would be out of the way. One of the owners asked if while I was there I would occasionally sweep the hair off the floor for her. She also asked if I would mind sitting in the back room when I was not sweeping the floor so that there would be more room for her and her clients. I agreed to both requests. Since this seemed fair to me, I also offered my services to the other hair salon owners, and they took me up on my offer. However, my presence was never concealed. Sometimes when patrons came in I would be in the back room and they would not know that I was there, but then I would come out, be introduced to them by the owner, sweep the floor, and return to the back room. Although I was not at the hair salons all the time, the fact that I was periodically there over a nine-year period made all the clients accept my presence as nothing out of the ordinary.

How could an academic integrate himself into long-term poor neighborhoods like these? To begin with, I am Latino, and each of the five neighborhoods contained a Latino population. Thus I did not particularly stand out from the other residents. Even in neighborhoods where there was conflict between Afro-origin groups and Latinos, the fact that I had gone to all the groups in the various local establishments to introduce myself and the project allowed the word to spread that although I was living in the neighborhood I was not an "official combatant" of the neighborhood. This provided me with a type of social pass to visit and interact with ethnic groups other than my own.

On a related methodological point, the fact that I had grown up in poor neighborhoods and conducted research among the poor for more than thirty years certainly aided me in being sensitive to certain cues that helped to determine the meaning of various behaviors, but I would emphasize that others not from this background could have observed what I did and identified the same meanings as I did if they had spent enough time observing in these areas. This is an important point because the book generalizes about poor neighborhoods and other researchers will want to replicate the study; many of them will be capable of observing what is reported in this book.

During the project I used the qualitative data analysis program askSam, which allowed me to systematically code and categorize the data for analysis.[56] Ultimately the data were analyzed to determine the generalized patterns of behavior and thought that directly related to the questions addressed. Therefore, the reader should assume that both the narrative examples and illustrative quotes used in the text are representative of the general patterns observed. Idiosyncrasies that were substantively important are reported and identified as such.

ORGANIZATION OF THIS BOOK

The first chapter of this book presents a theory of social change and preservation in poor neighborhoods in the United States. Some might consider it an example of the grounded-theory method eloquently described by Glaser and Strauss in their very important book on the subject, but such a conclusion would be misleading.[57] The present study is much more aligned with the positivist tradition of social research than with the grounded-theory tradition.[58] Although most of the relationships that are formally presented in the theory (chapter 1) emerge from the data of the study and are thus "grounded," the theory does not arise exclusively from the data. Rather, it emerges from a systematic examination of other theories concerning social change and stability more generally, as well as those that apply specifically to each of the neighborhood establishments mentioned above. As such, the theory in chapter 1 is a combination of the tenets of other related theories and the empirical findings of the present study. In a classical "scientific" format it would have been located in the conclusion, but I have chosen to forego this traditional presentation and bring it forward as a separate chapter. My rationale for doing so is threefold: (1) it offers a preview of the relationships I found, (2) it presents them as formal propositions that can be tested by other researchers, and (3) it provides a road map for what will follow in each of the substantive chapters.

After the theory chapter, the book devotes two chapters to each of the five neighborhood establishments: housing projects, grocery stores, barber shops/beauty salons, gangs, and high schools. The first chapter of each pair provides a sociological description of each establishment and an analysis of the functional role that it plays in the social structure and order of poor neighborhoods. The second chapter of each pair analyzes the mechanisms of social change and preservation operating on and within the establishment, as well as its impact on the overall structure and order in the poor neighborhoods studied. The empirical chapters are followed by a conclusion that provides a fuller sociological picture of poor neighborhoods in the United States and explores the possible implications of the findings for social policy. Although some readers may be concerned that larger societal institutions and forces are not at the center of the analysis, it should be noted that two of the five establishments studied (public housing and schools) are government run. Further, the involvement of larger institutions and forces with local establishments is explored in every relevant chapter.

A few caveats should be issued. First, a reader expecting to be presented with a history of all of the micro and macro social changes that occurred in each of the five neighborhoods over the nine years of research, or a "scorecard" for each neighborhood that gives its comparative standing, will be disappointed. What this book offers instead is an analytic description of the social change and preservation mechanisms that affected each of the five establishments within the five neighborhoods studied. No issue is more fundamental to understanding the life and death of any object than the mechanisms involved in maintaining or changing its present form and function. Thus I have made these mechanisms, rather than broad descriptive accounts of each neighborhood, the focus of this book.[59] In doing so, I engage, in a challenging and hopefully productive way, the paradigm of the Chicago School of Sociology.

I have tried to present as many descriptive examples of the various analytic points as possible while keeping the manuscript at a reasonable length; thus I do not offer examples for each point. Nevertheless, every point I make is based on patterned observations from my nine years of field research. I obtained the quotations in the text using a shorthand technique that allowed me to record nearly verbatim what people said. I may have missed a few prepositions, but the quotes are 98 percent verbatim and 100 percent accurate as to content and meaning. In sum, since the study's design used standard techniques to generate a sample that is representative of neighborhoods throughout the United States that have experienced long-term poverty, both the quotes and behavioral examples should be considered representative of how people in such neighborhoods think and behave under the conditions that are discussed.[60]

Finally, all the names used in the text to identify neighborhoods, people, and establishments are fictitious. I made them up so that I could fulfill my obligations to protect the anonymity and confidentiality of my subjects.

CHAPTER I

A Theory of Life, Social Change, and Preservation in Poor Neighborhoods

The virtue of adversity is fortitude.
> Francis Bacon, *Essays*
> (1625)

Although poor neighborhoods can be described as suffering from a constant condition of extreme scarcity, they are not socially static. Rather, issues surrounding social change are an integral part of the residents' daily lives. Yet it is impossible to appreciate the dynamics of social change or conservation in their lives without considering the context in which they occur, and doing that requires an understanding of poor neighborhoods' social structure. This chapter outlines the structural and cultural contours of poor neighborhoods and the social dynamics affecting them. It will provide a framework for understanding poor neighborhoods as complex, demographically heterogeneous habitats in which social change reflects more than just changes in poverty levels, the arrival of new groups, or the introduction of new products.

A PRELUDE

In the present study, Dory, a twelve-year-old girl, typifies the profound scarcity in income, resources, and space that the children of the urban poor, who inherit the hardships of their parents, experience. She has acute asthma but has been treated for it only at the county hospital's emergency room because her parents do not have health insurance. Her father has held five jobs in four years with significant periods of unemployment, and her family, now living in the Bronx's Palm Court housing project, has moved three times in four years because they could not pay rent. Like all children, regardless of class background, the children of the poor learn to depend on social institutions to help them navigate their world. Through institutions all people, including the poor, manage their lives.[1] Therefore, any effort to understand poor neighborhoods must begin with their institutional character.

As Douglass North has stated, "Institutions are the rules of the game in a society or, more formally, are the humanly devised constraints that shape human interaction. In consequence they structure incentives in human exchange, whether political, social, or economic."[2] However, Ronald Jepperson has added that "whether we consider an object an institution depends upon what we are considering to be our analytical problem."[3] To understand the dynamics of change and preservation in poor neighborhoods, this book addresses the two most salient institutional types that affect them: state institutions and neighborhood institutions. State institutions are governmental agencies that administer the legislative, executive, and judicial programs and directives determined to be in the best interests of the general society and/or state.[4] The administrative actions of the various state institutions are governed by a set of morals and values that stem from the dominant social norms of the nation, as well as norms derived from internal roles established by these agencies.[5]

Neighborhood institutions, on the other hand, are social organizations composed of people whose patterns of local morals and values are acted out in a consistent and ordered fashion within their local social arena and have over time evolved into a set of norms governing the interactive behavior of the neighborhood's residents. All neighborhood institutions embody, teach, and differentially reinforce local value orientations and social identities, their concomitant activity scripts, and social engagement etiquette. Thus institutions in certain social contexts, including poor neighborhoods, are not necessarily institutions in others.

Neighborhood institutions have three properties: (1) they have a primary orientation toward the local community or neighborhood (as opposed to the city, state, or nation); (2) they are confined to a particular geographic location (e.g., a building or an area of public space like a corner);[6] and (3) they form the primary elements of a local social structure by organizing social behavior both within their confines and in the neighborhood at large. Further elaboration of some integral components of these institutions is necessary for a full understanding of how state and neighborhood institutions affect social change and stability in poor neighborhoods.

MORALS IN THE POOR NEIGHBORHOOD

Institutions are composed of people who have developed morals and values that help them interpret, guide, and direct their lives.[7] For residents of low-income neighborhoods, morals are the big principles of "right" and "wrong" that form their individual or collective character.[8] Morality for the urban poor in the United States centers on the concept of "responsibility," with "responsibility" being considered moral and "irresponsibility" immoral. Every individual adopts a position as to the meaning of "responsible" and "irresponsible,"[9] although each position is influenced by the individual's condition of extreme material scarcity, his or her associations with particular religious traditions, and the American socioeconomic ideology that acknowledges and celebrates the existence of winners and losers in the competitive arena called the market.[10] Positions on the meaning of "responsibility" carry significant behavioral consequences when individual and local assessments of who is responsible and who is not follow an evaluative code that has been collectively defined and developed over a sustained period of time.[11]

VALUE ORIENTATIONS IN THE POOR NEIGHBORHOOD

The moral concepts of "responsibility" and "irresponsibility" provide the basis for the development of a set of value orientations that influence the daily behavior of the urban poor. Values are the "shoulds" and "should nots" that individuals internalize. For residents of poor neighborhoods a set of values is developed that defines what "responsibility" means. Although a number of value orientations exist among the urban poor, two are dominant. The first is focused on and designed to maximize personal and family socioeconomic and physical "security," and the second to maximize "excitement" and pleasure in personal life.

In the first value orientation, the individual seeks to live his or her life in a way that will maximize financial security and reduce economic hardship, personal injury, and physical discomfort. The result is a more guarded and measured lifestyle focused on employment, saving money, and staying out of harm's way.

Contrarily, individuals who possess a value orientation to live for excitement and pleasure make every effort to seek experiences for immediate and maximum enjoyment. Their quest is predicated on the idea that excitement, when available, must be had rather than deferred for the future. These beliefs and actions are not based on hedonism; rather, they are about living life to the fullest and seizing any opportunity for excitement because of the lack of such experiences in these individuals' socioeconomic environment. This position is consistent with their belief in a God who may not have given them everything in the world but who certainly wants them to use what has been provided.

At first these two orientations may recall Elijah Anderson's description of "street" and "decent" families in his study of poor African Americans in Philadelphia, as well as the general anthropological descriptions of people possessing variations in time orientation, with some oriented to the future and others to the present or past. However, there are some important differences.[12] First, both of the value systems in this study (maximizing security and maximizing excitement) are present oriented. When it comes to economic issues, future-oriented individuals engage in "deferred gratification." Their plan is to sacrifice fun, time, money, and material possessions in the present with the expectation that more fun, leisure time, money, and material possessions will become available later as their economic fortunes in the way of professional credentials and opportunities improve.[13] To most readers, the excitement-maximizing orientation might appear to be an obvious fit for a present orientation, but some might find it surprising or odd that the security-maximizing set of values is present oriented as well. Although by definition anything beyond the present involves some portion of the future, the scale of a person's time horizon must be considered. Security-maximizing individuals are looking to save money every day, but not because of a plan of deferring gratification to accumulate savings that could buy expensive goods and services in the future. They rarely enjoy the fruits of their labor. Rather, they feel incapable of spending because of their fear that when the disaster occurs—and to them it will occur—they will lose their ability to provide for themselves and their families. Their frugality becomes a lifestyle in itself, and they will continue to put away money and buy products on sale or the cheapest versions of them even if they have accumulated enough money to safeguard their present economic condition through at least one disaster. What separates them from the future-oriented individuals who work today for future rewards is the time frame for the work that they are doing. Security-maximizing individuals work for an impending disaster that they believe is always very close to happening. Any accident could be such an event, and when catastrophe does occur to a relative or anyone in the neighborhood it simply reinforces their nightmare. Thus, when future-oriented individuals go to school, study, and save money, they do so for purposes of professional and material consumption in the future, but a future reckoned most often in years. In contrast, security-maximizing individuals feel they may need to spend their savings in a future as early as tomorrow or later in the same day. Thus middle-class people who are future oriented have a positive view of their prospects, whereas people living in poverty and oriented toward maximizing security have a negative view of their prospects. Future-oriented individuals using deferred gratification are willing to deprive themselves today for the material rewards later, but security-oriented individuals among the poor are willing to deprive themselves today to avoid future suffering.

The differences between my typology of security-maximizing and excitement-maximizing value orientations and Anderson's typology of "decent" and "street" families to describe the moral orientations of poor African Americans in Philadelphia may seem slight, but they are significant. Anderson stated that these categories were not simply imposed by the researcher (in this case Anderson himself) but were often used by the individuals of his study. The "decent families" would be those viewed positively, in moral terms, by contemporary American society as a whole, and the "street families" would be those viewed negatively. It is difficult, given his description of the behavior associated with both, to see them as anything other than the "good" and "bad" families that exist among poor African Americans regardless of whether the researcher or locals use these terms.[14] In this regard Anderson follows a line of argument similar to that in Gerald Suttles's work on the poor, in which the individuals in poor neighborhoods adopt the values of the dominant society even if they fall short of acting them out.[15] In the present study, the categories of maximizing security and maximizing excitement are composites of beliefs about a number of life experiences that form a worldview. Although those who subscribe to each would argue that theirs is morally superior, both orientations have a logic that can be morally construed as "responsible." Both have strengths and weaknesses in helping residents in poor neighborhoods to negotiate conditions of extreme material scarcity and provide a meaningful life for themselves under those conditions. Further, unlike the typologies employed by Suttles and Anderson, these orientations are built without reference or deference to the dominant moral position outside poverty.

Another difference between Anderson's work and the present study is that Anderson makes no claim that the categories he uses for African Americans are generalizable to other ethnic groups, whereas I argue in this book that the two value orientations are generalizable to other ethnic groups living in poor neighborhoods. The present study employed a sample that included nine ethnic groups and empirically found patterns of behavior that allowed for generalizations across ethnicities.

Finally, for Anderson, whole families are oriented toward either "street" or "decent" morality. In the present study, however, it is individuals who adopt a security-maximizing or excitement-maximizing value orientation. They do so regardless of whether both parents have the same orientation because these individuals have determined their chosen orientation to be "more responsible" given the challenges and satisfactions they perceive for their lives. Therefore, the conceptual framework used here can better explain the differences that exist within families between husbands and wives, siblings, and parents and children, as well as between families. This conceptual schema is closer to that employed in Ann Swidler's cultural study of love in that both suggest that the frameworks used by individuals offer them alternative moral solutions to structural predicaments.[16] To analytically categorize these as "responsible" or "irresponsible" is to let the researcher's values infiltrate the research in the manner that Weber cautioned against.[17]

In brief, saving money and avoiding risky situations gives those with a "responsibility as security" orientation a sense of financial and physical security from predatory elements of the local marketplace and social environment. However, these individuals also recognize and resign themselves to the fact that successfully achieving their goal of security will not give them socioeconomic mobility. The "responsibility as excitement" orientation is predicated on the belief that the chance of living comfortably in the present environment is unlikely and that people should therefore find as much excitement as possible in such conditions, live each day to the fullest, and share their excitement and fun with friends and family because of the goodness of reciprocity. From this perspective, any other behavior is foolishly shortsighted and individually and socially irresponsible. As presented in this study, the two moral positions on responsibility have given rise to a complex set of values regarding various aspects or spheres of life that together express a worldview. The ten aspects of life most significant to the urban poor are (1) finances, (2) spirituality, (3) sex, (4) support/assistance, (5) desires, (6) self-expression, (7) love, (8) children, (9) dreams, and (10) fear.

Finances

Individuals who operate under the moral code of "responsibility as security" view their world as having limited resources that must be managed on the basis of the belief that the world is not fair and is not likely to change. Therefore, people should take care of themselves and their family, exercise frugality and sometimes stinginess, mistrust others' motives, and save for future disasters, which could occur at any time.[18]

Individuals who operate under the moral code of "responsibility as excitement" hold the same view of the world. But they believe that they should take care of themselves and their family today, spend money when they have it, consume when they can, share with others when possible, and not plan a great deal, if at all, for tomorrow.[19]

Spirituality

Those who live to maximize personal security follow the adage that "God helps those who help themselves." This belief follows the principles that "righteousness" begins and ends with taking care of family, being a member of a formal church, and attending church regularly (though that does not mean necessarily every week).[20] Those who adhere to these principles will be provided with good things on earth and in the hereafter.

Those who live to maximize excitement understand God as giving and taking away. They feel that people should go to religious services at least on occasion to profess their faith and acknowledge their weakness, but they do not see regular (e.g., weekly) attendance as necessary. Their emphasis on sharing and reciprocity forms the foundation for their beliefs on the afterlife.[21] In essence, their values center on the beliefs that people are not in total control of their destiny and that personal weakness is part of the human condition, so that one should not feel guilt over sinful lapses. Their God is a forgiving God who supports their views about human frailty and allows them to pursue life without much restraint.[22]

Support

Those who live to maximize security believe in dependence on themselves, support for members of their immediate family, and a duty to provide support to extended family. In return, they expect, when possible, to receive support from their families. Thus support, particularly financial, is focused on family, not friends. In fact, these individuals believe that friends should not ask friends for financial support because it could impose a burden. Additionally, asking for support from friends publicly acknowledges one's failure to maximize security, which to them is immoral and embarrassing.

Contrarily, those who live to maximize excitement believe that people should rely on themselves to some degree but should also share what they have. Giving support and assistance to others is a high priority, and reciprocity is expected. Their modus vivendi is to share what you have and take all that is given.

Self-Expression

Those with a security-maximizing orientation express themselves through a presentation of self-confidence, restraint, and modesty.[23] This presentation reduces their chances of offending people and risking physical retribution from those offended. Additionally, it garners respect and confidence from those with whom they interact, particularly those who are, or might be, in a position to either hire or promote them to a better occupational position.[24]

Those with an excitement-maximizing orientation present themselves in varied and sometimes "outlandish" ways to be less inhibited and to be introduced to a wider variety of experiences than may be available to those who are more focused and reserved. They believe that such a presentation emphasizes symbols of personal strength, thus reducing the likelihood that social predators will view them as potential prey.[25] Finally, outlandish or outrageous behavior reduces the likelihood that they will be anonymous and invisible to others.[26] Thus an individual's choice of clothing or hairstyle or a parent's decision to give a child a distinctive name is an effort to reduce the possibility that oneself or one's child will simply be another anonymous, nondescript person in the sea of the poor.[27]

Dreams

The dreams of poor people assume two divergent characters. Those who live to maximize security believe in dreaming about possibilities that are realistically within their grasp. Doing otherwise would only invite disappointment and lead to further failures, whereas dreaming about realistic possibilities provides a vision that can be used as a functional resource for eventual success.

On the other hand, people who live to maximize excitement believe in dreaming the "outlandish." Such fantasy provides rewarding experiences in a social environment that does not readily allow for such experiences in reality. In essence, for this element of the poor, outlandish dreams keep hope alive and help make their everyday routines manageable.

Desire

Related to dreaming is "desire." Individuals in poor areas reduce grand dreams to a series of everyday desires. For those trying to maximize their security, desires must be controlled because they have the potential to destroy a person's "realistic" life chances.[28] This view is predicated on an understanding that desires are emotional urges related to the concept of "lust."[29] Since lustful urges are usually directed toward affection, sex, power, protection, luxury, and leisure, these individuals believe that when such desires are acted out, they can, and usually do, create negative repercussions. Further, they believe that people who cannot control their desires will compromise the security they have worked hard to achieve and therefore must be avoided.

People who are excitement oriented believe in expressing whatever desires they feel, whenever they feel them and wherever they are. They believe that not expressing their desires will deprive them of an unspecified number of exciting experiences without increasing their likelihood of improving their life chances. In essence, for the excitement-maximizing person, those who deny their desires potentially lose out doubly because they do not allow themselves to live.

Sex

Differences in value orientations are also found with regard to sexual activity. Those who live to maximize excitement view sexual activity as the most pleasurable of human acts and thus as something that should be engaged in whenever one has the desire and the opportunity. They view sex as the one pleasure in life that is free and thus believe it would be foolish and irresponsible to themselves and their partners not to engage in it. Men with such values prefer to have sexual relations with as many women as possible. Women are more likely to embed sex in the desire that their partner love them and be committed to them and are less likely to engage in it merely for the physical pleasure of the act. Further, both men and women of this value orientation, though more commonly men, believe that a person need not be troubled about promises made in the heat of passion. Additionally, both sexes equally believe that people don't need to be anxious about the consequences of sexual encounters; they need only make the best of these consequences.[30]

Those who attempt to live life by maximizing security are more cautious in their sexual activity. Although they acknowledge that sex is pleasurable, they tend to view it as an activity that can reduce their chances of being economically secure and perhaps their chances of being economically mobile. Consequences such as pregnancy can cause economic vulnerability for women and can jeopardize the father's economic goals if he chooses to help raise the child. The consequence of infection from sexually transmitted diseases could compromise a person's health and impede efforts to achieve socioeconomic security. Sexual activity also runs the risk of increased conflict between people, which can reduce the probability of realizing the socioeconomic goals of the individuals involved.[31] Thus people should be cautious in their number of sexual encounters, and individuals can and should control their actions rather than being controlled by them. Most women with this value orientation do not use birth control, so they feel it is imperative that they be honest with their partners about their intentions to take extreme care to avoid the pitfalls that could compromise their efforts to pursue and acquire a more comfortable life. Thus a woman's honesty about her intentions inhibits sexual activity and deters interest in her as a potential partner. However, if a woman becomes pregnant, it is believed that she should bring the baby to term. This view is partially related to religious beliefs but primarily stems from the more general value placed on life.

Individuals subscribing to either value orientation believe that life deserves a chance. If life were fair, their present situation would be different, but all people must be given a chance to live the best life possible in their present circumstances. They acknowledge the difficulty of their lives but are thankful for the opportunity to live. Further, people of both value orientations believe that children, like death, are simply part of the life cycle that cannot be avoided. Thus giving birth is not a significant issue but merely an integral part of their physically oriented world.

Love

Closely associated with sexual relations is the concept of love. People who live to maximize security believe that love should be sought out, experienced, and expressed and that the term *love* should not be used loosely or falsely for the mere purpose of sexual relations. False expressions of love can result in disgruntled lovers, pregnancy, or health problems. Thus they inherently believe in committed relationships, but they take a cautious approach, since the emotional power of love can consume much energy that could otherwise be used in the pursuit of material goals.[32]

For people who have an excitement-maximizing orientation, a person should also be very guarded in expressing and experiencing love because if one does express and experience love, one leaves oneself vulnerable to being emotionally hurt.[33] In essence, excitement-maximizing individuals believe that love should be sought after but never emotionally offered. They also believe that while it is perfectly appropriate to verbally commit to another person, one should not commit emotionally. The advantage to evading emotional commitment is that it allows the pleasures of sex while avoiding the potential pain of rejection and/or ridicule by one's partner.[34]

Children

One consequence of desire, sexual activity, and love is children. People who live for maximum security think that children should be loved but view raising them as a chore because, under their conditions of extreme material scarcity, children make life more difficult to manage. Individuals who hold this value orientation are intent on managing their environment to maximize their own and their family's security within their existing economic parameters. Because these parents are so intent on providing security for their children, and because that security demands and often consumes considerable resources of time, money, and energy, they find it often difficult and sometimes impossible to fully enjoy the experience of child rearing. Thus they are more likely to try to limit the number of children they have.

Along with feeling the burden of children, people with a security-maximizing value orientation sense that children can potentially offer them immortality. Therefore, their feelings of anonymity, inadequacy, or even failure can be alleviated by the idea that their children will carry on the family name and memories of their parents' efforts to improve their lives. In addition, people operating within this value orientation often view children as a resource contributing to the family's economy in good times and bad.[35] Thus these individuals believe that if families are to maximize their security, children must be controlled at all cost, including physical domination.[36]

For the men and women with an excitement-maximizing value orientation, children are not only a consequence of sex but the result of the capacity of one individual to dominate another. The ability to procreate is understood as the main defining characteristic of what it means to be a man and as symbolizing the man's domination through power and virility. Women's ability to give birth is a sign of being wanted or desired and a symbol they use to define themselves as women. Even if a woman deludes herself about being wanted or desired, she views her decision to bring a child to term as a tangible sign of power. Ultimately, both men and women operating under the excitement-maximizing value orientation consider the act of impregnating and giving birth a significant step toward moral responsibility. Some consider having as many children as nature provides to be both positive and responsible. Further, they do not believe that biological parents, to be considered responsible, must manage the daily care of their children. Rather, in their view, children are simply a part of life and must, as their parents did, learn to fend for themselves. Hence parenting is as much a process of coexisting with children as it is providing them with material and emotional support.[37]

Fear

Those who operate under the security-maximizing value orientation believe that putting oneself in danger and thereby risking bodily harm is enormously foolish and irresponsible. Although they know it is impossible to control all the events that might negatively affect them, they feel they can avoid life-threatening situations if they act strategically.

Divergently, people who operate under an excitement-maximizing value orientation believe that depriving oneself of an exciting experience for fear of physical risk is foolish. Because they view life as fragile by definition, they believe that as much pleasure as possible should be had and that regrets about losing a chance for fun and excitement out of fear should be avoided. To these excitement-maximizing individuals, regret is a classic consequence of irresponsibly depriving oneself of life's exhilarating experiences out of fear.

In sum, these two value orientations dominate the low-income neighborhoods of this study, but they are not evenly distributed within each neighborhood; the proportion varies. Further, the initial value orientation an individual develops is not immutable: individuals can switch from one value orientation to the other, though this is extremely difficult and rare. Most importantly, individuals with either value orientation claim moral "responsibility" and assign "irresponsibility" to those operating under the other orientation. Further, both value orientations develop criteria to establish status categories and assess individual performances on the basis of these categories. The interactions of the two orientations and their respective status categories provide the substance of the social institutions within poor neighborhoods.

Finally, neither value orientation is strategically better able to obtain social mobility than the other. Neither has an intrinsic advantage, for both have strengths in dealing with the condition of poverty and weaknesses in achieving socioeconomic mobility. Initially it might appear that the excitement-maximizing orientation would be incapable of deferring gratification and investing in human capital to improve possibilities for economic mobility, whereas the security-maximizing orientation would be more compatible with both. However, since those who hold the security-maximizing orientation seek safety within their low-income environment, they are more prone to resisting certain risks that would increase their chances for socioeconomic mobility and thus are likely to restrict themselves to remain "safe." In contrast, those operating under an excitement-maximizing orientation are more likely to take entrepreneurial chances, but they often do so in the illicit economy, which carries much higher risks and rates of failure.[38]

TYPES OF POOR NEIGHBORHOODS

Within this study, a "neighborhood" is defined as an area of contiguous streets constituting eight to ten square blocks that is perceived by its residents, as well as those outside, as constituting a single unit of social identification. I have identified two general sociological types of poor neighborhoods, the "contested" and the "fragmented," distinguished by how their residents are socially divided. Despite the social divisions present in both types, each is a cohesive unit with its own specific set of regularized interactions. In this regard, the contested neighborhood is one in which social divisions are driven by residents' ethnic differences. However, social divisions can also occur between recent immigrants and second- and later-generation residents of the same ethnic group because of a distinct cultural difference between recent immigrants and those who have adapted to American culture (e.g., in the Mexican population). These divisions are structured by in-group solidarity and discipline and strong enmity toward the out-group(s). Such neighborhoods are characterized by hostility between groups and territorial behavior regulated by social separation, avoidance, and aggression.

The fragmented neighborhood is represented by social divisions based on the two value orientations discussed above, length of residence in the neighborhood, origin of birth, citizenship, employment status, occupation, and gender. These factors establish a status hierarchy according to which residents identify, label, and assign individuals. Within this system of division, a high rate of agreement exists among the residents as to the assignment of individuals to each substratum, but little agreement as to the status level (high/low) of a particular substratum. The system is characterized by (1) an acknowledgment of substrata divisions; (2) a propensity to subjectively view certain substrata as morally superior; (3) a preference to associate more with others in the same substrata; and (4) wariness of those in the substrata identified as morally inferior.[39]

Neighborhood types are not static but can evolve from one to another. Table 1 gives the changes in neighborhood type over the nine years of the study. Such changes depend on a number of demographic and social changes that internally alter the history of individuals and groups in the neighborhood. Thus a contested neighborhood that experiences competition between ethnic groups will evolve into a fragmented neighborhood if only one group remains in the neighborhood, leaving it ethnically homogeneous, or if competition and antagonism cease to regulate interaction and are replaced by a shared set of cultural rules governing internal divisions. The latter outcome ocurred in the late 1980s and early 1990s in the Bronx's highly contested Elmway neighborhood, where ethnic groups included African Americans, Puerto Ricans, Dominicans, and a small number of Irish and Italians. Over time nearly all the Irish and Italians moved out, and the other residents formed a hierarchy in which each individual's place was based on individual characteristics associated with a particular substratum. Likewise, when a significant number of people from a new ethnic group move to a fragmented neighborhood, abiding by their own cultural rules of internal division rather than those established and shared by the existing group(s), the neighborhood becomes contested. Brooklyn's Eagleton neighborhood experienced such a shift, with the rapid influx of West Indian residents into a stable population of African Americans and Puerto Ricans. However, both types of neighborhoods are structured, and the rules of interaction are identifiable and regularized. Therefore, no matter how much conflict exists between groups, neither type of neighborhood represents a condition of disorganization, and neither neighborhood type can be considered more developed than the other.

TABLE I. CHANGE AND PERSISTENCE OF NEIGHBORHOOD TYPE OVER TIME OF STUDY

	1991	1992	1993	1994	1995	1996	1997	1998	1999
Bronx									
Elmway	C	C	C	C	C	C	F	F	F
Monument	F	F	F	F	F	F	F	C	C
Brooklyn									
Eagleton	F	F	C	C	C	C	C	C	C
Los Angeles									
El Rey	C	C	F	F	F	F	F	F	F
Richardson	C	C	C	C	C	C	C	C	C

NOTE: C = contested neighborhood; F = fragmented neighborhood.

INSTITUTIONS IN POOR NEIGHBORHOODS

Through the neighborhoods' institutions, the two dominant value orientations are integrated to form the social order of a community. Further, the struggle between the dynamics of change and preservation in the neighborhood takes place within these institutions. Therefore, to best understand the dynamics of change and preservation, it is necessary to focus on the social arena of institutions in poor neighborhoods.

Institutions in poor neighborhoods are established through a set of social interactions within a physical place that gives them a consistent point of reference. While many other social interactions occur in the absence of a physical place, they cannot constitute the elements of a neighborhood institution as interactions within physical structures can. Without a physical place to form and to dispense and renew their functionality, social institutions in poor neighborhoods would be incapable of regulating societal behavior. To consistently affect the social order of a neighborhood, a physical location is needed to provide residents with an arena where social interactions can be systematically arranged and managed. Ultimately, physical establishments provide an environment in which social actors can develop, strengthen, and exhibit their moral and value orientations, launch efforts to maximize their interests, and host people from other establishments within the neighborhood.

Poor neighborhoods contain commercial, social, and governmental establishments. All of these can assume different dispositions, depending on the extent to which they are integrated into the neighborhood where they are located. Commercial establishments may be either what I have termed "enterprises" or "neighborhood institutions." An enterprise's interactions are primarily concerned with the exchange of goods, services, and money for the expressed purpose of serving personal, professional, or group economic interests. Interactions between patrons based on noneconomic interests do not arise from an enterprise's management and are discouraged while patrons are on the premises. Although the environment is not necessarily inhospitable, or managers or workers unfriendly, any friendly interactions are essentially associated with business concerns. Enterprises in poor neighborhoods are never local institutions because they are neither willing nor able to contribute to the existing neighborhood social structure. Although they may fit into the social structure of the larger society, they are not a fundamental element in the poor neighborhood's social structure. In contrast, when a commercial establishment is a "neighborhood institution," the everyday activities of both patrons and owners or managers express local values, the morals associated with these values, and local norms through a set of rules that facilitate order, producing regularized behaviors that influence and govern interactions within the establishment and the neighborhood. In essence, local institutions reinforce the existing value orientations, morals, norms, and interaction rituals in the neighborhood. Since they constitute the foundations of the local social structure, any change in the nature of a particular institution, or the removal of an institution altogether, creates important shifts in a neighborhood's social organization.

Social establishments, such as gangs and churches, also assume these two possible dispositions. As enterprises, they are business ventures that are merely located in the neighborhood as they go about their activities. As neighborhood institutions, they are an organic part of their neighborhood's social structure and order. Although the gang is examined in this book, the church is not; however, there are numerous examples of churches assuming these two dispositions.[40]

Governmental establishments in poor neighborhoods are establishments run by governmental agencies—for example, public housing projects and schools. I have labeled them "state institutions," and they take on an "enterprise" character when they are governed primarily by values, norms, and interests exogenous to the neighborhood and fulfill primarily the needs and interests of the state and the broader society or primarily their own bureaucratic interests, which generally focus more narrowly on aspects related to maintaining or expanding their budget or responsibilities. In either event, like commercial enterprises, they provide services in compliance with regulations (i.e., not qualitative criteria) and cost management. At times the objective of state institutions is to alter or undermine a neighborhood's existing social structure with the intention of improving the residents' condition. However, at other times these institutions simply conduct their business, and their actions innocently undermine the existing social structure. Because the state's agendas represent exogenous interests, they rarely support the local social structure and are generally resisted by the local residents.[41] When residents succeed in making housing projects and schools predominantly reflect and reinforce the neighborhood's values, norms, and interests rather than the state's, these establishments take on the disposition of neighborhood institutions.

THE PROCESS OF INSTITUTIONAL DEVELOPMENT

The process by which some local establishments become neighborhood institutions and remain as such is related to the issue of institutionalization. There is a good deal of literature on institutionalization, but the present study will differ significantly from a number of important works. Although much research on institutionalization concentrates on formal organizations, most institutions that operate and significantly contribute to poor neighborhoods are informal.[42] Thus it is necessary to focus on the dynamics of local institutionalization and not those of formal organizations. Further, some institutions, like the public housing authority, schools, the YMCA, Boys Clubs, and gangs, are organizations that operate at the community level, but by no means do they automatically become neighborhood institutions. Whether they do depends on a number of contingent factors, but at a minimum they must support the local norms of the two main value orientations that coexist within poor neighborhoods, even though their coexistence can be contentious.

The genesis of institutions has been a topic of much debate. Some researchers, subscribing to the "invisible hand" approach to institutional development, view it as a spontaneous emergence of voluntary associations in which people with no particular common goal engage in a series of self-interested activities.[43] However, other theories on institutional genesis are based on the premise that institutions emerge when people with a common goal group together and adhere to a set of self-imposed rules to realize their goals. Michael Hechter refers to this approach as the "solidaristic approach," explaining that the genesis of cooperative institutions is based on individuals' demand to acquire "private (i.e., excludable) goods" and their ability to keep fellow compatriots from free-riding.[44] Aspects of the solidaristic approach are adopted in this study, but with some important caveats.

One of the most important differences between the solidaristic approach and my approach is the assumption that institutions emerge from people acting with common goals. This assumption cannot be made for the residents of poor neighborhoods. The emergence of institutions in poor neighborhoods has three prerequisites and assumes two different trajectories. In each, those who participate in institutions do so for reasons that are devoid of a common goal. What binds people together are the value orientations, morals, and norms that provide the foundation for the status categories that they assume and use to navigate their daily lives. These status identities are either created by the individuals themselves or assigned to them by members of the local society.[45]

For an establishment to develop into a neighborhood institution, a status hierarchy must form on the premises, with a set of rules and norms to establish consistent expectations to govern beliefs and interactions among the holders of the status positions. These rules and norms must be clear to all participants of the institution to maximize compliance.[46]

Further, a "caretaker" is needed to establish the rules governing the behavior of individuals while in the establishment. The caretaker is also charged with disseminating information concerning the rules, monitoring norms, and managing conflicts that emerge inside or outside the establishment's walls. He or she is generally the owner or manager, since it would be difficult, if not impossible, for a local institution to exist without the owner or manager's cooperation.[47]

For institutionalization to progress, the regularized behavior that emerges from the norms and rules of the status hierarchy within the establishment must be strong enough to influence behavior outside the physical boundaries of the establishment.[48] That is, the status categories of the establishment must be integrated into the neighborhood in one of two ways. Either the actors must either hold status ranks complementary to those in the neighborhood, or they must integrate the status assigned to them in the neighborhood, which is based on the values, morals, and norms that gave rise to the status hierarchy and govern it, with the values, morals, and norms operating inside the physical bounds of the establishment. If the rules and consequent behavioral patterns do not influence the behavior of the establishment's actors on the outside, the establishment either is insufficiently institutionalized or is becoming deinstitutionalized.[49]

As previously mentioned, two trajectories of institution development are found in poor neighborhoods. The first, which I call the "demand trajectory," occurs when people in the community search for a place where they can have certain needs fulfilled. Some of these needs are (1) a desire for a shelter from the tension associated with the competition for scarce resources; (2) friendship and companionship to avoid loneliness and isolation; (3) respect, deference, and leisure; and (4) access to a quasi-economic safety net. The quest to satisfy these needs arises from a general scarcity of social space in poor neighborhoods to realize these needs.[50]

Within the "demand trajectory," individuals may initiate the start of a local institution, but their effort is insufficient for institutionalization to occur. Rather, the process is gradual, beginning with potential institutional actors frequenting an establishment and integrating themselves into a system of relationships that will ultimately form the institution's foundation. From this network of emergent relationships, a set of social statuses must be developed for the individuals of the institution.[51] Next, one or more persons (depending on the institution) must become the caretaker(s) of the institution. Finally, a set of rules related to the norms of the neighborhood must be set up to regulate individual conduct within the establishment. This process ultimately results in an institution that functionally serves the neighborhood.

I have termed the second trajectory of institution building in poor neighborhoods the "evolutionary trajectory." This form of development simply emerges when people routinely frequent a place near where they live for a purpose other than any desire or need to create an institution. Through the routine of visits and communicative and physical interaction, a set of mutually reinforcing relationships is formed and a local institution commences.

This uncomplicated model of institutionalization forms as people enter the establishment with their various neighborhood identities and statuses that have emerged from the routines of daily life. Such individual identities can include numbers runner, fast talker, con artist, good cook, good parent, joker, pimp, drug addict, information source, physically strong, psychologically strong, fighter, job contractor, good game player (cards, pool, dominos), good athlete (basketball, baseball, football), sensitive listener, comfort giver, money lender, and so on.[52] Of particular importance for the development of an institution is the accommodation of all these identities in the establishment. Such categories may seem too common and diverse to be able to systematize or order social relations in any type of establishment, but they are precisely what poor people rely on to craft and individualize social identities among their peers.[53] Thus a neighborhood institution emerges when residents interweave two sets of status categories in such a way that they complement each other: one, more important set emerging from the neighborhood and the other set emerging within the social and physical confines of the establishment.

Because the various statuses of individuals emerge from competing value orientations and interests, their accommodation has important implications for interaction within the establishment. Through regularized interaction, some individuals have their status immediately recognized because of their importance in the community, while others achieve their status through a consistent display of deeds outside or inside the establishment. Status identities are not necessarily based on actions viewed as positive; they can also be achieved by actions considered negative.[54] All that is required is that the actions be sufficiently clear to assign a status to the individual and place him or her within the ranking system.

Whether the two sets of identity statuses are complementary, and thus functional, depends on the willingness and competence of the designated caretaker of the institution. To achieve success, a caretaker must craft and enforce a set of rules and norms to regulate the behaviors of those inside the establishment. In addition, the caretaker must constantly inform the participants of the prevailing norms and rules.

The general process of institutionalization of establishments requires the social interactions of three broad groups: (1) regular patrons, (2) periodic patrons, and (3) occasional patrons. Regular patrons are those who frequent the establishment nearly every day, or, in the case of the housing units studied, those who live in the units. Periodic patrons frequent the establishment on a regular basis with standardized gaps, usually every four or five days, in their visits. Finally, occasional patrons frequent the establishment sporadically with significant time gaps between visits but are not strangers to the regular or periodic patrons and have good relations with them while present.[55] Although regular patrons are the foundation, the periodic and occasional patrons are critical in transforming the establishment into a local institution.[56] If an establishment is composed entirely of regulars, it becomes insular and assumes the sociological character of a private social club and not that of a neighborhood institution. The periodic and occasional patrons, many of whom are regulars of other institutions, link one establishment to the various others in the neighborhood, forming a network that reinforces the neighborhood's social structure.

Any process of institutionalization involves change. For an establishment to become an institution, a process of change is necessary, although ironically, seeds of preservation are also needed to maintain the establishment. When the owner and patrons of an establishment create a comfortable environment where residents want to spend their time, the norms of the neighborhood must be integrated into those governing social relations inside the establishment. When the cultural norms of the establishment mirror those in the neighborhood, it becomes a local institution. With this accomplished, the new institution assumes a strategic position to directly affect what Lynne Zucker describes as the three main aspects of cultural persistence: "transmission, maintenance, and resistance to change."[57]

NEIGHBORHOOD INSTITUTIONS
AND LOCAL SOCIAL STRUCTURE

Despite the consensus in the literature that poor neighborhoods are disorganized, they are in fact organized primarily by neighborhood institutions. Neighborhood institutions both support and are supported by the values and norms of their residents. How the various institutions in a neighborhood are linked defines the neighborhood's particular social structure.

The social structure in poor neighborhoods develops from those who frequent social institutions, what they do in them, and how each institution links to others. These links are formed and maintained when the neighborhood's residents interact in various local institutions through a process similar to cross-pollination. The result is the interconnection of various institutions in a way that structurally supports the daily lives of the neighborhood's residents.

Each neighborhood has a social structure that operates through its social order. This order is constructed from individual identities, the existing status categories assigned to these identities, and the rules and norms that regulate interaction within and between institutions of the neighborhood.[58] Thus the social order represents the normative positions of individuals within and among the various institutions through their interactions with each other, as well as defined appropriate and inappropriate behavior.

Gerald Suttles argued that the social order of poor neighborhoods centers on ethnicity, gender, and age and that the experiences associated with these ascriptive categories are responsible for the ordered segmentation existing in the "slum" community.[59] Certainly the factors that Suttles identified as part of the ordered segmentation in the Chicago neighborhood he studied are operative in most low-income communities in America today. However, with the exception of ethnicity, which plays a significant, though not determinative, function in contested neighborhoods, they play a subordinate role to other factors, such as the residents' (1) length of time in the neighborhood and the country (one's own, one's family's, one's ethnic group's); (2) economic standing; (3) personal attributes such as physical attraction, strength, the ability to think quickly, and the ability to persuade others to support their interests; and (4) social capital in the form of extensive personal networks. One of the major changes since the completion of Suttles's work in the 1960s is that these four factors have assumed a more dominant role in establishing social order in the contemporary poor neighborhood. The sections that follow describe the impact of these four significant factors on the establishment and operation of the social order in poor neighborhoods.

Longevity of Residence

In ethnically homogeneous poor neighborhoods, social order begins with the length of time a person or family has resided in the United States or the neighborhood, which I refer to as "generational factors." The most recent arrivals occupy the lowest rung of the neighborhood's social order, while members of succeeding generations assume higher ranks. In ethnically heterogeneous neighborhoods, the ethnic group that (as a group) immigrated or migrated to the neighborhood first, if it maintains significant numbers, assumes the highest position in the social order, whereas the groups that arrive later assume positions commensurate with their time of arrival as compared to the arrival of other groups. However, the social order is more complicated when multiple ethnicities and generations are present. In such situations, it is understood that immigrants of the most recently arrived ethnic group assume the lowest rung of the social order following the first, second, and third generations of their group and that they in turn are followed by the generations of the succeeding groups.[60]

Economic Standing

Although some people might view low-income neighborhoods as simple composites of homogeneous poor inhabitants, this is not the case. While nearly all have low incomes, variations exist within the low-income category.[61] Further, some inhabitants of poor neighborhoods are not poor. It is important to understand that the residents of these neighborhoods construct the hierarchy contributing to the development of the neighborhood's social order.

Within the poor neighborhood's social hierarchy, the lowest category is the "idle poor," which includes those who, for a variety of reasons, simply do not work. Some cannot work due to physical or mental disability, others are women unable to work because they have dependent children and receive public assistance,[62] and some are no longer willing or able to work because of drug or alcohol addiction.[63] Finally, the homeless find it impossible to obtain work because employers require a place of residence that they don't have.[64]

The second category is the "periodically working poor," composed of people who generally work in the secondary labor market, where wages are low and there is little security. Since many are employed in industries that are competitive and seasonal and have small profit margins (e.g., the apparel industry or construction day labor), industry managers and owners tend to cut their workforce during cyclical periods when sales are low. Thus workers in this economic sector experience structurally determined periodic unemployment.[65] Other periodically working poor are employed in the lower echelons of the underground economy, which have a very fast turnover rate, leaving workers in a constant state of uncertainty as to how long their jobs will last.[66] In addition, there are the obvious risks that the owners or managers of these underground businesses or the employees themselves may be apprehended by law enforcement at any time, in which case employees will lose their jobs.[67] Finally, some of the periodically working poor are physically and mentally incapable of keeping a job. Those who suffer from physical and psychological disabilities, many of which are job related, generally have a work life punctuated by long periods of unemployment. Those with alcohol and drug addictions find it difficult, if not impossible, to keep a job because their addiction usually leaves them physically and mentally incapable of consistently going to work each day or competently performing their job-related duties. Therefore, they are usually terminated and unemployed for significant periods of the year, and supporting themselves is generally a cyclical routine of hustling others until another employment opportunity arises, briefly keeping clean from drugs while they are employed, getting fired, and resuming drug use.

The third economic segment, or substratum, of the poor neighborhood is the "working poor," who are generally in the secondary labor market.[68] They hold steady jobs characterized by low wages, no benefits or advancement opportunities, and little job security.[69] In fact, because the firms that generate these jobs operate in the service industries, construction, or a very competitive area of the production sector, they require flexibility in their labor pool, which causes a great deal of worker movement from one firm to another.[70] Although the working poor are steadily employed, the community views those who remain in this economic sector as stuck because they lack either the initiative or the time to gain the human capital skills necessary to advance to the primary labor market.

The fourth substratum in the low-income community is the "working class," composed of individuals with steady incomes who hold traditional blue-collar jobs in the primary labor market, most of which provide respectable wages and benefits. Thus the working class are envied by the less fortunate members of the neighborhood. Workers in this segment view their situation as superior to that of most others because they work every day and more closely resemble what the wider society considers "responsible."[71]

The fifth substratum in low-income areas is the "middle class." Although middle-class residents are rare in poor neighborhoods, the few that exist do play a role in the neighborhoods' social order. A few are

remainders from when a particular neighborhood was socioeconomically mixed,[72] but the largest portion emerge from business dealings
associated with the illicit underground economy. These individuals live
in poor neighborhoods because their market is in the area or because
their neighbors give them security warnings regarding their various dealings with competitors who could physically harm them.[73]

Personal Attributes

In low-income areas, personal attributes substitute for material resources
and are important assets in defining and negotiating a person's social condition. Three personal attributes contribute to the social order in poor
neighborhoods, deriving from the comparative evaluation of a person's
particular attribute, the degree to which the person has it, and its quality
as evaluated by peers. The condition of the attribute is thus tied to the
community's social norms, giving it both a specific local substance and
the fluidity necessary for desired change.

The first personal attribute is an individual's physical attractiveness.
Since so much of the experience of people living in poor neighborhoods centers on the physical, it is not surprising that physical attractiveness plays an
important role in the social order. Both women and men direct much attention to judging and being judged as physically attractive, so objects that
accentuate this attribute, particularly adornments to one's body such as
clothing, are important. Although every segment of society is "clothes conscious," people living in poor areas are especially aware of their own and
others' clothing. Expensive and "stylish" clothing is desired, not simply
because it represents status, but because its quality is thought to enhance
one's attractiveness. Therefore, every effort is made to purchase it.[74]

The second personal attribute is physical and psychological strength. In
the case of the former, a physical world demands physical prowess in both
men and women, and those who develop it have power over others in the
community who have less. Essentially, they have more freedom to do what
they want and cause others to do what they would not on their own voli-
tion.[75] Certainly firearms reduce the impact of a person's physical strength,
but they do not eliminate it. Because brute strength, unlike a gun, can be
directly associated with a person's individual qualities, it is important
because, like physical attractiveness, it can affect the actions of others.

Those who possess psychological strength are powerful and are
viewed as such by those in the poor neighborhood. They can pursue their
economic and leisure interests without hesitation or fear; thus their psy-

chological strength is measured by their display of personal stability, responsibility, and resolve (tenacity) to pursue their interests despite the hardships that could demoralize them.[76] The more people demonstrate strength in these areas, the more power they have and the more deference they are granted by those in their community.

Quick thinking is another highly valued attribute and is used by individuals to entertain others, save themselves from embarrassment or physical harm (get out of trouble), and develop schemes to obtain money and/or material possessions. For instance, people who play well at a version of the game "The Dozens" or who succeed in a number of sophisticated scams gain deference and status.[77]

Finally, the ability to persuade others through conversational skills is thought to be an important attribute. Individuals with this attribute are used to being called "sweet-talkers," "con artists," or "foxes." Some people in the low-income neighborhood attempt to develop whatever abilities they possess in this area. Those who have a special capacity to be liked, thereby getting what they want, are acknowledged as special. The more a person demonstrates such abilities, the higher his or her neighborhood status ranking.

Social Capital

A final factor determining one's status in the social order is an individual's social capital—that is, the extensiveness and quality of the individual's personal networks. Thus individuals attempt to nurture personal relationships that they believe will secure the goods and services they might need in the future. Since most poor people think it is "who you know" that determines how well you will fare in life, relationships with individuals who will do one a favor at strategic times are seen as essential. Most residents of poor neighborhoods differ from those in the middle class in that (1) they believe that private and state bureaucracies cannot or will not give them needed help; (2) they have little or no knowledge of what specific bureaucracy would be most effective in helping them achieve a desired goal; or (3) they do not know how to get a particular bureaucracy to work for them. Therefore, they rely on personal networks, and the extensiveness of an individual's personal networks is a key ingredient in raising his or her status and power within an institution and the neighborhood.

To review, whereas Suttles found ethnicity, gender, and age to be the important factors segmenting poor neighborhoods in the 1960s, I found

that in contemporary poor neighborhoods ethnicity, ethnic generational factors, longevity of residence, value orientation, certain personal
attributes, and an individual's social capital emerge as the primary
determinants of social division and segmentation. Although age, gender, and sometimes territory complement these factors to form division
and segmentation, the status hierarchies that develop from the factors
mentioned above are the primary mechanisms that sustain segmentation in poor neighborhoods. Therefore, the configuration of social status has important implications in the arrangement of power in the
neighborhood, ultimately defining the social order. In turn, the social
order is important in understanding not only the social structure of
poor neighborhoods but the dynamics involved in their change and
preservation.

CHANGE AND PRESERVATION
IN POOR NEIGHBORHOODS

I begin with two strikingly different reactions to homecoming that were
expressed by returning residents within the same week in two different
neighborhoods. In the first, a former resident had just come home from a
stint in the military. Two days after his arrival he said to an army buddy at
a local bar, "I haven't been home for three years, and so much has changed.
There are new grocery stores and a whole lot more Mexicans here than
when I left." In the second, a former resident had just moved back to the
neighborhood after three and a half years away in Tennessee, where her
father had gotten a permanent job. She said to a friend at the community
basketball courts, "I can't get over it, nothing has changed in the neighborhood since I left. . . . The people and the stores are just the same!"[78]

Poor neighborhoods are constantly involved in processes of social
change and preservation. In fact, the competitive actions of social change
and preservation agents create the ongoing social condition of the neighborhood at any given time. Change agents can be defined as instruments,
or forces, of human, spiritual, conceptual, or material form that either
create conditions for change or directly or indirectly cause change. Alter-
natively, preservation agents are instruments that affirmatively retain the
existing social structure and culture. Both types of agents are active at
both macro and micro levels of urban society.

At the macro level, change agents affect, directly or indirectly, neighborhood institutions, which in turn affect, to varying degrees, the entire
structure of the poor neighborhood. These agents, usually coming from

outside the community, include demographic shifts in population density, as well as shifts in ethnic, social class (gentrification), and age populations.[79] Further, structural changes to the economy of the local neighborhood can result in profound changes in the neighborhood's population. Such changes as the opening of a once-closed illegal drug economy, the reduction of blue-collar jobs, or the expansion of occupations in the lower-level service sector affect the social composition of the neighborhood. Finally, alterations to the physical state of the neighborhood through disaster or urban renewal also affect social structure.[80] Thus changes in the socioeconomic and physical condition of a neighborhood directly affect the content, organization, and functioning of its various institutions in everyday life.[81]

Outside pressure has other effects on neighborhood institutions as well, such as changes in the personnel of an institution, which significantly affect the institution's internal operations. Further, changes in property taxes and wholesale prices affect the institution's ability to function, and changes in police, fire, and sanitation services directly influence the local institution's ability to perform. Because many neighborhood institutions are business establishments, changes that affect business operations invariably affect the establishment's institutional functions. Business pressures thus shift the establishment away from its institutional role and toward a more enterprise-oriented role. Although this shift seems subtle at first, it begins a process of patron disengagement, ultimately causing an establishment's institutional death.

Change agents that work at the micro level of the neighborhood are usually associated with behavioral changes within the neighborhood or within the institutions themselves. The three most prevalent and potent changes affecting the behavior of neighborhood residents are increases in robbery, vandalism, and violence, all of which produce change within neighborhood institutions. People who once were integral parts of an institution may patronize it less often because of the increased risk, causing an aesthetically less inviting environment or constraints on the various institutional actors' abilities to perform the routines that are crucial to the continued health of the institution.[82]

Social changes can also come from within the institution, and the agents of such change are the very people who form its core element. First, change agents can be the institution's in-group personalities. Each neighborhood institution is composed of people who know each other and have accommodated themselves to each other's personalities. Because of the wide range of personalities in any institution, formal rules and roles aid in the integration of different people.[83] To support these formal rules and roles, participants are asked to be tolerant of others' personalities, and this is accomplished through the development of institutional norms. Since these norms can be conceived of as group-accepted standards in behavior, individuals who come into an institution with a significantly different personality from those present can significantly change the institution's operational environment.

Second, the change can involve the institution's status hierarchies. Competition between the various institutional actors or the arrival of new actors necessitates change because it leads to shifts in the status hierarchy. Such changes modify the internal interpersonal interactions of the institution by forcing others to adapt to a familiar person occupying a new, unfamiliar (to both the person and themselves), or perceived illegitimate role in the established internal status hierarchy. In a situation that involves new actors, not only do new people occupy new positions, but people with different personalities are introduced as well. This presents a predicament for the people in the institution because they must now adapt to a new personality within the group or to a person whose personality creates a new set of role behaviors attached to a status position previously held by someone with a different personality.

Although changes of personnel inside the institution are important, none is more significant than a change involving what I call the institutional caretaker. Change occurs when the new caretaker of an institution is of a different age, ethnicity, gender, or personality than the previous caretaker. The institutional caretaker is greatly respected and often revered by the active participants in the local institution. Thus a change in the institutional caretaker requires significant adjustments on the part of the participants to simply maintain the institution. Such a change may also alter how the institution is perceived or functions in the neighborhood at large, causing important implications for change in the neighborhood's social structure and order.

Dynamics of preservation also occur in poor neighborhoods. Preservation involves residents' actions to keep the neighborhood operating at its present status. Those who act as agents of preservation actively engage in maintaining all, or most, of the neighborhood's social structure (configuration of institutions) and social order (status hierarchies). Three primary sets of individual and group interests are involved in preserving poor neighborhoods—*cultural, economic,* and *social.*

Concerning culture, preservation agents are aligned with the development and maintenance of a local subculture. Claude Fischer's subcultural theory of urbanism is an important conceptual tool for understanding much of this process. Fischer's theory postulates that the larger the city, the more apt it is to develop, hide, and protect subcultures; certainly this is the case for the subcultures within poor neighborhoods.[84] Fischer's theory provides insight into why a particular poor neighborhood, like the five studied, remains operationally consistent for over twenty-five years: the dynamics of urbanism (particularly size) keep a neighborhood hidden as a distinct ethnic, religious, and/or poor entity. The sheer size of a city or metropolitan area thus provides an optimal environment for developing and maintaining a local subculture that preserves the neighborhood's character.

Among the poor, preservation of the existing subculture arises from two similar but distinct experiences: living within the norms of a particular ethnicity and living with material scarcity. For instance, those who integrate their ethnic culture with the social conditions of the neighborhood can preserve that culture only if they and their neighbors maintain the existing social structure and social order, even if this means reducing their chances for economic mobility.[85] Agents of preservation then view their actions as a rational means of preserving a way of life that they believe is more important than economic gain, even if the neighborhood's ethnic culture has changed since they first arrived from the country of origin. Thus, whatever the state of their present ethnic subculture, the agents of preservation consider it an honorable enough form of the "mother culture" to be kept alive. Their meaning of life emerged from, and is predicated on, the form of ethnic culture that currently exists in their neighborhood, and this reinforces their desire to maintain the existing social structure and social order even if it is counterproductive to their economic mobility.[86]

For subcultural agents of preservation to succeed, they must be able to enforce neighborhood discipline, whether through appeals to ethnic group solidarity or through group sanctions.[87] In the case of the former, preservation agents gain control through positive reinforcement and achieve solidarity through the celebration of local ethnic culture by sponsoring ethnic cultural events and encouraging local residents to frequent and patronize institutions that support their ethnic culture in the neighborhood.[88] The most efficient means to secure neighborhood solidarity is through language. No matter what the local language is, it provides the mechanism by which people make sense of and give meaning to their world. Use of their ethnic language, which can be a combination of English and the native tongue or a lower-class version of English, is a public sign of group solidarity because whatever their generation in the neighborhood, formal English is constantly present as the dominant language of the larger community. The more local language is used as the primary means of communication, the more group solidarity will exist. Therefore, preservers of the neighborhood's subculture define their ethnic group as poor and promote the idea that they are not an element of an ethnic group socioeconomically left behind but a "true and pure" remnant of the ethnic group practicing the "old ways."[89] Further, they argue that the only "real" members of the ethnic group are those who think and behave in the ways that others in the neighborhood think and behave.[90] Since most neighborhood residents have low incomes, an unstated premise exists that this condition is advantageous in maintaining traditional culture and that those from the group who become economically mobile have been forced to abandon traditional culture and assimilate.

People intent on maintaining the existing social structure and order in the neighborhood also negatively sanction local residents who they believe threaten the existing condition. The tactic most commonly used is to socially "shun" those identified as deviant from the local cultural norms by excluding them from full participation in ritualized conversations and social activities viewed by the vast majority in the neighborhood as central to its identity. Such tactics are designed to stigmatize the deviants as "sellouts" of their culture.

Culture is also related to preservation through the effects of residents' immediate socioeconomic environment on the development of a distinctive culture. Research on poverty over the years shows the importance of structural conditions in creating inequality and poverty.[91] However, people living in poverty adapt to their circumstances by fashioning a social life with valued cultural meaning and symbols that, over time, are appreciated by the larger society in the areas of sports, clothing, speech, and entertainment. Many researchers believe that poor people are middle-class people without money,[92] a myth perpetuated by forty years of research that emphasizes the structural origins of poverty while attacking any suggestion that the poor have developed a culture related to deprivation.[93] The result has been the gross neglect of the existence and workings of a culture among the poor. Preservation within poor neighborhoods is predicated on a culture directly formed from the experiences of prolonged financial and material deprivation, a condition I have labeled the "subculture of scarcity."[94] Of course, the discipline of economics is the study of scarcity, so it should be made clear that I am referring to a subculture whose origins and operation involve managing daily life in a condition of extreme financial and material scarcity over a long period with little probability of significant economic improvement.

Because the United States is a nation of immigrants, and the newest immigrants are generally in the lower class and have little income,[95] some aspects of this subculture are ethnic in origin.[96] However, these ethnic aspects are merely the fringe of the subculture. The subculture of scarcity includes a worldview of material deprivation as the central organizing principle of life. In such a worldview, no matter how well off one is, a vulnerability to poverty with no safety net is always lurking in the future.[97]

The values and norms that emerge from this worldview are described in the preceding sections of this chapter and represent important agents in sustaining the social character of poor neighborhoods by providing the blueprints for its maintenance. The blueprints, on the other hand, establish the framework of what are considered the "appropriate" strategies and instruments for individuals to realize their interests. Of course, a group of people faced with scarcity could share the limited resources available rather than competing for them, but the prevailing "winner take all" ideology of the United States does not support sharing. Rather, this ideology supports only a sharing of misery and a belief that anyone who accumulates surplus wealth should consider giving a portion of it as charity to those less fortunate.[98] Hence, many of the strategies and instruments of choice used by poor people in the United States involve power, advantage, and physical force. Culture thus shifts from worldview and value orientations to what Ann Swidler calls the use of a "tool kit" to realize the value orientations engendered in the worldview.[99] Therefore, culture as described in this study incorporates two separate but complementary aspects. First, culture includes a set of morals and values that arise from a particular worldview that explains how and why the world operates as it does. Second, once this worldview is established, culture determines the *what, where,* and *when* of any particular social action, *how* an action is to occur, and its strategic importance to the individual, group, or society in general. Thus my concept of culture integrates the idea of "value orientations" in the work of Weber, Parsons, Clyde Kluckhohn, Florence Kluckhohn, and Fred Strodtbeck with the idea of culture as a "tool kit" advanced by Swidler, and draws on Fischer's "subculture of urbanism" framework to account for the subculture of scarcity's physical location and persistence within large cities over time.[100]

Through the interplay of the worldview described above, with its set of values and norms, and the strategies and instruments used to realize individual interests, a variety of status identities and social hierarchies are constructed to form a subcultural system that local participants value and want to pass on to succeeding generations. Nothing is more fundamental or normal to any cultural system than the desire and effort to pass on the present morals, values, and norms in the society or subsociety to the next generation. Most poverty researchers have failed to fully appreciate the degree to which this exists in poor neighborhoods. As a result, they have missed that the transfer of what is considered valuable to the next generation is accomplished through the everyday activities of local institutions, where young people and newcomers alike are formally and informally socialized into the subcultural world of the poor neighborhood.[101]

Another factor besides the subculture that works to preserve the status quo in a poor neighborhood is the economic interests of those dependent on the neighborhood for the well-being they have achieved or hope to achieve. The interests of these individuals vary a great deal. Some are owners of small businesses in the illicit economy,[102] others are small business owners in the legal economy,[103] and still others hope to enter the illicit economy, taking their chances for mobility within it.[104] Few people find the hope of entering the legal economy attractive because the types of economic establishments active in poor neighborhoods do not offer opportunities to increase a person's life chances.[105] Those who have economic interests in the low-income community are provided with employees, clients, and a protected environment from economic competitors and/or law enforcement. Thus these people resist social change because it has the potential to disrupt the prevailing operating system, introducing more uncertainty and greater risk to their economic life. Most of these people vigorously work to maintain the existing social order.

The last element of the poor community that works to preserve the existing social environment consists of those who find their social interests, and thus their lives, integrally tied to their neighborhood's present social structure and order. Over time, indigent people develop a subculture that facilitates their everyday activities and gives evaluative meaning to their lives.[106] The most important aspect of this subculture is the social statuses that have emerged from the prevailing values and social norms. These status categories give individuals a social identity and system that creates prestige, honor, and respect in their lives and establishes some attractive aspects of life for people who are marginalized by members of the wider society (but who may still be big fish in a small pond).[107] Thus the residents of these poor neighborhoods have a vested interest in maintaining the prevailing local social order. Of course, as in the wider society, those who occupy statuses with the most prestige have more interest in preserving the present system than those at the lower rungs, but surprisingly, they are not alone in resisting change and conserving the prevailing social system (and social order) in their neighborhood.[108] Even people at the lower rungs of the community try to preserve it because they have internalized the values associated with the existing socioeconomic conditions. It is for this reason that someone who left the community and has achieved more financial success will say, "Yeah, I have more money and don't live here anymore, but I really ain't any different, and I like coming here."

THE DYNAMICS OF CHANGE AND PRESERVATION

The term *social dynamic* is used in this study in reference to the forces that produce activities of change and maintenance in a given social arena. These forces, either competing and conflictual or consensual and complementing, are the mechanisms that create or maintain a particular society. The persistently poor neighborhood is a composite of activities producing a social equilibrium that forms the basis of a functionally reproducing neighborhood. Within this equilibrium exist agents intent on producing social change and agents intent on resisting it. This tension, or dialectic, produces a synthesis that becomes what people observe as the "existing neighborhood."

The dynamics of change in poor neighborhoods occur in four distinct patterns. In the first and most prevalent pattern, actions change a neighborhood institution into an economic enterprise (as when a grocery store that supported a variety of neighborhood interactions becomes an establishment run for profit only); in the second pattern, actions change a neighborhood institution into a state institution (as when a school reinforcing neighborhood norms becomes one that reinforces state/national norms). In both cases, change agents could affect either the institution as a whole or the institution's internal social order, beginning a process of internal decay that would eventually result in the establishment's collapse as a neighborhood institution and its assumption of the character of an "enterprise" or state institution. The outcome is ultimately a net loss of an institution in the neighborhood. Since the social structure of the neighborhood is composed of the interconnection of institutions, any institutional loss upsets and weakens the neighborhood social structure, creating instability. Neighborhood instability is a condition in which individuals' or groups' lack of a functional social consistency (routine) causes varied, random, and unpredictable behavior among the residents.

In such a condition, the mechanisms of social control cannot fully eliminate behavior that is socially detrimental to the maintenance of the
neighborhood's social structure. However, this situation should not be
confused with the elimination of behavior that the outside society finds
detrimental to the neighborhood or its interests (like violence or crime).
Although some might call this condition disorder, such a judgment
misses the fact that a number of preservation agents still operate to
reestablish the existing social order. In brief, only rarely does a particular poor neighborhood change from a condition of order to one of
disorder.[109]

Two additional patterns of change occur in poor neighborhoods: when
an economic enterprise becomes a neighborhood institution and when a
state institution becomes a neighborhood institution. Such changes occur
through instrumental acts of preservation intended to either restore the
prior structure and social order or maintain the existing one. These
efforts strengthen cohesion in the neighborhood, even though the economic, social, and physical condition of the residents remains the same.
A successful preservation effort revitalizes the existing social structure
and strengthens the subjective meaning that residents assign to their lives.
This meaning is not false consciousness on their part or that of an outside researcher "idealizing" poverty;[110] nor is it the residents' tolerance
of an intolerable condition. Rather, it is a meaning that develops from a
subculture of scarcity that is positive and strong enough to maintain loyalty to subcultural values and norms even when prior residents have left
the neighborhood and improved their economic status.

Because of the large structural arrangements of the society, residents
of poor neighborhoods confront extreme material scarcity and social
deprivation as an everyday condition. Within this condition they develop
a set of values and norms that produce the elements of a social hierarchy.
In turn, these elements are brought by individuals into local social institutions to be further developed and nurtured, forming a social order that
governs the behavioral interactions in the institution and, by extension,
in the neighborhood at large. Finally, the ways in which social institutions and their social orders are linked in the neighborhood define its
social structure.

Within this context the forces of change and preservation create constant tension in poor neighborhoods. The change agents (from outside
or inside the neighborhood) usually affect the external and internal environment of the social institution, modifying its content and character.
Such an alteration changes how the social institution relates to other

institutions, causing instability until institutional shifts patch any social damage to the overall structure.

Social maintenance occurs as a result of individual acts to protect the operative subculture. Because change agents challenge the existing subculture, instability occurs in social relations. In such cases, social institutions cannot work at full capacity to support the neighborhood's social structure, so people are less able to predict others' behavior, an uncertainty that significantly impairs social outcomes. Yet as preservation efforts progress, people's ability to predict behaviors and social outcomes improves because information regarding others' behaviors is integrated within the context of the existing subculture. When the local subculture is restored, equilibrium within the local social structure is reestablished.

Instability in the neighborhood's social order is not to be equated with disorder. Unlike other studies, this study does not define social disorganization as the number or density of networks. Rather, disorganization occurs when the neighborhood has no functional social order that addresses common local issues. This allows for a better appreciation of how the neighborhood is constructed and organized and focuses on the social issues of normal, everyday interaction rather than, as social disorganization theorists conceptualize, the neighborhood's ability to solve large social problems like drug addiction, litter, public intoxication, or prostitution.[111] Any neighborhood, or society, can have difficulty solving large social problems but still be socially organized.

My argument is not that social disorganization is nonexistent but that the criteria previously used cannot adequately determine it. Social disorder exists in poor neighborhoods, but only when there are too few people to support a functional institutional environment as described in this study and residents are consequently forced to find institutional affiliation outside their neighborhood. When consistent institutional affiliation outside the neighborhood is the modus vivendi of the few residents who still live within the geographic area of the old neighborhood, then and only then has the neighborhood become functionally disorganized or socially dead.

CHAPTER 2

Give Me Shelter

Competing Agendas
for Life in Public Housing

> The projects are hideous, of course, there being a law, appar-
> ently respected throughout the world, that popular housing
> shall be as cheerless as prison.
>
> James Baldwin, Nobody Knows My Name (1961)

The public housing project is a common sight in most of the geographic
areas where the American urban poor now live. This, however, has not
always been the case. For much of the twentieth century the poor resided
in various forms of private housing such as row housing, small single
homes, roominghouses, transient hotels, and tenements.[1] Those unable
to pay the minimum rents of tenement and flop housing were relegated
to the streets and alleys to find shelter.[2] Community aid for those unable
to afford housing came from private donations that funded what were
commonly referred to as "alms and poor houses."[3]

Around 1934 New York City began a daring effort in social intervention by establishing state-funded subsidies for housing. This bold effort
would not only relieve some of the poor from meeting the high rents of
an inadequate private housing market but profoundly alter the social
and physical landscape of urban America.[4]

As the problem of housing for the poor and working class grew, the
federal government created more housing units that provided rent subsidies to predominantly working-class families. This was largely the
case after World War II, when the men who had served in the armed
services returned to rebuild their lives. The state also loaned money to
veterans and other working- and middle-class families to buy single-
family homes. This gave former residents of state-subsidized housing
the opportunity to move to private housing in the less densely populated
suburbs.

Increasing numbers of the poor were now able to rent units in public housing buildings. As time progressed, the surrounding neighborhoods became less desirable residential areas for middle- and working-class people, who began to leave. As a result, these neighborhoods became more homogeneously poor in population and experienced a general economic decline.[5] By the 1970s most of the public housing across the nation had become dominated by families that were nonwhite and poor.[6] The housing units were not properly maintained, and increasing numbers of them became dilapidated. In fact, some of the federally funded housing projects, such as St. Louis's Pruitt-Igoe, became so dilapidated that they were evacuated and demolished by their local housing authorities.[7]

Public housing projects have significantly influenced the social lives of all people who live in the neighborhoods in which they exist. To date, there has been little systematic research, particularly ethnographic research, on social life within housing projects or poor housing generally, mostly because of researchers' difficulty in gaining both physical and social access to these places (i.e., being able to live there and being accepted by the residents).[8] From the little work that has been done, two very different portraits of "normal" life in housing projects have emerged. By far the most prevalent depicts life as so difficult that it is simply oppressive.[9] Yet one study, in what appears to be a reaction to the standard depiction, argues that life in large public housing units is comparable to life found outside and even that housing projects can be very positive places in which to live and raise children.[10] The obvious question is, What are we to make of these two widely divergent depictions of project life? Which is the more accurate? The short answer is that both have some degree of accuracy. To comprehend the sociological condition of housing projects and their contribution to the structure of poor neighborhoods in general, it will be necessary to understand how people are housed and how they make homes for themselves in a rather bleak environment. This chapter examines the factors that structure life in housing projects (see table 2 for a list of the five projects studied) and shows that an active struggle is being waged between the state and the neighborhood over what the institutional character of the housing project will be.

THE STATE AND PUBLIC HOUSING

State legislation created public housing, and state appropriations continue to support its operations. Therefore, public housing must be seen as an organ of the state and the people who administer it as agents of

TABLE 2. HOUSING PROJECTS
IN THE FIVE NEIGHBORHOODS STUDIED

Bronx
    Elmway
        Palm Court Apartments
    Monument
        Buckley Gardens
Brooklyn
    Eagleton
        Gardenia Avenue Apartments
Los Angeles
    El Rey
        Orchid Lane Apartments
    Richardson
        John C. Fremont Homes

the state designated to create and maintain the housing project as a state institution. In practical terms, this means the agents attempt to run the units within the parameters of the statutes and guidelines established by the federal government and the local public housing authorities.

The administrators for the five housing projects examined in this study expressed three fundamental objectives. The first was to operate within the officially defined guidelines of "administrative responsibility," particularly supervising revenues and managing costs, which translated into operating within the budget parameters established by local housing authorities. Since revenues were in part generated by the rents assigned to the occupants, monitoring rents was a priority and required a sustained effort to see that occupants consistently honored their responsibilities. In addition, it required the selection of new, employed people as tenants.

The priority to rent to employed tenants originated in a series of policies beginning in 1949 that addressed the escalating difficulties of an increasing number of urban poor in securing housing. Because these policies required that tenants' rents not exceed 30 percent of their "adjusted monthly income" or 10 percent of their gross income, whichever was greater, public housing operations were subsidized at a higher rate for unemployed tenants, resulting in a greater strain to operate within assigned budgets.[11] Therefore, the working poor were sought after as tenants.

In the five housing projects studied, administrators looked the other way when renters were employed but did not meet all the requirements for tenancy. Numerous families living in one of the housing projects of

Los Angeles were not citizens and thus were not entitled to be tenants. Although these families had some type of documentation indicating that they were citizens, the housing administration had every reason to believe, given the renters' low English language proficiency, their occupations (most reported being independent construction workers), and the existence of a large and sophisticated industry in forged documents, that they were in the country illegally. However, the administrators of both complexes chose to ignore these facts because the families paid their monthly rent, which helped meet the costs of running the units. For example, the administrator of the Orchid Lane Apartments in Los Angeles stated:

> There are people here who may be illegal, but we check to see that everyone has papers, and if they do and they meet the criteria for public housing we offer it to them. Now I know, or suspect, that a number of these people are here illegally, but they pay their rent every month. Since we have so many people that we don't get rents from, those people who do pay make a big difference toward us meeting our operating cost in the budget. . . . Hey, as I said, there may be people here who are illegal, but as long as they pay their rents and keep up their apartments, we're not going to be too concerned. We got enough deadbeats [nonpaying residents] who are here legally to worry about.[12]

The same view was expressed by many of the staff working in the projects. A custodian from the John C. Fremont Homes in L.A.'s Richardson neighborhood said:

> That family over there are illegals, but none of the big shots [administrators] here care about that, they only care if they pay the rent and don't cause any trouble. I told [the administrator] that they were illegal, but he told me, "They pay the rent and stay out of trouble. If we don't have people who pay the rent, we got trouble." So I don't tell him about all the people who're here illegally, and there are a whole lot, because he don't care about that. What he really don't like is the people who can't pay any rent at all, and most of them people is citizens.[13]

Another common situation in which people not eligible for tenancy were allowed to remain because the rent was paid regularly and in full involved residents of the buildings who allowed relatives, usually their children, who were unable to find work and housing to replace them as residents without informing the administration. Since the parents continued to pay the rent, administrators usually made no effort to evict the children. As an assistant administrator for Buckley Gardens in the Bronx's Monument neighborhood commented:

Sure, there are a number of people living in these units that are not entitled
to be tenants, but if they are paying their rents they will not be evicted. We
don't police people who are paying the rent. We're trying to create something good here, which also involves paying rents.[14]

Budgetary guidelines were also met by limiting the operating costs of
the buildings to the extent that no health code was violated. In numerous conversations with janitors of all the housing projects, I found that
this resulted in delays in repairs to tenants' units. Most of the delays were
correlated with the availability of funds; as the fiscal year approached
its end, fewer resources were available.

Administrators' objective of meeting organizational needs by running
operations within or close to budget led them to limit financial commit-
ments to residents who had shown little success or interest in becoming
employed while maintaining a modest commitment to the working poor,
whom they believed to be more deserving of help.[15] Thus the administration made a conscious effort to extend state ideology and values
regarding the poor.

Administrators' second objective was to ensure public safety, especially the protection of residents and their children from accidents that
could seriously injure and/or kill them.[16] In the high-rise buildings, window guards were placed on all the windows so that children could not
fall. Around the low-rise buildings of the L.A. housing projects, speed
bumps were raised to protect children from speeding automobiles. Lights
in public areas were continually replaced when they burned out. Large
items of discarded furniture were removed from high-rise stairwells so
that residents would have unimpeded fire-escape routes. Garbage was
collected regularly from the bins of each building to reduce the risk of
rodents and insect infestations, and when infestations were reported, a
relatively quick effort was made to control the problem. Inevitably, some
delays arose in the above safety procedures, but they were not indicative
of any attempt to avoid safety issues.

In addition, a priority was placed on protecting residents from robbery, assault, harassment, and shootings. The main responsibility for this
protection was assumed by the nearest precinct of the local police, even
though both the New York and Los Angeles housing authorities had
their own police. At times both police forces were reluctant or even
refused to enter a building they believed to be extremely dangerous, but
they generally patrolled the outside areas regularly. The securing of the
residents' safety was by no means achieved completely in all the buildings that I studied, but the administrators made a continuous effort. This

priority also served to support the public relations departments of the two cities' housing authorities in their function of countering possible negative publicity regarding any breach of safety.

For the state, public security served to establish social control over the inhabitants of the housing units as well as the larger community as a whole. The state's emphasis on social control is rooted in the desire to obtain what Weber described as the state's paramount symbol of authority over its citizens.[17] Each of the units constituted a significant amount of land and contained a significant proportion of the neighborhood's population, so social control was extended to the wider neighborhood as well. Although the administrators of the local housing units were unable to establish the desired level of social control, their superiors emphasized its implementation as a priority. As the administrator of the Palm Court housing project in the Bronx stated:

> I get messages from my boss all the time saying, "I hear there has been some violence in your buildings, you need to put an end to this quickly. We need to establish that we are in total control." He says, "Remember, we're the government and that means maintaining total control" [mimicking his superiors]. So of course I make a consistent effort, but it's a tough job to do.[18]

The third objective of the administrators was to implement a policy consistent with the values of both the dominant society and the state. This involved attempting to make the residents understand that the apartments in which they lived were not their property. Although residents might pay rent for the apartments, the property was owned by the state and as such was merely on loan. Furthermore, under normal circumstances no one was entitled to live in the units unless they qualified. Administrators publicly expressed the view that people should not live in public housing forever and should be encouraged to find work and housing in the private sector. The comments of the administrator of the Gardenia Avenue Apartments in Brooklyn are representative:

> There is no reason why people should live their whole lives in projects. The only reason they do stay is because we don't kick them out! People are not entitled to public housing just because they don't have money. The government or the general public didn't intend to have this happen. No one believes this is the best for the country or the individual. And at minimum, if we give public housing to people, we need to have them pay for what the bare minimum expenses are to operate the apartment. Giving people free apartments is just giving the wrong value message, and they won't appreciate it or even try to move even if they do get some money.[19]

Nearly all the administrators believed that public housing should be similar to the type of aid administered after a natural disaster—that it should be given to those who qualified for aid temporarily. Ironically, a financial disaster was seen as fundamentally different from a natural disaster. A financial disaster was viewed as an illegitimate or, at best, quasi-legitimate reason for assistance because it was considered to be a crisis caused in part by the victims, while suffering caused by a natural disaster was believed to lie completely outside anyone's control. However, quite the opposite is true, as most of the financial disasters that poor people suffer are outside their control, and most of the suffering caused by natural disasters could have been prevented (or mitigated) by better planning or engineering.[20] Nonetheless, administrators and staff shared a general prejudice toward people who lived in public housing for a long time. If the original concept of public housing as a rent subsidy program for the poor had not been replaced with the belief that housing projects were a place to "dump the poor," such prejudice would have never developed. Despite it, the number of people who live in public housing for long periods has continued to increase since the 1950s.[21]

The administrators and staff who worked in public housing had strong ambivalent feelings toward the tenants. I found that significant numbers of them felt that most of the tenants should not be allowed residency because they did not try to find work, had salaries that disqualified them from residence, or acted disruptively and destructively. The comments of the administrator for the John C. Fremont Homes in Los Angeles are representative of these attitudes:

> I don't think all the people who are tenants should be allowed to stay in these units indefinitely. Yes, there are people living here who deserve and need to have subsidized housing, but too many of the tenants here are just taking advantage of a good thing. They have money to move into private-sector apartments, but they have become so dependent on rent-subsidized housing they will not go out and look for a job or housing in the private sector. It really is difficult to serve them without showing anger sometimes.[22]

A janitor in the Palm Court Apartments in the Bronx said:

> There are too many people who live here that don't deserve to live here. They act like animals. I mean real animals. I have to clean up urine in the elevators, and sometimes I have to clean real human shit! Can you believe it? Real shit! They can't even go to their apartments and take a piss, they got to act like animals and do it in the elevators or hallways. I even found bloody sanitary napkins in the hallway or elevator. Shit, I can't even tell you how bad it is inside a whole lot of these apartments. You really

wouldn't believe it! These people got no respect for the fact that they be getting subsidized housing. They getting housing that a lot of working people like me pay for, and then they treat it like this. It's not even theirs and they treat it like this. They need to get rid of a lot of people in these units.[23]

These views are consistent with the standard ideology and cultural values espoused by the state and the wider U.S. public. Administrators attempted to make residents more economically and socially responsible by discouraging antisystem attitudes, values, and behaviors.[24] As a worker in the Buckley Gardens day care center said, "These people should pay their rent, be clean, don't cause any disturbance, get a job, save their money, and leave public housing."[25]

The actions of the housing authority and the local administrators in these five complexes were intended to create and legitimize the housing project as a state institution. By establishing conditions that supported their objectives without regard for the lives and interests of the people living in the projects, the housing authority endeavored to insert state interests into the institutional order and structure of the projects and, by extension, the surrounding neighborhoods.[26]

STRUCTURING INSTITUTIONAL LIFE

The housing project has become a locus of competition between the state and the local community over its institutional character. Conflict occurs as the state filters resources into the housing project, asserting its own interests, while the local community tries to claim the housing project as its own to meet its needs.

By housing large numbers of low-income people, the five projects studied provided a constant supply of poor people to the neighborhoods and socialized them to their public and physical environments.[27] Issues related to these factors determined whether the housing project would be a state institution or a neighborhood institution.

A housing project is an environment dominated by financial and resource scarcity, and residents learn to understand its nature, their own place within it, and how to sustain themselves within it. Inhabitants' lives and beliefs are influenced and dominated by the struggle to obtain resources in an environment of resource uncertainty and a psychological commitment to cope with these harsh conditions. David, a twenty-one-year-old African American living in the John C. Fremont Homes of Los Angeles, expressed this commitment:

> Hey, don't laugh, man, there ain't going to be big changes in the projects.
> There ain't much help in life, so you or me, or everybody really, has got to
> scrap for what there is here, man; and definitely forget getting down if
> things get tough, 'cause that won't get you shit![28]

Similarly, Ana, a twenty-six-year-old Puerto Rican wife and mother of
two who worked as a cashier for a local home video store in the Bronx's
Monument neighborhood and lived in Buckley Gardens, stated:

> Things ain't going to change in a hundred years in this neighborhood. I just
> got to find a way to help me get my son to day care. After I get that done, I
> can work more hours at my job to help get some things we need. But you
> know, everybody is trying to do this too, so I just got to keep trying to get
> this done. People tell me that I won't be able to do this or that, but I ain't
> listening to them, I can't listen to that because it won't help me get what
> my family needs.[29]

All the residents of the five housing projects had to negotiate four
environmental elements: high population density, limited and contested
space, dirt, and noise. Although these elements are present in every big-
city environment, they assume a specific physical and social form when
they are found within the general condition of material scarcity.[30] Further, these physical elements and the cultural views associated with them
attained a level within housing projects that facilitated their becoming
neighborhood institutions.

In the past, when public housing was simply subsidized housing, a
significant number of families who lived in it had incomes well above the
poverty level. Over time, however, public housing has become more of
a housing repository for the poor. This change has made the subculture
of scarcity associated with the poor a dominant feature of public housing; indeed, the housing project has acted as a beacon of this culture (see
chapter 1). For this reason, several values and behaviors that are found
throughout the five neighborhoods will be discussed here.

High Density

The housing projects are high density both in the sense that the buildings contain a great many housing units in one location and in the sense
that many people live in each unit. Density is physical, since it is calculated on the basis of the number of people occupying a specific amount
of space, and most people who live in an urban area, rich or poor, experience its effects to some degree. Yet density experienced in poor areas
has sociological properties that set it apart from density in more afflu-

ent neighborhoods, and these properties are important for understanding the thoughts and behaviors of those who live in public housing.

In housing projects, the physical contours of density that have sociological implications within everyday interactions are influenced by the number of people who operate within the subculture of scarcity outlined in chapter 1 (i.e., social density). As studies have consistently shown, the poor have more children and begin parenthood at a younger age. Thus children and young people numerically dominate older generations in the projects.[31] As Kristin Luker states in her book on teenage pregnancy: "Although poverty alone is a strong predictor of early childbearing, teenage parents, compared with people who don't become parents as teens, are much more likely to have many other problems in their lives even before they get pregnant: they are more likely to come from a single-parent family, to have trouble in school, to have been held back a grade, to come from a home that has been broken by divorce or separation, and to live in bad neighborhoods."[32] However, what causes more pregnancies in poor neighborhoods is not a set of problems or young girls' poor decisions. Women of all ages had babies for similar reasons that emanated from a particular worldview associated with the subculture of scarcity.

Some pregnancies were simply the result of unprotected sex. Since sex was one of the few things that involved fun and pleasure without requiring up-front money, it appealed to those who generally had little money for entertainment. A conversation between Celia, a sixteen-year-old Puerto Rican living in Brooklyn's Gardenia Avenue Apartments, and a young man named Malcolm illustrates this:

Malcolm: I see you're going to have a baby. When is it due?
    Celia: Yeah, I am due in three and half months.
Malcolm: You're pretty young to be a mom.
    Celia: Yeah, well, it was sort of a surprise, you know. I mean it was and it wasn't.
Malcolm: You getting some help from your partner?
    Celia: No, he ain't got no job and he is still in school [high school].
Malcolm: Is the dad the boy I would see you with in the stairwells of the building late, late at night?
    Celia: Yeah [laughing], that's him. He's my boyfriend and we would just hang there listening to CDs.
Malcolm: Well, you must have done more than just listen to CDs.
    Celia: [Laughing] Well, yeah. We didn't have money to go to the movies or things, so we just hung out with friends in the hallway. It's quiet after midnight and we like it, but I didn't intend to

get pregnant. Then this night someone had left a bed mattress on the stairs, so we laid down and listened to music, kissed, and things happened.[33]

Some young women engaged in sexual behavior to gain freedom from fathers who were overbearing in their efforts to protect their daughters.[34] One of these was Connie, a seventeen-year-old Mexican American living in the Orchid Lane Apartments of Los Angeles. Connie was never allowed to go out on dates, had a rigidly enforced curfew, and was always questioned by her father about looks she received from men. In time, she became pregnant as a result of a secret relationship. Connie stated:

My dad worked until 7:30 at night, so that meant that I could go to the reading program after school and then walk home with Eddie. So one day we were walking home and he kissed me. We were near the park, so we went there and started to kiss. I don't know exactly why I did it, I just was so tired of my father watching me and threatening me about boys and sex that I just didn't want to feel trapped all the time. I didn't get pregnant that time, but about two months later I did.[35]

Other women became pregnant because they were pressured into having unprotected sex by partners who sought to control them.[36] One of these was Safron, a twenty-four-year-old Jamaican American woman living in Brooklyn's Gardenia Avenue Apartments. Her lover Maurice constantly worried that Safron was seeing someone else despite assurances from others that he had nothing to worry about. He felt that he needed to "give her a child to keep things in order." After Safron became pregnant, Maurice said:

Yeah, I went and gave Safron a child. I got started making love and told her to not worry about putting anything in [a diaphragm], 'cause I'd be careful. She was worried and stuff, but you know the emotions and stuff kind of won the moment. . . . Well, I feel better now 'cause I know there ain't no way she can be without me. The kid is mine no matter what.[37]

Still another factor in women's pregnancies was the belief held by some men that their ability to get women pregnant was a sign of social status.[38] Veronica, a nineteen-year-old Puerto Rican who lived in the Palm Court Apartments in the Bronx, became pregnant by her twenty-two-year-old boyfriend, Marcos. Marcos left her after she became pregnant. Shortly afterward he said:

I got me so many ladies pregnant that there ain't no guy in this building that comes anywhere close. Some guys like to think they get a woman pregnant and they some kind of big man or something. Shit, anybody can get somebody knocked up, it's how many that says something about how good you is.[39]

One girl, Leticia, a seventeen-year-old Mexican national living in the El Rey neighborhood of Los Angeles, was convinced by her boyfriend David that she should have his baby early on in case he died:

> David wanted to have a baby, but I didn't really think it was a good idea right now while we're in school. . . . Well, we're talking about it and he said that he would like to have a baby because he might get killed in a gang fight, or something to do with gangs, and wanted me to be the one to carry his name [to the future]. I felt, I don't know, so special, I guess, that I just wanted to give him his baby. [Her two friends nod in support.][40]

Two months after I recorded this conversation, Leticia became pregnant with David's baby. She finished high school, but at the end of my fieldwork David was in jail and Leticia was caring for their two children while working part time at a local church.

There were also women who wanted to become pregnant to express their desire for their lovers. The hope was that pregnancy would prompt reciprocal acts of public and private displays of affection and ultimately marriage.[41] Julia, a seventeen-year-old Dominican girl living in the Bronx's Palm Court Apartments, is representative:

> Mario says he's happy with his new job, and likes to see me, but he never really kisses or hugs me when we're not alone. I wish he would do that more 'cause it makes me feel special. . . . Maybe if I have his baby he'll know how much I love him and do the public thing [affection] 'cause I'll be the mother of his child. [Her friends nod in approval.][42]

Within the subculture of scarcity, males believed that women were always attempting to entrap them. Throughout the nine years of this study I observed some women who attempted to establish control over their lovers by becoming pregnant. In nearly all these cases the women were afraid either of being left for another woman or of being strung along for a long time with unfulfilled promises of marriage.[43] The number of women who wanted to get pregnant for these reasons may have been small, but it was just enough to keep the myth and fear of entrapment alive in the minds of males. The comments of Renee, a nineteen-year-old African American living in the Bronx's Elmway neighborhood, exemplify the belief held by some women that pregnancy leads to commitment:

> Tyrell is playing me. I just know it. He don't admit it, but I just know. I love him so much that I can't stand to think what it would be like if he'd

go. I know this sounds bad, but I'm going to have his baby and make him
[be] always with me. [Her friends tell her they think this a bad idea.][44]

About a month after this conversation Renee became pregnant with
Tyrell's baby. At the end of my fieldwork, Tyrell was in the army and
Renee was living with another man.

Another dynamic that played a role in young parenthood was the
belief that by giving parents the grandchildren they wanted, one would
receive attention, adoration, and respect in return. The case of Monique,
an eighteen-year-old Puerto Rican woman from the Gardenia Avenue
Apartments in Brooklyn, is representative:

> I wanted to get pregnant with José's child because I knew it would be such
> a perfect gift to my parents. They always wanted lots of grandchildren, and
> giving them one would make them so happy. I love them so much and I
> know they will be happy with me.[45]

Many might find Monique's beliefs a rationalization, or even delusional,
but this would not be entirely accurate. Parents often expressed their
desire for grandchildren so that they could see the family into the next
generation. Sergio, for example, a forty-six-year-old Mexican American
father of two girls and two boys, constantly spoke of his kids "giving him
and his wife grandchildren so that we have a chance to love our next generation." He also said that he "looked forward to the time that one of my
children will present me with them."[46] A year after Sergio said this, his
eighteen-year-old son had a baby girl with his seventeen-year-old wife.

Some young men and women thought that if they married and had children their parents and relatives would hold them in high esteem and view
them as mature, unlike other, single members of their families who were
just looking to have fun. Kelley and Todd, first-generation Jamaicans who
lived in the Gardenia Avenue Apartments in Brooklyn, felt this way. When
the eighteen-year-old Kelley became pregnant by twenty-year-old Todd,
they decided to get married because Todd, who worked part time for a
heating company, wanted to do what was "responsible." Todd's two
brothers were unmarried and unemployed, and both had fathered children without marrying the mothers, much to the disappointment of their
parents. Todd said, "I want my parents to think of me as being responsible, and marrying Kelley will do that."[47]

The final reason for the large population of small children is that
within the subculture of scarcity women are more inclined to bring their
pregnancies to term than to get an abortion. Elijah Anderson claimed
that this was because most women in the "black underclass" were from

families with fundamentalist religious backgrounds that held prolife philosophies.[48] Yet religious belief cannot be the full explanation, for in each of the five neighborhoods studied some middle- and working-class women who came from religious backgrounds with strong "prolife" philosophies did in fact terminate their pregnancies through abortion, whereas the poor women mostly did not.

Many of the women in the present study, especially those living in the projects, came from a position associated less with a specific religious doctrine than with a more fundamental understanding that it was their responsibility to give life a chance no matter how hard life's circumstances. Since most of the women themselves had experienced difficult lives and already took care of younger brothers and sisters, they could not see how taking care of their own child could dramatically change life for the worse.[49] The comments of Andrea, a seventeen-year-old Mexican American living in L.A.'s John C. Fremont Homes, are representative:

> I know that I'm young to have a baby, but I would not think of having an abortion. When I went to the hospital for a checkup one of the counselors mentioned the option of an abortion, but I said, "I have nothing against life." My life has been difficult, but I'm glad I'm here and living. Me and my sister help take care of my little brothers and sisters, so me taking care of my own ain't going to make things any worse for anybody.[50]

Most of the women who became pregnant had parents or grandparents who provided a home for them and the baby and/or day care for their child while they were working. This safety net internal to the subculture of scarcity produced three significant results. First of all, it gave support to the worldview that bringing a baby to term was a natural and rewarding part of the life cycle. The comments of Loretta, a seventeen-year-old African American living in the Bronx's Buckley Gardens, are representative:

> When I first told my mother I was pregnant, I thought she would kick me out of the house, but she just looked disappointed and kinda shocked. . . . After she sat down and said that my grandma and her would watch the baby while I was at work, it just, I don't know, just made me feel like having the baby and keepin' it was the right thing.[51]

Second, it contributed to population density within the project units, which in turn influenced social behavior in both the projects and other parts of neighborhood life. Finally, it helped to produce a population in which children, who were the most vulnerable to all of life's forces, outnumbered adults, who because of their disadvantaged position in the labor market were the least able to support them economically.[52]

The density of people operating within the subculture of scarcity was what separated the housing project's environment from other parts of the neighborhood. Poor neighborhoods more generally have a small but sufficient number of working-class and middle-class residents to expose the other residents to a different set of values and norms associated with sex, marriage, and children. Only in the projects does the subculture of scarcity view of sex, marriage, and children dominate.

Physical density in housing projects also increased because relatives, most of whom were either elderly or unable to care for their children without help, often came to live with residents during times of economic difficulty. This further crowded the existing physical and social space of the projects.[53]

In places with a high population density, people are forced to interact with each other, thus affecting cultural density as well. There was little opportunity to isolate oneself from family, friends or neighbors, since both private and public space was used nearly all the time, so strategies were developed and used to minimize conflict. This required building a knowledge base about other groups, associations, bonds, and a sense of neighborhood identity.[54]

At its most fundamental level, the social implications of population density in the projects meant that normally two to three people lived in each bedroom. Since all the apartments in the five projects studied had only one bath, a small kitchen area, and a small living room, an enormous demand for and use of utilities, appliances, and common space put a great deal of strain on all three of these necessities, causing consistent deterioration, breakdown, and inconvenience. Thus people living in high-density environments had to learn to tolerate being consistently inconvenienced by circumstances such as broken elevators, too little space for family meals, and unavailable bathrooms.

Limited and Contested Space

During construction, the spatial dimensions of the projects were determined by the housing authority's need to keep building and maintenance costs within budgetary limits.[55] Thus the housing project's design reflected the institutional interests of the state more than the needs of the poor.[56] While the state's social meaning for the housing projects could be easily seen in their physical layout, the social meaning that the tenants assigned to them was less readily seen but no less influential.

The housing projects that I studied were of two general designs: vertical apartment buildings and horizontal row houses. Each contained two-, three-, and four-bedroom apartments that had a living room, a bathroom, and a kitchen, all designed to compress space. Because the majority of families that lived in the projects had two or more children, there was great demand for and competition over the limited space that existed. Therefore, nearly all space was considered open and legitimate to claim as one's own to use for a specific amount of time.

Since kitchens in the apartments were small, cooking began at a time when there would not be a constant stream of people (mostly children) coming in and out. Also because of a lack of space, dinner was typically informal and eaten in shifts rather than together as a family. Mothers adapted by cooking dishes that could be reheated and served whenever family members were both willing and able to sit down to eat.

The bathroom was also a hotly contested space. Rare was the opportunity to take a leisurely shower or bath or to have all the time wanted for grooming. In fact, simply going to the bathroom to relieve oneself required working into others' demands for the same space.

Finally, there was constant competition over the use of the living room. This was a source of constant bickering and occasional physical fights. Thus the living room, meant to be the main room for leisure, was anything but, making rest problematic for everyone. The comments of Donald, a fifteen-year-old African American living in Buckley Gardens in the Bronx, exemplify one of the many types of competitions that occurred over living room space:

> Jesus, did you see that shit? Justin and Kirk [his two smaller brothers, one six and the other seven], will you sit your asses down or go to the other room?! I can't see the damn game [he is trying to watch a football game] 'cause you keep standing up and talking. This is the reason Dad is at the bar, because there is no way to watch anything in this fucking house, ever![57]

An example of how parents dealt with competition over space and noise levels involved Raphael, a thirty-nine-year-old Puerto Rican car mechanic living in Brooklyn's Gardenia Avenue Apartments. Raphael decided that he was too tired after work to endure his four children fighting about what television program to watch or whether the television should even be turned on, so he went out and bought a television, placed it in his bedroom, and retreated there after dinner to relax. He always closed the door, but when he left it open just a crack, other family members knew that they could enter. When the door was completely closed, it signaled that no one was to disturb him and his wife. This tactic was an effective means to partially isolate Raphael and his wife from the trials and tribulations associated with space usage.

The scarcity of space permeated other social areas, reinforcing the physicality of life in poor neighborhoods and the culture that emerged from it. The lack of space had a profound impact on the individual's sense of privacy. People need time alone to rest, relax, reflect, develop secrets, or grapple with problems, but privacy was a rare commodity in the projects. Any need for privacy had to be contested with others. When two family members wanted to be alone and the only place available was the bedroom they shared, conflict could occur.

Intimate feelings associated with modesty were also challenged by the spatial environment in the housing projects. People constantly walked in on others in bathrooms and/or bedrooms. Therefore, dressing and using the bathroom had to be done quickly to avoid exposure, but discomfort was still often experienced.

Spatial arrangements also made it difficult to keep sexual activity private. Since rooms were arranged immediately next to each other, it was common to hear people engaged in sex. Thus it was necessary to deal with the question of behavioral appropriateness. In most cases, couples having sex considered decency to have been preserved if no one actually saw them engage in the act, and those who overheard integrated it into their sense of the ordinary, so that they too maintained their sense of decency. A conversation between Paco and Dina, both of whom were in their late twenties and lived in the Orchid Lane Apartments of Los Angeles, is representative:

> *Dina*: Do you think we were too loud for the kids? I think it was all right, 'cause we did have the door shut.
>
> *Paco*: Well, it's not like they saw us or anything, so it's okay. Everything will be fine.[58]

A conversation between two eight-year-old friends who lived in the Bronx's Palm Court Apartments, Darius, who was African American, and Dominic, who was Puerto Rican, illustrates the same principle. Both were playing at the kitchen table:

> *Darius*: What's going on in the bedroom? What's that noise?
>
> *Dominic*: Oh, that's my sister and her husband loving each other. They do that sometimes.
>
> *Darius*: Oh, okay.[59]

Maintaining decency is a very important personal attribute of both men and women because it involves morals, values, and identity. Modesty among the poor in the housing projects had broad parameters, allowing others to enter individual space in a way that avoided compromising people's sense of personal decency. This preserved a sense of self that incorporated both body parts and bodily functions into the "normal," making use of them in jokes and everyday conversation and thus changing the boundaries of what in the mainstream middle-class society would be considered socially taboo. For example, the constant use of *fuck* in the vernacular of the projects and neighborhoods made the use of a word for a bodily act commonplace in everyday life. In poor neighborhoods, unlike the general culture, which has been influenced more by the middle class, the word *fuck* is not crude, vulgar, or gross. It can refer to something bad or something good and can even be a mere conjunction to connect clauses in a sentence. Thus language, identity, and behavior were directly influenced by issues of modesty and decency that were in turn created by the compact spatial arrangements of the projects.

Spatial arrangements in the housing units also affected the residents' personal sense of freedom. This is clearly seen in many teenagers' and young adults' practice of putting old mattresses in the stairwells of the buildings in order to have sex late at night. Sometimes, however, if mattresses were left in the stairwells, tenants frustrated by the inconvenience of a blocked stairwell, or fearful of a blocked fire escape, would call the housing authority office to have them removed. If this was not done quickly, someone would light a fire to them. The fire department would then have to come and put out the fire before it threatened the entire structure. Then the fire department would formally instruct the housing authority to quickly remove debris from public spaces. This would be done for a month or two, but then the janitors would become more relaxed about, or fatigued with, picking it up in a timely fashion.

A further infringement on personal freedom arose because the scarcity of money and material possessions in poor neighborhoods encouraged the development of a large group of social predators. Consequently, residents were vigilant in public spaces both inside and outside the buildings. During some portion of the day, they could walk or sit in the common areas of the projects with little risk of being physically harmed. At other times, particularly early morning, late afternoon, and night, these same areas could be extremely dangerous.[60] Yet although the news media and some researchers have emphasized the restriction of residents' sense of freedom by the threat of physical violence, the organization of space and its concomitant social relations actually restricted residents' sense of freedom far more than the fear of harm did.

Dirt

One physical condition that permeates the entire social environment of the poor is dirt. The most important reason for the accumulation of dirt in housing projects was that population density overtaxed the space available and that the vast majority of people using space were children. Because space was so limited, children would play in all the rooms of the house, which made it impossible for parents to isolate dirt in one or two rooms. Furthermore, in the high-rise units, it was more difficult for parents to let their children play outside, so the children were confined to the apartment for most of the day, resulting in large amounts of dirt. Unfortunately, parents who lived in the horizontal units were not able to avoid this problem either, since after their children returned home from outdoor play they brought along large quantities of dirt. Thus the population density associated with the physical designs of the public housing units facilitated the accumulation of dirt, especially by children.

In the public areas of the projects, people often engaged in acts of bodily convenience that created dirt and filth. In one of the high-rise projects in New York, residents constantly urinated in the elevators, forcing others using the elevators to stand in urine. Although people in the projects often called those responsible "pigs," there was no intention to create filth; rather, the actions arose from various circumstances. Some people were simply too lazy to go upstairs to their apartments and use the toilet. Other people socializing in the lobby used the elevators because they did not live in the building and have access to an apartment. Finally, young people socializing in the stairwells used the elevator to urinate because if they returned to their apartments their parents would not allow them to leave again.

People were faced with the option of going back to their apartments, thereby interrupting the privacy they had just managed to establish, or using a public place. Once the decision was made not to go to the apartment, the elevator became a logical choice. It had a door that gave privacy to maintain modesty, and it was not any specific person's private domain but the domain of the housing authority (the state). The comments of Josh, a nineteen-year-old African American living in Buckley Gardens in the Bronx's Monument neighborhood, represent this point of view:

I got to go and make a quick pit stop. . . . I'm just going over here. [Some-
one asks if he used the elevator] . . . Yeah, I did use the elevator! Hey,
what's the problem? It's not like I went into someone's apartment and
watered the floor. Now that would be disgusting! I just used the housing
people's [housing authority's] fucking space! [Everyone laughs, and then a
new conversation starts.][61]

Thus the possibility of standing in urine became a part of people's common experience. Many researchers using disorganization theory would
have seen this and used it as evidence that the area had become socially
disorganized, but such a conclusion would have been totally inaccurate
because the building and the neighborhood were very organized.

The use of the elevator as a urinal is a prime example of how spatial
arrangements influenced behavior. Since space was in short supply, the
opportunity to use private places for private acts was extremely limited.
Residents then needed to use public places such as stairwells, lobbies, the
commons, fronts of buildings, or parking lots to gain privacy and freedom. Thus social life in the projects, much of which occurred for people of other social classes in the home, was transferred to public areas.

Dirt was also caused by people who considered the area a dump. The
comments of Reneirio, a twenty-one-year-old Mexican living in the
Orchid Lane Apartments of Los Angeles, are typical. After drinking a
beer in the common area of the project, he threw the bottle off to the
side under a small tree. When someone said he ought to wait and throw
all his bottles in the trash, he said:

Fuck it! Look at this shit here. Look at all this shit from the cars driving by.
I ain't waiting to throw this [the bottle] away, my fuckin' bottle is not going
to make a fuckin' difference. This is a shithole in a shitty place, an empty
bottle ain't going to change that. Pass me another one. [Everyone laughs.][62]

While dirt was a part of life in the projects, adults and young people
made a good deal of effort to keep themselves and those closest to them
clean (i.e., their bodies and their clothing) because this was one area individuals could reasonably control.[63] Further, they were continuously trying to keep the bathtub (or shower), sink, and toilet clean, as well as the
kitchen sink and stovetop. Although cleaning efforts were not always
completely successful, cleanliness was valued among the residents.

The same can be said about vermin and insects, which existed in all
of the projects studied. Residents took steps to eliminate them from
foodstuffs, eating places, and the bathroom. They set traps, and they
called the housing authority to spray pesticide. Still, residents knew that

pests would remain a part of their lives and had to psychologically accommodate themselves to their presence.

In middle-class areas dirt does not assume a significant social presence. It still exists, but it can be more easily eliminated. Middle-class families have fewer children and more space in which to live, both of which, as shown previously, are factors in the accumulation and elimination of dirt. Further, they often can afford to hire people to clean their homes or apartments. In contrast, although poor families in the projects worked to eliminate socially defined pollution, they had to learn to live with it as well. Thus, in the projects, dirt maintained a distinct social presence that affected many aspects of life.

Dirt reinforced the subculture of scarcity in these neighborhoods by encouraging and strengthening a local understanding of the world. The poor, mainly through TV and radio, were well aware of the middle class's views on cleanliness and knew that they, their families, and their community did not compare favorably to the middle-class standard. Yet they also understood that their living conditions were more difficult. The result was a sense of shared group experience, unique to them, that became an important ingredient of their subculture.[64]

Noise

The final physical feature of housing projects that residents had to negotiate was noise. Outside noise came from the constant police, fire, and ambulance sirens in all the neighborhoods studied, especially in the evening, when there was more activity on the street. In Los Angeles, there was the constant sound of police helicopters on patrol or in pursuit of a suspect. Because the projects contained and attracted so many people doing so many things, they saw a great deal of police, fire, and ambulance activity.

In addition, all the projects studied were close to major thoroughfares. Thus everyone was exposed to the constant monotonic buzz of tires and engines and the occasional sounds of tires squealing to a stop, engines accelerating, and the crunch of metal in accidents. There was also constant noise from car alarms.[65]

Finally, people were always talking, laughing, and yelling in the common areas of the building, and car horns were constantly beeping to signal arrivals. The continual noise could be irritating, but there were few, if any, complaints from the residents, who were capable of resting, sleeping, or listening to other things through noisy episodes.

Although noises generated inside the apartments and hallways of the buildings were mostly the same as those heard outside, the proximity made them more forceful: children crying and jumping on furniture; collective sounds from screaming, laughing, running, objects being thrown, and musical instruments being played; adults arguing; radios, televisions, and stereos playing loudly; and gunfire. Of all these, gunfire caused the least noise pollution because it was not long-lived or very loud. In the nine years of my research I heard and recorded some sixty-three shootings; only four involved shotguns that made a significant amount of noise.

In each of the buildings that I inhabited, the most disruptive noise came from the playing of musical instruments in adjoining apartments or those in close proximity. In a typical case, whoever shared a wall with my bedroom in the adjoining apartment would play the bongo drums from ten or eleven in the evening until one or two in the morning, four to five days a week. Noise from radios or stereo CD players with sound-enhancing devices ("woofers") was also present, making two of the Los Angeles and one of the Brooklyn apartments in which I was staying seem to vibrate. Despite the noise, people did not complain for reasons offered below.

Most of the time, noise in the projects was generated by a number of sources at the same time, creating three general reactions. First, people tried to reduce the level of noise they had to endure by going to a room as far from the source as possible. Then they would generally turn on another noise-generating machine like the television, radio, or stereo to a level that would drown out unwanted sounds. Others plugged in earphones to radios or stereo CD players to shut out the unwanted noise. All of these efforts buffered them from the outside world.

As a second response, people talked loudly. Because there was so much noise, it was difficult for people to know how loudly they should speak in order to be heard. Some people spoke loudly to aggressively become involved in conversation. At other times, people were just unaware of how loudly they were speaking, as they were so accustomed to speaking over all the surrounding noise.

Finally, people just left the premises of the housing project altogether. They would go to a park, an alley, or a local business that also functioned as a neighborhood institution, such as a local mom-and-pop store, a barbershop, or a church. The comments of Dorothy, a fifty-eight-year-old Dominican who had lived in the Palm Court Apartments all of her adult life, are representative of this response to noise overload:

Well, when the noise in the building gets too loud or just gets to me, I go to
the grocery store. There I can just sit for a while, and if I want to talk to
the owner I can, or I can just sit and be quiet. You have to pick the right
time because the store can get noisy too, but it is one of the places that I
can go. . . . You can also go to the church [local Catholic church], but it is
not always open because of vandalism.[66]

People in the projects were unable to control the noise level that they
were forced to endure. They could not ask neighbors or other people in
the building to lower their levels of noise because it would be seen as an
effort to curtail the freedom of others. Since so much individual freedom
was compromised by the living arrangement of the projects, attempts to
further limit freedom, even by other residents seeking their own rights
to peace, were met with extreme resistance and hostility. When people
called the police to reduce the noise generated by other residents of the
building, some form of retaliation would follow. Therefore, most of the
residents simply learned to endure the noise.

Most people experienced some degree of sleep deprivation, anxiety,
frustration, and anger because of noise. Noise also forced individuals to
reach inward for strength in an effort to mentally isolate themselves from
the intrusions, inconveniences, and discomforts of daily life and to become
more aggressive in establishing control over other aspects of their lives.

Thus, for residents of the projects, going inward and isolating were
not symptomatic of malaise or clinical depression originating from the
stresses of city life, as Georg Simmel and a number of Chicago School
sociologists suggested.[67] Rather, they were strategies using personal
strength to control the aspects of life that residents could manage in their
social environment.

THE DEVELOPMENT OF A WORLDVIEW

The conditions of scarcity that structured the lives of the people in the
housing projects gave rise to, or reinforced, a worldview that provided
an understanding of both the nature of life and the individual's place
within this universe. Since the material conditions in both the housing
project and neighborhood were dominated by scarcity, scarcity spawned
and maintained the basic value orientations of the neighborhood. The
particular worldview that dominated the neighborhood had five fundamental premises.

The first premise was that life was characterized by a scarcity that one
had to manage in order to survive and make life worth living.[68] The

comments of Sharon, a fifteen-year-old Jamaican American living in the Gardenia Avenue Apartments in Brooklyn, reflect this basic premise:

> Life ain't got enough for everybody. Some people will have a lot and some like us won't. It's just the way the world is, 'cause there ain't enough to go around for everyone.[69]

The second premise was that life had been unfair. The residents of the projects and neighborhoods thought of themselves as being unlucky enough to have been born into poverty. It was simply a function of chance. Supporting this notion was the belief that they were as smart as others in society who had money but that they did not have the same chances. The comments of twenty-year-old Ricardo, a Mexican American who worked part time at a laundry and lived in the Orchid Lane Apartments in Los Angeles, represent this perspective:

> Shit, I ain't any different than anybody else. I'm in this shitty place [the housing project] 'cause I never got a chance. If I'd been born to parents with money I'd be living in a good section of town with money too. . . . They [the people who have money] ain't no smarter than me, but just like I said, they got lucky 'cause they gots parents who gots money. So of course they gots better chances.[70]

The third premise was that life would remain unfair, there was little chance of escaping present circumstances, and individuals had to learn to deal with the unfairness of life. The comments of Tati, a twenty-six-year-old Puerto Rican waitress who lived with her family and son in Buckley Gardens, typify this view:

> Yeah, there been some real tough times for me and my son. There were lots of tough times for my parents too. We had such a big family that my folks couldn't help us. You know, I had to help them with translations and stuff. Life ain't really that fair to everyone, and that ain't going to change either, but that's what I got, so I got to work with that.[71]

The fourth premise was that everyone in society cheated. The rich cheated to remain rich, the middle class cheated to promote their interests and maintain their lifestyles, and the housing authority (the state) cheated to promote its interests without regard for the tenants. So the poor too had to cheat to get by in life. Life was a "hustle" for everyone. The comments of Carl, a thirty-six-year-old African American who worked part time as a laborer for a moving company in New York and lived with his wife, three sons, and mother in the Palm Court Apartments in the Bronx, are representative of this view:

The newspapers and television is always talking about how the people on welfare do this or that to cheats the government. Shit, that's a joke! Everybody cheats, and everybody knows it. Them rich peoples cheats all the time. They cheat on taxes and a whole lot of other things. Hell, I can't cheat on taxes, I ain't in no position to do it—I don't make enough. But in them areas that I can do some cheatin' too, I do. Hey, the hustle is what life is. You know?[72]

The last premise was the belief that social disaster was a constant part of life. The comments of Paloma, a twenty-four-year-old Mexican housekeeper who lived with her husband and three children in the John C. Fremont Homes in Los Angeles, express this belief:

One of my nephews got meningitis and is very sick in the hospital. My sister had to quit working with me to stay with him, and so I can only do about half of the houses I usually clean when she's helping. We both need the money, so this really hurts both of us. This week I had to cut back on my kids' school lunch because I couldn't afford to buy all that I usually do. If this keeps up, my husband and I will have some problem paying rent. Last month we just got some money together to get a new television, and then my husband got in a car accident and we had to take the television back. So no matter what, there's always going to be big problems in life.[73]

The significance of this worldview is that it emerged from experiences shaped by the condition of material scarcity, and it helped give the poor an understanding and explanation of (1) why *they* had to live and deal with this condition rather than others, (2) the natural order of life in this condition, and (3) how to manage living the lives that they were given. Their worldview was neither self-defeatist nor responsible for keeping them poor; rather, it provided the framework for a set of values and contributed to a local subculture that would establish the housing project as a neighborhood institution.[74]

The moral principles that prevailed in the projects, and the neighborhoods at large, centered on the concept of "responsibility." Contrary to all that has been written on the lack of personal responsibility as the root cause of the difficulties of moving out of poverty,[75] responsibility and the subculture that defines and supports it are precisely what helped shape the housing project as a neighborhood institution.

As described in chapter 1, the responsibility-centered morality in the five neighborhoods had two sets of value orientations ("maximizing security" and "maximizing excitement"). These value orientations could be seen within the housing projects in the individual's attitudes toward the ideas of "home" and "tenancy."

For those who adopted the security-maximizing value orientation, "home" was a haven from the trials of work and the street, a place to rest and seek comfort, and a shelter from the demands of social life. Others adopted the excitement-maximizing value orientation, in which "home" was a place to sleep or hang one's hat for a short time before going out to find amusement and leisure at another person's home, a movie theater, a bar, a restaurant, a pool hall, a nightclub, the street, a store, or a barbershop or beauty salon. In this orientation, home was merely a shelter from the physical elements.

The state's idea of tenancy incorporated the belief that all tenants in the projects should be appreciative of their publicly subsidized housing. Those with a security-maximizing value orientation partly believed that there was a benefit in not having to face all the uncertainties and costs associated with the private housing market. However, they also believed that the housing authority was fortunate to have tenants who followed the rules and paid their rents on time, especially when so many people would do neither.

Residents who held an excitement-maximizing value orientation viewed their apartments simply as a place of shelter from the physical elements. Further, they thought them to be in such poor condition that the housing authority was lucky to have anyone live in them at all. The comments of Jerry, a twenty-two-year-old African American living in the Gardenia Avenue Apartments in Brooklyn, are representative of this belief:

> They [housing authority] heard that I got this job, now they want me to pay more rent. Look at this place, it's a shithole of a place, and them people think I should pay more rent. They got to be out of their motherfuckin' minds! This place ain't worth nobody paying nothin'. They should be paying us motherfuckers to live in this shit.[76]

The housing authority determined a reasonable rent based on the income of each tenant. Yet the tenants were rarely honest in declaring their incomes or in divulging who lived in the apartments. Those who shared the excitement-maximizing value orientation viewed lying about their incomes as simply doing what everybody, including the state, did all the time. They nearly always mentioned the housing authority's failure to honor promises to repair specific objects by a particular time. Further, they did not see lying about their incomes as morally wrong because if they divulged their real incomes, they could be taken advantage of by state workers, whom they viewed as corrupt. The comments of forty-year-old Emmett, a Barbadian American who lived in the Bronx's Buckley Gardens, represent this line of thinking:

> If I was to tell the housing authority that I made some extra monies, they'd just take the money even though they don't need nothing extra to run the building. Then they'd just deprive me of my little extra for nothing but their own good time. Them people is corrupt, man.[77]

Those who adopted the security-maximizing value orientation also did not believe it was immoral to keep information from the housing authority about all the income in the home. Most thought that paying their rent on time satisfied their obligations to the state. Further, both groups doubted that the state would help them during difficult times, so they considered it irresponsible to reveal all of one's earnings, since any extra income could be used as needed in the future.

The people who assumed the security-maximizing value orientation rarely told the authorities who was living in the apartments, especially when it came to relatives. Divulging this information was viewed as morally irresponsible to one's family, whose interests had to be protected above all else. The obvious clash of rights between the state and the residents led to a disregard of the state's "ideals" and property and support for those ideals that were locally born.

PERSONAL IDENTITY IN THE FORMATION OF A LOCAL INSTITUTION

As discussed in chapter 1, for an establishment to become a local institution it must develop a set of identities that are recognized by participants while on the premises and are identified with the place itself. As these identities assume more formal roles, they become embedded in the establishment, thereby strengthening institutionalization and legitimacy in the neighborhood.

The social identities that emerged from the housing project were forged out of the conditions of scarcity, physical arrangements, and value orientations. Identity formation began with a set of behavioral traits that arose from the physical conditions in the housing project. These traits assumed psychological significance as individuals incrementally acquired attributes in an effort to construct their desired identities. In the vast majority of cases, chosen identities were linked to an image that conferred individuality, respect, and status. Most importantly, the individual identities of project residents played a role in making the project a local institution by integrating the individual's identity with that of the place and highlighting that an individual from such a living environment not only could be worth something but could be special in his or her own right.

Take Devon, a fifteen-year-old African American from Buckley Gardens in the Bronx. Devon not only played baseball very well but also read a lot about baseball and knew the statistics of players in the professional leagues. While he was having a conversation about baseball in the Town Barbershop with two friends, Stacy and Bill, he recited some statistics. Larry, another patron in the barbershop, overheard and said, "Hey, you know a lot about baseball, do you know who had the most pitching saves last year in the National League?" When Devon gave him the answer, Larry said, "Hey, you're like a library!" Stacy and Bill then said, "Yeah, he is like a library, we going to call him 'Bray!'"[78] They began referring to Devon as "Bray" in public, and explained the nickname to friends and acquaintances. Devon himself embraced the image and nurtured his identity by continuing to memorize facts. Devon later went on to play professionally for the Philadelphia Phillies, but he was still known as a kid from the projects and "Bray" in the neighborhood.

Perhaps the most important personal identity within the various housing projects was the person or persons identified as the institutional caretakers of the building.[79] As noted in chapter 1, caretakers are essential to the daily operation and survival of any institution. The caretakers acted as the institution's guidance system that welcomed and integrated individuals while regulating institutional life. The caretakers in the projects I studied were a varied group. Some presented themselves as empathetic to the tenants' needs by lending small amounts of cash. Others had connections to people who had money or political power and could help tenants with their needs. Still others, particularly among the various Latino groups, were thought to have healing powers, such as the folk medicine practitioners, who were referred to as *curanderos*.[80] Finally, some were leaders of a unit's self-help governance building committee (the equivalent of a block club).

Caretakers were never anonymous.[81] The residents of the buildings recognized the caretakers as people who gave of themselves in order to help others in the building and/or the entire complex. In return for their caretaking, residents offered them services such as providing meals, driving, helping fix their cars, helping remodel their apartments, and protecting them from predators.

A variety of identities were created within the projects, and through the daily interactions of the residents these identities filled a substantive social area, such as athletics, sexuality, comedy, music, or business. Individual identities were assigned a position within the status system of the substantive area (e.g., terrific, good, or fair basketball player) as well as within the housing units (e.g., respected, liked, and appreciated to different degrees). These personal identities were important in that they were created by the local environment rather than the outside community.[82] They gave the housing project an internal identification and status system that was not dependent on that of the general society, allowing the local residents to avoid issues concerning personal inadequacy.[83] The interaction of these identities with the social orders of other neighborhood institutions forms the substance of the local social system.[84]

SOME CLOSING REMARKS

The housing project has taken the place of the tenement as the major physical presence in most persistently poor neighborhoods in America. Because it houses the majority of the population in most persistently poor areas, it is the major player in the social life of these neighborhoods. How important it is and in what ways it becomes vital to the social structure and life of the neighborhood depend on the content of its institutional character. Competing with the residents of the housing project and the local community over its institutional character is the state. The state struggles to carry out its policies of isolating the poor in one geographic area, minimizing costs, and creating new behavior patterns that are more in line with those found among the middle class,[85] and the competition over the institutional character of the projects creates a constant tension between the state and the neighborhood. As we shall see in the next chapter, this tension sets the stage for understanding the dynamics of change and maintenance within both the housing projects and the neighborhoods of which they are a part.

CHAPTER 3

A Living Refuge

Social Change and
Preservation in the Housing Project

They passed and day grew, and with pitiless faces
The dull houses stared on the prey they had trapped;
'Twas as though they had slain all the fair morning places
Where in love and in leisure our joyance had happed.
> William Morris, *The Pilgrims of Hope* (1885–86)

The housing project was created by the state to subsidize disadvantaged families in securing adequate shelter. Despite state efforts to imbue tenants with state values, interests, and policies, the five housing projects in the present study (see table 2, p. 56) remained neighborhood institutions. Thus the most important dynamics of change and preservation are those that influence the character of the housing project as a local institution. This chapter focuses on the factors that affect change and preservation of social life in the housing projects.

SOURCES OF CHANGE

Social change occurred as a result of both deliberate acts and unintended consequences from agents outside and inside the various housing projects. Four factors most significantly led to change in the five housing projects: (1) labor market changes; (2) ethnic changes; (3) changes in the generational structure; and (4) groups involved in the illicit economy. Although these factors do not represent an exhaustive list, they were particularly influential in either the strengthening and development or the weakening and demise of the housing projects as neighborhood institutions.

Labor Market Changes

During the 1990s the country experienced impressive economic growth, but like most poor neighborhoods the five neighborhoods in this study were still dealing with the economic decline in production jobs that had affected the country in the 1980s.[1] Thus labor market changes significantly influenced the social composition of the various housing projects studied. As the local job opportunities in production declined, many people who held these jobs found themselves unemployed, underemployed, and/or without social and medical benefits. A significant number of these individuals were forced to move into the projects to compensate for income lost, or new expenses incurred from their loss of benefits. In addition, some people already living in the housing projects lost their jobs as a result of employers' efforts to reduce labor costs. Most of those affected were men working primarily, although not exclusively, in traditional blue-collar manufacturing occupations.[2] Many of these people were forced to find work in the secondary labor market.[3]

In New York and Los Angeles the decline in job opportunities increased demand for the already inadequate supply of low-income housing that was adequately maintained.[4] As labor market conditions worsened from 1991 to 1994 and the underemployed increasingly encountered difficulty in paying rent and maintaining their apartments and homes, landlords were faced with rising costs in upkeep and thus were unable to adequately maintain their property. Given that it was very difficult to evict a family with children even if they were delinquent in paying rent or maintaining the premises, landlords, especially in the Bronx and Brooklyn, found it more profitable to have their buildings burned down and to collect the insurance rather than continue to rent. The net result was a dwindling supply of minimally maintained housing (within the local building code) for the poor, making public housing an attractive alternative.[5] The comments of Ken and Claudia are representative of those who found public housing more attractive than what they found in the private market. Ken, a thirty-eight-year-old African American who had formerly worked on the production line of a metal can company but now worked as a doorman at a Manhattan office building, lived in the Bronx's Buckley Gardens with his wife and three children:

> Man oh man, I am so glad to finally get into these apartments because there ain't much I could afford in regular [private] housing. And the stuff I could afford was just so dangerous for my kids—they got rats and shit like

paint chips and stuff. I feel good [fortunate] to have gotten into these apartments [Buckley Gardens], to tell you the truth.[6]

Claudia, a twenty-seven-year-old Mexican American living in the John C. Fremont Homes in Los Angeles with her husband and five children, similarly stated:

My husband tried to find a house we could afford, but the ones he found were very bad and more expensive than we could pay. He was able to get into this public housing, but they told him that there was mostly blacks [African Americans] that lived there. They don't like us [Mexicans] and so they pick on us, but we thought it was better to put up with that than risk a fire in the houses we been living in, and so I'm glad we moved here.[7]

At the same time, changes in the labor market were bringing more low-level service jobs to Los Angeles and New York.[8] This attracted immigrants and migrants from areas that were experiencing even greater economic hardship. Securing public housing was a priority for them because it was less expensive than the private sector. They were also ideal candidates for the housing authorities because immigrants had a history of consistently paying their rent. This resulted in an observed rise in immigrant occupancy in the public housing complexes of both cities. Ironically, whereas the new changes in the economy meant increased hardship for many low-income families, for immigrants they meant mostly increased opportunities in available public housing.[9]

These changes in the labor and housing markets produced a larger demand for public housing because public housing appeared to be a shelter from the storm experienced in the private sector.[10] The greater demand for public housing produced some important changes. First, the projects filled to capacity, and as they did the number of people capable of contributing and becoming leaders there increased, strengthening the projects as neighborhood institutions. Second, the socioeconomic composition of the buildings' populations changed. In most accounts of poor areas, only one segment of society is represented—a group designated as poor. However, the population of the neighborhoods that most other researchers have simply considered and labeled "poor" or low income is actually composed of several stratified and identifiable groups: the traditional middle and working classes, the working poor, and the idle poor.[11] During the nine years of this study, the numbers of idle and working poor in the buildings of the Bronx increased, while the numbers having traditional working-class jobs decreased.[12] Brooklyn's Eagleton neighborhood experienced a somewhat different pattern. The numbers of the idle and working poor remained roughly the same while those of the working class increased slightly because of increases in Caribbean immigrants who had been able through the use of ethnic networks to secure working-class jobs.[13] In each of the Los Angeles neighborhoods, the housing project studied saw a steady increase in the numbers of the working and idle poor and a decrease in the numbers of working-class residents.[14] These observations caution against concluding that a low-income population consists entirely of those denominated as "poor." Particularly when the units appear to be the home of one ethnic group such as African Americans, the tendency is to merge ethnicity with poverty and to conclude, for example, that a particular housing project is composed solely of African American poor. Such a conclusion would underestimate the importance of the socioeconomic divisions within public housing, as well as the small but significant changes that may occur in projects' socioeconomic composition. In fact, a change in housing projects' demographic substrata has particular significance for the larger social structure of the neighborhood because it affects the internal divisions within a fragmented neighborhood or signals a structural change from a contested to a fragmented neighborhood, or both. (See chapter 1 for a description of these types of neighborhoods.)

Ethnic Changes

The ethnic composition of the various housing projects shifted over the nine-year research period. Not only did new ethnic groups emerge, but within ethnic groups the proportions of subgroups would change: for example, residents of Mexican descent born in the United States versus those born in Mexico, Puerto Ricans born in the United States versus those born in Puerto Rico, and residents of African descent born in the United States versus those born in other locales such as Jamaica, Barbados, the Bahamas, Trinidad, and Haiti.[15] To many outside observers the housing projects' populations might continue to be associated with the colors "brown" or "black." However, to the people living in the units, significant ethnic change was occurring that established the conditions for a contested or fragmented type of neighborhood.[16] It should be remembered from chapter 1 that changes in the population size of an ethnic group can create a contested neighborhood or change a contested neighborhood to a fragmented one. The comment of Humberto, a forty-seven-year-old Puerto Rican living in the Bronx's Buckley Gardens, was representative of the changes taking place in the units:

There's so many more blacks moving in this building it's just going to make everything worse, you watch! They just are bad news, so you'll see there's gonna be more trouble here, especially between us and them.[17]

Three months after he said this there was trouble and the neighborhood began to be contested.

Generational Changes

Some units saw slow but steady shifts in the population of different generations that descended from the immigrant or migrant experience. The migrant experience is included here because it usually had enough similarities with the immigrant experience to be comparable. In short, the migrant experience involved not only physically moving to a new area but making cultural, linguistic, and psychological adjustments to a new environment as well.[18]

The experiences of adult tenants who grew up in the housing projects and whose parents and grandparents had also lived in housing projects provided additional divisions in the tenant population. Therefore, shifts in the number of people with divergent generational experiences became another aspect of demographic change in the units, and its impact was the creation, or maintenance, of a fragmented type of neighborhood.[19]

Illicit-Economy Groups

Organized groups from outside the projects that were involved in the selling of illicit drugs, stolen contraband, and gambling establishments often saw the housing project as a fertile market to expand their operations. Many of these groups made a concerted effort to establish a presence in the housing projects and to protect their monopoly from competitors and the state. Success was a measure of their ability (i.e., power) to control the market and thwart the state's attempts to eradicate their market. Their presence significantly changed the social organization within the project units, most notably by adding another layer to the existing social divisions in both fragmented and contested neighborhoods.[20]

The State

As mentioned in the previous chapter, the state, through its agents (housing authority managers), made an effort to further its control by instilling in residents a mentality that was responsive to its interests. Although

it never fully achieved these objectives within the units studied, its decisions changed the projects in two general ways. First, the housing
authority's selection of tenants directly affected the demographic content of the units. As mentioned in the previous chapter, the housing
authorities attempted to meet budgetary expectations by giving tenancy
to applicants who could pay their rents, regardless of their eligibility in
terms of yearly income or legal status. Often they tried, in New York,
for example, to diversify the class composition of the tenant population
by bringing in more working-class residents, though they had no consistently effective means of doing this.[21] As more idle poor, or single mothers with children, came to live in the buildings, working-class families
began to move out. The comments of Michael, a sixty-year-old Italian
American construction worker living in the Bronx's Palm Court Apartments, are representative:

> My wife and I decided that we got to find another place to lie. Too many
> "lowlifes" are moving into the building. They don't work, they just hang
> out all day, and there is more drugs and crime since they started moving in.
> It's too bad, we been here for twenty-four years, but things is changing for
> the worse. You understand?[22]

Further, the state could select tenants on the basis of ethnicity and
thereby affect the ethnic demographic in the projects. The housing
authority was often concerned with the safety of families, so when they
believed that a particular ethnic group's safety was threatened, it limited their population. Consequently, some projects were slow to integrate in terms of ethnicity or nationality.[23] This occurred in both
neighborhoods of Los Angeles. In the John C. Fremont Homes of the
Richardson neighborhood, where tenants were homogeneously African
American, the housing authority was slow to allow tenancy to Mexicans because of already-existing tensions between the two groups. In the
El Rey neighborhood's Orchid Lane Apartments, where the population
was homogeneously Mexican American, there was an attempt to limit
the residency of Mexican nationals because of a history of antagonism
between Mexican Americans and Mexican national immigrants, in
which conflicts, especially when involving young people and gangs, had
often been quite violent. The housing authority's choice of tenants had
a direct impact on the social fabric of the buildings studied. The effects
were variable, but they included conditions that nurtured factions, central to fragmented neighborhoods, and conflict, fundamental to contested neighborhoods.

The second way the state acted as an agent of change in the housing projects was through its service policies. Policy decisions concerning the extent and timing of repairs to apartments, sanitation (garbage removal and pest control), upkeep of equipment such as stoves, refrigerators, boilers, and hot water heaters, and maintenance of the public areas and their equipment (e.g., for recreation) all had a significant impact on who would live in the buildings and on residents' everyday activities. For example, not having enough hot water limited bathing, dishwashing, and laundry. A lack of heat caused people to spend more time at the homes of others, affecting the schoolwork of children who could not be at their own homes. This, in turn, affected another state institution—the school. A broken stove meant limited cooking, leading to changes in the types of food served. All of these small changes created uncertainty among the residents, in turn reinforcing the two value orientations (maximizing security and maximizing excitement), since these were ways of coping with the uncertainty of living in an environment of scarcity.

Internal Agents of Change

Change within the housing projects also came from various internal factors. The emergence of internal groups involved in the illicit economy had the power to change an entire housing complex. In the Gardenia Avenue Apartments in Brooklyn, for example, a group of Jamaican residents formed a "posse" (syndicate) involved in the illicit drug trade. The group developed slowly but over a five-year period became the leading seller of drugs in the project. It had three significant impacts on project life. First, as a new group involved in the illicit economy, it competed with other groups for a greater market share, forcing the involvement of many other residents in its associated violence.[24] Second, it introduced a substantially greater volume of drugs into the complex with all the negative repercussions related to their use, such as an increase in robberies and physical fights. Third, it increased the number of people involved in the illicit economy by recruiting individuals from the projects, so that more people entered the criminal justice system or were shot and killed.[25]

Sometimes an internal group developed for social reasons and then "drifted" into the underground economy.[26] In the Orchid Lane Apartments in Los Angeles, for example, Mexican-national youth from illegal immigrant parents were constantly harassed by a gang of Mexican American youth. To defend themselves, they formed a protective group. Six months later, the group was contacted by an illegal drug ring from

Mexico and asked to be their distributor for drugs in the community. They agreed to be the outlet for this ring and became quite successful. They were also harassed less by the Mexican American gangs because they had the protection of an organized crime group. However, as their business operations grew, they recruited more people, and like the Jamaican posse in the Gardenia Avenue Apartments they became more enmeshed in violent confrontations with competing organizations. Over a two-year period, three members of the group were jailed, two were killed, and uninvolved residents had to adjust to the violence by changing their use of public spaces.[27]

The second internal agent of change involved the consumption of drugs.[28] When more people in the projects consumed more drugs, the social behavior of all residents changed.[29] Drug use caused alternating states of consciousness and influenced emotional states. The behavioral changes in drug users led to changes in the emotional dispositions of friends and family with whom they interacted.

Drugs also increased violence in the environment. This resulted from (1) the business practices of drug organizations; (2) the activities of addicts trying to gain the money needed to purchase more drugs; and (3) the random outbreaks of aggression caused by the effects of drugs on the users.[30] Residents then became more wary about the people they associated with and more acutely aware of signs of drug use or its support. The broader impact on the internal social order increased uncertainty in social relations and weakened the social fabric meant for support in managing environmental scarcity.[31]

Finally, the loss of institutional caretakers caused change within the projects. As noted in chapter 1, caretakers are very important in the daily operation and survival of any neighborhood institution. Caretakers act as the institution's guidance system by welcoming, integrating, regulating, and assisting those admitted into their social setting. They assume various nonexclusive forms. As mentioned in chapter 2, some of the caretakers in the projects studied were folk medicine practitioners, such as the Latino *curanderos*.[32] Others had connections to people with money or political influence who could help tenants with their needs. Still others were empathetic to tenants' needs and would lend out small amounts of cash. Finally, some were leaders of building committees (similar to block committees).[33]

Caretakers were not anonymous. In all cases, residents of the buildings recognized caretakers as people who gave of themselves to help others in the building or the complex. In return, the residents offered caretakers such services as meals, rides, car repairs, remodeling of their apartments, and protection from predators who could physically harm them or their families.

When the neighborhood and/or public housing complex was dominated by the social relations associated with a contested neighborhood involving Latinos and African Americans, some African American residents saw the *curanderos* as caretakers for various Latino groups (Mexicans, Central Americans, Puerto Ricans, or Dominicans) with whom they were in conflict and gravitated instead to the individuals whom they considered as "their" caretakers. However, in fragmented neighborhoods African Americans had strong relationships with the *curandero* caretakers in their units.

Caretaking responsibilities were very taxing on a person's time and money, so while each building within a housing project had caretakers, there were never many. Thus the loss of an institutional caretaker who played a particularly central role in the building's social relations resulted in significant social change among the residents. One illustrative incident occurred in Los Angeles, where David, a forty-three-year-old Mexican with a family of four, was an active caretaker of the Orchid Lane Apartments. David, who had lived in the projects for eight years, was employed by a furniture manufacturing company and was an excellent mechanic. He helped other tenants with their cars and was called upon at all hours for help. When people stopped by to talk while he was working on a car, he gave advice, mediated conflicts, or listened to a tenant's problems. David was known by many in the complex and received gifts from many of the tenants.

One day, while he was driving to work, he was killed in an automobile accident. This created a great void not only in his building but in the complex. There were six other caretakers, but they were unable to fill the gap left by David's absence because their resource networks were not as extensive as David's had been (they could not speak English well, whereas David could), and for various reasons they did not have relationships with as many people in the buildings as David had had. Thus David's absence created some important changes in the project. People had to have their automobiles repaired by other people in the community (primarily mechanics), and some residents who lacked the money for car repairs could not even drive to work. Most of these people now had to take public transportation. Increased conflict between the gangs in the projects also resulted because David, who had developed relationships with the gang members, was not there to mediate. Obtaining some services from the housing authority became problematic because David had built a special relationship with many of the office workers and could get them to quickly fix problems. Difficulties resulting from David's death continued for five months until Raymundo, a fifty-five-year-old former construction worker on permanent disability, took David's place as caretaker. Although Raymundo was not a mechanic, he had a very extensive network of friends inside and outside the project.

To sum up, a primary finding of the present study is that while many of the changes that occurred in poor neighborhoods were small, random, and not concerted, they nevertheless had a significant impact on the neighborhood's social structure. Neighborhoods required various institutional elements of the social structure to maintain the existing social order. These agents of preservation are discussed next.

SOURCES OF PRESERVATION

At the same time that agents of change created stress on the existing social order, other agents acted to preserve the existing social arrangements and thereby maintain the existing social values and order that had guided life in the neighborhood. Thus the primary goal of most people living in the five neighborhoods studied was to increase the amount of available money while keeping the existing subculture intact.

External Agents of Preservation

Although unintentionally, the state acted as the first external agent of preservation. The state has historically continued to build and maintain public housing in low-income neighborhoods rather than in more afflu-ent ones.[34] The effect has been to associate housing projects not only with low-income neighborhoods but with ethnic neighborhoods as well. Thus a set of demographic conditions was created that nurtured the maintenance of an independent subculture in these neighborhoods. As indicated earlier, the populations of the housing projects studied were not homogeneous in ethnicity (though ethnically homogeneous housing projects do exist in the United States), and, like most U.S. housing proj-ects, they were not homogeneous with regard to their substrata popula-tion either. However, as mentioned in chapter 1, heterogeneity (in ethnicity, economic status, generation, etc.) did not inhibit the formation of a social order and a set of values, norms, and personal identities that formed an integrative system accepted and appreciated by all residents.

The more value the residents of the projects placed on this system, the more invested they were in maintaining it. This process helped create a culture and concomitant social order that residents found worth working to maintain. The desire to uphold the social order contrasted with the state's intent to create a temporary living situation that residents would eagerly abandon for the middle-class values and lifestyle it tried to promote.

Public Housing as Haven

One of the primary reasons the residents supported preserving the existing social system was that they liked living in public housing.[35] The outside world might consider public housing a "hellhole," but the vast majority of its residents who were poor saw it as a haven from the unpredictable hardships associated with the private housing market.[36] The comments of Carmela and Dennis are representative. Carmela was a forty-two-year-old Puerto Rican housewife who lived with her husband and four children in Buckley Gardens in the Bronx:

> You can take that house [a single-family house being bought by another person from the building], because I sure don't want it! Why Juana wants that house I don't know, she'll have to pay all that money and then she's goin' to need to pay more money for all them repairs and stuff. And then she will be in a place where she doesn't have her friends either. No sir, I like it right here [Buckley Gardens] 'cause I got all my friends and stuff here in the building and the neighborhood, and I don't have to worry about how to pay for those expenses for repairs and stuff that Juana is goin' to have to.[37]

Dennis was a thirty-two-year-old African American father of two who lived with his wife in the John C. Fremont Homes in Los Angeles:

> Hey, they can say what they want to about the projects, but I ain't about to move anytime quick, I can tell you that. My family's comfortable and we gots our friends here in the neighborhood. Plus we don't pay nothing like you gots to pay for your rent on the outside. I ain't sayin' this is a palace, 'cause a palace it ain't, but I like the people here and the neighborhood around here, so I don't really want to move away. Hell, don't be telling the white folks what you just heard, 'cause they'd just say, "Yep, that's them niggers for you, they never want to get off that welfare shit!" [Everyone laughs.][38]

Often people from outside these communities have found residents' positive comments about living in the projects to be either disingenuous, rationalizations of their situation in life, or nonrepresentative.[39] Yet significant numbers of residents in this study did like living in the projects.

This does not mean that they did not want to improve their economic condition. They would have preferred more money, more comfortable housing, better health, and more safety, but at the same time they wanted to retain the values, norms, and personal identities that made up their present social life. In essence, few, if any, people like to be poor, but the vast majority of the poor value much (not all) of the lifestyle that has developed from this condition. The comments of Elizando, a thirty-four-year-old Puerto Rican from Brooklyn's Eagleton neighborhood's Gardenia Avenue Apartments, are representative:

> My cousin from Puerto Rico is got some business and travels to Miami and L.A. to sell these little fountains for desks that he manufactures. He always hires me to translate for him with, you know, his customers. He wants to hire me full time and, you know, travel between Miami and L.A. . . . I could live in either city with money too, but I don't like the lifestyle there. I like it here much more, I just do. The people here are just more fun and real, you know? [His friend nods in agreement.][40]

Those who find the lifestyle to have meaning and value make its preservation a priority, so at every opportunity they struggle to deflect or neutralize the actions of those who would change it. In a very real way, the people intent on maintaining the social life of the neighborhood act much as the human immune system does when confronting an injury.[41] They respond vigorously to any agents that intrude and threaten their world while also working to mend any wounds incurred. For example, at one point the housing authority tried to crack down on crime in L.A.'s John C. Fremont units and common area in order to eliminate drug sales. They sent a notice that there would be police sweeps throughout the units and asked the residents to be cooperative. However, a number of residents viewed the police presence as disruptive to their everyday lives, which included not only the sale of drugs but the sale of stolen electronic and home products that were in demand. In addition, many people were avoiding the authorities because they were delinquent on one or more of their payments or had too many nonfamily members living in their apartments illegally. To thwart the proposed housing authority action, an ad hoc group of individuals from the units formed and decided to undertake two activities. Half of the group went to the local legal services office and asked for help in initiating a legal challenge to keep the police from entering apartments without a formal search warrant or stopping and questioning residents without just cause. The other half approached the housing authority and offered to establish a residential council to draft a strategy for limiting drug sales without a large police presence. This two-pronged strategy to resist the state's plan to intervene in the project's everyday activities was successful, and the housing authority agreed to support a tenant council and adopt its suggestions.

The Caretakers

Of all the agents working to preserve the existing social arrangements in the housing project, the caretakers did the most. The caretakers in the projects contributed every day to the institution's preservation simply by performing their regular duties of facilitating social relations within the established rules of engagement that defined the social order of their buildings. As part of this effort, they helped people financially, gave them names and contacts for needed aid, and, most importantly, assisted in the development of personal identities while minimizing the amount of conflict with others attempting to do the same.[42] It was the caretakers who engineered and maintained the social order in their buildings and complexes.

Caretakers talked to everyone and knew all the gossip and news in the neighborhood. As highly sociable people, they organized the complicated circuitry of social relations in the units. They also connected and integrated the social identities of people in the wider neighborhood with those in the housing project. Such actions helped to preserve the housing project as an institutional element in the neighborhood's social structure.

When agents of change in the buildings altered the existing social order, the caretakers worked to preserve the system. The two examples that follow are representative of caretakers counteracting challenges to the institutional order in their buildings. The first example relates to ethnic change and the second to changes in the substrata discussed in chapter 1.[43]

Hector, a fifty-two-year-old Puerto Rican man who worked in a garment manufacturing shop, was one of the caretakers of the Palm Court Apartments in the Bronx. As such, he acted sometimes as a *curandero* and at other times as an informal job contractor for some of the Puerto Rican men in his building and some of the other units in the complex. In addition, he lent out small amounts of money and cigarettes to people. All the people in the building knew him and his wife and were always cordial in the public spaces of the complex. Hector was also well known in a number of social cliques in the neighborhood. His personal contacts were extensive, and he used them to help maintain the social order of the building. There was always tension in the social order, but Hector managed to adjudicate most conflicts.[44] One example involved an increasing number of African American residents in his building. Hector and the other caretakers faced the difficult problem of how to integrate these newcomers into the existing social order. This was not an easy task, since the building residents were primarily Puerto Rican; and while conflicts that had marked intergroup relations in the past were occurring less frequently, the existing social order was built around divisions based on value orientations and the amount of time a family had lived in the neighborhood. Since the newcomers would change the proportional composition of the building, there was a good deal of resistance to the newcomers from the Puerto Rican tenants. This resistance took the forms of shunning, refusing to talk by claiming an inability to speak English, and some fighting between the youth of the two groups.

Not wanting to change the existing social order, Hector went to the apartments of the resident African Americans to say they could call on him for help and to maintain peaceful coexistence between the two groups. By keeping communication open regarding potential conflicts, he and the other caretakers were able to moderate the situation. Each welcomed the newcomers and informed them about where they should socialize and with whom, as well as what they should avoid saying and doing to avert a confrontation. In addition, Hector, as a source of information on possible employment opportunities, assured the African Americans he spoke with that he would pass information on to them. It was understood that his first priority had to be the employment needs of the Puerto Rican tenants, but the African Americans appreciated his efforts. This helped stabilize the situation and allowed the new tenants the opportunity to establish their own identities within the neighborhood, which was evolving from fragmented to contested. While competition and varying degrees of conflict are the primary modus vivendi of contested neighborhoods, everyday interaction is characterized by an integration of identities and competitive engagements that creates a whole social system. The actions of Hector and the other caretakers managed to keep this intact. Thus Hector was conserving the institutional character of the housing project by allowing for some social change while maintaining the structural integrity of the neighborhood.

The second example involves Enriquetta, a forty-nine-year-old Mexican mother of two small girls and one of the caretakers of L.A.'s Orchid Lane Apartments. As newly arrived Mexican nationals took up residency in the units, relations between the nationals and the Mexican Americans became increasingly strained, since Mexican nationals were more economically disadvantaged and were recent immigrants. This situation added a new layer to the substrata of this neighborhood, which was fragmented at the time. This new strain manifested in the Mexican Americans' characterization of the newcomers as crude and ignorant and in the Mexican nationals' criticism of the Chicanos' incorrect use of Spanish.[45] Ironically, to the outside world both groups were Mexican, but inside the projects the differences were significant in establishing standardized social identities and rules of interaction within the complex and neighborhood. The caretakers were concerned that since the current social order was based on identities that emerged from the existing social divisions, it would be in flux until the newcomers were fully integrated.

Enriquetta made the Mexican nationals feel more comfortable about being in the buildings and told them that they could ask her for the things they needed. Once they felt more comfortable with her, she contacted some older Mexican Americans to see if they would be willing to help. Once she had secured a number of people who could act as resources, she provided the Mexican families with information on whom they should contact for help in such areas as education, employment, and health.

When conflict occurred between Mexican nationals and Mexican American tenants, Enriquetta interpreted and explained the nature of the conflict to the Mexican nationals, whether it was due to competition in the job market, the breaking of facilities due to overuse, or a culture clash. She then counseled them on mediating and avoiding conflict in the future. Her actions slowly socialized them to the norms of the building; and the more integrated the nationals became with the existing social order, the lower the level of isolation and conflict became.

The caretakers were not alone in their attempts to preserve the present social arrangements in each of the projects, but at this stage they were central to managing the preservation effort. They acted as brokers between the interests of those wanting change and the interests of those wanting to keep the status quo in a way that maintained the existing social organization in the buildings.

CHANGE AND PRESERVATION
FOR INSTITUTION AND NEIGHBORHOOD

Each housing project had its own unique configuration of economic substrata, and when changes were made, there were reverberations throughout the unit, complex, and neighborhood. A shift in the distribution of economic status categories in the population caused change in the distribution of the two dominant value orientations. When more working-class and working poor residents were present, the security-maximizing value orientation was quite prevalent; when more idle poor were present, the excitement-maximizing value orientation was prominent.[46] Because value orientations provide the cognitive map for behavior, changes in their distribution signaled a change in the criteria governing the social order. Such changes affected the functioning of the complex's utilities and the general structure of the buildings and grounds, yet physical change did not create social disorder.[47] As the number of idle poor residents in the Bronx's Buckley Gardens grew, the amount of trash in the building and the grounds, urine in the elevator, broken windows in the community center, and destroyed equipment in the playgrounds all noticeably increased.[48] Contrarily, an increase in the number of working-class and working poor residents in L.A.'s Orchid Lane units was accompanied by less trash in the common areas, new flower and vegetable gardens that were planted and managed by the residents, and public equipment in good working order. Yet even when broken windows and trash increased, the residents adjusted to maintain their routines of social interaction, indicating an arrangement of social organization despite the appearance of physical disorder.

Change in value orientations also brought about changes in the configuration of friendship networks and business establishments. Where friendship networks were composed of a mixture of people subscribing to either value orientation, changes that created a new network with more people from one camp or the other were followed by corresponding changes in (1) how money was exchanged (e.g., from checks and cash being used to cash only or vice versa); (2) when people lent money to each other, from whenever possible to rarely or vice versa; and (3) where people spent time, whether more in their apartments and less in public space or vice versa.

Changes to business establishments would alter the types of goods and services available. For example, increases in the excitement-maximizing value orientation meant an increased demand for, and a subsequently increased supply of, entertainment businesses such as gambling establishments, after-hours liquor stores, drug establishments (crack and heroin houses), bingo parlors, card clubs, and dog and cockfights. However, contrary to the conclusions of other studies, these changes did not spell the decline of the neighborhood because they did not diminish the existing institutions or residents' support for the local social order and culture.[49]

The second major change involved ethnicity. Shifts in ethnic composition within the projects caused a neighborhood to change from fragmented to contested, or vice versa. When an ethnically homogeneous population became more heterogeneous, there was a general change from fragmented to contested, leading to ethnic separation and limited contact between the groups. In this situation, people became reserved in the presence of competing group members and hostile when the equilibrium in resource access was compromised. A typical example occurred in the John C. Fremont Homes of L.A.'s Richardson neighborhood. A group of Mexican boys were playing at the basketball courts when a group of African Americans approached. Most of the African Americans felt that it was their court because they had lived there before the Mexicans moved in and that they should have priority since they believed the Mexicans didn't even know how to play. They asked the Mexicans how long they would be on the court and, when told that their stay would be indefinite, proceeded to throw trash on the court until the Mexicans attacked them and a big fight ensued. The fight ended with two arrests, one stabbing, and two concussions.[50]

Although violence to gain dominance within the neighborhood was common in this situation of social change, local knowledge concerning its timing and circumstances made it fairly predictable. For example, deadly violence with the use of lethal weapons was associated with late evening and early morning activity. It was more likely to occur in areas of drug sales and away from areas regularly patrolled by the police. Fighting could occur anywhere but was more likely in areas of greater socializing among residents, such as common areas where sports were played, laundry rooms, and parking lots, at the times when the most socializing occurred. Hence, even in times of considerable violence, this predictability permitted residents to avoid or lessen their exposure to it, so that social relations could be normalized and the housing project could remain a local institution that supported the more general elements of the neighborhood's social structure.[51]

Because ethnic groups have distinct cultures and languages, they pose a significant problem to be solved if the housing project is to become or remain a local institution. The most immediate problem was how to integrate the various groups to a level where they could form mutually beneficial and valued relationships. Only when this occurred could the housing project be a neighborhood institution that supported the local subculture and aided residents in everyday interactions. The greatest hurdle was communication. Since the ethnic groups in the projects studied spoke different languages, basic communication could be difficult.[52] When communication was difficult, people sought others from their own

ethnic group to socialize with. For example, Elsie, a fifty-five-year-old
African American woman had lived with her husband and raised three
children in the Gardenia Avenue Apartments in Brooklyn for twenty
years. Over those years, Elsie and her husband had developed many close
friendships with their neighbors. During most of that time the building
they occupied was mostly, though not exclusively, composed of other
African Americans. However, in recent years, more Puerto Ricans had
moved in. On Elsie's floor, Puerto Rican families came to occupy all the
other apartments. Two of the families could not speak English, and the
other two were uncomfortable with their English. Because of this language barrier, they were friendly and said hi to Elsie but then disappeared
behind their doors. In fact, because of their lack of fluency in English,
Elsie's presence made them feel uncomfortable, so they tried to avoid her.
At the same time, the Spanish-speaking neighbors carried on long conversations that Elsie could hear but not partake in. The entire situation
made Elsie feel rejected and more isolated than she had ever been, causing resentment. In a conversation with a group of African American
women, she articulated her feelings:

> I ain't got nothin' against them Puerto Ricans, but the government has got
> to do something about the number they're sending here. They just take
> everything over when they move somewhere. They only like their kind,
> look at my neighbor Diego, he is blacker than me. But he thinks he's a
> Puerto Rican, not a black. He and his wife don't speak English, they don't
> talk to me or nobody else who is American. None of them Puerto Ricans
> will talk to you much, they sure talk to themselves though. [Everyone says,
> "Amen."] I feel like a stranger in my own country, and I sure don't like it
> much. [They all agree by nodding their heads.] And, now I got Puerto
> Ricans on all sides of me, I don't have nobody to talk to any more, so
> thank God I got the telephone so I can talk to you all.[53]

The hostility felt by Elsie was echoed over and over again by other tenants who were in buildings experiencing similar changes in ethnic composition. Much of the frustration felt was expressed in a form of
xenophobia. This occurred most often between groups that spoke different languages. Members of each group thought that the other group was
talking about them, although this was almost never the case. Yet xenophobic responses also occurred between two groups that spoke the same
language. For example, it was common to hear Puerto Ricans complain
about Dominicans and African Americans about West Indians.[54]

Each of these general changes (i.e., value orientations and ethnic composition) affected the structure of the neighborhood. One way they did

was by affecting the types of businesses in the neighborhood. When a particular ethnic group's numbers increased, the number of businesses catering to its tastes increased while the number of businesses associated with the other group(s) declined. Although this was a simple market response to demand, the closing of businesses such as grocery stores, beauty salons, and barbershops altered the institutional configuration of the neighborhood. The remaining neighborhood institutions of the group who were losing neighborhood establishments bore the weight of supporting their group's functional and emotional interests. Since contested neighborhoods mutually support competing groups, there was no general decline in the social structure, but its elements were reconfigured.

Finally, there was the change from contested neighborhoods to fragmented neighborhoods. The ethnic divisions and hostilities that formed the basis of a contested neighborhood generally lasted for years, but change occurred when one of the competing ethnic groups came to dominate. This normally began with the numerical increase of one group and a corresponding decline of the other(s). When it occurred, group differences and the xenophobic suspicions that influenced interaction were gradually replaced by commonly held beliefs and behaviors and a rise in trust and respect. Divisions formerly based on ethnicity soon gave way to divisions based on value orientations. Thus a fragmented neighborhood was born, and stratification was structured primarily on value orientations, work status, generation, gender, and age.[55]

The third major change involved shifts in the number of people who had different generational experiences, such as the trials and triumphs associated with immigration to the United States, migration from one part of the United States to another, the length of time that a family had lived in the United States, and the length of tenancy in a family's present public housing unit. Changes in the number of immigrant tenants raised issues of ethnic identity, as discussed in the previous section. However, they also had an impact on which value orientation would dominate the complex.

Immigrants generally viewed living in a housing project as an opportunity to save money for their futures and were much more likely to have a security-maximizing value orientation. Second-generation individuals were divided between the two value orientations. Finally, individuals from succeeding generations often held an excitement-maximizing orientation.[56]

The migrant experience was similar to that of immigrants. As used here, the term *migrants* refers to people who had moved from one part of the country to another in search of a better life. As with immigrants, economic push and pull factors were usually instrumental in their decision to move.[57] Thus migrants generally operated within a security-maximizing value orientation, especially if they had moved from a rural poor area where economic conditions were harsh.[58]

When shifts in the number of residents representing different generational experiences occurred, they caused changes in the units' internal patterns of association and interaction. People associated more closely with those who held the same values and were more reserved with those holding the other value orientation, viewing them as morally "irresponsible." Thus changes in the distribution of value orientations within the unit or complex produced changes in the configuration of social cliques and their interactions with each other.

THE MEANING OF INSTITUTIONAL PRESERVATION

One might legitimately ask: Who would want to preserve the existing social relations in housing projects if they are so bad? The answer is that significant numbers wanted to preserve the projects as they were because they had managed to establish a meaningful life within a harsh environment.[59] There were those who valued the status of their personal identities and the camaraderie they found in their cliques. Some people were not completely satisfied with either their status or their personal identities but were afraid that any change to the existing social order might make their situation worse rather than better.

As with all the neighborhood institutions, the preservation dynamic was active at all times in the housing projects. During times when there was no apparent threat to the status quo, the everyday activities of people in the various social cliques and networks reinforced the existing roles, rituals, and routines that had come to be accepted as the dominant pattern of association. When these "normal" roles, rituals, and routines were challenged or interrupted, residents took a series of instrumental actions to preserve or restore the existing social order, primarily through the internal network system. Willy, a forty-eight-year-old African American who lived in L.A.'s John C. Fremont Homes and was employed in a local lumberyard, exemplifies how this system worked. Because he was considered to be an excellent cook, he was often asked to barbeque for people in the complex who were having a party for their friends and relatives. People would give Willy the food they wanted to serve a couple of days before the event, and he would have it ready for them when they needed it. For his work, Willy was given money and food. Because people from different cliques hired and liked Willy, he was associated with a number of cliques. Therefore, anyone who needed to get in touch with individuals in other cliques would call Willy, and he would make the necessary connections.

The housing projects were densely populated, so no individual could know or be closely connected to all the individuals in his or her complex. However, an internal network linked individuals in the various units through their membership in overlapping cliques. Individuals' personal identities were woven into a set of interconnecting group identities associated with each particular clique to which they belonged. Individuals needing the help of others in another clique went to people belonging to more than one clique, who provided the connections that formed the network system.

In times of institutional crisis, impulses of preservation took the form of five responses in the housing projects. First, friendships were greatly reinforced within cliques. During times of insecurity, people contacted their friends more often and spent more time together than they did on a regular basis. The purpose was to determine if their friends remained loyal and whether the patterns of association they had mutually developed were still intact. An example of this involved Alex, a twenty-eight-year-old Puerto Rican living in Buckley Gardens in the Bronx. For a seven- to ten-year period, Puerto Ricans were the primary ethnic group in Buckley Gardens. However, in a little over a ten-month period the number of African Americans moving into the units significantly increased. As the African Americans became a more visible presence, Alex increased his efforts to call his friends in the building. The issue for Alex and his friends was not that African Americans were moving into the units but that the new residents were moving in so fast they were developing their own set of cliques that were not yet integrated into the existing network system. This presented uncertainty for Alex and the others because so much of their own sense of self was related to their social clique and the existing network system in the neighborhood, which they felt could no longer exist in its present form.

In his effort to solidify clique relations, Alex contacted a number of friends on a daily basis. Jaime, one of his friends, suggested that they get together and go to the bar. Alex and Jaime went to the bar a few times during that week. The next week Alex called Jaime to go to the bar every evening, but Jaime could go only two evenings. Alex then called another friend in his social clique in the building and asked if he wanted to get together. At the bar the conversation was dominated by the topic of how the buildings were changing and the belief that this would cause a sharp increase in violence. Whenever there was uncertainty related to new residents, it was nearly always accompanied by the belief that life would become more dangerous.

During the succeeding weeks Alex continued to call his friends, and some of his friends called him. Although these activities appeared to be socially "needy," they were efforts to maintain the established social order. This went on for nearly two months until the number of new African American residents stabilized. Once the threat was lifted, everyone reestablished participation with the broader social network.[60] Alex and his friends returned to their old routine of getting together in the building and meeting people outside their immediate clique.

The second response was an increased effort to determine if internal solidarity remained strong within the social clique and network. People asked friends or clique associates for more help than usual, requesting favors that they rarely asked for during times of stability in order to test relationships' solidarity.[61] Because everyone was aware that any denial of a request would be seen as an affront to both the person making the request and his or her clique, those wanting to maintain solidarity offered some help rather than no help at all.

In addition, people tested the loyalty of a friend or clique associate by making negative comments about one of the change agents that they perceived as a threat to the status quo to see how their friend would respond. The sign of solidarity was to agree in principle, if not in degree, with their negative statement.

Third, during times of change, activity focused on identifying potential collaborators among the change agents. People would observe whom others in their cliques were socializing with. Gossip, not always the most reliable source, became the primary means of gaining and distributing this information,[62] since individuals in a clique could not observe the everyday activities of all their associates. People in the projects and poor neighborhoods more generally know that gossip can be unreliable, but they use it as a resource for social control.[63] Thus people tried to avoid being labeled in the gossip communication channels because once this had happened, the label was difficult to remove.[64] The comments of Elenor, a thirty-three-year-old Mexican American woman living in L.A.'s John C. Fremont Homes, illustrate the use of gossip:

> There's been a lot of break-ins lately, and they always come when someone is not home. Some people told a group of us that Chuy there [she points to

a man at the corner] has been talking to some of the dopers [drug addicts] in the yard, so my friends and me have been checking Chuy out to see if he's been telling some of the dopers when people go away from their apartments to shop and stuff. If he is, we'll deal with Chuy and get out the word, and people will be prepared. But it might be hard to tell now, 'cause Chuy knows that people are checking him out so he's just been watching who he's talking to.[65]

The fourth response was the labeling of any group that threatened the status quo as demonic, lacking the moral integrity to exist in the neighborhood. People used extremely crude and vulgar language to describe their identified nemesis, not because they were incapable of using other words to express their discontent, but because such language carried the anger they wanted to communicate.[66] Language was also used to strengthen solidarity in resisting any change, undermine the legitimacy of the opposing side, and establish a position of being on higher moral ground. The comments of Tony, a twenty-seven-year-old Puerto Rican living in Brooklyn's Gardenia Avenue Apartments, are representative:

> Fuckin' Dominicans, they been coming in the neighborhood, now there are some in the building. They also bought Sal's bodega with money that I don't know where they fuckin' got. I think it must be drug money 'cause they ain't got fuckin' nothing. They act like shit, they steal shit from you. But I don't care; I ain't letting their shit make me move. They try fuckin' with the neighborhood like they usually do, they got to fuck with all of us. And there's no way they can mess with all of us 'cause we'll kick their asses back to the DR [Dominican Republic].[67]

During times when the status quo was challenged, a fifth response was a greater reliance on other neighborhood institutions to aid in counteracting the impact of the change agents. For example, in the Gardenia Avenue Apartments there was a sudden increase in violence related to the competition between two local drug syndicates. This had an adverse effect on the housing project's role of providing recreation for the neighborhood because people were reluctant to use the complex's athletic facilities or the children's play structure. Community members, acting as agents of preservation, got the local high school to provide access to its facilities, which allowed the children to resume their play. In addition, two of the local gangs got the parks and recreation department to sponsor some events focused on children and young adults. Finally, in contested neighborhoods, there were times when it was difficult for cliques to associate with other cliques on the projects' grounds. Since clique interaction played a vital role in the housing projects, it moved to other institutions like the mom-and-pop grocery stores, beauty salons, and barbershops (see chapters 4–7).

STRATEGIES AND NEIGHBORHOOD TYPE

The activities involving change and preservation were of two general types: (1) quick action to address the situation; and (2) the investment of time to plan before taking action. Planning involves a strategy, and most strategy considers the environment in which it must operate. This section describes the strategies used by agents of change and preservation to achieve their goals within contested and fragmented neighborhoods.[68]

The first strategy was to interrupt the interaction pattern of the competitor. People used it whether they wanted change or preservation and whether they were operating in a contested or a fragmented neighborhood. It involved occupying public spaces within the housing complex that were considered to be central meeting places in order to deny one's rivals a place to socialize. In a nonviolent approach, members of one group made a consistent effort to occupy a particularly public space coveted by their competitors. In a violent approach, usually adopted by youth or young adults, physical force was used to intimidate rivals from frequenting their desired areas. Whatever tactic was employed, the desired effect was to make it difficult, if not impossible, for rivals to promote their cliques.

When successful, this strategy withered the communication network necessary to support a social clique. It was used by change agents to undermine the existing social order and by preservation agents to disrupt the efforts of those trying to create change. A representative example occurred in the Orchid Lane Apartments of L.A.'s El Rey neighborhood. Mexican Americans were the largest ethnic group represented among the tenants, but over a ten-month period increasing numbers of Mexican immigrants took up residence in the units. Mexican Americans resented the Mexican immigrants because they felt that the immigrants reduced the wages in many of the occupations that Mexican Americans held and because employers sometimes used the immigrants to replace Mexican American workers who would raise issues such as benefits. Mexican American workers and Mexican immigrants also had conflicts over cultural and personal identity. The Mexican Americans found the Mexican immigrants traditional and simple, while the Mexican immigrants considered the Mexican Americans to be Mexican in name only—that is, mostly assimilated into American culture.[69] The comments of Patricia and Ignacio are representative. Patricia, a forty-one-year-old Mexican American living in the Orchid Lane Apartments of L.A.'s El Rey neighborhood, worked in an industrial laundry that cleaned linens from hospitals and hotels:

> I really have grown to hate these people [immigrants from Mexico]. They are the simplest, most ignorant people I know. They'll do anything for the job no matter how dangerous or hard it is . . . and every time we bring up working conditions or getting benefits to the owners, they always say they are okay with things. Johnny [a Mexican American worker] used to work here, and she got a burned hand because of the way that they make us do things. When she wanted them [employers] to make some changes, they got rid of her and brought in another wetback [Mexican immigrant], and [the supervisors] told us there were lots of people who wanted to work here just like things were and threatened to let everyone who did not like it here go![70]

Ignacio was a twenty-nine-year-old Mexican immigrant who worked in a furniture shop:

> Yes, I know these *pochos* [Mexican Americans] won't give my kids a ride to school. They don't like us [Mexican immigrants], and Tomás [his son] told me that they get nervous around him because they know he speaks Spanish better than English and they don't speak that well. That's the main reason they won't give him a ride! It's a real shame they don't know their culture, but that's their fault for not keeping the culture! It's not mine or my family's fault.[71]

When Mexican immigrants, regardless of age or gender, used the common area, they spoke only Spanish. The Mexican Americans who spoke a combination of English and Spanish, regardless of age or gender, found this irritating and socially threatening because they felt that a lower-status group was dominating their physical and cultural space. Mexican Americans tried to occupy the most coveted public space before the Mexican immigrants got there or, failing this, simply tried to outnumber them in the same space. Their strategy was to crowd the same area, leaving inadequate social space for the immigrants to feel comfortable in their interactions. This action was fairly successful because the immigrants generally withdrew to another area that was more isolated from the main pathways in the complex.

This demonstrates the competition that exists between substrata in fragmented neighborhoods, a competition that is less about which group will dominate public space than about how the local social system will be organized. Will the social order be arranged in a way that privileges the immigrant or native criteria so that individuals from one of these groupings receive more social status than the other? Thus issues of identity, social status, and social ordering (standing) of individuals along a continuum dominated by criteria associated with particular substrata motivate strategic planning in fragmented neighborhoods. Issues of identity and culture, as well as space and resource use associated with specific ethnic groups, motivate strategic planning in contested neighborhoods.

A second strategy used was the imposition of one group's pattern of association on other groups. Three approaches were associated with this strategy. The most benign was an effort made by one party or the other (i.e., agents of change or preservation) to assimilate the leaders of the perceived threat into their group. Opposition leaders were invited to join their clique and, once active, were given a new nickname, identity, and position in the internal status hierarchy. Of the three approaches, this one was the most difficult to achieve, and it occurred only when members of one group had an already existing desire to be associated with the other group.

In the second and most Machiavellian approach, members of groups infiltrated one of the housing complex's official tenant organizations with the intention of influencing the organization's policies to support the desired change or preservation. An example of this strategy was employed in the Palm Court Apartments of the Bronx when a group of people formed a tenants' association intended to effect change by creating a better environment for all residents, primarily by beautifying the grounds and improving security. The head of the organization contacted the housing authority manager and asked for financial assistance in this effort. The manager provided assistance to purchase plants for the front of the building and installed a new set of mailboxes.

To reduce crime around the buildings, the group circulated a suggestion among the residents for the housing authority to dismantle the basketball courts, which were used frequently to sell drugs, and replace them with a children's play structure. However, the courts were also used by men from the entire neighborhood to play pickup basketball throughout the summer months, as well as by people who congregated to watch the games and socialize. Changing the basketball courts meant the removal of an important location for social interaction. Because this change would negatively affect the pattern of interaction for a significant number of tenants during the summer months, a few people joined the tenants' organization with the intent to sabotage the effort to remove the basketball courts. They constantly requested clarification and evidence that removal of the courts would really reduce crime rather than simply moving it to another area of the complex. In addition, they asked the housing authority to describe what kind of play structure would be built, how safety would be provided for the children, and how the structure would be maintained throughout the winter months. Finally, when the time came for a vote, members of their group offered amendments to the proposal that resulted in endless debate. As time wore on without any action taken, many proponents of the change simply grew tired and the whole idea died.

The most hostile of the three approaches involved the attempt of paramilitary groups to physically dominate their competitors. One set of these groups consisted of gangs or local organized crime syndicates intent on promoting their business and organizational interests.[72] Such organizations were involved in either instituting changes to realize their interests or preserving existing social arrangements that protected their interests.[73]

One such incident took place in Buckley Gardens in the Bronx. A local syndicate called the Fishmongers had established itself in the buildings and was operating a small "drug mill" (drug factory) out of one of the apartments. Many of the residents objected to the syndicate's presence in the buildings and were in the process of mobilizing tenants against its activities. The Fishmongers syndicate had been present in the buildings for more than a year and had become part of the existing social order, so in seeking to suppress its activities the tenants were attempting to initiate change. The syndicate first responded by consistently occupying the space in the lobby and the front of the building to intimidate the tenant association's members from disseminating information to recruit residents to support their efforts. In addition, the syndicate physically intimidated tenants who opposed them by openly carrying guns, threatening to physically hurt them, and physically bumping into them as they conversed. The syndicate's efforts to dominate the opposition and preserve the status quo proved successful, and the tenants' committee was never able to secure the support necessary to pressure the Fishmongers syndicate and its business into leaving the building.[74]

Another type of paramilitary group active in the five poor neighborhoods has been associated with the so-called "defended neighborhoods" conceptual framework, but many of the groups active in the neighborhoods did not neatly fit with the "defended neighborhood" concept. [75] Most of them would have been referred to as "vigilante groups" because they used force to maintain the status quo and operated outside official law enforcement establishments.[76] These groups could be involved in social change but were mostly involved in preservation, and though they were active in both types of neighborhoods they were mostly present in contested neighborhoods. One example, in the Gardenia Avenue Apartments of Brooklyn, was a group calling itself the JAS (Justice and Safety). It was first composed of about thirty-five African American men, but within a month it had grown to about sixty men, ranging in age from twenty to fifty-one. The group decided to reduce the amount of crime in their buildings by stopping the drug sales there; but because the housing complex was part of a contested neighborhood involving Puerto Ricans, Jamaicans, and African Americans, with the drug syndicate under the operation of Jamaican Americans, the attempt to control their activity was to a large extent part of the ongoing conflict between the three groups.

The JAS armed themselves with sophisticated weapons and intimidated people coming to buy drugs. This proved quite successful, so the Jamaican syndicate selling the drugs responded by shooting at some of the men as they made their patrol, wounding two. The JAS retaliated by shooting at some of the syndicate's men, wounding one. Since the JAS had more members and were well armed, and since the shootings brought more police to the area, the syndicate decided to withdraw from the buildings dominated by African Americans and reorganize its activities in Jamaican-dominated buildings. The African American vigilante group's strategy was successful, but it could patrol and control only the buildings and immediate surrounding areas where its members lived.

The last strategy used to implement a group's desire for change or preservation was to call upon the state for help. A group would go to the housing authority to ask for more police protection or would call the appropriate state authorities concerning various illegalities and health issues within the units. The tactical strength of this strategy was the threat that if nothing was done, news of the situation would be made public. It was a strategy used in both contested and fragmented neighborhoods to create change or preserve the social order within the complex. Although this method was not as effective as the others described, it worked in situations where there was no local group that could provide protection.

In sum, all the above strategies had a common thread. They all attempted to disrupt and isolate their opposition, forcing them to go to another area of the neighborhood or another neighborhood to realize their social goals. The strategizing group could then occupy the critical social space necessary to effect their desired change or preserve their preferred status quo. Whether they were successful depended upon contingencies not always under their control. More significant than a group's success or failure was the social jostling that helped maintain the social equilibrium necessary for institutional and neighborhood longevity. However, if these strategies failed, the group would seek the aid of the state to create their desired goal.

SOME CLOSING REMARKS

Public housing is the only form of housing that has assumed institutional status in the persistently poor neighborhoods of contemporary urban America.[77] Politics and state planning after the Second World War replaced the tenement with the public housing project and made it an institution in poor neighborhoods.[78] The battle over whether it will be a state or neighborhood institution is what frames dynamics of change and preservation.

The housing project was born as a result of state action and continues to be administered by state officials. It will always be a part of the state bureaucracy, but the chance that it will become a state institution, as defined by its ability to create and implement state policy and adhere to state ideology on issues of state and individual responsibilities toward destitution in poor neighborhoods, is remote at best. The material conditions in poor neighborhoods are simply too harsh and have created a social environment too austere to nourish such an institution. The housing project exists in an environment favorable to its being a neighborhood institution, but the exact content of its institutional character is determined by a persistent competition between agents of change, preservation, and (state) regulation.

Because housing projects serve such a large proportion of the neighborhood's population, they tend to have the most influence on social life in the area. Thus any social change that affects the housing project will reverberate throughout the neighborhood. In many ways the housing project is to the long-term poor neighborhood like a critical organ of the body. Just as understanding blood pressure within the human body would require one to consider the operations of the kidneys because they are the central organs regulating it, so understanding what regulates the social blood pressure of most persistently poor neighborhoods in the United States requires one to consider the operations of the housing project.

Finally, though outside observers of a particular public housing complex might see nothing happening there except the aging and deterioration of the buildings and a good deal of social pathology, they would miss the enormous amount of activity engaged in by agents associated with change, preservation, and regulation who are constantly busy trying to meet their goals. Thus observations of crime and violence in housing projects, though often interpreted as signs of decline or disorganization, are simply snapshots of life that fail to include the internal jockeying that occurs in an organized institution governed by the neighborhood's internally established mechanisms. Although life in housing projects is often violent and sometimes brutish, it is a mistake to think of it as unorganized.

CHAPTER 4

Provisions for Life

Making the Mom-and-Pop
Store a Neighborhood Institution

Trade may be oriented to the market or to customers.

Max Weber, *Economy and Society* (1958)

At one time in American history mom-and-pop grocery stores were ubiquitous in nearly every town and urban community. The advent of large retail stores has severely reduced their numbers, particularly in middle- and upper-class neighborhoods, but they still remain a significant presence in low-income neighborhoods.[1] Most studies on low-income and poor neighborhoods treat them as economic establishments and focus primarily on understanding their roles in facilitating economic mobility among various ethnic groups.[2] Yet as Herbert Gans and Gerald Suttles note in their studies of poor neighborhoods in Chicago and Boston, the mom-and-pop store is not only an economic establishment but an important arena for social relations.[3] Although not all mom-and-pop stores are neighborhood institutions, their physical location in the neighborhood strategically situates them to assume institutional status. Their status as a neighborhood institution and their contribution to the structure and life of the neighborhood depend on a number of factors discussed in this chapter.

A TYPOLOGY OF MOM-AND-POP STORE OWNERSHIP

An understanding of mom-and-pop stores in poor neighborhoods begins with the circumstances under which they were established. Although this might appear to be a simple issue of an owner's desire to earn money by offering products for consumption, it is more complex in poor areas. In his study of a slum neighborhood in Chicago, Suttles found that to residents the ideal form of commercial relations was for a particular ethnic group to frequent only establishments run by members of their own group and that when this was not the case commercial relations were distinguished by interactions he described as "seclusion/suspicion, guest/ host, mutual tolerance/mutual exploitation."[4] While I found that under certain circumstances social relations in stores could assume the forms described by Suttles, much of the stores' functions depended on their social origins, which I will categorize by their relations to the neighborhoods they existed in. Table 3 shows the stores studied and tracks ethnic changes in their ownership and clientele over time, as well as their type and the character of their operations.

Four types of mom-and-pop stores existed in the poor neighborhoods studied. The first of these I have provocatively termed the "imperialist" type to describe the specific social and economic presence in poor communities that they consciously assume.[5] Generally, this type of store is bought as a first step in realizing the "American dream" in terms of socioeconomic mobility.[6] It illustrates Waldinger's "niche theory," which argues that if a particular ethnic group has the capital to dominate a particular niche in the urban economy (e.g., small retail stores) its members can fill vacancies regardless of their physical locations. The sociological significance of the imperialist establishment is that its owners and customers have a divergent understanding of the economic interaction within the store. The store's owner, who is neither a resident nor an ethnic compatriot and has no socioeconomic connection to the neighborhood, views it as a means to make a decent living and accumulate capital and equity for socioeconomic mobility.

Though the neighborhood's residents find the store convenient, they are aware that the money they spend in the store goes to other communities rather than their own and that the prices they pay there are significantly and consistently higher than prices for the same products in larger retail stores. Both of these facts leave them resentful of the proprietor, who is a member of an ethnic group that does not live in the neighborhood and who is profiting from their consumption. Thus the residents feel they are being exploited by a foreigner to the community. It is worth noting that the symbolic power of money leaving the neighborhood far exceeds the significance of the cash flow itself. People in middle-class neighborhoods do not delude themselves into thinking that the stores in their area, such as major food and department stores, keep money in their neighborhoods, but they have secure enough lives that such activity loses its imperialist edge. The comments of Junior, a twenty-nine-year-old African American from L.A.'s Richardson neighborhood, are representative of attitudes toward the imperialist type of store:

> Yeah, shit, I seen it. I see them kids steal from that store all the time, but I don't tell nobody because they [the kids] just be evenin' the score. That shittin' Korean who owns it ain't nothin' but stealin' money from us and takin' it to K-Town [Korean Town]. You check out the fuckin' prices in this store? Shit, they is out of this world! Fuck him, let the kids steal his ass![7]

Similarly, DeeDee, a twenty-two-year-old Puerto Rican from the Bronx's Monument neighborhood, said to a friend about a store that the two of them had just left:

> Every time I go to that store I get mad. That Indian, or whatever he is, just charges so much for things. He and his brother are so unfriendly when you ask for something and especially when you check to see if the price is right. I heard them guys talking the other day about their home on the Island [Long Island]. You know them guys make so much money off us, and then they just take it to the Island [Long Island community] and spend it. They just take so much advantage of us. They're so disgusting![8]

The owners of the imperialist type of store came from a variety of ethnic groups. In the New York neighborhoods they were principally, though not exclusively, East Indian, Pakistani, and Korean, while in Los Angeles they were Chinese, Armenian, and Korean. Their ethnicity was significant only to the extent that it was not that of the general neighborhood population and that they did not identify with the neighborhood, which for them was simply a geographic location for business.[9]

In their study of Korean entrepreneurs, Light and Bonacich argue that Korean small-business owners should be understood as exploited workers rather than exploiters because their hard work, long hours, and low pay benefit their investors more than themselves. They argue that Korean small businessmen are not really the owners of their businesses but workers for the investment businesses that have fronted the money for them to start the business.[10] In the grocery stores that I studied in Los Angeles and New York, Korean owners did have to repay high-interest loans to their investors, but they made a modest profit from their business activities. In fact, their profits supported their families and provided money for their children's higher education. In some cases, they used their profits as seed money to become involved in another business when they eventually sold the grocery store and moved.[11] However, even in cases where store owners were exploited by their lending source, they

TABLE 3. MOM-AND-POP STORES' ETHNIC OWNERSHIP, ETHNIC CLIENTELE, AND ESTABLISHMENT TYPE OVER TIME IN THE FIVE NEIGHBORHOODS

City/Section/Store	1991	1992	1993	1994	1995	1996	1997	1998	1999
Bronx									
Elmway									
Finger's	C (Imp)Ar/AA[Ent]	C	C (Imp)Pak/AA[Ent]	C	C	C	F (Imp)Pak/AA,PR[Ent]	F	F
Mikey's	(H)It/PR[NI]			(T)PR/PR[NI]					(Ind)PR/PR,AA[NI]
Primo	(Ind)PR/PR[NI]				(T)AA/AA,PR[Ent]				(Ind)AA/AA[NI]
Isla	(Ind)PR/PR[NI]	(T)Dom/PR[NI]							
Monument									
B.J.	F (H)Ir/PR[NI]	F	F (Ind)PR/AA,PR[NI]		F	F	F (Ind)PR/AA[Ent]	C	C
Gordon St.	(Ind)AA/AA[NI]			(Imp)Ar/AA,PR[Ent]				(Imp)Kor/PR,AA[Ent]	
Tortuga	(T)PR/PR[NI]					(T)Mex-a/PR,Mex-n[NI]			
Brooklyn									
Eagleton									
Nino's	F (Ind)PR/PR[NI]	F	C (Imp)Kor/PR,AA[Ent]	C	C	C	C (Ind)PR/PR[NI]	C	C
Happy Gro	(Imp)Kor/PR,AA[Ent]				(Ind)PR/PR[NI]				
Shippley's	(Ind)AA/AA/[NI]		(T)Jam/Jam,AA[Ent]			(Ind)Jam/Jam[NI]			
Farragut St.	(H)Je/AA,PR[Ent]		(H)Je/AA[NI]		(Ind)AA/AA[NI]				

Los Angeles

	C	F	F	F	F	F
El Rey	C	F	F	F	F	F
Martinez	(H)Mex-a/Mex-a,Mex-n[NI]		(Ind)Mex-n/Mex-n[NI]			(Ind)Mex-a/Mex-a,Mex-n[NI]
Jalisco	(Imp)Ch/Mex-a[Ent]		(Ind)Mex-a/Mex-a,Mex-n[NI]			
Canal	(Imp)Ar/Mex-a[Ent]	(T)Viet/Mex-a,Mex-n[Ent]				(Ind)Mex-a/Mex-a,Mex-n[NI]
Richardson	C	C	C	C	C	C
Monitor	(H)AA/AA[NI]	(T)Nic/Mex-a,Mex-n[Ent]	(Ind)Mex-n/Mex-a,Mex-n[NI]			
Daddy G's	(Ind)AA/AA[NI]					
Treviño's	(T)Mex-n/Mex-n[NI]	(Imp)Ch/Mex-a/Mex-n[Ent]				(Ind)Mex-a/Mex-a,Mex-n[NI]
Top	(Ind)AA/AA[NI]	(Imp)Kor/AA[Ent]		(Ind)Ar/AA[NI]		

N = 18

NOTE: Symbols for Neighborhoods: C = contested; F = fragmented (for definitions, see chapter 1). Sequence of Symbols for Stores: (Character of store)Ethnicity of owner/Primary ethnicity of patrons[Character of operations]. Symbols for Stores: Character of store: Imp = imperialist; Ind = indigenous; H = holdout; T = trailblazer (for definitions, see chapter 4). Ethnicity: AA = African American; Mex-n = Mexican national; Mex-a = Mexican American; It = Italian; Ir = Irish; Pak = Pakistani; In = East Indian; PR = Puerto Rican; Dom = Dominican; Nic = Nicaraguan; Jam = Jamaican; Kor = Korean; Je = Jewish; Viet = Vietnamese; Ch = Chinese; Ar = Arab; Arm = Armenian. Character of operations: NI = neighborhood institution; Ent = enterprise (for definitions, see chapter 1).

neither identified with nor invested in the neighborhood, a fact that residents considered exploitative.[12]

In the second type of store, which I have labeled the "holdout" type, the owner had bought and run the store back when ethnic groups that now no longer lived in the neighborhood were the residents.[13] The owners themselves were usually members of the ethnic groups that had previously lived in the area and symbolized for residents both the change in the area's ethnic character and the fact that the old ethnic group did not want to live next to them. The owners who stayed did so for a variety of reasons. Many of the older owners thought it too onerous to raise capital and sustain enough energy to start a new business; and since they were not mentally or financially ready for retirement, they felt that their only option was to keep operating their business. The comments of Leonard, a sixty-four-year-old Jewish American who operated a store in Brooklyn's Eagleton neighborhood, are representative:

> I have owned this store for thirty-seven years, and I have done well until recently. I still do okay, but not like the past, when I could make a good living. Lately it has been hard to make money, but I don't mind. Hey, even if I did, what could I do about it? I couldn't sell the store for anything reasonable, so that is not an option. I really don't want to sit home and retire yet, so even if I did sell the store, who would give me the money to start a new one nearer to where I live?[14]

Many older owners also kept their stores because of their sentimental attachment to a time gone by when they had been younger and in the prime of their lives. Thus their stores kept a part of their own histories alive. The comments of Hector, the sixty-year-old Mexican American owner of the Martinez Grocery in L.A.'s El Rey neighborhood, are representative:

> To sell this store to someone right now would just kill me. I love this store. I been working here for thirty-two years. I still can remember when I got the loan to buy the store. I was so proud of the fact that I could own a business, since I came to the U.S. [from Mexico] with no money and just worked in a meat-processing plant until I had some money to invest. When I got this store and started to run it, it was the best time of my life. As a matter of fact, I married the daughter of one of the women who used to come into the store all the time. When I am in this store I have good thoughts.[15]

Finally, some people held on to their stores because of ethnic or family traditions. They came from families that had been running grocery stores for generations and did not want to give up their store because they were uncertain as to whether any new store they could buy was capable of sustaining itself. Some wanted to pass the business down to their children to maintain the family tradition, and others hoped that one of their children would be able to make a reasonable living from the store for their family. This latter group simply saw the business as a resource that could help one of their kids (usually the one their parents felt would have the most difficulty) make a comfortable living.[16]

Holdout owners in the five neighborhoods were of Jewish, Italian, and African American descent in New York and Mexican and African American descent in Los Angeles. Spike Lee's film *Do The Right Thing* vividly portrayed this group in the character of the pizzeria owner. Waldinger describes them as owners who, when they eventually give up their businesses, create a vacancy for a new ethnic group to secure a greater portion of the economic niche.[17]

The third type of store was the "trailblazer," acquired by someone who saw an emerging business opportunity from the neighborhood's changing population dynamics. For example, when a few members of an ethnic group moved to a new neighborhood, one of them opened a store to serve both the existing population and the future population anticipated from the group's expansion.[18] At first such stores were fairly isolated because their establishment as places for a particular group's needs distanced them from the neighborhood's dominant ethnic groups. Community members from their group saw them as invaluable resources, but other ethnic groups saw them as ominous, yet inevitable signs of neighborhood change. Josephine, a forty-year-old Jamaican who had just moved to the Eagleton neighborhood of Brooklyn, and Ella, a thirty-seven-year-old African American resident, represent these divergent views. Josephine told two of her friends, who also came from Jamaica,

> I am so glad to come here [Shippley's Grocery] to get the groceries I need for cooking. If I didn't have it I would have to travel by two buses to shop, plus I wouldn't get to talk much to you two.[19]

Ella, in contrast, told her friends,

> No, I ain't going to Shippley's anymore since it now is for them foreign blacks. They gots food and stuff for them, and I don't cook with that stuff. . . .Yeah, just like that there store, there is going to be lots of them [Jamaicans] coming here [Eagleton] to live, and that's a shame.[20]

The last type of proprietorship, which I have termed "indigenous," was the most "organic" in that the store owner currently lived in the neighborhood or had lived there in the past and was a member of one of the dominant ethnic groups. Owners of this type of store were socially integrated into the community, and although they might make a very modest living, they found satisfaction in their interaction with members of their community. Some of the establishments might well have been trailblazers in the past, but as the population of their group increased and their tenure in business lengthened, they became indigenous.[21]

THE SOCIAL MEANING OF ECONOMIC EXCHANGE

As part of its daily operations, every form of the mom-and-pop store engaged in economic exchanges whose social meaning was determined by the way and degree to which the store had been integrated into the social fabric of the neighborhood. When a store was completely integrated, it became a neighborhood institution, whereas a store that was not so integrated was an economic enterprise, defined here as an establishment run by an owner or manager whose sole motive was economic profit and the accumulation of wealth. Two processes existed through which a mom-and-pop store developed into either a neighborhood institution or an enterprise.

The Making of a Neighborhood Institution

In most cases, the trailblazer and indigenous types of ownership were more likely to achieve the status of a neighborhood institution. The imperialist type was more likely to be an economic enterprise, while the holdout type could assume the character of a neighborhood institution or an economic enterprise, depending on what set of roles the owner wanted to assume. A mom-and-pop store started becoming a neighborhood institution when the proprietor supplied the provisions that were in demand by the neighborhood's residents, the first of which were food and drink. Small grocery stores maintained ethnic and class culture by stocking their shelves with foodstuffs that the residents needed to cook in a way specific to their group.[22] Although some of the large and medium-sized supermarkets supplied ethnic-specific products, the proprietors of mom-and-pop stores, as members of a certain ethnic group, were often more aware of the specialty products residents required, so they made it easy for residents to acquire small quantities of these products.

In most cases, mom-and-pop stores specialized in the foods and drinks of the ethnic group to which the proprietor belonged, but sometimes they provided products needed by two, or occasionally three, of the ethnic groups in the area, thereby helping to establish the store as an important source of traditional culture.[23] Although the store itself was not a symbol of traditionalism, it served as an important cultural foundation because food plays an important role in any culture.[24] Thus, where traditional culture was constantly practiced as opposed to being merely symbolic, the store, among other institutions, accommodated the everyday cultural activities of various ethnic groups.[25]

Mom-and-pop stores also eased the transition of the immigrant poor from their country of origin by providing traditional food items that were also symbols of the familiar and dear while at the same time offering products associated with the new culture. The comments of Sharon, a thirty-seven-year-old Jamaican who had lived in the United States for only six months, are representative. She was talking to Irving, the owner of the Farragut Street Grocery, who was Jewish:

> *Sharon*: You got that turmeric from the Island I been looking for. What a nice surprise.
>
> *Irving*: Yes, it came in about two days ago. I had to call a couple of different distributors, but I got it.
>
> *Sharon*: You know, you made my day. I missed the home [Jamaica], and having the same ingredients to make my curry goat makes me just feel so good. You are such a dear for thinking of this, Irving. You just help [make] my move so much easier.
>
> *Irving*: Thank you, Sharon, but it's you good people that make things nice for me too. Remember, you need anything, just let me know and I'll try to get it.
>
> *Sharon*: You made my day, Irving, see you tomorrow.
>
> *Irving*: I'm glad, see you tomorrow.[26]

These stores also performed services for their patrons, often by delivering groceries ordered over the telephone. In addition, the store owner usually had someone available to help patrons who needed their groceries carried home. This was an invaluable service, especially to the elderly, because it enabled them to purchase more than they otherwise could and helped them feel protected during the time they were most vulnerable to being robbed.

Furthermore, mom-and-pop stores performed financial services for their patrons by allowing customers to buy goods on credit.[27] Credit was good until the end of the month, when it was assumed that patrons either were paid by their employers or had received their stipends from the various social service agencies. However, most stores extended the credit period for a customer who had consistently paid off past credit advances.

Other financial services performed by mom-and-pop stores were the cashing of personal and company checks and the provision of small loans. The poor often found it impossible to get to their bank before closing time and preferred not to use check-cashing businesses because of their high fees. Further, sometimes the poor did not have enough money in their accounts to cover their purchases and asked the owner to hold a check for a few days before cashing it—in essence, the equivalent of a quick loan. Finally, patrons sometimes asked the store owner for an outright loan, generally for less than $100, but at times for $500 or more.[28] These loans were not completely free; since they were outright cash loans, the store owner often charged a onetime fee.

Competing with the mom-and-pop store for business were the medium- and large-sized supermarkets. Their numbers were not significant, but at least one was near enough to the residents of these poor neighborhoods to present competition since some did part of their shopping at these supermarkets.[29] Further, although most of these stores would carry some ethnic products and set prices significantly lower than those in small stores, mom-and-pop stores survived primarily because of their proximity and the services they provided to the neighborhood. The location of the mom-and-pop store in the community, giving residents easy access, was crucial because poor people did not own or have ready access to a vehicle, making transportation difficult.[30] Thus a store in close proximity allowed them to secure products when they needed them, rather than estimating and procuring a week's rations, a task that raised difficulties for many residents because they lacked the physical and refrigeration space to store a week's worth of supplies or the funds to purchase them. A second factor that was particularly important for single parents who had to purchase some item but did not have anyone to watch the children while they went to the store was that it took less time to go to a local mom-and-pop store than to the supermarket.[31] Finally, because the adult residents knew the store's owner and workers, they could send their children to purchase products without worrying about whether they would be cheated or refused service when they asked for products like cigarettes.

SOCIAL INTERACTION IN THE STORE

Although a good deal of the mom-and-pop store's legitimacy in the neighborhoods came from its supplying of provisions, it also came from the owner's willingness to allow space for social interaction. The substance, strength, and quantity of these interactions were very important to the residents' everyday lives.[32] These interactions were related to the social subgroups in the community and their associated interests. The four important types of constituent groups that used the store were those of ethnicity, economic status, gender, and age, none of which can be understood in isolation. Even when the influence of these groups overlapped, interests were expressed through the medium of one of them.

Gender and age played the most important role in the institutionalizing process. Women, men, and youth all frequented the store, but generally at different times. Sometimes two or even all three groups were in the store at the same time, but this pattern was not typical (see table 4). In fact, the pattern of using the store at separate times was understood as a form of reservation by each of the constituent groups. It was not that any particular group was strictly forbidden to use the store during a specific time; rather, one of the groups dominated the social and physical space, making it difficult for the other groups to have the "quality" time they sought. Commonly, "reservation" times corresponded to the work or school schedules of each group, which appeared to be associated with some "natural rhythm" that the residents lived by. These perceived "natural rhythms" were actually the norms that provided ordered interaction.[33]

Women's use of the store was interesting because gender groups, like age groups, overlapped with the other groups observed. As table 4 indicates, women frequented the store primarily from 9:00 a.m. to 12:00 noon, arriving after their children had gone to school and their husbands to work. They shopped for provisions for lunch (if anyone came home for lunch) and dinner. Since many dinners required much preparation and their kitchens were small, it was optimal that the women get home and begin when the children would not get in the way. Women went to the store at other times, especially for a particular item that had run out, but they generally purchased the item and left immediately. This general pattern was observed in other constituent groups who needed to use the store outside their "scheduled" times.

Women in the Store. Women frequented a particular store for both practical and social reasons. For practicality, they went to the store to purchase supplies. As Pierre Bourdieu's work on social distinction points out, supplies purchased have social significance in that they are the artifacts of tastes manufactured from the social conditions of a particular

TABLE 4. PATTERNS OF TIME FREQUENTING MOM-AND-POP STORES BY GENDER, AGE, AND ECONOMIC STATUS

		Morning	Afternoon	Evening
Women		9:00–12:00	12:00–1:00	7:00–9:00
Kids		7:30–8:45	3:00–5:00	9:00–11:00
Men	IP	10:00–11:00	2:00–3:00	
	PWP	7:15–8:15	12:00–1:30	5:00–8:00
	WP	7:00–7:45		5:00–7:00
	WC	7:00–7:45		5:00–7:00

NOTE: Times given are the specific times when members of these groups were the dominant presence in the stores. IP = idle poor (unemployed); PWP = periodically working poor (periodically unemployed, wages below or near official poverty line); WP = working poor (steadily employed, wages below or near the official poverty line); WC = working class (working full time in occupations that pay wages that can produce a relatively comfortable living; although the exact incomes fluctuate in relation to the strength of the economy, particularly inflation, the range during the nine years of this study, from 1991 to 2000, was between $35,000 and $60,000).

social standing.[34] Supplies also provided the basis for the production of identity and social divisions within the five neighborhoods.[35]

Food purchases gave the women a means of building and maintaining the solidarity of their social cliques. Therefore, in each of the mom-and-pop stores, the foods available were those desired by the dictates of the local subculture, which were often displayed in the window or glass freezer to indicate the store's local orientation. Because these stores had limited space, the number of products offered was limited, and this encouraged different stores to offer modestly different food. People in the five neighborhoods studied were generally meat eaters, but the selection of meats, or cuts of meat, that they could afford was limited, as was the store's freezer capacity. Thus the mom-and-pop store would stock processed, sliced meats like sausages and turkey loaf, canned meats like Spam, and less desirable parts of animals like ox tails, feet, liver, intestines, stomach, brains, and tongues.

Food, or the topic of food, was an important factor in making the store a neighborhood institution because it helped integrate people of different value orientations through the formation of social cliques. Thus food like internal organs, feet, heads, and tails, consumed by the lower classes but considered vulgar and disgusting by the middle and upper classes, established a cultural bond among the poor of these neighborhoods.[36] The strength of this aspect of culture could be seen when the residents had enough money to eat "middle- and upper-class food" but chose the less healthy foods on which they had been brought up.[37]

Culture's role in poorer people's attachment to certain foods began with the process of socialization that transformed the material conditions of life into social taste.[38] Women using less expensive foods like intestines, stomach, pig and chicken feet, ox tail, tongue, and brains worked creatively to make their meals attractive by camouflaging their natural look, smell, and taste, by cutting certain organs into smaller, indistinguishable pieces, and by mixing them with other ingredients to make stews and soups. They transformed foods from merely palatable to desired dishes, such as *menudo* (cow's stomach), *barbaracoa* (meat shaved from the head of a cow), and *tripas* (pig intestines) in Mexican culture, chitterlings and hog maws (small and large intestines) and brains in African American culture, and *patitas* (pigs' feet) in Puerto Rican culture.[39]

That the lower classes' preference for their own particular foods rather than those of the middle and upper classes was based on social taste and not just on cost is clearly shown by an incident involving

Humberto, a thirty-four-year-old Puerto Rican who worked part time as a parking lot attendant, and his family, who had been on food stamps for a year. When he came into the Elmway neighborhood's Isla Grocery, Manny, the owner, greeted him with "I just got a small amount of center-cut steak that I will sell to you for the same price as strip steak." Humberto respectfully declined, saying, "I'd rather buy my wife those *patitas* [pigs' feet] so she can make *sancocho* [a Puerto Rican stew] that all of us like better." At one time he even complained about a free meal that his boss at the parking lot treated him and his co-workers to, saying, "The dinner was expensive and pretty good, but I didn't really care for the food that much because it didn't have a lot of good spices on it."[40]

The preference for certain foods, in addition to being a matter of taste, was a way to preserve culture. Many dishes were an integral part of ethnic identification, since class origins of food had to do with an individual's ethnic origins. For example, *menudo*, a dish made from cow's stomach, was a central element in Mexican culture even though middle- and upper-class Mexicans would not readily eat it. This gave lower-class Mexicans a feeling that they were the legitimate keepers of traditional culture and could maintain this aspect of group culture even under financial hardship, significantly contributing to the reproduction of both Mexican and lower-class culture.[41]

Food was a primary means through which people in the neighborhoods bonded while in the store. They often bought products associated with the lower class and then conversed about what they planned to eat for dinner, how to prepare it, and who in the family especially liked it. Take the comments of Gloria, a fifty-one-year-old African American resident of the Palm Court Apartments in the Bronx:

> I'm glad that Steve [the store owner] got some fresh innards in. I was going to make some chitterlings and hog maws this weekend. My husband likes them, and my boy's been complaining and complaining that he don't even know what they is. [Laughter between the two] I ain't been makin' them as much as I used to because of all that cholesterol and stuff the doctor be talking about, but my son be actin' like he don't get nothin' good to eat. I just made 'em four weeks ago! My, he does like them, and so I clean and boil 'em good. Then I try to sprinkle them with some spices and lemon. They be so tender by then, and I serve them with a hot sauce that I came up with—they be so good! When my boy starts requestin' them, then my husband gets goin' that he be starved for some hisself and that his color is getting lighter as a result! [There is more laughter because the comment implies that he is becoming white as a result of her not making African American food.][42]

Each aspect of these conversations (the dish, the recipe, and who liked it) communicated group membership and thereby generated the friendships of the store's social cliques.

Another important social contribution of food was the establishment of a special relationship with the store owners. Store owners let people know when they had a particular food in stock, and patrons asked them when they would have specific products. By providing the owners and patrons with evidence that the other was thinking of them, these interactions established a strong bond, as the prior conversation between Sharon and Irving, the owner of the Farragut Street Grocery, indicates. They also gave all those involved an opportunity to discuss their social lives, which, for many of these women, were so camouflaged by their routines that they might otherwise go unnoticed. Thus talk of food blended the routine of cooking with stories of family and a sense of group history through the dish's history, providing an important element in the store's development as a neighborhood institution.

Women's frequenting of a store and interactions there had important implications for the store's role in the structure of the neighborhood. This interaction was primarily verbal and involved "gossip." The words *gossip* and *rumor* are often used interchangeably, but in low-income or poor neighborhoods residents use them to denote two different concepts with different psychological and behavioral properties.[43] In this context, gossip was the reiteration of events that had occurred sometime in the past and was almost always laced with normative judgments. What separated gossip from nongossip was that the latter purveyed information to make a point, whereas gossip transmitted either factual or nonfactual information about another person's private affairs, for the purpose of entertainment and personal benefit, to people who might or might not want to know about it.[44] Rumor, on the other hand, was the reporting, without normative judgments, of events in order to communicate information about an action currently occurring, or projected to occur in the future, when the full accuracy of the report was questionable, although not necessarily meaningless.[45]

Gossip in the mom-and-pop stores was primarily associated with women and assumed certain forms, contents, and purposes. It had four forms. The first of these was a power-enhancing form: one person presented him- or herself as having information that should be known by others in the group lest they risk being labeled "foolish." Thus gossip was used to enhance a person's status within his or her clique and, more generally, in the neighborhood.

The second form of gossip was pseudosecretive. The person impart-
ing the gossip either clearly stated that information about to be made
public was to be kept confidential by the listener or used mannerisms to
suggest he or she was about to impart sensitive information that was
inappropriate for mass consumption. However, even when the messenger issued an official warning that the information was to be controlled,
he or she subtly implied that it could be passed on in situations that the
listener judged appropriate.

The third form of gossip was a communicative interaction as a symbol of friendship. Gossip was presented in a manner that symbolized a
close friendship with the listener and implied that for the listener to violate the messenger's trust by passing it on would put the messenger at
risk of retribution, thus violating the friendship. The comment of Hertha
in a conversation with Nancy in the Richardson neighborhood's Monitor Grocery represents this form of gossip:

> Yeah, can you believe it? I saw him [the man they are talking about] all
> over her, and with his little girl in the car! I don't know how he can show
> himself to his family. Now, don't tell anyone that I saw and told you
> because his wife and family might feel embarrassed and he'd be real pissed
> at me.[46]

The final form of gossip was an exaggeration of information. This
type of gossip consisted of stories whose events were elaborated upon to
make them more painful, strange, or awkward than they had been when
they were originally made public. This was done to (1) capture and sustain a person or group's attention; (2) authenticate the information and
its reason for being told; and (3) establish the importance of the person
telling the story.

The content of gossip among the women who frequented the mom-
and-pop stores could be categorized as comprising six conversational
topics. The first topic concerned bodily problems, such as a person's
health, appearance (shape, size, and age), and death. A second topic
focused on the problems of another's love life, centering on people in the
community who were no longer partners, or who in the community was
cheating on whom. A third topic was the problems of other people's children: being held back a grade in school, getting involved with drugs,
alcohol, or firearms, robbing from their parents, or getting pregnant.

Other people's troubles with the law were also an important subject
of gossip in the store. Since so many people from these neighborhoods
were arrested and sent to jail, the tone of the gossip was ominous, as

though the conversation were about a spreading epidemic. People gossiped about who in a family was incarcerated, often in a tone suggesting that any one of them could be next. The details of these discussions were all too familiar to the women participating but served as a reminder of their common vulnerability and their need for each other's support. The comments of Corine, a forty-year-old African American living in the Bronx's Monument neighborhood, are representative. She was talking to two friends at the Gordon Street Grocery:

> I just hear about Dahli's son being arrested for murder. I heard he is at Riker's Island [New York City's Detention Center]. My, this is going to be so, so hard on poor Dahli. She's worked so hard for all those kids and then this happens. We need to call her to see if she needs some help. [The two friends say "yes."] Gosh, what would we do without each other? [Everyone says, "You are so right!"][47]

The fifth topic of gossip in the store was the economic troubles of specific residents, such as how an individual or family had been evicted from their residence or had had their belongings repossessed. Empathy and fear underlay this gossip, as seen in the following conversation between Tati, Julia, and Nilda at the Monument neighborhood's Tortuga Grocery:

> *Tati*: Tony told me that Angela didn't have any place to live now that the building they were in burned down.
>
> *Julia*: Yeah, my boy Hector said he saw Donnie [Angela's son] huddled in one of the abandoned buildings over by the highway. Do you think they are living there?
>
> *Tati*: I'll bet they are, because Angela's two year old needs milk and Pat [a friend of Tati] said she saw her at the B.J. store [the store close to the abandoned building]. It's a shame!
>
> *Julia and Nilda*: Yeah, it is a shame![48]

The sixth, and final, topic of gossip was violations of local norms, primarily violations having to do with child neglect, abuse, and violence by residents toward vulnerable members of the neighborhood. A conversation between thirty-year-old Leonard, forty-two-year-old Mark, and thirty-eight-year-old Derek, three African American men at Finger's Grocery in the Elmway neighborhood, illustrates this type of gossip:

> *Derek*: Doc said he heard Jamaal was in trouble with Child Protective Services. Something about his young three-year-old being burned and taken to the hospital for treatment.

Leonard: They think it was done on purpose?
    Derek: I don't know, I guess, 'cause someone said that hot water spilled
            on him, and it didn't look like a water burn. Something like that.
    Mark: That's fucked up, man!
    Derek: Jamaal is fucked up![49]

Both the form and content of gossip in the mom-and-pop store furthered certain aims, the first of which was entertainment. This entertainment resulted from the nourishment of feelings of amazement. In most cases, stories were so exaggerated that their telling amused people.[50] Sometimes gossip stories were so funny that people could not help laughing. In each of these cases, people looked forward to discussions in the hope that normal conversation would give way to a piece of gossip that would offer amusement.

Gossip was also used to inform people. It was often, though not always, exaggerated, but at times it included some accurate information. Thus the fact that the information often did not have an "official" source and was disseminated by word of mouth did not disqualify it from being useful, but people had to pay close attention to determine what was "accurate" and what opened up interesting possibilities. For example, in Mikey's Grocery in the Bronx Elmway neighborhood, Tony told a group of men that he heard that the local numbers joint (illegal lottery business) had found three people cheating on their collections and had nearly beaten them to death as a result. This gossip proved useful in warning those who played the game to keep their receipts for more than a week to prove that they had paid for their card. After hearing the story, a man named Henry went to the owner of the numbers joint and asked to replace one of the three men who had been cheating. As it turned out, the story was a bit exaggerated in that only one man had been cheating, but Henry did get his job.

A third purpose of gossip was the psychological relief often provided by a comparison of the stories about other people with one's own situation. Thus people listened to stories of bad illnesses, injuries, confinement, and death, all common situations, with interest and relief that they did not have to deal with such problems at the moment and that, no matter how bad their situation, someone's was worse. The comment of Dona, a thirty-one-year-old Jamaican American living in Brooklyn's Eagleton neighborhood, is representative:

I'm going to see if I can visit Rupert today. His mom told me that the doctors thought he would not be able to walk again. I just can't believe it, he

just goes to work, trips and falls from the scaffold, and his whole life is forever the pits. I ain't ever going to worry about stupid stuff like getting
taken for that $50 by Jordan [a friend]. I been taking tunafish sandwiches
to work because of it, but that's okay given all that can happen.[51]

Finally, gossip was used as a means of social control. Gossip could
affect a person's or his or her family's identity positively or negatively
(i.e., by conferring stigma). Therefore, women who frequented the stores
put much effort into managing gossip in such a way that it regulated
behavior and contributed to social control and cohesion within the
store.[52] One example of gossip management involved Soledad, a twenty-
seven-year-old Mexican American living in the El Rey neighborhood of
Los Angeles:

He did what? He got Flora [his sister] pregnant and she got an abortion?
. . . I don't know about that. Who said that? I don't think that anybody
should say anything about this until someone knows more, 'cause it's not
fair to Hilda [the mother] and her family.[53]

In addition to purveying gossip and rumors, women in the store often
discussed entertainment, such as television, movies, and music. The
movies and television shows discussed were nearly always heavily laden
with emotion. In the Latino stores, an inordinate amount of discussion
was about the *novelas* (Spanish soap operas) that played on Spanish-
language television. These *novelas* were popular because they followed
a formula that included honorable and dishonorable people, love and
betrayal, sickness and health, and life and death, topics that the women
might think about privately but could not talk about with each other
except through the medium of the *novela*. Thus women shared their own
feelings and experiences through their discussions of the *novela*'s characters and situations. *Novelas* had certain advantages over English-
language soap operas because a typical *novela* lasted for a number of
months and then ended, to be followed by a new one, whereas typical
English-language soap operas went on for years. Thus, although the
women watching the *novela* had less opportunity to have an ongoing
relationship with its characters, the frequent introduction of new stories
provided fresh material for conversation.

Most of the women in these poor neighborhoods were religious, so
they often discussed church. However, despite their religiosity, they
rarely, if ever, brought religion itself (i.e., theological dogma) into their
conversations, focusing instead on the physical condition of their
church and the activities they were involved in. Conversations about

what a particular church was doing in the areas of remodeling, intra-congregational activities, and missionary initiatives were common.

Church activities were a prominent topic of discussion for three reasons. First, since women dominated the activities of their churches they had a common ground of shared experiences. Second, for many women, church activities were the primary social events of the week. Finally, women thought a lot about spiritual issues and the promise of the afterlife. Since the afterlife was predicated on redemption, becoming closer to God through the activities of the church was a means to that end.[54] The comments of Bertha, a thirty-three-year-old Jamaican woman who lived in Brooklyn's Eagleton neighborhood, are representative:

> We been working so hard at our church lately. We just started a new crusade, and so I been helping to get the church set up for the new people who will be joining us. We been cleaning, setting up tables, getting the nursery in order, and mimeographing things to hand out. . . . Yes, it is a lot of work, but I like working there with the people I know and like, and the Lord tells us to work for him and reap the glory of his kingdom in the next life. Amen! [All the other women say, "Amen."][55]

In sum, the small talk often taken for granted by people, including researchers, was in fact instrumental to the formation of social cliques that were necessary for the store to become a neighborhood institution since it provided the substance for close and continued relationships.

Men in the Store.   Men frequented the store at different times depending on their economic status. Those who worked full time generally frequented the store early in the morning before going to work. Some of them bought a pastry for breakfast, but most bought sandwiches, drinks, and various tobacco products to take to work (see table 4). Most employed men returned to the store after work, not to purchase supplies, but to socialize and relax. They generally came to the store at five in the afternoon, and a group of them (not the same people) remained until nine at night.

The periodically working poor and the idle poor frequented the store at different times. On working days, the periodically working poor came to the store at around 8:00 a.m. to pick up food to eat while on the job. On days when they did not work, they generally came to the store between 12:00 and 12:30 to buy lunch. Regardless of whether the men worked, they all came to the store between five in the afternoon and eight in the evening to interact comfortably with each other.

The idle poor frequented the store between ten and eleven in the morning, two to three in the afternoon, four to five in the late afternoon, and nine to eleven in the evening. They came to the store at these times for two reasons. First, many of them drank heavily and did not recover from the preceding day's drinking until ten or eleven in the morning. Second, they wanted to avoid contact with the working men because, even among the poor, unemployment was stigmatized and they did not want to face looks of disdain and pity when asking for money or beer.[56] A representative incident occurred at the Martinez Grocery in L.A.'s El Rey neighborhood when a group of working men were picking up some food for lunch before going to work. Umberto, a regular at the store who had been unemployed for more than five years and drank inexpensive wine throughout the day, was waiting with another unemployed friend on a corner about a block from the store. I came up to them, exchanged greetings, and asked, "Are you on the way to the store?" They answered, "Yes," so I said, "Let's go to the store." Umberto, who knew me best, said, "We're going to wait for a bit." I replied "Okay, I'll wait too." He must have felt awkward because he then said, "We don't want to go now, 'cause the guys [men who will be doing day work] buying their food now will give us a bad time for not working, and we don't want to deal with it again and again and again!" I acknowledged, "Oh," and he went on, "They ask if you got a job yet, or they just look at you like you're worthless, so we'll just wait till they're not there." We waited at the corner for forty minutes and then went into the store, where Umberto and his friend stayed for about three hours.

During the summer, employed men dominated the physical and social space of the mom-and-pop stores from five in the afternoon until nine at night, usually placing chairs outside the store or sitting on the trunks or hoods of automobiles, talking, and drinking beer. Five topics emerged as conversational patterns. The first of these was job-related issues. During these conversations the men nearly always talked about who in the community had jobs, what type of jobs they had, and how someone might move from one type of job to another. These talks were useful because they established networks that provided resources to secure employment and facilitated mobility within the limits of the men's highly stratified labor market.[57] Of particular interest was how important the men in the working class were to the working poor who were employed part time or worked in the secondary labor market or both. The working-class men helped people get jobs in their companies by introducing them to the hiring agents of the company or to people who had some influence to help them secure a job. They also taught men what to say during job interviews or what skills they would need for a particular job.[58]

Men in the stores also talked about money problems and their schemes to get out of them. A particular person's schemes demonstrated to the others that he was smart, creative, and enterprising, attributes that were considered desirable and given a good deal of status in these poor neighborhoods. Thus a man with these qualities could raise or maintain his status in the group regardless of whether he operated under the security-maximizing or excitement-maximizing value orientation.

Men who had been planning a scheme to make money generally spent some time immediately outside the store to see if any others would co-operate in the scheme. Since men came and went throughout a particular time period, there was ample opportunity to pitch ideas, often to those who had not yet heard of the plan, or to pitch a new version of the plan. The other men usually responded to a new scheme with genuine amusement and friendly kidding about why it would not work and were in return told by the planner of the scheme why it would work. Although some of the plans went from imagination to implementation, most failed. The very few that were successful only served to keep the scheming alive because they were rarely successful enough to achieve wealth. What was important was the camaraderie produced by these discussions, which significantly contributed to the building and maintenance of social cliques that were necessary to the store's becoming a neighborhood institution.

The fourth topic of conversation among the male patrons was entertainment such as sports, gambling, and the movies. Some stores posted schedules of the city's professional sports teams, and others had televisions that received the live game broadcast of professional teams from the patrons' country of origin. People often came by the store to see who had won a game that they had not seen. The stores also reported results of sports events in other countries, such as soccer from Mexico and Jamaica, baseball from Mexico, the Dominican Republic, and Puerto Rico, and boxing from Mexico, the Dominican Republic, and Jamaica, by posting them on a piece of paper by the door or behind the counter. This information precipitated discussions and arguments, building the camaraderie among the patrons that was necessary for clique and institutional development.

Some stores sold official tickets for the state lottery, while others were fronts for unofficial lottery games (i.e., numbers). Thus conversations in the store centered on what numbers to choose for the various official and unofficial lottery games, as well as who had recently won. Since games were constantly played, the men often talked about what they would do with the money if they won. The constant excitement surrounding these "dream lists" stimulated conversations about morals and commodities.

The men in the store also discussed rumors, often about someone's physical retaliation for an occurrence in which he believed he had been wronged. Such rumors warned patrons of potential danger and areas that could be a setting for retaliation. Rumors were different from gossip in that they provided information that men evaluated for accuracy and assessed for the level of danger to which they could be subjected if the rumor was accurate. A representative instance was a rumor that twenty-four-year-old Pablo passed on to four other Mexican American men at the Jalisco Grocery in the El Rey neighborhood of Los Angeles:

> Felix is going to get shot, and you better believe it! This is the second time a group of *mojados* [immigrants] has been caught at "K" Street [an immigrant day-laborer employment site], and everyone says Felix called the *migra* [the Immigration and Naturalization Service]. I sure don't want to hang [socialize] with him, 'cause anyone around him when it comes down [the shooting] is going to go down with him [be shot]![59]

Though men frequently discussed rumors at the store, they were less likely to engage in gossip there, particularly about women in the neighborhood, because it was not a private preserve for men since women sometimes frequented the store during the "men's time." Further, children in the store might hear something negative about a family member, and this was considered not only to be in "bad" taste but to invite physical retaliation if word got back to a family member. Thus gossip was avoided because it could compromise clique solidarity, as well as the social order in the store and neighborhood.

Youth in the Store.   Young people between the ages of five and twenty most often frequented the stores on weekdays, starting at 7:30 a.m. on their way to school to buy food for breakfast or for a morning snack at school. They also came to the store between 11:45 a.m. and 1:00 p.m. to buy food for lunch and then reappeared after school from 3:00 to 5:00 p.m. to buy snacks, finally coming back to the store between 7:00 p.m. and 9:00 p.m. In the evening, the five- to eleven-year-olds tended to come to the store between 7:00 p.m. and 8:00 p.m., whereas the twelve- to nineteen-year-olds came and went from 7:00 p.m. to the store's closing. During the week when school was in session, few youth of any age frequented the store in the evening, but on the weekends the older youth stayed until the store closed. In summer one would observe young people at the stores throughout the day and evening.

While at the store, the youth of these five neighborhoods had regular patterns of behavior that fell into two types. The first of these was the purchase and consumption of products in high demand by youth, particularly "junk foods" heavily saturated with fats, carbohydrates, and sugar, which though lacking in nutrition, tasted good, were temporarily filling, and were relatively inexpensive. Thus the mom-and-pop store was a primary place for youth purchases because of its great variety of such foods and the convenience of its proximity and business hours.[60]

Youth could occasionally purchase products at the mom-and-pop store that were prohibited by law. The most common product bought was cigarettes, although liquor and fireworks were also purchased. The store owner was lenient about selling cigarettes to youth, but if they wanted to buy liquor and fireworks they asked someone of legal age to be the official buyer. Although everyone knew what was taking place, it was generally understood that the store owner had to be protected.

Second, the store was a very important place for social relations among the youth of these neighborhoods, who came there to talk and play with others their age and ease the isolation and boredom that they felt in their generally cramped living arrangements. The comments of Ricardo and Jewel are representative. Ricardo was a fourteen-year-old Dominican from the Elmway neighborhood of New York:

> Yeah, I like going to the Primo Grocery and seeing who's around. Sometimes there ain't nothing to do in this apartment, and sometimes the building ain't got nobody around it too. But the store's got people to hang with if you go at the right time. Sometimes there is not that much to do at the store either, but at least there is other people you like that you can just talk with.[61]

Jewel was a sixteen-year-old African American from Brooklyn's Eagleton neighborhood:

> You want to go to Shippley's [the store]? There'll be somebody there for us to check out [see and talk to]. . . . Well, there sure ain't nothing happening around here, and I'm getting bored. Let's just go at five and see who's there and if there might be some party going tonight. . . . Janice and Myrna [friends] might not be there, but they might stop. They usually do, and if we don't see them somebody else will show up.[62]

Although the store was a place to meet other youth, it was not a neutral location for everyone. In both contested and fragmented neighborhoods, certain stores served as centers for fraternizing and information exchange for particular social groups. Everyone was welcome to use any store to purchase products, but only a specific group(s) had the authority to use a specific store as a social space. In contested neighborhoods this was enforced through verbal harassment and threat or physical confrontation.[63] In fragmented neighborhoods it was enforced through body language, the stopping of conversation, and the refusal to acknowledge the intruder's presence.[64]

During times of socializing, young people discussed recent social events that affected them. Gossip about who was sexually interested in or involved with whom was also a primary topic of youth conversation. Further, young people used the store as a staging area for social events in another part of the neighborhood. Most often, they met at the store to find out who was having a party, or who would provide a place for a party, and then moved on to that location.

In addition, the store was a site for sexual socialization. Although the barbershops, beauty salons, and gangs were the primary places where the learning of sexuality began (see chapters 6 and 8), young people practiced what they had learned in other institutional contexts at the store. Thus, in the store, they began a variety of rituals related to sexuality. For example, local norms of gender segregation while at the store were mediated by each gender group's occupation of a physical location that gave them the opportunity to observe and be observed by the opposite sex. This ritual generally played out after school, during which the physical posturing by both sexes was very important. Integral to the ritual was the presentation of what the youth believed were their "attractive assets," communicating that they wanted to be watched by one or more of the opposite sex in the store, followed by verbal overtures to the people of interest to them.

Although feelings about the opposite sex remained guarded to protect an individual's sense of private and public dignity, satisfying one's physical (sexual) and emotional (love) desires was still paramount. Kidding and playing games with those to whom one was attracted provided the substance of the young people's courtship rituals. In situations when a boy wanted only a sexual relationship, the kidding and the games played contained explicit sexual references. However, when a boy sought a long-term relationship, he avoided anything explicitly sexual in his kidding and game playing. These differences within the same ritual were subtle but effective in communicating intentions.

REGULATING SOCIAL INTERACTION

The store's development into a neighborhood institution was contingent on how its social interactions were managed. In this regard, social interaction within the store was molded into a specific form, regulated, and ultimately extended to other institutions in the neighborhood. Neighborhood residents in the store had a set of regularized interactions that established a pattern whereby they could easily predict the broad outline of social and economic exchanges to an extent that they felt comfortable with and excited about.

Establishing an Interactive Order.   The interactive order that provided one of the most essential elements of the store's emergence as a neighborhood institution was the development of social identities for its regular patrons. These identities were forged from the group's perceptions of each individual's history within the neighborhood. Although identity formation occurred for everyone, there were differences in both process and substance for men and women. Women based their identities on group-oriented criteria, particularly the exceptional qualities related to their everyday routines that made them, for example, a good mother, friend, cook and housekeeper, or church attendee. They shared the everyday events of their families, friends, and neighbors but avoided topics that would make their family, and thus them, appear idiosyncratic. They also made a concerted effort to be cordial to all the regulars in the store and to indicate an interest in becoming a member of the store's "inner group." Since their personal identities were group oriented, their institutional identities were based on their capacity for cooperation.

Identity formation of men in the store was very different from that of women. Men in each store went out of their way to emphasize their unique qualities, highlighting a unique feature of their physical appearance, behavior, and/or experience. These qualities often led to the conferring of nicknames. Nicknames became symbols of a man's "social self" and an image that they and their inner group represented in the neighborhood. A representative example occurred at the B. J. Grocery in the Bronx's Monument neighborhood. Richard, an African American who had grown up in the neighborhood and who frequented the store, worked nights as a doorman in a Manhattan apartment building and went to Fordham University during the day. While in the store, he often answered questions with some obscure fact he had learned; thus, although he did not have a degree and worked as a doorman, he was nicknamed "Doc," an affectionate term for "doctor." During conversations in the store, others deferred to him for "facts" they wanted to know. If he was not present, they said, "We'll have to wait until Doc gets here," "Doc will be able to answer that question," or "I wonder what Doc will say?"

Another example of identify formation through the use of nicknames involved a Mexican American man named Ernesto who was a regular at Daddy G's Grocery in L.A.'s Richardson neighborhood. He owned two motorcycles, one to ride in the city, the other to use in the country for recreation, both of which he rode fast. While riding one day on wet pavement he braked suddenly and flew off his bike into the windshield of a parked car, cracking the windshield and injuring himself, although not seriously. When he told friends at the store about the accident, someone asked if he had stopped riding motorcycles. He said, "Hell, no. I know I hit that windshield just like a BB [a round pellet shot from a gun], but I still ride my cycles to the limit."[65] Everyone laughed at his BB analogy and from that time forward honored his fearlessness by referring to him as "BB."

The social identities developed in the store were one of the features that structured the social interactions in these establishments and ultimately in the broader neighborhood. The other feature was the construction of a status hierarchy from the various identities and from the amount of time one spent at the store. This status hierarchy established a person as a regular, periodic, or occasional patron (see chapter 1 for definitions) and assigned the regulars the highest status, followed by the periodic and then the occasional patrons.[66] When the store owner was viewed as a member of the organic community, the person(s) closest to him or her assumed the highest status levels.[67] Someone close to the proprietor usually helped with odd jobs while providing friendship and company. In turn, the proprietors bestowed their favor on them, while others, including the regulars, deferred to them.

Position in the status hierarchy was based on four perceived aspects of an individual: (1) time spent in the store; (2) degree of closeness to the store owner; (3) personal resources; and (4) generosity in aiding other patrons of the store. The strength of an individual's reputation based on these qualities determined his or her status among the store's social cliques. The case of Josue, a forty-three-year-old Puerto Rican regular at Nino's Grocery in the Eagleton neighborhood of Brooklyn, is representative. He worked as a mechanic at a gas station not far from the store and had previously worked part time in a hardware store. Through his work he had accumulated a number of resources such as a knowledge of tools and products, skills in building and repairing, and a network of people with additional skills and knowledge. As a regular who frequently ate at the store, he was always being interrupted and asked questions by other patrons. Because he was a primary resource for all the social cliques, he was given one of the highest rankings in Nino's.

A variety of other criteria were used to establish status among the various people frequenting the store, but none was more important than the willingness to assist others who socialized there. For example, because of a general lack of money, some people generously offered their physical labor to help other patrons, some shared certain "treats" with others in the store, and some gave their time to listen to others and offer emotional support to those in need. Finally, some of the store's patrons, most of whom had successfully confronted extreme and/or constant difficulties with persistence, inspired others to persevere during difficult times. Ultimately, social hierarchy was established by assigning higher status to those who possessed higher quantities of these attributes.[68] It should be emphasized that the neighborhood residents who frequented the various stores were aware of the social hierarchy, the status of individuals within it, and the criteria used for placement. However, even though the social hierarchy had graded levels, it did not assume a pyramid formation.

Maintaining Ordered Interaction.   Three items regulated the social identities and their concomitant hierarchies in each of the stores. One of these was the behavioral norms that had developed out of the patrons' consistent interactions. These norms originated in the ethnic and substrata cultures of the five neighborhoods' residents.

Many of the social relations in the mom-and-pop stores were organized around the norms associated with the cultural concepts of honor and respect. Honor was operative in the stores where Mexican and Central Americans were the primary patrons, since these ethnic groups are oriented to that value, which derives from both the Spanish and Native cultures that formed each group's basic identity. In such cultures, a person's honor is bestowed at birth and is his or hers to protect and maintain. Honor can be lost but not gained, so its protection is valued. In stores that served Mexican and/or Central Americans, the preservation of honor governed social relations, so people were cautious not to offend other patrons.[69] Exchanges between all patrons who entered the store were characterized by a politeness and a fellowship not seen in stores operating under norms of respect. Newcomers were easily welcomed and incorporated into the group. Additionally, because everyday interactions were regulated by the cultural norms of honor, they were predictable, a characteristic essential to the formation and maintenance of the store as a neighborhood institution.[70]

In stores where honor regulated interaction, joking that connoted friendship, defused tension, and introduced new subjects in a manner that did not offend another's honor was common among people who knew each other. Gestures were used to signal a disclaimer of any damaging insinuation that might be implied by the joke. In many cases, whoever told the joke used an "affected" laugh in the middle or immediately after its telling to intimate that no one's honor was being targeted. Such general deference protected people's honor and established predictable behavior.

In stores primarily frequented by African Americans, Jamaicans, Puerto Ricans, and Dominicans, social relations were dominated by the norms of "respect." The concept of respect is different from that of honor because it is based on prestige that is earned rather than bestowed. Since respect is earned, it is sought after like a commodity that can be lost and regained, establishing fluidity in how and when it is obtained and to what degree. Because of its nature, one can gain and accumulate respect at the cost of another, thereby reducing the other's amount of respect.[71] In stores where these ethnic groups were most prevalent, respect was demanded through verbal and behavioral cues. The verbal means included aggressive orders to others in the store, accusations about the inadequacy of others' actions, and attempts to gain the group's esteem. The physical means involved carrying oneself with style and bravado. One gesture that challenged a person's respect was looking at the person for an extended period of time because it was intended to make him or her self-conscious and uncomfortable.[72]

Social Sanctions in the Ordered Interaction Process. A good deal of positive reinforcement was used in establishing and maintaining social control through the emotional satisfaction that people gained from friendship in the store's formal clique(s). Since most interactions in the store were face to face, positive feedback such as hugs, kisses, handshakes, and verbal gestures of appreciation was given immediately after one acted within the boundaries of the existing social norms. This created an environment where people wanted to act in accordance with the store's norms in order to be liked.

When positive reinforcement proved unsuccessful, negative sanctions were implemented to obtain the desired level of compliance with the existing norms. Members of a particular clique often used gossip and rumors to announce character flaws in individuals they saw as a threat to the equilibrium of the store's social relations. Such stories were used to send a message to targeted individuals that they had to either change their attitude and behavior or face a demotion in status that accompanied the stigma associated with the gossip and rumors. The case of Dora, who was

Barbadian and lived in Brooklyn's Eagleton neighborhood, is representative. Dora had been a regular in Shippley's Grocery and was forced to move from her apartment to one that was less expensive in a different section of the neighborhood. Although she lived closer to Nino's Grocery, she would occasionally take a bus to Shippley's. Formally she was now considered an occasional patron at Shippley's, whereas in the past she had been a regular. The move to the new apartment upset Dora a great deal, and every time she came into Shippley's she would start an argument with someone. These arguments would start rather benignly and then become increasingly aggressive. Each of her trips to the store became annoying and raised the level of tension while she was there. A number of regulars tried to tell her that she needed to stop acting this way because it made everyone uncomfortable. None of the interventions had the desired effect, so Roberta, a regular, decided to start a rumor that Dora had been so difficult with the owner of her last apartment that she had been asked to leave. After it was arranged for Dora to hear the rumor, she was noticeably upset and complained to everyone about it. Although the rumor was untrue, Dora realized that she needed to change. She did change, and when the regulars were sure that the change was permanent, they started another rumor that the previous one had been erroneous. This sent Dora and those in the other cliques the message that norms needed to be followed.[73]

The second mechanism used to reestablish social control was verbal confrontation, whereby those who violated the codes and expectations of the clique(s) were verbally assaulted. Since verbal confrontations were public and aggressive, they were very uncomfortable for the targeted individual. Given that people could say anything that was left to the targeted individual(s) to refute, such confrontations were effective deterrents. This tactic was used mainly in respect cultures because in honor cultures it would have produced a physical altercation that ended up lessening social control.

The third means to gain compliance was physical confrontation. Physical confrontation was an integral part of lower-class life in the neighborhood, but it was usually used in the store when all the other options were exhausted and only rarely employed immediately to achieve the desired outcome. Physical confrontation or its threat generally achieved compliance with the established norms of the store. An example involved Arturo, a twenty-seven-year-old Mexican construction worker living in the El Rey neighborhood of Los Angeles. Every afternoon around six Arturo would come after work and drink beer with the other regulars at the Canal Grocery. He had a drinking problem, so although he would be

very nice when he started drinking he would become increasingly bel-
ligerent, aggressive, and confrontational as he drank more. This would
inevitably end in some type of physical altercation. The regulars wanted
to avoid this, so they would go home before he got drunk. Everyone was
frustrated that he was ruining their good time socializing, so the owner
talked to one of his relatives who was very large and asked him to talk
to Arturo. The man came to the store, and when Arturo had just started
to drink his first beer, the man came up behind him and grabbed Arturo
under the chin and squeezed it so hard that his face became red and he
began to choke. The man told Arturo that he had to stop getting drunk
and starting fights or he was going to get hurt badly. Arturo left the store
immediately and stayed away for three weeks. Eventually, when he came
back, he would have two beers, talk, and then leave. The message had
been delivered and the social order was restored.

The last mechanism to create or maintain control in the store was
"shunning." This was an effective tactic in reducing a person's status and
socially isolating him or her. It was the most punitive sanction for an
undesired act because isolation was precisely what members of the various social cliques wanted to avoid.[74]

THE CARETAKER'S ROLE IN CREATING SOCIAL ORDER

The actions of the store owner significantly contributed to the creation
and maintenance of the store's social order.[75] The store owner set the
basic rules of engagement in the establishment, outlining what he or she
considered acceptable and unacceptable social and transactional behavior. All the store owners found fighting, physical play, screaming, and
yelling unacceptable behavior. In addition, stealing and trying to avoid
paying for goods were considered unacceptable. People who violated
these rules were not allowed in the store, and the store owner would call
the police to have the violators removed. The enforcement of these rules
helped make the store a safe and inviting environment. Take the comments of Rhoda, a forty-five-year-old mother of two who frequented the
Farragut Street Grocery in Brooklyn's Eagleton neighborhood:

> Yeah, you should come to the Farragut [Grocery] to shop. Irving [the store
> owner] don't take shit from all them fools who try to come in and make
> trouble, he calls the police and gets them out. I like goin' there 'cause I can
> shop and talk and not feel like I got to worry about who is coming to cause
> trouble. Plus, he don't give general loans to the street people, so they don't
> be coming to hassle him in the store for money either. It's a good place to
> shop and talk.[76]

However, another set of rules also existed in the stores: the codes established by the members of the social clique(s) to regulate interaction among themselves and nonclique members. Essentially these unwritten codes defined acceptable and unacceptable behavior and emanated from ethnic and substrata cultural norms, as well as the store owner's declaration of proper etiquette. For example, clique members were not to disrupt business or make it difficult for people to shop. Behavior such as staring at patrons or rudeness was considered unacceptable. Conspiring to disrupt the social hierarchy of the clique while its members were in the store was also inappropriate. Conspiring could be done, but not in the store. This kept the store from becoming an arena of conflict.

In fact, the codes required clique members to be instrumental in creating an environment that made people feel comfortable in the store. Clique members accomplished this by conversing in ways that invited others in the neighborhood to join. Kidding and friendly gestures were used to create a congenial environment and advertise that the store was socially open to everyone who wanted to interact within the established rules. When these codes were followed, the store's commercial activities, as well as its image as an important place for people from the neighborhood to socially congregate, remained healthy.

The store owner's actions as institutional caretaker were instrumental in regulating the codes and managing the interactions on the premises. As caretaker, the store owner informed people about the rules and codes by providing subtle reminders of the established etiquette of social interaction and forcefully expelling (by calling the police) those who violated his or her rules of conduct. The owner also provided information about people's whereabouts and their physical and psychological condition. Further, store owners acted as quasi-therapists for their patrons. Both men and women talked about various problems at the mom-and-pop store. A prominent and consistent topic was the money problems that most patrons dealt with. Some store owners felt that such talk was a way to lead up to requests for loans and credit. Yet store owners who acted as caretakers understood the divulgence of financial difficulties for what it usually was, a simple airing of one's financial anxieties. In these cases, the caretaker merely listened but offered little or no advice on how to improve the situation. What was important to the patrons was having someone listen to their troubles and show caring even if he or she could not offer any solutions.

Herbert Gans also reported that shopkeepers, as well as bartenders, acted as "internal caretakers" in the poverty community, providing psychological services to many of what he called their "peer group clients."[77]

How my findings differ from what Gans reported has to do with who the caretakers are and what they take care of.[78] I found that caretakers generally did not attend to all members of the neighborhood's peer group but were oriented primarily toward the regular patrons of their establishments. Further, they did not have to be, nor were they always, from the peer group they took care of. To be caretakers, store owners had to feel that their establishment was not just a business but also a neighborhood institution that they desired to maintain. Melvin, the owner of Daddy G's Grocery in L.A.'s Richardson neighborhood, is representative of owners who recognized the importance of the store in the community, as well as their role in maintaining it:

> I thought about selling the store to a real nice Indian man who made me a great offer, but I just couldn't do it. . . . No, I had not been thinking of selling, but the hours are long and it might be nice to spend a little more time with my wife. I just thought how much the people living here in the neighborhood depend on the store, and I was just a little worried that the new owner would not run the store like I do, and that would change it for everyone in the neighborhood. You know what I mean? [The two men in the conversation both nod their heads, and one responds with "I sure do know what you mean!"][79]

In addition to establishing and enforcing the rules and codes in the stores, store owners played a critical role as social mediators. Often they acted as interpreters for people, especially if one did not speak English while the other did, and their interpretations would generally soften any crude comments in order to maintain friendly relations.

The store owner continuously coordinated social relations and reduced conflict between patrons. Such conflict occurred for various reasons. Sometimes people who had a disagreement somewhere else in the neighborhood brought the conflict with them to the store, where the store owner tried to talk both parties into working out an equitable solution. This occurred in the Bronx's Monument neighborhood between Angel and Tomás, two regular members of a social clique in Finger's Grocery, over the use of a vacant garage to work on their cars and store some of their tools and equipment. Neither wanted to share the garage; both argued that the garage was too small and that since their work schedules overlapped, the garage would be impossible to share. As their dispute escalated, they started to solicit support from other members of the clique. Tensions began to increase between everyone, including neutral parties, who worried that a fight was imminent between those aligned with Angel or Tomás. Because of the increasing tension, the store owner became involved and called a friend who knew someone with two garages behind his house, one of which was unoccupied. The store owner asked his friend to ask the garage owner if someone could occupy the vacant garage. The owner agreed, on the condition that the occupier clean out the debris that had accumulated over the years and then keep the place clean. Since Tomás was closer to the store owner, the store owner asked him if he would like to take the new garage. Tomás agreed because the new garage was closer to his apartment. The store owner then contacted Angel, told him of the new agreement, and informed those who had taken sides that an amicable agreement had been reached, thereby defusing any hostilities that would have undermined the store's social relations and weakened its institutional character.

Although they occasionally had to arrange complicated solutions to mediate conflict among their regular patrons, store owners usually simply mediated minor disagreements. The degree to which the store owner was an effective caretaker of the everyday social relations in the store determined the strength of the store as a neighborhood institution.

In sum, some important aspects of the institutionalization of mom-and-pop stores in which the owner acted as caretaker must be highlighted. One aspect was identity formation among patrons of the store because a social order could not be developed without a set of personal identities that could be rationally arranged. Without this order there was insufficient structure to support an institutional status.

Further, a social order among the different personal identities was predicated on the assignment of status positions to those who were regular, periodic, and occasional patrons. Regulars were given the highest status because they saw themselves as part of a family. Regulars perceived those who frequented the store periodically as friends and those who frequented it only occasionally as guests.[80] The caretaker store owner kept all the identities and status positions straight and reminded patrons of this social order when disputes arose.

The Building of an Enterprise

Whereas some of the small grocery stores studied became neighborhood institutions, others underwent a different process that I have termed "the building of an enterprise." As stated earlier, I am defining an enterprise as an establishment run solely for profit. Thus economics shaped the dynamic regulating the store's daily operations whether or not the owner was present. In such establishments, social concern for the residents of the neighborhood and for those who patronized the store outside the confines of economic exchange was nonexistent.

In building an enterprise type of establishment, the owner's first strategy was to limit, and ultimately remove, group relations and social exchanges in the store. People who did not buy anything and simply hung around talking to each other were seen as loitering and inhibiting business. Those who bought products but also socialized in the store were also seen as inhibiting business. In each of these cases the owner tried to keep patrons moving in order to disrupt their social exchanges, most often by interrupting conversations with "Can I help you with anything?" If the first effort was not successful, other interventions were used, such as "Are you having any trouble finding anything?" and "Could you move a little, people might be having trouble seeing or getting the products they want." These tactics, if they did not end people's conversations, sufficiently disrupted them to force those who wanted to continue talking out of the store.

Another tactic used in enterprise establishments was to deny favors to the patrons. The refusal to grant social and economic favors limited social exchanges between patrons and owners or managers to simple acts of service such as finding the products that the patrons wanted and collecting the payment from them. Patrons' attempts to start personal conversations with the owner, or even conversations that approached anything personal, were abruptly and rudely terminated.[81] This also eliminated any reinforcement of the various value orientations and norms of the neighborhood.

Store owners of enterprise establishments assumed a particular demeanor with the customers. They actively minimized face-to-face relations and physically distanced themselves from the patrons. For instance, they often remodeled the checkout area by raising the floor behind the counter and installing bulletproof glass that extended two or three feet up from the counter top. This not only gave them a vantage point to watch for any vandalism or theft and provided protection from armed robbery but also expressed the owner's desire to have the store be simply a business.

Thus in an enterprise establishment owners watched customers without looking them directly in the face. This general mode of surveillance was intended to signal that unacceptable behavior would be seen but not tolerated. Further, owners' facial expressions exhibited little if any emotion. They showed no signs of happiness, sadness, depression, or friendliness. This promoted separation between the clients and the owners that reduced relationships to a set of economic transactions while removing any sense of social connection.

Enterprise establishments, then, provided their respective neighborhoods convenient services without having any neighborhood institutional properties. The imperialist and holdout types of stores were more likely to assume an enterprise character, whereas the trailblazer and indigenous types were more likely to be neighborhood institutions. The upshot was that enterprise establishments made no meaningful contribution to any of the five neighborhoods' social structures.

SOME CLOSING REMARKS

Although mom-and-pop stores are often institutions in poor neighborhoods, a mom-and-pop store in a poor neighborhood is not automatically a neighborhood institution. The achievement of neighborhood institutional status is based on the history of store ownership, the reinforcement of ethnic and class groups' social taste in food products, and social interactions that nurture individual identity and establish a status system. When all the above are present, the store is fully integrated into the subculture of the neighborhood.

The mere existence of establishments that sell grocery products in a poor neighborhood provides little information about the social health of the neighborhood. Studies that rely on the number of businesses to assess a poor neighborhood's social organization and quality of life are insufficient.[82] The character of these businesses has a greater impact on the neighborhood's social structure. Whether or not a neighborhood is structured and healthy depends on the functional quality, not quantity, of its establishments' institutional contents as described in this chapter.

CHAPTER 5

Taking Care of Business

Social Change and Preservation
in the Mom-and-Pop Store

Exchange is the purest and most concentrated form of interactions in which serious interests are at stake.

Georg Simmel, *The Philosophy of Money* (1907)

The last chapter discussed the process through which the mom-and-pop
grocery store became either an institution or an enterprise in the five
poor neighborhoods of this study. This chapter looks at the dynamics
through which these stores changed or maintained the status quo, a topic
that few studies of poor neighborhoods have addressed. The most recent
studies have assessed the economic health of a poor neighborhood by
the number and types of stores, assuming that a decline in their numbers
corresponds to a decline in the quality of the neighborhood's health.[1]
However, this approach is vulnerable to two errors. The first is overlook-
ing the character of life in the neighborhood and the changes it under-
goes: for instance, a neighborhood's conversion from fragmented to
contested, or vice versa, and its effect on the social life of the residents.
The second is misdiagnosing the neighborhood's general health and
sometimes prematurely predicting its extinction.[2] This is not to say that
the mom-and-pop store cannot be a key institution in producing and
reproducing the neighborhood social order, because when it functions
as a neighborhood institution it can. However, research that solely
focuses on the number of stores in a neighborhood neglects the mechanisms and meanings of neighborhood social change. From direct observation of neighborhood life, this chapter argues that the disappearance
of mom-and-pop stores does not produce social disorganization; it
merely initiates a reconfiguration of the social structure and order. Thus
any treatment of poor neighborhoods that simply takes the raw number

of stores as a proxy of neighborhood health and/or organization is making an unsound inference.

SOCIAL CHANGE IN THE STORE

Social change in the mom-and-pop grocery begins with the impact of two broad sets of agents: external (i.e., external to the social relations within the store) and internal. These sets could overlap, but for the purpose of analysis they will be separated.

External Change Agents

One of the most significant change agents in the stores was their physical layout. Changes in a store's dimensions affected social activity in the store. At times, store owners added shelving to stock new products that were in demand, thereby reducing the amount of physical space used for social interaction. This occurred in the Primo Grocery in the Bronx's Elmway neighborhood when the owner added shelving to accommodate his growing Puerto Rican clientele (see table 3, pp. 116–17). The change cut the square footage of aisle space by 20 percent, restricting social interaction to the checkout area. As more people conversed in the checkout area, other customers had difficulty buying products and began to frequent other stores. Because Primo's profits were negatively affected from the loss of customers, he limited conversations around the checkout area, forcing groups to meet outside the store. During cold weather this new policy significantly reduced social interaction. Consequently, many people began going to the Isla Grocery and integrated themselves into its cliques. As this continued, Primo's increasingly became an enterprise establishment where people simply bought products but did not socialize. Thus the neighborhood lost one of its important institutions.

An increase in physical space also affected the character of establishments, as was the case in the Farragut Street Grocery in Brooklyn's Eagleton neighborhood when Irving, the owner, increased space to add new products. After the store's remodeling was complete, new Puerto Rican and Jamaican clients from the neighborhood began to frequent the store. The added space made both shopping and conversing in the aisles easier. In addition, Irving fixed the soda fountain. The repair was not easy because parts for soda fountains were no longer manufactured, but Irving could do it because his father, the previous owner of a similar grocery, had bought and kept a number of spare parts in the base-ment of his store, and Irving had found them while cleaning it out. With the completion of the remodeling, his store became quite popular because of the larger variety of products and the novelty of being able to buy ice cream floats and the traditional "egg creams," which were becoming hard to find.[3] As more people frequented the store on a regu-lar basis, cliques began to develop with their coexistent identities and social orders, establishing the store as a neighborhood institution.

Increases in crime and social predators in the area of a store also resulted in behavioral changes and interactions of the store's patrons. Robbers, rapists, and drug addicts had the largest impact on patrons because they used physical force. Increased crime around a store changed the pattern of association among the "regular" patrons. In the case of the Jalisco Grocery in L.A.'s El Rey neighborhood, a local syn-dicate began to use the corner just outside the store to sell their drugs. Conflict between them and a rival syndicate resulted in an increase of drive-by shootings, killing two people and injuring eight. The increase in violence caused so much anxiety among the store's patrons that reg-ular and occasional patrons limited their time at the store to around fif-teen or twenty minutes, whereas before the shootings they had usually spent between forty-five minutes and two hours there.[4] This reduced interactions among clique members at the store, forcing them to frequent other establishments to socialize, such as the Mi Tierra pool hall for men and the J & L Laundry for women. Other institutions were also affected because they had to make "social room" for the new patrons in their existing social orders, and although the situation was uncomfortable, everyone tried to "make do" until conditions at the Jalisco improved.

After about five weeks, one of the drug syndicates won the struggle for control of the trade around the Jalisco area, and the store became safe again. Those who had migrated to new establishments returned and resumed their associations. This example shows how the number of stores in an area is not a reliable indicator of social order, for order here had never been compromised. Adjustments were made, and this allowed for a reestablishment of routines and a smooth restoration of the Jalisco Grocery as a neighborhood institution.

At times neighborhoods saw new or increasing populations of an eth-nic or socioeconomic group that had not previously constituted a signifi-cant presence, but it was the changes in ethnic composition that presented the most significant challenge to mom-and-pop stores. For an enterprise, new ethnic groups simply meant the addition of new patrons whose preferences had to be satisfied to optimize the store's business opportunities. However, for a store that was also a neighborhood institution, the owner had to decide whether to accommodate the newcomers or preserve the status quo: a difficult decision because any type of accommodation would change the social arrangements of the store as well as create instability during the transition period. Generally, accommodating newcomers was the most prudent action because it gave the owner new customers and the assurance that the store would remain in business if the newcomer population increased and became the majority. The comments of Reuben, the owner of Primo Grocery in the Bronx's Elmway neighborhood, represent the most common view of store owners during demographic changes:

> There are more and more blacks [African Americans] moving into this area. I decided to carry more of the products they want, 'cause it's good business for me. I know a lot of my Puerto Rican customers don't care for it much, so me and them will have to adjust.[5]

The first change to occur in the stores from the influx of new ethnic groups was the stocking of new products that were now in demand. Owners made room for new products by reducing the number of existing products, occasionally irritating the older customers when their desired products were out of stock. However, older customers also benefited from these changes because a decrease in the quantity of products meant they sold out more quickly and were stocked more frequently, making the store's general inventory fresher. Older patrons constantly told the owner how they enjoyed the better, fresher quality of products.

Changes in social relations in the stores that were neighborhood institutions were the most profound because now the old social cliques had to be reorganized to integrate members of the new ethnic group, or members of the new ethnic groups had to form their own cliques. Newcomers were integrated into the social structure of the store gradually. This process occurred in the Tortuga Grocery in the Bronx's Monument neighborhood, the Farragut Street Grocery in Brooklyn's Eagleton neighborhood, and the Monitor Grocery in L.A.'s Richardson neighborhood. All three neighborhoods experienced changes in their ethnic composition: Monument, a predominantly Puerto Rican area, saw increasing numbers of African Americans; Eagleton, dominated by African Americans and Puerto Ricans, saw increasing numbers of West Indians; and L.A.'s Richardson neighborhood, a traditionally African American community, saw an increase in Mexican Americans and Mexican nationals.

Because of the changing conditions of the neighborhood, the stores gradually integrated newcomers by socializing them into the norms that governed social interaction and making accommodations to the store's established social order. The first step in this process was to establish the social identities of the newcomers:[6] a difficult task because most of them spoke different languages than the existing patrons and were shy in this new environment.[7] Thus the process of establishing new identities was extremely tedious and lengthy. It began with the new ethnic group's formation of its own cliques while they shopped at the store. As they established a routine they began to talk to the owner more and, on occasion, to some of the long-term regulars, at which point they began to be integrated into the store's social order.

In the case of the Tortuga Grocery, Angel, the owner, asked some of the new African American women about themselves, their friends, and others to determine what their social identities had been so that he and the store's regulars could relate to them positively and productively. This took time for Angel because he needed to speak with them in normal, friendly conversation, and although he spoke English he was not totally comfortable with it as it was not his first language. Angel was both shy about speaking in a different language and anxious about understanding the subtle meanings expressed by the African Americans.

The same situation occurred in two other stores. In L.A.'s Monitor Grocery, Dwayne, the English-speaking, African American owner, had to interact with Spanish-speaking Mexican shoppers. Irving, the Jewish owner of Brooklyn's Farragut Street Grocery, could not sufficiently understand the West Indian dialect of his new customers. Furthermore, the regulars of his store were African Americans, who spoke their own English dialect, and Puerto Ricans, who spoke Spanish, so that all of them had difficulty understanding the West Indians.

Once language difficulties had been overcome and enough was known about the identities of the new patrons, the store owner slowly tried to establish a group of regulars among the newcomers and introduce them to a group of incumbent regulars. In stores of contested neighborhoods, the owner facilitated separate cliques for the different ethnic groups among regular, periodic, and occasional customers by persuading people from the new ethnic group who regularly came to the store to help him "understand" and "aid" the new patrons. By doing this, the owner created a group of regulars who now thought of themselves as leaders. He established relations of trust with them and taught them the store's norms of "proper" behavior to pass on to others of their group.

The new customers then formed their own cliques, generally over a six-month period, and were allowed to talk collectively regardless of whether it was interfering with business.

These norms established by the owner maintained a good business environment while keeping intact the informal rules established by the regulars that governed social interactions in the store.[8] Irving, the owner of the Farragut Grocery, taught the newcomers his rules of "proper" behavior in the store by telling funny stories of past incidents in which he had inflicted penalties on rule violators. He also informed the newcomers about the norms that operated among the store's regulars by telling entertaining and nonthreatening stories about misunderstandings that had occurred between people who spoke different languages. Other store owners followed similar strategies in setting behavioral norms. In general, when ethnic changes divided contested neighborhoods, the mom-and-pop store created an environment where the contested nature of the neighborhood was institutionalized with a minimum of open hostility and physical confrontation.

Market conditions also had an important role in producing change in the mom-and-pop stores. In *When Work Disappears,* William Julius Wilson argues that when demand for manufacturing and/or service labor declines, unemployment increases, reducing laborers' available capital to purchase goods and services from businesses in the neighborhoods where they live.[9] However, changes in the manufacturing sector affect ghetto areas more than poor neighborhoods because in ghetto areas residents from various socioeconomic levels work in various economic sectors, while in poor neighborhoods the majority of residents, when they work, do so primarily in the secondary labor market and in the lower levels of the service sector. In the poor neighborhoods of the current study two changes in economic activity affected the operations of mom-and-pop stores. The first was changes in the local food market. In three of the neighborhoods, the opening of new supermarkets immediately affected the business operations of the mom-and-pop stores because they offered a large variety of fresh foods at lower prices than the small grocery stores. Immediately following the grand openings of these supermarkets, regulars of the small stores began to shop at them to see the selection of products and their prices. Invariably, there were more products, some of which were new to the local residents, as well as familiar products that were fresher and less costly. Many locals began shopping at the new store for supplies and frequenting the small grocery only to socialize, greatly straining the small store owner's ability to stay open because the reduced business was insufficient to meet monthly expenses.[10] Some stores raised prices to recoup some of their losses, thereby further angering and alienating customers who were physically unable to get to the supermarket. When raising prices did not work, a few stores lowered their prices to what they had been, although neither strategy quickly brought back their customers. During this initial period, which generally lasted about three or four months, the mom-and-pop stores went deeper in debt, and employees who were not related to the owner were laid off. Then, if the store was a neighborhood institution, patrons slowly returned to shop. One reason for the return of the local store's patrons was inertia. Patrons rationalized that since they were already at the local store socializing, they might as well shop there rather than making an extra trip to the supermarket for goods that were slightly less pricey. As this pattern continued, the store owner reduced prices, encouraging others to return. In the case of enterprise-type local stores, however, the economic strains created by the new supermarket generally caused the business to change ownership or close permanently.

Another reason for the gradual return of patrons to the local store was that the new supermarket, unlike the local store, did not extend credit to customers and thus created hardship for many who shopped there. A conversation between two residents of L.A.'s El Rey neighborhood, Leonor, a twenty-seven-year-old Mexican American mother of three, and Francine, a twenty-four-year-old mother of two, reflects these attitudes:

> *Leonor*: Yes, I was going to the new Safeway [large food store in California], but I am going back to Martinez Grocery. . . . Yeah, I like seeing Esther, Connie, and Diana and you; and Hector [store owner] gives me the credit I need when Jorge [her husband] has not gotten his pay.
>
> *Francine*: Yeah, me too. I need the credit that Hector gives to me when my husband does not give me the money I need for food for the children.[11]

Another factor that could affect the economic operations of the stores was an increasing amount of crime and theft inside the stores. Although single incidents of theft were normally small, the accumulated losses could be substantial. To combat petty theft, the store usually hired additional help to watch for potential shoplifters, shelve products, and clean. In all but four cases, the store owners hired a young man from the neighborhood;[12] in the other four stores, the owners or managers hired relatives.[13]

Stores also experienced armed robberies and after-hours break-ins,[14] which caused much more substantial losses of cash and commodities as well as the loss of a few customers until they again felt safe in the store. Another expense generated from break-ins was the increase in insurance premiums. The comments of Jerry, owner of the B. J. Grocery in the Bronx's Monument neighborhood, represent owners' concerns over these situations:

> When shit like just happened happens [an armed robbery], it is such a pain in the ass! First, it is scary as you could see. Then you lose the cash, which isn't great, but at least you're alive. But then after it happens some of my customers don't come around for awhile 'cause they get a little scared about being here when a robber starts shooting or something. That hurts my business along with the increase of my insurance. I tell you, after it happens a couple of times, I know I shouldn't, but I don't think about losing my life, I just think of the business problems it causes.[15]

Increased costs to the stores from theft resulted in higher prices for the customers. Figure 1 shows the average amount of increase in prices following robberies in all the stores. The greatest increase occurred among stores that were neighborhood institutions because their owners consciously tried to keep prices at an amount that still generated profit without taking advantage of the customers. Since prices were generally set just above costs to support a modest profit, there was little room to absorb losses from insurance increases, so prices had to be raised to make up for the rise in costs. As Figure 1 indicates, enterprise stores had less of an increase in prices following robberies because their prices were on average fifteen to forty cents higher than those in neighborhood institutions, so insurance increases did not require an immediate rise in prices. Some stores had such high prices to begin with that even when insurance premiums increased after robberies, they could not raise prices and expect to keep customers.

In stores that were neighborhood institutions, prices were slightly reduced after three to six months without robberies, but enterprise establishments rarely reduced their prices. This was a general pattern because owners of neighborhood institution stores felt a personal responsibility to help neighborhood residents when possible, whereas owners of enterprise establishments did not share these concerns. The comments of J. J., the owner of Nino's Grocery in Brooklyn's Eagleton neighborhood, represent the sentiments of owners of a neighborhood institution:

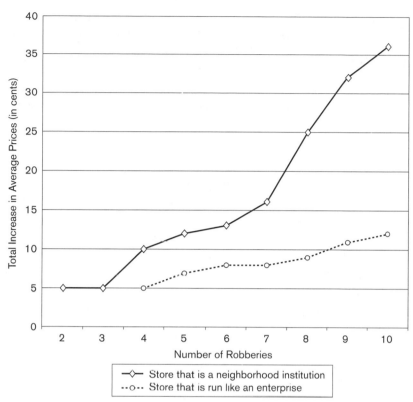

FIGURE 1. Increase in average prices following robberies at the stores studied within an average twelve-month period.

I really, really hate to keep raising prices because I like the people who come here, and this hurts a lot of them. As soon as I can make some of the money I'm out back, I got to reduce some of the prices in the store. I don't know if I can reduce all of them because some of the wholesalers have raised prices too, but I know I can begin to reduce some of the prices by a few cents. If it wasn't for all the trouble with the robberies and the insurance I wouldn't have raised prices more than a few cents. These fucking robbers just screw everybody.[16]

Increased robberies, higher insurance payments, and diminished business due to customer apprehension also forced some owners to eliminate the credit they extended to many of their customers. The comments of Thomas, owner of the Monitor Grocery in L.A.'s Richardson neighborhood, represent owners' feelings when they were faced with such situations:

Right now I got to stop giving credit to people. I don't like to do that because a lot of these people I give credit to are good folks who just ran out of money, and it makes it real hard on them. Also, when I do this it hurts my whole business 'cause other people get mad at me and don't come for awhile. And then there are some who don't come because the people they talk to are not here 'cause they got to go somewhere else to see if they can get credit there. No, I definitely don't like to do it, but I got no choice until I make some money back.[17]

Increases in wholesale prices also affected the economic activity of the store. When wholesale prices increased, the store's prices increased as well. The owners of neighborhood institutions tried to raise prices by very small amounts, but when increasing wholesale prices occurred simultaneously with rising insurance premiums and shoplifting (pilfering), owners had little option but to raise prices sharply.

Sharp price increases were accompanied by strained relations between the owner and the regular clients because clients felt frustrated by an added hardship to their lives and the fact that it came from one of their refuges from hardship.[18] They felt that the store's owner had broken some social contract between them, and as a result they would, for varying amounts of time, spend less time at the store until they felt better about this situation. The comments of Baltazar, a forty-year-old Puerto Rican regular at the Isla Grocery in the Bronx's Elmway neighborhood, are indicative of these feelings:

I can't believe that Manny raised these prices again. He says he ain't got no choice, but fuck, I hate paying more and more! It wouldn't be bad if me or everybody else was making more and more money, but we fucking ain't! This place was a good place to come because you got decent prices and could hook up with people from the neighborhood, but now I'm just fucking pissed as hell that even this fucking place is squeezing me! I may go back there, but right now I don't want to see Manny![19]

Another economic factor that produced change among the small neighborhood stores was the sale of illegal products and services. As previously discussed, many store owners sometimes had difficulty staying in business, which made them vulnerable to illicit opportunities that could generate additional profit. A significant number of customers constantly looked for ways to make money and devised moneymaking schemes where they tried to persuade others, including the store owner, to become involved. Poor neighborhoods created an environment of new ideas for potential business ventures and zeal to promote them to whoever was interested in investing money. Since "hustles" were very common, there was a large variation in the quality of these ventures.[20] The mom-and-pop store owners were constantly barraged with invitations to participate in these schemes, and some became involved in schemes that appeared, at least in comparison to most, to be legitimately capable of making money.

The two types of illegal activities most commonly found in the stores were selling illegal products and gambling. The illegal products sold to patrons from the neighborhood included homemade liquor, sometimes to minors, weapons such as knives and bullets, and pornography. Reuben, the owner of the Primo Grocery in the Bronx's Elmway neighborhood, described the selling of homemade liquor:

> I sell this moonshine to those who want a little with their Coke [Coca-Cola]. Some want to mix the two, others just want to drink it like a shot and then chase it with Coke. Either way they get a kick. This stuff is made from fermenting fruit and it's over one hundred proof, so you get a kick from it. I don't sell too much to any one person 'cause I make the stuff and I can't make it that fast. You know, I just use it to create a good atmosphere for my customers. I give some to the teenage gang members sometimes too. Don't get me wrong, I do make a good deal of money from sales, but I don't do it for that reason.[21]

The comments of Combs, the owner of the Gordon Street Grocery in the Bronx's Monument neighborhood, on the sale of knives and pornography are representative of the attitudes of other owners who allowed these activities:

> Shit, there's a lot of crazy drug addicts in this neighborhood, and most of us gots to look out for them or they'll attack you and take your money. Plus, most of the folks here don't got much money, so they don't wants to give it to a dopehead. So they looks for protection and I sell them protection. . . . Now the skin movies and books is another thing. I sell or rent them to whoever wants them. The government don't want me to do that shit, but shit, it's just some entertainment for guys, that's all.[22]

The most prevalent illegal activity in mom-and-pop stores was gambling.[23] Some owners allowed runners from the local numbers business to collect payments and distribute winnings in the store, some allowed runners for the local sports bookies to collect bets and distribute winnings in the store, and others allowed bookies to take bets on the local cockfights in the store. In each case, the store got some payoff for its involvement in these businesses. In Eagleton's Shippley's Grocery and the Bronx's Isla Grocery, the owners allowed gambling because of the extra money they could earn. The comments of Thomas, the owner of

Shippley's Grocery in Brooklyn's Eagleton neighborhood, are indicative
of this general pattern:

> Well, I can't say that I wanted to start selling numbers tickets in here, but
> when they [representatives of the local syndicate] came, I just said okay.
> Since they came in it has not bothered business at all, in fact it has
> increased business. Now more people stay longer to play and talk about
> their fortunes. So everyone just looks at being able to place a bet as an
> extra service that I'm providing, and my customers appreciate it.[24]

However, in the cases of the Bronx's B. J. and Mikey's Groceries and
L.A.'s Jalisco Grocery, local syndicates pressured the owners to let their
stores be used for collection and distribution activities. In these three
cases, the owners acquiesced and, as the syndicates determined, were
compensated with cash.

Internal Change Agents

Along with external agents, two agents internal to the store, the store
owners and the regular and periodic patrons, affected social change in
the stores of the neighborhoods studied. Each had the potential to disrupt social relations and cause the store to cease as a functioning establishment within the neighborhood. Critical to the store's neighborhood
institutional status was the social cliques' ability to create and maintain
social order, which depended on the composition of their members.
More than anything else, the mixture of the divergent social factions in
the store challenged the stability of the store's social order.

CHANGES IN THE PATRONS

In fragmented neighborhoods, the store was a primary institution that
integrated divergent substrata, but as with any institution in this type of
neighborhood, ethnicity was not a factor. However, when a neighborhood was in the first stage of changing from one type (fragmented or contested) to another, changes occurred in neighborhood institutional stores.
A change from a fragmented to a contested neighborhood was signaled
by a change in the internal functioning of the cliques:[25] where at first
cliques had been ranked and organized by substrata characteristics, now
quasi-independent social groups based on ethnicity emerged, as in accul-
turated social systems, and then cliques became rigidly segregated by ethnicity, as in "castelike" systems.[26] The Bronx's B. J. Grocery, located in a
predominantly Puerto Rican area with some African Americans, where

members from these groups made up the three social cliques in the store, illustrated this process. When an increasing number of Dominicans moved into the neighborhood, they began to shop at the store. The first contingent of Dominican patrons was friendly and deferential toward the Puerto Rican and African American members of the three cliques, some of whom wanted to incorporate them into their group. However, incorporation takes time as people get to know the newcomers, their value orientations and behavior, and how they will fit into their clique. During the initial period of incorporation, a few newcomers were invited to join the cliques. As Dominican patrons continued to increase in numbers, they innocently formed small groups to talk about common interests, such as foods of their own culture that the owner stocked for them, the Dominican Republic, and their experience of moving to New York.[27] Although they shared the same language as the Puerto Ricans, their accent was distinct, as were many of their customs.[28] As their associations became more regular, the group assumed a more formal character with its own criteria for creating identity and became a separate social clique in the store. This changed the store's internal social order. Although its role as a neighborhood institution was unaffected, the store altered its social order to accommodate growing group separatism.[29]

The same process occurred from changes in the number of people with different value orientations or changes in the times when different age groups frequented the store. Such intraneighborhood change occurred in the Gordon Street Grocery of the Bronx's Monument neighborhood, a fragmented neighborhood at the time where many of the residents were African Americans who held blue-collar jobs in small manufacturing plants. As racially based preferences in certain neighborhoods lowered the value of housing and rental prices, more housing became available to the poor, increasingly straining relations between those who had adopted a security-maximizing or an excitement-maximizing value orientation (see chapter 1).[30] Within the Gordon Street Grocery the primary clique blended people from both orientations, but the security-maximizing orientation was the more dominant. As this clique incorporated more of the new residents, the number of people with an excitement-maximizing orientation increased. Although this change did not affect the social identities of the group, it strongly influenced the social order because of a change in the store's social status hierarchy, causing some to gain prestige and deference and others to lose their higher status. While each value orientation was tolerated in the everyday life of poor neighborhoods, they were not equally respected. Each "value camp" saw the other as irresponsible and became intolerant of hearing the life stories that supported and legitimized the rival orientation, so that gossip and bickering between clique associates increased. Some clique members who felt that their camp was outnumbered even stopped frequenting the store regularly, significantly altering the environment that had made the store a neighborhood institution. Because of these changes, Gordon Street Grocery entered a kind of social purgatory between the revered "institution" and the reviled "enterprise," and its functional responsibilities toward neighborhood residents were temporarily passed on to other neighborhood institutions.

Changes in the times that young people visited the store also altered the social environment, making it difficult to maintain the existing social order. The case of the Jalisco Grocery in the El Rey neighborhood of Los Angeles typified this dynamic. Adults generally frequented the store in the early evenings to buy products that had been overlooked or already consumed earlier in the day. The largest group who came to the store at this time was the men, who generally bought beer to drink at the store while discussing the day's work and then bought beer to take home. The majority of this group consisted of Mexican national day laborers who either did not have a family to go home to or just wanted to have a beer before retiring to their generally small and confining living quarters.[31] During this time, a group of young high school students also came to the store to buy soda and snack food that they would take to the park two blocks away, where they would eat and talk for an hour or two during the school year and for three or four hours during the summer. However, a gang war broke out that was carried to the park where many of the nongang youth went to drink, take drugs, and party. Because of a shooting in the park during the gang war, the youth who were not directly involved felt vulnerable and scared and began to socialize at the store for safety. Their numbers increased as word spread that the store was "the safe place" to hang out, changing the social interactions of a primary clique of men who were regularly there to socialize. Some of the change occurred because several of the youth were the children of the men who frequented the store, and their presence restricted the men's conversation and behavior. In addition, the men were inhibited in their discussions because the youth group included a significant number of young women. The young people's presence was disruptive as they constantly shoved, spoke loudly, laughed, giggled, played their CD players, and honked their car horns, obstructing the men's conversations and causing them much irritation. As a result, a significant number of men stopped spending time at the store during the week and simply returned to their residences to drink.[32] This change weakened the cliques because the routine that had reinforced social identities and order within the store was partially removed. It also negatively affected family relations because the men, without having the store as a place where they could relax from a grueling day's work, now brought their frustrations home from work, mixed with the effects of alcohol. During this period women who frequented the store reported that physical violence in the home was increasing.[33] This result serves as a good example of the complicated and positive role that neighborhood institution stores played in the residents' lives.

CHANGES IN THE CARETAKER

A shift in the role of the store's institutional caretaker, which sometimes occurred when the caretaker sold the business, retired, or died, could radically affect the store's internal social order and environment. If the caretaker died and an immediate family member with experience in the store took over, as happened in Mikey's Grocery in the Bronx's Elmwood neighborhood and the Martinez Grocery in the El Rey neighborhood of Los Angeles, significant changes in the social order did not occur. However, if the caretaker left and was replaced by someone whose ethnicity differed from that of the patrons in the social cliques or the dominant ethnicity of the neighborhood, the store experienced serious repercussions in the maintenance of its established internal social order. In such situations, the new owner, like Shanku in the B. J. Grocery of the Bronx's Monument neighborhood, or Paul in the Top Grocery of L.A.'s Richardson neighborhood, did not know or care that a clique met at the store regularly because his sole intent was to run the store as an enterprise to make money. Thus, without a caretaker in these two stores, the social cliques had no one to coordinate and maintain social relations. As a result, the clique system died, the stores lost their status as neighborhood institutions, and ethnic antagonism was displayed toward the store owner.

For many observers, ethnic antagonism toward a new store owner arises from the patrons' belief that the new owner has had economic advantages (loans) to buy the store that are unavailable to them and other members of their group.[34] Although patrons of the stores in the present study often held this belief, they were resentful primarily because they had lost a neighborhood institution that had been a valued social space. They believed that the store's status would not have changed if someone from their own ethnic group had become the new owner.[35]

When new owners were members of an ethnic group either currently living in the neighborhood (indigenous owners) or just starting to live there (trailblazer owners), they took steps to develop close relationships with the patrons.[36] Although they were not trying to create a neighborhood institution, only to produce a profitable business, the reciprocity of these relationships established the foundations for what ultimately became a neighborhood institution. As the character of the store developed, the owner assumed and accepted the caretaker responsibilities necessary for any neighborhood institution.

Although the owners described above were active in the institutionalization of the store, some changes destabilized the store's institutional character. Those stores whose owners died or retired generally experienced difficulty in establishing and maintaining a caretaker to manage social relations. Sometimes new owners did not want to assume the burdens associated with being a caretaker and just wanted to operate an enterprise establishment. Some new owners were amenable to assuming a caretaker role but did not know the duties it entailed or how to administer them, as was the case in the Canal Street Grocery of L.A.'s El Rey neighborhood and the Gordon Street Grocery of the Bronx's Monument neighborhood, where the new owners had a different ethnicity than the regulars of the internal social cliques.

COMPETITION AMONG INDIVIDUAL MEMBERS

A person's place within the hierarchy of the social clique was predicated on his or her actions and how he or she was evaluated by peers. In this environment, members sometimes competed over their place in the hierarchy.[37] Two conditions stimulated individual competition. First, the arrival of new patrons incorporated into the status queue often created competition among members of the clique to maintain or improve their status positions. Competition primarily occurred among those considered regulars, causing unrest until the situation stabilized and there was consensus as to where people stood in the hierarchy.[38] A representative example involved a man named Jesús who had just come from Texas to live with an aunt in the El Rey neighborhood's Orchid Lane Apartments. He was particularly fit, very friendly, and articulate, and he used phrases and mannerisms that the patrons and caretaker (owner) thought were charming. As he continued to visit the store he was often deferred to in everyday conversation. His status soared above that of a number of regulars who had lived in the neighborhood all their lives. Jesús's status was directly attributed to his newness in the neighborhood and his idiosyncrasies. Although many of the patrons were intrigued with Jesús, three regulars who were being ignored began to resent him. They confronted the owner/caretaker after he had referred to something Jesús had said in a recent conversation. They told the caretaker that there was no reason to think Jesús was correct and "Who was this guy anyway? He just got here!" The owner, taken aback, said that Jesús was a nice guy and everyone was just trying to help his adjustment to the neighborhood. However, the offended regulars said he had been helped enough and they were tired of everyone thinking he was something special when he had not done anything for the neighborhood. They went on to remind the caretaker/owner that they had lived in the area all their lives and had done much to help the other people who lived there. They ended the conversation with "If people around here think Jesús is that great, then ask him for things instead of us!"[39] The caretaker/owner got the message and next morning began to downplay Jesús to everyone who visited. In the next two weeks the offended regulars resumed their previous status and Jesús assumed a more modest position.

The second circumstance involved competition between people who were already members of the social order and who for personal reasons wanted to improve their status within the clique. In most of these cases, those who wanted to improve their status had an identity that only partially corresponded to their own sense of self-worth. Thus, to improve their status, they needed to change their identities by forcing their peers in the store to think of them differently, a change that could occur only if they did something that others would consider extraordinary. Such an identity change was made by Vilma, a twenty-six-year-old mother of two who frequented Daddy G's Grocery of L.A.'s Richardson neighborhood. Both of her children had different fathers who were serving long prison terms for gang activity. Vilma was a regular at the store, but because she had never married and had used drugs she occupied a lower rung of the status hierarchy and was subtly marginalized by the older women. In an effort to improve her position by gaining respect, she began to help other women customers who had lost their governmental benefits because of changes associated with the Welfare Reform Act by showing them how they could acquire financial aid from various social agencies in the neighborhood. As she became more successful in her efforts to help these women, she rose in the store's social hierarchy, causing resentment among some of the women regulars, who reacted by spreading false rumors about her. In turn, the women whom Vilma had helped aggressively defended her, causing instability in the social order until Vilma's status was resolved and the hierarchy was repaired. Vilma's status did improve enormously, although she did not become one of the elite in the store. The case of Vilma shows the power of the existing network in establishing a status position for individual participants. It also shows how important the information that people provided for others in the store could be. The people that Vilma helped were like many other women in the neighborhoods who were no longer covered under the new TANF (Temporary Assistance to Needy Families) welfare reform program, which limited aid for low-income families to a period of two years, because they had not secured employment. These women needed information on where nongovernment services and resources could be obtained. In many cases the information they received in stores and hair salons mitigated the full negative impact of this change in social policy.

SOCIAL PRESERVATION IN THE STORE

As with all institutions in low-income neighborhoods, agents to preserve the social arrangements in the store were as active as agents of change. These preservation agents were motivated by a self-interest that considered the store's present social order to be equally beneficial for those who were directly involved in it and for the neighborhood at large. Thus they fully integrated their own interests with those of the group, whereas change agents were more inclined to separate the two. For example, people who actively tried to preserve the status quo nearly always argued that changing the present social order would be harmful to both the ethnic group and the neighborhood. Agents of change, however, argued that when their specific interests were realized everyone would benefit (though unequally) through some sort of "trickle-down" effect.

The Role of the Caretaker

Owners who also acted as caretakers were involved in the preservation of the store's social order since part of their duties was to manage social interaction there. The caretakers of the stores were so involved in the day-to-day business and social operations that they nearly always believed the existing social order was vital to the continued health of the store and community. The comments of Combs, owner of the Gordon Street Grocery in the Bronx's Monument neighborhood, represent this view:

I like the store and the people who come here all the time. They all support each other, and we all have fun here every day, or nearly every day. Everybody gets along with everybody, and people just have a nice feeling about being here. We had to work at it a bit, but now all the folks have their own thing [niche], and things run smooth for everybody. I like what we got here. If it was not like this it wouldn't be worth it to me to keep doing business here. It would be too hard for me to make any money, and there would just be too many hassles. . . . Like I always be saying, the neighborhood and store is one, what goes on in one goes on in the other.[40]

When agents tried to implement change in the store, the caretakers used a variety of strategies to neutralize their impact. Their main tactic was to isolate the change agent by influencing others in the establishment against the attempted change through rumors and gossip about those causing the social unrest. Mikey, the owner of Mikey's Grocery in the Elmway neighborhood of the Bronx, used this tactic when a new patron began to frequent the store and disrupted its social order. The newcomer was Puerto Rican and had been a patron of Finger's Grocery, but that store's dominant group was of a different ethnicity, so he came to Mikey's, where Puerto Ricans constituted the majority of patrons. Since he was an excellent dominos player and bodybuilder, he had the personal identity of a leader. In several attempts to assert himself as a leader of various cliques, he disrupted social relations so much that many regulars withdrew from socializing at the store. Mikey decided to isolate him by first asking him to do some tasks around the store in exchange for beer and then talking to him about following the customs of the existing social order, while at the same time telling the other patrons to avoid conversing with him until he gave the signal that it was acceptable. Each time the new patron joined a clique without asserting leadership, people spoke to him, but when he did not follow the established customs, he was avoided. After three weeks of this treatment, the new patron got the message and followed the established rules of conduct, and throughout the entire nine years of research he never became a clique leader.

The Role of the Patrons

Some of the store's patrons were preservation agents because they were happy with the existing social order in the store, particularly the services provided, such as loans, credit, social support, and camaraderie. Essentially, they wanted to maintain social relations because the social identities and norms within the store gave them status and a place of comfort in their local society. Like most social systems, the microsystem that developed in neighborhood institutional stores centered on a sense of predictability. It was predictability that buffered the structural insecurity that sprang from material scarcity, competition for limited resources, and individual anonymity. Thus preservationists vigorously protected existing social relations because they were predictable, as shown by the comment of Ramon, a "regular" in the Tortuga Grocery:

> The people who come here are good people, and now they got to worry about these assholes Juan and Richard who've been bothering people about starting a game of dominos in the side room here. We already have a domino game here, but it is just when people want to play. Now they want to set it up where people play for big pots but they got to pay a tax to play. Some of the money they say would go to Angel [the store owner] for letting them do it, but he don't want this fucking money. This would change things here, and me and most everybody who comes here regularly don't want things to change. We come here 'cause things will be the same, and everybody knows everybody and they know how everything works. But this new shit [the new game arrangements] will change everything! That's why we're going to stop it![41]

After Juan and Richard told a number of the patrons about their new idea, Ramón, Izzy, and Tomás immediately started a rumor that the type of game they were suggesting would be bad for the store and significantly change things for everyone. They went on to say that if the new game started and was profitable, new people from outside the neighborhood, some of whom could be members of organized crime looking to expand their business, would frequent the store. These arguments successfully alarmed the other patrons and mobilized them against Juan and Richard's plan, which died a week later.

The Role of Other Institutions

Another preservation mechanism used by members of the social cliques was to solicit another institution from inside or outside the neighborhood to help restore order, as was the case in an incident involving the Primo Grocery of the Bronx's Elmway neighborhood. During September and October of 1995 the store was robbed twice and three people were robbed after leaving because of a large number of predators operating in the neighborhood. As a result, people began to spend less time at the store, disabling its institutional character. To establish and maintain an environment where people felt comfortable and safe, the owner and some regulars continuously called the police to report suspicious behavior. Thus, through the cooperation of the police and their increased presence around the store, the police department became a preservation agent. This strategy effectively deterred crime around the store and reestablished a safe atmosphere in which the patrons could resume their roles in the store's social order.

Some neighborhood institutions acted as preservation agents because their members believed that changes involving the store would negatively affect their institution. A representative instance of this occurred in the Martinez Grocery of the El Rey neighborhood in Los Angeles, where immediately outside ten drug addicts used a back parking lot to inject themselves. As the number of addicts increased, they spent more time in the parking lot, a development that had several negative repercussions. First of all, the addicts used space generally reserved for older adults to socialize on summer nights, and as a result the older adults stopped coming. In addition, they left syringes behind, instigating fear that someone would contract AIDS or hepatitis. This concern was enough to provoke calls to the police, who occasionally chased the addicts away for a short time until they returned. The police presence also inhibited a local gang from using one of their spots to sell or exchange drugs. Consequently the gang confronted the addicts in the back parking lot with bats, clubs, and steel rods, telling them that they were not wanted there now or in the future and that they needed to find another place "to shoot up." When one of the addicts questioned the gang, the gang brutally beat the addicts, who then ran off and did not return. After the addicts were gone, the store's normal social operations returned and the neighbors were thankful.[42]

Preservation in the mom-and-pop stores assumed two strategic forms. The first was proactive, designed to keep the institution healthy and happy. Steps were taken to insulate the store from both predatory groups and a multiplicity of behaviors that could threaten the existing social arrangements and business operations. Requesting that the police increase their patrols around the store and remove suspected petty thieves was seen by the stores' owners and most regular patrons as useful in protecting the stores' environment. The second strategy involved using vigilante-type groups as deterrents to provide protection from many intruding elements that had the power to create change within the store.[43] Gangs and members of the local syndicate often wanted the store's help for their own business dealings, so there was a mutual interest to protect the store from change. The comments of Thomas, the owner of Shippley's Grocery in Brooklyn's Eagleton neighborhood, represent this strategy:

> Lucky we have the help of Milton's group [the local drug syndicate] to take care of the fucking stickup artists who've been snatching money from everyone and messing this place [the store] up. Milton's boys sure keep that shit away from us so we can keep the place the same as we like. But you know Milton's got uses himself for me store. Right now I plan to give him some space out in the back [of the store], and sometimes over there in the corner [of the store], to sell his stuff [cocaine]. It's a "you scratch my back and I'll scratch yours" thing.[44]

Another "proactive activity" that the owner and members of the store's social cliques used was to keep everyone reasonably satisfied with the establishment. This involved (1) maintaining the supply of products to meet the customers' demands so they would not have to shop elsewhere; (2) keeping, as necessity would allow, prices slightly lower than those of enterprise establishments in the neighborhood; (3) offering credit and occasional loans; and (4) maintaining the established social order and everyone's positions within it.

Although these strategies were generally successful in maintaining the store's health as an institution, at times a reactive strategy was needed to preserve the existing arrangements. As opposed to proactive strategies, which were put in place incrementally and involved a great deal of compromise, reactive strategies were generally assertive and confrontational. Reactive strategies assumed two basic forms. One form was simple noncooperation with the change agents, through passive-aggressive resistance to any effort that would significantly modify the workings of the store. For example, when the police department asked the owner of the Top Grocery to provide information about neighborhood crime in exchange for more police protection, the owner and his patrons did not reject the request, but they never provided the police with detailed information about specific individuals either.

Another reaction to change was to actively subvert the identified threat, as exemplified in an incident at Nino's Grocery. Because J. J., the store owner and caretaker, was having difficulty paying his bills, he offered the local bookmaker the use of the back of his store as a satellite operation in exchange for rent of the space. The bookmaker took the offer with the intention of expanding his business into the Eagleton neighborhood by first getting the patrons of the store to participate. The patrons thought that an influx of new people from outside the neighborhood would disrupt the store's social order, so they worked out a strat-

egy with J. J. to subvert the operation. They decided to modestly participate in the numbers business until J. J. had enough money to pay his
debts, at which point they would stop playing altogether. After four
months, they stopped playing and got most of the other residents to do
the same. This ultimately forced the "numbers joint" to close three
months later.

THE STORE AND THE NEIGHBORHOOD
SOCIAL STRUCTURE

The result of the store tug-of-war between change and preservation for
the neighborhood at large depends on the type of neighborhood and
how change and preservation agents affect the store's social environment. In contested neighborhoods, where conflict between different ethnic groups structures interpersonal relations, a store's change from an
enterprise to a neighborhood institution created an environment for
members of one ethnic group to socialize exclusively with each other.
Such change reduced overt conflict in the neighborhood.

In fragmented neighborhoods, a store's change from enterprise to
neighborhood institution increased the number of intergroup networks,
providing residents with more resources to secure needed goods and
services. This reduced psychological stress and strengthened the residents' sense of a neighborhood identity. Basically, in an enterprise-
oriented store groups were self-contained and separated, whereas in
stores that were neighborhood institutions the patrons within the different fragments interacted and received assistance from each other.

A store's change from neighborhood institution to enterprise in contested neighborhoods had two primary impacts. The first was a severe
reduction in resources available to the patrons, such as food items associated with particular groups, extensions of credit, and check cashing.
In addition, because the new owners wanted only to maintain an efficient business, they discouraged people from socializing in the store,
thereby suffocating the established networks that had previously acted
as a socially integrating device. Finally, since the owners had no alle-
giance to any of the competing groups, each declared equal rights to
shop there, increasing contact, social tensions, and conflict.

In fragmented neighborhoods, a store's change from neighborhood
institution to enterprise increased tension between socioeconomic groups
because the integrative aspect of the institutional store had been removed.
An example of this occurred in the Monument neighborhood's B. J.

Grocery when the owner, Jerry, sold it to an East Indian man named Shanku. Even though Jerry was Irish and the neighborhood was predominantly Puerto Rican and African American, the store was still a neighborhood institution because Jerry's family had owned the store for many years, and although the neighborhood was no longer Irish and Italian, Jerry worked hard to maintain the store as a neighborhood institution. Jerry was a "holdout" (see chapter 4 for a description), but he was a master caretaker, and as a neighborhood institution the B. J. Grocery was an important resource for many people. After buying the store from Jerry, Shanku changed the character of the store to make it a profit-oriented enterprise. He worked to establish a good business relationship with the customers, but he did not attempt to be socially friendly. People often asked Shanku for credit, and although he was reluctant to give it to everyone, he did extend credit to customers he judged as "trustworthy" to repay the debt. In nearly all of these cases, he extended credit to people of a particular economic status—generally working-class men and women who had steady jobs—and denied credit to unemployed or partially employed patrons. This created resentment among the customers, first toward Shanku and then to those who received credit, which grew to a point of constant tension between the groups as well as some verbal and physical conflict. The end result for the neighborhood was an increase in division and stress.[45] Further, patrons stopped socializing there and went more to the barbershop and beauty salon for that purpose.

Preservation agents, which existed only in stores that were neighborhood institutions, also affected both contested and fragmented neighborhoods, although in different ways. In neighborhoods that were being contested, preservation tended to have two divergent effects. In neighborhoods like Richardson, Eagleton, and Elmway, patrons tried to preserve the store by strengthening their group identity. The ethnocentrism and prejudice associated with the different stores of the neighborhood were strengthened through conversation. The comments of Dalton, a twenty-nine-year-old African American from L.A.'s Richardson neighborhood, are representative:

> With all these fuckin' Mexicans moving here, you know this store was just going to be one of theirs. I am glad we fuckin' held together and made it difficult for them to come in here. I knows Melvin here [the store owner] was important in makin' them know this [the store] ain't no place for their brown asses. We all held the line to keep this ours 'cause they take all the jobs and we don't want them to take over all our motherfuckin' neighborhoods and stores too![46]

Similar sentiments were expressed by Orlando, a twenty-seven-year-old American of Jamaican descent from Brooklyn's Eagleton neighborhood:

> We spent a good deal of time building this store into something we all enjoy coming to to get food. It's really a good place to relax and just talk. The whole group [those who were in the store's cliques] is so pleased that we're able to keep the store the way it is [it is a store that caters to Jamaican tastes] and not let blacks [African Americans] mess it up. They need to go to their own stores and let everybody be. Then there won't be trouble.[47]

At times when change agents came in from outside the neighborhood, preservation agents created solidarity among groups that had been relatively hostile to each other.[48] One such example involved Mikey's Grocery, which was located in a part of the Bronx's Elmway neighborhood where a local developer planned to clear most of the block and replace it with new housing. The owner, Mike, a forty-one-year-old Italian American, had inherited the grocery from his parents, who had owned the store when the neighborhood was mostly Italian with some Jewish and Irish residents. Though some Italian families still lived in the neighborhood, Puerto Ricans constituted the most significant presence, and a few African American families resided there as well. The store had been a bastion for the remaining Italian Americans, who used it as a place to congregate and talk about the invasion of "spics" (a negative term for Puerto Ricans) into their neighborhood.[49] As more Puerto Ricans moved into the neighborhood and more Italians moved out, the store had more Puerto Rican patrons than Italian, resulting in a social order dominated by two separate cliques and the loss of the store's Italian identity. Although tensions existed between the Italians and Puerto Ricans both outside and inside the store, Mikey effectively made the "new social order" functional for both groups. As the redevelopment plans moved forward, Mikey solicited people to help fight the plan. Mikey made it clear to the others that the only way to save the store from the redevelopment was to have a coalition of Italians and Puerto Ricans fight it. Mikey met with some resistance from the Italian patrons, but over a two-week period they agreed to work with the Puerto Ricans. Since most of the store's patrons had limited incomes and did not participate much in city politics, they had limited political power to stop the redevelopment plan, but they contacted their local representatives, two city council members, one state assemblyman, and a U.S. congressman to see if anything could be done.[50] Through Mikey, the politicians arranged to meet with a group of the residents and ended up agreeing to help. In the next month rumors spread about the development, but nothing official came from either the company chosen to do the work, the government, or the politicians. Then, about six weeks after the politicians became involved, Mikey heard from the office of the local councilman that the redevelopment plan had been postponed indefinitely. All the buildings would remain as they were.[51] Although no one definitively found out why the plan had been postponed, the rumor mill had it that the decision to stop the redevelopment had been made through a complicated agreement with the redevelopment company to redevelop another part of the Bronx that had been scheduled for work after Elmway. This decision kept the store intact, but it also kept the dilapidated housing structures as they were.

To resist the redevelopment project, the Italians, Puerto Ricans, and African Americans were forced to work with each other. As the regulars in the various cliques spent more time together, they got to know each other and much of the mistrust that had perpetuated hostility was eased. People felt more comfortable with each other, so intergroup relations became more civil. The process of preservation was instrumental in changing Elmway from a contested to a fragmented neighborhood.[52]

In fragmented neighborhoods, acts of preservation to thwart any threats of change created a sense of solidarity among all the separate groups because the solidarity that individuals felt within their particular cultural milieu was forged from the condition of scarcity and the divisions developed from it. Of course, once the threat was no longer present, life returned to its previous structured divisions. However, despite group divisions, preservation in fragmented neighborhoods nearly always reinforced each group's common identity by reinforcing the subculture of scarcity that permeated it.[53]

SOME CLOSING REMARKS

Changes to the institutional character of the mom-and-pop store had important implications for the structure of the neighborhood. In both fragmented and contested neighborhoods the institutional mom-and-pop store provided both social and material support for the residents, and while these elements assumed different forms they were functional to the neighborhood's structural integrity. In fragmented neighborhoods the store integrated people from divergent social groups by providing a meeting area where all the patrons felt comfortable interacting with each other. In essence, it was a physical place that people used to maintain previously established friendships.

The store also provided a social environment that facilitated the incorporation of recent arrivals to the neighborhood's existing social structure and order, helping to reinforce the social divisions of the neighborhood. This in turn contributed to the creation and maintenance of the residents' personal identities, which were instrumental in their efforts to establish meaningful lives. Both of these functions were particularly important for residents who were new to the area. The comments of Isidro, a thirty-year-old part-time worker in a garment factory living in the Bronx's Monument neighborhood, to his friend Juan are representative:

> You know that when my family first started living in this project, we didn't know anybody. We were lost and lonely and didn't know who to ask about getting things we needed. The whole building seemed real unfriendly, so we stayed in our apartment a lot. But then one of the people who my mother talked to in the hallway when she used to empty the garbage said that she should go to B. J.'s [Grocery] because it was a good place to meet people, even people who lived in the building. So she had us all go down there, and we did meet people. It was a great place 'cause everybody in the family got connected to people in the different groups and we all got help with a lot of stuff we needed help with. You tell your mother she should check it out. It'll help her real good.[54]

In contested neighborhoods, the store integrated people of particular ethnicities by uniting them against people from other ethnic groups so that they no longer got in conflicts with each other. An example of this occurred in L.A.'s Richardson neighborhood with the Mexican American and the recently immigrated Mexican national residents. Although conflict often existed between them, the hostility toward both groups by the established African American population united them through their association with each other at Treviño's (the Mexican store).

The store in contested neighborhoods also integrated groups into the general conflict condition that formed the basis of social interaction. Because the stores were generally the exclusive domain of particular ethnic groups, they provided a place and mechanism through which neighborhood residents of different ethnicities could be socially separated. The history of conflict established a set of appropriate behaviors in contested neighborhoods that gave residents the predictability they needed to negotiate the contingencies of their everyday lives.

Finally, the store provided a place for groups that were hostile to each other to meet and mediate a particular dispute. Because the store was an establishment that sold products, it could be neutral in bringing individuals together to negotiate a resolution to a dispute. A representative incident occurred in Brooklyn's Eagleton neighborhood, where some hostility existed between African Americans and Jamaicans. When a few Jamaicans had their car radios stolen in car break-ins, they blamed a number of African Americans, and the raised tensions led to confrontations on the street. Shippley's was a store in the neighborhood that catered primarily to Jamaicans but had a small number of African American patrons. The African American patrons were made to feel uncomfortable in the store, so they never developed their own social cliques there, preferring to socialize at the Farragut Grocery. Yet when it was suggested that a meeting be established to resolve the conflict, a regular customer at Shippley's asked the owner if he would help facilitate the meeting with appropriate African American representatives. Thus a meeting set up to discuss the recent thefts and tensions between the two groups resulted in the formation of a neighborhood watch group and relaxed tensions.

In sum, the mom-and-pop stores played a pivotal role in the five neighborhoods of this study. They supported ethnic cultures in the neighborhoods, but more importantly they reinforced, through the products that were sold and the various social networks that were nurtured, the lower-class variant of those cultures that emerged from conditions of long-term scarcity. The loss of neighborhood institution stores, either because they became enterprise establishments or because they simply went out of business, resulted in a strain on the neighborhood's social structure. Residents had to find another store or neighborhood institution if they were to receive the supporting benefits that they had lost from the change. In this regard, researchers' assumptions that strains in the social structure created by changes in the number and character of mom-and-pop stores lead to social decay and disorganization are mistaken. Structural strains created by such changes can be short term, lasting only until another store takes the missing store's place or until another institution assumes the responsibilities of the missing store and structural soundness is reestablished. Thus the meaning of change for the neighborhood depended on the establishment's character (i.e., whether it was a neighborhood institution or an enterprise), the strength of preservation forces, and the adaptive effectiveness of other neighborhood institutions to compensate for any structural weakness caused by changes to any one neighborhood institution like the store.

CHAPTER 6

Not Just a Clip Joint

Hair Shops and the Institution of Grooming

Fashion furnishes . . . on the one hand a field of general imi-
tation, the individual floating in the broadest social current,
relieved of responsibility for his tastes and his actions, yet on
the other hand we have a certain conspicuousness, an emphasis, an individual accentuation of the personality. It seems
that there exists for each class of human beings, probably for
each individual, a definite quantitative relation between the
tendency towards individualization and the desire to be
merged in the group, so that when the satisfying of one tendency is denied in a certain field of life, he seeks another, in
which he then fulfills the measure which he requires.

Georg Simmel, *Fashion* (1904)

Scholars have often mentioned the importance of barbershops and
salons to poor ethnic neighborhoods. Some scholars have considered
barbershops and salons as efforts by a particular ethnic group to build
and/or maintain an economic infrastructure.[1] In addition, a number of
researchers have identified barbershops and salons as important places
of social interaction.[2] Elijah Anderson, for example, writes in his study
of an African American bar on the south side of Chicago that "urban
taverns and bars, like barbershops, carry-out, and other such establishments, with their adjacent street corners and alleys, serve as important
gathering places for people of the 'urban villages' and ghetto areas of the
city. . . . They provide settings for sociability and places where neighborhood residents can gain a sense of self-worth."[3]

In grouping taverns with "barbershops, carry-out, and other such
establishments," however, Anderson overlooks the possibility that all
these establishments do not make the same contribution to the social

order of a poor neighborhood. This chapter provides a better understanding of the social meaning of the barbershop and hair salon for the
poor neighborhood, as well as their unique contribution to the neighborhood's social structure and order. Barbershops and salons play an
important role in the structure of poor neighborhoods, but its exact
nature and significance depends on whether they are neighborhood institutions and on whether they function within a contested or a fragmented
neighborhood.

Whether a neighborhood is fragmented or contested, its social structure depends upon internal institutions to reinforce the local culture
that regulate and reproduce social life. The functional roles that hair
shops provide when operating as neighborhood institutions can be broken down into four substantive areas: (1) socialization, (2) the creation
of fashion and style, (3) entertainment, (4) information exchange and
the creation of local knowledge. When a barbershop or hair salon per-
forms all these functions to a great degree and is recognized by the residents of the neighborhood as such, it is a mature neighborhood
institution. Table 5 shows, for each establishment (identified by a pseudonym), the neighborhood, neighborhood type, shop type, location, the
owner's ethnicity, the ethnicities of its most frequent patrons, its status
as either a neighborhood institution or an enterprise, and changes in
these factors over the nine years of the study.

SOCIALIZATION

A significant function of hair shops is the socialization of individuals to
the cultural norms governing social life in the neighborhood;[4] that is, the
process by which people learn the roles and norms of their society.[5] In
the barbershop and beauty salon small children learn what is expected
and acceptable, and these establishments play a role in either altering or
reinforcing expectations related to social norms. Socialization in the barbershops and hair salons was related to four primary areas of life: (1)
gender roles and identity, (2) sexuality, (3) community values, and (4)
social divisions and relations.

First, barbershops and hair salons profoundly affected identities and
behaviors related to gender and sexuality. Their importance in these
realms can be better understood in the context of the physicality of the
world in which the poor generally live. In this world where the physical
aspects of life play such a primary role, nothing has more physical meaning than the body. Since barbershops and hair salons are sex segregated,

and since they cater to care of the body (the head, and sometimes the face, hands, and nails), they provide a fertile social environment for developing, reaffirming, and disseminating normative sex and gender roles within the community. In barbershops and hair salons behaviors associated with men and women construct the identity of the other. Thus men and women can remain grounded in their specific gender identities, while conferring on the other gender a mythical character essential in the formation of a counteridentity.

Socialization in the Barbershop

For men in both fragmented and contested neighborhoods, sexual roles were defined in the barbershop. Masculinity assumed three similar characteristics in each neighborhood. First was the requirement to dominate both one's physical and social space. The dangerous environment in which men lived, characterized by competition for scarce resources, imbued them with the belief that they must either dominate or be dominated—a worldview that was articulated throughout the neighborhood and that permeated every institution, including hair shops. For the poor, domination means controlling what a person does, where, when, and how, and control of others is implemented physically rather than through thought, resource, or legal sense. Thus physical strength was ritualized, and men considered their bodies as a resource with which to compete in the world.[6] The comments of Henry, a twenty-year-old African American resident of the Eagleton neighborhood of Brooklyn, represent this view:

> Look at J's [a mutual friend] haircut. He got those lines cut into his hair and it looks really freaky. Can you imagine what he looks like in the dark? He can walk into the valley and fear no evil. . . .Yeah, I gots to get me one of them, 'cause when you look bad, you is bad, and when you don't, peoples is goin' to put you in a bad way![7]

The men from all five neighborhoods believed that in the natural state of the world man should dominate woman. The overwhelming consensus among them was that no matter what women said or how they acted, they both should be and really wanted to be dominated—the rationale being it made women feel important, wanted (on the rationalization that a man wouldn't waste his energy on dominating a woman if he didn't care about her), and protected. In part this view was an effort to deal with a context in which all men were continually threatened by the possibility

TABLE 5. HAIR SHOPS' ETHNIC OWNERSHIP, ETHNIC CLIENTELE, AND ESTABLISHMENT TYPE OVER TIME IN THE FIVE NEIGHBORHOODS

City/Section/Shop	1991	1992	1993	1994	1995	1996	1997	1998	1999
Bronx									
Elmway	C	C	C	C	C	C	F	F	F
Monte's	(B)It/It,Ir,PR[Ent]							(B)PR/PR,Dom[NI]	
E & M	(B)AA/AA[NI]								
Main St.		(B)AA/AA[NI]		(U)AA/AA,PR,Dom[Ent]					(U)AA/AA,PR,Dom[NI]
Jewel	(S)AA/AA[NI]						(S)AA/AA,PR[NI]		
Monument	F	F	F	F	F	F	F	C	C
Town	(B)AA/AA[NI]			(B)AA/AA,PR,Dom[NI]	(B)AA/AA,PR,Dom[NI]				
Playa	(B)AA/AA,Dom,PR[Ent]		(B)Dom/Dom,PR,Other[NI]					(B)AA/AA[NI]	
Best	(B)AA/AA[NI]			(U)AA/AA,PR,Dom[Ent]		(U)AA/AA,PR,Dom[Ent]			(B)PR/PR,Dom,Other[NI]
Angela's	(S)PR/AA[Ent]			(S)PR/AA,PR,Dom[NI]	(S)PR/AA,PR,Dom[NI]				(S)PR/PR, Dom, Other[NI]
African Sun								(S)AA/AA[NI]	
Brooklyn									
Eagleton	F	F	C	C	C	C	C	C	C
Hampton	(B)AA/AA[NI]						(B)AA/AA[Ent]		
Ellerby's		(B)Jam/Jam,WI,AA[NI]						(B)Jam/Jam[NI]	

Shop	Character	Shop ethnicity codes
La Perla	C	(B)PR/PR,Dom[NI]
Kendall	F	(S)AA/AA,PR[NI] · (S)PR/AA,PR,Dom[Ent]
Jean's	F	(S)AA/AA[NI]
Sea Breeze	F	(S)WI/Jam,WI[NI] · (S)WI/Jam,WI[Ent] · (S)PR/PR,Dom[NI]
Los Angeles		
El Rey	C	
Pepe's	C	(B)Mex-a/Mex-a[NI]
La Palma	F	(U)Mex-a/Mex-n,Mex-n[Ent]
Aguila	F	(B)Mex-a/Mex-a[NI] · (B)Mex-a/Mex-n[NI]
Mariposa	F	(S)Mex-a/Mex-a[NI] · (S)Mex-a/Mex-n[NI]
Richardson	C	
Harper's	C	(B)AA/AA[NI] · (U)AA/AA[Ent]
Castro's	C	(B)Mex-a/Mex-n[NI] · (B)Mex-a/Mex-a,Mex-n[NI]
Distinctive	C	(S)AA/AA[NI]
John's	C	(B)AA/AA[NI] · (B)AA/Mex-a,Mex-n,AA[Ent] · (B)Mex-a/Mex-a,Mex-n[NI] · (B)Mex-a/Mex-a,Mex-n,Other[NI]

N = 23

NOTE: Symbols for Neighborhoods: C = Contested; F = Fragmented (for definitions, see chapter 1). Sequence of Symbols: (Gender type of shop)Ethnicity of owner/Primary ethnicity of clientele[Character of operations]. Gender type of shop: S = hair salon for women; B = barbershop for men; U = unisex hair shop for men and women. Ethnicity: AA = African American; Mex-n = Mexican national; Mex-a = Mexican American; PR = Puerto Rican; Dom = Dominican; CA = Central American, including people from a variety of countries, but primarily El Salvador and Nicaragua; Jam = Jamaican; WI = West Indian, including a potpourri of nationalities from all of the Caribbean and excluding Spanish-speaking Puerto Ricans, Dominicans, and Cubans: Other = includes a potpourri of nationalities from South America. Character of operations: NI = neighborhood institution; Ent = enterprise.

of being dominated by other men. The comments of Felipe, a twenty-seven-year-old Puerto Rican resident of the Monument neighborhood of the Bronx, are representative of this prevalent belief:

> Hell no, she got two punches from me in the face and went down crying. She had some big swelling over the eye, but at least she knows I like her, and I know she knows I can protect her 'cause she is going to be sore tomorrow. [Three of his friends acknowledge that they understand and agree with his point of view by nodding and saying, "That's right."][8]

The male view on domination was predicated by the general idea that women were personal property to be acquired, consumed, maintained, protected, and evaluated (assessed as to their value).[9] Men operating under both security- and excitement-maximizing value orientations constantly referred to the home as their property and insisted that everyone who entered had to abide by their will and rules. Roderick, a forty-three-year-old African American mechanic from Brooklyn with a security-maximizing value orientation, expressed these views:

> Shit, I came home and my wife messed up. She was not home and there was no supper, and then when she came home and cooked she said she was tired and went to sleep without waiting for me. At breakfast the next morning, I told her that shit she pulled last night ain't acceptable because this is my house and those living here—and that meant her too—gots to take care of business [his needs] and that's it![10]

So did Hector, a twenty-nine-year-old Mexican American part-time construction worker in Los Angeles with an excitement-maximizing orientation:

> I work hard, so on the weekends when my girlfriend comes over to my apartment, I want to kick back, relax, and have some good loving [sex] and food. . . . This is my home, and when she's here this is the way it is going to be.[11]

In contested neighborhoods, domination was particularly crude. Stories in the barbershop centered on the conquest of women from the various out-groups. Men saw women from these groups as prizes that they could show off as personal and group conquests over rivals. Although they did not consider these women to be legitimate partners, they spoke of them as objects of sexual conquest and domination. If a man had personal feelings for a woman in an out-group, he kept them private. When men did become partners with women from competing groups, their choice was viewed as a repudiation of the women from their own group and was met with aggression by other male members of the group.

In fragmented neighborhoods, talk in the barbershop was a little more guarded so that open antagonism would be avoided. When the topic of women came up, men enthusiastically participated but refrained from giving names and ethnic affiliation or told stories about women whom no one knew so that civility could be maintained.[12] Higher-status men and boys believed that if they sexually penetrated a lower-status girl or woman they had done her a favor.[13] Because of their higher status, they viewed themselves as better than these women with whom they had sex and thus believed that these women achieved higher status by sexually submitting to them. Conversely, lower-status men spoke about sex with higher-status women as giving these women the physical satisfaction that the higher-status men could not provide. The comments of Alvin, a twenty-six-year-old African American from the Bronx's Monument neighborhood, are representative:

> Yeah, me too. There is this lady who's got to have me because her man don't satisfy her. She thinks she is classy, and gots all these men with money, but she got to have me to get her off. I ain't into her, but hell, she needs my dick. [Three other males laugh in agreement.][14]

In both types of neighborhoods men did not speak of women of their own economic, racial, or ethnic substratum, since any negative sexual talk about these women would reflect poorly on themselves. Further, women from their own subgroup were more likely to be related to someone within their circle, so speaking of them could provoke a violent confrontation.

The barbershop also functioned to socialize men to believe that masculinity involved the requirement to protect women, a requirement consistent with and integral to men's views of domination. The protection of women and children, considered to be the most vulnerable members of the community, was a primary topic of conversation in the barbershop. Although this value is shared by members of all classes, its implementation differs. While the middle and upper classes generally rely on their local law enforcement, in poor neighborhoods individual males assume the responsibility of protection. One reason for this difference is that poor neighborhoods are more physically dangerous and the police are less willing and/or able to provide timely service. In addition, the protection of women is a way to assume domination and maintain ownership. Within the social structure of the poor neighborhoods studied, women were viewed as objects to be dominated and protected from domination by a more powerful individual. Thus the protection of women was a symbol of possession.[15] This laid the foundation for the pervasive sexual double standard in these neighborhoods: it was socially accepted that men would always be in pursuit of sex with more than one partner while women were to remain monogamous.

While the protection and domination of women were discussed in the barbershops of both contested and fragmented neighborhoods, their implementation differed. In barbershops of contested neighborhoods, men were responsible only for protecting women of their own ethnic group. Conversations centered on stories of women from one's own ethnic group being stalked by men of other group(s). Horror stories were told about women who had been raped and then beaten by men of an opposing group, with the implication that competing group(s) in the neighborhood would, at every opportunity, add insult to injury when assaulting the most precious and vulnerable possessions of one's own group. Thus men had to protect the women of their own group from the predatory men of the other group(s) to maintain honor and respect and to avoid the threat that their objects of pleasure (women) would be taken from them.

A third characteristic of masculinity taught and reinforced in the barbershop's socialization process was the view that men should not be sexually monogamous. This view was predicated on the belief that women were in a constant state of sexual need. The comments of Pablo, a twenty-five-year-old Mexican American laborer from L.A.'s Richardson neighborhood, are representative:

> Man, you should have seen this woman, when I was just doing my job sweeping the hallways. She was doing some studies or something, and she would occasionally look up and smile as I went by. She was just pretending to want to study, you could just tell. Shit, she knew I was married, but man, she couldn't help herself, she just needed to have sex. I didn't do anything, but she's got to have it [sex], so next time I'll just give it to her.[16]

In the barbershops of fragmented neighborhoods men were socialized to believe that they should constantly look for sexual partners because it was natural for men to satisfy the sexual desires of many women. Contested neighborhoods added to this view the message that men should look for women of competing groups. A man who succeeded in seducing women from competing groups was seen as making a conquest that reaffirmed both his and by extension the group's stature. The comments of Emmett, a twenty-eight-year-old African American part-time worker in a commercial laundry in Los Angeles, are representative:

> Me and T. T. were just cruising, checking things out, and there was a lot of pussy walking on the street, man, there was this Mexican bitch—oh, sorry,

Gus [one of the older African American customers who looks with disapproval at him using the word *bitch*]—who looked at me, and I knew she wanted to have some black fun, you know? We stop and I talk to her, and we may meet at the grocery store and see where it goes. . . . Shit, I ain't saying she good enough to take to mama, but she good enough to let her experience the best, instead of that lame shit she gonna get with them wetbacks [Mexican males]. Shit! [There is good deal of laughter before they realize I am sitting in the back watching two people playing checkers. Then the laughter wanes and Emmett says to me, "Sorry, no offense, just playing," but everyone knows it's his way of getting out of an embarrassing situation.][17]

In the barbershops of both contested and fragmented neighborhoods, young men's talk was filled with bravado, particularly about the conquest of women. Older men tolerated this except when it strayed outside the norms of respect and honor (see chapter 4). In this regard, Latino men were not tolerant of any talk or behavior that would dishonor another person or family, including women, since women were integrated into men's honor systems. African Americans and West Indians were intolerant of young men showing disrespect to others, particularly older men. Women, however, were not offered the same respect, unless they were revered older women, because women were generally seen by African American and West Indian men as objects to be used in the acquisition of respect. They also were perceived as threatening a man's respect if they verbally insulted him. The conversation of Duke, a twenty-three-year-old African American, Simon, a twenty-five-year-old Jamaican American, and Logan, a twenty-three-year-old Barbadian American, in Ellerby's Barbershop in Brooklyn's Eagleton neighborhood is representative:

Duke: I just have to have Dianne for myself. She's so fine, and all you wolfs will be agonizing that I be getting her and you is not! [There is laughter from the others.]

Simon: No, no, fella, I be feelin' sorry for your ass because she be talkin' to you like you was some slime or something. That be too much to put up with so I can get me steady pussy. [Laughter from everyone in the shop]

Logan: Simon speaks the truth. Dianne be nice and all, but she does come along with edgy opinions about your ass, Duke! That's a mighty price tag there. [More groans from everyone in the shop]

Duke: I know, I know, but both of yous would love to take her shit to get what I'm gettin'! [More laughter and denials from Simon and Logan][18]

Since the barbershop was a place of entertainment, the men understood that displays of bravado merely consisted of made-up stories without substance. In the barbershops of contested neighborhoods, bravado was tolerated only if it did not violate ethnic norms. In fragmented neighborhoods it was tolerated only if it did not violate the norms associated with the excitement-maximizing and security-maximizing value orientations that structured their social order.

Supporting Agents of Socialization in the Barbershop

Many agents supporting socialization operated in barbershops. Some were explicit and direct, while others were more subtle and supplemental. However, within the two different types of neighborhoods they produced distinctive variations in thought and behavioral outcomes.

The most influential agents were the various symbols that played important, although divergent, roles in fragmented and contested neighborhoods. Because a major division within fragmented neighborhoods was between the excitement-maximizing and the security-maximizing value orientations, symbols displayed in the barbershops represented and reinforced images that were closely linked to these orientations.[19] The two types of symbols most important to the socialization of young men were the fixtures that adorned the walls of the shop and the various print media available.

In all the barbershops studied, a variety of pictures, calendars, and other decorations adorned the walls or hung from the ceilings, and a variety of magazines lay on the various counters. In fragmented neighborhoods, nearly every barbershop had pictures on the walls depicting women in ways that men with different values could easily incorporate into their fantasies. For men with the security-maximizing orientation, pictures depicted women dressed in expensively fashionable clothing. Although the pictures, most of which were advertisements for grooming products, revealed parts of the women's bodies, they portrayed women in a sexually "tasteful" manner. Such pictures appealed to men who had adopted a security-maximizing value orientation because they implied that conventional financial responsibility had its sexual rewards. A conversation between Orville, a nineteen-year-old African American, and Harold, a twenty-seven-year-old African American, at the E & M Barbershop of the Bronx's Elmway neighborhood exemplifies the influence of such pictures on those who held a security-maximizing value orientation:

> Orville: Yeah, I trying to take care of my business. I been at this job making parts for hand radar systems and been learning a lot. I'm about to get a small promotion, but the way I been learning I'll be

> moving up in the tech department quite fast. Right now I've been saving my money, and soon I'll be checking out a woman just like her [pointing to a picture of a woman hanging from the barbershop wall].
>
> *Harold*: Yeah, you sure are right about that, man, I myself found a lady just like her [nodding toward the picture], but that was after I got myself a steady, good-paying job. Them types of ladies is looking for men who got responsibility and nothing else.[20]

Other barbershops, in contrast, hung pictures of women who were either nude or nearly nude, many of which were liquor advertisements. These pictures appealed to men who held the excitement-maximizing value orientation and were often referred to in conversation. The conversation between three Puerto Ricans, eleven-year-old Nestor, thirteen-year-old Jaime, and thirty-two-year-old Ricardo, in La Perla Barbershop in Brooklyn's Eagleton neighborhood represents the appeal of such pictures.

> *Jaime*: Ness, [Nestor] did you see the body of that bitch over there?
>
> *Nestor*: You mean the calendar?
>
> *Jaime*: Yeah, check out the legs and ass, and tell me you wouldn't die for one jump?
>
> *Nestor*: No shit, I been looking for this pussy for some time now.
>
> *Ricardo*: Shit yeah, that's prime flesh, man, but let me tell you that this new chick Lydia I been seeing has got some great legs and ass just like you see. So it's out there, you just got to keep your eyes open and then when you see it, make the definitive move![21]

Some barbershops also featured pinup calendars that reinforced men's sexual identity, such as *Playboy* magazine's calendar with a nude "playmate" each month or *Hustler* magazine's nude calendars. Few patrons failed to take notice, and whenever the calendar page was turned for the new month it was always spoken of. Those holding the excitement-maximizing value orientation were more likely to make crude remarks about the pictures.

The Mexican barbershops of Los Angeles did not contain many *Playboy* or *Hustler* magazine calendars. In fact, I observed only one barbershop with a *Playboy* calendar, and it was up for only a year. Mexican barbershops tended to feature three types of calendars. One type pictured various myths about the Aztecs, such as an Aztec warrior deity rescuing a beautiful Aztec woman from impending danger. The imagery of him carrying her in his arms and her submission to his overwhelming power symbolized and reinforced the belief that women should submit to the domination of men. Thus, through such symbols, the barbershop

socialized young men and reinforced in older men views on the proper
roles of men and women, as shown in a conversation between Tito and
Jason at Pepe's Barbershop in L.A.'s El Rey neighborhood:

> *Tito*: My brother has been worrying about his girlfriend because her
> brother has been introducing her to some of his friends. So the
> other day somebody tells him that she is in the park with her
> brother and he goes and gets his gun and goes down there and takes
> her out of the park because there are a lot of shootings there. So I
> ask him what he is doing, and he says to me, "Being a man!"
>
> *Jason*: What's he trying to be, Quetzalcoatl [the Aztec deity]?
>
> *Tito*: I guess.[22]

Mexican barbershops also hung calendars that pictured the Virgen de
Guadalupe, patron saint of Mexico. Such calendars not only carried the
religious imagery of Catholicism but functioned as symbols of Mexican
identity. Mexican men generally marry women whom they find physically and culturally attractive, and it is understood in Mexican culture
that women are primarily responsible for raising the children, managing
the home, and teaching the children manners, ethnic culture, and religion.[23] Such responsibility is to be accompanied by a piety that to some
degree reflects the sacrifice and piety of *la Virgen*.[24] Thus calendars pic-
turing the *Virgen* complement the Aztec mythological calendars in suggesting that the "natural order" is for men to dominate and women to
submit, just as the *Virgen* willfully submitted to God and nurtured her
family. The comments of Amado, a nineteen-year-old Mexican American living in L.A.'s El Rey neighborhood, are representative:

> My cousin is having trouble with his girlfriend, who says my cousin needs
> to treat her more equally. He really doesn't like it when she starts this com-
> plaining and says that this is not the way it's supposed to be. He says he
> tells her that men are supposed to be the head and provide for women, but
> she gets mad at him every time he says this. I got to agree with my cousin,
> and I told him she must not have been raised religiously 'cause if she was
> she'd have been taught about *la Virgen* and then this wouldn't even be an
> issue. He agrees with me. I think he's going break up with her.[25]

A third type of calendar at Mexican barbershops such as Pepe's in the
El Rey neighborhood of Los Angeles featured elaborate "low-rider"
cars. Low-rider cars are usually older-model automobiles that have been
redone with elaborate detailing to the body and interior. They are
referred to as low-riders because the springs have been cut down or
removed so that the car rides very low to the pavement. Most are
equipped with hydraulic systems that allow the driver to make the car

rise from its low-riding position to a normal level. Low-riders are expensive to build and maintain and are seen as pieces of art. Calendars of low-riders depict attractive young women posing suggestively in seductive clothing by the car. Many other barbershops in Mexican areas also displayed exotic cars, often next to pictures of attractive women. Despite some differences in the items displayed in the barbershops, the symbolic message was the same. Conversations in the Aguila Barbershop in L.A. and the Hampton Barbershop of Brooklyn were typical in demonstrating the influence of these symbols. For example, at the Hampton Barbershop Drew, a fourteen-year-old African American, had the following interchange with two of his friends:

> *Drew*: I got to get me one of those new hogs [a name for a Cadillac], and then the ladies like that one there in the picture will be wanting to be riding with me in style.
>
> *The other two friends [in unison]*: You got that right!
>
> *The barber*: Yes sir![26]

Similarly, in the Aguila Barbershop, thirty-one-year-old Alejandro said to the barber:

> Jerry and me been working on this "rider" [low-rider car] for a while. It's so fine that there ain't a woman around that's more beautiful, not even Selma Hayek! [Everyone laughs] When we send it out for its first run, the *chicas* [ladies] will be lined up to get down with us. And I tell you, they got to give it up [have sex] if they want to stay with us and this car.[27]

In sum, the symbolic messages of the barbershops influenced the beliefs of young men that women were sexual beings to be pursued primarily for their sexual attractiveness. Further, men's own sexual identities and worth as "men" were judged to a large extent by their success in attracting and keeping "desirable" women. These beliefs reinforced the view that women were possessions to adorn a man's life.

Reinforcement of Value Orientations and Identity

Symbols associated with various magazines in the barbershops reinforced the primary social divisions in fragmented neighborhoods, beginning with divisions in value orientations delineated by the choice of articles that were read. African American barbershops carried magazines such as *Sports Illustrated* or the *Sporting News* that focused on a variety of sports, as well as magazines that specialized in a particular sport.

Different specialized magazines were clearly associated with differences in value orientation. Although all the men read about football and basketball, those with an excitement-maximizing orientation were far more likely to read magazines about boxing, wrestling, and weight lifting, and those with a security-maximizing orientation were more likely to read magazines about baseball and track.

This same pattern was seen in the Latino barbershops. Men with an excitement-maximizing orientation read about boxing and soccer, while men holding a security-maximizing orientation read about baseball, tennis, and golf. Mexican barbershops also carried automobile magazines, in which customers' reading choices also signified differences in value orientation. Men holding a security-maximizing orientation read magazines such as *Car Quest* or *Consumer Reports*, whereas those with an excitement-maximizing orientation preferred *Low Rider* or *Exotic Cars*. Age also played a factor in reading choices. Among younger men and boys, those with a security-maximizing orientation were more inclined to read *Car Quest,* while those with a excitement-maximizing orientation read *Low Rider.* Among older men, those with a security-maximizing orientation read *Consumer Reports,* and those with an excitement-maximizing orientation read *Exotic Cars.*

In sum, socialization in all of the fragmented neighborhoods was consistent with the two dominant value orientations. Socialization in the barbershops helped create identities that were closely associated with these two value orientations. The conversation between John, a thirty-two-year-old African American, and Emilio, a forty-eight-year-old Puerto Rican in the Bronx's Town Barbershop, exemplifies this pattern:

> *John*: You hear them guys [two other men talking about the nudes and fast cars in the different magazines], the way they be carryin' on about all this wild shit they be doing if they gots themselves one them ladies? They sure were carryin' on about all the good things they were goin' to buy and such. They ain't goin' to get anything because them guys all act crazy, livin' for today and not takin' care of tomorrow.
>
> *Emilio*: Yeah, I don't know why they have to think that way, they want all that flashy stuff, but they will end up with nothing but talk 'cause they don't think about anything but having fun. They're just a different class of person.
>
> *John*: You sure right about that, ain't it a shame?[28]

In contested neighborhoods the pattern of socialization was slightly different. The most influential symbols in the barbershops emphasized the differences between the various ethnic groups contesting for social dominance. Since most of the barbershops were ethnically segregated, pictures displayed women of a particular ethnic group.

This pattern was also seen in the magazines of these barbershops. Magazines about women featured women from the same ethnic group. Magazines about automobiles and sports varied according to the interests of the different ethnic groups. African American barbershops carried magazines featuring luxury cars like Cadillacs, Lincolns, and Mercedes, while Latino barbershops had magazines featuring old low-riders and trucks. Likewise, sports magazines highlighted the sports that a particular ethnic group identified with and excelled in. Hence magazines in Latino barbershops emphasized boxing, soccer, and baseball, while those in African American barbershops emphasized basketball, football, track, and baseball. Thus the symbols in the barbershops of contested neighborhoods not only emphasized ethnic differences but highlighted the unique attributes of specific ethnic groups. The overall impact of these symbols not only established women as sexual objects but taught and reinforced ethnic identities, social divisions, and boundaries in the neighborhoods.

Socialization in the Hair Salon

For the social system to work in poor neighborhoods, a socialization process must occur simultaneously among women that functionally complements that occurring among the men. The hair salon was one of the most important places where this parallel process took place. In these establishments the community norms of appropriate and inappropriate gender roles were reinforced, significantly contributing to the development of personal identities.[29]

The socialization process was less dramatic in the hair salons than in the barbershops because women were more likely to make appointments to have their hair done and to show up close to their appointment times.[30] This minimized the interaction between patrons that would have occurred (as in male barbershops) if women waited for service. Furthermore, women generally did not use the beauty salon as a social gathering place independent of the service it provided. Finally, the service itself involved more alone time with the hairdresser and less time with other women receiving or waiting for service. Despite these moderating circumstances, talk among the women in the hair salons did exist and produced a socialization process that affected both how women thought of themselves and how they behaved.

Women's sense of their gender role translated into four beliefs about the nature of men and women. The hair salon played an important role in the development and dissemination of these beliefs among the women of the neighborhood.

The first of these beliefs was that women's role was to sustain everyone in their immediate families and, where appropriate, to contribute to the sustenance of the broader community. During difficult times, they were to be the force binding everyone together. For Latina women, this meant assuming a "Madonna" persona in giving their husbands and especially their children comfort and unconditional love.[31] This role established women as a dependable refuge where a socially wounded person could regroup before making another effort to struggle with life's inevitable difficulties. The conversation in Brooklyn's Kendall Salon between Susana, a twenty-five-year-old Dominican with three children, and Lucia, a twenty-five-year-old Puerto Rican with two children and a third on the way, expresses this belief:

> *Susana*: I want my children to know that they can always come home no matter what trouble they're facing and I will help the best I can.
> *Lucia*: Absolutely, I tell my kids that life will be tough, but I will always be there to love them . . . just like the Virgin does for us.[32]

Interestingly, women operating under the security-maximizing value orientation emphasized to their families, and especially to the men, that everyone needed to be responsible in their work. The comment of Edna, a twenty-year-old Mexican American mother of two, to Marilucia, hairdresser of the Mariposa Salon in L.A.'s El Rey neighborhood, represents this vision:

> Oh yeah, I tell my boys that individuals must take pride in what they are doing regardless of the type of work and that all work has its own dignity. So showing up at the right time and doing the required tasks completely and good provides dignity and honor too. Anything less will dishonor the job and the individual.[33]

Women operating within the excitement-maximizing orientation viewed a man's work as simply a means to pay the bills. They did not see a job as worthwhile in itself or as needing to be long term. Demoralizing work, they felt, should not be done for long periods of time even if it paid well. Thus it was their position that their men (husbands or lovers) should be supported if they skipped work for a day or two or were sent home by their superiors for inadequate work. The comment of Regina, a twenty-nine-year-old Jamaican American from Brooklyn's Eagleton neighborhood, is representative of this position:

My husband works so hard at that clothing shop, and he sometimes breathes all that cotton dust from the machines and gets sick. So sometimes he says to me that he just doesn't feel like going to work, and I tell him, "Don't, then." So he says, "They'll get mad at me for missing, and when I go back [to work] they'll send me home without pay." So I say, "To hell with them! They don't pay you that much anyway!" I feel he needs my support. [The other patrons listening to Regina all nod and say they agree with her.][34]

Conversations among the women in the Latina salons celebrated and/or defended the occupational behavior of family members. Any deviance from presenting an understanding and appreciation of their family member's work efforts met with public disapproval, as shown by an unmistakable silence.

For African American women, the role of sustaining both family and elements of the broader community meant being a rock, someone willing to endure all the obstacles put in her way with confidence and resolve.[35] Within the conversations at the African American hair salons, this vision included love demonstrated as "tough love."[36] Women rarely expressed outspoken disapproval of others for their failure to live up to the vision; rather, they described particular instances of women handling a situation in accordance with it. In doing so, they both taught and reinforced the belief in woman's sustaining role in the community without hurting anyone.

A second conception of their role that women expressed was that women rather than men should direct most family and community activities and orchestrate everyday events. Conversations nearly always articulated the view that women were more competent and responsible and that men were incapable of coordinating family members' schedules and planning and cooking meals. A conversation between Josie, a twenty-nine-year-old Puerto Rican living with her husband and two children, and Ilda, a thirty-one-year-old Puerto Rican living with her husband and three children in the Bronx's Elmway neighborhood, is representative:

Josie: Yes, I am going to visit my mother in Puerto Rico for a week, and I got so much work to do before I go. I got to make a number of meals for my family and put them in the freezer, otherwise they will eat junk food, 'cause my husband has no idea about cooking. They'd starve if it were left to him. [Laughing from the other women in the salon]

Ilda: I went to see some of my family in Florida, and I had to make sure my sister had the kids' schedule and the date when the rent was to be paid, 'cause nothing would have worked right if I left it to him [her husband]. That man could not remember all those details! [More laughter from the other women in the hair salon][37]

A third belief expressed by the women was that they must be wary of men trying to take advantage of them. Although they wanted to believe men, they felt that initially no man should be taken at face value when presenting himself or his intentions. This view was fueled by the inordinate number of men who were simply after a woman's body or money.[38] Although the women knew that not all men were insincere, they found it initially difficult to separate men with bad intentions from men legitimately interested in developing a mutually supportive relationship. Thus women presented "a reserved persona" simply because it was the most strategic for a presentation of self.[39]

Although this belief was present in both types of neighborhoods, it was heightened in the contested neighborhoods, where men from other groups were seen as both "taboo" and predators.[40] The ethnic groups' desire to maintain internal solidarity established a social taboo concerning fraternizing with men from contending groups. The upshot was a heightened depiction of the predatory motives of men from competing ethnic groups. The comments of Laura, a twenty-two-year-old Puerto Rican living with her parents in the Eagleton neighborhood of Brooklyn, are representative:

> *Laura*: This black guy keeps talking to me every time that I go to the video store. He works there and he always leaves what he's doing and comes to where I am to talk. He keeps saying that he wants to get to know me better, but all that means is he wants to get me in bed. [Some giggles and everyone nodding affirmatively]
>
> *Gina (a friend of Laura)*: That's what all these black guys want from their own women, so what else would he want from a Puerto Rican?![41]

Interestingly, during this conversation, Afro–Puerto Rican and Dominican women who were in the hair salon talking did not find Laura's comments offensive in the least. Although they, and perhaps their husbands and family members, had African physical features, they were considered by themselves and others to be Puerto Ricans and Dominicans and not African American. In their view, what separated people was not color per se but ethnicity or culture.[42]

Dovena, a twenty-six-year-old African American living with her two sisters in the Richardson neighborhood of Los Angeles, expressed a similar suspicion about the motives of a man from a competing ethnic group:

I work at this store, and this janitor guy keeps on talkin' to me when he gets a break. He ain't said anything to me about going out, but he definitely be checkin' me out. He probably thinks we give better sex than his women, which he's probably right about [laughter from the other women in the salon], but there ain't no way that I am doin' anything with a Mexican guy![43]

The fourth belief articulated in the various neighborhood hair salons was that women themselves could not be completely trusted when it came to sexual relations with men. This belief was predicated on the assumption that women looked for attractive men and would go after them regardless of whether the man was married or seeing another woman. Thus all women should be vigilant of other women when it came to a man they loved. The comment of Margarita, a twenty-year-old Mexican resident of the El Rey neighborhood of Los Angeles, reflects this belief:

Yes, Lupe has been going around talking to people, being real nice to everyone, but if she gets alone with Tómas [Margarita's boyfriend] she will just try getting him in bed so she can have him. I been friends with her in school, but she will go after who she wants, so I know I need to watch all the time. [The others in the salon nod in agreement.][44]

So does the comment of Tarilyn, a twenty-five-year-old African American resident of the Bronx's Monument neighborhood:

That Rhonda is trying to slut around with my man [Tarilyn's boyfriend], and she better stop it 'cause I got my eye on her. I don't care what she says, you got to, 'cause she be moving her body around him like she some goddess or something. [Nods of agreement and some small laughter] . . . I know she knows he is with me, but you got to keep an eye open for people trying to take your man or you be left out. You know? [More nods of agreement] I remember watching that story on television when Mohammad Ali's wife's best friend took up with him, and she was the guest of Mrs. Ali in her own house, shee, you definitely got to keep your eyes open! [Everyone either nods in agreement or says "yes" in agreement.][45]

Both striking and important about this belief was how it complemented the men's idea of women. The men saw women as being in a constant state of "heat," always either wanting or needing sex, and thought that in having sex with women they were doing them a favor. Although both of these beliefs portrayed women as being in a constant state of sexual readiness, men believed that women just wanted sex, whereas the women felt that the men were the most focused on sex and women really wanted a relationship.

The different understandings that men and women have of themselves are intertwined. The independent social identities of men and women complement each other to form a mutually supportive system of gender stratification that is an important element in the social structure of the neighborhoods. This differentiation in gender creates an important status system. In more affluent areas, gender stratification often uses money and material objects to establish status and meaning, which can cause ambiguity in social roles. In poverty areas, gender stratification is predicated on physical attributes to establish and maintain identity, meaning, and social roles.

Supporting Agents of Socialization in the Hair Salon

As in the barbershops, specific agents socialized young women to the norms of the neighborhood and reinforced them in the older women. In the beauty salons of the five neighborhoods, no more than three pictures of men adorned the walls, each of which also depicted women. While the subject of women was present in the pictures of barbershops and hair salons, their symbolism was clearly different. Whereas the pictures in the barbershops showed significant parts of a woman's body, those in the hair salons simply displayed shots of women's heads or of women wearing different styles of clothing. Thus pictures in the hair salons emphasized the relationship between hair and clothing styles in helping women appear attractive.

Women's perceptions of sexual identity combined physical attributes with clothing that accentuated those attributes. Looking good involved grooming and expensive clothing. People cut back on other expenses to save money for one or two expensive items. Although there was some variation in this behavior among ethnic groups, being well dressed and groomed helped define identity.[46] The comments of Rosa, a twenty-one-year-old Dominican from the Bronx's Monument neighborhood, represent this general pattern:

> I got to get my hair done and then run in to Manhattan to get this dress I laid away at Bloomingdale's. I tell you it is a gorgeous dress and I'm going to be gorgeous in it! [Laughter from the hairdresser and two other women in the salon] Horace [her date] likes it when I turn heads, but he may get more than he likes. [More laughter from the women][47]

Although the content was different, the message was complementary to that in the barbershops. Men saw women as sexual objects to be pursued and conquered, and this understanding of women was not lost in the beauty salons. Women often talked, sometimes humorously, about how men thought of them. The conversation of Stephanie, twenty-three, Gina, eighteen, and Dori, twenty-two, in the Mariposa Salon of L.A.'s El Rey neighborhood is representative:

Stephanie: These *vatos* [men] are all the same. They smell a woman and right away they want her.

Dori: Not all of her, just sex. [Everyone laughs.]

Gina: It doesn't matter how old they are, they are all just like dogs! [Everyone again laughs.][48]

Their talk consisted partly of complaints about the nature of men and partly of discussions on how to operate in such an environment. The discussions, combined with the pictures, had a significant impact in socializing the young women who frequented the salons. The primary focus of socialization in the hair salons involved how young women should think about themselves. One theme was that women were primarily concerned about style, while men were primarily concerned about women's bodies. Another was that a woman should feel good about how she looked and that was dependent upon how other women viewed her looks. Men's views were important but were secondary to a woman's opinion because the prevailing belief among women was that their sense of style was superior to men's. The conversation between Carol, a thirty-eight-year-old Trinidadian, and Bianca, a forty-three-year-old of Jamaican descent, illustrates this belief:

Bianca: My husband only knows one hairstyle for himself, and all he wants is for me to have the same style as he is used to. He has no idea about style, what's in and what's not, so all he wants is for me to keep what I got. [There is snickering among the other women in the salon.]

Carol: My husband is the same. He wouldn't know something in style if it came up and hit him in the head [laughter among the other women in the salon]. The man has worn the same work clothes and got the same haircut since we got married, so who can listen to him? [More laughter in the salon, with a number of women nodding in agreement with what Carol and Bianca are saying][49]

Although some trends were seen in all the salons, others were associated with different types of neighborhoods. In fragmented neighborhoods pictures showed styles associated with the different social strata and immigrant factions of the neighborhood. This trend avoided alienating the different clientele while symbolically reinforcing the identities of the various factions. Women who held security-maximizing values talked about the various contemporary styles depicted and chose two or three they thought suitable. The hairstyles they chose were always a modest change from their present styles, consistent with their general tendency to assume an unpretentious and nonadventurist demeanor.[50]

Women with an excitement-maximizing value orientation talked about pictures of styles they thought interesting and attractive, and their decisions were not based on a consensus. Always willing to take chances, they prided themselves on choosing styles that were radically different from either their present styles or the general trend. A conversation in Angela's Salon in the Bronx's Monument neighborhood between Joellen, a twenty-year-old African American, and Marise, a thirty-year-old African American, represents this trend:

> *Marise*: What do you think of the style that that girl has? [She points to one of fifteen pictures on the wall.]
> *Joellen*: I like it a lot. It got "unique" written all over it. But I also like that one over to the left of that one.
> *Marise*: Which one? Two over?
> *Joellen*: Yeah, two over.
> *Marise*: Oh yeah, I like that, and I ain't seen nobody having that.
> *Joellen*: Yeah, that's going to be for me, I'll be the first.
> *Marise*: Uh huh, do it, girl, it will be exciting to have people checking you out.
> *Joellen*: You're right, girl. You seen some of these other pictures [of hairstyles]? There is some real boring stuff there! [Both laugh.][51]

In neighborhoods such as El Rey in Los Angeles, where Mexican immigrants formed one of the social strata fragments, pictures of hairstyles from Mexico adorned the walls of the Mariposa Hair Salon. Lucia, the owner of the hair salon, continually changed the pictures when new styles came to her attention. These pictures, along with pictures in magazines, helped these women remain identified with the cultural fashions of their home country and were an important socializing agent for their young daughters.

The owners of salons in both fragmented and contested neighborhoods were very conscious of their clientele. Thus they subscribed to magazines of various interests and tastes. Not only was this effort good business for the owner and appreciated by the clientele, but it socialized and reinforced the divisional identities of the neighborhoods.

Socialization in the hair shops was very important to the development of the social individual. Additionally, it reinforced the divisions within a neighborhood's social order. Thus the hair shops aided in teaching the norms of appropriate and inappropriate behavior regarding sexual identity, gender roles, and intra- and intergroup relations.

FASHION AND STYLE

Perhaps the most obvious role of hair shops was the creation of fashion and style. Hair is a focal point of style, particularly in low-income neighborhoods. Among residents of the poor neighborhoods in the present study, taking care of one's hair was important. Barbershops often featured the most recent hairstyles, as in African American barbershops, where posters often depicted fifteen to thirty different styles. They advertised some of the more popular styles and the barber's ability to cut them.

Style is a popular topic in most poor neighborhoods. What constitutes "style" in any neighborhood depends on the development of expressions of taste.[52] Within poor neighborhoods expressions of style associated with the body are more emphasized because much of the social world is focused on physical objects. Chapter 3 discussed the role of taste in people's food choices. Food assumes a unique relationship to the body by providing necessary sustenance while exhibiting an expression of taste.[53] Although the consumption of food can be private, the body is highly visible and requires individual management.[54]

Fashion and presentation of style were the main ways individuals could establish, define, and reinforce their private and public identities.[55] Thus the hair shops played a critical role in the personal development of the neighborhoods' residents. Identities formed and nurtured in the hair shops were manifested in the other institutions of the neighborhood.

A hairstyle makes a statement about an individual, representing a chosen or sought-after identity, and is thus different from cutting one's hair for the sake of comfort. Most individuals in the five neighborhoods studied put thought into their choice of hairstyle, which they subsequently communicated to the barber/beautician. Their decisions were based on two considerations. The first was the personal identity that had been bestowed upon them and their own image of that identity. Personal identities in low-income areas are often given by people closest to an individual, such as their parents, siblings, relatives, or friends. The origin of this identity is often a nickname that has emerged from a separate or series of behavioral incidents. Through this name and the incident(s) that gave rise to it, an individual develops an image of the type of person he or she wants to become. For example, some people desire an image of kindness, others of toughness, and others of sexiness or elegance. The case of Diego, a twenty-year-old Mexican American living in the Richardson neighborhood of Los Angeles and nicknamed by his friends as Snoopy, is typical of this process. The name was chosen not because he resembled the dog in the Peanuts comic strip but because he always asked questions. As one of his friends, Mateo, said while he and Snoopy were in Castro's Barbershop, "Snoopy, you are driving me nuts with all these questions. Do you have to ask a question about every shittin' thing? Don't you have any answers?" Everyone in the barbershop then laughed at Mateo's comment. Although Snoopy was named for a particular behavior, he chose his own image and personal identity. He chose to see himself as cute and curious, and he chose haircuts that he thought presented this image.

The second consideration in choosing a hairstyle was the individual's public image, into which the internal image of identity was transformed. The public image is what Goffman calls "the presentation of self in everyday life."[56] Yet the people of these five neighborhoods had both a primary public that included family, intimate friends, and neighbors, and a secondary public that included the rest of society. Each of these environments influenced which aspects of the internal self would be presented to the public.

Some individuals were remarkably consistent in all their interactions. Others, like Eddie, a seventeen-year-old African American living in the Monument neighborhood of the Bronx, developed a repertoire of selves to be utilized in different situations.[57] Eddie's nickname was "Eyes" because he always seemed to know what was going on with everyone in the neighborhood. He knew the latest rumors or gossip, so he was always asked for information. Most found this behavior amusing, and he was continually teased about it in a friendly manner. Thus the public identity he assumed in the neighborhood was positive and endearing. In the broader community, however, he nurtured an identity of vigilance and inscrutability. Outside the neighborhood he spoke only in response to questions and then did so cautiously. Most often, he simply watched people, and when getting a haircut he always chose a style that accentuated his eyes, which he considered his best feature.

This same pattern was seen in women. Rosa, for example, a twenty-four-year-old Puerto Rican living in the Eagleton neighborhood of Brooklyn, was nicknamed to show her fondness for *coquitos,* sweet drinks made with coconut and rum that are served during the Christmas sea-son. Her nickname was given to her by the women in her apartment because of her kindness and her efforts to cheer people up, as seen by her little jokes and mischievous playing with the other women at the Kendall Hair Salon. Even when she was not in the hair salon the other women spoke of her with affection, telling stories of her playfulness. Rosa was remarkably consistent in how she presented herself in the neighborhood, and everyone who knew her spoke of her efforts to make people happy. However, when outside the neighborhood she was anything but outgoing and cheery; instead she was withdrawn, shy, and sometimes even rude. When a young woman asked her for directions to the nearest subway station, Rosa very curtly responded, "I have no idea," and kept on walking, even though she knew the location of the station. At work, an office building where she did maintenance, she was shy and reserved with both her fellow workers and the professional occupants of the building. It was clear that the public self she presented outside her neighborhood maintained her sense of personal protection and security. Her choice of a public self in different environments was her attempt to integrate personal identity and social control; thus she chose hairstyles that gave her a "reserved" look.[58] Her standard line to the beautician was always "Nothing too radical, now."

Most people chose a public identity by combining their image of themselves with what they considered a culturally appropriate presentation.[59] This made it possible for others to understand them and choose appropriate communicative and behavioral responses. When people considered only their local culture, they were left vulnerable in a variety of contexts, especially those outside the neighborhood. Likewise, when people used an identity that was meaningful only outside the neighborhood, the local neighbors could not understand the behavior or considered it culturally inappropriate. Significantly, identities were sometimes either established in the hair shops or reinforced by the hairstyle that people chose and their interaction with others in the shop. The seemingly simple choice of hairstyle actually involved integrating within a lower-class context the individual's private and public identities with a style considered fashionable.

African American barbershops offered three to four times the number of styles that barbershops serving other ethnic groups offered. Thirty to sixty different African American hairstyles were available to customers. While some advertisements in non–African American shops had only sketches of people with different hairstyles, the African American barbershops usually had a poster of each style offered.

Over the nine years of the study African Americans initiated new styles very quickly because they stressed the creation of unique individual identities over fads that conformed to a specific style. This partly corresponds to Cornel West's argument that the everyday experience of African Americans within American society is one of social denigration and invisibility. In their hairstyles, as in their selection of unique and exotic first names, individuals sought ways to publicly declare, "I am! I exist!"[60]

Physically distinguishing oneself could take many other forms, including dress—wearing avant-garde styles of clothing or expensive clothes— and decoration of the body with tattoos. A more extreme form of bodily decoration, adopted primarily by men, was branding. A particular symbol (no single symbol was used) was burned into the skin, usually on the outside of the bicep, and when it healed, the raised scar tissue formed the symbol. A brand not only was artistic but represented the physical and mental strength of someone able to withstand the pain of acquiring it.[61]

The use of hair and grooming to establish individuality and avoid invisibility is prominent in low-income areas, from the shaved haircut for men and women to the use of straightening products and techniques to develop unique and stunning looks. Thus, in both the barbershops and the hair salons of poor neighborhoods, experimentation with new styles and knowledge of the most recent styles in the community are common. In fact, barbers and beauticians often tell customers about the most recent styles in an effort to have them try new ones.[62]

It is necessary to understand fashion and style in poor areas if one is to understand the role that hair shops play in group and neighborhood culture. People with low incomes, many of whom are officially listed as poor, are keenly aware of fashion, particularly fashion that has to do with the body, such as clothing and personal grooming. Most are aware of what is considered "in fashion" by people with money, and they try to emulate being fashionable. Thus it is not uncommon to find people with very little money buying very expensive clothing or cars. This has often led to much resentment from people with money because they consider it irresponsible. In their view, the poor should purchase modest, inexpensive clothing.[63] The comments of Andy and Sylvia represent this attitude. Andy, a twenty-nine-year-old Italian American from Stanton Island, was speaking to Phil, the Italian owner of Monte's Barbershop in the Bronx's Elmway neighborhood:

> Look at the way that the fucking niggers and spics live. They fucking got no money, a shit house, and yet they can buy new fucking clothes and shit! They shouldn't give these fucks welfare, or any other kind of money. If they

don't have any food, let 'em starve, because if you give 'em money they just spend it on stupid stuff.[64]

Sylvia, a twenty-three-year-old white woman from the Hollywood Hills section of Los Angeles, commented to her assistant Loren after delivering some grooming products to the Distinctive Hair Salon in the Richardson neighborhood:

> Did you see the clothes that the women in there [the salon] had on? If you think that those clothes were good, you should have been here a couple of months ago when I had to make a rush delivery. It was a late Saturday afternoon and some of the women had gotten their hair done and then changed in the back room into some of their good clothes. Boy, was there some expensive clothes being worn that day. I don't want to sound prejudiced, but I'll bet all of those women are poorer than hell, and still they'll go out and spend every last dime on clothing. This is why I can't feel sorry for them, because they will spend their money on their clothes and not on their children.[65]

To the poor, the purchase of expensive clothing has a variety of meanings. It shows that although they may be poor they have not lost their sense of "fashion." They too want to experience the feeling of expensive fabric and wear clothing tailored to fit them so that they will look the best they can.

Some ethnic groups living in poverty seem less focused on creating an individual "look" through fashion and style. Suttles reported in his study of a Chicago slum that African Americans were more clothes conscious than other ethnic groups living in the area.[66] Many African Americans considered this observation offensive because they thought it made them look irresponsible. However, Suttles's point was not that other ethnic groups were not fashion conscious but that they were less focused on fashions in clothing specifically. Some ethnic groups in the neighborhoods of the present study relied more on other objects like cars, furniture, televisions, and home decorations as means to establish individual identities, although they still used clothing, hair, and grooming as well.

In Mexican American areas a variety of hairstyles were present, each associated with a particular identity. In one style for men, the Mongolian, the hair was cut close to the skin except for a spot at the back of the skull left longer and a small tuft of hair left long enough to form a mini-pigtail. The ducktail style was similar to the Mongolian in that the hair was cut short, sometimes forming a crewcut on top, with a small tuft of hair left long enough to form a mini-pigtail at the very base of the hairline. In yet another style, the head was simply shaved to the scalp. Last was the fade style, a tapered look in which hair was cut somewhat long in front and progressively shorter toward the back of the head. Other styles were also seen in the neighborhoods, some of which were associated with a desire to be identified with gangs.[67]

These same barrios also featured other, more conventional hairstyles, the most common of which was a cut that allowed hair to be swept from the forehead to the back of the head. This style cultivated an image of conventionality and responsibility and, when worn by adults, was associated with the security-maximizing value orientation. The comments of Moises, a twenty-nine-year-old Mexican American, at Pepe's Barbershop in L.A.'s El Rey neighborhood are representative:

> *Moises*: I want it cut so I can sweep it back. When I was younger, I wanted it short so it wouldn't be so hot when I wore a cap, but now with the kids wearing theirs short, I don't want to look like I'm an old street wannabe.
>
> *Barber*: [laughs] Well, with this style everyone will know you're a guy who goes to work every day [others laugh].[68]

Hairstyles were thus a personal statement of identity that had both group and individual attributes, the sum of which was the desired public identity and response to this identity that individuals sought from others in the neighborhood. Individuals cultivated identities intended to cut across multiple publics, especially those of their neighborhood and close friends. The hairstyle chosen was a type of social mask that publicly presented an identity accentuating what the person believed to be positive while concealing vulnerable parts of the self. Once it was presented, individuals worked to develop other aspects of their presented self to correspond to the image desired.[69] Manuel, a twenty-year-old Mexican American living in the Richardson neighborhood of Los Angeles, showed this careful consideration of the implications of his hairstyle as a public presentation of self in a conversation with his brother Romeo in the family apartment:

> *Romeo*: Why did you get that *cholo* [gang] haircut?
>
> *Manuel*: 'Cause I'm trying to improve myself and I don't want to get hassled by every *vato* [gang member] in the hood. They will mess with me by taking my money 'cause they don't want me to be better than them.
>
> *Romeo*: You really think they care?
>
> *Manuel*: Hell yes they care, plus I don't want them to make fun of me going to night school to get my GED. They'll just call me stupid and things. It's just better if I don't look like I'm trying to improve myself so I can get a good job, and a haircut is the least I can do.
>
> *Romeo*: Okay, don't get so sensitive, I'm just asking.[70]

Dorothy, a twenty-year-old Jamaican living in Brooklyn's Eagleton neighborhood, showed a similar awareness in a conversation with her hospital co-worker at the Kendall Salon:

> I want to get my hair styled like that woman over there. Now, she got one of them styles that lets people know that she's elegant and responsible—you know, a serious person who is looking for a serious man, not some guy looking for a good time. I really am ready to meet a serious man, but the way my family acts, men around here just think I want only a good time. But that ain't me. I want a serious and successful man, and I going to give that message the best I can.[71]

The hair shops in the five neighborhoods studied provided a place where people's personal and public identities were forged, reinforced, or reinvented. The body was purposefully manipulated to communicate a message about an individual's "self" to both immediate and extended publics. When a person asks, "What's in a name?" or "What's in a haircut?" the most accurate answer is that both have many meanings that are very significant in everyday interaction. Since hair styling is done most often to create and maintain a physical attractiveness whose objective is sexual desirability and identity, the barbershop and hair salon are strategic in teaching the local wisdom about such roles and identities.[72]

A PLACE OF ENTERTAINMENT

In addition to serving the functional role of cutting and styling hair, the hair shops in poor neighborhoods are places of fun and entertainment. The type of entertainment provided in the barbershop varied depending on the amount of space and the desires of the clientele. The clientele provided the entertainment, while the barber merely provided the physical space.[73]

The most common type of entertainment was the verbal bantering that constantly kept up people's interest. Some bantering involved verbal games in which players attempted to one-up the others in the match, often through a series of arguments that everyone understood as nothing more than a play of words and wit. Making people laugh was what counted for both the audience and the speakers. Even when the bantering provoked some resentment among the players, monitors constantly reminded them that becoming serious, irritated, or mad was inappropriate and against the rules of engagement. Thus it was rare for a physical altercation to result from this type of playing.

More formal games were also played in the barbershops. In Puerto Rican, Dominican, and Mexican barbershops the clientele played dominos. Often multiple games were played simultaneously. Sometimes the barber did not even cut hair during the games and became an onlooker like the others in his shop. The comments of Jorge to Beto, the barber, while I was getting a haircut are representative of those who frequented the Aguila Barbershop in the El Rey neighborhood. Other than me, Jorge was the only customer in the barbershop.

> *Jorge*: Boy, I sure wish someone would get in soon. I'd like to have a game of bones [dominos]. What's going on, Beto? Is there some reason nobody's come in?
>
> *Beto*: No, it's just been a slow day.
>
> *Jorge*: This is crazy, ain't it?
>
> *Beto*: Yep.
>
> *Jorge*: I thought I'd come down for an hour or so and have a few games of bones and then pick up my wife at her sister's [place]. Fuck, this is disappointing that there ain't no one here to have a game. I guess I'll just stay and talk for a while and then head over to pick up my wife.[74]

In African American barbershops checkers or chess was often played. Even though only two people could play at the same time, many others watched (and commented). Everyone knew that chess involved strategy. However, most people believed that checkers was merely a game of fun, mainly because children played and because it seemed to present more limited move possibilities. Yet the rules in the barbershops studied made the game more complex and created, to varying degrees, the potential for strategy that always became part of the game.

The games of chess, checkers, and dominos always included onlookers who were never quiet. Onlookers sometimes commented about a play they would have made and kidded players about a move they had just made or the specific predicament in which they found themselves. At other times comments between the men, including the players, had nothing to do with the game itself. This was completely tolerated because the game was not more important than the neighborhood, of which the barbershop was an extension, and the camaraderie and companionship associated with the game.

INFORMATION EXCHANGE
AND THE CREATION OF LOCAL KNOWLEDGE

For groups to maintain internal cohesion, they need a common worldview. A common worldview allows individuals with different identities and experiences to interact with each other in a coordinated manner because it helps them predict the responses of those with whom they interact. A necessary step in creating and maintaining a particular world-view is the establishment of "local knowledge," which is predicated on the exchange of information, and no place was more important in this creation than the hair shops.[75] Individuals need information because it empowers them to take action that is most beneficial to them. In each of the five neighborhoods studied, everyone identified the hair shops as a continual source of information (even if it was not always accurate) on neighborhood, city, national, and international developments. The information circulating in hair shops covered five main topics: (1) social events; (2) employment opportunities; (3) safety; (4) residents' troubles; and (5) local and national politics.

The most popular type of information available at the hair shops was information about parties and other social events that either had occurred or were about to occur in the neighborhood. There was a great deal of interest in "comings and goings" in the neighborhood, and both young and old went to the barbershop to obtain this information. Upcoming parties, their hosts, and the possible attendees were the most sought-after information among men under the age of forty. Men over forty may also have been interested, but they generally showed few signs of this outside the normal interest in gossip; older men in the neighborhood considered the topics of parties, women, and drugs the domain of young men. Men stopped by the barbershop just to get information and talk about the possible social dynamics that might occur between those who were invited. People also talked about why certain people were not invited and the likely social ramifications for those responsible for the exclusion. These conversations became entertaining comic dramas that had everyone laughing because everyone got involved in speculation, much of it absurd. However, if those who had been excluded were present, such talk was avoided because it was considered socially inappropriate and potentially volatile under the codes of respect and honor. Nearly everyone in the barbershop knew most, if not all, of the people discussed, indicating a level of networking beyond that found in middle-class neighborhoods.

Safety was a much-discussed topic in the hair shops as well. Like other conversations, those concerning safety were slightly different in contested and fragmented neighborhoods. In contested neighborhoods, discussions of safety often centered on information that would enable patrons to avoid confrontations and violence. This was particularly important in the summertime when a party was being held in one of the public parks that competing groups used. An example involved Castro's Barbershop in the Richardson neighborhood of Los Angeles, patronized by both Mexican Americans and Mexican nationals. One week in July, a patron found out about a picnic and party in the local park organized by an African American social club. He passed on the information to the men in the barbershop, who then circulated it among the people who came in. Because there was a great deal of gang activity in the neighborhood and because members of at least one African American gang would be at the picnic, Mexicans needed to avoid the park on that day to prevent some type of violent confrontation. The police were also aware of the picnic and had planned for violence, but because the Mexicans had prior knowledge of the picnic, it occurred without incident.

Safety in contested neighborhoods was associated with defending members of one's group from other groups, and conversations nearly always depicted members of one's own group as victims and members of other groups as predators. This reinforced the need to bond together for protection, the moral superiority of one's own group compared to other groups, and the need to persevere. Group solidarity was both maintained and strengthened, as shown in a conversation between Rodolfo, a twenty-three-year-old Mexican American, and five other men at Castro's Barbershop in L.A.'s Richardson neighborhood:

> *Daniel [the barber]*: Hey Rudy, was that your cousin who got beat up last week?
>
> *Rudolfo*: It sure was! Them *majates* [literally "bugs," but used to refer to African Americans in a derogatory way] really hurt him. He was in the hospital for two weeks getting all kinds of blood and things. They wanted his money, but he wouldn't give it to them. These *majates* ain't getting me to give them anything either, and I ain't going to move because of them! [The other five men nod their heads in agreement.]
>
> *Daniel*: You better not, because I don't know how to cut blacks' hair. [Everyone laughs.][76]

In fragmented neighborhoods discussions about safety centered on controlling the "lowlifes" of the neighborhood. Most of the men in the barbershops associated crime, especially violent crime, with sick and irresponsible people who lived for today and did little to plan for tomorrow. They reasoned that people who lived for today set themselves up for involvement in crime. The comments of Claude, a thirty-six-year-old African American living in the Bronx's Monument neighborhood, are representative:

You see them guys who don't save nothing [people with excitement-maximizing value orientations] always be havin' scrapes with the law 'cause they wants good things, but they spend their monies as soon as they get it and then they got nothin' when they wants something else. So then they just try and take it, and that's how they in trouble with the law.[77]

However, when it came to law enforcement, both types of neighborhoods had similar views. They believed that the police were not interested in protecting them and that police viewed everyone in the neighborhood as a criminal or capable of becoming one. Most conversations centered on the police harassing them by giving undeserved citations, planting evidence for arrests, using unnecessary force to apprehend suspects, and using racial profiling to stop and search them. Since the police constituted the most basic level of state power, discussions of police behavior in the barbershops taught young boys that the state was malevolent toward poor nonwhites.[78]

Older men in the barbershop were intensely ambivalent. They acknowledged their dependence on the police and believed that police should be helpful and protective but also felt disappointment and contempt that police, instead of helping, simply wanted to control the local population. The comments of Dexter and Tito in the Bronx's Town Barbershop are representative:

Dexter: Fucking police! They could have stopped that harassment of Dino [a resident] by those drug addicts, but no, they just have to spend their time giving Alton [another resident] shit for not having a headlight on his car. So now Dino's had a heart attack and Alton's got to find money to pay the ticket.

Tito: They did the same shit in my building. They raid the place for drug dealers and then didn't come when my neighbor was being robbed in her apartment, even though she called 911 when the guy was trying to come in her window. I wish you could just trust the fuckers.[79]

One of the most important kinds of information provided in the barbershops was tips on employment opportunities that gave interested people a contact person who worked for the company. In fragmented neighborhoods this information was not disseminated to everyone in the barbershop because the patrons considered themselves to have different social positions. Rather, whoever had the information selectively disseminated it to those he thought appropriate, as determined by his assessment of the job and the people who were present. For example, if someone knew of a job that did not require a particular skill but did require general competency and consistency in coming to work, he passed on the information to those who met the job's requirements.[80]

The decision of whom to inform about a job opportunity was not easy, particularly when the person with the information was making value judgments on potential applicants' responsibility: it was important to avoid offending people, especially in fragmented neighborhoods, where value orientations expressed in differing moral definitions of "responsible" versus "irresponsible" were a major principle of division. Thus, to avoid offending anyone, the person who knew about the job presented just enough information about it so that the contact person got applicants who would be considered appropriate. Many times, he knew what duties the job entailed, how much it paid, whether it came with benefits, how many hours a day or week it involved, and when it would start. Furthermore, he usually knew of a contact person at the business who would help with the paperwork and talk to the boss for the interested applicant. Finally, he often knew who in the community had the skills required for the job and would be willing to give the prospective applicant a quick lesson.[81] Yet he passed on this additional information only to those he thought were responsible.[82]

Numerous researchers have described the importance of social networks in securing work, especially for immigrant populations, and barbershops in contested neighborhoods were primary locations for occupational networks.[83] In many of the barbershops, entire groups of patrons found employment in what Roger Waldinger has called sector niches in the urban economy.[84] For example, in Ellerby's Barbershop in Brooklyn, Jamaican American patrons had developed a network throughout a number of the hospitals in New York City. The men in the barbershop knew when a job opened up in one of the hospital departments and who in the local Jamaican American community should be contacted for help in getting hired.[85]

Likewise, patrons were informed about occupations controlled by ethnic groups other than their own. Thus, in applying for jobs, patrons knew which jobs were realistically available to them and which belonged to another group's niche. At John's Barbershop in L.A.'s Richardson neighborhood, the news spread that Hendricks Corporation (a pseudonym) was opening two new buildings and had a number of openings for janitors. It was known, however, that African Americans had a very poor chance of getting hired because Mexicans had established a strong network within the janitorial sector and greatly influenced the hiring process. Such information exaggerated the power of Mexican workers, but it illustrated the strength of the Mexican network, for nearly all the janitors at Hendricks's other establishments were Mexican.[86]

Hair shops also provided information about the troubles affecting community residents such as fires (how they had started, who had been physically and materially injured), evictions, contagious diseases, injuries, and, most of all, crime and law enforcement. The discussions had three functions. First, they passed on information that could help patrons comfort the victim or be respectful of another's tragedy. Second, the topics made the listeners realize that they had been spared a hardship and thus caused them to feel a little better about their present situation. Although the feeling only lasted for a few days or weeks, it provided a temporary sense of relief.

Many of the men were also entertained by another's tragedy in some way. Loïc Wacquant has theorized that the middle class often enjoy hearing about the "pathologies" taking place in ghetto areas.[87] The lower class and poor, too, are not immune to this phenomenon. Thus a tragic story could be intriguing enough to receive a good deal of attention and discussion.

Finally, conventional topics that focused on hardship and tragedy helped to socialize young patrons by introducing them to a life that would have its share of tragedies, which they would have to deal with so that life would not get the best of them. Young men were taught that those who succumbed to the difficulties of life were weak and destined to live in the gutter. In fact, many of the men in the barbershop believed that the male suicides in the neighborhoods were the result of the victims' inability to stand up and take what life had given them. The comments of Aureliano, a thirty-three-year-old Puerto Rican, to the barber and six other men in Monte's Barbershop in the Bronx's Elmway neighborhood represent this belief:

> Shit, that was something about Roberto [he shakes his head]. I knew he was having trouble with his job and his wife, but jumping in front of a bus is something. You know, everybody gets shit thrown at them in life, but you just keep going. I guess he did not have the balls to do that. [He shakes his head again, and the other men nod and shake their heads too.][88]

A fifth popular topic was politics. Much discussion of news concerning local and national issues took place in the barbershops and hair salons. These discussions were an attractive alternative to reading news magazines such as *Time, Newsweek,* and *U.S. News and World Report.* Conversing with others about the news was considered more exciting than reading it.

Discussions of the local and national news in barbershops and hair salons also functioned to teach, reinforce, and control public thought about politics. Conversations on national politics in contested neighborhood barbershops focused on candidates. During a presidential election year all the discussions were about the presidential candidates. If barbershops were patronized by one ethnic group, discussions were about which candidate would best help or hurt members of that group. Inhabitants of poor neighborhoods generally support the Democratic Party, so during the primaries a great many discussions were about which candidate within that party would best help them. After a candidate was chosen, discussions refocused on supporting the Democratic candidate and vilifying the Republican candidate. Men in these barbershops felt a socioeconomic vulnerability and displayed it by criticizing the campaign of their favorite candidate out of fear that they would lose the election and be left in even worse condition. The comments of Edgar, a twenty-four-year-old Puerto Rican, Jonah, a twenty-nine-year-old Dominican, and Marvin, a thirty-four-year-old Dominican, are representative of this response.

> *Jonah*: Shit, that Clinton is messing up. He makes all those statements that makes it look like he's going to create socialism! You know how all those middle-class people feel about that?
>
> *Marvin*: God, I hope he don't screw this up 'cause it will be piss awful for people like us.
>
> *Edgar*: That fucking jerk! What an asshole! He's going to lose and make it worse for us.[89]

Discussions in the barbershops usually focused on candidates' positions on economic issues that would affect neighborhood residents, but discussions in the hair salons were much more focused on candidates' personality and sense of compassion. Women saw the candidates' political positions on future issues as directly associated with their moral sense of compassion for those in need. The comment of Natalie, a thirty-four-year-old African American mother of two living in L.A.'s Richardson neighborhood, to two other women in the Distinctive Salon represents this pattern:

> I don't like them bills [legislation] to stop illegal immigrants from getting education or medical help. Them people is innocent, and that is just wrong to stop childrens from learning. . . . Yeah, can you believe somebody needin' medical help and they just say no? Them politicians should be very ashamed, and God will judge them.[90]

Women from contested neighborhoods focused on issues that affected their group. Many of the women from recent immigrant groups were very concerned about how the candidate would handle policies that affected immigrants, such as public school, health, and language. In some of the hair salons discussions were not very extensive, since for a good deal of the time clients were primarily interacting with the hairdresser. The modus operandi in the beauty salon made general discussion between all the patrons difficult, and discussions with the hairdresser alone were rather limited, usually serving merely to reinforce the patron's preferences.

In the hair salons of fragmented neighborhoods, discussions between beautician and client focused a great deal on issues of child care, religion, and health. The deep rift between women who identified with the security-maximizing and excitement-maximizing value orientations was not present because women in both groups recognized that they faced similar problems. They supported compassionate candidates who would try to help ease the burdens of their lives, which mostly meant helping their families survive the hardships of everyday life. Sometimes people with a security-maximizing orientation were more likely to support candidates who took a strong stand on drug use and violations of food subsidies. However, support for penalties regarding food subsidies usually stemmed from a belief that such policies would help the children who needed them most.

Of all the political discussions taking place in the barbershops, those involving local political issues were the most heated. During local elections, the political pulse of the neighborhood could be found in the barbershops. In contested neighborhoods, talk was dominated by rationalizing the importance of supporting candidates of one's own ethnic group. This was a consistent exercise in reaffirming group identity and reinforcing the group's sense of their local knowledge system.

This pattern can be seen in an exchange that occurred in Castro's Barbershop in the Richardson neighborhood of Los Angeles. Three Mexican patrons were talking about the upcoming election of an elementary school's parent association presidency.

> *Marco*: Magdelena Rosa is running for the association's board presidency.
> *Guillermo*: Carla Thomas [an African American] told people in the group [association] it would be better if the president was born in the United States.
> *Ignacio*: What a racist comment! They [African Americans] are so prejudiced against us because they don't want us to have any positions on anything that they had control of.
> *Marco*: I don't know if Carla is racist, she just wants an African American.

Guillermo: She sure is racist, she thinks that we are poor and ignorant because many of us have come from Mexico. I heard her use "wetbacks" [illegal immigrants from Mexico] when referring to us. She is no different from the other African Americans here. [Marco nods in agreement as Ignacio continues to give examples of acrimonious interactions with African Americans.][91]

This example indicates that the Mexican view of interethnic relations with African Americans is understood through a particular ethnic prism developed through experiences that color future experiences. In contested neighborhoods, this view nearly always is predicated on the likelihood of conflict.

Conversations also occurred when a particular ethnic group in a contested neighborhood did not have anyone of their ethnicity running in an election. In the barbershop, these discussions focused on supporting a candidate who would not hurt their group. At Monte's Barbershop in the Bronx's Elmway neighborhood, a conversation between three Italian Americans, Dante, Enrico, and John, about the local election for their district is representative:

Dante: What a fucking choice we got. There is a fucking spic for the Democrats and a fucking kike for the Republicans. We're going to get fucked no matter what, but I gotta go with the fucking Jew, 'cause at least he is Republican and he knows there is a lot of us [Italians] in the Republican Party.

John: Plus the fucking Jews ain't as bad to live next to as those fucking spics.

Enrico: Yeah, it's the shits to live next to those spics. They'll just have millions of fucking kids and smell up the entire community with that shit-food of theirs!

John: I don't know what this shittin' place is turning into. [Dante and Enrico shake their heads.]

Dante: A fucking asshole if we leave them [Puerto Ricans] have it.[92]

In the hair salons of contested neighborhoods, discussions of local politics centered less on candidates and broad community issues like economic development than on specific issues that residents and their families faced on a daily basis, particularly their own and their children's safety. The political context of public safety, seen as safety from the predatory behavior of members of competing ethnic groups in the neighborhood, was a constant topic of discussion. Women from particular ethnic groups discussed the lack of police effort to protect their children from attack by children from other ethnic groups. They viewed members of other ethnic groups as dangerous to their children, themselves, and the routines that they had established, even if there were few incidents of violence involving children of their group. The occurrence of just one incident of violence was seen as a sign of a perilous trend that would result in their children constantly having to cope with the threat of physical harm. Thus conversations centered on whose family members were attacked, where the attacks had taken place, and what the political authorities had done to protect their children.

In the barbershops and hair salons in fragmented neighborhoods, conversations about local politics centered on which candidates were politically responsible. What was considered responsible was highly debated, and the divisions were quite clear and predictable since opinions on responsibility were direct extensions of a person's value orientation. For those operating under the security-maximizing value orientation, conversations focused on benefit to the neighborhood. Responsibility meant a civic orientation toward the neighborhood, so politicians who were accessible to local people and worked to help residents with problems were verbally supported. Candidates considered irresponsible were seen as being more concerned for themselves than for the community, doing little to bring resources to members of the community, and being parasitic on the community.

Whereas political thinking among men was influenced by group pressure within the barbershop to conform to community norms, within the hair salon the hairdresser influenced individual women to conform to community political norms. This difference existed because female patrons were more involved with the hairdresser than with other patrons while in the salon. Thus the hairdresser was the primary source of community information. Patrons' discussions with the hairdresser were aimed at acquiring information to help them manage their economic and emotional lives. However, when it came to politics, the hairdresser passed on information she had heard from other women in the neighborhood, so she became an authority on what people in the neighborhood considered politically correct. When a client expressed a deviant opinion from the community norm, the hairdresser informed her of the dominant opinion in the neighborhood in order to let her know what was expected. The hairdresser's suggestion was nearly always gentle, but most of the women became quiet and appeared to conform.

SOME CLOSING REMARKS

Hair shops make important contributions to the social order and structure of poor neighborhoods. The barbershop and hair salon are two of the primary places where personal identities are generated and reinforced through the process of socialization and the creation of style. However, these personal identities do not stay within the confines of the hair shop but carry over to other social institutions. Ultimately, hair shops are places for leisure, information transfer, and social networking. At the most fundamental level, they help integrate a person's sense of individuality with a social identity. The intertwining of individual and social identities provides the elements organized by, and for, the neighborhood social order and structure.

CHAPTER 7

Life on the Edge

Social Change
and Preservation in the Hair Shop

There was a beauty parlor at the corner. She would get a
shampoo that she couldn't afford, but she would have people
around her and it would use up a lot of time.

Ann Petry, *The Street* (1946)

According to some researchers, barbershops and hair salons, like mom-
and-pop stores, are types of economic establishments that are disappear-
ing in the poorest urban areas of the United States.[1] Consequently, they
argue, these neighborhoods are losing the infrastructure that maintains
the social order residents need if they are to live a decent life.[2] However,
in persistently poor neighborhoods, a decrease in the number of economic establishments is not nearly as significant to the social order as
whether these establishments are neighborhood institutions or economic
enterprises, as defined in chapter 1.

Barbershops and beauty salons are similar to mom-and-pop stores in
that they are central elements in the structure of poor neighborhoods.
They differ in that the service they provide to residents is much more privately individual than that provided by the small corner grocery store
and is in steady demand. Yet despite this demand they sometimes face
difficulties that can change a neighborhood's status quo. The following
analysis identifies (1) agents that change the functioning of barbershops
and hair salons, (2) agents that preserve the status quo, and (3) the consequences of social change and maintenance for the structure and operation of the neighborhood. Thus this chapter will compare and examine
change and maintenance in barbershops and beauty salons of contested
and fragmented neighborhoods in relation to internal and external
dynamics that affect their status as neighborhood institutions or economic enterprises.

SOCIAL CHANGE IN HAIR SHOPS
OF CONTESTED NEIGHBORHOODS

Like all other neighborhood establishments discussed thus far, hair shops are subject to various change agents that can fundamentally alter their operations or render them incapable of operating. Some of the dynamics and results of these change agents are the same in both contested and fragmented neighborhoods, whereas others are different. The variation, however, provides a better understanding of the conditions that produce divergent results.

In contested neighborhoods changes often occurred in the population demographics such that increasing numbers of one ethnic group moved into the neighborhood while an equally increasing number of another moved out. This led to an increase of barbershops and hair salons that served some ethnic groups and a decline in those that served others. Although in this particular situation hair shops in contested neighborhoods were objects of change and preservation, it should be understood that they were also agents of change and preservation.

External Change Agents

Like any establishment, the barbershop or hair salon could be changed by a variety of forces, some of which were external. Shifts in population helped establish contested neighborhoods, but they also caused changes in establishments like barbershops and hair salons, the most obvious of which was the number of paying customers. Like all economic establishments, barbershops and hair salons ultimately depended on the number of consistently paying customers. A significant drop in this number created a budgeting crisis that was rarely remedied, resulting in bankruptcy. Although many neighborhood disorganization theorists would argue that the significance of a hair shop's closing is the loss of a neighborhood economic enterprise, its real significance is the loss of a social institution and the resulting strain placed on the neighborhood's social structure.[3]

Population shifts often caused a change in the number of customers that altered the internal dynamics of the barbershop, initiating a total transformation of the establishment. Monte's Barbershop in the Bronx's Elmway neighborhood, for example, was an institution that had served Italian and Irish residents for over two generations. When African Americans moved into the neighborhood and started their own barbershops, the Italians and Irish resisted this population change. As in most contested neighborhoods, a great deal of hostility existed between the groups, leading to rigid territoriality.[4] This territoriality lasted until Puerto Ricans moved into the neighborhood and started their own barbershop. As their population grew, their territory expanded into the area that had been occupied by the Irish and Italians, and they began to patronize Monte's Barbershop, since there were no Puerto Rican barbershops nearby. As increasing numbers of Puerto Ricans became loyal customers, the internal dynamics of Monte's changed, and the shop went from being a neighborhood institution for the Italians and Irish to being just another economic enterprise.[5] Thus population shifts in contested neighborhoods could change establishments from institutions to economic enterprises once they no longer were social bastions for one of the competing factions. This was because internal social order and dynamics could be based on the norms of only one ethnic faction if the establishment was to offer social support as an institution. When competing factions patronized a single hair shop, there was constant tension and conflict until either one faction became dominant or the shop was reorganized as an economic enterprise (see table 5, pp. 180–81).

Population shifts could also change a neighborhood's barbershop when residents moved away from the area to avoid negative social and economic repercussions associated with the arrival of a new ethnic group. This occurred in the Richardson neighborhood of Los Angeles when Mexicans (and some Central Americans) began to quickly move into the area. As they replaced the African American population, John Jackson, the owner of John's Barbershop, began to lose clients and feared bankruptcy if the current population trend continued. As a result, he sold his business to a Mexican American barber. The sale initially changed the establishment from a neighborhood institution to an economic enterprise. However, after the Mexican barber had been in business for a year and his clientele had become entirely Mexican, the barbershop again became a neighborhood institution. Thus population shifts can potentially change a hair shop from a neighborhood institution to an economic enterprise and vice versa, although in the latter case a longer time frame is required.

Economic forces were another set of external factors that caused change in hair shops. One of these was market competition. Syndicated enterprises sought a market advantage by serving people from all ethnic groups. No doubt, this strategy helped them secure customers they would not otherwise have, but in contested neighborhoods, when one ethnic group patronized these establishments, other groups did not. Even though an establishment might not have ties to any particular group, it de facto found itself allied to one group. Thus, instead of serving the entire neighborhood, it became an enterprise for one of the neighborhood's groups, compromising the economic viability of other hair shops that served the same population.

Examples of this trend occurred in both the Elmway and Richardson neighborhoods. In both of these contested neighborhoods, a hair shop chain opened in geographic areas dominated by African Americans and consequently attracted a large number of young African American men and women. Although all the shops in the chain had workers of all ethnicities, the fact that they were frequented by African Americans deterred other ethnic groups from going there. This market situation caused other African American hair shops to lose a portion of their clientele. Consequently, one barbershop and one salon in the Bronx's Elmway neighborhood and a barbershop in L.A.'s Richardson neighborhood were forced out of business.

Theoretically, the intrusion of a large, syndicated hair shop into the local economy should have a negative economic impact on all hair shops. In contested neighborhoods, however, the burden is assumed by hair shops that serve one, or at most two, ethnic groups and now have to share their clientele.

Another economic force affecting the operations of hair shops was rent. Rents were raised when landlords needed an increase in revenue to meet their economic objectives. Then establishments like hair shops had to either pass on the added expense to their customers or absorb it themselves. Problematically, however, their customers' incomes were generally not increasing at the same time to cover an increase in price. Further, these establishments were often places of camaraderie and solidarity, so an increase in their patrons' economic burden undermined their legitimacy as neighborhood institutions. This situation was quite critical for people in contested neighborhoods because each group had a limited number of hair shops. Thus the loss of a hair shop or two affected interactions within the group, within other institutions, or both.

A final external factor that created change in the hair shops was either anticipated or unanticipated disaster. Fire had the greatest impact because in nearly every case the physical structure was so severely damaged that it had to be completely rebuilt. In contested neighborhoods, a neighborhood institution was shut down by such a disaster while the owner processed a claim with the insurance company.

In Ellerby's Barbershop in Brooklyn's Eagleton neighborhood, for example, a fire started during the night and destroyed most of the barbershop. Until the shop was rebuilt, most of the Jamaican clients were forced to patronize another Jamaican barbershop on the edge of the neighborhood. This was an extremely difficult time for the neighborhood because the other barbershop could not integrate the new clients into its existing social order without causing strained relations. The arrival of the new people with their new identities presented a challenge as to who would occupy the top, middle, and lower levels of the internal status hierarchy. Consequently that barbershop was stressed as a neighborhood institution.

A fire that destroyed everything in Harper's Barbershop in L.A.'s Richardson neighborhood provides yet another example. The owner began working with the insurance company to start rebuilding, but the population of the area was shifting from African American to predominantly Mexican. While the owner was negotiating with the insurance company, more Mexicans moved into the area, so the barber decided to rebuild in another section of the city. This left the remaining African Americans in the neighborhood with one less institution and placed a great deal of strain on John's Barbershop, which had to integrate the additional clients into its social status hierarchy. Thus a disaster to one establishment stressed the African American population of the neighborhood.

Violent crime also altered the barbershops' functional operations. As in many poor neighborhoods, violence was an everyday occurrence in the five neighborhoods of this study. Although both barbershops and hair salons felt the effects of this violence in their everyday operations, the salons felt it the most.[6]

In barbershops, neighborhood violence was ordinarily a discussion topic that helped reinforce one of the practical functions of the shop as neighborhood institution. Nonetheless, when violence occurred in close proximity to a barbershop, patrons went there less often. This slowed down the barber's business and disrupted the everyday interactions of the shop, though it did not stop business or interaction.

The effect of violence occurring close to a hair salon was much greater: women were frightened away. This was especially the case in contested neighborhoods, where women felt that violence was not random but the result of intergroup antagonisms that were likely to occur as long as the current demographic conditions continued. For example, four shootings took place one summer between African Americans and Puerto Ricans, two of them near the Jewel Beauty Salon in the Bronx's Elmway neighborhood. Hostilities had been simmering for some time but intensified over a dispute concerning who had the rights to play and for how long on the softball field in a local park. During one of the many fights that occurred in the park, two Puerto Rican girls were seriously wounded. In retaliation, a number of drive-by shootings occurred along the street where the Jewel Salon operated, a street that was a primary walkway for both male and female African Americans going to the major shopping avenue. Although the shots could have been meant for either young men or women, many African American women, especially young women who frequented the hair salon, believed that they were the targets. Thus many of the women stopped going to the hair salon and did their hair at home, significantly reducing the salon's clientele. Business dropped so much that the owner seriously considered closing the shop and filing for bankruptcy.

The shootings not only drove down business but effectively blocked the social interactions that functionally contributed to the everyday operations of the neighborhood. Women who had frequented the hair salon diverted their energies to the local churches they attended, which consequently adopted some of the specialized social functions of the hair salon. Topics and issues such as family relations that had previously been discussed in the hair salon now took place at church, but women were inhibited from speaking freely because of the men present. Further, some women believed that sexual relations between husbands and wives, let alone unmarried individuals, were not appropriate conversation topics in the house of God. Those who thought these topics inappropriate saw the church as a spiritual place that was a retreat from the trials and tribulations of everyday life. As might be expected, the situation caused conflict among the parishioners and strained the church's operations as an institution. When violence along the street ceased, women returned to the hair salon, and the various churches that had served as replacements were able to return to their previous patterns of interaction. Thereafter, both the salon and church could perform their specific institutional roles, thus restoring the integrity of the neighborhood's social structure.

Internal Change Agents

Agents of change were also found within the hair shops. The most immediate impact was made by barbers and beauticians, who occupied a central position inside these establishments. Apart from providing service or organizing workers to provide it, when their establishment had become a neighborhood institution they assumed the role of institutional caretaker. Like caretakers of other institutions in the neighborhood, they promoted the functioning of the establishment as a social institution by ensuring that all the actors behaved in ways that supported the local community. This necessitated negotiating internal differences, determining individual needs, and providing functional (physical, psychological, and economic) support for their patrons.[7] In this way trust was gained and institutional legitimacy materialized or was maintained. Therefore, the death of a barber or beautician was very stressful to the people who personally knew that person or who knew him or her only more generally as the caretaker of the institution.

When a barber or beautician died, a relative often took over the business and did so with little disruption. However, if someone who had not worked in the shop assumed the responsibilities of the establishment, the transition was difficult. Furthermore, if the establishment was a neighborhood institution, it went through a transitional period until social relations were restored, functional needs were met, and trust was reestablished. If the new owner was not able to restore the establishment to its previous institutional state, patronage declined, at first slowly and then precipitously, until the shop was forced into bankruptcy, resulting in social change to the neighborhood. This occurred in the Hampton Barbershop of Brooklyn's Eagleton neighborhood. Richard M. Hampton, whom everyone called "Hamp," had owned the barbershop for thirty-eight years and had built it into a neighborhood institution. In fact, as a local resident, he was considered a neighborhood institution himself because he managed the caretaker duties of the barbershop so effectively that his influence was felt throughout the community. "Hamp" was greatly appreciated for being one of those people who made everyone feel worthy of attention. When he died suddenly of a heart attack in his home, everyone was shocked and saddened, including those in the neighborhood who patronized other barbershops.

"Hamp" had three girls, none of whom were interested in learning the business, and no one else in the immediate or extended family was willing, or able, to take over the business. That left a big void to be filled. A barber from a shop in Queens bought the business from "Hamp's" family, but he found it difficult to regain the previous number of patrons, so he had trouble meeting expenses. He struggled for about ten months but was finally forced to declare bankruptcy and sell the equipment. Thus Eagleton lost an institution, and additional pressure to assume some of the responsibilities of the Hampton Barbershop was placed on other institutions.

Sometimes the death of a barber or beautician created an immediate vacancy that no one wanted to fill, mostly because the neighborhood population of the group served by the hair shop was declining. This reduced the client base and made starting a new business a very precarious economic venture that attracted few, if any, applicants. Such was the case with Jean's Beauty Salon in Brooklyn's Eagleton neighborhood. Jean started the salon and built it into both a good business and a neighborhood institution. She was its caretaker for twenty-six years, but at the age of fifty-three she died of pancreatic cancer within two months of being diagnosed. Her clients were grief stricken over her passing because she had been so important in their lives for so long. Many of these women of the same age group had confided in her and had received psychological comfort, informational resources, and a temporary escape from the stresses of family life, work, and physical discomfort in a neighborhood with little empathy.[8] The hair salon had served the African American women of Eagleton, but the neighborhood's demographics had been changing for six to seven years. The number of Puerto Rican and Dominican inhabitants kept increasing, and as the trend continued the African American population began moving to other areas. This resulted in few African American women in the neighborhood and even fewer young women, so Jean's Beauty Salon was patronized consistently by only a few young girls and women over the age of forty. Even before her death, the hair salon's important role in socializing a new generation of African American women to the neighborhood had been waning.[9] Therefore, when Jean's son put the hair salon up for sale, no African American women offered to buy it. Potential African American buyers usually did not go forward with the transaction because the client base was small and the prospects for expanding it were slim. Thus Jean's death meant the loss of not only a revered person but also an institution that had maintained the African American community in what had been a contested neighborhood.

Another internal change that had an important and immediate impact on social change in the barbershop was the loss of a caretaker's desire or ability to control his or her patrons' behavior in the establishment. An important role of the caretaker was managing interpersonal relations in a way that promoted stability in the hair shop while contributing to social cohesion in the neighborhood. When the roles of individuals who regularly frequented the hair shops were not nurtured, some of the social functions of the hair shops were weakened. For example, a number of regulars in the barbershop had roles such as keeping the laughter going, mediating disputes, enforcing game rules in checkers and dominos, or collecting neighborhood information. If new clients began to compete for these roles, the caretaker ordinarily managed the situation by creating new roles for the challengers without taking away those of the regulars. When a caretaker could not manage the situation, however, conflict in the hair shop resulted, disabling the effective operation of the institution.

When individuals were unhappy with their roles in a particular hair shop, they began to frequent other shops to improve their status. This often created conflict in these institutions because they were not initially prepared to manage the increased number of patrons. Eventually, they were able to manage and the internal social order was repaired. Thus, when a barber or beautician no longer could or wanted to regulate social relations, social change was imminent.

Economic pressure also had an important impact on the caretakers. When the business was faltering economically and was in danger of shutting down, the barber or beautician was tempted to allow other ethnic groups to patronize the establishment. In contested neighborhoods, this had particularly devastating consequences for social relations inside the establishment. In such cases, the hair shop could no longer function as an institution. One of the defining features of institutions in contested neighborhoods was that they served only one group. If a hair shop was not able to do this, it did not contribute to the institutional structure of the neighborhood. An instance of this occurred in the Main Street Barbershop of the Bronx's Elmway neighborhood when the owner, Calvin, was experiencing financial problems. These problems had been increasing since the neighborhood had begun experiencing a greater influx of Puerto Ricans and Dominicans. As more members of these groups moved into the housing projects and surrounding tenements, fewer African Americans remained in the neighborhood, so that over the course of fifteen months the barbershop drew fewer and fewer customers. At first, the shop did not experience any change in financial or internal social dynamics; it just served as one of the primary meeting places for African American men to express their complaints about the newest residents in the area, voice their opposition to the influx of immigrants, and solidify plans for contesting the change. However, as time moved on and the population of the new groups grew, the barbershop saw a significant loss of clients, so much so that Calvin was faced with the choice of either advertising the establishment to all groups in the neighborhood or going out of business. Because Calvin was in his fifties and financially unable to retire, he decided not to go out of business, so he hired a Puerto Rican barber and paid him a small base salary with a commission on all the new business he brought in. The Puerto Rican barber solicited Puerto Ricans and Dominicans to come to the shop, telling them that Main Street was no longer solely for African Americans (i.e., an African American institution) but was open to the entire neighborhood. As Puerto Ricans and Dominicans began to patronize the establishment, the internal dynamics changed dramatically. African Americans could not speak freely since members of the competing group(s) were present. They also had to watch their behavior because the internal dynamics were no longer predicated on African American symbols, rituals, and status markers. In a short time, the shop's internal dynamics were completely transformed, and the Main Street Barbershop changed from a contested neighborhood institution to an economic enterprise. Ironically, the change in the Main Street Barbershop was eased by the E & M Barbershop, which still operated as an African American institution because it was in a section of the neighborhood that remained African American. Thus African Americans who did not like the fact that other ethnic groups were allowed to frequent "their" barbershop transferred their patronage and loyalty from Main Street to the E & M.

Although the E & M did not experience the radical changes of the Main Street Barbershop, it confronted a different set of challenges, namely the reorganization of the shop's internal dynamics. The new clients of the E & M brought with them their identities and social status rankings from the Main Street Barbershop. This led to minor internal conflicts as the new patrons managed their beliefs about themselves and where they should fit in the status hierarchy of the veteran clients at the E & M Barbershop. Individuals complained about the behavior of the new patrons, and the formation of cliques undermined what had been a homogeneous environment where everyone had interacted congenially. Over time, however, the internal status hierarchy was redrawn in a way that was acceptable to all patrons; this repaired the internal order and reestablished the neighborhood's structure.

SOCIAL CHANGE IN HAIR SHOPS OF FRAGMENTED NEIGHBORHOODS

Often, the same changes that occurred in contested neighborhoods had a different impact on the operations and social structure of barbershops in fragmented neighborhoods. This was because social divisions in contested neighborhoods were based on ethnicity, whereas those in fragmented neighborhoods were based primarily on value orientation.

External Change Agents

Population shifts occurred in fragmented as well as contested neighbor-hoods, but they mostly involved people of the same ethnic group oper-ating under different value orientations (excitement maximizing versus security maximizing; see chapter 1). Although population shifts could be multidirectional, in fragmented neighborhoods they generally showed a trend in one direction. In neighborhoods occupied by Latinos or Jamaicans, shifts were due to an influx of recently arrived immigrant families; in African American neighborhoods they normally involved an increase in unemployed residents with few possibilities of securing jobs to improve their economic situation, and thus a trend toward a poorer population.[10]

These population shifts inevitably changed the internal dynamics of the hair shops. Usually, residents whose weekly resources allowed them to purchase only the basic necessities operated under an excitement-max-imizing value orientation. Residents who were officially counted as poor but had resources modestly above a basic-necessity level operated under a security-maximizing value orientation. Under normal conditions, a neighborhood institution had a more or less even distribution of people operating under each value orientation. However, when the balance tipped significantly in favor of those with an excitement-maximizing ori-entation, people with a security-maximizing orientation started to leave. No matter how hard the barber or beautician tried to manage the insti-tution, patrons with a security-maximizing orientation did not feel com-fortable interacting with a group they saw as "irresponsible spenders" (excitement-maximizing people). Likewise, people with an excitement-maximizing orientation were antagonistic toward a group they believed to be "tightwads" (security-maximizing people). Thus when security-maximizing patrons became a small minority they were not able to speak freely because their views were not accepted or respected by the major-ity of the shop's patrons. The comments of Damon, a forty-two-year-old African American resident in the Bronx's Monument neighborhood, after leaving the Town Barbershop reflect the sentiments among those trying to maximize security:

> I am not going to come to this shop any more. It just has changed too
> much for me. It's not the same. You can't believe the bullshit that is passed
> out there. Ever since all those niggers came into the neighborhood, all you
> get to hear is long, long conversations of how they're going to spend money
> doing this and that and this and that. Then they talk about what they spent

their money on and how great it is. It is such shit to have to hear this shit
when there ain't none of them got any money anyhow. . . . I got to go to a
place where you don't have to constantly listen to that shit and then defend
yourself because you want to act more responsible and save your money.[11]

Rosa, a twenty-seven-year-old Mexican American resident of the El Rey
neighborhood of Los Angeles, shared this view:

I am sorry about the way Mariposa [Salon] has changed. I liked it so much
for the last nine years, but now there are just too many *cholas* [girls in a
gang] that come to it. All they want to do is talk about who is going to
jump who or who got jumped by who and stupid stuff like that. Then if
somebody asks them about their boyfriend they say something like "Oh,
he's in prison." But then if you start telling them about the job you got and
saving and stuff like that, they tell you, or make faces, like you're boring
and dumb. I like Lucia [the salon's owner], but it's not fun to go to anymore. That's why I go somewhere else now.[12]

While it might seem strange that macroeconomic changes would have
a significant impact on people already living in poverty, their impact can
be considerable. Poor people, especially recent immigrants, often have
jobs, but these are often temporary, low-wage jobs without benefits and
a chance for individual mobility.[13] Most of them are in the low-skill
building or service sectors, and when hard times hit the general economy,
people generally stop spending on goods and services that they believe to
be marginal in maintaining their lifestyles. Thus fewer goods and services
are consumed, particularly those produced and provided by people
employed in these sectors. This leads to a reduction in work hours, wages,
and disposable income for the working poor. Therefore, even the poor
are affected by the general economy and have less to spend on goods and
services, a trend that often negatively affects the hair shops.

During such hard times, residents of the five neighborhoods extended
the period of time between haircuts, and if the recession lasted a while
the barber or beautician was forced to raise prices. This resulted in continued socialization in the hair shop but fewer purchases of haircuts. The
impact on hair salons tended to be greater than on barbershops because
women's styles were more complex. In addition, women had their
friends cut and style their hair at home more often than men did, placing a great deal of stress on the salons' business. Although in the short
run this had little social impact on the institution, people gradually
became more self-conscious about postponing their haircuts and spent
less time at the hair shops, weakening them as functional institutions in
the neighborhood.

Rent increases and disasters also had an impact on hair shops in fragmented neighborhoods. When rent increased, the barber or beautician had little choice but to pass on the expense to the customer by increasing prices. As people purchased fewer haircuts, hair shops faced increasing financial difficulty and were often forced to take radical steps such as expanding services to both men and women to increase clientele. However, while unisex hair shops could generally increase their clientele and stay in business, the changes in their internal dynamics had social repercussions for the neighborhood. Men and women in unisex shops were not able to talk about gender-specific topics or frequent the shops for entertainment. As a result, the unisex shops became economic enterprises rather than neighborhood institutions.

Fires caused changes in the hair shops of fragmented as well as contested neighborhoods, but with some subtle differences in their impact. In fragmented as in contested neighborhoods, clients of a shop closed down by a fire were forced to patronize other establishments, but they had different effects on the social order of the shops to which they migrated. The Aguila Barbershop of L.A.'s El Rey neighborhood is a case in point. The building's faulty wiring went unnoticed for some time because it was between the walls, but eventually smoke appeared and the fire department was called. The firemen got there quickly and put the fire out in little more than an hour, but the fire greatly damaged the inside of the shop, forcing it to close indefinitely for repairs and forcing customers to find another establishment.

The shop's internal social divisions had been formed around two groups: immigrants from Mexico and first-, second-, and third-generation Mexican Americans. Immigrants who frequented the barbershop, like most (not all) immigrants in the neighborhood, held a security-maximizing value orientation, while many second- and later-generation Mexican American patrons operated under the excitement-maximizing value orientation. Because of the fire, the two groups, which had established a coexisting relationship in the barbershop, had to find another establishment where they could not only get a haircut but interact comfortably.

A small contingent of Mexican nationals began to frequent La Palma Barbershop, which had been patronized by a small group of immigrants for six or seven years. Although integrating themselves into the social structure of the barbershop took time, they managed it. The majority of immigrants, however, decided to patronize a newly opened unisex shop in the neighborhood, since it was easier for them to patronize an establishment that only provided haircuts than to become integrated into a place with an existing social structure. Although they did not receive the social benefits of an institutional neighborhood barbershop, such as a friendly and entertaining environment, information about the neighborhood, or leads on job opportunities, they felt they could get some of these benefits from other neighborhood institutions, and they preferred this alternative to the awkwardness of integrating into a new institutional environment.

The Mexican Americans were divided as to where they would transfer their patronage. Some chose Pepe's Barbershop, while others went to La Palma. This decision was based on where their closest friends were going and the proximity of the barbershop to their homes. As in the case of the nationals, their total integration into the status hierarchy of the two barbershops took time, but it did occur while the Aguila was being rebuilt.

Overall, the fire broke up the social hierarchy of the Aguila Barbershop and changed the internal structure of the other two barbershops. During the transition, tensions were heightened between individuals and between the two groups because the status hierarchy in Pepe's and La Palma had to be reorganized and the status of some clients lowered. For example, when people whose status had been high at Aguila's came into a new barbershop, their presence challenged the existing status hierarchy. Sometimes new patrons had to take a secondary role to one of the regulars of the barbershop, while at other times they were raised above a regular. If the individuals competing over status came from different groups (Mexican American and Mexican national), a competition between the two groups resulted, creating a less harmonious environment and compromising institutional effectiveness.

The change also affected the roles of entertaining and socialization. Since the regulars and new patrons did not know each other in this environment, neither felt comfortable initiating these roles. Mexicans, for example, whose honor culture sought to avoid insults in order to reduce violence, were cautious in the presence of newcomers, changing the barbershop's entire internal dynamic. In these situations behavioral changes caused establishments to operate less like neighborhood institutions and more like economic enterprises.

Internal Change Agents

In fragmented neighborhoods, internal dynamics were based on the social division between those operating under the two value orientations. Thus any changes affecting how these two groups interacted in one of the neighborhood's institutions affected the other institutions in the neighborhood as well. Changes with the most impact were associated with the barber or beautician.

Changes in the role of the barber or beautician as caretaker affected people's interactions. He or she made sure that everyone in the shop recognized individual patrons' status in the social hierarchy and took pride in the respect that patrons received from others in the shop. This regulation gave the barber or beautician reciprocal respect and power from patrons to maintain this arrangement. If an individual's identity, status, or place in the hierarchy was challenged, the barber or beautician had the institutional authority to recall where everyone fit. Thus the death or retirement of a barber or beautician created a major personal and institutional void.

Barber and beautician caretakers clarified intent, mediating conflict and confusion by restating the rules and supporting a patron's status, so their absence caused uncertainty in social relations. People no longer knew how others would interpret and react to their verbal or bodily communicative behavior—whether they would take offense and react aggressively or whether, as in the past, they would be amused and engage in mutually respectful bantering. This uncertainty made everyone reserved and self conscious, so that the shop became the antithesis of a vital and functional institution.[14]

The absence of a caretaker to negotiate the differences between the two value-oriented groups allowed one group to dominate social relations and encouraged the exit of the minority group, so that eventually the establishment became a place for just one group. Although this situation might appear to reduce competition and potential conflict between the two value-oriented groups, it destroyed integration of the various socioeconomic groups, a defining property of institutions in fragmented neighborhoods. The change intensified group separation, generating more conflict like that found in contested neighborhoods. This occurred at La Palma Barbershop in L.A.'s El Rey neighborhood, owned by Enrique for twenty years. La Palma was a neighborhood institution, and Enrique had been an astute caretaker, but when he developed cancer his family was forced to sell the business to a barber from another part of town. The new barber did not understand La Palma's institutional character or assume the caretaker role. A few weeks after he bought the shop, some young men, many of whom belonged to the local gang and operated under an excitement-maximizing orientation, began to patronize the La Palma. In the past, Enrique had made it known that only gang members whose parents already patronized La Palma would be welcomed. However, since the new owner was unaware of this, he viewed the influx of these new patrons as an economic gain. The new development immediately changed the internal interactions in the barbershop. Individuals with a security-maximizing orientation were now the minority, and those who had been on the top of the status hierarchy were now challenged by the excitement-maximizing majority. This challenge was not directed at any particular individual but was the result of a natural desire to elevate people who thought and behaved alike. With the new majority, much of the conversation in the barbershop focused on parties, sex, schemes and scams to make money, and the entertainment value of violence. At first, this was simply an annoyance to the security-maximizing regulars, but as many of them were demoted in the hierarchy they grew resentful and left La Palma for Pepe's and the Aguila Barbershop.[15] This created antagonism and the development of two clearly defined social cliques that had little interaction in La Palma, and the tensions carried over to other institutions like the local bar and the local Catholic church. The exit of the security-maximizing patrons marked La Palma's decline both economically and institutionally. Ultimately business became so bad that the new owner converted the barbershop to a unisex shop, finalizing the change of La Palma from a neighborhood institution to an economic enterprise.

PRESERVATION AGENTS

As in all other cases of neighborhood institutions, dynamics of preservation operate to resist change agents' intrusion, whether in fragmented or contested neighborhoods. The primary preservation agents in the hair shops were the patrons and the caretaker.

Preservation Dynamics in Contested Neighborhoods

Within contested neighborhoods, patrons and barbers or beauticians did five things to resist the challenges to their institutional operations. First, the barber or beautician asserted his or her commitment to the shop's traditional ethnic group by making it clear to members of the other group that the establishment was for one group only. Since a characteristic of contested neighborhoods was ethnic tension, members of each group attempted to minimize interaction with each other, and the barber or beautician had to resist entry by members of the new group to keep the shop from being threatened as an institution that served the prior group. The comments of Hank, the barber of Harper's Barbershop in L.A.'s Richardson neighborhood, typify this response. When two Mexicans came to the barbershop for haircuts, tension among the African Americans in the barbershop rose. Hank asked the Mexican men how they were, and after they said they were fine, he said:

> I only cut black hair 'cause that is all I know how to cut. You know, this barbershop is for blacks, Mexicans have their own barbershop four streets over. I don't get many Mexicans in here because the groups don't get along very much and I don't want to have any trouble in here. If something happens, I can't stop it very well, and the police take way too long to get here. So let others know they got to go to their barbershop 'cause I can't stop anything and I don't want to have trouble in my shop.[16]

A second tactic was for the patrons to assume an intimidating role by maintaining a strong presence in the establishment during most of the day. Often the barber or beautician alerted patrons when members of contesting ethnic groups were around the shop. In most cases, the patrons congregated around the door to send a message that only those they wanted in the barbershop were welcome and that if other ethnic groups tried to come in they risked being thrown out. Patrons also maintained a strong presence by locking up parking: the regulars would drive their automobiles up in front of the hair shop and take all the parking, or would double-park while they got out and talked moving their cars only for a person of their ethnic group. This frustrated and infuriated the contending group, but it underscored the existing group's resolution to keep its institution as an outpost in alien territory, while strengthening their solidarity to remain competitive in the neighborhood.

If all members of the group moved to other parts of the neighborhood or to another neighborhood, the barber or beautician had to rent a place in a part of the neighborhood where the group remained dominant if the shop was to avoid going out of business. Jasmine, the beautician and owner of the Jewel Beauty Salon of the Bronx's Elmway neighborhood, adopted this tactic. The shop had been operating in a predominantly African American part of the neighborhood, but when Puerto Ricans and Dominicans began moving there, tensions grew to a point where two Latina women were viciously attacked and robbed within a two-week period. When the women identified their assailants as young African American men, many Latinos publicly decried the attacks and threatened to use force on anyone who looked suspicious. The African Americans took the comments as an insult to the injury of having to share "their neighborhood" with groups they thought of as foreign, inferior, and illegitimately in the country. Tensions between the groups rose even further, erupting into three physical altercations in the subway station and video store. So when two Puerto Rican women who did not have African features came into the Jewel Beauty Salon to get their hair done, there was a great deal of tension.[17] When the first woman came into the shop, two African American women getting their hair done aggressively asked the woman why she could not go to "her own salon." The woman was taken aback and said, "Because this is closer." Jasmine was caught in a situation that she handled by serving the woman without being at all friendly, a tactic she also used with the second Puerto Rican woman. A week later, however, a Puerto Rican woman who looked very African came to the hair salon and was not recognized by Jasmine or the other women as Puerto Rican. Just as she got up to get her hair washed, three other Puerto Rican women came in and spoke to the first woman in Spanish, indicating to everyone in the salon that all four women were Puerto Rican. This event seemed to signal that the hair salon would no longer be exclusively African American. Three weeks later, Jasmine noticed that a number of her African American clientele were beginning to frequent another salon that remained exclusively African American. She understood that although her business would continue, the salon would no longer be a neighborhood institution for African American residents. Two months later she rented space in a section of the neighborhood that remained African American. While informing her loyal African American clients of the new location, she said nothing to the Puerto Ricans and Dominicans who patronized her hair salon. A week later she placed in the window of her old shop a sign saying that the shop was officially closed but not giving any information about her new location.

Jasmine moved to her new location and began her business, retaining most of her old African American clientele and attracting some new ones. She had developed a preservation strategy and executed it flawlessly, reestablishing the institutional aspect of the business. The Jewel Beauty Salon was again an African American establishment and an important institution in this contested neighborhood.

Barbers and beauticians faced with challenges to their institution's internal social order sometimes had recourse to the tactic of recruiting patrons to restore the shop's internal order by spreading gossip and rumors. This was clever because it tapped into the fuel that ran the internal engine of the institution—a person's character and reputation. However, it had to be delicately managed because it had the potential to explode in such a way as to destroy the very institutional structure it was trying to preserve.

A typical instance of the use of this tactic occurred in Castro's Barbershop in L.A.'s Richardson neighborhood. One day, in the middle of a dominos game and gossip about women, Humberto casually remarked that he had seen Diego the other night with a girl named Carla who looked like an African American and that, although he was not sure, they seemed to be on a date. His comment caught the attention of all the men in the shop, who asked, "Could this be true?" indicating their amazement that any Mexican they knew would date an African American. After the men had questioned Humberto, their fascination with the possibility that one of their friends was dating a person of a taboo group switched to various modes of disapproval. To the Mexicans, the African Americans had discriminated against them when they moved into the neighborhood and tried to physically intimidate them. Therefore, the Mexicans saw the African Americans as a hostile group and any sexual involvement with them as inappropriate. The comments of Raúl, a nineteen-year-old security guard, were typical of the comments that day:

> Chingao [fuck]! What is he doing, man? He shouldn't be fucking with those women. He can't find any *mujeres* [women, but he means Mexican women] to go out with? The *mayates* [literally, "bugs," but used pejoratively in reference to African Americans] jump us at school and on the street and take our money and he's going out with one of them? That's fucked up, man![18]

While many people in the barbershop agreed with Raúl, others did not want him to talk about one of their friends, believing it dishonored Diego, something that they would not allow. A very heated argument began about a week later that caused a lot of tension, but the barber was able to maintain control through diplomacy. He said that he did not approve of Diego's action, but he reminded everyone that no one knew whether the rumor was true. It was clear from ensuing discussions that the social order (not social control) within the shop was in danger of being significantly altered. Diego and his friends no longer held their status positions, and a variety of others on both sides of the debate no longer held their positions. If there was confusion as to where people fit in the order, there was no order, and that spelled difficulty for the institution and relations in the neighborhood. Tito, the barber, immediately recognized the significance of the situation and worried that it would spiral out of control to a point where the barbershop could no longer serve as an important meeting place for the Mexicans of the neighborhood.

Acting as caretaker, he began his efforts toward social preservation by soliciting patrons from both sides of the debate to make sure that it remained a debate and nothing more. He talked to various people, including Diego, about the debate over whether it was right to go out with an African American girl. On the basis of these conversations, he tried to determine how much of the objection was attributable to the competition between Mexicans and African Americans and how much was related to group identity and solidarity, but he found that it was impossible to separate the two issues because they were intertwined. Consequently he decided to handle the situation by discouraging Humberto from pursuing the topic. He called Diego and persuaded him to go along with a counter-rumor Tito would start that he was just having fun and that his relationship with Carla was just a friendship. Diego agreed in part because the rumor about him and Carla was causing difficulties in his budding relationship with Rosa, who was offended that he was dating other women while telling her that he wanted to see her exclusively. Since he wanted to go out with Rosa, he decided that it was best to stop confronting Humberto and Raúl about his personal freedom and honor and made it known that the rumor was untrue. His friends told him that this was best for everyone because it allowed them all to maintain honor without having to physically defend it.

Tito, the barber, managed the entire affair by spreading the counter-rumor as he saw fit to the men who had been upset by the original rumor. He knew that his assertion that Diego and Carla were just friends would be taken as more accurate than anyone else's statements on the subject, since everyone believed that he was in the best position to know the truth. In addition, by telling individuals separately and avoiding any mention of the incident in a group situation, he allowed everyone to maintain a sense of honor and escape any potentially escalating confrontations. Thus Tito's efforts prevented internal conflict that would have changed the shop's internal social order.

A final tactic used to preserve the internal social order of the institution was the manipulation of symbols to maintain identity and create solidarity: the barber or beautician developed new styles associated with the shop's traditional ethnic group, providing a resource for group identity. This occurred at Castro's Barbershop, where the barbers were Mexican American. Lupe, the second barber, thought he needed to take action to maintain his shop as a place for the use and socialization of

Mexican youth of the neighborhood. This was becoming more difficult, since many of the youth identified with the African American youth. He and the auxiliary barber, Rogelio, asked some of the youth for their input in developing new styles. Since no one seemed to agree on any one style, twenty-two-year-old Rogelio adapted his hair to a look he had seen in a recent samurai movie. Many of the youth liked it because it styled long hair in a unique way. So they followed Rogelio in having their hair shaved to the top of their heads and the remaining hair cut to a moderate length. The youth were attracted to this style because it capitalized on the fact that the texture of their hair was different than that of African Americans, and they used it to establish an identity that was both avant-garde and distinctive. This not only established a unique identity for the youth but strengthened group solidarity and the barbershop as an institution. In addition, it maintained the competitive dynamic of the contested neighborhood.[19]

Preservation Dynamics in Fragmented Neighborhoods

Besides the structural functions that shaped the everyday social order of institutional hair shops, four tactics contributed to the preservation of these establishments in fragmented neighborhoods. As mentioned earlier, it was sometimes extremely difficult to pay a shop's monthly bills, so the barber or beautician's first strategy was to take actions to ensure that the establishment remained in business. Price increases were the first consideration, implemented with great care at a level that all patrons could afford so they could continue their established patterns of service without alteration. When price increases were necessary, they were occasionally advertised as temporary, as was the case when prices increased at La Playa Barbershop. Daniel, the barber, made a concerted effort to tell all his loyal patrons that increases would be temporary until the shop acquired more patrons. In addition, he informed his customers that he had to raise prices to pay off a loan for the purchase of new sterilizing equipment required by the county health department. As soon as the debt was repaid, he told them, he would lower the prices. Like other barbers and beauticians who found themselves in such situations and implemented necessary price increases, Daniel did indeed reduce his prices once his loan was repaid. Although he was not able to bring them back to their original level because of an increase in rent, he did reduce them to eleven dollars. This indicated to the patrons that he was simply taking care of the establishment so that it could remain viable for their use.

As Carlos, a forty-two-year-old patron, told Pablo, a thirty-seven-year-old patron, "You know that Daniel is special, he only will raise prices when he has to, and he only does it to keep this place going for us. . . . That's why everybody would do anything for him."[20]

At other times, however, changes caused such financial difficulty for the barber or beautician that simply raising prices would not solve the problem, and other strategies had to be used if the shop was to remain in business. The strategy most often used if the owner was younger than fifty and easily able to find a day job was to open the shop in the evening. Although this situation was not optimal, it offered the possibility of saving the shop as an institution, although not to the level at which it had functioned previously. An example of this strategy involved Pepe's Barbershop.

Pepe's, in the El Rey neighborhood of Los Angeles, was owned by David, a thirty-nine-year-old Mexican American. The majority of his clients were second- and third-generation Mexican Americans, and David himself was second generation. After graduating from high school and attending barber school, he worked for two other barbershops before opening Pepe's, which he named after a cousin killed in an automobile accident. After two years of business, a small recession occurred, causing job cutbacks or losses for many residents of the neighborhood. Many men who normally had their hair cut every three weeks lengthened the interval to six or eight weeks. David noticed that some of the men appeared to be getting their hair cut in between visits to the shop and speculated that their wives were cutting it for them. This overall reduction in business made it difficult for David to pay his own bills, so he raised his prices, but this did not solve his business's problems. He contemplated closing his business but instead found a day job in the office of a trucking company and opened his barbershop from 5:30 p.m. to 9:00 p.m. Tuesday through Friday and 8:00 a.m. to 6:00 p.m. on Saturdays. This continued for ten months until his business improved to a level where he could return to barbering full time. This strategy was suggested to David by another barber who had done the same thing, and it allowed David, like the other barber, to keep his business. To highlight the effectiveness of this strategy, during the ten months that the barbershop was open only from 5:30 p.m. to 9:00 p.m., Pepe's remained a hub of social activity.

Another preservation strategy was the barber or beautician's maintenance of the social equilibrium that had developed in the shop. Nothing could be more challenging to an establishment's institutional character than a change in the internal social status hierarchy. Equally challenging was the barber or beautician's delicate role of maintaining or reinstating the established social relations once they had been altered by a change agent. Both fragmented and contested neighborhoods were characterized by a relatively stable balance between the excitement-maximizing and security-maximizing value orientations that, although never exactly fifty-fifty, prevented either orientation from dominating the entire population. In fragmented neighborhoods, the most pressing priority for the barber or beautician was to maintain this balance among patrons. Therefore, the first action he or she took was to organize patrons to resist changes that could potentially alter it. If it had already been altered, regulars were solicited to reestablish the preexisting social order.

In the former situation, the barber or beautician made sure that all patrons felt that the hair shop remained "their" place. When external economic shifts created economic difficulties for the business and some new initiative had to be adopted, he or she was careful to avoid altering the internal equilibrium by chasing away patrons who subscribed to one value orientation or the other. Thus, if a price increase was necessary, it was set at a level that all patrons could afford so that no one had to limit the number of haircuts obtained each month. This allowed the barber or beautician to keep the existing mix of patrons from the two value orientations and to avoid any suggestion of favoring one group over another. Such a suggestion would have the same destructive impact on the internal order as changes in the social equilibrium because the barber or beautician's authority as caretaker would be compromised. The comments of Jordan, the beautician at the African Sun Salon in the Bronx's Monument neighborhood, are representative:

> I just have to raise my prices to pay my increasing expenses, but I don't really want to. I just don't know how much I need to go up, but whatever it is, I gots ladies who feel they need to save all the time [security maximizing] and so I can't raise it so that they have to wait longer to get their hair done; and then I gots other ladies that when they gots money they don't care how much the price is [excitement maximizing]. But them ladies is more spotty about when they'll get their hair done. So really I got to get a price everybody is okay with. If I don't, people will complain, boy, will they complain, and there'll be bad feelings in the shop, and folks won't like to come and socialize and stuff.[21]

When a change agent had disrupted the internal social order, the caretaker took steps to restore it. This occurred at the Town Barbershop in the Bronx's Monument neighborhood, which was experiencing economically hard times because considerable gang violence on the shop's street was changing who came into the shop and how often, causing a breakdown in normal social relations and order. Once the violence sub-sided and things calmed down, Evan, the caretaker/owner, had to reor-ganize the patrons into a hierarchy that would reconstruct the internal social order. He began by dividing them into regular and occasional patrons. He then persuaded the regulars to assume various functional roles such as "neighborhood information source," "referee" of games played in the shop, "jokester" to keep everyone entertained, and "bouncer" for physical disputes. He accomplished this by suggesting a role to an individual and praising his talent in that area, simply appoint-ing a task to someone, or asking a patron to do him a favor by taking on a specific role, like bouncer, when that was necessary. He did not need to intervene in the formation of the remaining status hierarchy because it was completed through the normal interactions within the shop. As a result of Evan's efforts, the social order was reconstituted within three weeks and the Town Barbershop was once again a smooth-running neighborhood institution.

Sometimes the caretaker had to integrate both new immigrants and migrants into the social hierarchy of their shop. This was not an easy task because many "old-timers" were antagonistic toward the new-comers of the neighborhood and treated them like social pariahs. The barbers and beauticians understood that since pressure on new residents was unlikely to make them leave the neighborhood they needed the new-comers as loyal clients if their businesses were to remain economically strong. Thus one of the strategies that barbers and beauticians used was finding interesting or unique qualities for all the new residents who came to the shop and giving them a social identity through nicknames to help legitimize their presence to the incumbent residents. Integration into the institution and neighborhood took time because new residents had to find a place in the status hierarchies of the various institutions, but obtaining an identity in the hair shop began the process.[22]

Barbers and beauticians also needed to keep economic competitors from changing the social order of their establishment. The most formi-dable adversaries were corporate chains because these were designed to attract both male and female customers with generally lower prices than any local shop could offer. Their competition put stress on barbers and beauticians both as business people, because of loss to the business, and as institutional caretakers, because of disruption in the social order when people went to the chain shops for haircuts and spent less time at the neighborhood hair shop. To counteract this problem, barbers and beauticians organized some regulars to maintain the operation of all functional activities and to highlight that a core group remained regulars. This maintained a portion of the business, participation in the institution's social activities, and the stability of the internal social order. In doing so, it socially benefited the neighborhood because men and women could go to the shop to seek emotional support from the trials and tribulations of life, avoid social isolation, receive entertainment, and obtain information.[23]

Corporate hair shops also affected the local hair shops by forcing some of them to become unisex establishments. As previously mentioned, this change not only altered the gender composition in the shop but changed the establishment from a neighborhood institution to an economic enterprise. Therefore, neighborhood preservationists aggressively attempted to thwart this development by encouraging patrons to remain loyal to the shop. Their arguments had almost nothing to do with supporting a neighborhood business; instead, they focused on loyalty to the owner of the business who had been their friend and on the benefits the shop provided in comparison to corporate and unisex shops. Loyalty to these traditions proved an effective resource when it was invoked.

In sum, the preservation dynamics in hair shops can be best understood as part of these institutions' immune system. They were very effective in protecting most institutions. Thus the closing of a hair shop that had been a neighborhood institution was a sign that the shop's immune system was in a weakened state, or simply overwhelmed.

SOME CLOSING REMARKS

Researchers have often treated the barbershop and hair salon as establishments that contribute to the economic infrastructure of urban neighborhoods. In their analysis, the barbershop and salon are important for providing residents with convenient services that make their lives easier. They also keep some of the residents' money in the neighborhood, allowing for a more vibrant community. Thus changes in the number of businesses like the barbershop and hair salon are taken to indicate economic decline and a more stressful existence for the residents of the neighborhood. However, this approach is too one-dimensional because hair shops are more than economic establishments: they can be social institutions in poor neighborhoods. Therefore, the loss of a barbershop or hair salon that is an institution in the neighborhood is less important to residents for what it offers the neighborhood's economy than for what it contributes to the social order of everyday life.

This chapter has identified how these neighborhood institutions are vulnerable to change. Large changes can threaten the economic existence of the hair shop or its status as a neighborhood institution and the concomitant functions it serves. Significant changes in neighborhood institutions shift some of the hair shop's responsibilities to other neighborhood institutions, thereby causing small but important internal changes in the social interactions of each. Changes that transform a neighborhood institution into an economic enterprise damage the neighborhood's social structure, thereby diminishing residents' quality of life. People lose a place in which to relax, receive emotional comfort and entertainment, socialize and avoid isolation, and obtain functional information. Thus the existence of a profit-making economic enterprise in a poor neighborhood is not an indicator of neighborhood improvement, and the number of neighborhood businesses in itself says nothing about residents' quality of life.[24] Far more important is these businesses' institutional content.

How barbershops and salons change has been a focus of this chapter, but another objective has been to provide an understanding of the social forces that resist change. A major argument of this book is that social forces in poor neighborhoods are engaged in maintaining the status quo. This does not mean that a poor neighborhood's residents want to keep it poor. Nearly all residents of poor neighborhoods would like to have more money, but they do not want to change the social structure that they have created. Their effort to maintain the neighborhood is an attempt to keep the social structure and the system of social relations that have been established. All the communities in this study were engaged in this effort, and all, to varying degrees, were successful. The dynamics of preservation were strong and formidable opponents to agents of change. Efforts to maintain the social structure strengthened people's commitment to the cultural norms and behaviors of their neighborhood.

In the broader context, when change agents were successful in incapacitating an institution, other neighborhood institutions adjusted to take on the social functions that the incapacitated one had provided. If these situations lasted for a long time, social interactions within the neighborhood were altered. However, the institutional crisis was most often short-lived, producing only a temporary change within the other institutions until the affected hair shop reorganized itself or a new one assumed its responsibilities. Three local institutions that often assumed some of the social responsibilities of the hair shop were the gang, the mom-and-pop store, and the tavern.[25]

CHAPTER 8

The Gang's All Here

Fathering a Bastard Institution

Truth never comes into the world but like a bastard, to the
ignominy of him that brought her birth.

John Milton, *The Doctrine of Discipline and Divorce*
(1643)

A prominent public image of poor neighborhoods in the United States
is that they are infested with gangs, so much so that the two seem to naturally go together. TV and movies have been instrumental in establishing this image.[1] However, among gang experts, there is some debate over
the relationship between gangs and poor neighborhoods.

Some researchers view gangs as predators of the residents of their
communities, a malignant artifact of poverty, and symptomatic of the
neighborhood's social disorganization and decline.[2] Others find that,
rather than being a menace, gangs assume various roles within their
neighborhoods, many of which are positive.[3] A primary reason for this
divergence has to do with the various researchers' foci. Criminologists,
who view gangs primarily as a menace to neighborhoods, generally use
large data sets to explain crime and violence in poor neighborhoods.[4]
Sociologists and anthropologists who use direct observational data to
analyze the social dynamics of poor communities have more often found
that gangs contribute to their neighborhoods both negatively and positively.[5] This chapter evaluates both the depictions of gangs and how and
under what conditions gangs become functional institutions within the
social structures of poor neighborhoods.

THE SOCIAL BASIS OF GANGS

Researchers and the general public usually address the phenomenon of
gangs when something is seriously amiss in the neighborhood, since

gangs have been identified as one of the most important contributors to social problems. Generally, most research on gangs is directed toward antisocial activities.[6] Researchers intent on explaining crime in poor neighborhoods find it difficult to understand gangs in any other way than their contribution to the total number of criminal activities taking place there. This has kept them from seeing gang activities that contribute to neighborhood cohesiveness.[7] Yet it is precisely the functional aspects of the gang's everyday activities that provide the basis for their existence in poor neighborhoods.[8] The exact nature of their functionality varies depending on whether the neighborhood is contested or fragmented.

One of the primary functions of gangs is the socialization of young men and women to the norms and worldviews of the adults living in their neighborhoods. In fragmented neighborhoods, gangs teach youth about the intraneighborhood division between excitement-maximizing and security-maximizing value orientations, starting with individual association with a particular peer group.[9] Adolescence is a time for much experimentation, resulting in unpredictable behavior.[10] One might guess that young people whose parents operate under an excitement-maximizing value orientation would be more likely to join a gang than those whose parents hold a security-maximizing value orientation. However, during this crucial time of development many youth are much more influenced by their peers than their parents. Therefore, nearly as many kids brought up in an environment of maximizing security join gangs as those brought up in an environment of maximizing excitement. Further, most youth, rather than viewing gangs as dangerous, view them as a means to maximize their security, since the gang can protect them and their families from local predators, as well as provide them with resources to secure money.[11]

The comments of Tobias, a fifteen-year-old Mexican American resident of L.A.'s El Rey neighborhood, are representative of youth in fragmented neighborhoods who decide to join a gang. Tobias was brought up by his father, a short-order cook, and his mother, a housewife, both of whom operated under a security-maximizing value orientation.

> No, I don't think we should think that way [be worried about going to prison as a result of gang activity]. If we do things the right way, we're going to make some big money. All of us would be definitely hurting if we hadn't jumped in [joined the gang]. Now we don't have to worry if we got enough money to do what we want to because the money we make [in the gang] is there for us.[12]

The comments of T. C., a sixteen-year-old African American living in the Monument neighborhood in the Bronx (at the time another fragmented neighborhood), are also representative. T. C. had been brought up by a father who worked part time as a janitor and a mother who was a housewife, and his parents, like Tobias's parents, both had a security-maximizing orientation:

> Yeah, my sister got attacked by some nigger druggie wanting her money last night. He smacked her pretty good and took her jewelry and thirty something dollars. That shit happened to me a couple of times, but it ain't fucking going to happen anymore to either me or my family, 'cause I hooked up with the Toppers [the local gang], and everybody knows that if you fuck with me you got to fuck with them. And that means you going to get jumped by lots of motherfuckers [guys in his gang].[13]

In such fragmented neighborhoods, physical confrontation and threats between the various segments are rare, and most attacks come from elements outside the neighborhood. Thus the neighborhood gang can offer some protection from these threats.[14]

The decision to join a gang in contested neighborhoods is related to social conflict between local ethnic groups. The comments of Eduardo, a fourteen-year-old Mexican American resident of L.A.'s Richardson neighborhood who lived with his mother, are representative. Both he and his mother had a security-maximizing orientation:[15]

> Ah, come on, it's not that I want to bang [gang fight]. I don't even fight that good, it's just . . . it's just that I don't want to get jumped going home all the time from these fucking *majates* [literally, "bugs," but derogatory in reference to African Americans]. . . . [One girl responds that his fear of attack doesn't mean he has to join a gang.] Easy for you to say, but I get shaken down every day on the way home, and if I ain't got anything they really let me have it. . . . No, I joined Fulton [the Chicano gang] so I could get to go home, or anywhere else, without trouble, that's all.[16]

Jamaal was a sixteen-year-old African American resident of the Bronx's Monument neighborhood after it had become a contested neighborhood. His parents worked part time in lower-level service jobs and held a strong security-maximizing value orientation.

> You should see all the stuff that we [the gang] get involved in. It sure is much more than we was doing a year ago. . . . Yeah, we're getting big-time now. Fuck, that's why I joined last year, I could tell there was goin' to be some good money available sometime down the road, and it's about to happen. But if we don't guard against those fucking spaghetti heads [Italians] or P-Ricans [term for Puerto Ricans, pronounced "pee-ricans"] they'll take it all away from us. I hate those bitches [referring to his male competitors].[17]

Many individuals whose parents held an excitement-maximizing value orientation decided to join gangs for the increased excitement of the value orientation to which they were accustomed. Their attraction to gangs was based on more parties, the exhilaration of successfully confronting and defeating gangs of the rival ethnic group, and the accumulation of money to be used for fun and excitement.[18] The comments of Lucy, a seventeen-year-old member of the Ladies BV, the female auxiliary of the East Birdville gang of L.A.'s Richardson neighborhood, who lived with her excitement-maximizing parents, are representative of this attraction:

> We are kicking it all the time, man. . . . It's a rush most of the time with everything going on like it does. Ain't no time to get bored with us, and that's what's for me, you know? . . . This neighborhood would be real fucked up without us [the gang], you know? . . . Yeah, it be one big-time sleep around here, and I can tell you that would be just like it was when my father kept me under his total control. That just about finished me, but being in BV [Birdville gang] is a lot of fun and like freedom, you know? Plus, we can kick the fucking T-Street's [African American gang] ass when they try to harass us. You know what I mean?[19]

The above observations might seem to indicate that youth's decision to join gangs in these poor neighborhoods would be based on their own rational choices, absent any cultural influence. However, while many of those who join gangs did use a rational calculus, it was not devoid of cultural influences.[20] Rather, their decision to join gangs was based on both individual rationales and the cultural values and norms of the neighborhood.[21] Therefore, despite the dangers of gang life, the fact that significant numbers of people in one's neighborhood and family belong to a gang can make the decision to join seem the best option for remaining part of the neighborhood.[22]

Gang researchers often view culture and neighborhood as different, with the neighborhood as the result of structure, and culture as the product of social interaction. With regard to neighborhood, they separate what they understand as its elements and attempt to measure the impact of each element on certain socioeconomic outcomes.[23] This approach is problematic not only because it separates the specific elements of a neighborhood but because it usually finds that only some of them have an influence and then refers to this finding as a "neighborhood impact." However, a "neighborhood impact" occurs when all elements of structure and culture in the neighborhood work together to psychologically affect an individual or group. Thus the combined neighborhood factors create and recreate local conditions that allow gang involvement to be a legitimate option to remedy circumstantial problems. A shared worldview springs from the structural conditions present in the neighborhood and the strategies used to navigate them, and the culture associated with this worldview teaches normatively appropriate thought and action for both general and specific situations. Culture in this context sets the parameters in which most people, especially the young, make choices about appropriate and inappropriate behavior (in both normative and strategic terms) through the structural filter of the neighborhood's institutions.[24]

Often young people, especially young men, choose to join a gang because it is appropriate within the culture of poor neighborhoods, even though it is not appropriate in middle- and upper-class society.[25] Despite the prominence of the gang culture in poor neighborhoods, many alternatives existed that were often exercised.[26] Joining a gang was simply a legitimate option for residents of poor neighborhoods, just as joining the military is for young men and women within the broader American culture. The military is designed to protect the interests of the nation by training people to kill, either directly or indirectly, and socializing them to violence—means and aims that are both tolerated and rewarded by the broader American culture.[27] Thus joining the military is not seen as a deviant act because young people within the larger community are socialized to view it as appropriate despite the risk and danger it carries. In direct contrast to both gangs and the military, Quaker and Amish subcultures view any type of violence as inappropriate.[28] These examples highlight the power of cultures and subcultures to legitimize all types of thoughts and behavior, including those that involve violence. In sum, cultures and people's thoughts and behaviors are mutually reinforcing.[29]

In poor neighborhoods, the decision to join a gang is rational within the context of the choices that the structure and culture present. When a person joins a gang because "it's just what a person does," the decision is influenced solely by the local subculture. However, when one joins a gang for greater economic and social benefits, as is usually the case, the decision is based on an individual rationale within a particular subcultural framework. The comments of Rufus and Antonio are representative of these two influences. Rufus, a sixteen-year-old African American living in the Bronx's Monument neighborhood, said of his decision to join the Toppers gang:

> Yeah, I got jumped in two weeks ago [went through the gang's initiation ritual], and now I be just hangin', you know. I was thinkin' of doin' it for a while, my brothers and uncle had joined, so it's how it is here. Ain't no big deal, just be what you know.[30]

Antonio, a fifteen-year-old Mexican American living in L.A.'s El Rey neighborhood, said about joining the Zapata Park gang:

> When I decided to hook up with the Zapatas, I just saw they had a lot of parties and stuff, and they also made some good money too. Shit, that was a lot more than what I had, so it was good, real good for me.[31]

Gangs have been a constant presence in poor American neighborhoods for more than 150 years and have existed in the poor neighborhoods of the present study for as long as twenty-five years. Despite the high risks associated with gang involvement, it remained a "legitimate" option for the young men and women of these neighborhoods and was one of the major socialization agents of the neighborhood. Some researchers see the gang's socialization process as antisocial, arguing that attempts to render it obsolete depend on neutralizing its influence on young kids. These researchers view the gang as similar to a cult because it indoctrinates youth from poor neighborhoods with the belief that the gang is glamorous despite the reality that gang life is detrimental to the heath and well-being of its members.[32]

Such depictions of gangs and their members are faulty because they are inconsistent with historical evidence. If poor communities viewed the gang as detrimental, the overwhelming majority of residents would have vigorously resisted and eradicated it. Yet evidence including that from the present study indicates that generations of poor people have been actively involved in gangs and that the gang is one of the most stable features of poor neighborhoods rather than an obsolete phenomenon.[33] Thus it is relatively clear that the gang does not represent the menace identified by many researchers. Further, it is neither, as many researchers influenced by the Chicago School of Sociology have argued, an undermining agent of social organization in urban neighborhoods nor a consequence of an already disorganized community.[34]

Gangs in the past were social institutions in low-income neighborhoods, where residents found them functionally relevant, and many gangs still are today. More fundamentally, residents understand them not as antisocial subcultures but as collectives of local boys that affect the community both positively and negatively. In essence, they are seen as natural and functional elements of the community.[35]

Much debate exists over what constitutes an accurate, or at least a reasonable, definition of a gang. Many researchers define gangs as loose associations of individuals that engage primarily in criminal activity. Malcolm Klein states that gangs are "groups of young people who may range in age from 10 to 30 or occasionally older, whose cohesion is fostered in large part by their acceptance of or even commitment to delinquent or criminal involvement. . . . Street gangs are delinquent groups that have passed a 'tipping point' in their confrontational stance as a group. They have set themselves apart from their neighborhoods in their own perceptions, and many members of the local community have come to see them as a group apart. In other words, the street gang comes to see itself as such, and so does the community."[36] For Klein, the gang's "commitment to delinquent and criminal involvement" separates it from the community by its own and the community's desire: the gang is a criminal collective that does not see itself as part of the community and is not seen as such by the community.

Yet the gang is not merely an association of individuals who congregate to commit a crime and have no connection or commitment to their immediate community. Any gang may exist for a particular amount of time, but all gangs develop and maintain some level of organization that distinguishes them from other forms of collective behavior. The collective behavior of crowds, mobs, and bands differs from that of gangs because the actions of these groups are spontaneous and occasional with less organizational integrity in pursuing their goals.[37] Because of the sociological difference between gangs and the other forms of collective behavior mentioned above, I have defined a gang as

> an organized social system that is both quasi-private (not fully open to the public) and quasi-secretive (much of the information concerning its business remains confined within the group) and one whose size and goals have necessitated that social interaction be governed by a leadership structure that has defined roles; where the authority associated with these roles has been legitimized to the extent that social codes are operational to regulate the behavior of both the leadership and the rank and file; that plans and provides not only for the social and economic services of its members, but also for its own maintenance as an organization; that pursues such goals irrespective of whether the action is legal or not; and that lacks a bureaucracy (i.e., an administrative staff that is hierarchically organized and separate from leadership).[38]

This definition emphasizes that a gang is an organization rather than a loose association of people. While gangs vary in their type and degree of organization, this definition both distinguishes them from other forms of collective behavior and allows them to be understood as a collective form of behavior operating in opposition to the societal mainstream.[39] However, organized as they are to pursue economic and social advantages for themselves, they maintain identification with the people and interests in their communities, and this separates them from crews and syndicates, which are two other organized groupings in poor neighborhoods. A crew is a small group of three to five individuals who work together for the sole purpose of robbing people, and a syndicate is a formal organization designed to participate primarily in illegal economic activity for profit. Crews or syndicates reside in a particular neighborhood but do not consider themselves part *of* it. As such, their pursuits of their own interests are independent of those associated with the individuals living in the neighborhood, and they feel no obligation or desire to aid residents.

As was mentioned earlier, some research on the relationship of communities and gangs found gangs to be a menace to their communities, while other research found social integration between gangs and their communities.[40] Klein suggests that research findings on social integration between gangs and their communities are more ideologically than empirically based; but given that his assertion presents no evidence, and that observational data are so consistent in the other direction, the foundational basis of his contention is at best weak.[41] Long-term ethnographic studies using direct observations of behavior in poor neighborhoods and discussion with their residents have consistently found that gangs are an integral part of their communities.[42] However, how gangs become an integral part of the community is often more complicated than has been reported in this research. The remainder of this chapter specifies the functional activities through which gangs integrate themselves into their neighborhoods and mutually reinforce other neighborhood institutions.

THE GANG AS AN AGENT OF SOCIALIZATION

Like other organizations in society, gangs play an important role in socializing people in poor neighborhoods. Many researchers and community activists who have identified gangs as important socialization agents in these areas have also tried to warn of gangs' harmful influence on young people's attitudes and behavior.[43] Within this framework, gangs are seen partly as an organization that brainwashes young people to a life of antisocial behavior. While the gangs in this study did socialize many young people into illegal activities, they also socialized them into social roles within both the gang structure and the more general cultural norms of their poor communities. Additionally, the fact that gangs could have a significant influence on nongang youth from middle-class communities reinforced and validated a gang's position within its own neighborhood's social structure. Although residents were concerned about the possible death or incarceration of local youth, they knew that the gang was an enduring element of their community.

Gangs socialized young people in five areas of social norms: (1) the understanding of one's place in the larger society; (2) gender stratification; (3) ethnic stratification; (4) social stratification; and (5) violence, pain, and suffering. Each set of norms affected both gang members and nonmembers and proved essential to the neighborhood's existing social order.

One's Place in the Larger Society

As part of the neighborhood, the gang, like other elements of the community, both reflected and regenerated social norms governing everyday life. The gang offered to those associated with it a comparative understanding of the neighborhood's social standing within the broader society. Most gang members did not consider themselves marginalized, but they were aware that their community was at the bottom of the social status hierarchy.[44] They took pride in the fact that they lived in a ghetto or barrio, understood by them as a slum, and verbally stressed this to any young person who did not acknowledge the nature of the area as a slum. Their pride in coming from a slum was often influenced by their belief that it made them tougher than, and thus morally and physically superior to, more affluent social groups. This understanding provided the poor of these neighborhoods with a positive self-image rather than one of self-hate. A situation involving Bony (a.k.a. LeRoy), a fourteen-year-old African American from the Bronx's Elmway neighborhood who was in the process of joining the Jinx Inc. gang, reflects this socialization process. (For a list of gangs in this study as well as associated information, see tables 6 through 8.)

While Bony and six friends, all members of the Jinx Inc., had been in Manhattan, they had gone into an electronic store to look at cell phones. In the store, they had been watched closely by the store owner. This bothered Bony, who felt that he was constantly under surveillance. When he asked the owner a question he was given a very curt answer, which further annoyed him. However, when he mentioned this to his friend Horn, Horn just shrugged his shoulders and kept looking at the phones. Upon leaving, Bony complained again, saying, "Did you see that fucking Ahab [slang for Arab] look at us while we were in there?

TABLE 6. DEMOGRAPHIC CHARACTERISTICS OF LOS ANGELES NEIGHBORHOOD GANGS OVER TIME

	1991	1992	1993	1994	1995	1996	1997	1998	1999
Neighborhood type	C	C	F	F	F	F	F	F	F
					El Rey Neighborhood				
Zapata Park									
Ethnicity[a]	Mex-a	Mex-a	Mex-a	Mex-a	Mex-a	Mex-a	Mex-a	Mex-a	Mex-a
No. in gang[b]	39–43	42–45	35–45	27–35	33–36	31–35	29–33	32–34	31–34
No. of girls in auxiliary	8–10	7–9	5–8	7–9	9–11	6–10	8–12	7–8	8
Group age range	14–27	14–25	14–25	14–23	14–24	14–24	14–26	13–26	13–22
No. imprisoned[c]	7	1	10	2	2	4	4	2	5
No. injured	4	1	6	4	2	2	1	2	2
No. killed	0	1	0	2	1	1	0	0	0
Organization type[d]	H	V	V	V	V	V	V	V	V
Cactus Vatos									
Ethnicity[a]	Mex-n	Mex-n	Mex-n	Mex-n	Mex-n	Mex-n	Mex-n	Mex-n	Mex-n
No. in gang[b]	24–29	29–34	32–39	23–28	20–25	20–23	23–25	23–26	24–25
No. of girls in auxiliary	0	5–6	6–8	7–8	6–8	4	0	0	0
Group age range	14–26	14–25	15–24	14–25	14–26	14–26	15–26	16–27	17–28
No. imprisoned[c]	3	2	1	2	2	2	4	5	5
No. injured	2	4	5	2	2	1	6	2	3
No. killed	0	0	1	0	1	0	1	1	0
Organization type[d]	I	H	H	I	I	I	I	I	I

Richardson Neighborhood

Neighborhood type	C	C	C	C	C	C	C	C	C
Trail Street									
Ethnicity[a]	AA	AA	AA	AA	AA	AA	AA	AA	AA
No. in gang[b]	78–80	71–76	63–70	61–66	60–63	59–65	50–59	48–52	49–52
No. of girls in auxiliary	9–10	10	7–8	7–8	6–8	6–10	8–10	7–10	10–12
Group age range	15–30	14–28	15–29	15–30	14–30	15–27	16–28	16–30	15–31
No. imprisoned[c]	2	2	5	1	1	2	4	1	3
No. injured	3	2	3	3	2	4	1	3	5
No. killed	0	1	1	2	0	2	0	1	1
Organization type[d]	V	V	V	V	V	V	V	V	V
East Birdville									
Ethnicity[a]	Mex-a,n	Mex-a, n,CA	Mex-a, n,CA	Mex-a, n,CA	Mex-a, n,CA	Mex-a, n,CA	Mex-a, n,CA	Mex-a, n,CA	Mex-a, n,CA
No. in gang[b]	25–28	34–38	35–31	30–35	34–37	30–36	34–40	36–42	31–36
No. of girls in auxiliary	9	7–8	6–8	6	6–8	6–7	7–8	10–12	7–10
Group age range	14–27	14–28	13–29	14–27	15–26	14–27	15–30	15–31	13–28
No. imprisoned[c]	3	2	2	5	2	4	6	4	4
No. injured	0	8	5	4	2	2	1	4	1
No. killed	0	2	2	0	0	2	0	0	0
Organization type[d]	I	H	V	V	V	V	V	H	I

[a] AA = African American; Mex-n = Mexican national; Mex-a = Mexican American; CA = Central American (Nicaraguan and Salvadoran).
[b] This number includes the number of members in the gang who dropped out, were imprisoned, or were killed during that year.
[c] *Imprisoned* includes both those placed in a correctional facility and those jailed and awaiting trial with no bail posted or granted.
[d] I = influential model (one or a small number lead because they are considered charismatic by the rank and file); H = horizontal model (a commission of leaders represent and are elected by a clique of their immediate rank and file); V = vertical model (leadership has a corporate structure of authority, consisting of a president, vice president, secretary, treasurer, and defense minister, each with his own rank, powers, and specialty). For a full discussion of these organizational types, see Sánchez-Jankowski, *Islands in the Street*, 64–67.

TABLE 7. DEMOGRAPHIC CHARACTERISTICS OF NEIGHBORHOOD GANGS IN THE BRONX OVER TIME

	1991	1992	1993	1994	1995	1996	1997	1998	1999
Neighborhood type	C	C	C	C	C	C	F	F	F
				Elmway Neighborhood					
Spice Kings									
Ethnicity[a]	IT/PR	PR	PR	PR	PR	PR	PR	PR/Dom	PR/Dom
No. in gang[b]	20–22	19–22	21	20	20–23	23–25	25–30	43–57	43–51
No. of girls in auxiliary	0	0	0		6	7–9	6–10	9	5–8
Group age range	15–19	14–24	14–25	13–26	14–25	15–26	14–25	14–29	14–30
No. imprisoned[c]	1	1	1	0	2	0	2	1	1
No. injured	5	3	2	4	2	1	3	3	2
No. killed	0	1	1	0	1	0	1	1	0
Organization type[d]	I	I	I	I	I	I	I	V	V
Jinx Inc.									
Ethnicity[a]	AA	AA	AA	AA	AA	AA/PR	AA/PR	AA/PR	AA/PR
No. in gang[b]	27–31	28–35	28–30	28–33	24–30	22–26	37–38	29–32	28–30
No. of girls in auxiliary	0	0	4–6	5–7	6–7	4–7	4	0	0
Group age range	14–25	15–26	15–28	15–27	16–28	15–27	16–28	14–29	15–31
No. imprisoned[c]	2	1	1	2	5	3	1	3	2
No. injured	3	3	2	4	2	5	3	6	3
No. killed	0	2	0	1	0	1	0	2	1
Organization type[d]	V	V	V	V	V	V	V	V	V

Monument Neighborhood

Neighborhood type	F	F	F	F	F	F	C	C
Toppers								
Ethnicity[a]	AA/PR	AA/PR	AA/PR	AA/PR	AA/PR	AA/PR	AA	AA
No. in gang[b]	24–28	27–30	32–34	31–34	27–30	29–31	26–28	28–29
No. of girls in auxiliary	0	7–8	6–10	4–7	2–6	0	0	0
Group age range	15–22	17	15–24	14–25	15–26	14–25	14–27	15–28
No. imprisoned[c]	0	0	0	2	3	2	2	0
No. injured	4	1	3	3	4	3	2	3
No. killed	0	1	0	1	0	1	0	1
Organization type[d]	H	V	V	V	V	V	H	H

[a] AA = African American; It = Italian; PR = Puerto Rican; Dom = Dominican.

[b] This number includes the number of members in the gang who dropped out, were imprisoned, or were killed during that year.

[c] *Imprisoned* includes both those placed in a correctional facility and those jailed and awaiting trial with no bail posted or granted.

[d] I = influential model (one or a small number lead because they are considered charismatic by the rank and file); H = horizontal model (a commission of leaders represent and are elected by a clique of their immediate rank and file); V = vertical model (leadership has a corporate structure of authority, consisting of a president, vice president, secretary, treasurer, and defense minister, each with his own rank, powers, and specialty). For a full discussion of these organizational types, see Sánchez-Jankowski, *Islands in the Street*, 64–67.

TABLE 8. DEMOGRAPHIC CHARACTERISTICS OF NEIGHBORHOOD GANGS IN BROOKLYN OVER TIME

	1991	1992	1993	1994	1995	1996	1997	1998	1999
Neighborhood type	F	F	C	C	C	C	C	C	C
					Eagleton Neighborhood				
Falcons									
Ethnicity[a]	AA/PR	AA/PR	AA	AA	AA	AA	AA	AA	AA
No. in gang[b]	26–32	26–30	25–28	26	34–36	40–41	39	25–30	28–29
No. of girls in auxiliary	0	0	2–6	4–9	0	0	0	3–6	0
Group age range	16–25	14–26	15–27	14–28	15–29	16–28	16–29	17–31	15–30
No. imprisoned[c]	1	1	1	0	2	1	2	3	1
No. injured	2	2	4	2	5	4	4	6	4
No. killed	0	1	0	0	1	0	1	2	0
Organization type[d]	I	I	I	I	H	H	H	H	H
St. James Place									
Ethnicity[a]	Jam	Jam	Jam	Jam	Jam/WI	Jam/WI	Jam/WI	Jam/WI	Jam/WI
No. in gang[b]	37	46	39	36	40	39	37	39	39
No. of girls in auxiliary	6–11	7–12	6–10	4–10	5–8	4–10	4–9	6–11	6–9
Group age range	16–25	15–26	15–27	16–28	16–29	16–30	15–30	14–30	15–28
No. imprisoned[c]	0	1	4	2	1	2	1	2	1
No. injured	5	6	5	6	1	3	5	3	5
No. killed	1	1	0	1	0	1	1	0	1
Organization type[d]	V	V	V	V	V	V	V	V	V

[a] AA = African American; PR = Puerto Rican; Jam = Jamaican; WI = West Indian, including a potpourri of nationalities from all of the Caribbean and excluding Spanish-speaking Puerto Ricans, Dominicans, and Cubans.

[b] This number includes the number of members in the gang who dropped out, were imprisoned, or were killed during that year.

[c] Imprisoned includes both those placed in a correctional facility and those jailed and awaiting trial with no bail posted or granted.

[d] I = influential model (one or a small number lead because they are considered charismatic by the rank and file); H = horizontal model (a commission of leaders represent and are elected by a clique of their immediate rank and file); V = vertical model (leadership has a corporate structure of authority, consisting of a president, vice president, secretary, treasurer, and defense minister, each with his own rank, powers, and specialty). For a full discussion of these organization types, see Sánchez-Jankowski, *Islands in the Street*, 64–67.

He's such a fucking racist! I would like to fuck him up!" His friend J.C. interrupted with:

> You dumb fucking nigger, what would you do if you saw six niggers from a slum go into your store? You got to know where we come from and what we look like—we're niggers from a slum, got it? We live the shit that they couldn't even dream of, and we do it without being fucking hypocrites like all them rich assholes. We're tougher than them, we have more fun than them, and we fucking can outsmart them to get some of their money. [The others laugh.] Don't forget that shit or you going to get caught up with this trivial ass-shit all the time and fuck your own self up!

Everyone agreed with J.C., and Bony just said, "Oh man, shit, okay. I just didn't like his shit, that's all." The message delivered was simple; we are African Americans from a slum, and not only is there nothing wrong with that, but it is our strength, and it makes us physically, morally, and mentally superior to middle-class people.[45]

Through this interaction, Bony began to learn about the prevailing morality of the neighborhood that would be reinforced in other conversations and behaviors for much of his life.[46] Over the nine years of this research, Bony, like others in the neighborhood, adopted the morality that J.C. had articulated. While other associations such as local sports teams and some church groups provided the same message of the moral superiority of poor people, the gang was a major contributor.[47]

Gender Stratification

The gang made a significant contribution to the neighborhood's socialization in gender roles and stratification. Although the larger society has undergone significant changes in gender roles, these have been only marginally realized in poor communities, except for more female participation in the labor force, because the social world of these communities is very different.[48] In an environment where opportunities to strengthen formal intellectual competence are severely limited, a person's body is the primary resource to be exchanged for capital.[49] Hence physical strength and beauty are the primary currency of power in everyday relations. Since any gang is composed mainly of youth in their formative years of psychosexual development, during which gender identity is in some respects fluid, the gang is able to influence the shape and content of the gender stratification system.[50]

Like gangs in general, those in the five neighborhoods studied were composed of young people of varying ages and, depending on the gang, were sometimes separated into age-specific groups. Whether or not they were separated, all were subject to the authority of an umbrella leadership, generally composed of older members who had been in the gang longer. Thus older members were the primary socializing agents who taught and reinforced beliefs and behaviors that emphasized the importance of the body and cunning in extracting material, emotional, and social advantage. Men had to develop and maintain their physical and mental strength in order to fulfill their responsibility to provide material sustenance and physical protection for the women and children of their family and inner circle and to defend their self-esteem. Gang members were taught to defend their self-esteem by demanding (as opposed to earning) the "respect" of others. As noted earlier, cultural orientations differed in emphasizing either honor, as in Latin American and Asian cultures, or respect, as in African American and North European cultures.[51] In the present study, gang members, regardless of their ethnic backgrounds, used the word *respect* to demand the deference associated with either the honor or the respect system. Gang members coming from honor systems were usually from non-English-speaking cultures, so in order to fit into the dominant English-speaking culture, they publicly used the word *respect* when they actually meant *honor.*[52] Although *respect* and *honor* had different cultural dynamics associated with them, both formed the emotional basis of interpersonal relations among gang members, as well as between members of different groups from the neighborhood. Since men in poor neighborhoods were the primary custodians of the honor and respect systems, the gang, as a male-dominated organization, played a critical role in socializing young men and women to the moral codes of these stratification systems.

Gangs have traditionally been associated with socially defined male activity such as interpersonal violence, extortion, robbery, and other criminal behavior, activities that were considered inappropriate for young, respectable women, especially poor women who had only their reputations to uphold their status. Today, as in the past, gangs are male-dominated social entities for men to initiate, develop, and support their identities. Many researchers view gangs as remedial organizations for personal identity crises.[53] However, gangs in these five neighborhoods functioned more to cultivate gender identity than to form individual identity.

In general, men were socialized to think of themselves as strong and able to withstand pain, and since most gangs in poor areas were physically oriented, they magnified this form of male identity. Both physical and mental toughness were stressed as necessary if one was to keep from being victimized by stronger individuals and succumbing to the environment. Weakness was detrimental not only to the individual but to those in poor communities considered "naturally weak," vulnerable, and in need of protection, such as women, children, and the elderly.[54] If men in their prime were physically able to defend the naturally vulnerable but did not do this, their inaction was considered ethically shameful. Further, a man who was physically and mentally unable to defend the vulnerable was considered "morally shamed" because of the belief that every man had the responsibility to become capable of defending others rather than being vulnerable himself. In either case, male identity was in a state of normative crisis, and although young men were socialized to views on gender roles and identity before joining a gang, the gang reinforced and solidified these beliefs. The comments of Pocket, a fifteen-year-old Puerto Rican from the Bronx's Elmway neighborhood who belonged to the Jinx Inc. gang, are representative:

> Yeah, a couple of weeks ago I was talking to my cousin's friend and he was saying that he was coming home one night two weeks ago and he heard this woman screaming in front of the pizza place that was closed and he said he didn't know what to do. He knew the girl was in trouble, and he saw that it was Debra, and, ah, he says that he decided that she was probably in a fight with one of her male pickups [someone who she had a date with]. If you can believe that! So, now he [his cousin's friend] was tired and didn't want to get involved 'cause it would have taken an hour or more to settle things if the police got called, so he decides to go home. I listened, but I'm thinking, what a fucking asshole! This is a guy who is six foot two and built like a rock, and carries a Bowie knife, and he doesn't go to see if Debra needs some help? That fucking idiot has got no heart, no balls, no nothing! He's not a man, just filth! The kicker is, she was jumped by a doppy [drug addict] and got her face all messed up.[55]

Leafy, a member of the Birdville gang and Mexican American resident of the Richardson neighborhood in Los Angeles, expressed a similar attitude:

> You know that guy named Jesús? He is that young guy who looks like he is just a normal guy, but hey, looks is all it is, man. You can't believe it, he so weak that if his wife was being killed in front of him, he would have to call the police. I mean the guy has nothing, man. He is so lame it's unbelievable. An old guy was getting mugged and he said he didn't want to get involved. Now he complains that the blacks are picking on him and wants to know if we can help him from getting beat up all the time. Can you believe it? He even complains that no girls will go out with him. I don't fucking give a shit what happens to the *puta* [whore]. And I really don't want him to have any girl, 'cause he ain't even a man; he is nothing but a fucking *maricon*

[homosexual]. He definitely ain't worth any woman, he ain't worth saving
or anything—he's just garbage.[56]

Because of their sociocultural environment, gangs adopted a worldview that men were physically stronger than women and thus should
have more status and deference. They socialized young members and
other youth to the meaning of being "a man" and what "a man" should
expect from women. They believed that the role of women was to provide men with sexual pleasure and unlimited emotional sustenance. The
gang also taught that married women should teach their children the religious and cultural traditions of the family's ethnic group, keep a clean
house, and cook the family meals. Most of these discussions on women's
responsibilities identified women who failed to maintain this standard;
thus they taught young men what to look for in a woman and, in the
context of gender stratification, what they must demand of women.
Women who deviated from this standard lowered the status of the men
they were with. Thus status achieved through the system of gender stratification in poor neighborhoods can be likened to the status acquired by
the nonpoor through money or material possessions. The comments of
Arnaldo, a twenty-year-old Puerto Rican member of the Spice Kings
gang, illustrate this system:

> Janet is history, man! She thinks she's some queen or something. She can't
> do this for me, or that for me. No, I ain't having no woman that can't take
> care of my house! [By "house" he means himself.] Them that can't do that
> ain't nothing but pussies waiting for a fuck; and if they think they getting it
> someplace else, they gonna take it! . . . Shit, they just whores with attitude!
> [The other three men laugh.] Hell, any of you want that kind of respect?
> [Everyone indicates they do not.] Me neither, it ain't worth nothing to me!
> [Everyone nods in agreement.][57]

Women clearly understood their roles within the gender stratification
system;[58] thus they did not need to be physically coerced to accept their
subservient position because they were socialized to these norms and to
the belief that these norms created a "positive" and "normal" social system.[59] Women commonly assumed their subservient roles vis-à-vis men
and professed an attachment to such a system, much of which was an
expression of their desire for a loving relationship with a man. The comments of Veronica, a sixteen-year-old Mexican American resident of
L.A.'s El Rey neighborhood, represent this view.

> My parents asked me if Ricardo is in a gang, and I told them he was. . . . I
> like him a lot. Sometimes he hits me when he is mad that I don't do what I

am supposed to. My mom would tell us when my dad hit her that when a man hits you, you can tell he loves you 'cause he wouldn't bother if he didn't—he'd just leave. I wish he didn't do those things, but I know you [the girl she is talking to] are right, he ain't going to stop because that would look bad in front of his friends. . . . Yeah, I love him and I know what I should do because it makes me feel good doing things for him.[60]

Women were also willing to comply with the unequal gender stratification system because it was the accepted norm of their community's world. To live in the world they had to navigate the existing social system by either accommodating themselves to the existing order, changing the existing social order, or leaving their community.[61] The second option was very unlikely to occur in their lifetime, and the third presented them with the possibility of an unknown, unfamiliar stratification system that might not be any more liberating or any more capable of improving their economic opportunities.[62] Therefore, the vast majority found it easiest to accommodate to a world and its norms to which they were already socialized. The comments of Rosa, a sixteen-year-old Dominican from Brooklyn's Eagleton neighborhood are representative of this way of thinking:

That fucking Daniel is a fucking dog! He will fuck any bitch who will let him! [laughter from the other women listening] Yeah, my cousin saw him with Julia two weeks ago and told me, and when I asked him he said he was sorry about it but he couldn't help it, it was just the way men are. And I say to him, no, that's just the way you are! Then he says, no, look at all the guys in this 'hood, tell me what one does anything different? [The other girls agree]. . . . Yeah, so they're all fucking dogs, I hate 'em all! . . . I could get the hell out of this neighborhood, but other neighborhoods got the same shit to deal with, even the white neighborhoods. So I might as well just stay here. Right now I just feel like shooting the son of a bitch! [More nods of agreement and quiet laughter from the other girls present][63]

Recent interest in female participation in gangs comes primarily from reporters trying to find a "human interest story."[64] Empirical studies on women in gangs report that their roles are varied and purposefully nontraditional.[65] Such findings have influenced many in the media to think that women are, or are becoming, a significant part of the gang phenomenon.[66] Yet the data used in these studies have tended to overestimate the number of girls formally involved in gangs. In my prior research on thirty-seven gangs in three cities over the course of ten years, I found that the number of girls directly and consistently involved in gangs was quite small, and subsequent research on gangs has not produced evidence to challenge this finding (see tables 6 through 8).[67] Despite the small number of girls in gangs in the present study, they contributed to the gangs' reinforcement of gender roles in the social structure of poor neighborhoods because they assumed subservient roles to men.

Social Stratification

Gangs also socialized young people to the neighborhood's stratification system. In fragmented neighborhoods, whose structure was based primarily on socioeconomic stratification, the gang contributed to the structure by identifying where in the neighborhood's social order their members were placed. This helped distinguish the various social categories in the neighborhood. The gang taught, by providing criteria for sorting, how to identify and place people in the various social categories, allowing its members to determine their competitors, enemies, and friends as well as the appropriate response to specific situations.

Through everyday conversations among gang members and potential members, the subjective rankings of the various neighborhood groups and those who belonged to them were communicated and legitimized. Various neighborhood associations, such as church groups, gambling groups, the Elks and Moose clubs, veterans' groups, social clubs, and social cliques, were dominated by people holding one of the primary value orientations, and they would collectively rank themselves vis-à-vis others. Such rankings established a constantly debated hierarchy, but they formed the fragments of a social order that created status-based identities for the neighborhood's residents. The gang was yet another group in the hierarchy system that gave its members a status, and although these rankings were generally biased, they were no more so than those provided by the other groups to their members. In sum, this subjective system gave residents an understanding of their neighborhood's social world, pride in belonging to their specific social fragment, a greater sense of solidarity within their group, a strengthened intraorganizational bond, a better understanding of the social space between groups, and a greater ability to self-regulate social interaction with other groups.

Ethnic Stratification

In neighborhoods characterized by competition between ethnic groups for sociocultural dominance, the gangs socialized their members to the existing ethnic divisions. This process vastly helped new residents because they did not yet know the divisions and dynamics of the neighborhood. The gang informed them of the establishments they could and "should" frequent, how and with whom they should interact, and who they could depend on for protection. Such information also helped longer-term residents of the ethnic group because locations associated with particular ethnic groups often changed. Thus, when a gang consistently frequented certain areas, residents of the same ethnic group knew them to be safe locations.[68]

An example of a gang socializing residents to the dangers of the neighborhood involved the Birdville gang of L.A.'s Richardson neighborhood and the Guzmán family, who were recent immigrants from Mexico temporarily staying with relatives. One day, Mr. Guzmán asked his sixteen-year-old son to go and get some groceries for the aunt they were staying with, and without being told where to go, the son just went out the door and started to walk westward toward the intersection of two main streets. On the way, he met a young member of the Birdville gang, who asked him for the time and a cigarette. After the Guzmán boy had given the gang member both, the two of them continued to walk down the street until they reached the bus stop, where four other gang members were waiting. The young gang member introduced the Guzmán boy to his friends, who began a discussion of their rivals, the African American Trail Street Gang, in which they frequently noted streets that the gang and other Mexicans should avoid. Since the Guzmán boy was headed to Daddy G's store, near one of the streets mentioned, he asked if it would be safe. The Birdville members warned him that he would be robbed and possibly beaten and told him to change directions toward Treviño's store, owned by a Mexican family. He did, and upon returning to his aunt's he told his brothers what he had learned. His aunt agreed, telling them to listen to the gang members since they knew what places to avoid in the neighborhood. After the Guzmán family got their own apartment, relatives arrived to temporarily stay with them, and all the young relatives were informed of the gang members' warnings and advice.[69] Thus the gang's contribution to the awareness of social space continued to be passed on.

Another socialization function of the gang in contested neighborhoods was the promotion of ethnic solidarity, especially in terms of interethnic dating. Most gang members primarily dated girls of the same ethnic group and stigmatized or shamed those who violated this norm. Girls who violated this norm were often referred to as whores and ethnic traitors. However, sex, rather than relationships, with girls from other ethnic groups was acceptable for boys, particularly gang members, because it was seen as an affront to males of the competing group. In this respect the gangs were simply following the norms of their ethnic group in the group situation, but their deviance in rudely vocalizing them made them invaluable agents of ethnic solidarity in the neighborhood.[70]

Violence and Pain

Much of the gangs' socialization function in the neighborhood was in teaching or reinforcing the prevailing norms, particularly in terms of how individuals should experience violence, pain, and suffering. Since the constitution of violence and pain differs among cultures, individuals learn to identify violent or painful occurrences, as well as the appropriate cultural response, through their culture.[71] Because cultural viewpoints and responses are learned in youth, and because gangs are dominated by young people, the gangs were influential teachers.

As in most poor neighborhoods, so much aggressive behavior occurred in the five neighborhoods studied that much of it was categorized as "normal" rather than "violent." "Normal" behavior either was not considered aggressive (in terms of local criteria, although other cultures might consider it so) or was considered aggressive but not excessively so. An instance of behavior not considered aggressive was the physical disciplining of children. If a child behaved in a way that was unacceptable to parental authority, such as "talking back" when given a direct order, the parent might repeatedly and forcefully strike the child and tell him or her never to violate the parent's authority again. These actions were considered normal ways to discipline a child: even if the child suffered bruises, the word *violence* would never be applied.[72] Acts considered aggressive but not excessively so would include physically attacking or injuring someone who made a sexual pass at another's date or attacking a female partner found cheating with another man and physically injuring both offending parties in "righteous retribution."[73] The comments of Cover, a nineteen-year-old member of the Falcons gang in Brooklyn's Eagleton neighborhood, represent the tolerant attitude generally taken toward aggression in such circumstances:

> Dish [a former member of the gang] was with his girlfriend, and these two guys call her out [make rude remarks to her]. Dish ain't happy about that at all, so he goes over to the two and tells them to shut the fuck up and get the hell movin'. Ain't none of them doin' a thing but laugh and call his bluff. Then out of nowhere Dish does what he ought to have done. He pulls a

knife and slashes one of them across the face and then grabs the other and puts the knife to his throat. Tells the guy to move out of there and slashes him on the shoulder and back of the neck. The guy runs and he goes back to the guy bleedin' from the face who was doing the talkin' and slashes him again across the front his chin. That guy ran too. . . . Hell, he [Dish] should have done more. [Everyone nods in agreement.] . . . Yeah, I seen it all, I was sittin' on my car talkin' when the whole thing came down.[74]

Acts of aggression that were considered "violent" included the use of illegitimate (inappropriate) or excessive force as defined by neighborhood residents. One instance was an attack on Eugenio, a sixteen-year-old Mexican American, while he was walking home from school in L.A.'s Richardson neighborhood. Eugenio was not fluent in English, so when three African American boys tried to rob him he did not produce the money fast enough because he didn't know what they were saying. They beat him with metal sticks, and he was left with bruises all over his face, shoulders, and legs. Stitches were required for his face and shoulders, and he could not open his left eye for eighteen days. Both African American and Mexican American residents considered this a violent act, not because of the injuries incurred, but because someone's inability to understand what was being asked of him made the use of any force illegitimate.

The reproach of excessive violence was reserved for instances in which the police used force that caused serious injuries to apprehend a neighborhood resident and was made in such cases even by those who supported the police. An example occurred when Tony, a young member of the Toppers gang in the Bronx, was walking home from a party where somebody had been stabbed during a fight. The police were called to the party and, after having the victim taken to the hospital, began a search for the assailant. They stopped Tony about a block from his apartment, checked to see if he was carrying any weapons on him, and put him in their car for questioning. He told them that he had witnessed the stabbing but did not know the perpetrator. The police did not believe him, however, because they had been told by someone at the party that the assailant was associated with the Toppers gang. Hoping to force the information out of Tony, the police struck him with nightsticks on his arms, back, and head each time he said he knew nothing, but when he persisted in that response they finally let him go. The next day, when Tony told other residents how he acquired the bumps and bruises, they agreed that Tony had been a victim of excessive violence.[75]

Gang members' use of the word *violence* was very selective, reflecting the norms of the community; thus to them even the most aggressive and brutal acts might not signify "violence." Phrases such as "defending myself," "taking care of business," and "doing what was needed" described the use of force and, more importantly, conceptually buffered gang members from the harsh reality of aggression.[76] Gang members reinforced among themselves and the residents of the neighborhood the view that the maximum use of force was always required to neutralize any threat; and since it was difficult to determine when an adversary had been neutralized, those involved in a physical confrontation needed to use too much force rather than too little in order to remain out of danger.

Because experiences of physical and psychological pain are abundant in the social environments of poor neighborhoods, residents must learn at a young age how to protect themselves and deal with pain in order to manage life and avoid mental breakdown. Gangs helped socialize youth to this environment by providing them with two general means to psychologically deal with pain. To buffer themselves from the psychological or emotional pain of disappointment caused by others, gang members held onto the belief that no one could be trusted completely. This guarded strategy did not allow them to fully experience and appreciate another person, but it reduced the pain associated with a trusted person's betrayal or the emotional wounds inflicted by another. An example of this guarded approach to relationships is seen in an interaction between Juan, seventeen, and Oswaldo, sixteen, Dominican residents of the United States since birth: Oswaldo said he was sorry that Juan's girlfriend of three years had left with her family for another city, but Juan only shrugged his shoulders and said, "There will be another hole."[77] To deal with physical pain from injury, gang members held and transmitted the belief that any show of pain was an indication of vulnerability and weakness that could lead to further injury. This aspect of the socialization process can be seen in an exchange between Gonzo, a member of L.A.'s Zapata Park gang, and Honey, a young, recent recruit. While Fang, a fellow member just released from a three-year stay at the state penitentiary, was giving Gonzo a tattoo at his home, Gonzo asked Honey if he wanted a tattoo. Honey responded in the affirmative, but with little conviction. When Gonzo asked, "Do you have a problem with pain?" Honey answered, "No" with conviction, so Gonzo again suggested that Honey get a tattoo. Honey consented, and Fang started one on his chest. To all the young boys present, a clear lesson was taught that no self-respecting male should show any fear of pain. Thus, when

Dagger, another gang member, flinched and made a noise indicating pain while he was getting his first tattoo on his neck, his young relatives and friends called him names that implied weakness.

In sum, gang members had to maintain the pose that pain had no influence on them. Thus they socialized themselves to pain through various designed activities, beginning with "jumping" a new recruit into the gang, which involved having everyone physically attack him to teach that pain was now a part of the recruit's life that he had to embrace. Getting tattooed on all parts of one's body, especially one's neck, a very nerve-sensitive area, also indicated gang members' ability to embrace pain. Finally, gang members had to refrain from expressing much emotion, whether about the possibility of dying, incarceration, or the loss of a close friend or family member, except when they were defending their honor or respect.[78] To authorities and the general public their demeanor might appear callous, ruthless, and even pathological, but inside the neighborhood it was simply seen as a "normal" presentation of self in the environment.[79] Even the prospect of dying did not keep gang members from using violence to gain advantage, although gang members from different ethnic backgrounds approached the issue of death differently. Those from African American backgrounds viewed death as a normal occurrence but believed that they themselves were too smart to be killed. The comments of Curly, a twenty-year-old member of the Bronx's Toppers gang, represent this view:

> You got to be out of yo' fucking mind if you think I ain't goin' to take that dope away from that Italian Mafia guy. . . . No, there ain't no reason to worry about dying, everybody does it, but most of them who got it lately is dumb motherfuckers, and I ain't one of them. Ain't nobody going to get me like that, I'm too good for that shit.[80]

Interestingly, this view on death incorporated the Protestant idea that individuals can manipulate their worlds. However, the comments of Rugs, a nineteen-year-old Mexican American member of L.A.'s Zapata Park gang, represent an alternative view of death held by those from Latino backgrounds:[81]

> Shit, I almost got hit when they [a rival gang] rode by and started shooting. It hit Jockey, who was right next to me, and he is still in the hospital. I'm going with Hotsy, Duke, and Shell to shoot whoever we can find in their neighborhood. . . . No, we ain't worried about getting shot, 'cause that ain't up to me. When God wants you dead, you're going to die, so there's no reason for me to worry.[82]

THE GANG AS PROTECTOR

An important function of the gang is protecting the community. The mere suggestion that gangs perform any positive role in the community has been rejected by some researchers.[83] However, it is precisely this role that binds most gangs to the community. Although not all the time, the gang protected three social constituencies within the neighborhoods: (1) women, children, and older men vulnerable to the extraction of money or sex by a variety of predators; (2) young men often terrorized by other gangs; and (3) small shopkeepers vulnerable to persistent theft. Without the protective contribution of the gang, each of these neighborhood constituencies would have been in added danger of physical harm, and their patterns of moving throughout the neighborhood would have been significantly limited. Any social entity requires an immune system, and the gang was one element of such a system in the five poor neighborhoods of this study.[84]

Many criminologists who study gangs have difficulty in conceiving the gang as a natural protector of the neighborhood. They often cite "gang-related" homicides in the very neighborhoods that gangs are meant to protect. Because most of these researchers do not directly observe gang behavior, they cannot determine when the violent actions of gangs involve protecting the community and when they are entirely unrelated.

A representative example of gang protection occurred in the Richardson neighborhood of Los Angeles, where a group of young men wearing clothing associated with the African American Crip gangs infiltrated the neighborhood and robbed older residents.[85] The police were notified and increased their patrols, stopping young men who lived in the neighborhood to ask questions. Yet despite this increased effort the robberies continued over an additional two-month period. Since most of the victims were Mexican Americans known to members of the Birdville gang, the gang decided to stop the robberies. Thus, when a member of the gang saw some African American youth whom he did not recognize sitting in a car at a liquor store, he called other members of his gang, who got into their cars and parked on each of their families' streets. When the African Americans drove onto one of the streets, some Birdville gang members sitting in their cars shot at the car and hit one of the tires, but the car drove off. The police quickly arrived at the report of gunfire, talked to witnesses, and reported the incident as a "gang-related shooting."[86] However, it was not a "gang-related shooting" but an act of vigilantism involving gangs.[87] No one was ever arrested, but the robberies abruptly stopped, indicating the success of the gang's attack, and the Latino community was very appreciative. The comments of Rogelio, a forty-eight-year-old Mexican American in Treviño's Grocery, are representative of this appreciation:

> My mother is sure glad that the robberies have stopped, and she's glad that the boys in the neighborhood looked out for the older people. . . . I tell you, the police tried to help, but it was BV [Birdville gang] that made it happen. [The six men and women in the store nod in agreement.][88]

THE GANG AS ENTERTAINMENT PROVIDER

The gangs in the communities studied, much like other fraternal organizations, provided multiple benefits to their members, one of the most important of which was entertainment. In poor areas, entertainment was not taken for granted, so those who sought entertainment had to provide it. Gangs used the collective skills of their members to make their everyday activities entertaining in order to help perpetuate the organization. The gangs' abilities to provide entertainment were influential in determining the strength of their internal structure and their place within the neighborhood.

Within each of the five neighborhoods, the gangs provided their membership with several types of entertainment. Six of the gangs from New York had modest clubhouses with makeshift bars to provide daily entertainment to members and a few guests. Drinks were not free, but they were cheaper than alcohol sold at commercial bars and were available to minors. Several of the clubhouses also had dartboards, card or domino tables, pool tables, various electronic game machines, and pinball machines. Thus they were hubs of entertainment at all hours of the day or night for youth who could not travel far or pay much money. Of course, not all gangs had elaborate entertainment facilities, but all attempted to provide some of these to their members.

Another type of entertainment was gang-organized parties, either exclusively for their members or for other neighborhood residents. Some parties were held at the clubhouse, and others were at additional venues like public parks. The private parties were very similar to those found among fraternities and sororities and bolstered group solidarity and recruitment, while the public parties promoted community solidarity. The private parties offered drugs, alcohol, and dancing, while the public parties offered beer, soft drinks, food, and music. Occasionally the gang hired a live band that played traditional music for the neighborhood guests at public parties, but most of the music played was prerecorded.

Since most gangs were composed primarily of young people, they provided many of these young people exactly what they were looking for.
Those who sought to eradicate gangs because of their negative activities
were at a disadvantage, since they could not provide the entertainment
that many of the young people in the neighborhood desired. The gang's
advantage was predicated on young members' immediate identification
of existing fads and their use of those fads to entertain themselves and
other neighborhood youth.

The gangs also established counterculture fads in the adult world that
gave other adolescents pride in their neighborhoods. This pride was
related to middle-class youth's emulation of the fads of low-income
youth, such as gang-type clothing or modified gang customs like tattoo-
ing, wearing baseball hats backwards, and listening to rap/hip-hop music.
The comments of Gabby, an eighteen-year-old member of the Trail Street
gang in L.A.'s Richardson neighborhood, represents this view:

> Did you check out those fucking whites at the concert? They do what we all
> do. They wish they could be in a gang, but they're too fucking weak. [The
> other members laugh.] We set all the fucking standards for them, and they
> know it! I wouldn't change [being in a gang] for what they got because they
> don't have nothing—we set everything. [The others all nod in agreement.][89]

THE ECONOMIC BASIS OF GANGS

The environment of poor neighborhoods also provided an economic basis
for the gangs, composed of three fundamental elements. As a type of collective behavior, gangs have been, and remain, a primarily lower-class
phenomenon. Thus the material basis of poor neighborhoods provides a
fertile environment for germinating and nourishing gang organizations,
which can be found among the working class as well.[90] Of course, middle-
class neighborhoods also have youth organizations that involve collective
behavior, such as fraternities/sororities, social clubs, and cults, but gangs
are very rare.[91] This is because poor and middle-class neighborhoods
have different economic and social bases. In the five poor neighborhoods
of this study, the economic bases came from a lack of material resources
at the individual and community level. Residents of these neighborhoods
wanted many of the comforts of life found in higher-income neighborhoods, but they did not have the resources to obtain them. Thus gangs
emerged and lessened the burden created by this condition by providing
an organization to obtain material possessions that could secure more
comfort.

Most individuals in low-income neighborhoods are socialized to cope with material scarcity, but some individuals are highly competitive, with an insatiable desire to succeed at any cost—a psychological character trait I have in previous research identified as "defiant individualism."[92] The gang organized those with this "defiant individualism" into an effective economic organization by selling products, goods, and services. Goods sold included stolen electronics, car parts, jewelry, and art, while products sold included illegal drugs like crack and crank produced in a "drug mill" that the gang operated and/or distributed. The gangs also offered and provided protection to businesses in the neighborhoods through service contracts, obtained sometimes through extortion and sometimes at the request of the establishments. In both cases they were monetarily successful, with the organizationally strong gangs in New York and Los Angeles grossing hundreds of dollars a month.[93]

Other services the gangs provided included arson for hire; transportation of drugs; and collections for loan sharks, independent drug dealers, and illegal lottery ("numbers") businesses. In the case of arson, business owners often hired gangs to set fire to their establishments in order to collect insurance money. To transport drugs from one geographic area or organization to another, the gangs used younger members (juveniles) and women in auxiliary groups.[94] To collect debts, the gangs used intimidation and force to secure the money owed to the lender. These services allowed other organizations to save money and forego the risks of arrest or physical injury. Through these economic activities, individual gang members acquired money that enabled them to buy items that provided convenience, pleasure, and entertainment.

The gangs' economic activity also benefited other members of the community. The families of gang members sometimes shared in stolen goods or were offered loans to pay off a debt. The comments of Alma, a thirty-one-year-old Jamaican American mother of four children, represent the general attitude regarding benefits received:

> Don't get me wrong, I ain't happy that Ricky [her son] is hanging around with St. James Place [the local gang]! But he been able to get some loans from them that help me pay the phone bill and school expenses until I turned the corner. So they do help some too.[95]

Hannah Arendt made an important philosophical distinction between labor and work. Both involve bodily activity, but work clearly results in an identified product, whereas labor is activity whose result (product) cannot be identified.[96] Her treatise on this difference shows that although the two terms are generally used interchangeably, they in fact denote separate actions. Gangs provide youth with what Arendt would label "work," which is why individuals in the neighborhoods studied found gang-associated economic activity more attractive than traditional, legitimate occupations that carried the psychological alienation associated with "labor" and the stigma of servitude.[97]

The primary economic activities of gangs are supplying drugs, providing services, and affording entertainment. This allows some youth to become economically active who might otherwise be idle, and it provides them with more than they had. However, in this highly competitive environment coupled with limited resources, youth must be creative in their strategies for success. Thus the economic schemes that gangs carry out are often the result of a clever deception, a "con job," or daring in the face of bodily and/or legal risk. These activities do not simply carry excitement, as Jack Katz has argued (although excitement is present); they provide satisfaction in knowing that something is being built and, if successful, in producing something that will provide financial and entertainment dividends. In brief, the youth of these poor neighborhoods felt that legitimate jobs—characterized by the alienating qualities of repetitiveness, low pay, and disconnection from the final product— were not as worthy of investment as the activities of the gang. The comment of Daddy Dee, an eighteen-year-old African American resident of the Bronx's Monument neighborhood and member of the Toppers gang, is representative of these views:

> Yeah, me and Crypto and Dimples dealt this college student some speed and Ecstasy. He was scared, but we worked with him for close to three days, and he finally paid the money. He didn't want the speed, but we had so much of that shit, we had to get him to take some, and he did. Today we is feeling great, and about to set out to do some more deals. . . . No, I ain't fucking with that office job downtown anymore. It's too fucking boring filing shit all day![98]

Equally representative is the comment of Red Eyes, a seventeen-year-old Mexican resident of L.A.'s El Rey neighborhood and a member of the Cactus Vatos gang:

> I quit that car wash 'cause I just couldn't stand how boring it got. The next time there is a deal to bring in those goods [drugs] from México, count me in? Beto told me about all the stuff you guys did to get in the last shipment, and that sounded good. I mean, it sounded good how everybody had to work out the problems to get the job done. . . . I know I'd like both the money and figuring how to make the deal work. Can you get me in?[99]

In sum, the gangs' abilities to act as a conduit to opportunities in the underground economy contributed to their economic basis within the neighborhood.

SOME CLOSING REMARKS

The social science literature on gangs has more often than not understood them as parasitic on their communities and society at large. Many parasitic economic establishments operate in poor neighborhoods: bail bondsmen, pawnbrokers, check-cashing businesses, numbers outfits, and the various grocery stores, hair shops, and tenements that have taken what I have described as the economic enterprise route. Gangs, on the other hand, are rarely parasitic within their own neighborhood. They often raid and are thus parasitic upon other neighborhoods, but they are one of the social groups least likely to prey on the residents of their own neighborhood.

Gangs often engage in aspects of the underground economy where violence is the medium to realize objectives, but they can also provide both social and economic benefits to the neighborhood's residents. In this latter role, they become functional elements of the neighborhood and assume institutional status and legitimacy there even though they lack legitimacy in the larger society. They can look much like the "bastard institutions" described by Everett Hughes. However, the larger point is that they are recognized as legitimate in the neighborhood and contribute to its social structure; thus their illegitimate status in the eyes of the larger society is irrelevant.[100]

CHAPTER 9

All in the Family

Mothering the Gang as a Bastard Institution

Bastard begot, bastard instructed, bastard in mind, bastard in valour, in everything illegitimate.

William Shakespeare, *Troilus and Cressida* (1601–2)

As mentioned in the previous chapter, the public often views gangs and poor neighborhoods as naturally going together.[1] In most scholarly or journalistic popular accounts, gangs spring up simply because of a neighborhood's poverty,[2] and they are viewed as a dysfunction of material want or as a dysfunctional contributor to community decay.[3] However, gangs often assume a functional position within the neighborhood's social structure that does not symbolize or cause neighborhood decay, though this position is seldom understood by researchers. Whether the gang is a contributor to neighborhood decay or a positive structural property of the poor neighborhood is determined by several contingent factors.

How and when do gangs negatively affect low-income neighborhoods? How and when do they help maintain the social fabric of poor neighborhoods? The first question focuses on how and under what circumstances gangs worsen the condition of poor neighborhoods and thus in a sense addresses the "broken windows" theory described by Wilson and Kelling.[4] The second question concerns how and under what circumstances gangs contribute to the neighborhoods' cultural and structural well-being.[5] This chapter addresses both of these questions as well as how gangs contribute to the dynamics of social change and persistence within poor neighborhoods.

GANGS IN THE CHANGE PROCESS

One demon of the modern metropolis is the gang.[6] Since the nineteenth century, gangs have been depicted as social vermin afflicting the environment of America's cities.[7] Although some researchers argue that gangs are not a low-income phenomenon, evidence shows that they are rarely found among the middle class and never found in the upper class.[8] Middle-class groups identified by researchers as gangs consistently lack the full panoply of sociological characteristics of a gang in that their only resemblance to the sociological "gang" is engagement in "ganging" behavior: joining together to undertake some desired goal. Research that conflates gangs with loose and temporary associations for the purpose of occasional criminal activity misidentifies two separate forms of collective behavior while adding to the negative mystique of gangs. This mystique, which has contributed much to the view of gangs as a sign, or agent, of neighborhood decay, has also obstructed the development of a sociological understanding of the gang's role in the life of poor neighborhoods.

Deindustrialization

Like other social entities, gangs affected and were affected by the processes of social change in the five neighborhoods of this study. To best understand the gang's role in the neighborhoods over time, it is necessary to begin with how the gangs, as establishments, were agents of social change.

The macroeconomic conditions identified by William Julius Wilson as affecting the poor neighborhoods of Chicago were particularly relevant to the five neighborhoods of New York and Los Angeles throughout the duration of the present study.[9] Essentially, Wilson argued that macroeconomic changes in the production sector caused a shift to an economy that specialized in technical services. This resulted in increased economic difficulty among the working class and poor because they had little chance of employment in either the technical service sector or the shrinking production sector.[10] Strong evidence from the present study supports Wilson's assertion as applied to gangs and to poor youth in general, whose employment options were limited to three sectors.[11] In the first sector, the secondary labor market, production still went on but under harsh working conditions, with low wages, no benefits or advancement opportunity, and long hours.[12] These conditions made this sector the least appealing option to native-born workers,[13] and they had two effects on gangs. First, immigrant youth attempted to postpone entry into this sector because of the associated drudgery and limited opportunity for mobility;[14] thus many looked to gangs as a means to money and fun. Since employment in a well-paying occupation for these youth was nonexistent, many saw the gang as an attractive interlude before they had to assume the adult responsibilities of marriage and the support of a family from a job with low wages, bad working conditions, and no benefits. The comments of Miguel, a sixteen-year-old Puerto Rican resident of the Bronx's Monument neighborhood, to two friends are representative of this viewpoint:

> My dad has been working for one of them cement factories in Brooklyn for about twenty-six years and he is tired out—fucking tired and he is only forty-four years old! He wants me to get a job when I get out of school like he's got, and that ain't a very pretty sight, you know? . . . Yeah, he is just like your dad [his friend's father] when it's about getting a job, and don't get me wrong, I want to work and get some money, but not at a job like that. . . . JoJo [a leader of the Toppers gang] has been telling my sister that I ought to join up and make some good money without having to go to work at one of them slave jobs [manual labor in a factory]. After my dad's last talk, I think I'm just going to check out JoJo's story. [Four weeks later Miguel joined the Toppers and took on the nickname Midnight.][15]

The service sector as well as the production sector was affected by the changing macroeconomic conditions. Its occupations were concentrated at two extremes. One set consisted of very technically oriented occupations designed to support the communications, management, and activities of large multinational corporations.[16] They required much training and commanded large salaries as a result, but youth from poor neighborhoods were poorly equipped with the skills necessary to successfully compete for these jobs. The other set of occupations required little technical capacity; it included housekeeping, gardening, day care work, janitorial work, stocking, shoe shining, filing, courier work, and other jobs to provide low-level support to business or government segments of the economy. Although there was an increasing demand for these jobs and many youth applied for them, they found them unattractive for either short- or long-term employment. Consequently, they tended to hold these jobs only for short periods with the intention of looking for another job with better pay. Few, if any, ever found jobs in the legal economy that paid what they desired, so they looked to the illegal economy to fulfill their monetary dreams.[17]

Gangs offered youth the chance to earn the amount of money necessary to maximize entertainment, although, as often stated by James
Short, they were rarely able to deliver on all their promises for the "good
life."[18] However, gangs' successes, even if modest, influenced potential
recruits much more than their failures. This highlights the importance of
two interdependent conditions for gangs' successful recruitment of neighborhood residents: the lack of employment opportunities with good pay,
benefits, and possible advancement and the ability of some gang members to accumulate significant amounts of money and status in poor
neighborhoods. While most gang members do not acquire large fortunes,
enough do to convince possible recruits that the potential exists and that
it is worth their investment of time and talent in gang activities. The comments of Carlos, a fifteen-year-old Mexican American resident of L.A.'s
El Rey neighborhood, are representative of this way of thinking:

> A cop came into our school today to talk about all the bad things that
> happen to you when you join a gang, but hey, ain't too many people lis-
> tenin' to that in this school. I mean, he goes and tells us all the kids that's
> been killed in gangs from this here school. But who fuckin' cares about
> that! There was a shitload of money made by Chuckie, Ant-Man, and
> Fats in Z Park [Zapata Park gang], and I'd like some of that too. I know I
> can make it happen in Z Park for me, so who cares if you got to serve a
> little time.[19]

The response of Larry, a sixteen-year-old African American resident of
the Bronx's Elmway neighborhood, to one of his former teachers from
junior high school is similar:

> Oh, come on, Mr. X [teacher], I know that getting involved with gangs is
> bad for one's health, but it does have its sugar [good things] too. . . . Well,
> regular jobs gots their own dangers [responding to Mr. X's warning of the
> danger associated with joining a gang]. Mr. Prince [a neighborhood resi-
> dent] got himself killed when one of the other workers at the factory he
> works at accidentally ran into him with a fork truck. So spending some
> time with Jinx Inc. ain't that more dangerous and could even pay some
> good dividends in a short time. You know that Jimmy joined, and look at
> that car he drives around in—tell me that ain't some real money. And hey,
> if I die, which I ain't, 'cause I'm too smart to get that, well hell, it was
> worth the chance—you got to die of something, so you might as well be
> trying things.[20]

In sum, deindustrialization had an impact on poor youths' involvement in gangs because it eliminated a significant number of blue-collar
(semiskilled) occupations, making employment options for poor youth

very limited. Therefore, some youth who might not otherwise have associated with gangs decided to join despite the risks because they knew members who had obtained money and status through their involvement.[21]

Changes in the Drug Economy

In the five poor neighborhoods of this study, the greatest increase of job opportunities was in the drug industry. This occurred as a result of two economic processes: an increased demand for drugs and a major change in the structure of the drug industry. The drug industry had been monopolized and controlled by the Italian Mafia for years in both the wholesale and retail sectors and thus from production to consumption. When the Italian Mafia lost their monopoly by the 1990s, an open market was created; new actors flooded into the business, and competition was intense.[22] Organizations like gangs no longer acted simply as training grounds for the larger syndicates but became active in a variety of wholesale/retail activities, dramatically increasing economic opportunities for both youth and adults in poor neighborhoods.[23]

All the gangs in the five neighborhoods studied saw the advantage of a hierarchical organization to establish greater control over potential profits within this new economic environment. No organization could hope to compete in the drug market without a formal internal structure capable of planning and executing a business strategy to gain and hold a portion of this market. Therefore, the gangs in the five neighborhoods studied were pressured to change their own internal structures. Most of the gangs found greater capability for internal control when leadership was hierarchically organized and aggressively punitive to rank-and-file failures in executing duties. Thus they sought to establish a rigid rank-and-file structure so that their drug business could run more effectively.[24]

Greater opportunities in selling drugs entailed an equal need to develop and protect markets. Some of the gangs' markets were geographically small, like that of the Cactus Vatos, which constituted only two blocks. Others, like Trail Street and the St. James Place gang, began small but enlarged their markets to a half-mile area. Gang leaders learned that to be successful they had to plan and execute policies that would expand their market share while protecting whatever share they had secured. In this regard, all the gangs were aggressive in efforts to expand and protect their market share because negotiation was not a viable option for obtaining advantage.

Many researchers as well as the public consider gang violence as merely an indication of members' personal deficiencies. Malcolm Klein, for instance, lists eleven negative personal traits or criteria of those inclined to join a gang, two of which are a prior history of violence and poor impulse control.[25] This assessment is problematic, however, because it underestimates individuals' ability to make rational decisions in determining what course of action best serves their economic interests.[26] Because gangs use violence, and researchers view violence as pathologically antisocial, self-destructive, and sadomasochistic, gang members are assumed to be irrational. However, this assumption disregards the unregulated nature of the markets in which gangs are engaged. Physical force (i.e., violence) is the only currency that can acquire advantage in these markets.

The gangs of the five neighborhoods studied had to grapple with extreme scarcity and aggressively compete to secure the most desirable objects within a winner-take-all environment, resulting in a general resistance to sharing with competitors. In this context, the poor were not greedier than other social classes; sharing was just not possible if they were to experience economic gain.[27] If sharing did occur, it was never during the acquisition process.

Gang members acting together as agents of the organization also used violence to meet their objectives, a behavior that stemmed from both the cultural norms governing competition between individuals and the structure of the illegal economy in which gangs were involved. Within this economy, the ability to gain control over the supply of products increased the probability that a desired economic goal would be achieved, and to secure this control no resource other than sheer power was available. As Hannah Arendt has stated, violence is simply the multiplication of physical power.[28] Thus, since no independent authority existed to mediate business disputes, the use of violence was the gangs' only option. In contrast, nearly all markets in the legal sector of the economy have outside authorities to resolve disputes, such as government, courts, and official boards of regulation; without these authorities, disputes are subjected to the calculus of "goodwill" or power. Certainly, if businesses throughout the world did not have independent authorities to mediate disputes they would resort to violence. Throughout history this has occurred in management-labor disputes and in international relations, as when the Japanese decided to attack the United States to secure economic goals they believed were systematically being threatened by the government of Franklin Delano Roosevelt.[29]

The macro changes discussed above in these and other poor neighbor-hoods and their impact on gang operations were followed by a govern-ment effort to curb gang activity and its impact. In California, for instance, the state passed a law that increased the incarceration rate of gang mem-bers and lengthened their sentences. Known as the Street Terrorism Enforcement and Protection Act (STEP), it established criteria to define a "criminal gang" and the activities that determined if an individual was a member. Therefore, any individual convicted of a "gang-associated" crime could serve a lengthier sentence in the state penitentiary.[30] In addition, an attempt was made to streamline existing laws to efficiently pick up gang members who were violating their paroles. These laws often violated indi-vidual rights, but the goal to reduce gang activity, especially violence, took precedence.[31] The policy resulted in fewer young gang members and their associates on the streets for greater periods of time. In the Los Angeles gangs of the present study, one significant change found was in the age dis-tribution of gang members. Members between the ages of twelve and six-teen and twenty-nine to thirty-six became more prominent, since most incarcerated members were between the ages of seventeen and twenty-eight. An unintended consequence was the undertaking of risky activities by younger boys that would have been denied them by the older members if their gang had had an even age distribution.

In addition, state initiatives in both New York and California allowed juveniles who committed particular violent acts to be tried as adults. Local law enforcement was encouraged by state and local authorities to aggressively apprehend and prosecute gang members who broke the law, resulting in the incarceration of gang members at a faster rate and for longer periods of time. In all the neighborhoods studied, the number of gang members arrested and convicted, as well as their sentences, in-creased. The state also attempted to cut off the head of the organization by targeting gang leaders for arrest and prosecution. In the present study, the number of neighborhood gang leaders incarcerated increased, but within months of their jailing, gang violence increased as well. This unin-tended consequence of the incarceration policy resulted from the cre-ation of three power vacuums. The first of these occurred within the gang through competition over leadership positions, which increased violence between various members of a single gang. The second occurred because with an absence of leadership it became difficult to control mem-bers. Thus many became rogue members, aggressively pursuing their own agendas and thereby increasing violent confrontations with mem-bers of other gangs. Finally, with the imprisonment of the leadership of an established gang, other gangs found an opportunity to increase their own power and attempted to take over the vulnerable rival. Further, gangs had difficulty controlling their drug markets when their leadership was removed, causing other gangs to quickly seize what they could of their market share. The result was an increase in violence, as it was the only means to secure a market advantage.

The increased availability of guns also affected violence in the neighborhoods, which in turn significantly affected the internal composition of the gangs as well as their business activities.[32] Weapons were a large component of gang behavior in the five neighborhoods not because they signified psychosocial perversion or deviance but because they were considered necessary tools for everyday life. The use of weapons (which would include aggressive dogs) was almost as common among non–gang member residents of these neighborhoods as it was among gangs. Thus the lack of some type of a weapon was deviant, since weapons were an established means to achieve advantage in a dispute as well as the psychological foundation for freedom of movement. Fishhook, an eighteen-year-old Jamaican in the St. James Place gang of Brooklyn, expressed this view:

> Yeah, I do definitely pack [carry a gun] when I go to the streets. If I didn't do that, I wouldn't feel right about going anywhere away from my street. . . . It just makes me feel I can go most anywhere.[33]

So did Hank, a thirty-year-old Puerto Rican non–gang member living in the Bronx's Monument neighborhood:

> Oh yeah, I have a gun. Ain't no way I'm walking these streets with nothing. With all the fools around here that want to take what you got and hurt you too. No, no, if they mess with me they going to have their hands full.[34]

It is ironic that gangs are considered one of the most armed elements in society, for weapons ownership is commonly found in middle-class communities as well. The difference however, lies in the use of weapons among these groups. The middle class possesses weapons for motives of self-defense, whereas the gang members studied used weapons both to defend themselves and to achieve desired socioeconomic goals. Middle-class people do not use weapons to obtain personal advantage or adjudicate disputes for two reasons: the availability of organizations to mediate their disputes and their fear of losing their freedom and material wealth if they are convicted of a violent crime. In contrast, gangs and other members of poor neighborhoods are little deterred by potential loss of freedom and material possessions. Some may dispute the lack of organizations to mediate disputes in poor neighborhoods, citing the police, courts, and family counseling and crisis intervention centers as potential resources. Precisely this argument forms the foundational basis of social control theory in criminology.[35] Further, this aspect of control theory is used by social disorganization theory to argue that the lack of organization in poor neighborhoods causes higher levels of violent crime.[36] However, fewer mediating organizations exist in poor neighborhoods, and residents lack the knowledge or ability to access them at the precise time when service is needed. Additionally, residents, including gang members, generally feel their freedom is already confined by their poverty, and their material possessions are too minimal to be of importance. Therefore, the use of weapons to achieve goals was a functional response within the environment in which residents operated. A representative example from the Eagleton neighborhood in Brooklyn involved Hot Rod, sixteen years old, and two other members of the Falcons gang. When four men began selling marijuana across the street from where the Falcons sold their drugs, Hot Rod said, "Fuck, these guys just show up and start selling their shit across the street from us." The three members got together, and Hot Rod told one of the men, "This is our place, so you got to move." The men, all over the age of twenty-five, replied, "There's enough room for everybody here," to which Hot Rod responded, "No there ain't." The men were indifferent, so Hot Rod told his fellow members that he was "going to see D-Man" (the Falcon leader) and left. About ninety minutes later he returned with three other members, Hatchet, Ziggy, and Hotel, who told the men, "Either you stop selling here or there's going to be trouble." When one of the guys responded, "We don't want trouble, we'll be done here soon," Hot Rod, Hatchet, Ziggy, and Hotel left, but twenty minutes later there was gunfire. Two of the men seemed to have been injured in the leg, and all three quickly drove off.[37] The police soon arrived to question the witnesses, all of whom told the police that they had not seen the shooting and had merely seen men who had been selling drugs on the corner drive off in their car. When the police then asked if anyone had been hit, the witnesses told them that they thought two had been hit in the leg. The police took notes and left, and nothing was heard of the incident again.[38]

Opportunities in the underground economy, where only organized groups operated and no existing group like a local syndicate held a monopoly, increased the number of gangs in each neighborhood studied.[39] The availability of weapons to youth of all ages enabled them to become active. Indeed, access to weapons changed many simply "delin-quent" groups that had been primarily composed of minors and involved in relatively minor crimes such as vandalism and petty theft into organized syndicates involved in grand larceny, auto theft, armed robbery, and large-scale drug sales.[40] Thus the availability of weapons was a significant factor allowing young gang members to realize economic success before adulthood.[41] The increased availability of weapons profoundly affected how and in which domains the gangs in this study chose to participate.

Demographic change from the influx of new residents to the neighborhoods studied also affected gangs, producing two significant results. In the first stage the incumbent residents physically harassed and attacked the newcomers. Because of their small numbers, the newcomers were unable to adequately defend themselves and thus were forced to endure the attacks. As their numbers grew, the attacks also grew in numbers and intensity, causing many new residents to organize for defensive purposes. The rise of gangs was one organizational response because gangs could effectively deter aggression. Therefore, the newcomers viewed gang membership and organization positively, as a necessary and welcomed response to persistent danger. The comments of Susana, a seventeen-year-old Mexican American living in the Richardson neighborhood of Los Angeles, express this attitude:

> Every day we come home and get beaten up by the blacks. It is so scary that I hated to go to school and I wanted to tell my mother that I'm sick so I didn't have to go. Finally, some of the boys formed a gang and they walk with us home so we won't get attacked. The gang boys say, "If they want one of us beans [name for Mexicans because they eat beans], then they're going to get the whole enchilada [confrontation with the whole group of Mexicans]." So I don't think the gang guys are messed up because they're the only ones keeping us safe.[42]

The second change caused by the influx of new residents was a significant rise in the anxiety level of the incumbent residents, generally because the cultural differences of the new residents were perceived as physically threatening. Thus the incumbent residents solicited the existing youth gangs to keep them safe from the new threat. The gangs then prioritized defense of the neighborhood over their economic activities, causing a strain on their financial resources, a halt in material benefits to members, and an increased risk of physical injury. Although none of the gangs were happy with the new situation, they had to vigilantly protect the neighborhood to maintain their institutional status.[43]

THE PATH OF CHANGE

As previously mentioned, gangs in these neighborhoods were influenced by macroeconomic changes that created fewer opportunities for youth to gain economically and led them to see gang participation as a more attractive option to secure money. The first repercussion of this change was a shift from individual entrepreneurial competitive behavior to group competition (gangs, crews, and syndicates) for market dominance.[44] This created a very tense situation in contested neighborhoods, particularly in public areas. Because of urban density, each neighborhood had a finite amount of public space in which to compete. When competing gangs with a history of antagonism were involved, territorial conflict was far more intense because scarce public space became a value-heightened commodity. A common behavioral pattern observed in contested neighborhoods was residents' avoidance or use of an area on the basis of the ethnic composition of the gang occupying it, creating either a safe area for ethnic compatriots or a hostile one for ethnic outsiders. Thus macroeconomic changes that affected gang competition also affected individual residents' personal security and their use of public space.

As new opportunities emerged in the drug industry in contested neighborhoods, the gangs also attempted to secure larger portions of the market by producing a market of ethnic-specific drugs. In Los Angeles, the African American gangs marketed cocaine and crack cocaine; because the latter was inexpensive, selling for five dollars a bag, it was in high demand in poor African American areas. Mexican Americans refused to market crack cocaine, preferring "crank," a mixture of cocaine and methamphetamine. Ethnic identity was extended to drug consumption, with consumption of white heroin and crack by African Americans, and crank and black heroin by Mexican Americans.[45] The development of ethnic-specific drugs by gangs produced a market but contributed to the ongoing ethnic conflict by strengthening ethnic solidarity through the selling and consumption of particular drugs and thereby accentuating even further the public differentiation of the two groups.

Changes in macroeconomic conditions also influenced gang formation in fragmented neighborhoods by giving higher status to gangs that could produce more economic benefits for their members. The gangs formed status hierarchies between themselves and among their own membership. Further, gangs and gang leaders that were unable to produce the material benefits for their members at a level competitive with other gangs were relegated to the margins of the neighborhood's status hierarchy.

Some marginalized groups were not gangs but bands of youth wanting to form a gang. Most of these bands were just starting off, encouraged by the rapidly expanding market in drug sales and gang formation during the late 1980s and early 1990s. Forming an organized gang was difficult during this period because the intense competition between groups often inhibited efforts to recruit enough members and create a formal infrastructure. Increased competition produced more violence, although it did not result in social disorder because the situation was stabilized by the existing formalized gangs. Gangs that were present for a number of years were large and powerful enough to maintain their existence and social position in the neighborhood while the fledgling gangs fought to merely exist. The larger gangs were above the fray, so beneath the surface they provided stability to what appeared to be a chaotically disorganized situation.

Gangs in fragmented neighborhoods competed over social status in the neighborhood rather than over the use of public space for business ventures or the establishment of "safe zones" for members of their ethnic group. Thus members committed violent acts, sometimes deadly, to achieve status.[46] Many of these violent encounters seemed senseless and could have been perceived as "stupid," but they followed a logical understanding that material wealth, used in the general society to establish social standing, could not be used for that purpose among the poor. Therefore, social status was worth fighting over as the only positive resource that youth could reasonably hope to gain. The comments of Bouncer, a seventeen-year-old member of the Falcons gang in Brooklyn's Eagleton neighborhood, represent this attitude:

> People who want to put us [the Falcons] down are going to get fucked up [physically hurt] by me and the rest of us. They [those critical of the Falcons] wish they had the respect we got, but they ain't; so they got to be dealt with, you know what I mean? If you ain't got a good reputation [status] you got shit! People think you ain't nothing [low status]. You know?[47]

In fragmented neighborhoods, the competition that increased violence over status originated from the macroeconomic changes that prevented poor individuals from pursuing economic interests in the traditional production sector.[48] The lack of manufacturing work influenced the involvement of youth in gangs and other organizations operating in an illicit underground economy that was itself undergoing major change.[49] As the underground economy attracted more people, resulting in intense competition, many organizations were unable to secure benefits for their members. To compensate for unsuccessful ventures, many organizations established a status system based on the desirability of the geographic location where they congregated and strengthened or weakened their status through territorial fighting. The impact on noncombatant residents resulted in their changing individual patterns of public movement by avoiding particular streets during certain times and finding new routes.[50] This situation increased their social anxiety until a new routine could be reestablished, which usually occurred in a few weeks, and the general social order was not compromised.

Guns, Gangs, and Neighborhoods

While guns increased the power of gang members and gang organizations, they caused significant changes within the broader population of the five neighborhoods. In contested neighborhoods, gun violence caused increased segregation among the resident ethnic groups. The fear of injury or death from gunfire between feuding gang members caused increased prejudice toward people (both gang and nongang members) who were not of one's own ethnic group.[51] Residents commonly complained that members of a competing group were "simply violence prone." Thus neighborhoods saw, instead of increased social integration, a general decline in social contact among members of competing ethnic groups outside some public spaces, economic enterprises, and neighborhood institutions.

One benefit of handguns was that they could cause serious injury or death but be easily concealed. Since guns were used not only for defensive purposes but to extract benefits from people in contested neighborhoods, two negative consequences resulted. The first was an increase in interethnic robbery because guns provided the means to coerce money from people of other ethnic groups. In turn, increased interethnic violence produced more anxiety among residents, elevating the general fear level within the neighborhood and inhibiting the cooperation necessary to initiate and sustain community development projects. Thus, although the residents in contested neighborhoods were no less impoverished than those in fragmented ones, these neighborhoods were more run down because the community involvement needed to improve physical conditions could not be generated among groups that were so fearful and resentful of each other.[52] Nonetheless, it would be inaccurate to think of these neighborhoods as unorganized in this situation: their organized elements just could not work with each other at that moment.

Gun ownership in the gangs of fragmented neighborhoods increased social distance between residents who operated under security-maximizing and excitement-maximizing value orientations. As gangs used more guns for business, more casualties occurred, some involving nongang members, a result that particularly upset most adult residents. A significant number of the adults operating under the security-maximizing value orientation thought that joining a gang was irresponsible, as was the use of guns. Since many youth of their neighborhoods were either in gangs or associated with them, residents found it difficult to identify who was involved in each shooting. They were, however, able to determine with much certainty who among the general population operated under the excitement-maximizing versus the security-maximizing value orientation. Residents who held a security-maximizing value orientation blamed neighborhood violence on the parents and youth who held an excitement-maximizing orientation. Thus, during periods of increased gun violence, security-maximizing residents were so angry that they were more resistant to helping excitement-maximizing residents financially and socially even if they were related. Under normal conditions, security-maximizing people were reluctant to provide unlimited assistance to excitement-maximizing individuals, but they would provide some aid. However, during times of increased violence reluctance was replaced by aggressive resistance. Thus such periods resulted in decreased tolerance of individuals with different values, strained social interaction, and increased residents' anxiety in conducting their daily routines.

Changes in Law Enforcement Strategy

As previously discussed, law enforcement establishments have implemented important changes in recent years. During this research period a concerted effort was made to penalize those who violated laws, especially in cases of drug activity and violent crime. Efforts were made to more tenaciously apprehend suspects, streamline their trials, incarcerate them for longer periods, and more efficiently revoke parole if they were delinquent. These changes significantly aided the police in what they labeled "gang-related crimes."[53] Prosecuting attorneys aggressively fought cases that involved gangs and, in Los Angeles, used STEP to increase the sentences of individuals found guilty of committing crimes for the benefit of a gang. In addition, if previous gang members associated with gangs while on parole, an effort was made to revoke their parole and send them back to prison. This policy incarcerated larger numbers of each neighborhood's active gang member population for longer periods but produced some unintended consequences that affected the various neighborhoods.

Rather than destroying gangs, the increased incarceration of young men in fragmented neighborhoods strengthened them. Before the new policy, prison gangs, which were basically organized crime groups, had continually tried to solicit the street gangs to join their organizations. The street gangs consistently resisted for a number of reasons, the most prevalent of which was that the rank-and-file street gang members did not want to be controlled by people from other neighborhoods. In an act of adolescent rebellion, they also did not want older men to take over their organizations. This situation was stable for the first two years of the study because most gang members were not arrested, tried as adults, or sent to adult prisons. Rather, they were usually sent to youth authority holding facilities, and even when they were sent to an adult prison they were usually given parole that was rarely revoked. With the implementation of the new policy, however, youth who committed violent crimes were sometimes sent to adult prison, and their parole was revoked if they continued to hang around gang members. Young gang members in prison who associated with and promised association with organized crime syndicates in prison in exchange for protection had to break their promise of association when they were released if they were to maintain their parole or resist having their group be controlled by the prison gang. However, with the state's new effort to impose more prison sentences for gang crimes, the chances of recidivism for active gang members increased. This led them to abandon the strategy of breaking their association with prison gangs after their release because they knew that the next time they went to prison they would not be protected by the prison gangs from the institution's social predators. Therefore, the new policy succeeded in securing continued cooperation with the prison gangs after release, and that in turn served to strengthen the larger organized crime syndicates. These changes made gangs even more attractive to many youth from poor neighborhoods because they now saw the possibility of making significantly more money from gang involvement and knew that if they were caught for some illegality the prison gangs would provide them (although not necessarily their families) with a safety net while they were in prison.

In contested neighborhoods, gang members who competed on the streets found themselves in prison with gang members from both their gang and their rivals', and the conflict that occurred between gang members on the street was reproduced in prison. Further, gang members from these neighborhoods left prison with a greater hatred for members of rival gangs and in general members of those gangs' ethnic groups. During such times, conflict between gangs became more intense, causing all residents to feel a greater sense of danger. Conversations in the hair shops and grocery stores focused on how unsafe everyone felt because of the increased conflict between the gangs. Yet rather than viewing the gangs as the cause of the conflict, people tended to blame the other ethnic groups and the gangs with which they were associated, thereby fueling the general ethnic competition and conflict in the neighborhood. The comments of Antonio, a thirty-six-year-old Puerto Rican living in the Bronx's Monument neighborhood, are representative:

> Oh yeah, the gangs been at it the last few nights. I really can't stand them Dominicans. Ever since they started to live in the area there's been more shootings and stabbings. Everywhere them people live this happens. [The others in the conversation all nod in agreement.][54]

Changes in law enforcement policy produced two additional unintended outcomes. The incarceration of more gang members decreased each neighborhood's gang membership, so vacancies were filled by preteens who otherwise would not have been able to join the main gangs until they were older. Thus gangs recruited younger members, a group that authorities particularly attempted to dissuade from gang involvement.

Another unintended outcome of the policy was increased rates of pregnancy among young girls from the neighborhoods. Because young gang members were spending more time in prison, young girls felt that they had to engage in sexual relations with boys or young men whom they loved sooner rather than later. Thus the girls, their friends, and some of their family members justified early sexual activity. Further, young girls had more incentive to avoid birth control because a baby fathered by their men enabled them to hold onto their men while they served their time. The comments of Lisa, a sixteen-year-old Dominican immigrant residing in Brooklyn's Eagleton neighborhood, are representative. She was five months' pregnant with her boyfriend's baby:

> No, I hope he [her boyfriend] gets to see the baby before he gets sentenced. My mother has been giving me all kinds of shit about having this baby while he is in prison for so long, and she is so mad at him for getting me pregnant. But I told her that it was me who wanted to get pregnant, and I told Jorge [her boyfriend] that I wanted him to give me a baby so that he knew that he had something waiting for him when he got out.[55]

Tawana, a fifteen-year-old African American lifetime resident of L.A.'s Richardson neighborhood, expressed similar sentiments:

> All the guys in this neighborhood is goin' to jail so fast there ain't going to be any of 'em left [laughter]. I been dating Leon for three months, and he is more serious than I thought. . . . I know he's older than me, but hey, he is so cute! [more laughter] He wants me to have his baby, but says that's not a good idea now 'cause he is going to be going to jail for the drug business that the Trail Street [gang] been running. . . . Don't be laughing now! The police came up to us yesterday when we was out getting an ice cream and said he was going down real soon. He laughed, but told me that they was probably right. . . . He didn't tell me to, but I going to have his baby now, 'cause who knows, with the police and all, when we'll get to live together.[56]

Gangs could become economic enterprises just like any other institution in poor neighborhoods. This happened when a gang decided to develop into an organized crime syndicate, as in the case of the St. James Place gang in Brooklyn's Eagleton neighborhood, which in the last three years of the study became so involved in the underground economy that their business extended far beyond the neighborhood and had to involve people from other neighborhoods. As the focus of the organization changed exclusively, or nearly so, to making money, it began to develop into an organized crime syndicate. In situations like this the organization remained in the neighborhood, but it ceased to think of itself as being *of* the neighborhood. It did physically stay in the neighborhood and rarely terrorized residents, but it remained there as a means to protect itself from competitors and made little effort to help residents. Like other enterprises, it did not functionally contribute to the neighborhood's social order or structure as it had when it was a gang.

AN INSTRUMENT OF PRESERVATION

In addition to acting as agents of social change, gangs were very important to each neighborhood's ability to resist change and maintain their structure and culture. As preservation agents, gangs generally affected both fragmented and contested neighborhoods in various ways. The role of the gang as a preservation agent is the least understood, yet it is vital for understanding the social dynamics operative in America's poor neighborhoods.

The Gang as a Preservation Agent in Poor Neighborhoods

Gangs acted as agents of preservation in three broad ways. First, they responded to neighborhood residents' solicitations to represent their interests in various socioeconomic and political domains. One of these domains was housing conditions. It is no secret that housing in poor neighborhoods is inadequate in size, structural integrity, and maintenance. At times already bad conditions continued to deteriorate, making life for the residents of the five neighborhoods studied barely tolerable. During these times residents complained to their managers, who passed on their concerns to the various landlords. When landlords refused to respond, or responded only cosmetically, residents became frustrated and on some occasions asked the gang for help. Residents often had problems with private landlords as well as the public housing authority. One gang response was to try to destroy the landlords' properties without inconveniencing the residents. Sometimes they wrote graffiti on the outside and inside walls, burned a vacant apartment, or broke windows. Such destruction of property had the greatest impact on the public housing authority, whose managers had to account for the appearance of the premises as well as manage their budgets.[57] Gangs also personally threatened landlords. This tactic had a larger impact on owners/managers in the private housing sector, since most were financially protected with insurance from destruction of property.

Residents also asked gangs to manage disputes with local business establishments. Whether the dispute involved an individual, a group of individuals from the neighborhood, or another local business, residents solicited the gang to threaten the business's owner or manager to achieve an equitable settlement. Such threats were usually successful because even if they were reported to the police, the police could not provide the amount of protection necessary to prevent retribution.

Gangs were asked to settle disputes between residents and various businesses in the illegal underground economy. This occurred in the Bronx's Monument neighborhood when a local numbers joint had collectors physically bully residents who were delinquent in their payments. These residents were attacked with so much force that their injuries kept them from work, so they requested the Toppers gang to intervene. The gang then asked the owners of the numbers establishment to allow residents to pay off their debts over time. When the owners refused, replying that harassment would continue if total payment was not received, the gang ambushed and physically assaulted the two collectors when they next came to collect.[58] They then told them to tell the owner that if his policy continued they would escalate retaliation and put him out of business. This resulted in a compromise such that residents were able to place bets without fear of physical harassment for late payments.[59]

Further, residents asked gangs to contact community leaders on their behalf when they felt that leaders were out of touch with the needs or desires of their constituents. In some cases the leaders were not aware of a new position emerging from the residents; at other times the leaders prioritized their own interests and desires over those of the residents' lives. In either situation, the gangs were called upon when the residents' other efforts to gain the leaders' attention were unsuccessful. Such a situation occurred in L.A.'s Richardson neighborhood when African American residents systematically harassed a number of the Mexican residents. The Mexican residents discussed their constant state of fear at the hair shops and grocery stores. They agreed that more police were needed for protection, but when they asked the leader from the area to request an increased police presence, he simply replied that everything that could be done to rectify the situation was being done. The leader was reluctant to push for more police intervention because he was a member of the greater Los Angeles Democratic Party and sought more power. Since African Americans assumed powerful positions within the party, he was afraid that a request for greater police protection for his Mexican constituents would be seen as anti–African American and that he would be "blackballed" within the party as a result.[60] The residents grew more fearful and desperate, since some of their children were being robbed on their way to school, so they asked the local Mexican East Birdville gang to ask the local leader to take action. The gang contacted the local leader and threatened to harm him and his family if something was not done. Fearful of injury and of losing a significant portion of his voting bloc if he requested a police crackdown on the East Birdville gang, the leader decided that the best course of action was to immediately call the police chief and request additional officers in the area. The police chief responded by promptly assigning more officers to the neighborhood. The gang's action resulted in decreased harassment, which significantly improved the lives of the Mexican American residents.

Land developers often view poor areas either as zones to be avoided or as locales of opportunity. Developers who had the skill to lure businesses to invest in the area by convincing them that the area was stable enough to produce the necessary customers for significant profits over time held the latter of these two views.[61] Social conditions were particularly important criteria for local investment, so two strategies were used by the private and public sectors to produce "security." First, residents had to be relocated from the direct area of redevelopment. Whether redevelopment was financed primarily by private investors or the public sector, the government was involved in the removal of build-ings and people.[62] Within the public sector the local government would condemn property that was inhabited, and sometimes owned, by the res-idents. The government was legally obligated to offer only what was determined to be a "fair value" to landowners, not the land's potential value. Renters were given the option to move either to public housing when available or to another low-income neighborhood.[63]

The gangs played an important role in helping neighborhood residents resist the threat of redevelopment and relocation. Although most resi-dents knew their neighborhood was run down, they valued it as "their community." During my research, I recorded nine occasions on which gangs, using several tactics, defended the neighborhood against potential redevelopment and relocation when asked for assistance by the residents. When a few businesses were first encouraged to start a redevelopment project through tax incentives offered by the local government, gangs developed a deterrent strategy of vandalizing new businesses, thus rais-ing costs and lowering profits. If this strategy was unsuccessful, they used various forms of violence such as shootings to deter people from patron-izing the business. When the city government announced the possible removal of some residents to make room for new business construction, the gangs attempted to raise the area's official crime rate so that busi-nesses seeking to invest large amounts of capital for new ventures in the area would be discouraged from doing so. They started by vandalizing cars to raise the general crime rate and then moved on to firing shots in the area and calling the police or having other residents call the police so that the violent crime rate would be raised as well.

In each of the five neighborhoods studied, the gangs succeeded in all nine of their efforts to deter development. If the government had been able to remove the area's entire population, the gangs would not have succeeded. However, because each neighborhood had public housing that could not be removed easily, even by law, government officials could not remove all the residents, and the gangs that had become a part of the neighborhood's social life were able to stay and resist.[64]

Thus the gangs maintained the communities' social conditions, and the residents were grateful even though the neighborhoods remained poor. This was because the residents valued the norms, values, and social life of their neighborhood much more than the material resources, serv-ices, and convenience that economic development would have pro-vided.[65] Such development would have destroyed a community with a familiar and functional social system and made the residents apprehen-

sive about an unpredictable future.[66] If forced to leave, they would face
the uncertainty and fear associated with moving to a new neighborhood
with a new social system. The comments of Evan, a twenty-four-year-
old Jamaican American resident of Brooklyn's Eagleton neighborhood,
reflect this sentiment:

> Yeah, I hear they [the city and a Manhattan developer] want to tear down
> all them buildings on Monroe Street [pseudonym] to build shopping and
> some expensive apartments. There goes the neighborhood [everyone
> laughs]. . . . No, seriously, I can't move to another part of Brooklyn no
> way. Who knows how they live there. I'd rather go to jail. [Everyone
> laughs, but shakes their head in agreement.][67]

Olivia, a twenty-nine-year-old Mexican American resident of L.A.'s El
Rey neighborhood, expressed the same attitude:

> Okay, say that I'm right and they force us to go live somewhere else. . . .
> Yeah, I'm nervous about leaving because I like this neighborhood even if
> it's not great, and I feel comfortable here. [Everyone nods in agreement.][68]

Poor communities in large cities have traditionally developed an
underground economy that serves the middle and upper classes while
providing employment for the residents of these areas. Gangs preserved
this economy by producing and distributing illegal products and services. They also played an important role in providing a pool of employment for various illegal enterprises.[69] Interestingly, the gangs were a vital
element in building human capital for many illegal enterprises like drug
syndicates by training individuals in production and sales. Further, by
increasing each member's social network, they gave them the means to
build the social capital necessary for advancement in this economy.[70]
Thus, by supporting the traditional economy of poor areas, the gangs
helped preserve the existing social order.

Finally, the gangs created a popular youth culture of rap and hip-hop
music and a style of dress that first influenced other members of their
community and then spread throughout U.S. society and around the
world. Historical examples of this influence in dress include zoot suits,
"satin and leather club jackets," Pendleton shirts and khakis, sleeveless
jean jackets with gang names, stocking cap beanies, and baseball caps
of certain colors. All of these styles, first identified with gangs, were
absorbed by the larger youth population. Other symbols of gang culture
like writing styles, art forms, and language that gang members developed to communicate with each other have also spread to other sectors
of the general society. In fact, police manuals include gang terms so that

police can identify gang members and understand their forms of communication.[71] This has carried over to gang graffiti seen on the buildings and signs throughout low-income areas, as well as buses and subway trains. A leader of a youth gang outreach organization even concluded that people who did not understand gang graffiti were at risk of serious injury when in low-income areas.[72] Although this may be an exaggeration, gang graffiti and the "tagger" art form that followed are significant cultural markers within the more general youth culture of the United States and the world.[73]

Tattoo forms specific to gangs developed from their lack of materials due to impoverished conditions and managed to become an important cultural expression. Gang tattoos were generally blue or black, due to lack of other colored ink, and either spelled out the gang's name, showed its specific symbol, or featured various caricatures of women. Tattoo themes were often elaborated upon when a gang member was imprisoned and joined a prison gang. For instance, some added tears to an existing tattoo of a woman's eye for every year they were imprisoned, every time they returned to prison, or every time they killed someone. Thus gang members wore tattoos both as an expression of art and as an identification of activities of honor, much like military men's ribbons indicating their engagements.[74]

The gangs' role in the development and maintenance of a distinct cultural form within poor neighborhoods cannot be overestimated.[75] The gangs in the present study were one of the institutions that significantly contributed to the youth culture of these neighborhoods, affecting both the youth and adult residents. Some residents operating within the security-maximizing value orientation viewed gangs as one of the problems of their neighborhood, but everyone took pride in the gangs' development of a popular culture that had significantly influenced the youth culture of the larger society. Calvin, a forty-one-year-old African American resident of the Bronx's Elmway neighborhood and doorman of a Manhattan apartment building, expressed this view:

> I was watchin' this television show last night and it had somethin' on gangs in the city. There was people on the show, mostly white people, talkin' all kinds of shit. [everyone laughs] They were sayin' things like the gangs is parasites of society, they just take and don't give anything to society and stuff like that. I'm like sitting there sayin', "You fools! While you be talkin' this shit, you kids be out there buyin' and listenin' to gangsta rap and wearin' clothes just like the gang kids do." [Everyone agrees] What do these fools mean about not givin' society nothin', the kids from neighborhoods like ours is creatin' culture for society! [Everyone laughs and agrees.][76]

Teresa, a thirty-seven-year-old Mexican American mother of two boys from the El Rey neighborhood of Los Angeles, held the same view:

> I never want my kids associated with gangs, but they still wear clothes like the *cholos* [gang members] do. I don't like it, but this is the fad now. I wish it weren't like this, but the gangs have a big influence on all youth today whether they are in a gang or not. You have to hand it to them [gang guys], they're creating new styles all the time.[77]

Gangs as Preservers in Particular Types of Neighborhoods

Gangs' preservation activities differed somewhat in fragmented versus contested neighborhoods. In fragmented neighborhoods gangs acted to preserve the community norms associated with socioeconomic group values and gender stratification. A good number of gang members and the girls associated with them seemed to operate within the excitement-maximizing value orientation. Residents who held a security-maximizing value orientation viewed these individuals as lacking in "moral strength," which to them meant inferiority, and conferred on women associated with gangs the added stigma of moral disdain for what they viewed as these women's promiscuity. Ironically, even gang members stigmatized the women with whom they associated, prejudicially viewing them more as sexual objects than as women they would one day marry. The comments of Estevan, an eighteen-year-old Mexican American resident of L.A.'s El Rey neighborhood who operated within the security-maximizing value orientation and had never been a gang member, represent these perceptions. He said about a girl who lived in his housing project building:

> Ay, no way! I ain't havin' nothin' to do with her. She hangs with the CV [Cactus Vatos gang]. What would I want to go around with her for, she's gotta be a slut hangin' with them guys. . . . I don't care how fine she is, there ain't no way in this life I'm goin' to be with someone like that![78]

The remarks of Cat-Dog, a seventeen-year-old Puerto Rican gang member from the Bronx's Elmway neighborhood to two fellow members, Click and Donut, at the Playa Barbershop, also reflect this view:

> I ain't trying to hit on Sosy! Who would want to do that? She's just pussy for anyone who gives her money and attention. She been hanging around the clubhouse [gang's official place] too long, ain't nobody who's going to take her home to mama! [There is laughter] If you want to take someone home to mama, that would be Lena, 'cause she stays home with her parents. . . . I know she's taken by Pato [an officer of the gang], but she'd be the one to take home, not Sosy.[79]

Thus gangs in "fragmented neighborhoods" preserved the existing internal social strata divisions of the two dominant value orientations, as well as those associated with the existing gender stratification system. For this reason, in fragmented neighborhoods one often found gangs with multiethnic memberships.

In contested neighborhoods, gangs played an important role in maintaining the existing ethnic separation. The gangs in these neighborhoods were nearly always ethnically homogeneous and assumed a well-defined ethnic identity. The constant conflict between different ethnic gangs in contested neighborhoods, some of which was lethal, reinforced the animosity their compatriots felt toward the other group(s). Group conflict not only separated people by renewing and strengthening animosity but also strengthened group solidarity.[80] Hence the gangs' continual conflict was an act of preservation because it significantly contributed to the existing social order of these neighborhoods that all the ethnic groups accepted as "normal."

SOME CLOSING REMARKS

Gangs have been portrayed in sociological literature as a symbol of social disorder in poor neighborhoods. As such, their emergence is seen as a change for the worse and their absence as a reprieve from social turmoil. However, this portrayal misunderstands both the nature of gangs and the constitution of a poor neighborhood's social order. Gangs can contribute to a decline in the neighborhood's social structure and its concomitant social order, but their mere presence is not the deciding factor. Rather, their influence on a neighborhood depends on whether they assume the social role of an institution or an enterprise.

Gangs that took on the character of a neighborhood institution accomplished two important feats. They performed important functional roles that supported the residents and other institutions of the neighborhood, and they actively preserved the basic social order of the neighborhood and the norms governing its system of social interaction.

Thus, while residents held a complex view of gangs, they qualitatively condoned their existence. In interviews by various outsiders regarding their views of gangs, they inevitably answered with what they believed the outside community wanted to hear and, to avoid stigmatization and marginalization, most often disavowed any tolerance of gangs. However, in conversations among themselves the residents continually offered qualified support for the gangs of their area. Their support sprang from the gangs' contributions in protecting them and the empathy they felt for the social plight of the next generation, some of whom were their own children, or the children of relatives and friends.

Some gangs that wanted to become syndicates assumed the character of an economic enterprise rather than that of an institution. These gangs did not necessarily prey on the residents of their neighborhood, but like other enterprises they were focused on their own needs and not on the fundamental interests of the community. They pursued their own interests and were involved in activities that overtly hurt some residents. The result was reduced solidarity, increased distrust, and increased self-isolating behavior among the residents that undermined the integrity of the neighborhoods' social structure.[81] Under such conditions other institutions had to make the necessary adjustments to reconstitute the social structure. However, these changes did not create social disorder, as argued by many urban sociologists. Residents often responded to gangs viewed as a threat by cooperating with the police or other law enforcement authorities to force the gangs to alter their behavior and be more cognizant and sensitive to their needs. These actions, through the police and the courts, wounded the gang's organizational integrity. Sometimes the wound was fatal: the gang was eradicated, and a new gang was born that saw the faults of its predecessors and assumed a role the community saw as positive. At other times the wound was serious but the gang recovered and as part of its healing process involved its members in functionally supporting the community. Finally, the gang's role in creating employment opportunities for the neighborhood's youth gave it a structured routine that allowed participants and nonparticipants alike to predict each other's behavior. This structure of predictive behavior played an important part in creating and maintaining the community's social order.

CHAPTER 10

Whither the Neighborhood High School?

Contending Roles and Functions

Now, what I want is Facts. Teach these boys and girls nothing but Facts. Facts alone are wanted in life. Plant nothing else, and root out everything else. You can only form the minds of reasoning animals upon Facts: nothing else will ever be of any service to them.

Charles Dickens, *Hard Times* (1854)

American society has long believed that for every individual the institution of school-based learning is the key to economic success. In this regard, most U.S. citizens view school as a place where their hopes for the future lie, and they expect, and in some cases demand, it to be the engine of their desired social mobility. It has become accepted that this single institution is essential for socioeconomic advancement.[1]

In a controversial book about inequality in American urban society, Edward Banfield argued more than thirty years ago that American education is generally ineffective in producing socioeconomic mobility for the urban poor, especially for the urban African American poor. Banfield rejected the idea that racism was a factor in school inequality and suggested instead that the culture of the lower class was the primary agent: schools dominated by lower-class pupils, regardless of race, ended up being run in response to the way pupils and their families acted. The result, in his view, was an operating condition that was ineffective in building the skills pupils needed to better their economic opportunities. Banfield labeled it "schooling": unlike the operating condition he called "education," which made the school a place where necessary skills were learned for success in the labor market and in society, "schooling" made the school a mere holding place for its students that offered them no opportunity to improve their chances for socioeconomic advancement.[2] Although research on poor schools rarely mentions Banfield or his argument, his distinction between schools as places for learning versus schools as mere holding places is still frequently invoked.[3] Researchers on the school's role in reproducing inequality reject Banfield's contention that the inadequacies of lower-class students make the school ineffective, pointing instead to the state's unwillingness to support its own institution at the level required for greater success.[4] However, proponents of both positions agree that many schools in poor neighborhoods have merely become holding places for the disadvantaged rather than centers of learning, even though they are not sure how it has worked out that way.

Research on how schools serve the poor has often claimed that schools give impoverished youth the basic skills necessary for acquiring further skills (human capital) that will enable them to become successful occupationally and thus are their greatest hope for achieving economic mobility. It has also contended, however, that schools reproduce the social inequalities present in the larger society—whether because market requirements associated with a capitalist economy have necessitated the development of an internal structure in schools to support that economy's needs[5] or because of a divergence between what the school expects and the inherent skills, ambitions, and behavior of underprivileged youth.[6] Yet no detailed evidence shows that all of the independent school districts in the United States have the intention, or the ability, to construct institutions to support the existing needs of the economy at the expense of the lower classes. Further, no consistent evidence supports the idea that impoverished youth resist the school's efforts on the basis of a rational assessment and determination that they have a low probability for economic mobility. Nonetheless, there is evidence that some youth from lower-class backgrounds support a counterculture that is at odds with the school system and thus resist what the school offers.[7] This chapter addresses the role of the high schools in the lives of the poor in the present study, portraying the high school as a site of struggle between, on the one hand, school authorities and some students who want the school to further the goals of the state by providing the education and skills for obtaining gainful employment and economic mobility and, on the other, students (usually the majority) and local residents who want the school to be an institution that promotes local values supporting the neighborhood's subculture. In the neighborhoods studied, those who wanted the school to be a neighborhood institution were not so much resisting the school as a state institution as affirming a subculture (in this case the "subculture of scarcity" outlined in chapter 1) that they valued for the lifestyles it shaped and supported.[8]

A number of studies on education in low-income areas describe students' resistance toward school authorities and their established codes and curricular activities. There is an important difference between the concept of "resistance" or "rejection" used in other studies of low-income students and the concept of "affirmation" used in this study. "Resistance" or "rejection" has been used to describe students' conscious effort to rebuff the initiatives of school officials as illegitimate, whereas I use "affirmation" to describe the proactive engagement by many students of the present study in activities consistent with the cultural beliefs, customs, and actions of the "subculture of scarcity" that they valued.[9] Thus, when a teacher tries to gain students' attention and the students continue to talk about their immediate lives and subculture, they are not resisting the school and teacher's efforts; their minds are simply focused on local cultural issues rather than on what is being taught. However, if a teacher aggressively interrupts their actions and forces them to pay attention, the students do resist, not because of the teacher's desire to teach, but most often because of the intrusion or the manner of intrusion. Further, their resistance is temporary until they are able to reestablish the preferred behavior related to the values of the local culture.

Since some of the schools studied were in contested neighborhoods, one might ask whether students there were affirming their specific ethnic cultures or the culture common to the neighborhood. Although ethnic conflict existed in the contested neighborhoods, the cultures present were all lower-class variants of each ethnic group. Further, because the neighborhood residents were constantly confronted with scarcity, all the groups in these neighborhoods had more in common with each other than with the middle and upper classes of their own ethnic groups who lived in other neighborhoods. The shared experience of adaptation to constant material scarcity bound all the ethnic groups to the local subculture. Thus, as in fragmented neighborhoods, students of contested neighborhoods affirmed their shared local subculture of scarcity, albeit with some modest ethnic competition and conflict.[10]

Thus, in the schools of this study, a struggle was taking place between two sets of interests for the hearts and minds of the students. Which set of interests prevailed depended upon whether the state authorities in the high school could make the school a place of formal education and learning or whether students and other residents could make it a place of local knowledge and custom.

THE HIGH SCHOOL AS A STATE INSTITUTION

The school is one of the most important institutions within American society. Historically, it has been instrumental in relieving children and parents from the burdens of the industrial labor market (forced child labor); it has contributed to an artificial regulation of wages by removing children from the supply of labor; it has provided the nation with a constant source of human capital that could be utilized to maintain economic growth; and it has aided in the socialization of the nation's next generation. In the present study, the state had three objectives for all five schools that structured their official, daily activities and were implemented by the faculty and staff through the directives of the district superintendent, principal, or department head of the school. (See table 9 for a list of the five schools studied.)

The first of these objectives was the teaching of literacy and other skills needed for economic improvement. This was accomplished primarily through a curriculum of reading, writing, and abstract thinking (math and analysis). Many students were deficient in a number of these areas, so the school administration was obligated to bring them up to standards determined by policy makers. The importance of this goal rested on the state's understood obligation to give all individuals the ability to pursue their interests in the labor market without disadvantage.

In each school, the curriculum was supposed to ensure that the students had the same institutional experience as those in all the other schools of the district. Many of the students' daily routines were dictated by the state's goal of achieving literacy or competency in the substantive areas of reading, writing, and analysis (math and problem solving). Thus students' time was entirely regulated by mandatory schedules that matched, at least in theory if not in content, the type of instruction necessary for successful completion of the competency requirements set by the legislature. Of course, for various reasons, the five schools did not always meet these requirements, yet all the students had a mandatory schedule of classes that dictated at least seven hours of their daily activities.

The most important function of the education system in poor neighborhoods is in theory the development of individuals' skills to improve occupational opportunities.[11] Although the five schools tried mainly to improve literacy and academic competence, they also offered classes in certain manual skills such as carpentry (wood shop), printing (print shop), drafting (design shop), and auto mechanics (auto shop).[12] In all of the five schools, the state's commitment to building human capital in

TABLE 9. NEIGHBORHOOD HIGH SCHOOLS

Bronx
    Elmway
        Lenape High School
    Monument
        Van Twiller High School
Brooklyn
    Eagleton
        Knickerbocker
Los Angeles
    El Rey
        James K. Polk High School
    Richardson
        Chester Himes High School

NOTE: All names are pseudonyms.

these ways was limited: the classes were elective and did not constitute a full curriculum, so students were unable to specialize in manual skills, at least through school. Nonetheless, these courses symbolically acknowledged the state's effort in aiding local youth toward vocations.

Although the word *track* was not used in any of the high schools, each school had at least two tiers of instruction: the first included students who scored at grade level or above on standardized tests used to assess student achievement, and the second included students who scored below grade level in one or more subjects. The first tier provided students with instruction that could make them eligible for college, while the second tier provided the instruction necessary to correct students' educational deficiencies. Every school viewed these tiers as a means to create opportunities for its students. However, all the schools lacked a plan to move students who had overcome academic deficiencies to the upper instructional tier. In addition, an individual's documented deficiencies in certain areas were often translated into, or treated as, a student's complete lack of capabilities.[13] Thus many students in the lower tiers could not obtain access to the upper tiers.[14]

The second objective of the schools was to teach students the norms and etiquette of adult American society. In all five schools the first goal of this objective was to teach English to immigrant children. Each school had an English as a Second Language (ESL) program to educate students in their native tongue for part of the day and in English for the rest of the day. Most of these ESL programs used a bilingual approach designed to transition children from competency in their native tongues to the dominant English language of U.S. society. ESL teachers and school administrators emphasized in formal meetings the need for every student to become competent in reading, writing, and speaking English.[15] Thus ESL programs promoted academic competence and the socialization of students to U.S. culture.[16]

The schools' social studies curricula were designed to socialize students to the existing political system and its norms. Books about the nation's origins and history as well as the workings and components of the political system were systematically emphasized in each school. Every social studies teacher in each school also tried to describe and reinforce what it meant to be a U.S. citizen.[17] The theme that anyone could achieve wealth in America if he or she had the desire and worked hard (i.e., the American dream) was predominant in each school, as was the view that the political system was structured to help people attain their life goals.[18]

The state's third objective in the five schools was the students' socialization to the societal requirement of self-control. Like most Western, liberal-democratic societies, the United States relies on the self-control of its citizens to maintain the social order required for political-economic stability, so the school helps teach self-control through formal codes of conduct and penalties for their violation.[19] Such codes included dress codes for boys and girls prohibiting clothing that could be deemed sexually suggestive and rules about when a student could be out of class, weapons in the school, language, student-teacher interaction, possession of drugs, vandalism of school property, and much more. Penalties for code violation included detention, parental meetings, fines, suspension, transfer, and dismissal from school. The principal, assistant principal, counselors, and attendance officers were charged with monitoring school codes and enforcing penalties; in addition, school police, hall monitors/security personnel, and probation officers had the responsibility of monitoring students for criminal behavior and enforcing societal laws as well as school codes. The overall message of the monitoring of behavior was that if students did not control themselves, the state would restrict their freedom. Nearly every student understood the message that self-control had to come from an internal sense of acceptable and unacceptable behavior. The comments of Lyza, a sixteen-year-old African American student from Brooklyn's Eagleton neighborhood who attended Knickerbocker High School, are representative:

> Shit, I was just going to talk to this friend on the way back from the bathroom when this security guard asks for my pass and says that I am over the time limit for going to the bathroom. I look at him and say, "What do

mean, over the limit?!" and he says, "You got ten minutes and this shows you been gone eighteen. You know that [the principal] told everybody about this rule." Now, you know he took me to the counselor and I had detention for three days after school! I thought I could just hang for a while after the bathroom, but I ain't doing that shit anymore 'cause I don't want any of that detention shit! [Everyone nods in agreement.][20]

German, a fifteen-year-old Mexican who lived in L.A.'s El Rey neighborhood and attended James K. Polk High School, expressed a similar attitude:

> I got trouble with the law 'cause I took that metal shank [small metal object that has been made into a sharp weapon] to history and one of the teachers saw it stick through my pocket. I wasn't even in that bitch's class and she comes and asks if she can see what's in my pants pockets. I take it out, and that's when she calls security and they take me to the dean. He talks to me and then says he's got to turn this in to the school police. . . . Yeah, I knew the school had a law against carrying weapons, but that fucking *pocho* [cultural sellout] Andrés [another person in the school] has told people he's after me. I didn't think they would be checking after the door. The police took me to their station and booked me. I was kinda worried, but I got out after a few hours. . . . I got the picture now and I ain't fucking up no more![21]

So did Curtis, an eighteen-year-old African American resident of L.A.'s Richardson neighborhood who attended Chester Himes High School:

> Thomas is like acting out, and I tell him to stop that shit or they going to come down hard on you. He knows that too, but he wants to get all the attention and starts teasing a guy who starts a fight with him, and they get picked up by the security guards and police. The police check his record and call the probation guy in the school, who cashes in his parole [revokes it], and now he's back at CYA [California Youth Authority, the penal system for juveniles]. He is got to be retarded, man, because if you get out of line them school officials is gonna fuck you up [punish you]![22]

The American school was never conceived of as an academy of knowledge and learning, as in ancient Greece. Once education became a right of citizenship, the state assumed responsibility for educating society's youth, and the school became an arm of the state. From that point on, the state incrementally added new goals for its educational institution. Although the school is designed to introduce students to knowledge, it also plays a role in weaving the social fabric of society. In the poor areas of this study the existing social fabric was often coarse and unruly, so the role of weaving it into a unified pattern was difficult. Yet each of the five schools made a consistent effort to implement state goals.

THE HIGH SCHOOL
AS A NEIGHBORHOOD INSTITUTION

One of the most important factors in deciding to buy a house in a particular neighborhood is the quality of its local schools. Residents of middle-class neighborhoods determine the quality of a school by whether it is a safe environment for children to learn, whether it reinforces the values of the parents, and whether it provides the skills necessary to maximize professional opportunities for their children. Although poor families do not have this luxury, since they must find basic housing that they can pay for, in the five neighborhoods of this study parents consistently declared that they wanted their children to be given the values, skills, and knowledge that would allow them the opportunity to leave the neighborhood. However, most students operated within the norms that governed the social order of the neighborhood, a set of values, skills, dispositions, and knowledge that were at odds with those of the school. Thus the high school was a place of conflict and struggle.

The youth of these neighborhoods viewed the high school as a temporary, four-year situation before adult life began. Thus for them school was not a place for work but a place for fun. This view was most clearly acted out among students with an excitement-maximizing value orientation. The comments of Tobias, a fifteen-year-old Mexican American sophomore at James K. Polk High School in the El Rey neighborhood of Los Angeles, are representative:

> Fuck no, I ain't studying for that assignment tonight! I got to go to gets some *mota* [marijuana] with Salt and Pepper [two of his friends]. . . . What you getting all upset about an exam for? It's not like it means anything. . . . Don't get so focused on school shit, just kick back and have as much fun as you can now. You got plenty of time to work.[23]

A similar attitude was expressed by Myesha, a sixteen-year-old African American junior at Knickerbocker High School in Brooklyn's Eagleton neighborhood:

> I hate school. I just go because my mom says that she wants me to, but I really hate it except for meeting up with everyone and having a good time. . . . My mom is always telling me that I need school and should be studying, but the only thing that's good about school is getting together with Donnell and Jeter. They're crazy and I love having fun with them. . . . I don't want to work like the teachers want, 'cause I'll be working the rest of my life and I want to have fun now.[24]

Students with a security-maximizing value orientation also sought fun at school, even though they were less reckless than those with an excitement-maximizing value orientation because of their awareness that they had to avoid trouble if they wanted to secure the best job possible in the labor market. The response of Maria-Elena, a sixteen-year-old student at Van Twiller High School in the Bronx's Monument neighborhood, to a question from a friend about the future represents this view:

> I don't know what I'm going to do next year after graduation, but I'm really not going to think about it now, and you shouldn't either. Why you talking about it anyway!? There is too much going on now for you or me to bother with anything else. . . . Hey, no one got to be like Lucy [another girl in their circle of friends] to have fun. Each of my classes have crazy fun things going in them—you know, boys acting up, and you know, girls carrying on that drives the teacher nuts—I have fun just sitting there. . . . I just laugh a lot, but I don't do anything that will get me in trouble. That's the way I just enjoy everything and not worry.[25]

Daryl, a seventeen-year-old junior at Chester Himes High School in L.A.'s Richardson neighborhood, expresses a similar viewpoint:

> Did you see that fuckin' Tyrell in the hall today? He was just cutting up, man. I couldn't stop laughing, man, it was too much. The teachers came by and stopped him from swinging around on the banister and we all were laughing so much. That's why I like coming to this place, it's crazy every day. . . . No, I ain't doing nothing like that, or anything that's going get my mom to have to come to get me, 'cause if that happens I get it from her. . . . Plus, I don't want get a bad mark on my record, 'cause that won't help me get any recommendation from the counselors for jobs that I want.[26]

Of course, middle-class students also seek fun at school, but they combine this urge with both their parents' and their own desire to gain the skills necessary to attend college because college graduates obtain increased status within the larger society.[27] This is fundamentally different from what was found in the five poor neighborhoods of this study, where the students viewed their high school years as their last chance for leisure and fun before they would be stigmatized as "idle" adults who simply wanted to take advantage of the welfare system.[28] The comments of Lovelle, a sixteen-year-old African American at Van Twiller High School in the Bronx's Monument neighborhood, are representative:

> I plan to have fun while I at this fucking school. Shit, when we get out of this place we'll have to find a job, and if there ain't none and we don't get any, people won't think we should have fun. So I tell my mom I going to

party now before everybody talks about us being lazy when we ain't got a job. I think she understands, but she always says to keep studying anyway.[29]

Marta, a sixteen-year-old Mexican at James K. Polk High School in L.A.'s El Rey neighborhood, expressed the same attitude:

> Come on, Emma [one of her friends], let's go to the next two parties. . . . No, I don't think it's bad to go to these parties. We have to now 'cause when we get out we won't be able to have as much fun 'cause we'll be working or married and can't . . . and also if people see us having fun they'll think we're getting welfare or something like that. [Emma laughs and agrees.][30]

In the high schools of the present study, the value orientations that permeated the neighborhoods were brought into the school, and the more these values could influence the thoughts and behaviors of the students, faculty, and administration, the more the school reinforced the neighborhood's social structure.

The value orientations of the neighborhood coexisted with a well-developed status structure that students operated under and were familiar with. The dominant value orientations (maximizing security and maximizing excitement) were integrated into status hierarchies that were in competition with the value orientations the schools attempted to promote. These hierarchies prioritized physical attributes, physical activities, and the associations and social events in which these were highlighted (e.g., parties, gangs, sports teams) more than intellectual performance, intellectual activities, or civic engagement.[31]

For those operating under the security-maximizing value orientation, status was arranged along a continuum that prioritized behavior maximizing opportunities to secure a job after completing high school. Most of these individuals took vocational classes, stayed out of trouble, were generally conservative in their public behavior, and tended to associate with others holding the same values. They were intent on doing what was necessary in school to either leave the neighborhood or improve their opportunities to make life more economically, physically, and socially secure.

The general value systems provided a broad umbrella that organized the various specific status criteria into a meaningful hierarchy that everyone understood and in which everyone participated. Since status in poor neighborhoods was organized around physical markers, such as looks, strength, skin color, and gender, those who possessed more of the valued traits of these physical characteristics obtained higher status, while those with fewer had lower status. What is more, those students who were good scholars became socially invisible. This does not mean they were stigmatized; they simply were not significant players in the dominant social cliques.

Status in the high schools, as in other institutions of these poor neighborhoods, was also influenced by actions. A person could achieve higher status by helping others in the neighborhood, performing daring and sometimes illegal activities, serving time in prison, having a baby with a high-status person in the community, performing record feats in sports, and so on. For the school to become a functioning neighborhood institution, these actions had to first occur outside the school and then be brought into the school's social milieu so that it was consistent with the organization of the neighborhood.

Peer associations played an important role both in making the school a neighborhood institution and in conferring status on individuals. Adolescence is a time when peer associations have a significant impact on individuals, and many of these are formed or solidified for life in the school. Many researchers recognize the influence of peer groups in structuring interactions in communities.[32] Although some peer associations are consistent with the school's role as a state institution, such as academic clubs like Spanish or French clubs, debating club, and chess club, as well as clubs associated with the arts like theater, dance, and choir, others, such as gangs, cults, sports teams, and social cliques, are much more allied with the neighborhood's institutions.

Peer associations were not gender specific in the five neighborhoods. For instance, in the gangs, boys formed the core, but some young girls belonged to their auxiliaries or to a clique informally associated with a particular gang.[33] Sports teams included both boys and girls, though on separate teams. They too were important peer associations both for participants and for those who socially attached themselves to the participants, since poor children dream that sports can lead them to a more affluent life.[34] Members of high school sports teams, including girls, who excelled at sports received higher status from their peers and adults in the neighborhoods because they might receive a college sports scholarship and improve their life chances.[35]

During adolescence, peers are of critical importance, so the formation of cliques is an activity that attracts all adolescents. The status system that emerged from peer cliques in the poor neighborhoods of this study was complex and highly differentiated both within and between the existing cliques. In local terms, the status system identified cliques that were "in-groups" and those that were not. This assessment was subjective, and most groups assumed a position in the middle of the scale, while only a few were considered "elite" or "losers." Cliques in the middle of the scale were more subjective because individual rankings were vague, creating an effective hierarchy system since individual clique members could claim a status position that only they recognized. Thus cliques in the middle of the spectrum reduced conflict and sustained the entire system. In many ways this system mirrored the social and status structure of the larger American society, in which "losers" (usually the poor) and "winners" (the rich and famous) held positions recognized by everyone, while individual members of the larger middle group assumed their own desired social status.[36] This provided self-respect for the majority in the middle without the need to challenge the elite and thus the entire system's legitimacy.

As in most poor neighborhoods, some people in the present study were recent immigrants to America, and their personal immigrant experience had a significant influence on the status position assigned to them by others. Some aspects of immigrants' experiences and identities, such as their birthplaces and names, their surnames in particular, played a critical role in determining their assigned status position. In the schools of these poor neighborhoods, personal status often emerged from group status that was formed through the evaluation of the circumstances through which members of a particular group became residents of the neighborhood. Groups that had resided in the neighborhood the longest naturally awarded themselves the highest status ranking, and each succeeding group held a lesser status commensurate with the length of their residency. For example, in Chester Himes High School in L.A.'s Richardson neighborhood, African Americans were the dominant group because they had lived in the neighborhood before the Mexicans and Central Americans, who constituted the other dominant ethnic groups. When Mexican immigrants moved to the neighborhood and began attending the school, the African American students declared that they had the highest status and enforced it through their numbers and physical intimidation. Then, as the number of Mexican residents increased, Central Americans began attending the school, giving the Mexicans a middle status and Central Americans the lowest. Thus the students constructed a group-status hierarchy in the school that mirrored that of the neighborhood.[37]

Proper names were also a factor in establishing status. Parents generally chose names that gave their children both a familial identity and a public identity. First names established an individual's identity by indicating how long he or she had lived in the United States as well as the prevailing views on what constituted group identity during a specific period of time.[38] Among immigrant groups, the second generation chose names distinct from those of the first or immigrant generation. This established markers for identifying individuals from the various generations and assigning status.[39]

Surnames were an additionally important factor in establishing status in all the neighborhoods, particularly in New York, where many residents had Afro-Latino backgrounds. Dominicans and Puerto Ricans used their Spanish surnames to identify themselves as Latino rather than African American. Most Afro-Latinos did not want to be associated with African Americans both because they took pride in their Spanish-speaking and Latin cultural heritage and because they wanted to avoid the stigma associated with African American identity, of which they were well aware.[40] Alano, for instance, an eighteen-year-old Afro-Dominican resident of Brooklyn's Eagleton neighborhood, wanted his father, Ysidro, to consider himself "black" rather than Dominican. During a discussion, Alano became frustrated with his father:

Alano: You may think that you are Dominican, but the white society only sees you as a "nigger."

Ysidro: Black is my color, but I am not like African Americans. I am from the Dominican Republic and its culture, and African Americans are from theirs. They are different, and their history with whites is different, and that is why they don't get along with whites and get ahead here [the United States] in life.

Alano: You are just buying what whites think about them [African Americans].

Ysidro: No, I am not, but at my work they [African Americans] skip work all the time and always complain about the job, and I want people to know I am not them and I will work hard every day for my pay.

Alano: There are differences, but I don't think whites can tell the difference, and that's why I think it's better if we all stick together.

Ysidro: Then we all will be worse off.[41]

A name was a social identifier with important functions for the organization of these poor neighborhoods because it provided a marker of a family's social position there. Nonetheless, a name associated with an ethnic group or the generation of a particular family in the neighborhood established a status position for the individual even before any other criteria could be used. Schools helped reinforce this pattern because students' names (first and last) were a matter of official record and constantly referenced. To combat this, young people often used nick-names that originated from their interactions with family and friends as part of their neighborhood and social identity. These nicknames estab-lished social identity for the individual and the social meaning of the iden-tity for others. They were used in the school and supplemented or supplanted the "official" surname on the school roster that identified individuals outside their local society. Therefore, nicknames were part of the neighborhood and functioned as symbols competing with those ema-nating from the values and mores of the outside society.

Individuals of any society use nicknames as social identifiers, but there is a difference in what nicknames represent for poor youth in terms of personal and social identity because poor neighborhoods are not fully economically or socially integrated into the larger society. Identification with a neighborhood nickname symbolically undermines the state's institutional authority and replaces it with that of the neighborhood. Although nicknames were common throughout the poor neighborhoods studied, name choices were the most unusual and colorful among gang members, who referred to their nicknames as "monikers." "Dopey," "Sneezy," "Sleepy," and other such names that originated from the comics or fairy tales like *Snow White and the Seven Dwarfs*[42] were used as the individual's primary identifier. Thus students' use of nicknames in school strengthened the school as a neighborhood institution because these names were associated with the neighborhood as opposed to the wider society that the school officially represented.

Finally, language use in the school had communicative and political significance for administrators, teachers, students, and community lead-ers. One language problem was students' inability to understand instruc-tions or academic material, particularly when teachers spoke in a manner that was foreign to some or all of the students—for example, using English when students spoke only their native language or using a formal dialect of English when students spoke an imprecise, incorrect, or different dialect of English.

In such cases, teachers' language use is not a functional form of com-munication and instead reflects social inequality. Thus the form of lan-guage used in schools becomes an educational and political issue. An example is the controversy over Ebonics.[43] Many linguists view Ebonics as an imprecise, lower-class dialect (patois) of English rather than a for-mal language. However, many African American community leaders and educators and some white academics view it as a separate, legitimate lan-guage that should be used in teaching African American children.

In the past, the use of foreign languages in public schools was typically discouraged except for communicating with non-English-speaking parents. At the beginning of the twentieth century, so many ethnic groups populated urban schools that it would have been technically impossible and educationally ineffective to teach in any language other than English. Further, most immigrant parents wanted their children to speak English because they would then have more opportunities in the labor market. These factors facilitated the use of formal English throughout the school system.

After the 1920s, the immigrant population declined significantly enough that language ceased to be a major educational concern. In the 1980s and 1990s, however, as the African American and Latino populations increased and their socioeconomic position remained close to or at the bottom of the scale, more attention was directed to schools' effectiveness in developing students' human capital skills.[44] Because in the nineteenth and early twentieth centuries the educational system had been relatively successful in providing the skills necessary for immigrant children to obtain jobs with higher pay and status, the gradual decline in socioeconomic mobility over the later twentieth century was attributed to the workings of the educational system rather than the market.[45] One area of concern was the large number of immigrants who held fast to their mother tongue. Belief that competence in English was essential for economic mobility prompted many schools to implement both bilingual and "total immersion" approaches to educate immigrant children. The total immersion approach was an effort to reestablish the state's interest in creating an English-speaking population integrated into its social and political customs and capable of securing employment.[46] The controversy over whether public high school instruction should be English or in students' primary language of communication continues today. In the high schools that I studied, the more English was used in a particular school, the more the school operated as a state-oriented institution. Conversely, the more students used, formally and informally, their native language or English dialect, the more the school assumed the character of a neighborhood institution.

Cursing is common in every class, but the degree and context of its use differ by class. Among the students in the five neighborhoods, cursing was constantly used to express a wide range of emotions. In addition, students cursed in both formal and informal contexts. The schools were places where cursing was used despite its prohibition. Students cursed in defense against what they believed to be unfair accusations, or in confrontation with each other, as well as when interacting with teachers, school administrators, and the police. By cursing in the schools, students brought the neighborhood vernacular into the formal environment of the state, creating a confrontation with the state's ideology of appropriate language. As in the case of foreign language, improper grammar and cursing in school brought neighborhood mores into a state institution, and the more this occurred, the more the school became a neighborhood institution.[47]

So far no reference has been made to an institutional caretaker in the public school. This is because, as in public housing, schools that are neighborhood institutions generally have more than one caretaker. Caretakers are generally faculty members who have been at the school for a long time and have grown comfortable with the norms of the local subculture. Such individuals receive a great deal of praise and status from students and residents for their apparent willingness to help students navigate the system and to advocate for them with school officials. Their consistent efforts to support students and resist changes that would cause the school to operate in a more controlled, education-oriented way (i.e., less like a local institution emphasizing local knowledge and values) make them caretakers of the school as a neighborhood institution. Further, these faculty members are conscious of their caretaker role, and while school administrations may not appreciate their behavior, they are protected from dismissal by the teachers' union.

SCHOOLS AND NEIGHBORHOOD TYPE

To become a neighborhood institution, a school must reinforce the social structure of one of the two types of poor neighborhoods. In contested neighborhoods, the existing ethnic stratification must be reinforced in the school. In such a situation, each ethnic group recognizes specific locations as the domain of a different group. Students of different ethnic groups at L.A.'s Chester Himes High School gathered in separate areas of the schoolyard, occupied separate tables in the cafeteria during nutrition periods, and congregated in sections of the schoolyard exclusive to them. At Lenape High School in the Bronx's Elmway neighborhood, Italian and Irish students occupied particular sections of the school during free time, and the Puerto Ricans occupied other sections. In Brooklyn's Eagleton neighborhood, Knickerbocker High School was divided primarily between African Americans, Jamaicans, and Puerto Ricans. In Chester Himes High School in L.A.'s Richardson neighborhood, public space was divided between African Americans and Latinos (Mexicans, Nicaraguans, and Salvadorans). The separation of different ethnic groups in these schools and its recognition by the students reinforced the legitimacy of the geographic segregation that existed in the neighborhood.

In addition, conflict occurred over school sponsorship of celebrations identified with particular ethnic groups, such as Black History Month and Cinco de Mayo in Los Angeles. If the school sponsored an event that featured the music of one ethnic group, members of the other group(s) would often cause interruptions. Such conflicts began with insults and eventually developed into physical confrontations, as occurred in Chester Himes High School over an event featuring a popular Mexican youth band sponsored by a Latino student organization. When the band began to perform, a group of African American students made fun of the music and were confronted by a group of Latino students, resulting in a fight and an abrupt end to the performance.

Conflict also occurred between the Irish, the Italians, and the Puerto Ricans over St. Patrick's Day and Columbus Day. On St. Patrick's Day, Irish students suffered insulting accusations of foolish and drunken behavior from the other groups, which inevitably led to fights in the halls and in the schoolyard. The same held true on Columbus Day, celebrated by the Italian students, who met with insults and sometimes attacked the hecklers. However, criticism of the cultural activities of students from another ethnic group did not have to lead to a physical altercation to reinforce the ethnic separation and competition present in contested neighborhoods. Everyday talk could provide enough information to all parties to maintain the patterns that existed in these neighborhoods.

In fragmented neighborhoods, as in contested neighborhoods, schools became neighborhood institutions when they supported the neighborhood's existing social divisions. In fragmented neighborhoods, social divisions were based on three criteria: (1) the length of time a person and/or family had lived in the United States; (2) the number of years of a family's residency in the neighborhood; and (3) the value orientation of the family or individual.

If the neighborhood's social structure was to be reinforced in the schools, members of the various social divisions had to relate to each other while reinforcing their own pride and identity. This was accomplished in two ways. The first involved joking about other fragments. The jokes, generally used between students of different immigrant generations and/or length of residency in the neighborhood, were often socially benign in that they noted differences without suggesting superiority or inferiority. Thus divisions were reinforced, but in a respectful way. For example, at Knickerbocker High School in Brooklyn's Eagleton neighborhood, Rupert, a sixteen-year-old Jamaican, was explaining a math assignment that was due the next day to three African Americans, a Puerto Rican, and another Jamaican when Jason and LaKeisa, two of the African Americans, interrupted him:

> *Jason*: LaKeisa, what did he say?
> *LaKeisa*: I really couldn't tell you, I didn't get any of it.
> *Rupert*: What's wrong with you people? Are you deaf?
> *Jason*: Hey, I speak English, but I didn't understand a word you said!
> *Rupert*: That's because you speak American and I speak the Queen's English.

Everyone laughed and Rupert repeated the information, but the interchange served as a reminder of the fragmented divisions in the school and neighborhood.[48]

Social divisions were also reinforced through small but symbolically powerful comments about the different value orientations (maximizing excitement and maximizing security). A representative example occurred at James K. Polk High School in L.A.'s El Rey neighborhood in a conversation between three seniors, seventeen-year-old Aureliano, eighteen-year-old Erlinda, and seventeen-year-old Susana, about Veronica, a friend of theirs:

> *Aureliano*: Veronica is hanging around with Armando, and he is just going to get her in trouble.
> *Susana*: *Y que?* [And so?] I don't know why you're surprised; they're both alike.
> *Erlinda*: Yeah, how do you know she won't get him in trouble? They both go for anything that's exciting to them, so they probably get each other in trouble. They are so stupid and irresponsible! [They all nod in agreement, laugh, and change the subject.][49]

These types of comments establish the superiority of one value orientation over another, in this case the security-maximizing value orientation of the people talking over the excitement-maximizing value orientation of the people they are talking about, thereby reinforcing the divisions that dominate the fragmented neighborhoods.

Additionally, extracurricular activities encouraged and supervised by the school's faculty played an important role in reinforcing the social divisions within the school. One such activity was sports, where recent immigrants of both genders were more likely to play soccer and baseball/

softball, while students of the second or later generations were more likely to play football and basketball. Immigrant and first-generation students tended to listen to music from their native country and participate in school clubs like folk dancing from the country of origin, whereas students of the second and later generations were more likely to participate in debate and chess clubs. Likewise, immigrant students were more likely to participate in poetry/creative writing clubs in their first language than were students of the same ethnic group born in the United States. At the same time, nonimmigrant students were more likely to engage in inter-school scholastic games. Generally, the divisions that formed from these extracurricular activities had to do with students' level of competency in English and the language of their country of origin. In sum, the factors influencing different students to engage in different activities served to recreate in the school the same fragmentation that existed in the neighborhood, contributing to the school's functioning as a neighborhood institution.

SOME CLOSING REMARKS

The school, whether an elementary, middle/junior high, or high school, is a product of the state, built and maintained with state revenues. People hired by the state developed the school's curriculum with the goal of developing and reinforcing the values and skills that contribute to the development and maintenance of the greater society. While the school has always played a critical role in implementing society's interests, the question of which segment of society will have its interests reinforced in the school has long been contentious, as shown by numerous publicized events of recent history: the battle over racial desegregation during the 1950s in the southern United States; the clash over community control that raged during the 1960s; the resistance by the Amish to sending their children to public school; the hostility over school busing during the 1970s; and the fight over the content of school curriculum waged by Hasidic Jews in upstate New York and African Americans in New York City during the late twentieth and early twenty-first centuries.[50]

In schools of lower-class neighborhoods there has been a continuous struggle over the social character of the school, and while it has been less subtle than the more publicized educational conflicts, it has been more continuous and socially profound. Although the school is a state institution by design, the people who interact within it every day are involved in a constant struggle over whether it will be an institution that supports the functional interests of the state, epitomized by the ideal of the "American dream," or the functional interests of the poor neighborhood.

One obvious question is whether the school can function as both a state and a neighborhood institution, the way it does in middle- and upper-class neighborhoods. In poor neighborhoods it is very difficult for the school to function as both because the values and goals of the community are incompatible with those of the state, resulting in a struggle where the winner takes all. Much more will be said about the nature of this struggle in the next chapter, but it is important to realize that the schools in the poor neighborhoods studied played an important and supportive role in the structure of these communities. When the school was a neighborhood institution it provided support for the existing social values and behaviors within the neighborhood. Whether the neighborhood was fragmented or contested, the school, when it was functioning as a neighborhood institution, reinforced the values and behaviors supportive of that type of neighborhood.

The question addressed by Edward Banfield at the beginning of the chapter, regarding whether lower-class schools are places of education or simply places of schooling, is complex. Evidence suggests that both elements are present but masks the struggle that exists in the school over its institutional character. The state sees the school as a place of learning that gives each individual the opportunity to gain the skills necessary for socioeconomic mobility, provides society with a ready source of expertise, and reduces potential discontent and political unrest by providing equal opportunity. However, because teachers and school administrators face so many problems in their efforts to create an institution of learning, the state settles for being an establishment of "schooling" that will at least obtain social control over a population (poor youth) that would otherwise create additional social problems.

Some education takes place in these schools because some teachers and students engage in learning the intellectual skills necessary to go to college, but their numbers are quite small. The vast majority of these youth are simply "schooled" in the sense that Banfield identified. Yet contrary to his view that "schooling" has no redeeming qualities, the condition of "schooling" is a consequence of the students' efforts to make the school an institution that supports the neighborhood's social structure and not their effort to resist the culture of the broader society.[51] These findings strikingly contradict other researchers who argue that the behavior of students in poor neighborhoods is merely the combination of the inherent psychosocial difficulties of adolescence with the difficulties specifically involved in moving from youth to adulthood while living in poverty, and those who suggest it is a form of resistance to the conventional cultural norms of middle-class society.[52] In the case of the former, it is not that youth during adolescence experience psychosocial development issues that are accentuated by lower-class culture, but rather that lower-class culture (in the form of the subculture of scarcity identified in this study) is the primary motor influencing behavior and it is accentuated by issues related to adolescent psychosocial development. In the case of the latter, there is a fine distinction, but a very large empirical and theoretical difference, between actions that resist an institution's policy and actions found in this study that simply affirm one's own culture.[53] The vast array of behaviors that are termed by researchers as either "resistance" or "supportive" of the dominant culture will be taken up in more detail in the next chapter on social change and persistence in these neighborhoods.

CHAPTER 11

School Works

The Dynamics of Two Production Lines

The ominous schoolhouses from which the child may emerge
maimed, blinded, hooked, or enraged for life.
            James Baldwin, *Nobody Knows My Name* (1961)

No institution has been considered more important in moving people
out of poverty than the school. The Chinese proverb "Give a man a fish
and he'll eat for a day; teach him how to fish and he'll eat forever"
expresses the conventional wisdom on the power of formal education in
improving people's opportunities and lives, and especially in lifting the
poor out of their plight. Schools provide the human and social capital
necessary for success in the labor market.[1] Thus American society has
consistently called for the improvement of the instructional conditions
and techniques in schools with high numbers of students from poor
backgrounds. No one has articulated the importance of schools in building human capital more forcefully than James Coleman. His studies of
public and private schools influenced most policy makers to invest in
schools to rectify problems of inequality and poverty.[2] Further, Coleman, along with Pierre Bourdieu, advanced views on the importance of
social capital for socioeconomic mobility.[3] Most researchers believe that
human, social, and cultural capital are fundamental for mobility and
that the school plays both a central role in the creation of human capital and a supporting role in the acquisition of social and cultural capital.[4] Because American ideology focuses on equal opportunity more
than equal outcomes, it is no surprise that the school, which provides
the technical expertise associated with higher-paying occupations, is
viewed as the central institution to address inequality.

Since it assumes a critical position in American society, agents both inside and outside the school attempt to make it a place where disadvantaged youth can obtain the skills necessary for success. Yet the view of the school as a means of becoming upwardly mobile in the broader society is not shared by all. As chapter 10 indicated, the school can also be a place where students learn and refine local values and skills to achieve success within the subculture of the neighborhood, and agents both inside and outside the school attempt to make it such a place.[5] This chapter will look at how all these agents attempt to realize their competing visions of the school in their daily activities.

THE DYNAMICS OF CHANGE IN SCHOOLS

Thus far it has been shown that considerable social change can occur in the establishments of poor neighborhoods for various reasons, and the school is no exception. In the local high schools of the five neighborhoods studied, two broad sets of factors created change. The first of these was demographic change in the neighborhood. Families come and go in poor neighborhoods just as they do in more affluent ones, but ethnic change in poor areas stresses the existing social order and initiates conflict as the incumbent group tries to exert control over the newcomers.

Changes in the ethnic composition of a neighborhood generally signaled that it was in a contested state, thus influencing the social order of all the neighborhood's institutions, including the local high school. The most common change that resulted in the high schools was the domination of specific locations by each ethnic group. When geographic boundaries were violated, physical fights followed. Nothing disrupted the everyday operations of the school more than a fight and the aftermath of rumors that kept tensions high. During these times students focused more on the conflict and how it could potentially harm them outside the classroom than on their studies. In the classrooms, students talked about the risks they might run later when they would move from one classroom to another or when they would be in the common area eating. An example of such tension occurred at Chester Himes High School in L.A.'s Richardson neighborhood (see table 9, p. 303). Here the population was initially overwhelmingly African American, but as the Latino population in the school and neighborhood increased (primarily Mexican with a significant contingent of Central Americans), the new Latino students met with both physical and verbal harassment by many African

American students. The Latino students were mocked for their clothing and accents, were physically confronted or attacked, and had money extorted from them by threats of further harm. All of these incidents placed them in a constant state of fear. Not surprisingly, the absenteeism and dropout rate among Latino students during this period were exceedingly high. Their academic performance varied widely, and although poor academic performance cannot be attributed solely to a preoccupation with fear, the environment of harassment by African Americans affected all the Latino students in some way.[6]

Since the 1960s, the schools have viewed issues of ethnic identity with sensitivity, believing that a positive ethnic identity enhances students' sense of self and helps their academic performance. In response to the lagging performance of poor, nonwhite, ethnic students, schools increased their efforts to incorporate specific ethnic histories into the curriculum. However, the matter of what and how much to incorporate led to intensified arguments over curriculum. While these debates, labeled "multiculturalism debates," were occurring at the district level of the five schools studied, principals and teachers continued to support efforts to celebrate the ethnic heritage of their students.[7] Thus the schools changed their curriculum and everyday operations in various ways to accommodate ethnic change. For instance, with the introduction of a new ethnic group, a curricular adaptation was developed that promoted tolerance and educated the faculty and students about the holidays of the new group. Schools also took measures in preparation for possible intolerance and confrontation during ethnic celebrations, such as occurred in the Eagleton neighborhood's Knickerbocker High School over a Puerto Rican Christmas dance. After obtaining permission from the administration, some Puerto Rican students advertised the event with the mention of traditional Puerto Rican food and drink like *sancocho* and nonalcoholic *coquito* along with salsa music.[8] The Puerto Ricans and school officials wished to promote camaraderie between the different ethnic groups, but because of the contested nature of the school and neighborhood the African and Jamaican Americans were resentful of another group's celebration.

Thus problems began even before the event. Some African Americans circulated a rumor that the celebration had been canceled, causing a great deal of confusion. After they circulated another rumor that insinuated trouble at the dance, a number of parents would not allow their children to attend. The dance began as scheduled but was disrupted when a number of African Americans loudly complained that they were tired of salsa music. This led to verbal exchanges and pushing and shoving among Puerto Rican, African American, and Jamaican students. Because tensions were increasing, school officials ended the event early before the situation worsened. However, tensions were still running high among the Puerto Rican students, who were disappointed and angry. Consequently students on their way home got in a number of physical fights and fired a few gunshots. Nobody was injured by the gunfire, but some students were injured while fighting, including two who were hospitalized for treatment. The end result was the continuation of violent confrontations for a month and the blatant failure of the school to create a climate of tolerance among the ethnic groups.

Ethnic changes in the student body also led to adjustments in social studies curricula and the development of ESL courses. The curricular changes often caused difficulty for other students in their course selection and disruption in the learning process because teachers were transferred to satisfy the new demand for ESL classes, and the content of courses such as literature and history was changed to accommodate the interests of the new students. Incumbent students' resistance to these changes also compromised some of the educational objectives of the staff for an indeterminate period. This occurred, for example, in the Chester Himes High School in L.A.'s Richardson neighborhood when school officials, in response to a demographic change that shifted the student body from primarily African American to primarily Mexican, quickly established a number of ESL programs and integrated Mexican history into the social studies curriculum. The changes met with opposition from the African American students, manifesting in their interruption of the new course content with laughter, talking, and refusal to complete assignments. This further resulted in a lower grade point average, as only a few students did well on the exams, and ultimately contributed to a significant number of students scoring low on the social studies section of the state high school exit exam.

Demographic change in fragmented neighborhoods could also cause social conflict when it altered the distribution of people operating under the two dominant value orientations. An example of such a shift occurred at James K. Polk High School in L.A.'s El Rey neighborhood because of a recent influx of immigrants from Mexico. Although the new immigrants were of the same social class as the majority of Mexican American residents, many held a different value orientation. Like other immigrants, the new Mexican residents came to America with hope and optimism, believing that their new country would provide economic opportunities unavailable to them in Mexico. This point of view was compatible with the security-maximizing value orientation because it valued the management of limited resources to save money for the possible fulfillment of dreams of socioeconomic mobility. For the mostly second- or third-generation Mexican American population of the El Rey neighborhood, however, hope of economic mobility had faded and been replaced by a desire to make the best of the difficult circumstances of their lives.[9] Many of these residents, especially the youth, held an excitement-maximizing value orientation. These divergent value orientations between Mexican immigrants and Mexican Americans produced the primary social divisions in the neighborhood.[10]

Generally, changes in the proportions of the student population operating within the two value orientations caused a change in the curriculum. So when the majority of students operated under a security-maximizing value orientation, the amount and complexity of information taught by the teachers increased, and when the majority of students operated under an excitement-maximizing value orientation, the curriculum's amount and complexity of information decreased. These differences in curriculum were due in part to the divergent patterns and behaviors of students operating within the two value orientations. Students with an excitement-maximizing orientation were less interested in planning for the future than in having fun and were more inclined to aggressively go about having fun in the classroom. Although students with a security-maximizing orientation were not necessarily more concerned about their education, their behavior in the classroom was more passive aggressive, giving teachers a false impression that they were interested in developing formal educational skills. The different approaches to education by students with differing value orientations were based on their views of what social and human capital they intended to use to achieve success. Excitement-maximizing students were attracted to the underground illicit economy or entrepreneurial endeavors that generated "quick money" from little investment, whereas security-maximizing students saw the local secondary labor market as the road to a modest but steady income.[11]

Much of school administrators' effort to accommodate immigrant students was predicated on the belief that because the students were new to the country they simply needed the resources to succeed in the labor market in order to move out of a temporary condition of poverty. The administration did not view the condition of immigrant children as endemic to the structure of their families or culture, as they did with students who had been in the United States for multiple generations. The comments of a vice-principal at the Bronx's Van Twiller High School in New York are representative:

> We need to work with the recent immigrant students to make up for what they didn't get before coming to the U.S. We certainly have to try and help them before they get influenced by the students who have lived here all their lives. They are just "ghetto," and their "ghetto culture" will hurt the immigrant students.[12]

Nonimmigrant students often interpreted the school's efforts to accommodate the educational needs of immigrant students as overt favoritism and felt that the faculty and administration's extra aid to the immigrants was illegitimate because most of the immigrant students had not been in the country long enough or were illegal. Thus school administrators' changes aimed at helping a segment of the student body also created conditions of potential social irritation and conflict.[13] The comments of Lana, a sixteen-year-old African American student at Chester Himes High School in L.A.'s Richardson neighborhood, are representative:

> Shit, I don't see why the teachers have to give them Mexican students so much help. They ain't helpin' us at all, and we is here legally. This ain't right, they help illegals more than us citizens. This is just shit![14]

Physical Changes in the Community

The two most prevalent physical conditions affecting the school were disasters and new housing construction. While disasters occur in all communities, their impact on poor communities is greater because they have fewer resources with which to respond and rebuild.[15] The primary disaster that affected the urban poor in this study was fire. The prevalence of fire and the destruction and injury that it leaves in poor areas are due to various conditions. First of all, housing structures are older, and the wiring in them more worn, causing malfunction. Second, many of the escape routes are deficient and children are often left unattended. In addition, property owners sometimes intentionally burn down their properties to collect insurance rather than keeping their buildings maintained or rebuilding after a fire.

Fires in the five neighborhoods studied had the largest impact on schools in contested neighborhoods because they inevitably changed the ethnic balance. When housing structures burned down, residents had to find new homes, often in a new neighborhood. In cases where a significant fraction of one ethnic group was affected in relation to other groups, demographic changes shifted the balance of power throughout the neighborhood, including the school. For example, in the Bronx's Elmway neighborhood a fire began in an apartment complex and quickly spread to the adjoining buildings. Although the exact number of families affected was unclear because some apartments were illegally shared, many families were forced to find housing in other sections of the Bronx. As a result, the neighborhood's majority population shifted from African American to Puerto Rican, causing a similar shift in Lenape High School. These changes initiated a round of open conflict between the two groups in and around the school as Puerto Ricans began to occupy geographic areas that had previously belonged to African Americans. Thus the increased conflict that resulted from the fires significantly compromised the teaching efforts of the faculty.

The physical change that had the largest impact on schools in fragmented neighborhoods was the building of new housing. Contrary to conceptions that poor areas are composed solely of dilapidated housing, new construction does occur when urban renewal projects and/or fires remove some dilapidated housing, making room for new developments. Construction was undertaken or supported by the government to provide decent and affordable housing for the poor, as well as to stimulate the development of private-sector buildings by entrepreneurs.

The development of new housing significantly changed the composition of the high school's student body. This occurred, for example, in the Bronx's Monument neighborhood when the government tore down tenement buildings that were not up to code. The government then rebuilt housing that could be used under the Department of Housing and Urban Development's Section 8 Housing Program. This government-subsidized program had an immediate impact on Van Twiller High School because only families with some income and savings were eligible for new housing. Monument was a fragmented neighborhood, and when the new housing program began the majority of students at Van Twiller High School held an excitement-maximizing value orientation. However, when the old tenements were torn down and replaced with new housing, more security-maximizing families moved into the neighborhood. As a result, students with security-maximizing value orientations began to have more influence at Van Twiller High School. Because students with security-maximizing orientations were less disruptive, school officials interpreted the change as a sign that the students wanted more education and were optimistic about it, viewing it as an opportunity to provide students with more skills and knowledge (i.e., human capital).[16]

The administration cautiously introduced changes in the curriculum to include more complex material and reported a modest improvement in test scores and graduation rates.[17]

State Agents of Change

The previous section described the state's indirect role in effecting change in schools by accommodating to changes that were taking place in the neighborhood. However, the school could also directly initiate change through four agents and one affiliate of the state: upper-level administration, principals, teachers, the state department of education, and teachers' unions.

School districts in large cities like New York and Los Angeles consist of a central administration and subadministrations in various subdistricts, called "district administrations" in Los Angeles and "borough administrations" in New York. These local subadministrations are responsible for managing the education of their students within the specified budget provided by the central administration. Therefore, when the subadministrations believe that change is required, they have the authority to take the necessary actions within their budgets. In the current study, some of their most common actions involved the quality of education delivered to students and were initiated in meetings with school principals through demands for the improvement of education and/or safety. Their demands required principals to change many safety procedures and modify the existing curricula. Because these changes altered individual behavioral patterns of the students and faculty, they created unease and resentment among teachers and students toward the new policies and the principals who initiated them.

Since principals were responsible for the educational and physical well-being of their students, they were agents who ordered and managed many types of change that affected people in the local school. Sometimes the principals merely followed the orders of higher-level administrators; in other instances they themselves presented the initiatives of change. In the latter case, principals took the risk of being removed from the school if their changes were ineffective. Initiatives created by principals could create significant changes, but they were rare: throughout the nine years of the current study, principals initiated only seven changes in the five high schools. Generally, principals were not inclined to initiate change unless they believed it would lead to their promotion or unless their jobs were in jeopardy because of significantly poor test scores, graduation rates, and/or truancy. In such cases, initiatives often were broad in scope, involving changes in philosophy, goals, and procedures, forcing the faculty to revise curricula, and requiring harder work by students and faculty; none of this was well received by either group. When principal-initiated changes were successful, a new culture was created in the school, but in most cases internal resistance prohibited implementation of the full plan. For example, it was often found that students in the various high schools were not given schedules on time so that they fell behind, became frustrated, and decided to drop out of school rather than taking the required classes out of sequence. Therefore, when principals wanted to improve graduation rates, they pressured counselors to ensure that students took all their required courses in the appropriate year. They also required attendance officers to be more aggressive in dealing with truancies on a daily rather than a weekly basis, a change that helped decrease low grades and the number of dropouts. However, if the principals did not continually direct a new policy's implementation so that it remained in place, no improvement was found in its success rates. In sum, whether or not principal-initiated measures succeeded, they caused significant change in the everyday operations of the schools.

Teachers, as the primary implementers of the curriculum, were also agents of change within the school, since they were in a particularly strategic position to influence student behavior. When teachers sought change, they employed new methods to disseminate information, increased students' problem-solving skills, and committed more time and energy to implement these changes.[18] However, although these changes could affect individual students, they could affect the entire school only if the whole faculty made the same commitment to prioritize the education of their own students.[19]

The state could directly affect change in a school when the state department of education wrested control from local authorities and assumed the responsibility for everyday operations. Because these measures radically departed from the local line of authority, they were taken only when representatives of the school district were no longer capable of running the school in accordance with the state department of education's guidelines. When this course of action was taken, the schools underwent significant internal change in all their procedures, and these changes remained in effect until conditions in the schools, including behaviors, were evaluated as complying with state guidelines. In L.A.'s Chester Himes High School, these extreme measures were taken due to daily fights and scores below the minimum level on state academic achievement tests. The school was considered such a problem that the school district sent their own authorities to assume its everyday management. A number of changes were implemented, including increased school police on campus; the restructuring of the attendance office to better monitor truancy; the restoration of bookkeeping by the assistant principal in charge of finances to account for missing funds; constant observation of teacher and student behavior in the classroom; and the reassignment of the principal. While these changes did not have an immediate impact, over the course of the year they significantly affected the operations of the school.

Teachers' unions, by negotiating and monitoring the teachers' contract with the school districts, also acted as change agents and significantly influenced the operations of each school. In the Bronx's Lenape High School, for instance, the union demanded safer conditions for their membership when six teachers were seriously assaulted by students within a three-month period. When the school administration did not provide increased protection from students at the request of the teachers, the union intervened and pressured the district administration to implement a new set of procedures to increase protection. These procedures increased security in the hallways at all times and in the parking lots after school and provided for strict disciplinary action toward any student who assaulted a teacher. Because of these initiatives, teachers felt safer in the school and were able to concentrate on the educational needs of their students rather than worrying about whether they had offended a student who would later attack them with impunity. Many teachers also felt a new commitment toward the school and their teaching efforts because of support from the school administration. Additionally, teachers felt safer to stay after school, an improvement that allowed them to offer students more educational activities.

The objective of the various change agents was to maintain or reestablish the school as a state institution and align it with the interests of the state.[20] Nonetheless, these change agents always operated in a hostile environment.

THE DYNAMICS OF PRESERVATION IN SCHOOLS

A general frustration associated with poor neighborhoods, often expressed in the larger society, is the question of why schools in these neighborhoods cannot provide the necessary education (human capital) to better the lives of their children. The answer is complicated, but one of the primary reasons for the schools' difficulties in this study was the presence of preservation agents that sought to maintain their own value systems in the schools even at the expense of a chance for socioeconomic mobility within the framework of the larger society. Agents that promoted this status quo emerged primarily from the neighborhood but were inadvertently supported by the state as well.

Neighborhood Agents of Preservation

Four neighborhood agents worked to counteract initiatives to change the existing social order in the schools. The first of these was the school's current and past students. Although current students were the school's primary preservation agents, past students who continued to hang around the campus were also involved. Each of the schools' present students had two roles: one was to function as an organic social entity of the neighborhood, a vital contributor to the neighborhood's social life, and the other was simply to function as a student. These two roles were generally in conflict because they had divergent values and goals. Thus, while in school, students had to decide which role to assume and had to accept the responsibility that the role demanded. Most students assumed a role that functionally supported the social order of the neighborhood, blocking the efforts of school authorities to effectively execute and achieve their duties and goals. As previously mentioned, one of the state's objectives in dealing with structural inequality among its citizens was the attempt to create students in the schools who thought and acted alike so as to maximize everyone's opportunities for socioeconomic mobility regardless of their social class backgrounds.[21] However, structural inequalities in the five poor neighborhoods studied produced a functional social order incompatible with that of the middle class. This incompatibility is emphasized throughout this book and applies here because acts that might at first appear to be *resistance*, or rejection of the dominant culture, were actually acts of *realization*, or an embrace of the local subculture.

Students used three actions to counteract and neutralize the state's attempt to create and maintain the school as its own institution. The first of these was their classroom behavior. While the state was attempting to teach literacy and instill social control, most students were trying to teach and reinforce the local knowledge with its concomitant social order. This created a situation of mutual intolerance in which the state attempted to impose its will over the students and vice versa. Teachers tried to invoke the "official power" mandated by the state to initiate procedures leading to state-imposed penalties. New York and Los Angeles school districts had their own security force (called hall monitors), and L.A. had a school district police force as well. These officials were powerful resources in helping the state to create the social control it required to achieve its objectives.[22]

Just as the state attempted to create conditions to accomplish its goals, the students acted in ways that were organically linked to the neighborhood, talking to each other about subjects related directly to their everyday lives. Although this may seem like innocent, "normal adolescent" behavior, their discussions in school not only centered on the local subculture but also disrupted instruction. While students within the general society were likely to discuss exams, grades, course content, and plans for future economic success in some of their conversations, students from poor neighborhoods discussed the activities of their locale, such as residents who had been hurt or killed, fights or potential fights among people, local gang activity, police activity and arrests, the tough girls or boys, the selling of drugs by classmates, crazy behavior among peers, class disruption by certain individuals and how it was handled by the teacher, and pregnancy among students.[23]

These discussions often interrupted and compromised the teacher's classroom duties and their desired educational goals, causing them frustration. Generally, student disruptions were not intended as malicious behavior toward teachers but were simply attempts to discuss "peer-oriented" interests and issues of the neighborhood subculture at inappropriate times.[24] Likewise, students moved around in class because they had trouble sitting for long periods of time or because they were reacting to the movement of other students. These cases, resulting in the decline of classroom control and formal learning, imply a clash of culture that few who have studied these schools have recognized.

At other times, however, disruption was intentional, particularly when teachers effectively created control in the classroom or when the administration invoked a schoolwide action to establish control through classroom observation. After a while, the students perceived that their school as a local institution was in the process of becoming a state institution, a trend they usually described as "becoming a normal school." Although not all students objected to this condition, the majority who were culturally attached to the local neighborhood were unhappy and bored with traditional reading, writing, and math associated with it. These students found this new environment stifling and developed ways to disrupt class to make it more interesting for them or retaliate for having been made to sit still and not talk. They did this by ceasing to pay attention and putting their heads on the desk in mock sleep; whispering jokes that caused laughter; giving silly answers to questions to make others laugh; asking to use the bathroom in order to fool around in the hallway; getting up to sharpen pencils; starting a fight in the classroom; throwing paper; and spitting on other students. [25] These tactics were intentionally used to force teachers to stop instruction and restore order, thereby undermining the school authorities' efforts to create their desired environment.

A representative example of this occurred at the Bronx's Lenape High School. A required class for graduation there was taught by a respected teacher who was dedicated to providing students with the skills necessary to pass the state exit exam. When the course was about 40 percent complete, the teacher, who was generally liked despite students' belief that she required too much work, had them working on a ten-page paper on an approved topic. One Monday, the class, unwilling to settle down to work, proceeded to talk and move around, causing the teacher to raise her voice in order to get their attention. When the students stopped their disruptive behavior, she asked them what the problem was. Two of her better students answered that they were having difficulty because along with learning the material in their textbook they were also required to complete the paper. When the teacher said she understood and asked them to keep working to become stronger students, they did not answer and instead seemed to resist her position by continuing to talk and move around until the period ended.

The next day the students began talking in class, much to the frustration of the teacher, who was trying to teach them a topic covered in the text. When she mentioned that no one seemed to be able to answer her questions, a student said that they did not have time to do both the paper and the reading. The teacher responded that they would have to do both and then asked a student to answer a question on the topic being taught. When the student replied, "I don't know," the teacher said, "Oh, come on now." A male student loudly passed gas, resulting in laughter throughout the class and causing a chain reaction of male students passing gas to continue the disruption. At this point the teacher panicked, lost concentration, and became quiet. She appeared very stressed and said nothing to the students for the remainder of the period. Within a week she requested reassignment to an upper-track course. When she informed the class that she was leaving, a student said, "Now we can get back to normal," and nearly everyone laughed and nodded in agreement. [26]

Another way that students counteracted attempts to make the school a state institution was to disrupt the administration's policies during free time, most often through food fights in the cafeteria and regular fights between students. Such fights affected a large number of students besides the participants, causing them difficulty in reestablishing a normal schedule to get to class on time. Disruptions outside the classroom interfered with instruction because students continued to talk about the fights and their potential after-school repercussions in class. Some of these disruptions were spontaneous extensions of the students' acting out the values and norms of the community; others were planned to reestablish the students' control of the school.[27] Representative incidents occurred at James K. Polk High School in the El Rey neighborhood of Los Angeles and Van Twiller High School in the Bronx's Monument neighborhood.

During a typical lunchtime at Van Twiller, an argument between two girls at a table became heated to a point where each student's friends intervened to hold them back from fighting. Normalcy seemed to return when one of the girls involved in the argument and her group moved to another part of the cafeteria. When two girls told her that her antagonist was spreading rumors about her, however, she said, "That fucking bitch, I'll show her!" She then picked up a tray of food and dumped it on her antagonist and her friends. The attacked girl's friends threw food back, hitting some of the targeted students as well as innocent bystanders, and a full-scale food fight ensued. School security restored order, but rumors about after-school fights continued during class and interfered with the remainder of the day's instruction.

At Polk High School, students caused intentional disruptions to regain their control during an assembly for freshman and sophomores about when the PSAT test would be offered to those who wanted to practice for the SAT test and what was expected of them at the school. As the assistant principal presented the information to those in attendance, two students opened one of the main doors and threw smoke bombs down each of the auditorium's three aisles. The noise was loud, the smoke was thick, and everyone got out of their seats and ran to the doors screaming and laughing, causing total confusion that continued even after the students had gone outside into the open schoolyard. Because the incident had occurred in the middle of the assembly, the students had nowhere to go, since the school schedule had been arranged to accommodate the presentation. The administration tried to reestablish a new schedule and send the students to their next class, but the new schedule compromised instruction by reducing each class by fifteen minutes.[28]

A final way that students disrupted the efforts of the state to maintain the school as a state institution was by roaming around the campus and not attending their assigned classes. Generally the "walkers" wandered the halls, talking loudly and/or throwing things that disrupted classroom activities. For example, at Knickerbocker High School in Brooklyn's Eagleton neighborhood, three boys walked the halls, trying to hide from the hall monitors who constantly patrolled each building wing. When a monitor came near, they quickly moved to another area, continuing this pattern until they were eventually caught and sent to the counselor's office. However, until they were caught, they opened classroom doors and screamed into the rooms, giving some students in the classroom the opportunity to disrupt instruction that they found irrelevant and/or boring. It took the teacher about five minutes to silence the students and more time to reestablish their concentration on the course material, resulting in the loss of about fifteen minutes of the fifty-minute period to teach substantive material.[29] School authorities generally did not view these actions as particularly problematic, but they disrupted learning for portions of each period, and their toll over the course of a day, not to mention a semester, was significant. In addition, when students saw other students roaming around out of class, it reinforced their sense of power over the school officials' loss of control.

Another agent preserving the neighborhood's social order in the school was the various parent groups that became involved with the general educational operations in the school. In each of the five schools studied, some parents met informally to discuss the school's actions in educating and protecting their children. At these meetings they often shared certain beliefs about unsatisfactory actions of the school and made suggestions for correcting the situation. Eventually, they met with the administration to discuss these issues, and although not all of their suggestions were taken, the parents still influenced every school administration through their aggressive and vocal presence. Throughout the period of this study, parent groups continued to recruit parents and community leaders to remain active and influential in neighborhood affairs. These organizations normally advocated for greater neighborhood participation in the school's operations, as well as for the students when they (the students) were unhappy about the school administration's attempts to institute a change that would significantly alter the current operating culture of the school. Generally, these organizations tried to maintain the school's operations in a way that the students found acceptable, which was nearly always within the norms of the neighborhood. Thus they acted as preservation agents for the neighborhood's local subculture within the school.

Parents were also concerned with increased violence at school or their children's involvement in violent activity (as either perpetrators or victims). In one representative instance at the Chester Himes High School in L.A.'s Richardson neighborhood, at least three fights occurred daily for a month. When one resulted in injury to a student's eye from a thrown textbook, the student's parent requested that the president of the school's parent association do something about the violence. The president contacted the school's principal and was told that he was trying to get the district to pay for more security guards but that a decision had yet to be made. The president then contacted the local county supervisor, who called the superintendent of schools, telling him that the issue of violence would be brought to the attention of the board of education at their next meeting. The superintendent replied that he would look into the issue of school violence, and within two weeks funding for additional security was approved.[30]

Finally, parents were concerned that their children graduate with a diploma, but there was little criticism of the fact that scores on the standardized tests were some of the lowest in the city or that the number of students eligible for four-year colleges was very low. Most parents were content if their children received a high school diploma, but local politicians focused primarily on issues related to low test scores and student eligibility for four-year colleges. However, any changes in the schools that caused parents additional problems, such as being called to the school because of a disciplinary problem, their child's transfer to another school, and or their child's temporary expulsion, drew criticism, a reaction that discouraged school efforts toward radical change and reinforced the schools' ties to the local culture.

Another agent of preservation was the local politicians, who either wanted to become more influential in the community or had aspirations for public office and needed the majority support of the neighborhood residents. If a person wanted to become, or remain, a political actor in the local community, nothing was more symbolically powerful than the issue of local education. As far as education was concerned, local politicians usually took the lead from parents so that they would appear to be responsive to neighborhood issues, and this worked to support local values and norms.[31]

The final preservation agent of the neighborhood's subculture in the schools was the gang. The gang resisted efforts toward state institutionalization of the school because if these were successful, the gang would be affected by (1) difficulty in protecting its members while they were in school; (2) reduction in the ability to maintain internal group discipline, since many gang members were split up for six hours a day, nine months of the year; (3) difficulty in securing information from members because they were isolated amid a number of state authorities; and (4) increased ability of the state to apprehend their members.[32]

The gangs worked to make the school an extension of the neighborhood by dividing the common areas into discrete geographic domains so that each gang had an identified area that the other gangs avoided.[33] Defined areas of congregation promoted solidarity and group cohesion while minimizing conflict between gangs during school. In some schools, gangs were divided by the domination of certain floors in the building. This was done to counteract state efforts, particularly by school security and the police, to stop drug sales on campus or, in contested neighborhoods, to protect members of the gang's ethnic group from attack by members of the competing group(s). Since the gang assumed a paramilitary character that was important in protecting the neighborhood, parents were generally reassured by its presence because they believed the gangs protected their children better than the authorities. The comments of Paloma, a thirty-six-year-old Mexican American from the Richardson neighborhood of Los Angeles, represent this position.

> I know that sounded odd, but I just feel that my daughter is safer when the EB's [East Birdville gang] is around when she's coming home from school. . . . I am not saying that I like gangs, 'cause I wish the kids would join something else, but there is so much trouble with blacks beating up kids on the way home and the police not helping, I feel she is just safer from these things with the gang around. [Three women nod in agreement, although they say they wish they did not have to admit to this.][34]

State Authorities as Neighborhood Preservation Agents

Although it seems contradictory for state authorities to play a role in opposition to their official position, they did so at each level of the school bureaucracy. Since teachers were the most involved in the students' everyday activities, they played the most important role in preserving the school as a neighborhood institution. In the previous section, teachers were described as agents of change or, at least, representatives of state interests. However, most teachers at these schools acted as change agents only when they were new to the profession and/or the school. Their initial interest and excitement as educators gradually waned as they became frustrated and tired from the constant strain of teaching in an environment that was indifferent or hostile to their efforts. Eventually they were likely to become apathetic and antagonistic toward the students. The comments of Dawn, a ninth-grade English teacher at Lenape High School in the Elmway neighborhood of the Bronx, are representative of this response:

> These kids just can't focus on academic issues. They are always talking, moving around, playing pranks on each other, and making such noise that it is practically impossible for me to try to have any meaningful discussion about the material. I have tried and tried to do this [have a discussion of the material], but if I do that there is so little time to teach that I now just give them a written assignment to turn in at the end of the period. . . . Yes, I know that they don't get much out of this, but at least they get something and it does keep the chaos down. [Three listeners nod in agreement.][35]

Richard, an eleventh-grade social studies teacher at James K. Polk High School in the El Rey neighborhood of Los Angeles, held a similar view:

> You know how I get them to sit down and keep quiet? I show them movies during class. They seem to pay attention, and those not interested just put their heads down on the desk and sleep. Any way you look at it, it's a win/win situation because they can get some good things out of the movie and they keep quiet, and I know everyone likes that. [The two male teachers addressed shake their heads and laugh.][36]

Such teachers, to make their lives easier, ceased their efforts to motivate the students and instead entered into an unspoken agreement that if they required little or no work from their students in or out of the classroom, the students would not cause problems during class. In essence, they capitulated to the pressures of the neighborhood school culture, relinquishing their roles as agents of the state and its objectives.[37]

The second set of state authorities to contribute to the preservation of the local subculture was the administrators at both the school and district level. Both the school principal and his or her immediate staff of vice-principals and counselors found the state's interests of teaching human and social skills difficult to achieve and decided to concentrate instead on the state's objectives of maintaining order and practicing fiscal accountability. To meet these objectives, the administrators in each school attempted to reduce or eliminate violence on campus and required that all the faculty and staff be financially accountable for all the public resources under their control.

Likewise, the district superintendent and administration were concerned first and foremost with ensuring the safety of all students in their schools. This was manifested in their efforts to keep the level of violence to a minimum so that it did not receive the attention of the press. Since district administrations had little power over everyday learning, they protected their own positions by creating the impression that schools within their district were operating "normally." While their strategy involved the interpretation of "normally" as "educationally effective," they attempted to maintain order in the school, without which education could not occur. Indeed, in the everyday operations of each school, social order was maintained but within a mix of state and local norms. The focus on order made teachers and school administrators susceptible to accepting order without questioning its basis.

The third state agent that aided the neighborhood's preservative effect in the school was the custodial staff, whose services helped maintain instructional equipment as well as the general educational environment. All the teachers depended on the custodial staff to daily provide a clean and usable physical environment conducive to learning. When the facilities were not tidy and familiarly ordered, routines were broken and students acted undisciplined in the classroom and/or the school's common space.[38] School custodians also kept instructional equipment in good working order and fixed broken equipment or electrical systems, an especially important task given the widespread use of educational technology to aid instruction. Therefore, when the custodians were unwilling or unable to maintain the services required for the teaching-learning process, they inadvertently reduced formal instruction and thereby contributed to the local preservation agents' efforts to keep the school within the neighborhood's cultural domain.[39]

The security guards, who were generally from the immediate or nearby area, were essential in providing a safe environment for the students and teachers. An integral part of their jobs involved supporting the objectives of the state, yet they came from environments where the dominant values were in competition with those of the state. The security guards often resisted the directives of the administration because they either disagreed with the administration or were afraid that if they followed these directives they would face consequences in the neighborhood. The conversation of Terry, Jack, and Ernie at James K. Polk High School in Los Angeles is representative:

> *Ernie*: Shit, [the principal] told me that we need to start telling the campus police who is selling *mota* [marijuana] on campus. I ain't going to do that, 'cause everybody at Pepe's [the local barbershop] will be on my case if I start helping the police lock up kids around here.

Jack: Plus, I ain't doing it 'cause I don't think smoking pot is that bad. Hell, I do it too. [There is laughter]

Terry: Yeah, they're making too big a deal out this and I ain't going to take it too seriously. . . . I'm just not going to see anything happening, that's all.[40]

In addition, some of the guards were disgruntled with the administration's directives to increase their surveillance activities for the same pay, so they did not fully or aggressively complete their duties. The conversation of Albert and Josh at the Eagleton neighborhood's Knickerbocker High School in Brooklyn is representative:

Albert: Can you believe they [the administration] want me to pick up kids for smoking [marijuana] on the campus and take them to the police?

Josh: Yeah, they told me that too, but I say to meself, "Hey, they want me to do more work for the same pay, no way!"

Albert: Exactly, they want us to put ourselves out there to be hurt for the same pay [referring to the job being more dangerous if they do what is asked]. No, no, that ain't happenin'. Now I ain't sayin' I would never do what they want, but I ain't puttin' myself in danger or people criticizin' me in the community for what they be payin' me now.

Josh: That's it![41]

By compromising the school's control, security guards increased violence and unruly behavior, making the state's effort to give students an optimal learning environment ineffectual. Thus the security force was often a conduit of the local subculture's control over the everyday operations of the school.[42]

Finally, the faculty members who were caretakers in the school acted as preservation agents by working with the various school personnel to resist significant changes in the way the school operated. They did this by supporting teachers, with the aid of their union, in resisting certain work-related procedures that were not in their contract; encouraging students to voice their opposition to the imposed changes; and soliciting community leaders to voice their opposition to the changes.

THE CONSEQUENCES OF CHANGE AND PERSISTENCE

The struggle to create social change or preserve neighborhood subculture in the five schools studied had reverberations throughout the entire social structure of the neighborhood. When local knowledge was not reinforced in the schools, the neighborhood's order was stressed because if one institutional element of its social structure was temporarily incapacitated, other elements had to compensate by assuming some, if not all, of its responsibilities.[43] Within the five neighborhoods, stress caused by a diminishment of a school's role as a neighborhood institution was first felt by the mom-and-pop stores. If students were less involved with the local subculture during school, they socialized at the mom-and-pop stores after school for much longer than they did when the school was aligned with neighborhood norms. When the school was more an extension of the neighborhood, the average time students spent at the local stores on a daily basis was between ten and twenty minutes. During New York winters students spent only about ten minutes in the stores because the stores were small and would be congested. They just bought what they wanted and were then forced outside to talk, and since the weather was cold they would not spend much time outside talking. However, during the milder weather of spring and fall, students spent about thirty minutes socializing outside the store before going home or to the home of a friend.[44]

When the school became more state oriented and restricted, the average time spent at the store increased to forty minutes during the winter and sixty minutes during the spring and fall. While at the store, students were able to engage in activities that reinforced the norms of the neighborhood's subculture, such as conversing more with each other about activities in the neighborhood, engaging in physical play, and acting out adolescent sexuality rituals that would have been stopped by authorities for being inappropriate at school.

A second neighborhood institution that assumed more responsibility when the school functioned more as a state institution was the barbershop or hair salon. In the hair shops, students could exchange information about upcoming social events, rumors about different people, and important neighborhood topics that included the prevailing opinion about them. During these times, the shop owners (i.e., the caretakers) as well as the adult patrons made more of an effort to bring issues directly related to the youth into the general conversation. These factors gave the youth a place to socialize and strengthened the neighborhood subculture. Thus when the high school operated more as a state institution the neighborhood stores and hair shops together took up its role and provided youth with the necessary space to behave in accordance with neighborhood norms and reinforce their neighborhood identities.

A third neighborhood institution to aid sociocultural preservation in times of change was the gang. The gangs' resistance to changes that occurred during school gave them the legitimacy to be more effective after school in teaching, reinforcing, and enforcing local values and behaviors. Their actions were especially important when the school increasingly became a state institution, making school life less relevant and fun for the students. During these times, student absences and dropout rates increased, and students felt a greater need for fun. Gang members often planned weekend parties and impromptu "get-togethers" during the week. These events helped disseminate information, reinforced local rather than societal identities, and managed internal divisions within both fragmented and contested neighborhoods.

Finally, the housing projects' social organization assumed a greater role in supporting the neighborhood's subculture. The projects undermined the state's efforts to make the school a vehicle to achieve its goals even though they themselves were state run establishments. As discussed in chapters 1 and 2, a variety of factors contributed to the housing projects' position as a neighborhood institution, such as the harboring of organizations that employed residents in the illegal economy; the exchange of information to help individuals obtain more economic relief services for themselves and their families; and activism for resident rights. When the school was more state oriented, youth from the units and neighborhood spent more time in the complexes' public spaces, particularly their social and athletic facilities. While some youth formally played games, others used the time to informally watch, talk, and play social games. This increased social interaction in the housing project helped reinforce the subculture and compensated for the local social structure's weakened condition caused by the demise of the school as a neighborhood institution.

SOME CLOSING REMARKS

Social change in schools occurs in either one of two directions, from neighborhood institution to state institution or vice versa. In either case, alterations in the school's social order are experienced. Since the schools' operations have changed, students and members of the neighborhood respond in ways that attempt to restore everyday interactions to a condition of preferred predictability consistent with the local subculture.

When the school becomes more state oriented, the equilibrium of the neighborhood's social structure is affected, prompting those tied to the local subculture to take action in order to reinstate the school as a neighborhood institution. Over the nine years of my research, the five high schools acted as neighborhood institutions most of the time. Although this maintained a life that was familiar and comfortable to the vast majority of the schools' students, a casualty of its preservation was the development of human capital that could have provided them with greater opportunity for economic mobility.

Conclusion

Yet nought else seemed happy; the past and its pleasure
Was light, and unworthy, had been and was gone;
If hope had deceived us, if hid were its treasure,
Nought now would be left us of all life had won.

William Morris, The Pilgrims of Hope (1885–86)

I have covered a great deal of terrain in describing how the dynamics of social change and preservation operate in poor neighborhoods. As with most studies, much more could have been included, but even in its present form this is a rather long book, and chapter 1 has already presented the major theoretical conclusions emerging from the study's findings. Thus I have limited my conclusion to a discussion of the theoretical and policy implications of the findings on issues affecting those who live below or near the official poverty threshold in neighborhoods where the majority of residents are in a similar situation and there are few resources.

INDIVIDUAL MORALS AND VALUE ORIENTATIONS

In the preface I mentioned that this study owes much to three "giants" of urban ethnographic research: William Foote Whyte, Herbert J. Gans, and Gerald D. Suttles. With regard to individuals living in a poor neighborhood, many of my findings and conclusions have corroborated or built on theirs, particularly those of Gans and Suttles. Like Suttles, I found that morals were important among the poor, and like Gans, I found that the residents of poor neighborhoods were stratified both by demographic categories and by two distinct behavioral styles. However, some of my findings modify or diverge from those of Gans and Suttles. Suttles found that poor people espoused a morality similar to that found within the general society but that because of their difficulty living up to these standards, they adopted morals that were a more relaxed version of the general type he called "provincial."[1] I too found morals to be an important influence on behavior, but unlike Suttles, I did not find them directly related to the morals of the general public. Rather, the morals I found most important in establishing generalized behavior patterns emerged directly from the meaning of "responsibility" within the stark material conditions in which the residents lived. In the present study, individuals' decision to adopt a particular moral code depended on their calculus of life chances within their environment. Thus the morals operative in poor neighborhoods were not a reflection of the wider society but were based on what "should be" the proper way to live one's life within a social environment dominated by scarcity. In this context, I found two broad moral approaches: (1) "maximizing excitement," or trying to find enjoyment every day and take advantage of any opportunities presented because they most likely would not be presented again; and (2) "maximizing security,'' or trying to protect oneself against hardship and disaster and keep what one had by saving money, staying employed, and staying out of harm's way. I have termed the value judgments and behaviors that emanated from these morally reasoned positions "value orientations."

Those familiar with Herbert Gans's work will note some similarities between his categories of "action seekers" and "routine seekers" and my categories of "maximizing excitement," and "maximizing security." However, the difference between Gans's analysis and my own, though somewhat subtle, is important because whereas Gans associates his categories of behavioral styles with different social strata within a neighborhood (e.g., "action seekers" with the lower class and "routine seekers" with the working class), I found the two dominant value orientations associated with deep-seated moral beliefs unspecific to any particular social class.[2] These value orientations and their concomitant morals were spread throughout these neighborhoods, and it was just as likely that each could be found among members of the same family as between families.[3] The significance of these findings lies in the fact that the two sets of morals and value orientations were deeply ingrained in those living in poor neighborhoods; thus individuals, even when their economic circumstances changed for the better, behaved much as they had when they were poor because what was directing their behavior were the ingrained principles that defined what was "righteous and responsible" as well as a set of value orientations that could transcend particular temporal and social conditions.

CULTURE AND STRUCTURE IN POOR NEIGHBORHOODS

Long-term poor neighborhoods are not insular entities but geographic areas with inexpensive rental housing that continually attract individuals new to the city as well as those from other areas of the city who are in financial need of such housing.[4] Thus some people come and leave while others remain for their entire lives. This process brings life, death, and renewal to both contested and fragmented poor neighborhoods. When new people arrive, the neighborhood is sociologically contested until one group numerically dominates and is able to culturally define the operative norms and social relations that signal the neighborhood's shift to being fragmented. This process is renewed when a new ethnic group(s) moves into the neighborhood or when members of the present minority group increase their numbers and challenge the status quo.[5]

People form the heart of any neighborhood, so any analysis of neighborhoods must begin with its residents. The organization of individuals determines the ultimate shape a neighborhood assumes, and it both influences and is influenced by the local social structure and culture. Structure and culture provide the basis for understanding the dynamics of change and preservation in poor neighborhoods, so it is useful to briefly describe their contributions.

No subject has been more controversial in the study of poor people than the concept of culture. Since culture is directly associated with a group, the use of culture to explain behavior among the poor has more often than not been criticized as "blaming the victim."[6] This was particularly true for the work of Oscar Lewis, which boldly advanced the "culture of poverty" theory.[7] It is interesting that any use of the concept of culture since Lewis has been greeted with both criticism and hostility.[8] Yet although the "culture of poverty" was rejected as a cause of people remaining in poverty, Gans, Miller, Suttles, and others have used the concept of "lower-class culture" to describe the values and behaviors of people living in poor neighborhoods. None of these researchers have argued that poverty exists because of culture.[9] There has been a consensus— which would include this study—that large socioeconomic structures establish the conditions for some people to be economically poor and others wealthier and that the position of a person and his or her family in the inequality queue has a great influence on their chances for socioeconomic improvement. Yet the dismissal of culture from the explanatory framework has greatly inhibited a more complete understanding of poor neighborhoods and the mechanisms that operate to keep them socially alive. The present study found culture alive and thriving in poor neighborhoods, blending elements of ethnicity with elements of a condition of constant material scarcity. This culture holds the neighborhood and community together and makes life meaningful and rewarding. Although it may be true that this culture is not strategically capable of increasing an individual's chances for socioeconomic mobility, it has "use value" for the poor in navigating their existing conditions of material scarcity and "worth value" in making life enjoyable.

What separates the present study from other studies of poor neighborhoods is that in the present analysis a culture is present in poor neighborhoods that is (1) neither bad nor good, even if both elements are present; (2) partially transmitted intergenerationally; (3) durable beyond a person's immediate socioeconomic status; and (4) transmittable from one geographic location to another. Although this formulation might appear to be very close to what Oscar Lewis and Daniel Patrick Moynihan report in their studies of the poor, there is an important distinction. While they were attempting to understand why people remained poor, I am attempting to explain how poor people have produced a life for themselves within the structural conditions of material scarcity.[10] Further, and most important, Lewis and Moynihan thought the "culture of poverty" produced social disorganization, whereas I found the subculture of scarcity to support social organization in poor neighborhoods.[11]

People who have lived with long-term poverty have developed a culture that is both economically and socially functional. It provides the means to economically persevere, while creating a system that allows people to enjoy life rather than simply tolerating it. The problem with most recent writing on the subject of poverty in the United States is that it depicts the condition as so intolerable that people stuck in it simply live miserably and depressed.[12] This is not to say that some people living in poverty are not miserable and depressed; rather, it is to maintain that a cultural system is operative in poor neighborhoods that goes beyond the mere toleration of deprivation and establishes enjoyment and pleasure in life within the condition of deprivation. Because this cultural system is strong enough to persuade the vast majority of the poor that it is morally and experientially superior to the culture associated with the dominant middle class of the United States, it is doggedly resilient. It should not be assumed that my conclusion blames the victim or could be construed as doing so, for it could equally be used to raise the poor to the status of heroes. There is no blame or hero-worship in the present analysis; rather, I argue that researchers must understand that a culture emerging from difficult socioeconomic conditions has both positive and negative elements, just as cultures emerging from more affluent economic conditions do. Thus it may be true that people can live a more comfortable life in middle-class conditions, but inferior economic conditions do not make it impossible to live a more fulfilling or enjoyable life.

It should also not be assumed that I am concluding, as Pierre-Joseph Proudhon did, that the condition of poverty is in some experiential way superior to the experiences of other social classes.[13] I am neither glorifying poor people nor theorizing, as Proudhon did, that living in poverty is spiritually more fulfilling than living with plenty. I am merely asserting the existence of a subculture associated with economic deprivation that is in many ways more functional than dysfunctional.

Past researchers have reported a subculture within the working-class population.[14] The primary difference between the working-class subculture they observed and the subculture observed in this study is that their findings on working-class culture included morals, norms, mores, and behaviors emerging from the material conditions produced through work in the manufacturing sector of the economy. In the present study, in contrast, the culture that emerges from living in, or near, a condition of poverty includes the development of morals, norms, mores and behaviors associated less with employment in a particular sector of the economy than with the incapacity to meet minimal needs in housing, food, and clothing for oneself and family for the indefinite future while still making life enjoyable. This difference can appear subtle but is substantively significant for understanding the attitudes and behaviors of those who have lived in a constant state of poverty or near-poverty, as well as those who contend with regularized spells of poverty. Further, it provides a basis for understanding the origins of attitudes and behaviors that appear to be both self-destructive and resistant to society's attempts to provide opportunities for economic mobility. Certainly the findings of Sampson, Wilson, Massey, Anderson, and Duneier come into better focus.[15] Instead of being at odds with the findings reported here and the work of Whyte, Gans, Suttles, Bourgois, and Wacquant, they are in part complementary. The fact that Sampson and others documented behaviors that make it difficult to be successful in the present structure of the society does not mean that the subculture that spawned these attitudes and behaviors must be inherently dysfunctional. Rather, the findings here, along with those of Whyte et al., offer a more complete picture of life in poor neighborhoods, thus documenting the functional basis of life.

It is true that the behaviors seen in the context of this culture of scarcity may be detrimental at times to economic success within the wider society, but the people engaged in these behaviors are living in their present world and not one that might be. Thus these behaviors are dysfunctional in one world and functional in another, and both worlds have their own legitimacy in time and place.

Finally, the subculture of scarcity found in the poor neighborhoods of this study is not the sole determinant of whether those who live within its norms remain poor. It powerfully reinforces the values that make life meaningful within the particular structural conditions of poverty, though at the expense of values found in the larger society that would improve a person's chances for obtaining and maintaining socioeconomic mobility. Further, the evidence from this study found the subculture to be dynamic rather than immutable. It has changed as social conditions within poverty have changed, suggesting that it is continually renewed as the material conditions that gave it birth evolve. Therefore, as conditions of extreme scarcity remain, the subculture wedded to them continues to evolve and assume new forms, proving that it is both resilient and a worthy foe to policy makers dedicated to improving the life chances of the poor.

The issue of structure in poor neighborhoods, while not as controversial as the issue of culture, has been disputed in the form of the question of whether persistently poor neighborhoods are organized or disorganized. A host of researchers have found that poor neighborhoods have a variety of social problems that are different in kind and degree from those found in both working- and middle-class neighborhoods. This has led most of these researchers to conclude that these neighborhoods are disorganized, lack social control, and ultimately are socially dysfunctional.[16] Yet this study has found that social structure and organization exist in persistently poor neighborhoods, creating a social order that allows social life to reproduce itself. While the social conditions considered "problematic" within a certain analytic and political context are not absent from these neighborhoods, their presence does not automatically constitute, or indicate, an absence of structure, order, and functionality. The poor neighborhoods in this study exhibited all the conditions (e.g., crime, public intoxication, uncared-for public spaces, and limited participation in formal voluntary organizations) that other researchers found to be detrimental to what they defined as a healthy "organized" neighborhood. However, these conditions were integrated into an existing structure and order that supported social life through times of social change and stability.

I found that the social structure of poor neighborhoods is formed by the interconnection of local institutions that individually provide services for the residents and collectively provide the edificial integrity to support the weight of local social life. Further, the social structure in these neighborhoods is held together by a number of centrifugal dynamics with the strength to provide an order capable of sustaining and reproducing social life: in the case of the individual, the moral tension between worldviews that encourage the maximization of excitement or security; for neighborhoods, the tension emanating from "fragmented" and "contested" social relations; and for social structure, the tension of local activities to create social change or preservation.

The fact that structure generally exists in poor neighborhoods even when social problems are present raises a question as to whether my analysis allows for any poor neighborhood to be unstructured, disorganized, and dysfunctional. Put bluntly, my findings are not so theoretically all-encompassing that a neighborhood could never be considered unstructured, disorganized, and dysfunctional. Unstructured, disorganized, and dysfunctional neighborhoods do exist, but in physical areas with few inhabitants. At one time these areas were neighborhoods that experienced structure, organization, and functionality, but over time they underwent depopulation that left vacant buildings and open spaces. In these neighborhoods, the decline of structure and organization was signaled by a decrease in both the number of habitable housing units and the amount of social contact among the residents that remained. Often this was the result of (1) fires (both accidental and arson) that destroyed housing;[17] (2) a decreasing number of available rental units accompanied by a decreasing number of renters capable of paying market rates;[18] (3) the abandonment of housing condemned by state authorities;[19] or (4) the razing of dilapidated structures by the state for purposes of redevelopment (urban renewal).[20] These events leave fewer people in the neighborhood and a declining need for commercial establishments that could be used as institutions for the local residents to build a structure.

When the number of people and resources fall below what is critically necessary to build a structure, disorganization commences and the neighborhood becomes socially dysfunctional. This occurred in the Bronx's Monument neighborhood, which for nearly five months was in a state of social dysfunction. The population had steadily declined to a point where small numbers of people lived in each area, and the remaining residents were so isolated from each other that they were forced to go outside the neighborhood to shop and socialize. In sum, the social death of a neighborhood (i.e., social disorganization and dysfunction) occurs when the neighborhood can no longer reproduce itself through the regularized and mutual supporting interaction of its inhabitants and institutions.

SOCIAL CHANGE AND PRESERVATION

Much of this book has been concerned with the mechanisms of social change and preservation within poor neighborhoods. It should be clear that much more social change occurs in poor neighborhoods than simply an increase or decrease in poverty rates or the number of existing social problems. One of the more important findings in this study is the existence of social forces, generally exogenous to the neighborhood, that seek to change or do change the social order, and their continual confrontation by endogenous forces attempting to maintain the status quo even if the changes would improve the general living conditions of the neighborhood's population (although more often they would not). A fundamental feature of this struggle occurs over the character of the various establishments in the neighborhood. One such struggle is whether these establishments will be "enterprises" intent on maximizing their private economic or political interests or "neighborhood institutions" that maximize the ability of local interests to support the social life they inherently identify and are comfortable with. The second struggle centers on whether a particular establishment will be a "state institution" or a "neighborhood institution." In the case of the former, the establishment attempts to realize the interests of the state, whereas in the latter it supports the structure and social order of the neighborhood. The result of this struggle is critical because it dictates the condition of the neighborhood's social health.

No conclusion is likely to be more important, and perhaps controversial, than the finding that poor neighborhoods, even those with significant social problems, remain structured and functional. Skeptics may ask how structure can exist without an apparent ability to organize and effectively control the population; isn't the lack of social control indicated in the number of social problems found in these neighborhoods? It is true that the residents of poor neighborhoods desire less crime, less drug use, and fewer deaths from weapons, but these conditions do not threaten their way of life. Such events are aspects of low-income neighborhood life and have been around for a very long time. The types of crimes, drugs, and weapons used may have changed over time, but the activities themselves have not. In fact, the only way that social life has been able to sustain itself over time has been through the building of a structure that accommodated these events. For instance, earthquakes in California are often seen as an ominous condition by people outside California, but the overwhelming number of Californians have built physical, social, and mental structures that help accommodate their occurrence.

Another example might be the attempt to convince a resident of a poor, rural area that dirt in the house poses a health problem. Residents do not view this as a problem because they have lived with it all their lives and find no way to effectively remove dirt from their environment. What they might see as problematic is their inability to borrow equipment from neighbors, or count on their help with needed construction, planting, or harvesting, but not dirt, which remains a constant of their experienced environment.

I have found it more reasonable to liken the social structure of poor neighborhoods to the anatomy of the human body. Some people's anatomics are close to the "ideal type" found in human biology textbooks, others are born with congenital flaws, and still others have deviated from the "ideal type" as the result of adapting to a hostile environment. In other words, some people, in order to survive and thrive, have developed "flaws" that actually enable their bodies to function under adverse circumstances. The social systems in poor neighborhoods have done likewise.

A different analogy to the human body can be used to understand how the structure of poor neighborhoods confronts and deals with threats. First, when an alien organism enters the body, an immediate response from the immune system confronts the intruder(s) in an effort to thwart any interruption to the general system's operation. While the immune agents act, certain organ(s) are occasionally incapable of working at full capacity, so other organs try to compensate. Likewise, intruders in poor neighborhoods are met with resistance within the embattled establishments, resulting in a struggle in which other neighborhood institutions assume the duties of the establishment under attack.

Second, sometimes an agent outside the body, or even within the system, attacks and permanently damages an organ's ability to function. The system then adapts its own structure and tasks to assume the function of the inoperative organ(s), as in the case of kidney failure, when the remaining functioning kidney assumes the work of both. This was seen in the present study when a neighborhood institution like a mom-and-pop store disappeared and its responsibilities were assumed by another mom-and-pop store until the creation of a new institution that could perform the duties of the deceased institution.[21]

Finally, alien agents often enter the body and the immune system does not have the power to remove them. With no help exogenous to the system (e.g., the surgeon or, in the case of poor neighborhoods, the police), the body is stuck with this alien object, whereupon the only option available is to isolate the agent from contact with other tissue. For instance, when a parasite enters the body and burrows into the tissue of an organ, the body sometimes encases it with a substance that isolates it from further contact. In the present study, the same tactic is used when residents from the neighborhood stop patronizing economic enterprises that threaten the social life of the neighborhood.

In sum, the long-term poor neighborhood, like any living organism, consists of a number of functional institutions (organs) that are interdependent and guard against agents that would attack and threaten the equilibrium it has established by taking steps to preserve its structural integrity and existence. When researchers of poor neighborhoods fail to understand this process, they often misdiagnose the patient (i.e., the poor neighborhood) with a fatal disease (i.e., disorganization, dysfunction, decline) when the patient is simply less healthy. Thus such research cannot explain how poor neighborhoods function long after they have been diagnosed with the disorganized/dysfunctional terminal condition.

POLICY

Neighborhoods have been very important in the history of American urban development, so it is not surprising that sociologists and urban planners have focused on them. For sociologists and planners, the urban neighborhood is the unit of urban space used to measure the social health of cities.[22] Those influenced by the Chicago School of Urban Sociology's paradigm consider the poor neighborhood a physical space that is both socioeconomically and culturally underdeveloped. Interestingly, a general trend in the urban literature has been to go one step further by observing poor neighborhoods and analytically categorizing them as either "healthy" or "disorganized and dying" entities.[23] While it may be true that poor neighborhoods experience social change that includes the death of certain social groups and the birth of others in the same space, the problem with using a "healthy/diseased" conceptual framework is the criteria used to determine whether a neighborhood belongs in one category or the other.[24] These criteria typically focus on the number or amount of (1) crimes committed; (2) debris existing in public spaces; (3) loitering; (4) substance abuse; (5) high school dropouts; (6) youth pregnancy; (7) gangs; (8) people living below the poverty threshold; (9) people receiving public assistance; (10) operating businesses; and (11) physical and social isolation from more affluent segments of the society.[25] To this list, William Julius Wilson and Robert Sampson creatively added the number and strength of social networks, the degree to which residents address social problems, and the rate of resident participation in voluntary formal organizations.[26] Most often, neighborhoods that experience the negative social conditions mentioned above are designated "disorganized," whereas those that lack these conditions or have them to a lesser degree are identified as poor but "functional."[27] One of the primary conclusions of the present study is that the Chicago School paradigm is prone to error because its analytic criteria are insufficient for assessing whether a poor neighborhood is organized (i.e., "healthy") or disorganized (i.e., "dying"). The present study found poor neighborhoods to be organized despite experiencing all of the conditions listed by the Chicago School paradigm as indicating disorganization—a finding supported by the studies of Whyte, Gans, Suttles, and recently Small.[28] Of course, poor neighborhoods might not be organized in a way that the general public or policy makers prefer, but a close look at their everyday operations demonstrates the presence of structure and organization that functionally manage the daily stresses associated with social and economic deprivation.

In relation to organization versus disorganization in poor neighborhoods, there is a consistent difference in the research findings emanating from aggregate survey data and direct observation studies. Studies using large aggregate data sets, most notably survey data, have provided important documentation and analyses concerning the broad socioeconomic contours of various social problems associated with poverty.[29] However, these studies have also produced a view of poor neighborhoods as socioeconomically barren environments with various defects.[30] The defects can be seen metaphorically as social cracks and crevices in a concrete structure. However, these cracks and crevices are not life threatening to the structure of which they are a part, nor are they symptomatic of the structure's imminent decline and collapse. More accurately, they are scars associated with the structure's responses to stressful events and the structure's ability to counteract such stress and maintain its integrity. Further, these cracks and crevices allow us the opportunity to directly observe how the elements composing the structure are created. Any reasonable hope of programmatically dealing with poverty requires the use of data from both approaches.

In sum, significant differences are found between the present study and many studies recently published, but to focus solely on these differences would unnecessarily distract researchers from the innumerable findings that support or complement each other. Clearly, progress in what Alice O'Connor calls "poverty knowledge" has been made.[31] Planners intent on creating policy initiatives to address issues within poor neighborhoods will need to use the results from both micro- and macro-level studies. In so doing, they can appreciate that people living in poverty do not have the luxury to simply let social forces continually act on them. They can hope that political and policy change might dramatically improve their lives, but they must still manage their present circumstances. Pursuing that end, they make lives for themselves that are, to varying degrees, satisfying. Finally, the lives that the poor build include structure and order that will prove resilient to policy initiatives intent on immediately changing them. Nothing can be more frustrating to people who wish to improve the lives of the poor than a resistance to their efforts. An effective initiative that goes beyond treating symptoms requires strong resolve because the irritating resistance that will be encountered is a reaction to past policy neglect, which has resulted in the poor's construction of cultural and functional structures that are quite durable despite any cracks that may appear.[32]

Methodological Appendix

The overarching focus of the study was on the dynamics that affect social change and preservation in poor neighborhoods. Four areas were addressed: (1) What dynamics or mechanisms of social change and stability affect poor neighborhoods? (2) How do these mechanisms work? (3) When do they occur? and (4) Why do they occur as they do? To pursue the investigation, a strategy was designed and executed to draw a sample, gather and record data, and analyze the data. What follows is a description of this strategy. However, before discussing the sample of neighborhoods and how I selected them, I will clarify the concept of "the neighborhood" as used in this study. The term *neighborhood* is used to refer to a geographic space of contiguous streets, ranging from eight to ten square blocks, that is perceived by its residents and those outside this area as constituting a single unit of social identification and that sometimes has a local or citywide name.

SAMPLE

To address what mechanisms affect social change and preservation in poor neighborhoods, a representative sample of poor neighborhoods was required. Previous research suggested that the following factors could affect the dynamics of social change and stability in neighborhoods: (1) the concentration of families below the poverty level; (2) the

length of time of residency by a large concentration of poor; (3) ethnic
and racial composition; (3) the presence or number of immigrant residents; (4) the regional location, climate, and political structures of the
cities to which these neighborhoods belonged; and (5) housing type and
population density.

To analyze the impact of concentrated poor neighborhoods, I sought
neighborhoods in which at least 50 percent of the present residents lived
at or below the official poverty level and had done so for at least twenty-
five years. In addition, I sought neighborhoods that were destination
points for newly arrived migrants to the city, both from other parts of
the United States and from other countries. Further, I wanted a sample
of neighborhoods composed of different types of housing structures,
such as apartment buildings, houses, and duplexes, with different levels
of population density. Finally, I sought neighborhoods in cities that were
located in different climatic zones and political cultures to see what, if
any, effects these factors might have on the behavior of those living in
long-term poor neighborhoods.

I used the two standard sampling techniques of clustering and strati-
fying to draw the sample.[1] My first step in securing a representative sample was to decide on the cities from which the neighborhoods would be
drawn. Los Angeles and New York were chosen because they were the
two largest cities in the United States, were in two different climatic
zones, and had two distinct political cultures. Although both cities have
a "strong mayoral system" of local governance, New York's came from
a tradition of patronage politics, whereas L.A.'s emerged from the
"reform movement" that campaigned against patronage politics.[2]

Having decided on the cities from which to draw the sample, I developed a list of possible neighborhoods with as many of the attributes
mentioned above as could be found. I visited the city planning departments of both New York and Los Angeles with my list of criteria and
asked them to identify all the neighborhoods that met these conditions.
After compiling a list, I used demographic data from the 1970–90 U.S.
Censuses to recheck whether the neighborhoods identified by the planning departments should be included in a list of potential sites.

From data provided by each planning department, I identified twenty-
seven potential neighborhoods for New York and twenty-four for Los
Angeles. I visited each neighborhood on the list to observe the physical
environment and talk to locals about who lived in the neighborhood and
for how long. I then reduced the list to twenty neighborhoods for New
York and eighteen for Los Angeles. The list of eligible neighborhoods for

each city was then subdivided into one group that included all the attributes desired and another that included some but not all of the desired attributes. I decided that the sample should include two neighborhoods from each city that included all the preferred attributes and one from either city that included a portion of those preferred. I drew one neighborhood with only some of the preferred conditions for use as a quasi-control neighborhood to assess whether the social dynamics operative in it were different from those with the preferred conditions.

I began selecting a sample by putting the names of all the neighborhoods from Los Angeles and New York with the preferred attributes into an empty wastebasket, mixing them, and randomly drawing two for each city. The fifth neighborhood was selected from all the neighborhoods in New York and Los Angeles that included only some of the preferred criteria. Since this neighborhood was to be used as a type of control neighborhood to assess any bias to the sample drawn of neighborhoods with all the preferred criteria, I placed the list of eligible neighborhoods from each city in a wastebasket and randomly selected one.

The neighborhoods selected from Los Angeles included one from the eastern section of Los Angeles and one from the section of the city known as South Central. The two neighborhoods from New York were both from the Bronx: one from the South Bronx and one from the East Bronx. The fifth neighborhood (the quasi-control neighborhood) chosen was from Brooklyn. A demographic description of these neighborhoods follows.

DEMOGRAPHIC PROFILE OF THE NEIGHBORHOODS

Three neighborhoods were selected from New York, two located in the Bronx and one in Brooklyn. The one I called "Monument" (a pseudonym) was located in the South Bronx and had been known as a poor neighborhood for more than twenty-five years, with the vast majority of its residents living below or near the poverty level and a large number of female-headed families (see table A1). The largest ethnic groups living in the Monument neighborhood were Puerto Ricans, African Americans, and Dominicans. The Monument neighborhood is one of the primary destination sites for newly arrived immigrants and migrants.

The second neighborhood, in the East Bronx, called the "Elmway" neighborhood (a pseudonym), had an overwhelming majority of residents living below or very near the poverty level, had been known as a poor neighborhood for over twenty-five years, and had a large percentage of female-headed families. The largest ethnic groups living in Elmway

TABLE A1. FIVE NEIGHBORHOODS

Neighborhood	Poverty Rate[a] (%)	Median Family Income[b] (%)	Black (%)	Hispanic (%)	Single-Female Households with Children[c] (%)
New York City	18.5	$41,877	24	27	20
Bronx: Monument	56	$13,499	26	72	41
Bronx: Elmway	61	$23,821	35	58	40
Brooklyn: Eagleton	62	$23,593	74	22	49
Los Angeles	18.3	$39,942	11	47	15
L.A.: El Rey	57	$21,853	4	90	17
L.A.: Richardson	52	$21,080	43	56	55

[a]These figures provide the weighted proportion of individuals that fall into each category for the census tracts that intersected the neighborhood. This composite measure deliberately reflects a broader geographic area than the neighborhood studied in order to protect the confidentiality of the neighborhood, its institutions, and residents.

[b]I provide the mean population-weighted median income for the multicensus tract area in which the neighborhood is located. For cities, I simply provide the citywide median income.

[c]The measure I use here is the number of female householders with related children under age eighteen with no husband present, divided by the total number of families with related children under eighteen.

at the start of the project were Italian, Irish, Puerto Rican, and African American. A significant number of Elmway's residents had immigrated to the U.S. mainland from Puerto Rico. Elmway had typically been the second destination for immigrants after they had secured low-wage jobs and saved some money, but that is no longer the case. At the time of the study it was an area of primary destination for migrants and immigrants. However, the housing is slightly more spacious and better maintained than in the Monument neighborhood, and there is less density among the housing units. The neighborhood in Brooklyn that I labeled "Eagleton" (a pseudonym) served as the quasi-control neighborhood. In 1985, six years before the start of the study, Eagleton had been known as a poor neighborhood, with a majority of its population living below the poverty level and a significant percentage of female-headed families. The largest ethnic groups living in the area were African American, Puerto Rican, and West Indian. Although some immigrants lived in Eagleton, immigrants did not consider it a neighborhood they could afford when they first arrived in the city. However, once they had found employment and saved a little money, it was a neighborhood to which they relocated. Thus Eagleton was the second destination site for people having come to New York.

The decision to study neighborhoods in New York City and Los Angeles was partially predicated on the variation in the architectural styles of living units and the density that such housing, including public housing, produced. In New York, private housing assumed a variety of styles and was present in all three neighborhoods. Single-family duplexes generally had three bedrooms, and single-family units stood as solitary structures. Private housing also included small two- to three-story buildings with each single-family unit making up one floor, often referred to as "walk-ups" because they had no elevators. In addition, there were apartment buildings with a large number of units that generally had one bath and one to three bedrooms. Many of these were referred to by the general public as "tenements," but although they were physically run down, as most tenements are, they were not technically tenements.[3] Finally, there were the public housing complexes in the New York neighborhoods, designed as high- and medium-rise structures. Both designs were vertical but differed in the amount of space they occupied on the ground and in the air. Some buildings were ten to fourteen floors high and others were three or four stories.

One of the neighborhoods selected from Los Angeles, which I called "El Rey" (a pseudonym), was located in the eastern section of the city. It had been known as a poor area for over twenty-five years, with an overwhelming number of its residents living at or below the poverty level and a significant number of single-parent families. Mexicans were the single dominant ethnic group living in El Rey, some of whom had recently immigrated from Mexico and others of whom were second, third, or fourth generation. Of course, residents varied from recent arrivals to those who were second to fourth generation living in the neighborhood. El Rey was a neighborhood where newly arrived Mexican immigrants could find affordable housing.

The second neighborhood in Los Angeles, which I called "Richardson" (a pseudonym), was located in the South Central area of Los Angeles. It too had been known as a poor area for over twenty-five years, with an inordinate number of its residents living below the poverty level and a large percentage of families headed by a single parent. The dominant ethnic groups living in Richardson were African American, Mexican, Salvadoran, and Nicaraguan. The neighborhood had a significant number of immigrants, as well as people who had lived in the United States for generations. In L.A.'s private housing market, single-family units were generally constructed of stucco and consisted of one bath and one to three small bedrooms. These small "bungalows" generally included a living room and either a small dining room and a small separate kitchen or only a kitchen where people both prepared and served food. Private housing also consisted of small one- or two-bedroom units in two rows, with each unit aligned to the next moving inward from the street, and usually had a driveway or walking path between the rows. In structure they often resembled motels. Additionally, there were small one-family units with two bedrooms, a small bathroom, a living room, and a kitchen. Families living in these units would sometimes add another bedroom or, generally in violation of the city's housing code, would convert the garage into another small apartment with one bedroom, a multipurpose space for gathering and eating, and a small bathroom attached outside the structure.

The Los Angeles neighborhoods also included apartment buildings, but they differed significantly from those in New York. The older apartment buildings were generally two to three stories high with approximately six to ten two-bedroom units. These units included a kitchenette, a small eating area, and a living room with one bath. The newer apartment buildings had two stories with ten to fourteen units that consisted of one or two bedrooms, one bath, a kitchenette, and a combined eating and living area.

Finally, the public housing projects in the L.A. neighborhoods were composed of one-story multiple attached units with two to three bedrooms, a kitchen, a living room, and one bath. Because these projects were horizontal structures, they tended to occupy more space than the public housing units in New York. Generally, Los Angeles public housing occupied multiple blocks and appeared to be less densely populated. However, while the density between buildings was less than in New York, the reality was that the density within each unit was equal to, or greater than, that of the units in New York.

GAINING ACCESS

A new study intending to use participant-observation methodology always involves gaining access to observe the individuals needed to address the research question. This is a critical period because until access is gained the research cannot proceed. I gained access in two general stages. First, I went to each of the five neighborhoods and established a presence by contacting people who could tell me of places to rent. In each neighborhood my housing question was greeted with caution since I was not from the neighborhood and since in New York my accent was clearly not local. Most often, the people I spoke to either told me that they did not know of any rentals or asked why I wanted to live in the neighborhood rather than a nicer one. I answered, "I am a college teacher who's taking time off from teaching to do some writing. I thought that I would like to write about life in different city neighborhoods and that I wanted to write about this neighborhood." I went on to say that I knew there were better neighborhoods, but this one just felt good to me. I then said that since I did not have much money, I figured I could find affordable housing in the area. In nearly every situation, someone provided me with at least one lead. However, despite these leads, my strategy was to continue asking, since optimally I wanted to stay with a family that lived in the neighborhood to provide me with the legitimacy necessary for access to local social life. The strategy worked, because in every neighborhood I became friendly with people who offered me space in their apartment or house. Generally, I offered to pay them for my stay, but in each case no one wanted to take money, so I was given a place to stay for free. Nevertheless, to contribute toward the household economy, I purchased staples at various times, indicating that I cared and did not want to take advantage of them.

Once I had secured a place to stay in each neighborhood, I visited the targeted establishments of my research design: (1) housing projects; (2) small grocery stores; (3) hair shops; (4) gangs; and (5) high schools.

With the exception of the local high school and housing project, each establishment had a relatively small number of regular patrons, so they knew that I was new and inevitably regarded me cautiously. In every case, I tried to start a conversation by volunteering that I was a college teacher on leave to write about different neighborhoods in the United States. I told them that I did not know if anyone would really read what I wrote, but I just enjoyed having the time to write. Some people asked if I would use any of them in my "stories," to which I replied, "I usually just make up people's names in my 'stories' so that people can keep their privacy, but if any of you want to read what I write and want me to use your name, I'll consider it." Most said nothing after my offer, though they made courteous gestures indicating that they were honored to be asked to read and decide. Throughout the research I would ask people if they wanted to read what I had written, yet no one ever asked to read either my notes or any of my finished chapters, even when they had seen me taking notes or knew that I had finished my writing.

In the mom-and-pop stores I targeted for study, my strategy was to continue to patronize each place and introduce myself to the owner as someone new to the neighborhood, mentioning whom I was staying with and saying that I was a college teacher who wanted to write a book about life in the neighborhood. This began the process of my acceptance in the neighborhood as a "local." The owner of the store often helped legitimize my status by telling patrons who I was and where I was staying. This validated my presence to the patrons and gained their trust, for almost immediately after his introduction they became more friendly and talkative toward me. This process of inclusion was not quick; it took a number of weeks, during which I took meticulous notes so it would be apparent when I was accepted and what changed as a result. In general, as people became comfortable with me they became less concerned about speaking and acting "properly," "intelligently," and "interestingly" and reverted to their regular routines of speech and behavior.

The barbershops and hair salons required my use of two different strategies to gain the necessary access. In the case of the barbershops, I simply began to patronize them and then continued to make regular visits to socialize. In those barbershops that were associated with an ethnic group I could not pass for, generally shops serving African Americans and West Indians, I first approached the barber and indicated that I wanted to write about barbershops as part of a book on different neighborhoods in the United States and asked if I could sit and write about the occurrences in his shop. Barbers usually answered that they first had to make sure their clients had no objections and that if not I could start coming in and they would introduce me to everyone, letting them know that I was temporarily living in the neighborhood to write a book about neighborhoods. They said they had no problem allowing me in because I was only living in the neighborhood temporarily and therefore was not "involved" in the current conflicts.

The hair salons presented some challenges for data gathering. My initial contact with each owner of the salons went remarkably well. I told the owners that I was writing a book on neighborhoods in the United States and wanted to write some chapters on hair salons and barbershops. They were all interested, but I told them that I did not want my presence to interfere with their natural routines. One of the owners asked if I would mind cleaning the hair from the floor while I was there and if, when not sweeping the floors, I would sit in the adjoining back rooms while clients had their hair done so that I would not interfere with the salon's work. I agreed to both of the owner's requests. Believing that it was only fair to help out while I was in the beauty salons, I asked the owners of the other salons I wanted to study if they would like me to do the same. They all accepted my invitation, so in all the beauty salons I would come out periodically to sweep and be introduced to the patrons as a person who was living in the neighborhood and writing a book about the neighborhood including beauty salons. I would then return to the back room to get out of everyone's way. Luckily, the back rooms were very close to where the clients sat and were separated off by a cloth or bead curtain hanging from the door frame. This allowed me to observe the clients and the beautician and to hear everything that was said in the establishments, since they were all relatively small.

Gaining access to gangs was not as difficult as one might imagine. My research question was focused, not directly on the internal workings of gangs, but on how gangs interacted in the community through the prism of the community. Thus I did not have to ask the gangs to allow me to hang around with them as I had done on a previous research project.[4] Given my age, it would have been impossible to hang around with the gangs and blend in, but it was easy for me to observe and interact with gang members in various neighborhood venues, particularly establishments, as someone merely living in the neighborhood who was writing a book about the area. In the entire nine years of research I only twice had difficulty with the gangs, and in both situations I overcame the difficulties very quickly. Therefore, I was allowed to freely observe the gangs as they interacted in the neighborhood, and they all allowed me to accompany them if I wanted as well as to visit their "official space," which could be a clubhouse or a geographic area.

The last establishment I researched was the local high schools in the neighborhoods. These were the hardest to gain access to because they required formal permission from school officials. In each school, I told the principals that I was a teacher from the University of California doing a book on neighborhoods and that part of the research was on the local high schools that served them. The officials wanted to know what I wanted to learn in the schools, so I told them that I wanted to record the everyday activities of schools that served low-income communities throughout the country. I then told them that I would like to have access to walk around their campus and take notes and observe classroom interactions. I said that I did not seek any interviews but just wanted to quietly observe in the common areas and occasionally the classroom. We came to an agreement that I would be allowed to observe all common areas on my own but that if I wanted to observe a particular classroom I needed to make the request a day before my visit and have it approved by both the administration and the teacher. This formal contract was agreed upon, but both the administration and the teachers eventually relaxed the formal protocol and just asked me to seek permission from the teacher before entering the classroom.

RECORDING DATA

Data were drawn primarily from two sources: direct observation and statements made by the subjects in normal, noninterview conversation. Direct observation constituted the primary data of this study, gathered through as systematic a "note-taking process" as I could invoke, namely writing down the data in small three-by-five notebooks while I was observing. To record observations, and some of the conversations that I heard, I used a shorthand technique that I had learned and adapted to this type of note taking. This method allowed me to record more completely and accurately the behavior and conversations of the subjects while protecting the notes from being read by a third party.

The second source of data was conversations I was in or was privy to. These conversations were recorded to establish people's views on a particular topic or person and were matched to how the people behaved. This allowed me to strengthen the validity associated with the subjects' thoughts and behavior by matching the consistency between the two.

At the end of each day, I transcribed my handwritten notes to a computer file using a computer-assisted program for qualitative data organization. The program that I used was askSam, an early-generation program for qualitative research that allowed data to be recorded, indexed, and coded. I developed an indexing format that provided easy access to data for the desired substantive topics associated with the various research questions. I also developed a rather elaborate coding system that allowed the data to be more finely organized around smaller substantive areas. The coding and indexing systems I developed aided in retrieving data and analyzing the general trends within the data.

DATA ANALYSIS

The goal of the participant observation approach taken in this study was to establish generalized trends in the ways people behave in particular contexts and situations. To establish these trends, it is necessary to quantify (i.e., counting the times under certain conditions) when a particular behavior is initiated, its average duration, and when it ends. In addition, it is imperative to understand the factors that influenced the behavior's life course. In the present study this was done with the aid of the computer-assisted program askSam. Although this particular program has been replaced by more powerful ones such as Ethnograph, FolioViews, and Atlas TI, it was a pioneer in the field when I was first looking for a computer-assisted data management program.[5]

The use of askSam proved to be an efficient and effective means of analyzing the data. Its search capacity enabled me to ascertain how many times a particular behavior occurred and under what conditions. The program was very effective in finding patterns of attitudes, beliefs, and values that were expressed orally in everyday conversation and matching them to behaviors. Further, the use of this computer-assisted program aided in establishing internal and external validity in the analysis and thereby greater reliability in the findings reported.

Finally, the results presented here are intended to be generalizable to other long-term poor neighborhoods in the United States. The study was designed to present results in a manner that allows its replication by other researchers. When such replication occurs, it will be possible to determine the behaviors and dynamics that maintain themselves and why, as well as those that have ceased and why. Only in this way can progress be made in understanding the life cycle of poor neighborhoods.

Notes

INTRODUCTION

1. The term *Anglo-American* refers to a variety of European groups who viewed themselves as the first Americans and were responsible for forging the "nativist movement," which discriminated against and excluded subsequent immigrant groups. Thus it refers primarily, though not exclusively, to white Anglo-Saxon Protestant groups. For the experience of the Africans, see Ira Berlin, *Many Thousands Gone: The First Two Centuries of Slavery in North America* (Cambridge, MA: Harvard University Press, 1998), and Robert William Fogel, *Without Consent or Contract: The Rise and Fall of American Slavery* (New York: Norton, 1989); for that of the Jews, see Irving Howe, *World of Our Fathers: The Journey of the Eastern European Jews to America and the Life They Found and Made* (New York: Simon and Schuster, 1976); for that of the Irish, Italians, and other European ethnic groups, see Matthew Frye Jacobson, *Whiteness of a Different Color: European Immigrants and the Alchemy of Race* (Cambridge, MA: Harvard University Press, 1998).

2. See W. E. B. Du Bois, *The Philadelphia Negro: A Social Study* (1899; repr., Philadelphia: University of Pennsylvania Press, 1996), 305–9. Also see Noel Ignatiev, *How the Irish Became White* (New York: Routledge, 1995), 40–43. Both of these studies report that the Irish and African Americans lived in the same neighborhoods because they were both poor and considered inferior to other ethnic groups.

3. Many of the investigative journalists who wrote about the plight of the poor were called muckrakers. The best examples of this body of work are Jacob Riis, *How the Other Half Lives: Studies among the Tenements* (1890; repr., New York: Dover Publications, 1971), and Upton Sinclair, *The Jungle* (1906; repr., New

York: Bantam Books, 1981). There were also works by people providing services to the poor, such as Jane Addams in Chicago. See her *Twenty Years at Hull House* (1910; repr., New York: Signet, 1960). For a very early journalistic exposé on the London poor of the nineteenth century, see Henry Mayhew's *London Labor and the London Poor* (1861–62; repr., London: Penguin Books, 1985).

4. See Robert E. Park, "The City as a Social Laboratory," in *Chicago: An Experiment in Social Science Research*, ed. T. V. Smith and Leonard D. White (Chicago: University of Chicago Press, 1929), 1–19, and Robert E. Park, Ernest W. Burgess, and Roderick D. McKenzie, *The City* (1925; repr., Chicago: University of Chicago Press, 1967), 1–46. Also see Louis Wirth's classic "Urbanism as a Way of Life," *American Journal of Sociology* 44, no. 1 (1938): 3–24.

5. See the work of Robert Park, who was joined by his colleagues and students. For the first formal discussion of the logic of urban growth, see Park et al., *City*, 47–79.

6. See ibid., 47–62.

7. See ibid., 63–79, and Harvey Warren Zorbaugh, *The Gold Coast and the Slum: A Sociological Study of Chicago's Near North Side* (Chicago: University of Chicago Press, 1929).

8. See Park et al., *The City*, 57.

9. The period of disorganization produced generations that were in neither the cultural world of the "old" country nor the cultural world of the "new." These people were labeled "marginal men." They usually belonged to the second or third generation, and while these generations were in some particular social and psychological way lost, the succeeding generations were fully assimilated citizens. See Robert E. Park, "Human Migration and the Marginal Man," *American Journal of Sociology* 33 (May 1928): 881–93.

10. The classic description of both the creation of an ethnic enclave and its gradual demise as a result of the natural process of urban development is Louis Wirth's *The Ghetto* (Chicago: University of Chicago Press, 1956).

11. See Milton Meltzer, *Brother, Can You Spare a Dime? The Great Depression, 1929–33* (New York: Knopf, 1969); James Agee and Walker Evans, *Let Us Now Praise Famous Men* (1939; repr., Boston: Houghton Mifflin, 1988).

12. William Foote Whyte, *Street Corner Society: The Social Structure of an Italian Slum* (Chicago: University of Chicago Press, 1943).

13. St. Clair Drake and Horace Cayton, *Black Metropolis: A Study of Negro Life in a Northern City* (New York: Harcourt, Brace, 1945).

14. See Loïc Wacquant, "Three Pernicious Premises in the Study of the American Ghetto," *International Journal of Urban and Regional Research* 21 (June 1997): 341–53.

15. Drake and Cayton, *Black Metropolis*, 202–13, 564–57.

16. William Julius Wilson would rely heavily on the Drake and Cayton study to document that African American poverty in the 1990s was substantively different from that of previous periods. See his *When Work Disappears: The World of the New Urban Poor* (New York: Knopf, 1996), 3–24.

17. Herbert J. Gans, *The Urban Villagers: Group and Class in the Life of Italian-Americans* (1962; repr., New York: Free Press, 1981). The study was conducted from October 1957 through May 1958.

18. See Herbert J. Gans, "Urbanism and Suburbanism as Ways of Life: A Re-evaluation of Definitions," in *Human Behavior and Social Processes,* ed. Arnold Rose (Boston: Houghton Mifflin, 1962), 625–48. In this article he convincingly argued against Louis Wirth and the Chicago School's claims that urbanism had the power to assimilate ethnic groups to a common culture even if individual ethnic groups tried to resist. See Wirth, "Urbanism," for the classic statement of urbanism's power. Gans's study also challenged the findings of Walter Isaac Thomas and Florian Znaniecke in their classic study *The Polish Peasant in Europe and America* (New York: Dover Publications, 1958).

19. Gerald Suttles, *The Social Order of the Slum: Ethnicity and Segmentation* (Chicago: University of Chicago Press, 1968).

20. Ibid., 3–12. His ideas were very similar to those advanced by Robert Merton on social anomie. See Robert Merton, *Social Theory and Social Structure* (1957; repr., New York: Free Press, 1968), 185–249.

21. Gans, *Urban Villagers,* 323–77; Suttles, *Social Order,* 21–22, 100, 224.

22. Oscar Lewis, *Five Families: Mexican Case Studies in the Culture of Poverty* (New York: Basic Books, 1959) and *La Vida: A Puerto Rican Family in the Culture of Poverty—San Juan and New York* (New York: Random House, 1965), xlii–lii.

23. For example, Lewis's premise that the culture of poverty was passed from generation to generation through children who felt hopeless to better their lives was reiterated by Michael Harrington in his *The Other America: Poverty in the United States* (New York: Macmillan, 1962), a book that influenced President John Kennedy to initiate a policy that would effectively give hope to the hopeless by providing government-sponsored programs to increase education, skills acquisition, and financial aid for housing and food. This policy would become known as the War on Poverty. For a history of social policy regarding the poor that includes a discussion of the War on Poverty's origins, see James T. Patterson, *America's Struggle against Poverty in the Twentieth Century* (Cambridge, MA: Harvard University Press, 2000), 122–49.

24. For critiques of the culture of poverty concept, see Charles A. Valentine, *Culture and Poverty: A Critique and Counter-Proposals* (Chicago: University of Chicago Press, 1968), and William Ryan, *Blaming the Victim* (New York: Pantheon Books, 1971).

25. Several popular policy studies did invoke a version of Lewis's theory. They were generally conducted by conservative right-wing scholars who were intent on showing that the poor were caught in a welfare culture that encouraged them not to work and be productive. The most famous of these was Charles Murray's *Losing Ground: American Social Policy, 1950–1980* (New York: Basic Books, 1984).

26. Regarding African Americans and the housing market, Melvin L. Oliver and Thomas M. Shapiro were the first to document the importance of a house in determining a family's net wealth in their *Black Wealth/White Wealth: A New Perspective on Racial Inequality* (New York: Routledge, 1995); a later investigation of the same issue is Dalton Conley's *Being Black and Living in the Red: Race, Wealth and Social Policy in America* (Berkeley: University of California Press, 1999).

27. The concern over housing values accelerated "white flight" from the city to the suburbs. For a good description of an extreme case of this fear affecting urban economic development, see Thomas J. Sugrue's *The Origins of the Urban Crisis: Race and Inequality in Postwar Detroit* (Princeton: Princeton University Press, 1996).

28. See Ida Susser, *Norman Street: Poverty and Politics in an Urban Neighborhood* (New York: Oxford University Press, 1982), and Jonathan Rieder, *Canarsie: The Jews and Italians against Liberalism* (Cambridge, MA: Harvard University Press, 1985).

29. Ruth Horowitz, *Honor and the American Dream: Identity and Culture in a Chicano Community* (New Brunswick: Rutgers University Press, 1983).

30. Horowitz's study supported Suttles's findings that ethnicity could structure a community, but whereas Suttles found that ethnic solidarity was produced through resistance to the cultural intrusion of other ethnic groups, Horowitz found that ethnic solidarity could be produced as a result of an intragroup struggle between the culture associated with the country of origin and that of the country of destination. In addition, Horowitz's and Suttles's work supported many of the earlier findings of Elliot Liebow, *Tally's Corner: A Study of Negro Street Corner Men* (Boston: Little, Brown, 1967), and Ulf Hannerz, *Soulside: Explorations in Ghetto Culture and Community* (New York: Columbia University Press, 1969).

31. Although William Julius Wilson's *The Declining Significance of Race: Blacks and Changing American Institutions* (Chicago: University of Chicago Press, 1978) was the intellectual root of the analysis, his book *The Truly Disadvantaged: The Inner City, the Underclass, and Public Policy* (Chicago: University of Chicago Press, 1987) was the work that would articulate what became known as the "urban underclass" thesis.

32. W. Wilson, *Truly Disadvantaged,* 134–35.

33. See Douglas A. Massey and Nancy A. Denton, *American Apartheid: Segregation and the Making of the American Underclass* (Cambridge, MA: Harvard University Press, 1993).

34. See W. Wilson, *When Work Disappears.*

35. Ibid., 25–110.

36. His findings about the Latino poor have been supported by the findings in Joan Moore and Raquel Pinderhughes, eds., *In the Barrios: Latinos and the Underclass Debate* (New York: Russell Sage Foundation, 1993), and Erik Klinenberg, *Heat Wave: A Social Autopsy of Disaster in Chicago* (Chicago: University of Chicago Press, 2002), 79–128.

37. W. Wilson, *When Work Disappears,* 25–50. Wilson's subsequent book on neighborhood change in Chicago maintained the disorganization conceptual schema. See William Julius Wilson and Richard P. Taub, *There Goes the Neighborhood: Racial, Ethnic, and Class Tensions in Four Chicago Neighborhoods and Their Meaning for America* (New York: Knopf, 2006), 9–13.

38. In addition to the research by William Julius Wilson and by Massey and Denton, see Paul A. Jargowsky, *Poverty and Place: Ghettos, Barrios, and the American City* (New York: Russell Sage Foundation, 1997), and Elijah Anderson, *Streetwise: Race, Class, and Changes in an Urban Community* (Chicago:

University of Chicago Press, 1990). The one exception to this depiction was Carol Stack's *All Our Kin: Strategies for Survival in a Black Community* (New York: Harper and Row, 1974), which found within the black community she studied a systematic organization to deal with problems associated with poverty and discrimination. However, her unit of analysis was not the neighborhood but the broader community.

39. Several studies have shown that as poor neighborhoods become marginalized they become more vulnerable to destruction and replacement by upper-income housing, universities, hospitals, or factories. On replacement by upper-income housing, see Gans, *Urban Villagers;* on replacement by universities and hospitals, see Suttles, *Social Order;* on replacement by factories, see Jeanie Wylie, *Poletown: A Community Betrayed* (Urbana: University of Illinois Press, 1989).

40. For studies using survey-level data, see Jeanne Brooks-Gunn, Greg J. Duncan, and J. Lawrence Aber, eds., *Neighborhood Poverty,* vols. 1 and 2 (New York: Russell Sage Foundation, 1997). For ethnographic studies, see Elijah Anderson, *A Place on the Corner* (Chicago: University of Chicago Press, 1978), *Streetwise,* and *Code of the Street: Decency, Violence, and the Moral Life of the Inner City* (New York: Norton, 1999); Jagna Wojcicka Sharff, *King Kong on 4th Street: Families and the Violence of Poverty on the Lower East Side* (Boulder, CO: Westview Press, 1998); and Scott Cummings's *Left Behind in Rosedale: Race Relations and the Collapse of Community Institutions* (Boulder, CO: Westview Press, 1998).

41. See Daniel Dohan, *The Price of Poverty: Money, Work, and Culture in the Mexican American Barrio* (Berkeley: University of California Press, 2003); and Mario Luis Small, *Villa Victoria: The Transformation of Social Capital in a Boston Barrio* (Chicago: University of Chicago Press, 2005).

42. Small's book is a study of what he calls "social capital" in poor neighborhoods, which he defines as including "the number of middle-class friends and acquaintances poor individuals have, the trust they have toward others in their neighborhood, and the amount of time they devote to local volunteer activities." See Small, *Villa Victoria,* 1.

43. On the subject of the Latino community being more organized than the African American community, see Klinenberg, *Heat Wave,* 109–28.

44. On the ways people respond to living in persistent poverty, see Small, *Villa Victoria.*

45. See W. Wilson, *When Work Disappears,* 20; Robert J. Sampson and William Julius Wilson, "Toward a Theory of Race, Crime, and Inequality," in *Crime and Inequality,* ed. John Hagan and Ruth D. Peterson (Stanford: Stanford University Press, 1995), 37–54.

46. Wesley Skogan's *Disorder and Decline: Crime and the Spiral of Decay in American Neighborhoods* (Berkeley: University of California Press, 1990) is one of the works that interprets social problems observed in poor neighborhoods as the result of social disorganization. It also could be said that the work of Elijah Anderson, especially *Streetwise* and *Code of the Street,* suggests that social ills in poor neighborhoods are the result of some form of social disorganization.

47. Innumerable cases throughout the United States could be cited. A few examples include Boston's West End in Gans's *Urban Villagers,* Chicago's Taylor Street area in Suttles's *Social Order of the Slum,* and Detroit's Poletown

community in Wylie's *Poletown*. See also Melvin King, *Chain of Change: Struggles for Black Community Development* (Boston: South End Press, 1981), on Boston's South End, and Thomas Hines, "Housing, Baseball, and Creeping Socialism: The Battle of Chavez Ravine, Los Angeles, 1949–1959," *Journal of Urban History* 8 (1982): 123–44, on Chavez Ravine in Los Angeles.

48. Innumerable middle- and working-class neighborhoods have died and been taken over by the poor. Much of this has been discussed by Jane Jacobs in her *The Death and Life of Great American Cities* (New York: Vintage Books, 1961), 270–90. A few specific examples include Hillel Levine and Lawrence Harmon, *The Death of an American Jewish Community: A Tragedy of Good Intentions* (New York: Free Press, 1992), on social change in Boston's Roxbury district, and Cummings, *Left Behind in Rosedale,* on social change in Dallas's Rosedale area.

49. See William Sewell, "A Theory of Structure: Duality, Agency, and Transformation," *American Journal of Sociology* 98 (1992): 1–29; Clyde Kluckhohn, "Values and Value-Orientations in the Theory of Action: An Exploration in Definition and Classification," and Talcott Parsons, Edward Shils, and James Olds, "Values, Motives, and Systems of Action," both in *Toward a General Theory of Action,* ed. Talcott Parsons and Edward A. Shils (New York: Harper Torchbooks, 1962), 388–433 and 53–109 respectively; Ann Swidler, "Culture in Action: Symbols and Strategies," *American Sociological Review* 51 (April 1986): 273–86; and Claude Fischer, "Toward a Sub-cultural Theory of Urbanism," *American Journal of Sociology* 80 (May 1975): 1319–41.

50. Fischer concentrated on the issue of ethnicity because it provided the most difficult case for his theory. Although he did not specifically address long-term poverty, he intended the theory to apply to a variety of social situations. See his "Toward a Subcultural Theory" and his twenty-year reassessment, "The Subcultural Theory of Urbanism: A Twentieth-Year Assessment," *American Journal of Sociology* 101 (November 1995): 543–75. See also his empirical findings in *To Dwell among Friends: Personal Networks in Town and City* (Chicago: University of Chicago Press, 1982).

51. See Lewis, *La Vida,* xliii.

52. See Max Weber's thoughts about maintaining value neutrality while engaged in systematic analysis. Max Weber, *The Methodology of the Social Sciences* (New York: Free Press, 1949).

53. See the classic work of Eugene D. Genovese, *Roll, Jordan, Roll: The World the Slaves Made* (New York: Pantheon Books, 1974). A useful comparison of the conditions of slavery and those of serfdom can be found in Peter Kolchin, *Unfree Labor: American Slavery and Russian Serfdom* (Cambridge, MA: Harvard University Press, 1987). For comparative studies of slavery and the urban poor in the United States during the same time period, see Robert William Fogel and Stanley L. Engerman, *Time on the Cross: The Economics of American Negro Slavery* (Boston: Little, Brown, 1974). The present study will not compare forms of servitude but will simply concentrate on the lives of poor people living in neighborhoods in which they dominate.

54. The official poverty line for a family of four can be found in the U.S. Census. For the years of the present study the rate, based on annual income, was as follows: 1990 = $13,359; 1991 = $13,924; 1992 = $14,335; 1993 = $14,763;

1994 = \$15,141; 1995 = \$15,569; 1996 = \$16,036; 1997 = \$16,400; 1998 = \$16,660; 1999 = \$17,029; 2000 = \$17,603.

55. It is important to point out that I became friendly with a number of people in the five neighborhoods, but I resisted becoming their friend so that I would not overidentify with my subjects and thereby compromise my ability to conduct the study as value-neutrally as possible. A number of these people were hospitable enough to offer me a place to stay in their public housing apartments. In those cases I was always respectful, appreciative, and as helpful as I could be, but I acted like the guest that I was. Herbert Gans speaks of doing the same thing in his methodological appendix to *Urban Villagers*, 402–6. Many researchers have argued against the possibility of what Max Weber called "value-neutral" research. It is true that it is difficult to be completely value-free while conducting fieldwork, but in my effort to reduce (not eliminate) error I did attempt to be as value neutral (particularly in judgments of "good" and "bad") as I could.

56. A number of better programs were developed for ethnographic data well after the project had started, but I was not able to utilize them because the data program I used made it too difficult to transfer data to a new program. Although the askSam program allowed me to organize and analyze my data more systematically than I could have from simply reading over hundreds, or thousands, of notebook pages, it was a first-generation program for participant-observation research and was rather clumsy compared to the next generation of programs. Nonetheless, at the time it was "state of the art" and proved to be quite useful in data analysis.

57. See Barney G. Glaser and Anselm L. Strauss, *The Discovery of Grounded Theory: Strategies for Qualitative Research* (Chicago: Aldine, 1967).

58. My colleague Michael Burawoy has categorized grounded theory within the broad positivist tradition, but Glaser and Strauss seem to think of it within the more "symbolic interactionist" tradition. Burawoy also assigns my earlier work to the tradition of "grounded theory," but I think he may have done so because my theory chapter was positioned as a separate chapter at the beginning of the book rather than as part of the conclusion, where a more conventional positivist analytic presentation would have placed it. See Michael Burawoy, "The Extended Case Method," *Sociological Theory* 16 (March 1998): 4–33.

59. Jane Jacobs is most associated with issues related to the life and death of cities, but her approach was much more concerned with cities and the contribution neighborhoods make to them than with neighborhoods per se. The present study concerns neighborhoods, specifically poor ones, not cities, and this focus distinguishes it from the work of Jacobs and more recently Mitchell Duneier, who in his study of street life in New York's Greenwich Village challenges some of Jacobs's premises. See J. Jacobs, *Death and Life*; Mitchell Duneier, *Sidewalk* (New York: Farrar, Straus and Giroux, 1999); and Mike Davis, *Dead Cities, and Other Tales* (New York: New Press, 2002).

60. For the purposes of this study, long-term poor neighborhoods have been defined as neighborhoods that have had 50 percent of their population below the official poverty level for more than twenty-five years. A more thorough discussion of these neighborhoods and the sampling technique used can be found in the Methodological Appendix.

1. A THEORY OF LIFE, SOCIAL CHANGE,
AND PRESERVATION IN POOR NEIGHBORHOODS

1. This point was made forcefully by Robert Bellah et al. in "We Live through Institutions," a chapter in their book *The Good Society* (New York: Knopf, 1991), 5–18.

2. See Douglass C. North, *Institutions, Institutional Change, and Economic Performance* (Cambridge: Cambridge University Press, 1990), 3.

3. Ronald L. Jepperson, "Institutions, Institutional Effects, and Institutionalism," in *The New Institutionalism in Organizational Analysis,* ed. Walter W. Powell and Paul J. DiMaggio (Chicago: University of Chicago Press, 1991), 146.

4. Most of the social programs administered by government agencies are governed by the dominant social norms of the time. Certainly those associated with poverty have been especially influenced by values and norms such as the belief that it is better for people to work regardless of how low the pay is and that it corrupts people to give them the material resources necessary to make their life comfortable. For an account of these values in relation to poverty, see W. Wilson, *When Work Disappears,* 149–82. On how the state acts on its own set of values and norms associated with its desire to protect its own interests, see Theda Skocpol, *States and Social Revolutions: A Comparative Analysis of France, Russia, and China* (New York: Cambridge University Press, 1979), and Frances Fox Piven and Richard Cloward, *Regulating the Poor: The Functions of Public Welfare* (New York: Pantheon Books, 1971).

5. Max Weber regarded the morals and values generated within the institution as institutional roles because they had the power to structure interactive behavior within the bureaucracy as well as between agents of the bureaucracy and the people they served. See Max Weber, *Economy and Society: An Outline of Interpretive Sociology,* ed. Gunther Roth and Claus Wittich (1921; repr., Berkeley: University of California Press, 1978), 49, 218, 956–1003.

6. Gangs often have a formal clubhouse or particular building that they will use as a formal meeting place. So in the case of those gangs that do have a building, their institutional setting is that building; for those that do not, it is the specific geographic area where they consistently meet.

7. Edward Banfield was the first researcher to apply the concept of "amorality" to an entire group of people when he introduced the concept of "amoral familism" to describe the peasantry of southern Italy. Although he was attempting to describe the value orientations of these Italians, it is very unlikely that they were "amoral" in any meaningful way. It is more likely that Banfield was unable to determine what moral code was driving their emphasis on the family. See his *The Moral Basis of a Backward Society* (Glencoe, IL: Free Press, 1958).

8. See C. Wright Mills and Hans Gerth, *Character and Social Structure* (New York: Harcourt, Brace, and World, 1953).

9. The terms *moral/immoral* and *responsible/irresponsible* are used in poor areas, but other words and phrases are also used to convey the same meaning: for example, among African Americans, *decent/indecent* and *righteous/unrighteous,* and among Latinos, *honorable/dishonorable.* Whatever the exact words used, most people in poor areas are sensitive to issues of morality and responsi-

bility, since they are aware of having been labeled by the media and popular opinion as immoral and irresponsible because of being poor. Further, most poor people will use the various moral words to categorize the degree to which they and others in their social circle are "responsible" to themselves, their families, and their community.

10. See Steve Derné, "Cultural Conceptions of Human Motivation and Their Significance for Culture Theory," in *The Sociology of Culture*, ed. Diana Crane (Cambridge, MA: Blackwell, 1994).

11. Gerald Suttles recognized the importance of moral codes in the lives of the urban poor. In fact, he placed morals at the center of his structural analysis of the urban poor. See his *Social Order*, 4–6, 223–34. Other researchers have also reported the importance of morals in the everyday behavior of the African American poor. See Anderson, *Code of the Street*.

12. There is a large literature concerning the various time orientations of people and groups. For a classic discussion of "present orientation," see Florence Kluckhohn and Fred Strodtbeck, *Variations in Value Orientations* (Evanston, IL: Row, Peterson, 1961). Also see Alfred Gell, *The Anthropology of Time: Cultural Constructions of Temporal Maps and Images* (New York: St. Martin's Press, 1992), and John Hassard, ed., *The Sociology of Time* (New York: St. Martin's Press, 1990).

13. See Max Weber, *The Protestant Ethic and the Spirit of Capitalism* (1938; repr., New York: Scribner and Sons, 1958).

14. For an empirical and theoretical critique of Anderson's use of "decent" and "street" family categories, see Sudhir Venkatesh, *Off the Books: The Underground Economy of the Urban Poor* (Cambridge, MA: Harvard University Press, 2006), 37–38, 60–61; Loïc Wacquant, "Scrutinizing the Streets: Poverty, Morality, and the Pitfalls of Urban Ethnography," *American Journal of Sociology* 107 (May 2002): 1468–1532; and Elijah Anderson's exchange with Wacquant in the same volume of the journal.

15. See also Merton, *Social Theory and Social Structure*, 185–249; and Liebow, *Tally's Corner*, on this issue.

16. Ann Swidler, *Talk of Love: How Culture Matters* (Chicago: University of Chicago Press, 2001).

17. See Weber, *Methodology*, 1–47, 49–112.

18. See Weber, *Protestant Ethic*, 41–42.

19. This value orientation has much in common with what James Scott labeled "moral economy" and associated with peasant societies. See James C. Scott, *Moral Economy of the Peasant: Rebellion and Subsistence in Southeast Asia* (New Haven: Yale University Press, 1976).

20. These values are also similar to the religious values that Max Weber identified with Protestantism. See Weber, *Protestant Ethic*, 176–77. There is also a version of the Protestant ethic that involves the proposition that the righteous display God's favor in their frugal but comfortable lifestyle.

21. For an excellent example of people developing strategies during their lives to get to the afterlife, see Samuel K. Cohn Jr., *Death and Property in Siena, 1205–1800: Strategies for the Afterlife* (Baltimore: Johns Hopkins University Press, 1988).

22. In many ways, this belief structure is closer to that found in some forms of Catholicism. See Andrew Greeley, *The Catholic Imagination* (Berkeley: University of California Press, 2000), 159–70.

23. One sees this in the description of the African American men in Mitchell Duneier's *Slim's Table: Race, Respectability, and Masculinity* (Chicago: University of Chicago Press, 1992).

24. See Anderson, *Code of the Street*, 37–45.

25. See Martín Sánchez-Jankowski, *Islands in the Street: Gangs and American Urban Society* (Berkeley: University of California Press, 1991), 141–44, 162–64; and Konrad Lorenz, *On Aggression* (London: Methuen, 1966).

26. The theme of invisibility is developed in two classic novels, Ralph Ellison's *Invisible Man* (New York: Random House, 1952) and James Baldwin's *Nobody Knows My Name: More Notes of a Native Son* (New York: Dell, 1961).

27. Cornel West, in a public lecture on African Americans and multiculturalism, stated that African American parents used unique names for their children precisely because they wanted to avoid being socially invisible. Also see Stanley Lieberson, *A Matter of Taste: How Names, Fashions, and Culture Change* (New Haven: Yale University Press, 2000).

28. See Ralf Dahrendorf, *Life Chances: Approaches to Social and Political Theory* (Chicago: University of Chicago Press, 1979).

29. See Simon Blackburn, *Lust* (New York: Oxford University Press, 2004).

30. On sexual behavior among the poor, see Liebow, *Tally's Corner*, 143–60; Anderson, *Streetwise*, 137; Hallowell Pope, "Negro-White Differences in Decisions Regarding Illegitimate Children," *Journal of Marriage and the Family* 31 (1969): 756–64; Nancy Scheper-Hughes, *Death without Weeping: The Violence of Everyday Life in Brazil* (Berkeley: University of California Press, 1992), 330–39.

31. See Kristin Luker, *Dubious Conceptions: The Politics of Teenage Pregnancy* (Cambridge, MA: Harvard University Press, 1996).

32. Although not identical, this is close to Swidler's conception of the "prosaic-realistic" view of love and marriage. See Swidler, *Talk of Love*, 118.

33. See ibid., 125.

34. While many may think that men are more likely to evade commitment, women do it too, especially as they grow older. Value orientations are not fixed but can change over the life course. For example, African American women are likely to adapt their value orientation as the number of eligible men declines.

35. For an excellent analysis of the changing value of children in the United States, see Viviana A. Zelizer, *Pricing the Priceless Child: The Changing Social Value of Children* (New York: Basic Books, 1985). Zelizer points out that value of children has fluctuated from useful to useless and back to useful. For the poor, such changes have doubtless been less dramatic because economic conditions have remained difficult and children have been able to make money for their parents.

36. See Melvin Kohn, *Class and Conformity: A Study in Values* (Homewood, IL: Dorsey Press, 1969), 93–103.

37. For a good discussion of this value orientation, see Scheper-Hughes, *Death without Weeping*, 342–53, 357–64, and Annette Lareau, *Unequal Child-*

hoods: Class, Race, and Family Life (Berkeley: University of California Press, 2003), esp. 30–31 for an overview.

38. See Anderson, *Code of the Street,* 35–65, and Venkatesh, *Off the Books,* 91–213, 278–365.

39. The development of social differentiation and the process of establishing solidarity between various elements or groups is discussed by Georg Simmel, "Group Expansion and the Development of Individuality," in *Georg Simmel: On Individuality and Social Forms,* ed. Donald N. Levine (Chicago: University of Chicago Press, 1971), 252–57.

40. For a description of churches assuming these types of dispositions, see Omar M. McRoberts, *Streets of Glory: Church and Community in a Black Neighborhood* (Chicago: University of Chicago Press, 2003).

41. State institutions have difficulty serving the interests and needs of the residents living in poor neighborhoods, but they do serve the interests and needs of people living in the more affluent neighborhoods by keeping the poor away from them. It is not necessary to look any further than the differing attitudes toward the police in poor and affluent neighborhoods—the poor see the police as simply intent on controlling them, while the affluent see the police as there to aid and protect them.

42. For a good discussion of institutionalization as it relates to organizational research, see Powell and DiMaggio, *New Institutionalism,* especially ch. 1.

43. E. A. Hayek's "Notes on the Evolution of Systems of Rules of Conduct," in *Studies in Philosophy, Politics, and Economics* (Chicago: University of Chicago Press, 1967), 66–81, and his *Law, Legislation, and Liberty,* 2 vols. (Chicago: University of Chicago Press, 1973–76), as well as Robert Nozick's *Anarchy, State, and Utopia* (New York: Basic Books, 1974), have been most associated with this approach. A good description of it is provided in Jack Knight, *Institutions and Social Conflict* (New York: Cambridge University Press, 1992), 9–13, 94–97.

44. See Michael Hechter, "The Emergence of Cooperative Social Institutions," in *Social Institutions: Their Emergence, Maintenance, and Effects,* ed. Michael Hechter, Karl-Dieter Opps, and Reinhard Wippler (New York: Aldine de Gruyter, 1990), 13–33, and his earlier work *Principles of Group Solidarity* (Berkeley: University of California Press, 1987).

45. See Harrison C. White, *Identity and Control: A Structural Theory of Action* (Princeton: Princeton University Press, 1992), 5–14.

46. See Knight's *Institutions and Social Conflict,* 73–80, which discusses the importance of information on an institution's rules and norms for the maintenance of the institution itself.

47. See Herbert J. Gans, *Urban Villagers,* 142–62. Gans also uses the concept of the "caretaker," but somewhat differently than I do here.

48. White, *Identity and Control,* 116.

49. See Ronald Jepperson on deinstitutionalization in "Institutions, Institutional Effects," 152–53.

50. This is very close to the dynamic that James Coleman theorized about in his exposition of the generation of norms. For Coleman's discussion of the role of individual demand in establishing norms, see his *Foundations of Social Theory*

(Cambridge, MA: Harvard University Press, 1990), 241–65, and his "The Emergence of Norms," in Hechter, Opps, and Wippler, *Social Institutions,* 35–59.

51. White, *Identity and Control,* 160–63.

52. I have purposely chosen each of these examples to indicate that men do not have more roles available to them than women. All of the roles I gave could be used by both men and women, with the exception perhaps of the "pimp" role, which is dominated by men. Empirically, women and men have an equal number of roles that can be used to generate a social identity.

53. See Anderson, *Place on the Corner,* 31–53, 179–206. He also made this observation, but in his study the status categories emerged from interactions inside the establishment, and I found that this was insufficient for an establishment to become a local institution.

54. When individuals are assigned an identity status that is understood to be negative, it usually results from people in the community feeling fear, envy, or a perverted sense of admiration for an activity(ies) whose ultimate consequence is evaluated as being negative.

55. See Elijah Anderson, *Place on the Corner,* 31–53. Anderson's description of the social formation in the bar and liquor store he studied is similar to many of the observations in the present study, but there are some important differences as well. First, although Anderson describes the social actors in a particular establishment, he makes no claims that this establishment is an institution, whereas I am explaining how establishments become social institutions and how the dynamics of change and preservation are affected by them. What makes an establishment an institution is the power of its internal dynamics to influence people's behavior both inside and outside its confines. Thus, if one is interested in understanding the impact of institutions on the structure of local neighborhoods it is necessary to describe and analyze the social relations inside the institution and their interconnectedness with the social order of the neighborhood.

56. See Mary Douglas, *How Institutions Think* (Syracuse: Syracuse University Press, 1986), 58–61.

57. See Lynne Zucker, "Institutionalization and Cultural Persistence," in Powell and DiMaggio, *New Institutionalism,* 87–88.

58. See Jon Elster, *The Cement of Society: A Study of Social Order* (New York: Cambridge University Press, 1989). Elster has argued that a social order is *the* factor that holds society together, "the cement of a society."

59. See Suttles, *Social Order,* 3–36.

60. Oliver Zunz, *The Changing Face of Inequality: Urbanization, Industrialization, Development, and Immigrants in Detroit, 1880–1920* (Chicago: University of Chicago Press, 1982).

61. See David Matza, "Poverty and Disrepute," in *Contemporary Social Problems,* 2nd ed., ed. Robert K. Merton and Robert A. Nisbet (New York: Harcourt, Brace and World, 1966), 619–69.

62. See Katheryn Edin and Laura Lein, *Making Ends Meet: How Single Mothers Survive Welfare and Low-Wage Work* (New York: Russell Sage Foundation, 1997), 60–87.

63. See Christopher Jencks, *The Homeless* (Cambridge, MA: Harvard University Press, 1985).

64. See David A. Snow and Leon Anderson, *Down on Their Luck: A Study of Homeless Street People* (Berkeley: University of California Press, 1993).

65. See Roger Waldinger, *Through the Eye of a Needle: Immigrants and Enterprise in New York's Garment Trades* (New York: New York University Press, 1986); for day workers, see Abel Valenzuela Jr., "Day Laborers as Entrepreneurs?" *Journal of Ethnic and Migration Studies* 27, no. 2 (2001): 335–52.

66. See Dohan, *Price of Poverty,* and Mercer Sullivan, *"Getting Paid": Youth Crime and Work in the Inner City* (Ithaca: Cornell University Press, 1989).

67. See Philippe Bourgois, *In Search of Respect: Selling Crack in El Barrio* (New York: Cambridge University Press, 1995).

68. See Frank Munger, ed., *Laboring below the Line: The New Ethnography of Poverty, Low-Wage Work, and Survival in the Global Economy* (New York: Russell Sage Foundation, 2002).

69. For a description of the secondary labor market, see David M. Gordon, Richard Edwards, and Michael Reich, *Segmented Labor, Divided Labor: Historical Transformations of Labor in the United States* (New York: Cambridge University Press, 1982).

70. Roger Waldinger and Michael I. Lichter, *How the Other Half Works: Immigration and the Social Organization of Labor* (Berkeley: University of California Press, 2003), 38.

71. The envy and inferiority that the poor feel toward the working class and the superiority that the working class feel toward the poor are discussed in Duneier's *Slim's Table* and Anderson's *Place on the Corner* and *Code of the Street.*

72. See Mary Patillo-McCoy, *Black Picket Fences: Privilege and Peril in the Black Middle Class* (Chicago: University of Chicago Press, 1999). She provides an analytic description of the process whereby the African American middle class tries to separate itself from the lower class but is unable to do so. Eventually the middle-class area becomes first a mixture of middle and lower class and then predominantly lower class.

73. See Bourgois, *In Search of Respect,* 105–13.

74. See Suttles, *Social Order,* 67–71. Suttles did not observe all of those living in a slum neighborhood dressing in expensive and "stylish" clothing; Italians, for example, did not dress stylishly. However, he did observe African Americans doing so, as well as Mexicans and Puerto Ricans. The African Americans wore stylish clothing within the broad range of conventions governing what was "stylish" in contemporary American society, whereas the Mexicans and Puerto Ricans wore clothing that mixed the conventions of what was considered "stylish" within each of the countries of origin.

75. For a more elaborate definition of power, see Herbert A. Simon, "Notes on the Observation and Measurement of Political Power," *Journal of Politics* 15 (November 1953): 504; and Felix Oppenheim, "'Power' Revisited," *Journal of Politics* 40 (August 1978): 590.

76. For a description of an extreme example of psychological strength and resolve in pursuing one's goals, see Sánchez-Jankowski, *Islands in the Street,* 23–28.

77. See Roger D. Abrahams, "Playing the Dozens," *Journal of American Folklore* 75 (1962): 209–18. "The Dozens" is a verbal game where each player

attempts to better the other's last disparaging remark about oneself or one's family and friends with the use of clever sentences, concepts, and words that are often rude or crass.

78. I took both these quotes as I listened to the two individuals talk to their friends. In neither case was I part of the social group in which the conversation was taking place.

79. On gentrification, see John P. Logan and Harvey L. Molotch, *Urban Fortunes: The Political Economy of Place* (Berkeley: University of California Press, 1987), 107–10; 115–17; Gans, *Urban Villagers,* 281–335.

80. On issues of urban renewal, see King, *Chain of Change,* 22, 64–72, 73–78, 203–10; Logan and Molotch, *Urban Fortunes,* 114–15; Gans, *Urban Villagers,* 323–95. On issues surrounding disasters, see Mike Davis, *Ecology of Fear: Los Angeles and the Imagination of Disaster* (New York: Metropolitan Books, 1998).

81. Suttles, *Social Order,* 23–24.

82. North, *Institutions, Institutional Change,* 36–53, has conceptualized institutional constraints as formal and informal. When I speak of constraints, I am including both. These agents of change have affected both the formal and informal constraints of local institutions to the point that they are not capable of sustaining their institutional character.

83. See Daniel Katz and Robert L. Kahn, *The Social Psychology of Organizations,* 2nd ed. (New York: John Wiley and Sons, 1978), 385–94.

84. See Fischer, "Toward A Sub-cultural Theory," and "Subcultural Theory of Urbanism."

85. Some in the neighborhood, given the size of the ethnic group in the area, might argue that this strategy is important for all members of the group in the entire city, not just for those in a particular neighborhood. Louis Wirth was one of those sociologists who saw ethnic traditions in decline when the original community began to disperse to other sections of the city. See Wirth, *Ghetto.*

86. An example of this would be the experience of the Gypsies and the Jews, both of whom found themselves without a homeland, despised, and prohibited from owning property in many countries for centuries. Subgroups within these two ethnicities would be the purest examples of the process that I am talking about, but other groups have also experienced this process on a more limited basis. For a history of the Jews, see Lloyd P. Gartner, *History of the Jews in Modern Times* (New York: Oxford University Press, 2001), and S. N. Eisenstadt, *Jewish Civilization: The Jewish Historical Experience in Comparative Perspective* (Albany: State University of New York Press, 1992); for the Gypsies, see Jean-Pierre Liegeois, *Gypsies: An Illustrated History* (London: Al Saqi Books, 1986), and David M. Crowe, *A History of the Gypsies of Eastern Europe and Russia* (New York: St. Martin's Press, 1995). Other groups, like the Chinese and Latvians, could be included as well. Also, the Italians found it valuable to maintain the lower-class adaptive culture they had rather than to give it up.

87. Hechter, *Principles of Group Solidarity.*

88. African American preachers would be a good example of preservation agents within this context.

89. See LeRoi Jones (a.k.a. Imamu Amiri Baraka), *Home: Social Essays* (New York: William Morrow, 1966), 101–4, which makes this argument about "soul food" among African Americans.

90. See Whyte, *Street Corner Society,* 104–8.

91. A great many studies have relied on a structural analysis of poverty. Some that incorporate aspects of the structuralist position are Thomas J. Sugrue, "The Structure of Urban Poverty: The Reorganization of Space and Work in Three Periods of American History," in *The Underclass Debate: Views from History,* ed. Michael B. Katz (Princeton: Princeton University Press, 1993); Peter B. Doeringer and Michael J. Piore, *Internal Labor Markets and Manpower Analysis* (Lexington, MA: D. C. Heath, 1971); Claude S. Fischer et al., *Inequality by Design: Cracking the Bell Curve Myth* (Princeton: Princeton University Press, 1996), 70–101; and W. Wilson, *Truly Disadvantaged.*

92. Conservative and liberal approaches to the condition of poverty both assume that people living in this state hold the same values that the more affluent elements of the society have; however, the liberal approach focuses on structural impediments to opportunities or on misfortunes arising from physical/mental disabilities that prevent people from leaving poverty. See Rebecca Blank, *It Takes a Nation: A New Agenda to Fight Poverty* (New York: Russell Sage Foundation, 1997); Glenn Loury, *The Anatomy of Racial Inequality* (Cambridge, MA: Harvard University Press, 2002). For conservatives a lack of initiative and government policies that encourage it are at the core of poverty. See Murray, *Losing Ground,* and Lawrence Mead, *The New Politics of Poverty: The Nonworking Poor in America* (New York: Basic Books, 1992).

93. Oscar Lewis's *Five Families* and *La Vida* had reported a culture among the poor that was related to their condition of deprivation. This finding was attacked by Ryan, *Blaming the Victim;* Valentine, *Culture and Poverty;* and Eleanor Burke Leacock, ed., *The Culture of Poverty: A Critique* (New York: Simon and Schuster, 1971), who argued that Lewis's concept of culture was flawed and that he had mistakenly attributed the predicament of the poor to their behavior rather than to structural conditions.

94. I do not mean to suggest that I am using *subculture* here in the same sense as that implied by phrases like "religious subculture" or "bohemian subculture"; I am positing something more general that includes a logic of scarcity, rationality of scarcity, worldview of scarcity, etc.

95. The majority of immigrants arrive with little more than muscle and drive. Some are celebrities and a sizable minority are highly educated and talented, but this latter group rarely start from, or find their way into, the poor neighborhoods of America.

96. See William A. V. Clark, "The Geography of Immigrant Poverty: Selective Evidence of an Immigrant Underclass," in *Strangers at the Gates,* ed. Roger Waldinger (Berkeley: University of California Press, 2001), 161; and Waldinger and Lichter, *How the Other Half Works,* 167, 236, 239.

97. My "subculture of scarcity" has some commonalities with previous studies' descriptions of the elements, conditions, and experiences of lower-class life. Many of these studies have used the concept of "lower-class culture" as their primary analytic tool. See, for example, S. M. Miller and Frank Riessman, "The

Working Class Subculture: A New View," *Social Problems* 9 (1961): 86–97; Lee Rainwater, *Behind Ghetto Walls: Black Family in a Federal Slum* (Chicago: Aldine, 1970), ch. 13.

98. See Janet Poppendieck, *Sweet Charity? Emergency Food and the End of Entitlement* (New York: Viking Press, 1998), on the use of private charity as a substitute for government-run programs that could serve as a permanent safety net. The ideology of charity for the poor that dominated social thought before the Great Depression has waned over time but never really been replaced.

99. See Ann Swidler, "Culture in Action: Symbols and Strategies," *American Sociological Review* 51 (1986): 273–86.

100. See Weber, *Protestant Ethic;* Talcott Parsons, *The Social System* (Glencoe, IL: Free Press, 1951); C. Kluckhohn, "Values and Value-Orientations," 388–433; F. Kluckhohn and Strodtbeck, *Variations in Value Orientations;* Swidler, "Culture in Action"; and Fischer, "Subcultural Theory of Urbanism."

101. See Lewis, *La Vida,* xlii–lii. Lewis recognized this principle, and his description of the "culture of poverty" included the passing of behaviors and values from one generation to another. Without such a process, he could not have fully considered the phenomenon he was analyzing as a "culture."

102. For an example of drug dealers, see Bourgois, *In Search of Respect,* 105–13.

103. For Korean businesses that received their "start-up" monies from Korean banks or loan associations with high interest rates, see Jennifer Lee, *Civility in the City: Blacks, Jews, and Koreans in Urban America* (Cambridge, MA: Harvard University Press, 2002), 37.

104. See Dohan, *Price of Poverty,* 103–53.

105. The jobs in the legal economy are usually secondary labor market jobs, which offer low wages, no benefits, and little opportunity for mobility. They may be in the legal economy, but they are what is often referred to as "dead-end jobs." See Waldinger and Lichter, *How the Other Half Works,* 219–20.

106. Even in the most restrictive environments, people build social systems with social status hierarchies that give meaning to the lives of those who are confined to such conditions. For example, on the existence of such social systems among slaves in the United States, see Genovese, *Roll, Jordan, Roll.*

107. See Martin Gilens, *Why Americans Hate Welfare: Race, Media, and the Politics of Antipoverty Policy* (Chicago: University of Chicago Press, 1999), on the attitudes of average Americans toward those who are poor and on welfare. Also see Loïc J.D. Wacquant, "The Rise of Advanced Marginality: Notes on its Nature and Implications," *Acta Sociologica* 39 (1996): 121–39.

108. Those who are actively resisting change may not succeed in their efforts. See Elijah Anderson's vivid description of how "old heads" were being displaced by "new heads" in the poor Philadelphia neighborhood he studied in *Streetwise,* 69–76, 242–43.

109. See Dennis Wrong, *The Problem of Order: What Unites and Divides Societies* (New York: Cambridge University Press, 1994), 202–43.

110. See Wacquant, "Three Pernicious Premises," 341–53.

111. Most of the researchers using the concept of social disorganization use the inability of local residents to work together to solve common problems as

the criterion for labeling the neighborhood as "disorganized." See, for example, W. Wilson, *When Work Disappears,* 20–21; Robert J. Sampson and W. Byron Groves, "Community Structure and Crime: Testing Social-Disorganization Theory," *American Journal of Sociology* 94 (January 1989): 774–802, esp. 777–82; and Skogan, *Disorder and Decline,* 21–50. This approach, however, fails to recognize that the local residents do indeed work together to solve common problems that involve managing functional needs within their everyday social interactions. The fact that they cannot solve larger problems affecting them does not mean they are disorganized. Canada cannot solve issues having to do with acid rain, not because it is disorganized, but because it cannot get cooperation from other governments like the United States.

2. GIVE ME SHELTER: COMPETING AGENDAS FOR LIFE IN PUBLIC HOUSING

1. For a discussion of the poor and a description (with pictures) of the housing they were relegated to live in, see Riis, *How The Other Half Lives.* Also see the discussion of these various housing types in poor neighborhoods in Zorbaugh, *Gold Coast.*

2. Riis has pictures of the homeless adults and children who were relegated to these areas. See his *How The Other Half Lives,* 153–69.

3. The work of Jane Addams was a prime example of a private citizen using private donations to house the poor. See her *Twenty Years at Hull House.* Also see Michael Katz, *In the Shadow of the Poorhouse: A Social History of Welfare in America* (1986; repr., New York: Basic Books, 1996), 3–116, and Lawrence J. Vale, *From the Puritans to the Projects: Public Housing and Public Neighbors* (Cambridge, MA: Harvard University Press, 2000), 1–92.

4. See Richard Plunz, *A History of Housing in New York City* (New York: Columbia University Press, 1990), 209.

5. See Douglas S. Massey and Shawn M. Kanaiaupuni, "Public Housing and the Concentration of Poverty," *Social Science Quarterly* 74 (March 1993): 109, 111; Adam Bickford and Douglas S. Massey, "Segregation in the Second Ghetto: Racial and Ethnic Segregation in American Public Housing, 1977," *Social Forces* 69, no. 4 (1991): 1011–36; for Chicago, see "High Rise Brought Low at Last," *Economist,* July 11, 1998; for Detroit, see "Motor City Money," *Michigan Daily,* October 15, 1996; and for St. Louis, see Alexander von Hoffman, "High-Rise Hellholes," *American Prospect,* April 9, 2001, 40–43.

6. See Arnold Hirsch, *Making the Second Ghetto: Race and Housing in Chicago, 1940–1960* (New York: Cambridge University Press, 1983); John F. Bauman, Norman P. Hummon, and Edward K. Muller, "Public Housing Isolation, and the Urban Underclass: Philadelphia's Richard Allen Homes, 1941–1965," *Journal of Urban History* 17 (May 1991): 264–92.

7. See Rainwater, *Behind Ghetto Walls.*

8. Two recent studies that have dealt with life in housing projects and tenements are Sudhir Venkatesh, *American Project: The Rise and Fall of a Modern Ghetto* (Cambridge, MA: Harvard University Press, 2000), and Dwight

Conquergood, "Life in Big Red: Struggle and Accommodations in a Chicago Polyethnic Tenement," in *Structuring Diversity: Ethnographic Perspectives on the New Immigration,* ed. Louise Lamphere (Chicago: University of Chicago Press, 1992), 95–144.

9. See the very important work of Lee Rainwater and associates analyzing the Pruitt-Igoe Projects of St. Louis, Missouri. The research project was directed by Alvin Gouldner while he was a member of the sociology department (when there was a sociology department) at Washington University in St. Louis. Much of the work, though not all of it, was summarized in Rainwater, *Behind Ghetto Walls.*

10. See Terry Williams and William Kornblum, *The Uptown Kids: Struggle and Hope in the Projects* (New York: G. P. Putnam and Sons, 1994).

11. See Paul H. Messenger, "Public-Housing Perversity: A View from the Trenches," *Public Interest* 108 (Summer 1992): 133–42. In this article, Messenger, who was an administrator of a public housing complex, discusses the legislation that has contributed to the difficulties that public housing administrators must confront. He also argues for a fundamental change in the role of public housing.

12. This quote was part of a conversation between the administrator and three employees who worked in the complex's community center. I was playing solitaire at the table next to where they were having the conversation.

13. The custodian told another worker this while I was waiting for him to clean the floor of the elevator I wanted to take.

14. The assistant administrator was conversing with two new workers at the community center. I was helping a resident fix his boy's baby carriage outside the door of the community center.

15. See Matza, "Poverty and Disrepute," 619–69.

16. If one image dominates academic and popular press descriptions of life in housing projects, it is that they are notoriously unsafe places for anyone to be in. While most of these accounts greatly exaggerate the danger of living in public housing, there can be a significant amount of risk, so it should come as no surprise that risk reduction would be one of the primary objectives of the administrators. For a depiction of housing projects as danger-ridden, see Alex Kotlowitz, *There Are No Children Here: The Story of Two Boys Growing Up in the Other America* (New York: Anchor Books, 1992).

17. See Weber, *Economy and Society,* 54.

18. The administrator was conversing with workers in charge of constructing the units' new play area. I was sitting on the public benches outside the play area reading the paper and listening to their conversation.

19. The administrator was conversing with one of his subordinates as they were reviewing the construction of a handball court in the public space of their complex. I was sitting on a bench watching the construction and listening to their conversation.

20. See Klinenberg, *Heat Wave.* Significant segments of society are frightened of natural disasters because they feel helpless. Ironically, the middle class, who see natural disasters as affecting them independent of wealth, are more likely than the poor to have this fear, which is very similar to the poor's feeling about

financial disasters. On the fear of natural disaster among the middle class, see
M. Davis, *Ecology of Fear.*

21. For studies that found patterns similar to my observations, see Raisa
Bahchieva and Amy Hosier, "Determinants of Tenure Duration in Public Housing: The Case of New York City," *Journal of Housing Research* 12, no. 2 (2001):
307–48, and, for Boston, Lawrence J. Vale, "Empathological Places: Residents'
Ambivalence toward Remaining in Public Housing," *Journal of Planning Education and Research* 16 (1997): 159–75.

22. The administrator was conversing with two people in a restaurant during lunch. I was in the booth behind them.

23. The janitor was talking with two of his friends who had come to visit him
at work. He was cleaning the elevators, and I was sitting out of their sight on
one of the inside fire escape steps, waiting for a friend to come down.

24. See Lawrence J. Vale, *From the Puritans,* 295–97.

25. The day care worker was talking to two of her co-workers in the day care
center. I was there checking on one of the children in the center. They did not
know that I was listening to them.

26. See Venkatesh, *American Project,* 124, for a description of the housing
authority's efforts to create a voluntary "identification system" in which residents carried identification cards and reported visitors to housing authority officials, as well as the housing authority's strategies for eviction.

27. See Hirsch, *Making the Second Ghetto;* John F. Bauman, *Public Housing, Race, and Renewal: Urban Planning in Philadelphia, 1920–1974* (Philadelphia: Temple University Press, 1987); and Massey and Kanaiaupuni, "Public
Housing," 109–22.

28. David was talking with his friends while waiting to get a haircut in
Harper's Barbershop in the Richardson neighborhood. I was in the barbershop
just listening to everyone's conversations.

29. It was snowing outside, and Ana was talking to her mother and two
friends in the lobby of Buckley Gardens while they waited for her cousin to pick
them up and drive them to work in a Brooklyn clothing factory. I was in the
lobby talking with the custodian and a friend.

30. Urban sociologists of the early Chicago School identified these conditions
as defining what it meant to be an "urban environment." See Wirth, "Urbanism." Also see Claude Fischer, *The Urban Experience,* 2nd ed. (San Diego: Harcourt Brace Jovanovich, 1984), 28–32.

31. See Lee Rainwater, *And the Poor Get Children* (Chicago: Quadrangle
Books, 1960). The U.S. Census Bureau's *Current Population Survey,* June 2000,
shows that as annual family income goes down, the number of births per thousand women increases: for incomes of $50,000 and up, it is 60.6; for $30,000
to $49,000, it is 63.6; for $20,000 to $29,000, it is 77.5; for $10,000 to $19,000,
it is 74.8; and for under $10,000, it is 86.8.

32. See Luker, *Dubious Conceptions,* 113.

33. Celia and Malcolm had this conversation while they were walking back
from a video store where they had just rented some movies. I was walking in
back of them.

34. Joan Moore also found that the Mexican women she studied often ran away from home as a result of being dominated or violated by male family members. See her *Going Down to the Barrio: Homeboys and Homegirls in Change* (Philadelphia: Temple University Press, 1991), 92–100; also see Horowitz's discussion of sexuality in *Honor and the American Dream*, 114–36.

35. Connie was talking with a friend at school. I was in the cafeteria at the next table. I also observed her relations within the family.

36. As noted in chapter 1, men believed that women were always trying to entrap them and were promiscuous.

37. Maurice was talking with another friend at a local laundromat. I was there waiting for my clothes to dry.

38. See Anderson, *Streetwise,* 112–15, who also found this to be a factor.

39. Marcos was conversing with four other young men at the basketball courts. There is good reason to believe that he had fathered a number of children. I was able to document through the use of three independent sources that he was the father of four other children.

40. Leticia was talking with two of her friends at the housing project's community center. I was sitting on a bench in the center.

41. This finding is similar to that of Anderson in *Streetwise,* 117–19.

42. Julia was talking to two of her friends in front of the Isla Bodega in the Bronx's Elmway neighborhood. I was sitting at a table that the owner had put out front for summer customers. Two months later, Julia was pregnant.

43. See the confirming evidence in Anderson, *Streetwise,* 118–19.

44. Renee was conversing with four of her friends at the community center of the Palm Court Apartments. I was waiting my turn to play table tennis.

45. Monique was talking with her brother and a friend of his at a local bar. I was sitting next to them at the bar.

46. Sergio was interacting with his family during a Sunday gathering. I was an invited guest of Sergio, whom I had met while playing dominoes at Pepe's Barbershop in the El Rey neighborhood of Los Angeles.

47. Todd was conversing with two friends at a laundromat near the Gardenia Avenue Apartments in Brooklyn's Eagleton neighborhood.

48. Anderson, *Streetwise,* 136.

49. Nancy Scheper-Hughes found this tendency to give life a chance even in the most difficult of physical and material conditions among the poor women of northeast Brazil. See her *Death without Weeping,* 333–39. The pages listed give some data on the thinking of women as it concerns birth control, but the entire book reflects a prevalent belief about a woman's responsibility to provide life to the world.

50. Andrea was conversing with a female worker at a bus stop in front of the day care center in the John C. Fremont Homes of L.A.'s El Rey neighborhood. I was there waiting for the same bus.

51. Loretta was talking to three friends at the community center. I was there socializing with a number of women who were trying to start a building advocacy organization.

52. See Lee Rainwater and Timothy Smeedling, *Poor Kids in Rich Countries* (New York: Russell Sage Foundation, 2003).

53. See Venkatesh, *American Project,* 47; and Martín Sánchez-Jankowski, "The Concentration of African American Poverty and the Dispersal of the Working Class: An Ethnographic Study of Three Inner-City Areas," *International Journal of Urban and Regional Research* 23 (December 1999): 619–37.

54. Much of what I observed concerning density is similar to Richard Sennett's observation that people in densely populated cities like New York are forced to learn about other groups in their or other neighborhoods in order to survive. See Richard Sennett, *The Uses of Disorder: Personal Identity and City Life* (New York: Knopf, 1970).

55. See Plunz, *History of Housing,* 236–37, and Jacqueline Leavitt, "Women under Fire: Public Housing Activism in Los Angeles," *Frontiers* 13, no. 2 (1992): 116.

56. Roger Montgomery has written a brief but wonderful discussion of the issues related to architecture's relationship to the poor and especially the poor living in housing projects. See his "Comment on 'Fear and House-as-Haven in the Lower Class,'" *Journal of the American Institute of Planners* 32 (January 1966): 31–37.

57. I took down this quote while I was visiting the apartment to see Tyler, the husband and father of the family. Tyler and I had made arrangements to meet at his apartment after he got out of work. I was in the kitchen reading the paper at the table when the conversation between Donald and his two brothers occurred. Their mother was next door visiting her neighbor.

58. Paco and Dina were talking at the kitchen table. I was in the living room watching television, waiting for Paco to go with me to see the illegal cockfights in the neighborhood. The kids were playing in the same room I was in, so Paco and Dina may have thought that their conversation was more private than it was.

59. During this conversation, I was in the living room watching television and waiting for Dominic's mother and father to return from visiting another family in the building. The boys were in the same room playing.

60. See Sally Engle Merry, *Urban Danger: Life in a Neighborhood of Strangers* (Philadelphia: Temple University Press, 1981), 153–55.

61. I listened to this conversation while sitting on the steps used for emergencies when the elevators were not working. The steps were located on both sides of the lobby where Josh and his friends were talking.

62. I took down this quote while talking with a group of unemployed males as they drank in the common area of the Orchid Lane Apartments.

63. Of course, it was not always possible to keep children clean, since they did little to control the amount of dirt in their lives. See Mary Douglas, *Purity and Danger: An Analysis of Concepts of Pollution and Taboo* (New York: Praeger, 1966), 2–5, for an analysis of the origins and meanings of rituals related to pollution, purification, and the concept of danger related to them.

64. Suttles, *Social Order,* 3–38, discusses the same attitude in the poor neighborhood he studied in Chicago.

65. Fischer, *Urban Experience,* 54–55, reports that the evidence concerning noise in cities suggests there is increased noise in urban settings but not measurable health effects. His data do address the impact of noise in low-income neighborhoods, where the variety of noise can create a good deal of stress. Further, it

may be true that people adapt, but this does not mean that noise has no impact on their stress level and ultimately their behavior. The evidence from the present study of five poor neighborhoods indicates that it does have an impact on most people and their behavior.

66. Dorothy was talking to a lady who had recently come to live in the housing project. They were both in the laundromat washing clothes. I was also there washing clothes when I took down their conversation.

67. See Georg Simmel, "The Metropolis and Mental Life," in *Georg Simmel: On Individuality and Social Forms*, ed. Donald M. Levine (Chicago: University of Chicago Press, 1971), 324–39; Park, "Human Migration," 194–206.

68. The concept of a worldview is a fundamental part of culture, and in this case it is a fundamental part of the local lower-class culture. Some of what I am describing within this culture was reported in earlier studies on lower- and working-class populations. See S. Miller and Riessman, "Working Class Subculture"; Walter B. Miller, "Lower Class Culture as a Generating Milieu of Gang Delinquency," *Journal of Social Issues* 14, no. 3 (1958): 4–19; and Rainwater, *Behind Ghetto Walls*, ch. 13 ("Negro Lower-Class Identity and Culture").

69. Sharon was talking with two friends in the common area of the project.

70. Ricardo was conversing with two friends while sitting in the common area of the project drinking beer. I was next to them with three other people who were having their own conversation.

71. Tati was talking to the cook while the two of them were on their break at the restaurant where they worked. Ironically, the cook could not speak English, as he had recently immigrated from Nigeria. I was listening and having a cup of coffee.

72. Carl was drinking beer and talking with three friends while they waited for their turn to play handball. I was there watching the handball game at the Palm Court Apartments' outdoor handball court.

73. Paloma was conversing with her friends Margarita and Susana as they watched their children play in the playground. I was sitting watching parents and children interact.

74. See the work of Oscar Lewis on the Puerto Rican and Mexican poor, particularly *La Vida,* and *Five Families.* Nancy Scheper-Hughes's work among the Brazilian poor indicates similar worldviews; see her *Death without Weeping.*

75. On the conservative side are the analyses of Murray, *Losing Ground* 180–91, and Mead, *New Politics of Poverty,* 145–51. On the liberal side are the analyses of Christopher Jencks, *Rethinking Social Policy: Race, Poverty, and the Underclass* (Cambridge, MA: Harvard University Press, 1992), 122–36, and W. Wilson, *When Work Disappears,* 70–86.

76. Jerry was talking to friends before playing a pickup basketball game at the complex's basketball courts. I was just sitting watching the games.

77. Emmett was talking to two of his relatives while they were walking home from church. I was walking with them.

78. This conversation took place while I was in the Town Barbershop socializing.

79. See Gans, *Urban Villagers,* 142–45.

80. *Curanderismo* is a traditional folk medicine approach to public health and is still practiced in Latino areas. For a description, see Ari Kiev, *Curanderismo: Mexican-American Folk Psychiatry* (New York: Free Press, 1968).

81. Gans, *Urban Villagers*, 145.

82. Both Elijah Anderson and Ruth Horowitz have provided important contributions to the understanding of identity formation in low-income neighborhoods. For Horowitz, identity formation was the result of residents' struggle to reconcile the values and identities of the American society with the values and identities of Mexican society. Because her work focused on the issue of ethnicity in identity formation, she emphasized what she found to be the two large and competing identity-forming systems—"the American dream," associated with the American host society, and "honor," associated with Mexican immigrant society. For Anderson, identity emerged from the competition within the primary group of an establishment (in his case, the patrons of a local bar in Chicago) to develop and maintain an identity. Although I found evidence to support the contentions of Horowitz and Anderson in some substantive areas that will be discussed later when I turn to other institutions, I found that social identities in the housing projects, and neighborhoods at large, were more varied and extensive than the ones Horowitz and Anderson reported. See Anderson, *Place on the Corner*, esp. 31–53, and Horowitz's *Honor and the American Dream*.

83. Suttles, *Social Order*, 3–12.

84. These findings support the theoretical propositions advanced in White's *Identity and Control*, 3–21, concerning the importance of identity and identity networks in social structure.

85. In some ways the efforts of the state and its agents, in this case the managers of the public housing units, are similar to the efforts of religious missionaries to bring their religion to the inhabitants of another area. Most often the environment is out of sync with the theology that is being proselytized and competing religions in the area that are established seem to have an advantage, but the missionaries continue because they are true believers and/or it is their paid profession. Over time the appeal of the theology (to provide support in life) and missionaries' offer to help in that process produce some successes. This encourages the missionaries (and their superiors) to keep trying and renews the competition for participants.

3. A LIVING REFUGE: SOCIAL CHANGE AND PRESERVATION IN THE HOUSING PROJECT

1. See W. Wilson, *When Work Disappears*, 3–50, and *Truly Disadvantaged*. Also see John Kasarda, "Structural Factors Affecting the Location and Timing of Urban Underclass Growth," *Urban Geography* 11 (1990): 234–64, "Inner-City Concentrated Poverty and Neighborhood Distress: 1970–1990," *Housing Policy Debate* 4, no. 3 (1993): 253–302, and "Cities as Places Where People Live and Work: Urban Change and Neighborhood Distress," in *Interwoven Destinies: Cities and the Nation*, ed. Henry G. Cisneros (New York: Norton, 1993), 81–124.

2. See Martín Sánchez-Jankowski, "Concentration of African American Poverty."

3. See corroborating evidence in Williams and Kornblum, *Uptown Kids,* 71.

4. Douglas Massey and colleagues have researched and written extensively on the cause of ghettoization in American inner cities. They have questioned the conclusions advanced by William Julius Wilson that inner-city segregation and poverty among African Americans are the net result of joblessness and have instead argued that segregation and the increasing concentration of African poverty in inner cities are primarily the result of aggressive and systematic racial discrimination in the housing market and only secondarily job loss, which has simply concentrated the African American poor in an already confined social area. The evidence that they have brought to bear on the question is extensive, and their argument has had a significant impact on the sociological understanding of concentrated poverty in African American areas. See Douglas Massey and Mitchell L. Eggers, "The Ecology of Inequality: Minorities and the Concentration of Poverty, 1970–1980," *American Journal of Sociology* 95 (1990): 1153–88; and Massey and Denton, *American Apartheid.* W. Wilson has written a response to Massey and his colleagues in *When Work Disappears,* 15. Yet how neighborhoods become concentrated with high numbers of poor is much more complicated than simply racial discrimination in the housing market, as advanced by Massey and Denton, or joblessness, as advanced by Wilson. See Sánchez-Jankowski, "Concentration of African American Poverty."

5. Williams and Kornblum, *Uptown Kids,* 21–22.

6. Ken was talking to his neighbors Edgar and Jesse at the Gordon Street mom-and-pop grocery store (see table 3 for a description of grocery stores in each neighborhood). I was in the store when their conversation occurred.

7. Claudia was talking to two of her co-workers at the bus stop in front of the John C. Fremont Homes. I was standing waiting for the bus as well.

8. In Los Angeles there is evidence that manufacturing jobs actually increased between 1980 and 1990, but jobs in the service sector increased significantly. See Allen J. Scott, "The Manufacturing Economy: Ethnic and Gender Divisions of Labor," in *Ethnic Los Angeles,* ed. Roger Waldinger and Mehdi Bozorgmehr (New York: Russell Sage Foundation, 1996), 215–44. For changes in the New York economy and the rise of the service sector, see Roger Waldinger, *Still the Promised City? African Americans and New Immigrants in Postindustrial New York* (Cambridge, MA: Harvard University Press, 1996), 33–56.

9. Many immigrants had entered the country legally and were entitled to public assistance if they were economically qualified. However, a significant number were in the country illegally. These people had managed, through contacts and a lively market in illegal documents, to purchase official-looking documents that were taken to be proof of legal residency or citizenship itself.

10. See Williams and Kornblum, *Uptown Kids,* 195.

11. See chapter 1 for a fuller discussion of these groups and their characteristics.

12. On the decline in working-class jobs, see W. Wilson, *When Work Disappears.*

13. See Suzanne Model, "Where New York's West Indians Work," in *Islands in the City: West Indian Migration to New York,* ed. Nancy Foner (Berkeley:

University of California Press, 2001), 61, table 2.4. Her data show nearly as many foreign-born West Indians as African Americans in construction and manufacturing (traditional working-class jobs), and foreign-born West Indians, if combined with native-born West Indians, form a clear majority over African Americans in these jobs. Thus the contribution of the foreign born with the skills and desire to enter this sector of the labor market is significant.

14. These observations support the findings of James H. Johnson Jr., Walter C. Farrell Jr., and Jennifer A. Stoloff, "African American Males in Decline: A Los Angeles Case Study," in *Prismatic Metropolis: Inequality in Los Angeles,* ed. Lawrence Bobo et al. (New York: Russell Sage Foundation, 2001), 315–37.

15. There are of course Puerto Ricans and Dominicans of African descent, but they are not included in the "African descent" category because they both identify with and are identified by members of the group as Puerto Rican and Dominican. This is not to suggest that there is no discrimination against darker individuals in each group, because there is. It is merely to acknowledge that both groups have found a way to incorporate individuals to a point that they consider themselves Puerto Ricans and Dominicans (albeit dark and light ones) and not Afro-Puerto Ricans and Afro-Dominicans. On identity and discrimination in Puerto Rican society, see Clara E. Rodriguez, "Racial Classification among Puerto Rican Men and Women in New York," *Hispanic Journal of Behavioral Sciences* 12 (1990): 366–80; and Nancy A. Denton and Douglas S. Massey, "Racial Identity among Caribbean Hispanics: The Effect of Double Minority Status on Residential Segregation," *American Sociological Review* 54 (1980): 790–808.

16. This dynamic was also at play in Boston, where, in addition to the groups mentioned, there were shifts in the population of public housing units from solely Irish American to multiethnic. There was great conflict at first, but as this chapter will show, the transition of neighborhoods from fragmented to contested was eventually followed by a transition back to fragmented. See Vale, *From the Puritans,* 267–346.

17. Humberto was talking to three friends at the units' outside handball courts. I was there watching the game that was being played.

18. On the issue of poor migrants changing the composition of the public housing population, see Nicholas Lemann, *The Promised Land: The Great Black Migration and How It Changed America* (New York: Vintage Books, 1992), 274–75.

19. For a description of variations in the cultural "action strategies" of different generations of Mexican Americans, see Dohan, *Price of Poverty.*

20. See Venkatesh, *American Project,* 131–52; and Nicholas Lemann, *Promised Land,* 226–29.

21. Kornblum and Williams also report that the New York Housing Authority preferred to maintain a distribution of employed and unemployed tenants. See their *Uptown Kids,* 212–15. Also see Lee Rainwater, "Lessons of Pruitt-Igoe," *Public Interest* 8 (Summer 1967): 116–26.

22. Michael was talking to the owner of Mikey's Grocery Store. I was in the store socializing.

23. *Nationality* here refers primarily to the Mexican population, in which some individuals are from Mexico and others were born in the United States.

There has been social conflict between the groups for some time, and during the early 1990s this conflict escalated. For an example of ethnic conflict in Boston public housing, see Vale, *From the Puritans,* 301–7.

24. Venkatesh, *American Project,* 131–52.

25. Venkatesh, *Off the Books,* 302–3, 349.

26. I use the word *drift* here to indicate a particular group's movement into the illegal economy as a result of either seeing opportunities that did not exist before or being recruited to participate by other operators in this economy. This usage is very similar to David Matza's in his classic *Delinquency and Drift* (New York: Wiley, 1964), 29.

27. See Merry, *Urban Danger,* 194–96.

28. Elijah Anderson also found drugs to be a major factor in the change of the neighborhood that he studied. See his *Streetwise,* 77–111, and *Code of the Street,* 107–41.

29. See Williams and Kornblum, *Uptown Kids,* 94–96, and Clarence Lusane, *Pipe Dream Blues: Racism and the War on Drugs* (Boston: South End Press, 1991). Lusane also saw the devastating impact that drugs, particularly crack cocaine, have had on the African American community and especially poor African American neighborhoods. He controversially argued that the drug problem in the African American community originated with the U.S. government, which was bringing in and selling the drugs to African Americans to finance its covert war in Central America.

30. See Sullivan, *"Getting Paid,"* 172–73.

31. There are few direct-observation or long-term studies of public housing to draw on, but the two main ones over the last fifty years both observed that crime makes it difficult for the people living there to manage their everyday affairs. See Venkatesh, *American Project,* 111–237, and Rainwater, *Behind Ghetto Walls,* 40.

32. *Curanderismo* is a traditional folk medicine approach to public health and is still practiced in Latino areas. For a description, see Kiev, *Curanderismo,* 22–32, 124–47.

33. See Gans, *Urban Villagers,* 142–45. He extensively discusses the importance of caretakers in poor communities but uses the concept somewhat differently than I do. Although Venkatesh reports on people who were leaders of the project units he studied in Chicago, these people were not identified as caretakers. Some of them could have been, but certainly not all. See Venkatesh, *American Project,* 1, 54, 55, 76, 90. Williams and Kornblum also report the existence of tenant associations; most of the people on these associations were not caretakers as I have used the concept here, but some could have been. For example, in their description of project life, Ms. Carmen Montana would appear to be a caretaker as I have used the concept in this book. See Williams and Kornblum, *Uptown Kids,* 196–200. It is important to point out that the caretakers do not have to participate in the local tenant association.

34. Several studies have indicated that public housing was put in poor black areas because whites had organized to fight politically any policies that would lead to the building of public housing in their areas. See Martin Myerson and Edward Banfield, *Politics, Planning, and the Public Interest: The Case of Public*

Housing in Chicago (Glencoe, IL: Free Press, 1955); Gregory D. Squires et al., *Chicago: Race, Class, and the Response to Urban Decline* (Philadelphia: Temple University Press, 1987); Hirsch, *Making the Second Ghetto.*

35. Williams and Kornblum, *Uptown Kids,* 195–96.

36. See Montgomery, "Comment," and Williams and Kornblum, *Uptown Kids,* 20–23, 195–96.

37. Carmela was talking to her friend Alana at the park while they watched their children play.

38. Dennis was talking to Jason and Carl, his two friends, in a booth next to mine in a small restaurant in the neighborhood.

39. Sometimes researchers' misunderstandings of the poor and/or misrepresentations are the result of their own ideological blinders (i.e., what they think the poor should want) or of their desire to help the poor improve their lives and their consequent disinclination to present any findings that might suggest the poor were not discontented with their lives.

40. Elizando was conversing with a friend in La Perla Barbershop. I was sitting in the barbershop socializing.

41. I use the analogy of the immune system's response to injury rather than the immune system's response to disease because the two represent quite different processes. In the case of injury, the immune system rushes to the site of the trauma and first attempts to eradicate the potential for infection. Then it starts its work to heal the traumatized area(s). In the case of disease, the immune system attacks the foreign elements in an effort to eradicate them. Failure to eradicate these elements will cause the affected organ to malfunction while raising the risk that the entire body will shut down. The injury analogy is more appropriate for neighborhoods because when a change agent does cause an existing institution to alter its existing relationships or to simply die altogether, the structure of the neighborhood is in danger of collapsing. However, in most cases, the other institutions compensate for the embattled institution (injured part) and begin to mend the structure by rearranging elements (institutions) and/or creating new ones.

42. They helped to develop residents' personal identities by keeping track of their current identities and publicizing them to others.

43. Substrata could be differentiated according to immigrant generation in the country and/or neighborhood, gender, value orientation, institutional participation (regulars, occasionals, etc.), or age.

44. There were always some people who did not like their position in the social order and complained about how they were treated, or people who thought they were not getting the respect they deserved from others in the social order. Hector would massage egos, maneuver individuals with their statuses intact to different positions within the social order through praise, and mediate conflict when that was called for.

45. For a discussion of language shift among Latinos in Los Angeles, see David E. López, "Language: Diversity and Assimilation," in Waldinger and Bozorgmehr, *Ethnic Los Angeles,* 139–64.

46. By this observation I do not mean to imply a strong correlation between types of poor and value orientations, only a tendency.

47. For a critique of the logic associated with those who equate physical disorder with social disorder, see Duneier, *Sidewalk*, 287–89, 315.

48. See Rainwater, *Behind Ghetto Walls*, 20.

49. For studies that have stressed the "decline of community" thesis, see Skogan, *Disorder and Decline*; W. Wilson, *When Work Disappears*; and Anderson, *Streetwise*.

50. I was at the basketball court watching the game when this confrontation occurred. I was in position to overhear the African Americans talk among themselves, and I noted their conversations as well as the ensuing events. Also see W. Wilson and Taub, *There Goes the Neighborhood*, 117–19, which reports ethnic conflict over the use of public spaces in Chicago.

51. North, *Institutions, Institutional Change*, 23; and Knight, *Institutions and Social Change*, 73–74.

52. W. Wilson and Taub, in *There Goes the Neighborhood*, 99–101, also report language issues.

53. Elsie was one of a group of African American women meeting in a community center who were talking about issues related to changes taking place in their buildings.

54. See Suttles, *Social Order*, 63–67. However, whereas Suttles identifies the factors that caused the community that he studied to remain permanently segmented, the present study found evidence that multiethnic poor neighborhoods can become integrated neighborhoods.

55. It is important to reemphasize that this research project is about social change and stability within neighborhoods that have remained poor and not about social change in neighborhoods that are making a transition out of poverty. Thus the changes in poor neighborhoods that I am studying are changes in neighborhood type, from contested to fragmented or vice versa, rather than changes in the neighborhood's economic status from poor to nonpoor. Though a poor neighborhood can change and become nonpoor, such a change is outside the power of the poor neighborhood's residents to bring about.

56. See Alejandro Portes and Rubén G. Rumbaut, *Legacies: The Story of the Immigrant Second Generation* (Berkeley: University of California Press, 2001), 49–54. They find that socioeconomic status has an impact on aspirations and that the type of acculturation does as well. Since the present study is on the poor, the findings are consistent with what Portes and Rumbaut call "dissonant acculturation."

57. Important historical studies of this experience are Neil Fligstein, *Going North: Migration of Blacks and Whites from the South, 1900–1950* (New York: Academic Press, 1981); Zaragosa Vargas, *Proletarians of the North: A History of Mexican Industrial Workers in Detroit and the Midwest, 1917–1933* (Berkeley: University of California Press, 1993); and Todd Gitlin and Nanci Hollander, *Uptown: Poor Whites in Chicago* (New York: Harper and Row, 1970).

58. For early American portraits of rural economic hardship, see Agee and Evans, *Let Us Now Praise Famous Men*, and Harrington, *Other America*. On the migration of people from these areas to what they hoped would be a more prosperous life, see Nicholas Lemann, *Promised Land*, and Douglas S. Massey

et al., *Return to Aztlan: The Social Process of International Migration from Western Mexico* (Berkeley: University of California Press, 1987).

59. Here it is important to point out that while establishing a socially meaningful life in a harsh environment can have the connotation of "survival techniques," it is less negative than that concept generally implies. Survival techniques associated with particularly difficult situations like imprisonment or being lost in an alien and hostile environment are different from the survival techniques adopted by people living in the subculture of scarcity. The social relations that have developed are positive for the individuals involved because they allow people to approach their life situation positively and not simply to endure it. One of the classic statements of the social survival thesis is Stack's *All Our Kin*.

60. I accompanied Alex and his friends on a number of these ventures to the local bar for drinks and was present for their conversations concerning the changes that were occurring in the building.

61. Examples of favors requested were the use of an associate's car, electric kitchen tools, weapons, musical instruments, or help in moving something or bringing groceries from the grocery store to an apartment.

62. Although I have used the word *gossip* to signify a particular mode of communication, Suttles used the word *rumor*. The two terms may not be exactly the same. See Suttles, *Social Order*, 195–202.

63. Merry, *Urban Danger*, 187.

64. The power of labeling has been consistently observed. See the classic on labeling theory, Howard Becker's *The Outsiders: Studies in the Sociology of Deviance* (Glencoe, IL: Free Press, 1963).

65. Elenor was at the laundromat, talking to her friend and neighbor Catrina about the recent break-ins in the units. I was there doing my own laundry.

66. Of course, in most of the cases I observed, fear and anxiety were fueling the anger. Thus the level of anger that residents expressed in their language was also a measure of the degree of fear and anxiety they were feeling about the conditions they were facing.

67. Tony was talking with Ricardo and Felipe, who were from his building, and Jorge and Alberto, who were from the neighborhood, while all of them were standing watching a handball game in the common area of the units. I was there waiting to play a game of handball.

68. Some of the agents of change do not seem to be trying to move the neighborhood anywhere; they are merely causing instability by doing what they do. However, change agents are of both sorts: those who start a new business in an area that has not had such a business before and who in the process create the neighborhood change required for their business to prosper, and those who take a certain action that has consequences they did not intend.

69. The Mexican immigrants would refer to the Mexican Americans that they thought were assimilated as *pochos*, a pejorative term for people considered to have given up their identity as a Mexican and become primarily American.

70. Patricia was conversing with two other women in the El Rey neighborhood's Mariposa Beauty Salon. I was sweeping the floor before the conversation started and was sitting in the back room when it was occurring.

71. Ignacio was talking to two other men and the owner of the Canal Grocery. I was standing talking with the owner when the conversation started.

72. Sociologically, there is a difference between a syndicate and a gang. A local crime syndicate is organized solely around economic interests, and its activities are focused on realizing these interests, primarily in markets that are producing and selling illegal or stolen products. In contrast, gangs are organized around both social and economic interests. The activities of gangs involve participation in the same illegal markets that syndicates operate in, but gangs are also social clubs that attempt to provide social entertainment and other social services to their members, their families, and members of the community. For a discussion of the differences between these two types of collective behavior, see Martín Sánchez-Jankowski, "Gangs and Social Change," *Theoretical Criminology* 7 (May 2003): 191–216.

73. Venkatesh, *Off the Books,* 278–302.

74. Five months after the tenants' committee ceased their efforts to remove the syndicate from the building, the housing police raided the drug mill and effectively removed it. See Venkatesh, *American Project,* 130–52, which describes a similar situation.

75. For a discussion of the concept of the "defended neighborhood," see Gerald D. Suttles, *The Social Construction of Communities* (Chicago: University of Chicago Press, 1972), 21–43; Donald P. Green, Dara Z. Strolovitch, and Janelle S. Wong, "Defended Neighborhoods, Integration, and Racially Motivated Crime," *American Journal of Sociology* 104 (September 1998): 372–403; Judith DeSena, *Protecting One's Turf: Social Strategies for Maintaining Urban Neighborhoods* (Lanham, MD: University Press of America, 1990).

76. For a discussion of vigilante groups as they relate to the local community, see Suttles, *Social Construction of Communities,* 189–229.

77. There are exceptions, but they are very few. For a good description of an exception, see Conquergood's "Life in Big Red," 95–144, which found a long-term tenement building in Chicago to be a local institution.

78. See Meyerson and Banfield, *Politics, Planning, and the Public Interest;* Hirsch, *Making the Second Ghetto,* 10, 268–69; Ira Goldstein and William L. Yancey, "Public Housing Projects, Blacks, and Public Policy: The Historical Ecology of Public Housing in Philadelphia," in *Housing Desegregation and Federal Policy,* ed. John M. Goering (Chapel Hill: University of North Carolina Press, 1986), 262–89; Vale, *From the Puritans,* 182–89.

4. PROVISIONS FOR LIFE: MAKING THE MOM-AND-POP STORE A NEIGHBORHOOD INSTITUTION

1. See Howard E. Aldrich and Roger Waldinger, "Ethnicity and Entrepreneurship," *Annual Review of Sociology* 81, no. 4 (1990): 117; Jennifer Lee, "Retail Niche Domination among African American, Jewish and Korean Entrepreneurs," *American Behavioral Scientist* 42 (1999): 1402–3; Anderson, *Streetwise,* 152–53, 220; Nancy Abelmann and John Lie, *Korean Americans and the Los Angeles Riots* (Cambridge, MA: Harvard University Press, 1995), 138–40.

2. There is a good deal of literature on small business and its impact on ethnic mobility. Some of the most significant books on this subject are Ivan Light's *Ethnic Enterprise in America: Business and Welfare among Chinese, Japanese, and Blacks* (Berkeley: University of California Press, 1972); Ivan Light and Edna Bonacich's *Immigrant Entrepreneurs: Koreans in Los Angeles, 1965–1982* (Berkeley: University of California Press, 1988); Roger Waldinger, Howard Aldrich, and Robin Ward's *Ethnic Entrepreneurs: Immigrant Business in Industrial Societies* (Newbury Park, CA: Sage Publications, 1990); and Waldinger's *Still the Promised City?*

3. See Gans, *Urban Villagers,* 117–19, and Suttles, *Social Order,* 46–54.

4. Suttles, *Social Order,* 47–54.

5. Some might find my use of the term *imperialism* provocatively reminiscent of Marxism. Whether or not the term has Marxist connotations, I am using it here merely in a technical sense to designate an economic activity and relationship that has been described by both Marxist and non-Marxist social scientists, namely business ventures in a geographic area that is not inhabited by those who own the businesses and the removal of profit from the geographic area where it was generated to a geographic area inhabited by the owners (investors) of the business.

Usually the concept (and analysis) has involved the relations between countries and has been described and analyzed by both Marxists like Lenin and Mao and non-Marxists like Thucydides and Hobson. Variants of this classical model have included concepts like "internal colonialism," in which the relationship is between a particular nation's dominant city and its hinterland, or between a dominant ethnic group in its primary location of settlement and subordinate ethnic groups inhabiting its outer rim.

6. See Light and Bonacich, *Immigrant Entrepreneurs,* 366–70.

7. Junior was speaking to Alice, a forty-three-year-old mother of two kids who lived in the John C. Fremont Homes, outside the store where they both had just been shopping. The conversation started when Alice asked Junior if he had seen four kids stealing some candy. I was outside with a group of men who were drinking beer and talking.

8. DeeDee and her friend Queta were talking at the bus stop about a half-block from the store. They had just stopped in the store on their way to work. I had been in the store and followed them to the bus stop to take a bus myself.

9. See Edward T. Chang, "Jewish and Korean Merchants in African American Neighborhoods: A Comparative Perspective," *Amerasia Journal* 19, no. 2 (1993): 9, 12–14; Illsoo Kim, "The Korean Fruit and Vegetable Business: A Case Study," in *The Apple Sliced: Sociological Studies of New York City,* ed. Vernon Boggs, Gerald Handel, and Sylvia Fava (New York: Praeger, 1984), 115–16; and Abelmann and Lie, *Korean Americans,* 122–23, 137–40, 155.

10. Light and Bonacich, *Immigrant Entrepreneurs,* 355, 354–400.

11. See I. Kim, "Korean Fruit and Vegetable Business," 107–17.

12. Gerald Suttles found a similar situation in his study of a Chicago slum. In one particular type of situation involving whites and African Americans that he included under the heading of "mutual exploitation," he described how African Americans came to see white-run businesses in their neighborhoods as stealing from them and how the businesses came to see the African Americans

as doing the same thing to them (by shoplifting, not paying their bills, and burglarizing the store). While the businesses that he described were similar to the "imperialist" type that I have just described here, the neighborhood residents' relationships to the businesses in his study and mine were not identical. In the present study the residents did not see anything "mutually exploitative" about the relationship. To them it was one-way exploitation, with the proprietor exploiting them for his or her own benefit. See Suttles, *Social Order,* 52–53.

13. See Yona Ginsberg, *Jews in a Changing Neighborhood* (New York: Macmillan, 1975), 104; and Lee, *Civility in the City,* 37.

14. Leonard was conversing with a deliveryman. I was sitting in the store listening.

15. Hector was talking with two longtime regulars as I sat in his store listening.

16. Lee, *Civility in the City,* 37–38.

17. Waldinger, *Still the Promised City?* 258–61.

18. See John Horton, *The Politics of Diversity* (Philadelphia: Temple University Press, 1995), 28–30; Howard E. Aldrich and Roger Waldinger, *Ethnic Entrepreneurs* (Newbury Park, CA: Sage Publications, 1990), 124; Louis Winnick, *New People in Old Neighborhoods* (New York: Russell Sage Foundation, 1990), 150–52; and Illsoo Kim, "The Koreans: Small Business in an Urban Frontier," in *New Immigrants in New York City,* ed. Nancy Foner (New York: Columbia University Press, 1987), 219–42.

19. Josephine was talking to her friends in Shippley's Grocery. I was sitting next to the owner reading a magazine.

20. Ella was talking to a group of her friends at the Farragut Street Grocery. I was standing with one of the young boys who helped the owner stock.

21. See Anderson, *Streetwise,* 63–64; Peter Kwong, *The New Chinatown* (New York: Hill and Wang, 1997), 37–39; and Lee, *Civility in the City,* 40–41, 52, 82–83.

22. On class consumption patterns, see Pierre Bourdieu, *Distinction: A Social Critique of the Judgement of Taste* (Cambridge, MA: Harvard University Press, 1984), 179–200.

23. The act of stocking a store with products associated with the cuisine of a particular ethnic group has been noted by a large number of researchers on ethnic businesses, but what is less known is how stores wanting or needing to provide for more than one ethnic group manage this situation. One of the first researchers on ethnic businesses was Ivan Light; see his *Ethnic Enterprises in America.*

24. See Mary Douglas, "Standard Social Uses of Food: Introduction," in *Food in the Social Order: Studies of Food and Festivities in Three American Communities,* ed. Mary Douglas (New York: Russell Sage Foundation, 1984), 1–39; Clifford Geertz, *The Interpretation of Cultures* (New York: Basic Books, 1973), 90; Eliot A. Singer, "Conversion through Foodways Enculturation: The Meaning of Eating in an American Hindu Sect," in *Ethnic and Regional Foodways in the United States,* ed. Linda Keller Brown and Kay Mussell (Knoxville: University of Tennessee Press, 1984), 195–96.

25. See Herbert Gans, "Symbolic Ethnicity: The Future of Ethnic Groups and Culture in America," *Ethnic and Racial Studies* 2 (January 1979): 1–20.

26. Sharon and Irving were talking at the checkout counter. I was in the store at the meat counter.

27. See Charles Choy Wong, "Black and Chinese Grocery Stores in Los Angeles' Black Ghetto," *Urban Life* 5 (January 1977): 439–64, specifically 445; Abelmann and Lie, *Korean Americans,* 139; Lee, *Civility in the City,* 4, 183.

28. Over the nine years of the study I recorded forty-four times that a patron requested a loan of $500 or more.

29. In both New York and Los Angeles large and medium-size supermarkets in or near the neighborhood studied offered a broader range of products for lower prices than those found in the mom-and-pop stores.

30. This generally occurred because the family had only one vehicle, which was in constant demand by all the members, or because the vehicle the family had was not in working order.

31. Abelmann and Lie, *Korean Americans,* 138–39; and Paul Ong, Kyeyoung Park, and Yasmin Tong, "The Korean-Black Conflict and the State," in *New Asian Immigration in Los Angeles and Global Restructuring,* ed. Paul Ong, Edna Bonacich, and Lucie Cheng (Philadelphia: Temple University Press, 1994), 269.

32. See Suttles, *Social Order,* 49, 83–85, 87–88, which also describes this.

33. See J. Coleman, *Foundations of Social Theory,* 241–44.

34. See Bourdieu, *Distinction,* 177–208.

35. On the importance of food for group and personal identity, see the essay "Soul Food," in L. Jones, *Home,* 101–4.

36. The importance of food in establishing the everyday culture of groups cannot be overemphasized, yet this aspect of culture has been understudied. See Paul DiMaggio, "Culture and Economy," in *The Handbook of Economic Sociology,* ed. Neil Smelser and Richard Swedberg (Princeton: Princeton University Press, 1994), 41–46.

37. For a related point that people use food to categorize others, and that moral judgments of others differ depending on the food they eat, see R.I. Stein and C.J. Nemeroff, "Moral Overtones of Food: Judgments of Others Based on What They Eat," *Personality and Social Psychology Bulletin* 21 (1995): 480–90.

38. See Mark Conner and Christopher J. Armitage, *The Social Psychology of Food* (Buckingham: Open University Press, 2002), 127.

39. All the groups in this study had dishes that used marginal food products.

40. Both of Humberto's statements were in the Isla Grocery. I was in the store but not part of either conversation.

41. See Richard D. Alba, *Ethnic Identity: Transformation of White America* (New Haven: Yale University Press, 1990), 85–93. Although he reports that food is important for ethnic identity, he also notes that its salience has been gradually diminishing as intermarriage among white ethnics continues. However, his study does not control for class on this point.

42. Gloria was talking with Maxine, a friend who lived in one of the tenements in the neighborhood. Both women were shopping at the Gordon Street Grocery in the Bronx. I was there talking to the owner.

43. When referring to psychological properties associated with the concepts of "gossip" and "rumor," I have morals, values, attitudes, and beliefs in mind.

44. See Ralph L. Rosnow and Gary Alan Fine, *Rumor and Gossip: The Social Psychology of Hearsay* (New York: Elsevier Scientific Publishing, 1976), 4, 84–85, 131.

45. Gordon W. Allport and Leo Postman, *The Psychology of Rumor* (New York: Russell and Russell, 1965), viii–x; and Rosnow and Fine, *Rumor and Gossip,* 4, 131.

46. This conversation occurred in the Monitor Grocery at the meat counter. I was talking to the owner as he stacked canned food.

47. Corine and the two other patrons were having their conversation. I was in the store talking to the owner when the conversation began.

48. During this conversation I was looking at a magazine while the store owner was talking to his milk deliveryman.

49. Mark, Leonard, Derek, and I were having a beer in front of the grocery.

50. I concluded this from observing that individuals would ask the talker questions to get him or her to say more, that their eyes would widen as they became more interested, that they would begin to smile, and that they would be very focused on the person telling the story.

51. Dona was talking to two of her friends, Judy and Sarah, in Shippley's Grocery. I was with the owner, who was participating in the conversation.

52. Suttles also discussed the contribution of community rumors to social control, but he emphasized more the social control exerted indirectly by outside agents such as the police (e.g., by their mere presence) and local street workers (by services they provided such as keeping people busy with sports or helping them with job applications). My study, however, found that the people who were directly interacting in the store and community made a more important contribution to social control than any outside actors did. For Suttles's findings, see his *Social Order,* 195–98, esp. 198.

53. Soledad was in the store talking with two other women, the store owner, and me.

54. The women's behavior was no different from that of people of former times who tried to secure a place in the afterlife. For a vivid sociohistorical description of strategizing for the afterlife, see Cohn, *Death and Property.*

55. Bertha was talking to two of her friends at the Farragut Street Grocery.

56. See Sandra Susan Smith, *Lone Pursuit: Distrust and Uncooperativeness among Black Poor Jobseekers and Jobholders* (New York: Russell Sage Foundation, 2007).

57. Some excellent studies on the importance of networks in securing employment in low-income communities are, for Mexicans and Mexican Americans, Dohan's *Price of Poverty,* 70–98; for Puerto Ricans, Small's *Villa Victoria,* 123–44; and for African Americans, Smith, *Lone Pursuit,* which discusses why African American networks are limited.

58. Sánchez-Jankowski, "Concentration," 619–37.

59. I was visiting the Jalisco Grocery and talking to the owner and another customer at the time.

60. Junk food from a variety of countries was available at the stores.

61. Ricardo was talking with his cousin from the Dominican Republic in the Palm Court Apartments. I was at the dinner table with them when the conversation began.

62. Jewel was talking to her friend Michelle in the hallway of an apartment building in the Eagleton neighborhood of Brooklyn. I was in the hall waiting for the elevator, which took a very long time to come.

63. See Suttles, *Social Order,* 49–54.

64. See W. Wilson and Taub, *There Goes the Neighborhood,* 129.

65. This conversation occurred in front of Daddy G's Grocery. I was listening to it while sitting on the hood of a car drinking a cola.

66. See Anderson, *Place on the Corner,* 179–206, for a discussion of the development of a social hierarchy in a bar using the internally developed categories of "regulars," "wineheads," and "hoodlums."

67. I am using the concept "organic community" in the way Durkheim established when he used the term *organic solidarity* to designate how specialized units were functionally interdependent and hierarchical in the formation of the social order. See Emile Durkheim, *The Division of Labor in Society,* trans. W. P. Halls (Glencoe, IL: Free Press, 1997), 68–87.

68. I determined a person's position in the social hierarchy in the store and the various social clique positions in the social hierarchy of the store and neighborhood through (1) the everyday conversational statements of the individuals concerning their own and other people's rankings of people in the neighborhood; (2) the mapping (sociometry) of whom they would associate with, where, and for how much time; and (3) the evaluation during everyday conversations of the status of various social cliques in the neighborhood.

69. Honor has been identified by anthropologists as an integral part of the cultures of Mediterranean Europe, various North African and Middle Eastern cultures, and many East Asian cultures. See J. G. Peristiany, ed., *Honor and Shame: The Values of Mediterranean Society* (London: Weidenfeld and Nicolson, 1965). Also see Ramon Gutierrez, *When Jesus Came, the Corn Mothers Went Away: Marriage, Sexuality, and Power in New Mexico, 1500–1846* (Stanford: Stanford University Press, 1991), 176–80. For a discussion of historical-cultural contributions to group identity, see Harold Isaacs, *Idols of the Tribe: Group Identity and Political Change* (New York: HarperCollins, 1975), 115–43.

70. See North, *Institutions, Institutional Change,* 22–24, and Knight, *Institutions and Social Conflict,* 56, for a discussion of the need and desire to control behavioral uncertainty in the building of institutions.

71. This does not happen in honor cultures because individuals cannot gain more honor by making others lose theirs. See Julio Caro Baroja, "Honor and Shame: A Historical Account of Several Conflicts," in Peristiany, *Honor and Shame,* 81–137.

72. See Anderson, *Code of the Street,* 34. This behavior is often referred to as "mad-dogging."

73. After the second rumor was started, there were numerous conversations among individuals in the various cliques about the message that this rumor was meant to convey. The topic of the conversation was that people had to abide by the rules of "proper" behavior.

74. On shunning as a mechanism for social control, see Reinhold Zippelius, "Exclusion and Shunning as Legal and Social Sanctions," *Ethology and Sociobiology* 7 (1986): 159–66.

75. See Gans, *Urban Villagers,* 160–61. Gans also reports that storeowners played a very important caretaker role in working-class neighborhoods.

76. Rhoda was talking to a friend of hers named Milly while they waited for a subway train. I was standing waiting for the train too. I knew Rhoda because

I had been in the Farragut Street Grocery when she came to purchase goods and interact with the others in her clique.

77. See Gans, *Urban Villagers,* 145, 161.

78. Ibid., 160–62.

79. Melvin was talking with me and two other men in Daddy G's Grocery when he brought up that he had received an offer for the store.

80. See Suttles, *Social Order,* 49–52, who observed similar issues related to neighborhood conceptions of "guests" and "hosts."

81. See Lee's *Civility in the City,* 85–86, which reports on how negatively neighborhood people viewed this coldness.

82. For examples of such studies, see Robert J. Sampson and Stephen W. Raudenbush, "Systematic Social Observation of Public Spaces: A New Look at Disorder in Urban Neighborhoods," *American Journal of Sociology* 105, no. 3 (1999): 603–51, and W. Wilson, *When Work Disappears,* 34–35.

5. TAKING CARE OF BUSINESS: SOCIAL CHANGE
AND PRESERVATION IN THE MOM-AND-POP STORE

1. W. Wilson, *When Work Disappears,* 35; Scott Cummings, *Left Behind in Rosedale,* 43; Skogan, *Disorder and Decline,* 50, 65.

2. The work of Jane Jacobs is vulnerable to this error; see J. Jacobs, *Death and Life,* 286, 270–90.

3. Egg creams are a drink made of milk, vanilla or chocolate syrup, and seltzer water. They were very popular throughout all of New York's neighborhoods for decades in the twentieth century but started dying out once these small stores became unable to repair their soda fountains. Although there are no eggs in an egg cream, according to Richard Wurman's *NYC Access,* 6th ed. (New York: Access Press, 1994), the syrup that was used in the original egg cream was made with eggs, and cream was used to give it a richer taste. Later milk and regular syrup were used, but the name was kept. Another version of the egg cream's origin says the term came from Jewish customers who would order "a cream soda" with a guttural accent that sounded like "egg cream" rather than simply "a cream." However, the fact that all the stores and luncheonettes offered egg creams, even the Italian delis that served an Italian clientele, casts doubt on this story.

4. I computed the average time individuals spent in the store by timing them with multiple stopwatches that I carried for this specific purpose. I began using stopwatches in the beginning of the research to help me identify the properties of the patrons who were "regulars," "periodics," and "occasionals." I then used the data I obtained as a baseline for later comparisons.

5. Reuben was speaking with one of his deliverymen. I was in the store talking to Reuben when the deliveryman came.

6. Identities were established through the highlighting of some personal attribute to create the necessary divisions in the store's social hierarchy. For example, if the members of the community thought of an individual as athletic, sympathetic, tough, cunning, attractive, or thoughtful, that trait would be used to establish the individual's social identity.

7. See Lee, *Civility in the City,* 60.

8. Jennifer Lee also found this in her study. See ibid., 75–79.

9. See W. Wilson, *When Work Disappears,* 28–33.

10. See Wong, "Black and Chinese Grocery Stores," 439–64.

11. The two women were talking as they sat watching their children in the play area of the Orchid Lane Apartments (public housing project). I was sitting in the play area drinking a soda.

12. Even among those stores where under normal conditions owners would have hired from their own families, like the Koreans, there was a tendency to hire someone from the community for both symbolic and practical reasons. Symbolically, it was hoped that such a hiring would indicate to the residents that the owner was willing to give something back to the community. Practically, the hire was advantageous because it brought into the store someone who could make a less prejudiced decision about who might be a potential robber or shoplifter. See Lee, *Civility in the City,* 100–110; Anderson, *Streetwise,* 63.

13. Arabs and East Indians usually hired more of their family or people from their immediate homelands to watch over the store for potential shoplifters.

14. Owners had to deal with shoplifting as well as armed robberies. See Ong, Park, and Tong, "Korean-Black Conflict," 277.

15. Jerry was conversing with one of his patrons. He had just been robbed for the third time in four months. I had been in the store when the robbery happened.

16. J. J. was conversing with two of his friends from New Jersey. He had been robbed for the seventh time in eleven months, which was a record for him. I had been in the store for one of the robberies.

17. Thomas was talking with a friend who had come from out of town to see him. He had just been robbed for the fifth time in six months. I was sitting outside having coffee.

18. See Ong, Park, and Tong, "Korean-Black Conflict," 277.

19. Baltazar had just been in the store to buy some products and had seen that the prices had been raised. I walked with him and his friend Ignacio all the way to his house, where he continued to complain to both of us while drinking a couple of beers.

20. See Loïc J. D. Wacquant, "In the Zone: The Social Art of the Hustler in the Black American Ghetto," *Theory, Culture and Society* 15, no. 2 (1998): 1–36.

21. Reuben was talking to a relative from Puerto Rico while he was serving some of his homemade moonshine to some of the teenage gang members who had come into his store to purchase it. I was in the store socializing. Earlier in the evening Reuben had served about six glasses to some of the adult men who were at the store playing dominos.

22. Combs was conversing with a friend he sometimes played cards with. He had just finished selling some bullets when he began to talk. Later he sold some pornographic magazines. He kept both products under the counter, so customers had to know he had them and ask for them directly. I was in the store socializing with two other patrons.

23. Illegal gambling in mom-and-pop stores was also reported in Bourgois, *In Search of Respect,* 72.

24. Thomas was speaking to his auto mechanic, who just brought him his car that had been in the shop getting fixed. Thomas did receive payment for his cooperation, and the runners gave it as they made their rounds. For a discussion of the numbers game in poor neighborhoods, see Sharff, *King Kong,* 24–25, and Ivan Light, "Numbers Gambling among Blacks: A Financial Institution," *American Sociological Review* 42 (December 1977): 892–904.

25. Suttles, *Social Order,* 49, describes a similar process.

26. See Michael Banton, *Racial Theories,* 2nd ed. (New York: Cambridge University Press, 1998), 118–25; John Dollard, *Caste and Class in a Southern Town* (Madison: University of Wisconsin Press, 1988).

27. For a discussion and analysis of Dominican migration to the United States, see Sherri Grasmuck and Patricia R. Pessar, *Between Two Islands: Dominican International Migration* (Berkeley: University of California Press, 1991).

28. See Harold Isaacs, "Basic Group Identity: The Idols of the Tribe," in *Ethnicity: Theory and Experience,* ed. Daniel Patrick Moynihan and Nathan Glazer (Cambridge, MA: Harvard University Press, 1975), 29–52.

29. For examples of social environments where the dynamic defining the social order involves group conflict, see Suttles, *Social Order,* and Sennett, *Uses of Disorder.* For examples of poor areas being mutually reinforcing, see William Kornblum's *Blue-Collar Community* (Chicago: University of Chicago Press, 1974).

30. Jacobs, *Death and Life,* 283–88; David Harris, "'Property Values Drop When Blacks Move In, Because. . .': Racial and Socioeconomic Determinants of Neighborhood Desirability," *American Sociological Review* 64 (1999): 461–79; W. Wilson and Taub, *There Goes the Neighborhood.*

31. For research on day laborers, see Abel Valenzuela Jr., Jennette A. Kawachi, and Michael Marr, "Seeking Work Daily: Supply, Demand, and Spatial Dimensions of Day Labor in Two Global Cities," *International Journal of Contemporary Sociology* 43, no. 2 (2002): 192–219.

32. On the weekends this was not an issue because the men would frequent another neighborhood institution—the bar. For the importance of the bar in low-income communities, see Anderson, *Place on the Corner,* 1–7.

33. I obtained this finding by listening to women's conversations and recording an increase in their talk about husbands becoming violent at home.

34. See Lee, *Civility in the City,* 152–53.

35. The finding that conflict comes from the everyday operations of the store and not the larger issues of racial deprivation is supported by evidence in Clair Jean Kim, *Bitter Fruit: The Politics of Black-Korean Conflict in New York City* (New Haven: Yale University Press, 2002), 116–18, although the incident she describes is not specifically about the loss of social space.

36. It should be recalled from chapter 4 that when the owner was a member of one of the ethnic groups living in the area, the character of the store was what I have called "indigenous." When the owner was a member of an ethnic group that was just starting to live in the neighborhood, I labeled the character of the store as "trailblazer."

37. A good example of this is described by Anderson, *Place on the Corner,* 100–107. In this section Herman wants to be looked at differently because he fears that his place in the social order is beginning to be tenuous. So he engages

in an extramarital affair to reestablish his place in the eyes of the other members of the social order.

38. It is necessary to remember that although the "regulars" constituted the main participants in, and thus the foundation for, the store's social order, or that of any neighborhood institution for that matter, the people categorized as "periodic" and "occasional" customers were also fundamental contributors to that order. Anderson's analysis of social order in the bar (Jelly's) that he studied in Chicago is different: he describes his three social groups (regulars, wineheads, and hoodlums) as rigidly segregated from each other and only minimally interacting, and he seems to overlook the fact that the structure of the institution (which includes the social order) must be the result of the interdependency of all three of these groups—that functionally all three are needed for the creation and re-creation of a social identity. See Anderson, *Place on the Corner.*

39. I took down this conversation as the owner and the two "regulars" discussed Jesús in the store. I was in the store socializing when the conversation began.

40. Combs was speaking with a "regular's" relative who was visiting the neighborhood. I was in the store socializing.

41. Ramon was speaking with Julio, Izzy and Tomás at the Tortuga Grocery in the Bronx's Monument neighborhood. I was in the store socializing.

42. See Sánchez-Jankowski, *Islands in the Street,* 178–211, for a discussion about how local gangs act to protect their neighborhoods while advancing their own interests.

43. See Suttles, *Social Construction of Communities,* ch. 8, and Cummings, *Left Behind in Roseville,* 103.

44. Thomas was speaking with two patrons, Jimmy and Sam, about why recent crime had stopped. I was in the store socializing.

45. When I say there was more stress in the neighborhood, I mean that people in the neighborhood were more worried than they had been about aspects of daily life. They would express this worry in conversations by complaining about the things that were bothering them, or they (mostly women) would simply acknowledge this anxiety in an effort to be reassured or comforted.

46. Dalton was speaking with Melvin, the owner of Daddy G's, and two regular patrons of the store named Kim and Earl. I had been in the store talking to Melvin for about two hours and was looking for some soda to take with me, so I was in an aisle when Dalton and the others started to talk. Since I am Mexican, the situation was awkward. I wrote down their conversation and then decided to leave without a soda just to ease the situation. I walked out and said nothing. They all saw me leave, but for whatever reason they never brought up this conversation with me again.

47. Orlando was speaking with Thomas (the owner of Shippley's Grocery), Richard, Preston, Sally, Dorothea, Oliver, and me.

48. This is a point made in Georg Simmel's *Conflict,* trans. Kurt H. Wolff (Glencoe, IL: Free Press, 1955) and Lewis Coser's *The Functions of Social Conflict* (New York: Free Press, 1967), 139–49.

49. See Whyte, *Street Corner Society,* 255–56, on the importance for Italians of congregating on street corners or establishments outside the home, and

Suttles, *Social Order,* 50, 51, 54, on how Italians congregated at stores they considered "theirs" as a way to isolate themselves from the new ethnic groups moving into the neighborhood.

50. It has been documented that lower-class individuals generally feel a lack of political efficacy and participate less in politics than middle- and upper-class individuals. See Sidney Verba, Kay Lehman Schlozman, and Henry Brady, *Voice and Equality: Civic Voluntarism in American Politics* (Cambridge, MA: Harvard University Press, 1995), 28; Steven Rosenstone and John Mark Hansen, *Mobilization, Participation, and Democracy in America* (New York: Macmillan, 1993), 236–42; and Sidney Verba and Norman H. Nie, *Participation in America: Political Democracy and Social Equality* (New York: Harper and Row, 1972), 125–37.

51. Similar results have not been obtained in some other documented cases. See Gans, *Urban Villagers,* 323–77; Suttles, *Social Order,* 21–22; King, *Chain of Change,* 207–10; and Wendell Pritchett, *Brownsville, Brooklyn: Blacks, Jews, and the Changing Face of the Ghetto* (Chicago: University of Chicago Press, 2002), 239–70.

52. A good example of this process in the literature is the Brooklyn neighborhood of Canarsie. Here the Italians and Jews, two groups that were not the friendliest toward each other, joined to resist the influx of Puerto Ricans and African Americans to the area whom they both perceived as a common threat. Through the act of resistance the neighborhood assumed a fragmented character. For a description of the resistance engaged in by the Italians and Jews of Canarsie, see Rieder, *Canarsie.*

53. Though most of the people in the subculture of scarcity are poor, that subculture is not to be confused with the "culture of poverty"; as I indicated in chapter 1, there are important differences between the two. The most important is that the subculture of scarcity does not *in toto* carry forward from one generation to another even when the conditions of extreme scarcity have been removed. Some traits remain among some of the first generation that lives outside conditions of extreme scarcity, but succeeding generations will lose all of them. Second, there is within the literature on a "culture of poverty" an emphasis on traits that keep people poor, whereas my concept of a subculture of scarcity emphasizes traits that allow people to construct meaningful lives for themselves within the constraints of extreme material scarcity. Their lives may not be comfortable, but people do find a way to live and enjoy parts of what they do have, no matter how meager and objectively oppressive their condition may be. This subculture is similar to that developed in other extreme environments where survival requires the routine of struggling for physical necessities as well as the establishment of a symbolic system to acquire the psychological necessities to persist.

54. Isidro and Juan were conversing while they waited for a bus together. I was waiting for a bus as well.

6. NOT JUST A CLIP JOINT: HAIR SHOPS
AND THE INSTITUTION OF GROOMING

1. W. E. B. Du Bois was one of the first to point out the importance of barbershops to the African American population in Philadelphia. His study found

that next to undertakers, barbers were the most prevalent business in the "Negro seventh ward." For Du Bois their importance was tied to the fact that they had dominated this sector of the service economy for whites as well as African Americans. He bemoaned the fact that they were declining as a result of a reluctance of young African Americans to take a job associated with slavery, as well as the competition from German and Italian barbers. He worried that African Americans would lose one of the few "niches" in the economy that they had, so that they would later have more difficulty becoming integrated into the larger economy. See his *Philadelphia Negro*, 115–16. Some forty-six years later, St. Clair Drake and Horace R. Cayton also identified barbershops and salons as central businesses within African American communities. They stated that African American barbers had a monopoly within the African American community because white barbers would not, or, as they said, did not know how to, cut African American hair. See their *Black Metropolis*, 460–62. Thus Du Bois's fear that white barbers would take over the "hair market," including that involving African American hair, much as they would take over the grocery business, did not come to fruition.

2. See Anderson, *Streetwise*, 58; Clyde W. Franklin II, "The Black Male Urban Barbershop as a Sex-Role Socialization Setting," *Sex Roles* 12 (May 1996): 965–79; and Melissa Harris-Lacewell, *Barbershops, Bibles, and BET: Everyday Talk and Black Political Thought* (Princeton: Princeton University Press, 2004). In many ways the recent analysis of poor neighborhoods in Chicago by W. Wilson, *When Work Disappears*, is influenced by Drake and Cayton's *Black Metropolis*, as is Anderson's *Streetwise*, which observed that the black ghetto of the past had an institutional structure including such businesses as barbershops and salons that produced healthier communities even if these communities were poor.

3. Anderson, *Place on the Corner*, 1.

4. Franklin, "Black Male Urban Barbershop," 965–79; Harris-Lacewell, *Barbershops, Bibles, and BET*, 162–203.

5. See Alan C. Kerchoff, *Socialization and Social Class* (Englewood Cliffs, NJ: Prentice-Hall, 1972), 1–2. Although Kerchoff looks at the family and the school as major agents of socialization, he does not look at other institutions that are primary agents, like the hair shops and gangs. Nonetheless, his book provides important insights into the socialization processes of different social classes.

6. Franklin, "Black Male Urban Barbershop."

7. Henry was talking to two of his friends as they were walking from the lobby of an apartment building toward the Hampton Barbershop. I was sitting on the front step waiting for a person in the building to come down to go hang out at Shippley's Grocery.

8. Felipe was speaking to three other people and the barber in the Playa Barbershop. I was there socializing.

9. See Pierre Bourdieu, *Masculine Domination*, trans. Richard Nice (Stanford: Stanford University Press, 2000).

10. Roderick was talking at the Hampton Barbershop in the Eagleton neighborhood of Brooklyn.

11. Hector was conversing at Pepe's Barbershop in the El Rey neighborhood of Los Angeles.

12. See Lee, *Civility in the City,* 182.

13. People from families that were highly respected in the neighborhood were given high status. Likewise, people considered to be more admirable because of their physical and character attractiveness within neighborhood norms were given more status. The different levels of status on this normative determined continuum constituted the hierarchy of the social order.

14. Alvin was talking in the Town Barbershop. I was there playing checkers.

15. See Bourdieu, *Masculine Domination.*

16. Pablo was talking in Pepe's Barbershop in the El Rey neighborhood of Los Angeles.

17. Emmett was talking in John's Barbershop in L.A.'s Richardson neighborhood.

18. I was in the barbershop socializing when this conversation took place.

19. Although the barbers would not use these value orientation concepts themselves, they did recognize how the men who frequented their shop thought differently about things, and they used various symbols to appeal to that difference.

20. During this conversation between Orville and Harold and a third man, Josh, I was in the barbershop reading a newspaper.

21. During this conversation I was in the shop watching a checkers game.

22. During this conversation I was in the barbershop socializing.

23. See Nathan Murillo, "The Mexican American Family," in *Chicanos: Social and Psychological Perspectives,* ed. N.N. Wagner and M.J. Haug (St. Louis, MO: C.V. Mosby, 1971), 97–108; Alfredo Mirandé and E. Enriquez, *La Chicana* (Chicago: University of Chicago Press, 1979).

24. The Virgen of Guadalupe is so important that December 12 in Mexico is a day devoted to her. See John H. Bushnell, "La Virgen de Guadalupe as Surrogate Mother," *American Anthropologist* 60 (1958): 261–65.

25. Amado was talking to the barber in the Aguila Barbershop. I was there reading the newspaper.

26. During this conversation I was in the barbershop watching a checkers game.

27. While Amado was talking I was sitting in the barbershop listening to the conversation.

28. I was sitting in the Town Barbershop listening to the conversation.

29. Gerald Suttles also talked about the division of gender roles in the slum neighborhood he studied in Chicago. What is so striking about studying slum neighborhoods today is how similar they are in creating and maintaining clearly defined male and female roles. The gender roles I found were not identical to those found by Suttles, but they still flourished in the five neighborhoods that I studied, and all of these neighborhoods would have been considered "slums" as Suttles had used the term to designate the neighborhood he studied. See Suttles, *Social Order,* 88–90.

30. Michele A. Eayrs, "Time, Trust, and Hazard: Hairdressers' Symbolic Roles," *Symbolic Interaction* 16, no. 1 (1993): 19–37.

31. See Horowitz, *Honor and the American Dream*, 70–73, who also found this.

32. The two women were talking while they had their hair done. I was listening to the conversation in an adjacent room, where I had gone after sweeping up the cut hair from the floor.

33. I had just placed the hair I had swept up in a wastebasket and was listening to the conversation.

34. Regina was talking to four women at the Sea Breeze Salon in Brooklyn's Eagleton neighborhood. I was in the back room trying to fix the vacuum cleaner, which had broken while I was attempting to vacuum up hair that the beautician had cut.

35. Any time I use the term *African American,* I am referring to those who are of African heritage who have been born and raised in the United States, most of whom would have been the descendants of slaves in the United States. Of course, Afro-Caribbeans live in the United States—Jamaicans, Trinidadians, and some Dominicans, Cubans, and Puerto Ricans, to name a few. However, the term *African American* in this book does not include individuals of African origin who are from these groups.

36. African American men also saw African American women as demonstrating "tough love," although they articulated it as being domineering. See Harris-Lacewell, *Barbershops, Bibles, and BET,* 183.

37. The women were conversing at the Jewel Salon in the Bronx's Elmway neighborhood. I was in the back room, where I had gone to dump the hair I had swept from the floor into a wastebasket.

38. The money that men would be after was from welfare support provided to women with children. See Dohan, *Price of Poverty,* 24, 29–32, 157–58.

39. See Erving Goffman, *The Presentation of Self in Everyday Life* (New York: Anchor Books, 1959), 22–30, for a discussion of "fronts."

40. On the topic of taboo, see Douglas, *Purity and Danger.*

41. This conversation was taking place in the Kendall Salon in Brooklyn. I was in the next room, having gone there after sweeping up hair from the floor.

42. Michele Lamont, *The Dignity of Working Men: Morality and the Boundaries of Race, Class and Immigration* (Cambridge, MA: Harvard University Press, 2000), 162–214, who finds this for her French case.

43. Dovena was talking to others in the Distinctive Salon. I was in a back room, having gone there after sweeping up hair from the floor.

44. Margarita was speaking in the Mariposa Salon in the El Rey neighborhood of Los Angeles. Occasionally I would come out and sweep the floors and then go to the back room.

45. Tarilyn was talking in Angela's Salon. I was observing from the side room, where I had gone after coming out and sweeping the hair that had just been cut.

46. See Georg Simmel, "Fashion," in *Georg Simmel: On Individuality and Social Forms,* ed. Donald N. Levine (Chicago: University of Chicago Press, 1971), 315.

47. Rosa was in Angela's Salon. I was listening behind the beaded curtain to the back room, where I had gone after coming out and sweeping the hair that had just been cut.

48. This conversation took place in the Mariposa Salon. I was in the back room, where I had gone after coming out and sweeping the hair that had just been cut.

49. This conversation took place in the Sea Breeze Salon, located in the Eagleton neighborhood of Brooklyn. I had just returned to the back room after sweeping up the hair that was on the floor.

50. See Debra Gimlin, "Pamela's Place: Power and Negotiation in the Hair Salon," *Gender and Society* 10 (October 1996): 505–26, who discusses how some hair styles are thought of as being more serious than others.

51. Joellen and Marise were conversing as they waited their turn with the beautician in Angela's Salon. I was in the back room, where I had gone after coming out and sweeping the hair that had just been cut.

52. Bourdieu has written the most exhaustive treatise on the social origins of "taste." See Bourdieu, *Distinction,* 173–75, for a short description of taste; the entire book looks at "taste" and social class.

53. Ibid., 183–200.

54. On the importance of the body and its management, see Loïc Wacquant, *Body and Soul: Notebooks of an Apprentice Boxer* (New York: Oxford University Press, 2004).

55. Anthony Synnott, "Shame and Glory: A Sociology of Hair," *British Journal of Sociology* 38 (September 1987): 381–413.

56. See Goffman, *Presentation of Self,* 15.

57. See Douglas E. Foley's *Learning Capitalist Culture: Deep in the Heart of Tejas* (Philadelphia: University of Pennsylvania Press, 1990), which talks about the importance of using multiple selves to be successful in school.

58. See White, *Identity and Control,* 200–201, 307–9. White does not use the term *identity* as I have used it here, but his theoretical concern is specifying the relationship between identity (personal and organizational) and social control more broadly understood (i.e., on a societal level) than what I have just described, which is a single person's control over his or her immediate environments.

59. Synnott, "Shame and Glory," 381–413.

60. West made this observation at a conference at the University of California, Los Angeles, that I attended. In a sense his argument at the conference complements the position he put forward in the chapter "Nihilism in Black America," which appears in *Race Matters* (Boston: Beacon Press, 1993), 11–32.

61. Omega Psi Phi is an African American college fraternity well known for having the Greek letter for Omega branded on the arms of its members. Some of the people in the neighborhoods may have been influenced by them.

62. Gimlin, "Pamela's Place," 505–26, reports that hair professionals tried to present themselves as experts on style and suggest particular styles for customers. The middle-class clients often rejected the advice, as did individuals who had become middle class and who had come back to their neighborhood for a visit and gone to the salons to get their hair done and socialize, but the residents of the neighborhood seldom resisted the advice of the beauticians.

63. See Gilens, *Why Americans Hate Welfare,* 62, 102–73.

64. I was sitting in the barbershop listening to the conversation. There were two other customers in the shop at the time.

65. I was leaning against the outside wall of the salon listening to the conversation. An African American owned the salon and the clientele was African American, and since I was Mexican and most of the Mexicans in the area spoke little English, I did not inhibit their conversation. In fact, at one point Sylvia said to Lorne, "Don't worry, he [Sánchez-Jankowski] probably doesn't speak English well enough to get what I'm talking about."

66. Suttles, *Social Order,* 68–72.

67. See Synnott, "Shame and Glory," 397–400.

68. I was socializing in the barbershop at the time.

69. Mary Douglas argued that the physical body is often used to manage the social body. She even went on to talk about how the social body influenced the appearance of the physical body, most especially as it applied to hair. See Mary Douglas, *Natural Symbols* (New York: Pelican Books, 1973).

70. During this conversation I was in the apartment waiting for their father to accompany me to the store to socialize.

71. During this conversation I was in an adjoining room of the salon that was separated from the main room by a hanging cloth. I had gone there after coming out and sweeping the hair that had just been cut.

72. The idea of local knowledge was vividly described by anthropologist Clifford Geertz in *Local Knowledge: Further Essays in Interpretive Anthropology,* 3rd ed. (New York: Basic Books, 2006), 167–234.

73. Harris-Lacewell, *Barbershops, Bibles, and BET,* 202.

74. I was getting a haircut during this conversation. I wrote it down as soon as my haircut was finished.

75. The important role of a worldview in establishing and maintaining a culture is discussed extensively in anthropology. More recently, Clifford Geertz has discussed a number of important issues surrounding a local worldview and its contribution to culture. See his *Interpretation of Cultures,* 126–41, and *Local Knowledge.*

76. I was in the barbershop socializing when this conversation took place.

77. Claude was talking to three friends waiting for a haircut in the Best Barbershop. I was there watching a checkers game.

78. For an older but still relevant discussion of the socialization of poor children toward the police, see Dean Jaros, Herbert Hirsch, and Frederic J. Fleron Jr., "The Malevolent Leader: Political Socialization in an American Sub-culture," *American Political Science Review* 62 (June 1968): 564–75.

79. I was in the shop socializing at the time of this conversation.

80. It should be remembered that in fragmented neighborhoods the various institutions, like the barbershop, are used by residents representing different social strata (or positions) because these neighborhoods are more integrated and less antagonistically divided than contested neighborhoods.

81. See Sánchez-Jankowski, "Concentration of African American Poverty," 619–37.

82. This is similar to the findings in Smith, *Lone Pursuit.*

83. See Alejandro Portes, "Economic Sociology and the Sociology of Immigration: A Conceptual Overview," in *The Economic Sociology of Immigration: Essays on Networks, Ethnicity, and Entrepreneurship,* ed. Alejandro Portes (New York: Russell Sage Foundation, 1995), 8–23.

84. Waldinger, *Still the Promised City?* However, Tarry Hum's "A Protected Niche: Immigrant Ethnic Economies and Labor Market Segmentation," in Bobo et al., *Prismatic Metropolis,* 279–314, found that the ethnic economy is not a protected niche that offers economic advantages but rather a place where immigrants find themselves because other alternatives are not available.

85. Networks have been shown to be important for immigrants and those living in immigrant communities. This certainly was the case in the Jamaican community in Brooklyn. For the importance of networks on Latino earnings, see Abel Valenzuela Jr. and Elizabeth Gonzalez, "Latino Earnings Inequality: Immigrant and Native-Born Differences," in Bobo et al., *Prismatic Metropolis,* 249–78.

86. A paper that describes the niche that immigrants can create for themselves is Jacqueline Maria Hagan's "Social Networks, Gender, and Immigrant Incorporation: Resources and Constraints," *American Sociological Review* 63 (February 1998): 55–67.

87. See Wacquant, "Three Pernicious Premises," 347.

88. The conversation occurred while I was sitting in the barbershop.

89. This conversation took place in the Playa Barbershop, which is in the Bronx's Monument neighborhood. I was there socializing.

90. During this conversation, I was listening behind the bead curtain to the back room of the Distinctive Salon, where I had gone after sweeping the hair that had just been cut.

91. This conversation occurred in Castro's Barbershop while I was there reading the paper.

92. This conversation occurred in March 1991, when Monte's was patronized primarily by Italians and some Irish. I was in the barbershop waiting to get a haircut.

7. LIFE ON THE EDGE: SOCIAL CHANGE AND PRESERVATION IN THE HAIR SHOP

1. Some examples of other types of economic establishments are dry-cleaning businesses, auto repair shops, hardware stores, clothing stores, and shoe repair shops.

2. W. Wilson, *Truly Disadvantaged;* Denton and Massey, *American Apartheid.*

3. On social disorganization, see W. Wilson, *When Work Disappears,* 35, 44.

4. This is similar to the dynamic reported by Suttles in his *Social Order,* 13–38.

5. Later Monte's redeveloped into a neighborhood institution once the Italian and Irish patrons left and the Puerto Ricans and Dominicans became the dominant customer base.

6. See Sharff, *King Kong,* 147–57.

7. See Eayrs, "Time, Trust and Hazard."

8. Emory L. Cown et al., "Hairdressers as Caregivers: A Descriptive Profile of Interpersonal Help-Giving Involvements," *American Journal of Community Psychology* 7, no. 6 (1978): 633–48.

9. Here is an excellent example of the effect that Elijah Anderson documented in his study of a poor neighborhood in Philadelphia. See his *Streetwise*, 73–76, where he discusses the importance of the decline in influence of "old heads" in neighborhood culture.

10. This trend matches the growing concentration of disadvantaged populations reported by W. Wilson, *Truly Disadvantaged*, and Denton and Massey, *American Apartheid*.

11. Damon was talking to a friend on the corner while the friend waited for his turn in the barber's chair. I was sitting on a bench in front of the barbershop reading the paper.

12. Rosa was talking with two other women at a taqueria. I had observed Rosa in the Mariposa Salon many times and had noticed from her demeanor an increasing disenchantment with new young clients: she was more reserved, showed no emotion when the young women thought something was funny, and frowned when they mentioned something they thought was positive.

13. See Hum, "A Protected Niche?" and Valenzuela and Gonzalez, "Latino Earnings Inequality."

14. This point has been made by North in *Institutions, Institutional Change*, 6, 22.

15. Reduction of status occurred when individuals who had previously been deferred to in conversation were no longer treated this way, or when people simply ignored the individual while he or she was there, no longer seeking that person's advice and changing the subject while he or she was talking on a particular subject.

16. At the time I was sitting in the barbershop playing checkers with one of the patrons. I was allowed in because everyone knew I was not a resident of the neighborhood. Also, I had already introduced the fact that I was writing a book.

17. Many Puerto Ricans have African features, since the island was dominated by an African slave population. However, before the Spanish arrived, the island was inhabited by an indigenous group called the Tainos who had maintained a presence there for some time. Even today a formal group of Puerto Ricans claim to be descendants of the Tainos. Undoubtedly, there was some mixture involving Tainos, Africans, and Spanish. Nonetheless, Puerto Rico is often referred to as a mulatto nation since the population is a mixture, to varying degrees, of African and Spanish people. While the history of the Dominican Republic is similar to that of Puerto Rico, and the nation would be considered mulatto as well, more Dominicans than Puerto Ricans have African features.

18. At the time I was sitting in the Castro Barbershop listening.

19. A newly formed fragmented neighborhood can be either ethnically homogeneous or multiethnic but dominated by the culture of one group. In either case, the neighborhood is no longer defined by the conflict between ethnic cultures but is instead defined by the conflict between the two value orientations of maximizing excitement and maximizing security. In multiethnic fragmented neighborhoods, members of each ethnic group adopt one of the two value orientations,

and the divisions that occur are articulated as differences between lifestyles rather than ethnicity.

20. Carlos and Pablo were talking outside the local numbers joint (i.e., illegal lottery). I was standing there with two other men.

21. Jordan was conversing with a hair cosmetics supplier from whom she had just ordered some products. I was in the African Sun Salon sweeping the floor for her.

22. See White, *Identity and Control*, 23.

23. See Anderson, *Place on the Corner*, 179–206, who discusses similar processes in the development of social order in the Chicago bar he studied.

24. See W. Wilson, *Truly Disadvantaged* and *When Work Disappears*. Also see Sampson and Raudenbush, "Systematic Social Observation."

25. This study does not include an analysis of the local bar or tavern. These establishments have been significant institutions in poor neighborhoods for centuries, but because the scope of this project was already so large, and because bars and taverns had already been studied, I decided not to include them. Nonetheless, the evidence on them reinforces their importance as major sources of social support within poor neighborhoods. Certainly they have been important places for entertainment and leisure. However, when some of the responsibilities offered by other institutions like the hair shop are no longer provided, the tavern assumes this responsibility. See Roy Rosenzweig, *Eight Hours for What They Will: Workers and Leisure in an Industrial City, 1870–1920* (New York: Cambridge University Press, 1983), 35–64, and Anderson, *Place on the Corner*, esp. 31–53, although much of the book is an applicable elaboration.

8. THE GANG'S ALL HERE:
FATHERING A BASTARD INSTITUTION

1. For a description of gangs and the media, see Sánchez-Jankowski, *Islands in the Street*, 284–309.

2. On disorganization, see Sampson and Wilson, "Toward a Theory of Race." On neighborhood decline, see Skogan, *Disorder and Decline*, 23–26; Malcolm W. Klein, *The American Street Gang: Its Nature, Prevalence, and Control* (New York: Oxford University Press, 1995), 66; Irving A. Spergel, *The Youth Gang Problem: A Community Approach* (New York: Oxford University Press, 1995); and Scott H. Decker and G. David Curry, "Gangs, Gang Homicides, and Gang Loyalty: Organized Crimes or Disorganized Criminals," *Journal of Criminal Justice* 30, no. 4 (2002): 343–52.

3. The early work included Whyte, *Street Corner Society*, and Suttles, *Social Order*. Later work included Sánchez-Jankowski, *Islands in the Street*; Carl S. Taylor, *Dangerous Society* (East Lansing: Michigan State University Press, 1990); Felix Padilla, *The Gang as an American Enterprise* (New Brunswick: Rutgers University Press, 1993); and Venkatesh, *American Project*.

4. For example, see George Tita and Greg Ridgeway, "The Impact of Gang Formation on Local Patterns of Crime," *Journal of Research in Crime and Delinquency* 44, no. 2 (2007): 208–37; Klein, *American Street Gang*; Cheryl Maxson

and Malcolm W. Klein, "Street Gang Violence: Twice as Great, or Half as Great?" in *Gangs in America*, ed. C. Ronald Huff (Newbury Park, CA: Sage Publications, 1990), 71–100; and Jeffrey Fagan, "The Social Organization of Drug Use and Drug Dealing among Urban Gangs," *Criminology* 27, no. 4 (1989): 633–67.

5. See Whyte, *Street Corner Society;* Suttles, *Social Order;* Venkatesh, *American Project.*

6. See Travis Hirschi, *Causes of Delinquency* (Berkeley: University of California Press, 1969); Robert J. Sampson, *Juvenile Criminal Behavior and Its Relation to Neighborhood Characteristics* (Washington, DC: Department of Justice, Office of Juvenile Justice and Delinquency Prevention, National Institute for Juvenile Justice and Delinquency Prevention, 1981).

7. Contemporary sociology does not care to use terms like *functional* to describe roles that individuals or institutions play for fear that it will be taken as embracing the structural-functional theoretical agenda advanced by Talcott Parsons in *The Social System*—a theoretical perspective that has at present been abandoned by most of the sociological community. Despite many valid critiques of the structural-functional conceptual framework, there are functional aspects to every society, and the gang, like any organization, can indeed be functional in poor neighborhoods.

8. For works that have described the functional aspects of gangs in their communities, see Whyte, *Street Corner Society;* Suttles, *Social Order;* Horowitz, *Honor and the American Dream;* Sánchez-Jankowski, *Islands in the Street;* Venkatesh, *American Project.*

9. On the importance of the peer group in low-income neighborhoods, see Herbert Gans, *Urban Villagers,* 197–226.

10. On adolescence in the scheme of human development, see Erik H. Erikson, *Identity, Youth and Crisis* (New York: Norton, 1968), 91–141.

11. See Sánchez-Jankowski, *Islands in the Street,* 40–42; Padilla, *Gang as an American Enterprise.*

12. Tobias was talking with friends in Pepe's Barbershop. There were many people in the shop that day, making private conversations much more possible than when there were few people in the shop.

13. T. C. was speaking to two older boys at the Gordon Street Grocery.

14. Sánchez-Jankowski, *Islands in the Street,* 180–88.

15. I interacted with Eduardo and his mother on a variety of occasions, so I had the opportunity to observe that she operated under a security-maximizing value orientation.

16. Eduardo was talking to three friends at school while I sat at the table next to them. Eduardo did belong to the Fulton gang, and I consistently observed him with them over the next two years.

17. Jamaal was talking with another teenager in the Gordon Street Grocery.

18. Much of the data would suggest that gang members operating under the excitement-maximizing value orientation join and stay in gangs to satisfy purely emotional needs, a thesis advanced by Jack Katz in his book *The Seductions of Crime: Moral and Sensual Attractions in Doing Evil* (New York: Basic Books, 1988). However, it should be pointed out that excitement-maximizing individuals who join gangs do so because they think the gang can provide them with

material benefits first. These individuals would not join merely for emotional benefits. Thus there is a rational calculus to their decisions to join, stay, or even leave.

19. Lucy was talking to four friends, one of them a member of her gang, at the side of the basketball courts of the John C. Fremont Homes housing project.

20. In previous research I argued that the majority of those who joined gangs made the decision as a rational choice. This argument should not be understood to mean that culture did not play a part in the calculus, only to indicate that the logic used was a rational choice computation. See Sánchez-Jankowski, *Islands in the Street*, 23–34.

21. See J. Coleman, *Foundations of Social Theory*, 241–65; Sánchez-Jankowski, *Islands in the Street*, 39–47.

22. Many of the researchers who have stressed culture over rational choice have failed to fully appreciate the complete rational choice theory or the decision-making process of those choosing to join a gang. For the best examples of research using culture to explain gang involvement, see Joan Moore, *Homeboys: Gangs, Drugs, and Prison in the Barrios of Los Angeles* (Philadelphia: Temple University Press, 1978) and *Going Down;* James Diego Vigil, *Barrio Gangs: Street Life and Identity in Southern California* (Austin: University of Texas Press, 1988) and *A Rainbow of Gangs: Street Cultures in the Mega-City* (Austin: University of Texas Press, 2002).

23. See James P. Connell and Bonnie L. Halpern-Felsher, "How Neighborhoods Affect Educational Outcomes in Middle Childhood and Adolescence: Conceptual Issues and an Empirical Example," and Margaret Beale Spencer et al., "Neighborhood and Family Influences on Young Urban Adolescents' Behavior Problems: A Multisample, Multisite Analysis," both in *Neighborhood and Poverty,* ed. Jeanne Brooks-Gunn, Greg J. Duncan (New York: Russell Sage Foundation, 1997), 1:174–99 and 200–218 respectively.

24. See Ruth Horowitz and Gary Schwartz, "Honor, Normative Ambiguity and Gang Violence," *American Sociological Review* 39, no. 2 (1974): 238–51.

25. See W. Miller, "Lower Class Culture," the first work to report the importance of lower-class culture in stimulating gang behavior. Miller emphasizes the influence of economic structural conditions on gang participation.

26. Some examples of alternatives to gang participation are involvement in sports (organized and ad hoc), car and motorcycle clubs, social clubs like the Boys Clubs, the YMCA/YWCA, the Boy and Girl Scouts, associations based on low-skilled work, computer hacking with others, and, to a very limited extent, deviant groups like "goth" cliques, which have been primarily a middle-class phenomenon. In addition, there are the legitimate societal activities associated with school, like academic clubs.

27. On this point, see the work of Richard Slotkin, *Gunfighter Nation: The Myth of the Frontier in Twentieth-Century America* (New York: Atheneum, 1992).

28. For the Amish, see John Andrew Hostetler, *Amish Society,* 4th ed. (Baltimore: Johns Hopkins University Press, 1993; for the Quakers, see Thomas D. Ham, *The Quakers in America* (New York: Columbia University Press, 2003).

29. See Orland Patterson, "Taking Culture Seriously: A Framework and an Afro-American Illustration," in *Culture Matters: How Values Shape Human*

Progress, ed. Lawrence E. Harrison and Samuel P. Huntington (New York: Basic Books, 2000), 202–30.

30. Rufus was talking to two young men and a young woman at the Gordon Street Grocery. I was there socializing.

31. Antonio was talking to a male acquaintance from the neighborhood in La Palma Barbershop. I was there reading a magazine.

32. Many researchers have used this line of argument, so I will mention just a few. The research of Klein is especially interesting because he has had a long and distinguished career studying gangs. Klein, *American Street Gang,* 74–80. In addition, see James Diego Vigil, "The Established Gangs," in *Gangs: The Origins and Impact of Contemporary Youth Gangs in the United States,* ed. Scott Jennings and David J. Monti (Albany: State University of New York Press, 1993), 99–100.

33. See Christopher Adamson, "Defensive Localism in White and Black: A Comparative History of European-American Youth Gangs," *Ethnic and Racial Studies* 23 (March 2000): 272–98.

34. See Alice O'Connor, *Poverty Knowledge: Social Science, Social Policy, and the Poor in Twentieth-Century U.S. History* (Princeton: Princeton University Press, 2001), 45–54.

35. Suttles, *Social Order,* 155–73; Ruth Horowitz, "Community Tolerance of Gang Violence," *Social Problems* 34 (December 1987): 437–49; Sudhir Venkatesh, "The Gang and the Community," in *Gangs in America,* 2nd ed., ed. C. Ronald Huff (Newbury Park, CA: Sage Publications, 1996), 241–56; Sánchez-Jankowski, *Islands in the Street,* 178–211.

36. Klein, *American Street Gang,* 75.

37. See Sánchez-Jankowski, "Gangs and Social Change." The problem with many definitions of gangs is that they tend to confuse sociologically divergent forms of collective behavior. For example, a band of people who attack an individual are involved in "ganging behavior," but that does not mean this group is a gang.

38. Sánchez-Jankowski, *Islands in the Street,* 28–29.

39. For a detailed account of the various organizational forms that gangs assume, as well as a more detailed analysis of gang and community relations, see ibid., 63–78, 178–211.

40. For those that see gangs as a menace to their communities, see Cummings, *Left Behind in Roseville;* Daniel J. Monti, *Gangs: The Origins and Impact of Contemporary Youth Gangs in the United States* (Albany: State University of New York Press, 1993); Robert J. Bursik Jr. and Harold G. Grasmick, *Neighborhoods and Crime: The Dimensions of Effective Community Control* (New York: Lexington Books, 1993); Sampson, *Juvenile Criminal Behavior.*

41. Klein, *American Street Gang,* 84.

42. See Whyte, *Street Corner Society;* Suttles, *Social Order;* W. Miller, "Lower-Class Culture," 52; Horowitz, *Honor and the American Dream;* Sánchez-Jankowski, *Islands in the Street;* Padilla, *Gang as an American Enterprise;* Venkatesh, *American Project.* These studies represent direct observations of gangs and their communities for each decade from the 1940s to 2000. Also see Jerome Skolnick, "The Social Structure of Street Drug Dealing," *American Journal of Police* 9 (1990): 1–41.

43. See Frederic Thrasher, *The Gang: A Study of 1,313 Gangs in Chicago* (Chicago: University of Chicago Press, 1927); Lewis Yablonsky, *The Violent Gang* (New York: Macmillan, 1962), 195–205; Rachel A. Gordon et al., "Antisocial Behavior and Youth Gang Membership: Selection and Socialization," *Criminology* 42, no. 1 (2004): 55–88.

44. See Loïc Wacquant, *Urban Outcasts: A Comparative Sociology of Advanced Marginality* (New York: Oxford University Press, 2007).

45. I was with Bony and the other members of the Jinx Inc. gang on their excursion into Manhattan. J.C. was twenty-five years old and had been in the gang since he was fifteen. He had served one year in a youth detention center for theft, but since then he had not been caught in any illegal acts.

46. There has been a history of poor people thinking they were smarter than the rich. This idea permeating poor and disadvantaged communities has many sources, but its overriding premise is that the rich can never get anything done by themselves: they may come up with plans, but they don't know how to implement them and must call on the other classes to figure it all out. Like the Br'er Rabbit story in Harriet Beecher Stowe's *Uncle Tom's Cabin* (1852; repr., Englewood Cliffs, NJ: Prentice Hall, 2003), this line of thinking suggests that although the master sees himself as superior, he is being played with by the slave or by any subordinate member of society who, despite every social disadvantage, can outsmart him.

47. This finding is slightly different from Suttles's finding in *Social Order*, 3–6, that the slum residents he studied would publicly endorse the morals of the wider society but would privately "take a more relaxed view as to those they expect[ed] to observe." He seemed to suggest that the local residents he studied knew the moral code of the wider society and were unable to successfully abide by it. In contrast, I found in my study that the residents knew the moral code of the larger society but considered it inferior to the operative code within their own neighborhoods. Some might say that this finding only indicates that the residents I studied were defensive about lacking the discipline necessary for abiding by the larger society's moral code, but I found very few residents to be defensive about not following the moral code of the larger society. Some people, of course, were defensive for this reason, but most young and old residents were not.

48. The only significant change is that women from poor communities work more in jobs outside the home than they did before.

49. By *formal intellectual competence* I am referring not to intelligence but to intellectualism associated with an interest in abstraction and abstract concepts that is learned or nurtured in formal educational environments like schools.

50. Freudians have long led the way in exploring psychosexual development. See Erik H. Erikson, *Identity, Youth, and Crisis,* and his *Childhood and Society* (New York: Norton, 1950).

51. I have written on the role of "respect" and "honor" among gangs in *Islands in the Street,* 141–42; for others who have written on the effects of honor cultures, see Julian Pitt-Rivers, *The Fate of Shechem: or, the Politics of Sex: Essays in the Anthropology of the Mediterranean* (New York: Cambridge University Press, 1977), and Gutierrez, *When Jesus Came,* 176–240.

52. Briefly, the primary difference between honor and respect has to do with the amount of time that a person has to endure shame. In honor cultures, honor

is bestowed at birth to every individual; it is the equivalent of a gift from God for life. In this culture, honor is finite and must be protected against all who would take it away. Thus people in honor systems can only lose honor, not work hard to gain it, and when a person loses all of it, it is gone forever. Therefore, it is guarded at all times, and enormous amounts of aggression are expended to keep it. Respect, on the other hand, is gained through one's actions. It can be lost but can be regained with good deeds. In this way, a person wants others to recognize his or her respect because that involves recognizing the effort that went into gaining (or regaining) it. For a study that shows the situations when violence is used for reasons of honor, see William B. Sanders, *Gangbangs and Drive-bys: Grounded Culture and Juvenile Gang Violence* (New York: Aldine de Gruyter, 1994).

53. Many works on gangs have emphasized that gangs are a place where kids with low self-esteem and a crisis in identity formation gravitate in order to obtain an identity that they feel good about. See, for example, Vigil, *Barrio Gangs*, 152–61; Horowitz, *Honor and the American Dream*, 27–29, 169–70, 177–97; Scott Decker and B. Van Wincle, *Life in a Gang: Family, Friends and Violence* (New York: Cambridge University Press, 1996), 67, 72–75.

54. People who were mentally feeble or physically impaired (e.g., having limited use of a limb) were not always classified by residents as "naturally vulnerable." Instead, they were classified in some conditional category because it could be difficult to determine whether they were vulnerable until they did something to show that they were in this category, and that took time.

55. Pocket was speaking to two friends in front of Monte's Barbershop. I was in the barbershop listening to the conversation.

56. Leafy was speaking to Juke Box, a fellow gang member, and his friend Julio in the Birdville gang's clubhouse. I was there talking to a few members.

57. Arnaldo was talking to two male friends in the gang's clubhouse. I was there socializing.

58. Mark D. Totten, *Guys, Gangs, and Girlfriend Abuse* (Peterborough, Ontario: Broadview Press, 2000). What he found in the Canadian context is also present in a more exaggerated form in the United States.

59. This discussion in many ways parallels the studies of thought reform ("brainwashing"). The difference between socialization and brainwashing is that the first involves attitude formation whereas the second involves attitude change. The literature on thought reform is extensive, but two classics are Robert Jay Lifton's *Thought Reform and the Psychology of Totalism: A Study of "Brainwashing" in China* (New York: Norton, 1969) and Edgar H. Schein, Inge Schein, and Curtis H. Barker's *Coercive Persuasion: A Socio-Psychological Analysis of the "Brainwashing" of American Civilian Prisoners by the Chinese Communists* (New York: Norton, 1961).

60. Veronica was talking to two of her friends in the Mariposa Hair Salon. I was in the back room after I had swept up the hair from the floor.

61. These options are very similar to those discussed by Albert O. Hirschman in his classic *Exit, Voice, and Loyalty: Responses to Decline in Firms, Organizations, and States* (Cambridge, MA: Harvard University Press, 1970).

62. The issue of changing gender stratification systems and the concomitant roles is nicely described in Pierrette Hondagneu-Sotelo's study of women who

come from Mexico to the United States to work. See her *Gendered Transitions: Mexican Experiences of Immigration* (Berkeley: University of California Press, 1994), 53–97, 98–148.

63. This conversation was taking place in the Kendall Hair Salon in Brooklyn. Five women were present, three of them getting their hair done and two waiting their turn. I was in the back room after having just swept up the hair from the floor.

64. See, for example, Maudlyne Ihejirika, "Girl Gang Stalks S. Side School's Halls," *Chicago Sun-Times*, April 30, 2004, 11; Cynthia Shepherd, "It's Hard to Exit a Female Gang," *Salt Lake City Desert News*, October 4, 1999, C1; Michael O'Connor, "Female Gang Members Rising in Bellevue, Groups Are Told," *Omaha World Herald*, October 25, 1994; Anastasia Hendrix, "Hill Girls' Gang Preys on Women: Police in S.F. Surprised by the Savagery of Attacks," *San Francisco Chronicle*, September 3, 2003, A11.

65. See Ann Campbell, *Girls in the Gang*, 2nd ed. (New York: Blackwell, 1991); Moore, *Going Down*; Joan Moore, James Diego Vigil, and J. Levy, "Huisas of the Street: Chicano Gang Members," *Latino Studies Journal* 6, no. 1 (2001): 27–48; Sudir Venkatesh, "Gender and Outlaw Capitalism: A Historical Account of the Black Sisters United," *Signs: Journal of Women and Culture in Society* 23 (Spring 1998): 683–709.

66. On the media's portrayal of girl gang members, see Meda Chesney-Lind, Randall G. Shelden, and Karen A. Joe, "Girls, Delinquency, and Gang Membership," in Huff, *Gangs in America*, 2nd ed., 205–21.

67. See Klein, *American Street Gang*, 64–67. In his survey of girls in gangs, he reports that girl gangs are "more common than might be thought" (59), but later in the chapter, when he discusses them in more detail, he cites only one study of a gang in Honolulu from the 1960s that was male/female integrated with thirty-six girls and sixty-six boys. He mentions reports from Rochester, Denver, and Pittsburgh that girls may be giving up their traditional roles as members of auxiliary support groups to the male gangs and becoming more autonomous, but there are many problems with accepting this as a potential trend. First, none of these three cities has a history of a large number of gangs with significant numbers of people involved in them; second, Klein does not offer any data from the "reports" he refers to; and last, he does not even formally cite the reports whose information he is using to make this claim. The data from the present study indicate that women have remained overwhelmingly in an auxiliary role.

68. Suttles, *Social Order*, 157–220, also found this.

69. I was socializing with the Guzmán family at the time, and I went with the young relative to the store. I was actually going to see a basketball game at the local playground, but I decided to stay with the relative to record his interaction with the Birdville gang, who knew me. Later, when the Guzmán family had relatives visiting and passed on the gang warning, I was again at the Guzmán house for dinner.

70. Gangs are one of the fundamental institutions in the neighborhood that promotes and protects the formation of basic group identity. For a powerful

statement concerning the elements in the formation of basic group identity, see Isaacs, *Idols of the Tribe,* 38–45. Also, for a very insightful statement on the dynamics of group solidarity, see Hechter, *Principles of Group Solidarity.*

71. On pain differences among cultures, see Sangeetha Nayak et al., "Culture and Gender Effects in Pain Beliefs and the Prediction of Pain Tolerance," *Cross-Cultural Research* 34 (2000): 135–51; Prithvi Raj, Ilona Steigerwald, and Stefan Esser, "Socioeconomic and Cultural Influences on Pain Management in Practice," *Pain Practice* 3 (2003): 80–83; Gary Rollman, "Culture and Pain," in *Cultural Clinical Psychology: Theory, Research, and Practice,* ed. S.S. Kazarian and David R. Evans (New York: Oxford University Press, 1998), 267–86.

72. For one of the most important studies examining the social class differences in the use of physical force to discipline children, see Kohn, *Class and Conformity,* 95–99.

73. See J. Katz, *Seductions of Crime,* 12–51.

74. Cover was talking to three young men, two of whom were gang members, at the handball courts in the Gardenia Avenue Apartments. I was standing next to them watching the handball game.

75. When Tony was stopped for questioning by the police, I was outside on a balcony that gave me a direct view of the incident. I could watch and listen to the whole interaction without being noticed. The next day Tony was hanging around the Primo Grocery when people asked him about his bumps and bruises, and I took down what was said. Tony's description of the incident spread throughout the neighborhood.

76. Hannah Arendt forcefully brought attention to the power of language as mediator of cruel physical events in her *Eichmann in Jerusalem: A Report on the Banality of Evil* (New York: Viking Press, 1964), 80.

77. This conversation took place at the Isla Grocery in the Bronx's Monument neighborhood. On the issue of men not showing that they love a woman for fear of being seen as weak, see Herman Schwendinger and Julia R. Siegal-Schwendinger, *Adolescent Subculture and Delinquency* (New York: Praeger, 1985), 167.

78. The only emotion that could be legitimately expressed was anger because it could be used for retaliatory purposes. Retaliation was considered the only effective means of preventing harm.

79. See Sánchez-Jankowski, *Islands in the Street,* 23–30, for a discussion of the "defiant individualism" that most gang members assume. Although gang members all have this "defiant individualism," many other men living in poor neighborhoods also have it.

80. Curly was talking to six men in front of the Gordon Street Grocery. I was sitting inside by the door while they were standing just outside it.

81. The ethnic differences were influenced by each group's more general religious orientation. Those who were from Protestant backgrounds believed that the world could be controlled, whereas those from Catholic backgrounds believed that the world acted on them and that its impact could only be accepted. Interestingly, these sets of beliefs are similar to the findings in Weber's *Protestant Ethic.*

82. Rugs and two other gang members were sitting in the stands watching a soccer game at the James K. Polk High School and talking. I was sitting in the row in front of them.

83. See Klein, *American Street Gang,* 84–85.

84. Much of the gang's role in providing protection is documented in Sánchez-Jankowski, *Islands in the Street,* 178–211, and mentioned in Venkatesh, *American Project,* 179.

85. The clothing consisted of shirts and various headgear colored blue.

86. I was at the gang's clubhouse when they decided to take action, and I was on a porch of a house that was two doors from where the shots were fired at the car carrying the African Americans. I saw the whole incident, including the police interviewing of witnesses.

87. See Suttles, *Social Construction of Community,* 189–229.

88. I was in Treviño's talking to the owner of the store when the conversation began at the checkout stand.

89. Gabby was talking to four other gang members. They had all just come back from a concert featuring rap artists and were hanging out in a parking lot drinking beer. I was hanging out with them.

90. See Walter Miller's seminal article "Lower-Class Culture," esp. 52.

91. Daniel Monti studied what he called gangs in a middle-class school in St. Louis, Missouri. Part of his argument was that gangs were in all types of neighborhoods, but this argument had no foundation. Certainly some groups in middle-class neighborhoods are involved in collective behavior that is unlawful and/or antisocial, but they are rarely "gangs" as this and most other studies of gangs would define the term. Thus arguments like Monti's erroneously specify the sociological basis of gangs and produce additional confusion about the gang phenomenon. See Daniel J. Monti, *Wannabe: Gangs in Suburbs and Schools* (New York: Oxford University Press, 1994).

92. For a very detailed description of this personality type, see Sánchez-Jankowski, *Islands in the Street,* 23–29.

93. Venkatesh, in *American Project,* 180, reports that the gang he studied would use coercive tactics to force small businesses to subscribe to its services.

94. See Carl S. Taylor, *Girls, Gangs, Women and Drugs* (East Lansing: Michigan State University Press, 1993), who also observed women being used to transport drugs.

95. Alma was talking with Jasmine and Lois at a laundromat. Ricky, Alma's son, was in the St. James Place gang, which operated in Brooklyn's Eagleton neighborhood. He was sixteen years old and had been in the gang for about five months.

96. See Hannah Arendt, *The Human Condition* (Chicago: University of Chicago Press, 1958), 79–174.

97. See Bourgois, *In Search of Respect,* 114–73. The struggle with the stigma of legal jobs that involve labor and not work is also highlighted in the findings of Catherine Newman, *No Shame in My Game: The Working Poor in the Inner City* (New York: Knopf, 1990). Although Newman does make the distinction between the concepts of work and labor, she describes the youth who are prepared to "labor" in fast-food jobs as understanding that the jobs carry stigma. It is precisely this stigma that gives rise to the title of her book.

98. This conversation took place between Daddy Dee, Conga, Deputy, and Tank at the Toppers' clubhouse.

99. Red Eyes was conversing with Cactus Vatos members Cubby, Juice, Wolfy, and Blue in a community park.

100. Everett Hughes coined the concept "bastard institution" to refer to society's "illegitimate" institutions, those not sanctioned by the dominant society. See Everett Hughes, *Work, Race, and the Sociological Imagination,* ed. Lewis A. Coser (Chicago: University of Chicago Press, 1994), 192–93.

9. ALL IN THE FAMILY: MOTHERING THE GANG AS A BASTARD INSTITUTION

1. See Herbert Asbury, *The Gangs of New York: An Informal History of the Underworld* (1898; repr., Garden City, NY: Garden City Publishing, 1928), 1–20.

2. There are numerous examples, but I will mention only two: on the scholarly side, John Hagedorn, *People and Folks: Gangs, Crime, and the Underclass in a Rustbelt City* (Chicago: Lakeview Press, 1988), and on the popular journalistic side, Léon Bing, *Do or Die* (New York: Harper, 1991).

3. On the gang as the dysfunctional product of material deprivation, see Albert K. Cohen, *Delinquent Boys: The Culture of the Gang* (Glencoe, IL: Free Press, 1955); Whyte, *Street Corner Society;* Suttles, *Social Order;* Sullivan, *"Getting Paid."* On the gang as a dysfunctional contributor to community decay, see Skogan, *Disorder and Decline;* Sampson and Wilson, "Toward a Theory of Race," 37–54.

4. See James Q. Wilson and G. Kelling, "Broken Windows," *Atlantic Monthly,* March 1982, 29–38. Along this line of argument, see also Skogan, *Disorder and Decline.* Although neither of these works portrays gangs as the sole reason for the disorder and subsequent decline, both point to gangs as a factor that indicates and accelerates decay.

5. The work of Elijah Anderson is relevant here because he addresses the issue of what contributes to and what hinders neighborhood well-being. His position is that struggle goes on between the "decent" and "street" elements of an inner-city neighborhood and that whichever element becomes triumphant has an important impact on whether a neighborhood will become a slum or one that has limited resources but is socioeconomically vibrant. His most relevant works on this point are *Streetwise* and *Code of the Street.* The work of William Julius Wilson is also germane to this issue. See W. Wilson, *When Work Disappears,* 21.

6. On social demonology, see Michael Rogin, *Ronald Reagan, the Movie and Other Episodes in Political Demonology* (Berkeley: University of California Press, 1988), xiii.

7. See Asbury, *Gangs of New York.*

8. Daniel J. Monti, in *Wannabe,* has argued that gangs are not merely a lower-class phenomenon. He studied a middle-class community school and identified a number of groups as "gangs." These groups, however, lacked much of the group and organizational substance that other research has identified with gangs.

9. W. Wilson, *Truly Disadvantaged,* 20–62.

10. W. Wilson, *When Work Disappears*, 25–34.

11. See Sullivan, *"Getting Paid."*

12. On the characteristics of the secondary labor market, see Doeringer and Piore, *Internal Labor Markets*.

13. See Bourgois, *In Search of Respect*, 114–73.

14. This finding was reported in Sánchez-Jankowski, *Islands in the Street*, 45–46.

15. Miguel and his friends were talking at the basketball courts in the Buckley Gardens housing project. I was sitting on a bench watching the pickup basketball game.

16. See Manuel Castells, *The Rise of the Network Society* (Oxford: Blackwell, 1996), 201–326.

17. Bourgois, *In Search of Respect*, 4, 114–73; Sullivan, *"Getting Paid,"* 58–105; Dohan, *Price of Poverty*, 47–49; Padilla, *Gang as an American Enterprise*, 37–42.

18. James Short, past president of the American Sociological Association and noted sociologist and criminologist, made this comment at a session of "The Author Meets Critics" at the American Sociological Association's annual meeting in 1992.

19. Carlos was speaking to a cousin and neighbor. The three of them were eating in a small local restaurant. I was also in the restaurant eating, but not with them.

20. Larry and the teacher were talking in front of a small newspaper stand. The teacher was trying to convince him that joining a gang was very dangerous and that he could get killed. Two weeks after this conversation, Larry decided to join the Jinx Inc. gang. He stayed in the gang for five years. During that time he was shot once in the shoulder but recuperated and made a significant amount of money selling drugs in the gang. When the present research project ended, Larry was serving time in the state penitentiary for selling drugs.

21. The effect of deindustrialization on gang membership was reported in Hagedorn, *People and Folks*, and Alford A. Young Jr., *The Minds of Marginalized Black Men: Making Sense of Mobility, Opportunity, and Future Life Chances* (Princeton: Princeton University Press, 2004), 48–49.

22. The breakdown in the drug monopoly occurred as a result of the traditional Italian Mafia's loss of control over organized crime in nonwhite ethnic areas in the United States and its inability to control the source of production for cocaine, heroin, and marijuana. See Francis A.J. Innai, *Black Mafia: Ethnic Succession in Organized Crime* (New York: Simon and Schuster, 1974).

23. Malcolm Klein has argued that gangs are not very involved in the drug wholesale-retail business: gang members working alone may be, but not their gang organizations. Gangs may not be the prime actors in the drug industry, but during my more than twenty years of research with multiple gangs in multiple cities, I found that all of them were involved in various levels of the drug industry and all benefited from that involvement. All the gangs in the present study were thoroughly involved in production and wholesale and retail sales. What is more, all the direct observation studies report gangs being integrally involved in

the drug economy. The only way to explain the discrepancy between Klein and the participant observation studies is that Klein uses large survey data sets rather than directly observing gang behavior. Surveys simply give a snapshot at one time with a group of people who have more to lose by answering survey questions truthfully than not. For recent research on gang involvement in the drug economy, see Sudhir Venkatesh, *American Project* and *Off the Books,* which support Sánchez-Jankowski, *Islands in the Street,* and Taylor, *Dangerous Society,* about gangs' active involvement in the drug economy. Malcolm Klein and Cheryl Maxson, in their *Street Gang Patterns and Policies* (New York: Oxford University Press, 2006), 187, have completely distorted and misused the findings of Venkatesh to support their point by referring to the gangs in the Venkatesh study as "specialty gangs," even though in fact these were simply the same type of gang that has been commonly observed again and again over time and in different contexts.

24 . Klein and Maxson, *Street Gang Patterns,* 170–71, contend that gangs are generally not organizationally structured and are instead just loose associations of small groups (cliques). Yet a wealth of direct observation research has consistently documented that gangs have organizational leadership and that this leadership can be sustained over time. That the authors ignore this finding suggests that they are more interested in sustaining their opposition to it. Studies from 1969 to 2006—R. Lincoln Keiser, *The Vice Lords, Warriors of the Streets* (New York: Holt, Reinhart and Winston, 1969); Walter B. Miller, *Violence by Youth Gangs and Youth Groups as a Crime Problem in Major American Cities* (Washington, DC: Department of Justice, 1975); Horowitz, *Honor and the American Dream;* Taylor, *Dangerous Society;* Sánchez-Jankowski, *Islands in the Street;* Venkatesh, *American Project* and *Off the Books*—have all found gangs to be organizations with identifiable and defined leadership.

25. Klein, *American Street Gang,* 80.

26. For findings indicating entrepreneurial skills and rational decision making among gang members, see Sánchez-Jankowski, *Islands in the Street,* 101–13; Padilla, *Gang as an American Enterprise,* 104–9; and Venkatesh, *Off the Books,* 278–365.

27. In this environment negotiation was not viewed as a viable option because negotiating for portions of an object(s) was thought to be the equivalent of not having any of it. That is, any amount less than the total object was so small as to make the act of securing a portion not worth the effort.

28. Hannah Arendt, *On Violence* (New York: Harcourt, Brace and World, 1969), 35.

29. On labor-management disputes, see Louis Adamic, *Dynamite: The Story of Class Violence in America* (New York: Chelsea House, 1931); on Japan's decision to attack the United States, see then–Secretary of State Cordell Hull, *The Memoirs of Cordell Hull* (New York: Macmillan, 1948), 2:982–1105.

30. STEP, Section 186.20 of the California State Penal Code, was first passed in 1988. Since then several provisions have been added. If a jury finds that an individual committed acts for the benefit of a gang, the court can add years to each count that the individual was found guilty as charged.

31. The right to association was compromised because the police could use sweeps to round up documented and suspected gang members if they were found to be congregating in public areas.

32. See the work of Franklin E. Zimring and Gordon Hawkins, *Crime Is Not the Problem: Lethal Violence in America* (New York: Oxford University Press, 1997).

33. Fishhook was talking to a friend in front of Shippley's Grocery. I was in front of the store with two older men who were sitting and drinking beer.

34. Hank was talking to three men at the Tortuga Grocery. I was in the store socializing with the owner at the time.

35. For an overview of social control theory, see Ruth Kornhauser, *The Social Sources of Delinquent Theory* (Chicago: University of Chicago Press, 1978), 51–138.

36. For an overview of social disorganization theory as it relates to the slum, see Kornhauser, *Social Sources*, 134–38; for a specific example of the use of control and disorganization theory to explain crime in poor areas, see Sampson and Wilson, "Toward a Theory of Race."

37. See Bruce A. Jacobs and Richard Wright, *Street Justice: Retaliation in the Criminal Underworld* (New York: Cambridge University Press, 2006), 54–58.

38. This incident took place on the corner just outside Nino's Grocery. I was able to hear all the conversations but was in the store when the shots were fired. I came out to see the men limp to their car and drive off. The police questioned all of us.

39. During the time of the research numerous groups that formed in each neighborhood tried to become gangs, but most either failed to become formal gangs or died as formal organizations. This occurred for a number of reasons: some were taken over by competing gangs that were stronger; others simply had most of their members in the penal system or killed and so were absent a critical number of members; and still others simply could never get enough members to establish a gang organization. Although this chapter has focused on the gangs that were recognized as dominant in each neighborhood, I recorded twenty-nine groups that tried to form a gang, or formed one and died, over the nine years of the research.

40. See Sánchez-Jankowski, "Gangs and Social Change," 191–216.

41. See Jeffrey Fagan and Deanna L. Wilkinson, "Guns, Youth Violence, and Social Identity in Inner Cities," *Crime and Justice* 24 (1998): 105–88.

42. Susana was talking to her friend Carla during lunch hour at Chester Himes High School in L.A.'s Richardson neighborhood. I was at the table next to them eating.

43. Howard Pinderhughes, *Race in the Hood: Conflict and Violence among Urban Youth* (Minneapolis: University of Minnesota Press, 1997); Sánchez-Jankowski, *Islands in the Street*, 183–92.

44. For a description of these types of collective behavior, see Sánchez-Jankowski, "Gangs and Social Change," 198–201.

45. Crack cocaine is cocaine that has been processed into crystals or rocks, which are then sold and smoked by the consumer in a pipelike apparatus. Crank cocaine is a cocaine and methamphetamine mixture that is consumed

by sniffing. White heroin is heroin that has been refined, whereas black heroin is unrefined.

46. See Horowitz, *Honor and the American Dream*, 89–97.

47. Bouncer was talking to two other males in the neighborhood while they watched a handball game at a park. I was there waiting to play with three other members of the Falcons gang.

48. Hagedorn, *People and Folks*, 41–50, 110–28.

49. Venkatesh, *Off the Books*, 283–90, also finds this.

50. See Patrick Sharkey, "Navigating Dangerous Streets: The Sources and Consequences of Street Efficacy," *American Sociological Review* 71 (October 2006): 826–47.

51. See Cummings, *Left Behind in Roseville*, 50–51.

52. See Bursik and Grasmick, *Neighborhoods and Crime*, 104–9.

53. Probably no social issue has better illustrated labeling theory than gangs. When police are unsure about a crime, they often label it as "gang related." For example, when gang members are involved in a robbery or some form of violent assault, the incident is almost always described as "gang related," yet in most of these cases the crime, though committed by a gang member, had nothing to do with his association with the gang or the formal gang organization. In essence, the crime was individual and would have happened even if the individual had not been associated with a gang. For a discussion of the tendency of the police to overlabel crimes "gang related," see Maxson and Klein, "Street Gang Violence," 71–100. The best statement of labeling theory is H. Becker, *Outsiders*.

54. Antonio was participating in a general discussion in the B. J. Grocery.

55. Lisa was talking to her friends Francesca and Nora in the lobby of the Gardenia Avenue Apartments housing project. I was in the lobby waiting for a friend to get his mail from the building's mailboxes. Lisa's boyfriend, Jorge, received a sentence of ten years for armed robbery in which the victim was injured by gunshot.

56. Tawana was talking to her friends Dora, Rene, and Ingrid in front of Daddy G's Grocery. I was in the store. Two months after this quote was taken, Tawana became pregnant and Leon was arrested for the sale of crack cocaine, convicted, and sent to prison for five years.

57. Venkatesh, in *American Project*, 78–80, 174–78, found the gangs in the Chicago Housing Authority's Robert Taylor Homes to be generally antagonistic toward the resident's interests for a better life, but this was not the case in the housing projects of this study. However, in one instance Venkatesh found that the gangs helped residents resist a housing authority change that the residents thought made their life more difficult.

58. Jacobs and Wright, *Street Justice*, 49–54, describe similar behavior.

59. See Sánchez-Jankowski, *Islands in the Street*, 180–201, and Venkatesh, *American Project*, 179.

60. See Raphael J. Sonenshein, *Politics in Black and White: Race and Power in Los Angeles* (Princeton: Princeton University Press, 1993), and Nicolás C. Vaca, *The Presumed Alliance: The Unspoken Conflict between Latinos and Blacks and What It Means for America* (New York: HarperCollins, 2004), 85–108, 127–45.

61. See Mary Patillo, *Black on the Block: The Politics of Race and Class in the City* (Chicago: University of Chicago Press, 2007), 113–47.

62. See ibid., 217–57.

63. I shall mention only a few of the many books on redevelopment in low-income areas and the government's involvement in that process. See Gans, *Urban Villagers,* on the redevelopment of the poor Boston neighborhood known as the West End; King, *Chain of Change,* on the redevelopment of the poor neighborhood in Boston called the South End; and Wylie, *Poletown,* on the redevelopment of the poor Detroit neighborhood called Poletown.

64. See Venkatesh, *American Project,* 44; and Sánchez-Jankowski, *Islands in the Street,* 191–92.

65. Patillo, *Black on the Block,* 72–73.

66. See Gans, *Urban Villagers,* 325–95; Suttles, *Social Order,* 20; and King, *Chain of Change.*

67. Evan was talking to his friends Janice and Roy outside the Farragut Street Grocery. I was just inside the front doorway talking with the owner. Evan had been in the Jamaican St. James Place gang when he was sixteen and had left the gang to go into the army. When this quote was taken, Evan was starting to hang around with the gang again.

68. Olivia was talking to three other mothers at the children's play structure in the Orchard Lane Apartments public housing complex. I was there eating lunch and watching the children play.

69. There has not been much sociological work on this area of the economy. See Venkatesh, *Off the Books,* 278–365, and Dohan, *Price of Poverty,* 120–29.

70. Social capital has been one of the important subjects addressed by economic sociologists analyzing an individual's socioeconomic destination. For example, see Nan Lin, *Social Capital: A Theory of Social Structure and Action* (New York: Cambridge University Press, 2001), 102–23; and Susan Saegert, J. Phillip Thompson, and Mark R. Warren, eds., *Social Capital and Poor Communities* (New York: Russell Sage Foundation, 2001); Smalls, *Villa Victoria.*

71. See the NYPD manual by H. Craig Collins, *Street Gangs: Profiles for Police* (New York: City of New York Police Department, 1979), and the L.A. Sheriff's Department's manual by Robert K. Jackson and Wesley D. McBride, *Understanding Street Gangs* (Costa Mesa, CA: Custom Publishing, 1985), 59–80.

72. The person making this statement was V. G. Guinses, executive director of Say Yes, Inc. of South Central Los Angeles, in a conference on youth gangs. See Robert L. Woodson, ed., *Youth Crime and Urban Policy: A View from the Inner City* (Washington, DC: American Enterprise Institute, 1981), 25.

73. In California, Mexican gangs have developed a distinctive print form that is referred to as *cholo* script (*cholo* being the word for someone in a gang), as well as a variety of words like *moniker* for a gang person's name, *placas* for gang symbols or tattoos, and *kites* for messages sent between gang members. This has made it clear that gangs are important actors in continuing to create cultural symbols. On Mexican American *cholo* script and words associated with gangs, see Susan A. Phillips, *Wallbangin': Graffiti and Gangs in L.A.* (Chicago: University of Chicago Press, 1999), 188–92, 198–210. For Chicago gangs, see George Knox, *An Introduction to Gangs* (Berrien-Springs, MI: Van de Vere, 1991), 455–86.

74. See Susan A. Phillips, "Gallo's Body: Decoration and Damnation in the Life of a Chicano Gang Member," *Ethnography* 2 (September 2001): 357–88.

75. See Eric C. Schneider, *Vampires, Dragons, and Egyptian Kings: Youth Gangs in Postwar New York* (Princeton: Princeton University Press, 1999), 137–63. Schneider wrote about the making of gang culture, but gang culture was in most ways a subculture of that found in poor neighborhoods. Also, Schneider's history of gangs and their culture after World War II did not recognize that gangs were both producers and propagators of culture to their own and the larger community.

76. Calvin was talking to three other men in the E & M Barbershop. I was sitting in the shop watching a checkers game.

77. Teresa was conversing with two other women and the owner of the Jalisco Grocery. I was in one of the aisles looking at products.

78. Estevan is in the Zapata Park gang and was speaking to two friends, Pablo and Joaquin, in front of the Canal Grocery. I was in front of the store watching a dominos game between four adult men.

79. This conversation took place in La Playa Barbershop. I was in the shop watching television.

80. See Simmel, *Conflict*, and Coser, *Functions of Social Conflict*. Simmel was the first to theorize about the role of conflict in promoting social bonding, and Louis Coser extended Simmel's thought by identifying how conflict functionally operated within societies.

81. Sánchez-Jankowski, *Islands in the Street*, 201–11; Venkatesh, *American Project*, 110–52; Dohan, *Price of Poverty*, 124.

10. WHITHER THE NEIGHBORHOOD HIGH SCHOOL? CONTENDING ROLES AND FUNCTIONS

1. The American people have tended to confuse two concepts of the school's role, the provision of equal opportunity to learn and be socioeconomically mobile and the actual production of learning and socioeconomic mobility for all citizens. Between the two, the concept of equal opportunity has dominated, and as a result nearly every presidential election from 1960 on has seen each major candidate include as part of his platform a commitment to do everything possible to support the schools in their efforts to educate the country's youth so that youth may have the opportunity to be economically successful in realizing their dreams.

2. See Edward Banfield, *The Unheavenly City Revisited* (1970; repr., Boston: Houghton-Mifflin, 1974), 148–78.

3. Some research blames the disadvantaged students for not taking advantage of opportunities to improve their own chances. On this, see Shelby Steele, *The Content of Our Character: A New Vision of Race in America* (New York: Harper, 1991); Thomas Sowell, *Inside American Education: The Decline, the Deception, the Dogmas* (New York: Free Press, 1993); John McWhorter, *Losing the Race: Self-Sabotage in Black America* (New York: Free Press, 2000).

4. See, for example, Jonathan Kozol, *Savage Inequalities: Children in America's Schools* (New York: Harper Perennial, 1992); Pedro Noguera, *City*

Schools and the America Dream (New York: Columbia Teacher's College Press, 2003).

5. See Samuel Bowles and Herbert Gintis, *Schooling in Capitalist America* (New York: Basic Books, 1976).

6. For a recent study that identifies this mismatch, see Lareau, *Unequal Childhoods*, 14–32, although the entire book reports on the elements of the mismatch. Previous studies that identify and analyze various aspects of this mismatch are Basil Bernstein, "Social Class, Language, and Socialization," in *Power and Ideology in Education*, ed. Jerome Karabel and A.H. Halsey (New York: Oxford University Press, 1977), 473–87; Henry A. Giroux, *Theory and Resistance in Education: A Pedagogy for the Opposition* (London: Heinemann Educational Books, 1983); Paul Willis, *Learning to Labor: How Working Class Kids Get Working Class Jobs* (New York: Columbia University Press, 1977); Jay MacLeod, *Ain't No Makin' It: Aspirations and Attainment in a Low-Income Neighborhood* (Boulder, CO: Westview Press, 1995).

7. See Willis, *Learning to Labor,* MacLeod, *Ain't No Makin' It,* and Giroux, *Theory and Resistance,* all of which find resistance and rejection to be a factor in student behavior.

8. See Prudence L. Carter, *Keepin' It Real: School Success beyond Black and White* (New York: Oxford University Press, 2005), who in a recent study using data from sixty-eight in-depth interviews also found culture to be a factor in explaining why children from low-income families did more poorly in school than those from middle- and upper-income families. Carter's findings about the importance of culture support in part the findings in this study, but there is an important difference between her findings and those found here. This difference centers on the nature of culture itself. The students in Carter's study whom she labels "noncompliant believers" are individuals who use their ethnic culture as a resource to "critique and cope" with inequality. However, in the present study the students' beliefs about education and their behaviors in school affirm not so much their specific ethnic cultures as the culture and values that have developed from their impoverished environment. The students in the present study, unlike those in Carter's study, are less resistant to what she calls the "dominant achievement ideology" of American society and more affirmative in embracing, celebrating, and acting with the dictates of a local culture that has emerged and been nurtured from persistent material scarcity.

9. One of the best studies to illuminate acts of resistance in lower-class schools is Willis, *Learning to Labor.*

10. This finding is what separates the present study from that of MacLeod's *Ain't No Makin' It.* In his study ethnicity was a major explanatory factor in how the groups of individuals he studied reacted to the school, albeit in directions opposite to what would be predicted by conventional wisdom. MacLeod found that the black students whom he labeled "the Brothers" believed in the "American dream" ideology of economic mobility and the use of the school in that effort, whereas the group he labeled "the Hallway Hangers," who were composed of Italian and Irish youth (the exception being one black and one youth of mixed race), were not believers in the ideology that economic mobility was possible for everyone if they studied in school and worked hard. In the present

study ethnicity was not a major factor in the student's beliefs about education and economic mobility or their behavior in the schools as it related to affirming the local subculture.

11. On the concept of "life chances," see Dahrendorf, *Life Chances,* 21–96.

12. These efforts by the school were aimed at building human capital in the students. For the classic statement of human capital in relation to education and life chances, see Gary S. Becker, *Human Capital: A Theoretical and Empirical Analysis with Special Reference to Education* (1964; repr., Chicago: University of Chicago Press, 1993), 51–53.

13. The term *capabilities* implies something genetically based and immutable. Standardized tests are the general mechanism used to assess academic competence and capabilities. Basically two types of tests are used: (1) those intended to measure a person's intellectual ability, which are referred to as "intelligence tests" (IQ tests), and (2) those intended to measure an individual's knowledge base, which are referred to as "aptitude tests." For a broad statement on the importance of IQ tests, see Richard Herrnstein and Charles Murray, *The Bell Curve: Intelligence and Class Structure in American Life* (New York: Free Press, 1994). For a critique of this book and *The Bell Curve*'s argument that intelligence structures American life, see Claude S. Fischer et al., *Inequality by Design: Cracking the Bell Curve Myth* (Princeton: Princeton University Press, 1996). For a history of these tests, see Nicolas Lemann, *The Big Test: The Secret History of American Meritocracy* (New York: Farrar, Straus, and Giroux, 1999).

14. For a discussion of the impact of tracking on students in general and poor students in particular, see Samuel Roundfield Lucas, *Tracking Inequality: Stratification and Mobility in America's High Schools* (New York: Columbia Teacher's College Press, 1999).

15. See Jack Citrin et al., "The 'Official English' Movement and the Symbolic Politics of Language in the United States," *Western Political Quarterly* 43 (September 1990): 535–60; Carol Schmid, "The English Only Movement: Social Bases of Support and Opposition among Anglos and Latinos," in *Language Loyalties,* ed. James Crawford (Chicago: University of Chicago Press, 1992), 202–9.

16. Early in the Republic the school was supposed to teach immigrant children the language, society, and political system. See Carl F. Kaestle, *Pillars of the Republic: Common Schools and the American Society, 1780–1860* (New York: Hill and Wang, 1983).

17. T. H. Marshall stressed the importance of having full citizenship in a country, arguing that without it individuals had diminished life chances in the society and constituted a serious challenge to the existence of the state that was unwilling or unable to provide it to them. See T. H. Marshall, *Citizenship and Social Class, and Other Essays* (New York: Cambridge University Press, 1950).

18. See John U. Ogbu, *Black American Students in an Affluent Suburb: A Study of Academic Disengagement* (Mahwah, NJ: Lawrence Erlbaum, 2003), 52–54, 145–56, which discusses how immigrant minorities and African Americans view the "American dream" as it relates to school.

19. Michel Foucault, *Discipline and Punish: The Birth of the Prison* (1975; repr., New York: Vintage Books, 1979), has described the shifts in establishing social control from an external to internal locus. In the present study the school

authorities first tried to encourage internal social control, and if that failed they shifted their efforts to external sources of control.

20. Lyza was talking to her friends during lunch hour in the cafeteria. I was sitting at the table next to them eating with two male students.

21. Germán was talking with three of his friends while standing in the lunch line. I was in line as well.

22. Curtis and two of his friends, one male and the other female, were talking about Thomas later in the day after the incident. The conversation was taking place at the gym, where Curtis and his friends were getting ready to watch the varsity basketball team. I was in the stands behind them watching the players warm up.

23. Tobias was talking with his friends Edna, John, and Roberto during the official school nutrition period break. I was at the table next to theirs.

24. Myesha was talking with her friend Elenor and Aline, Elenor's new neighbor, while the three were standing in line waiting to use the public telephone. I was sitting in the counselors' office next to the phone.

25. Maria-Elena, who is Puerto Rican, was conversing with four of her friends during lunch hour. I was at the next table eating some lunch.

26. Daryl, who is African American, was talking with two friends in front of the Monitor Grocery in the Richardson neighborhood. I was in front drinking a soda.

27. I could see this class difference in the schools of this study that had a very small number of middle-class students (at least middle class as determined by income) in them. Also see Judith Lynne Hanna, *Disruptive School Behavior: Class, Race, and Culture* (New York: Homes and Meier, 1988), 80–82.

28. See Gilens, *Why Americans Hate Welfare;* James R. Kluegel and Eliot R. Smith, *Beliefs about Inequality: Americans' Views of What Is and What Ought to Be* (Hawthorne, NY: Aldine de Gruyter, 1986), 78–83.

29. Lovelle was talking to three of his friends during lunch. I was at the table next to him eating my lunch.

30. Marta was talking in the hall before class. I was at the door waiting for the students to come into the classroom, which was a few feet away.

31. See Judith Torney-Purta, "The School's Role in Developing Civic Engagement: A Study of Adolescents in Twenty-Eight Countries," *Applied Developmental Science* 6, no. 4 (2002): 203–12; Daniel Hart and Robert Atkins, "Civic Competence in Urban Youth," *Applied Developmental Science* 6, no. 4 (2002): 227–36.

32. Regarding adolescence in general, the work of Erikson has been particularly influential. See his *Identity, Youth, and Crisis* 128–35, 155–58, and *Childhood and Society*, 262. There is a large body of research on the importance of peer groups among the poor, but none more important than that of Herbert Gans. See his *Urban Villagers*, 74–94. In many ways the combination of findings in these two seminal works provides the empirical basis for understanding the importance of peer associations in the schools of low-income communities. This is not to say that associations in middle-class schools are not important for the youth who attend them, but the social meaning is different for both the individuals and the communities of which they are a part.

33. Much of the role of girl gangs has already been discussed in chapter 9. The point here is that some girls find it important to be associated with gang members both formally (in auxiliary gangs) and informally (in cliques).

34. Throughout American history, sports have been a vehicle for the lower classes to become socioeconomically mobile. Not everyone in the ethnic working class has used this avenue, but a significant number have, and all types of sports have been used for this purpose. For example, Jews are now thought of as an ethnic group that specializes in business and various professional occupations, but when they immigrated to the United States in the nineteenth and twentieth centuries they were largely uneducated and poor. During this period they participated in the sport of boxing just like other ethnic groups in the same socioeconomic position. They also were actively involved in gangs. See Howe, *World of Our Fathers;* Jenna Weisman Joselit, *Our Gang: Jewish Crime and the New York Jewish Community, 1900–1940* (Bloomington: Indiana University Press, 1983).

35. Girls have options in basketball, soccer, and Olympic sports. A number of girls from poor backgrounds have succeeded in using sports to improve their life chances, and the residents of poor neighborhoods recognize this. For this reason more attention is given to these young women than those who are not as gifted in sports.

36. Richard P. Coleman and Lee Rainwater, *Social Standing in America: New Dimensions of Class* (New York: Basic Books, 1978). Some research has found the middle class to be of critical importance in maintaining a strong liberal-democratic system; see, for instance, Seymour Martin Lipset, *Political Man: The Social Basis of Politics* (Garden City, NY: Doubleday, 1960).

37. On interethnic competition and the attitudes that emerge from it, see Lawrence D. Bobo and Vincent L. Hutchings, "Perceptions of Racial Group Competition: Extending Blumer's Theory of Group Position to a Multiracial Social Context," *American Sociological Review* 61, no. 6 (1996): 951–72; Lawrence D. Bobo and Michael P. Massagli, "Stereotyping and Urban Inequality," in *Urban Inequality: Evidence from Four Cities,* ed. Alice O'Connor, Chris Tilly, and Lawrence D. Bobo (New York: Russell Sage Foundation, 2001), 89–162; Mary R. Jackman, *The Velvet Glove: Paternalism and Conflict in Gender, Class, and Race Relations* (Berkeley: University of California Press, 1994).

38. Names in all cultures go through changes. See Lieberson, *Matter of Taste.*

39. Portes and Rumbaut, *Legacies,* 189–90, report that new second-generation immigrants face a more lenient environment in accepting names associated with their country of origin. They use the fact that in the states of Texas and California the most popular name in 1998 was José and not Michael, John, or David; however, on an informal level, the present study found the second generation adopting first names that were more American.

40. Mary C. Waters, *Black Identities: West Indian Immigrant Dreams and American Realities* (New York: Russell Sage Foundation, 1999), 287–90; Alex Stepick et al., "Shifting Identities and Intergenerational Conflict: Growing Up Haitian in Miami," in *Ethnicities: Children of Immigrants in America,* ed. Rubén Rumbaut and Alejandro Portes (Berkeley: University of California Press, 2001), 229–66, esp. 253–54.

41. Alano and his father had this conversation in a local restaurant where they were eating. I was in the booth immediately behind them. The conversation is very similar to the one that Piri Thomas reports he had with his father about whether to identify as Puerto Rican or "black." See Piri Thomas, *Down These Mean Streets* (New York: Knopf, 1967), 145–54.

42. One of the jokes I often heard among police officers was that if you were interrogating a group of Mexican gang members and wanted to find out some information about a particular member and didn't know his "street name," you should just start off using one of the names of the seven dwarfs, since you would be bound to get a response from one of them and you could then proceed from there.

43. On the Ebonics controversy, see Theresa Perry and Lisa Delpit, eds., *The Real Ebonics Debate: Power, Language, and the Education of African-American Children* (Boston: Beacon Press, 1998).

44. Charles Hirschman and C. Matthew Snipp, "The State of the American Dream: Race and Ethnic Socioeconomic Inequality in the United States, 1970–1990," in *A Nation Divided: Diversity, Inequality, and Community in American Society*, ed. Phyllis Moen et al. (Ithaca: Cornell University Press, 1999), 89–107.

45. On mobility, see Michael Hout, "More Universalism and Less Structural Mobility: The American Occupational Structure in the 1980s," *American Journal of Sociology* 93 (May 1988): 1358–1400.

46. Jennifer L. Hochschild and Nathan Scovronick, *The American Dream and the Public Schools* (New York: Oxford University Press, 2003), 149–59.

47. Hanna, *Disruptive School Behavior*, 99.

48. I was listening to the conversation at a lunch table next to the participants'.

49. The students were having lunch; I was at the lunch table next to them.

50. On racial desegregation, see George R. Metcalf, *From Little Rock to Boston: The History of School Desegregation* (Westport, CT: Greenwood Press, 1983); on community control, see Mario Fantini, Marilyn Gittell, and Richard Magat, *Community Control and the Urban School* (New York: Praeger, 1970); Lisa W. Federico, "Hasidic Public School Loses Again before U.S. Supreme Court, but Supporters Persist," *New York Times*, October 13, 1999, 5; James A. Banks, "The Canon Debate, Knowledge Construction, and Multi-Culturalism," *Educational Researcher* 22 (1993): 4–14.

51. For a discussion of the school, see Banfield, *Unheavenly City Revisited*, 148–78.

52. See Willis, *Learning to Labor*; MacLeod, *Ain't No Makin' It*; Bourgois, *In Search of Respect*; Giroux, *Theory and Resistance*; John Devine, *Maximum Security: The Culture of Violence in Inner-City Schools* (Chicago: University of Chicago Press, 1996).

53. See Salvatore Saporito and Sohoni Deenesh, "Coloring Outside the Lines: Racial Segregation in Public Schools and Their Attendance Boundaries," *Sociology of Education* 79 (2006): 81–105. In this article the authors focus on private, charter, and magnet schools in large school districts with significant racial diversity. They find that the public schools are more segregated than they would be if all the kids in these neighborhoods attended them. In other words, the private,

charter, and magnet schools seem to be overenrolling whites and in so doing increasing segregation. Why do white parents who are given a choice avoid schools in poor areas? The answer is in this chapter: the white parents see a distinction between schools that are dominated by a local lower-class culture and schools that are run in accordance with the state's goals, which match their own values and goals for their children. Thus they avoid the neighborhood schools and choose the magnet, charter, or private schools.

11. SCHOOL WORKS:
THE DYNAMICS OF TWO PRODUCTION LINES

1. There is a large literature on the importance of building one's human and social capital to become more successful in the labor market. Two classical studies articulating the importance of human capital for everyone are G. Becker, *Human Capital*; Theodore W. Schultz, "Investment in Human Capital," *American Economic Review* 51 (March 1961): 1–17. In addition, Conley's *Being Black*, 55–107, is very important in analyzing the importance of human capital.

2. James S. Coleman and Thomas Hoffer, *Public and Private High Schools: The Impact of Communities* (New York: Basic Books, 1987).

3. See James S. Coleman, "Social Capital in the Creation of Human Capital," *American Journal of Sociology* 94, suppl. (1988): S95–S120; Pierre Bourdieu, "Cultural Production and Social Reproduction," in *Power and Ideology in Education,* ed. Jerome Karabel and A. H. Halsey (New York: Oxford University Press, 1977), 487–511.

4. See Lin, *Social Capital,* 133–36; Conley, *Being Black*, 55–107; and the various papers in Saegert, Thompson, and Warren, *Social Capital.*

5. In addition to the data presented in chapter 10, see Allison Davis, *Social-Class Influences upon Learning* (Cambridge, MA: Harvard University Press, 1948), 22–37.

6. Other factors also had the potential to contribute to the Latino students' poor performances in their academic courses. Language competency was certainly one, but so were all the issues related to lower-class culture. See Bernstein, "Social Class, Language," 473–86.

7. There is a considerable literature on the debates over issues related to multiculturalism, but in my judgment a book that successfully analyzes the underlying impetuses of these debates is Todd Gitlin's *The Twilight of Common Dreams: Why America Is Wracked by Culture Wars* (New York: Metropolitan Books, 1995). See also Hochschild and Scovronick, *American Dream,* 168–90.

8. *Sancocho* is a Puerto Rican stew-type dish that combines a number of ingredients, including chickpeas, pig's feet, pumpkin, and onions. *Coquito* is a drink made during the Christmas holidays and is a mixture of coconut milk, spices, and rum. The rum was removed from the *coquito* served for the high school dance.

9. See David E. López and Ricardo Stanton-Salazar, "Mexican Americans: A Second Generation at Risk," in Rumbaut and Portes, *Ethnicities,* 57–90.

10. See Dohan, *Price of Poverty,* 89–98. Here Dohan describes the immigrant-dominated Guadalupe barrio as oriented to strategies of "overwork" and

the second- and later-generation Chavez barrio as oriented to strategies of "hustling." This discussion taps the divide in value orientations between immigrant and succeeding generations of Mexican-origin populations.

11. See Carla O'Connor, "Dreamkeeping in the Inner City: Diminishing the Divide between Aspirations and Expectations," in *Coping with Poverty: The Social Contexts of Neighborhood, Work, and Family in the African-American Community,* ed. Sheldon Danziger and Ann Chih Lin (Ann Arbor: University of Michigan Press, 2000), 105–40.

12. The vice-principal was talking to a group of math and science teachers as they met to discuss changes in the curriculum. I was attending the meeting.

13. See Stepick et al., "Shifting Identities," 239–40, which describes the conflicts due to ethnic prejudice that Haitian students have with other students of minority and white backgrounds when they first attend their local high school.

14. Lana was talking after school to three friends at the Monitor Grocery in L.A.'s Richardson neighborhood. I was in the store talking to the owner.

15. There is no more important study of natural disaster than Klinenberg's *Heat Wave.* Klinenberg documents why disasters, even natural ones, affect the poor more and demonstrates that within the poor population the elderly and the very young are most vulnerable. More recently, Hurricane Katrina's disproportionate impact on the poorest areas of New Orleans illustrates Klinenberg's point.

16. Students operating within a security-maximizing value orientation are less disruptive in class. This is often interpreted by teachers and administrators as a sign that the students want more education or that an environment now exists where more education can be offered. It is true that some of these students would like more education, but others are passive aggressive toward the teachers' efforts, and still others are totally uninterested.

17. The role of housing in creating wealth and wealth's impact on school performance (i.e., building human and social capital) can be seen in Conley, *Being Black,* 68–79, 86–95.

18. Ann Swidler used the symbolic label of a "tool kit" to talk about culture. Her use of this symbolic label was particularly instructive because it emphasized the need to understand culture as having practical aspects. Education, which can be considered an integral part of culture itself, has practical as well as intellectual elements. See Swidler, "Culture in Action," 273–86.

19. See Noguera, *City Schools,* 149–51, 154.

20. See Bowles and Gintis, *Schooling in Capitalist America,* 53–101. In this work Bowles and Gintis pointed out that the school serves the interests of the American capitalist system. However, while the school certainly helps the economic system, it is an agent of the state and its first interests are to aid it. Of course, the state's interests are often allied with those of the business community, but at times there are differences, and in those cases the school system will be allied with the interests of the state first.

21. See MacLeod, *Ain't No Makin' It.* MacLeod apparently mistakenly saw the behaviors that he labeled "leveled aspirations" as emerging from the structure of school, when these behaviors were not "leveled aspirations" at all, simply aspirations toward obtaining what was valued within a different cultural

system. In this case, what I have labeled the "subculture of scarcity" produced these behaviors.

22. The schools in both Los Angeles and New York also had a group of security guards that were often employees from the local areas. Therefore, most schools had these security guards, the local police, and/or school police. See Devine, *Maximum Security*, 75–100.

23. Students have often labeled some of their colleagues as "acting white." This is less an issue of color than an issue of culture. Students use the label to identify the behavior of students they believe are acting in the way the society and state want students to act. Their use of this label is an attempt to pressure these students to return to behaving in accordance with neighborhood class values. See Signithia Fordham and John U. Ogbu, "Black Students' Success: Coping with the Burden of 'Acting White,'" *Urban Review* 18, no. 3 (1986): 176–216; Ogbu, *Black American Students*, 203–10.

24. See Gans, *Urban Villagers*, 218–23.

25. See Hanna, *Disruptive School Behavior*, 90–104.

26. During these two incidents I was in the back of the classroom on a computer. The students had ceased to pay any attention to me.

27. Devine, *Maximum Security*, 103–29.

28. I was in the auditorium and saw the two boys throw the bombs and then followed the students as they dispersed.

29. The fifteen minutes consisted of ten minutes related to the incident and five minutes that the teacher allowed at the end of class time for the students to write down the assignment for the next day. This incident happened while I was walking the hall observing these students. They knew that I was not part of the faculty or staff and as a result did not worry that I would turn them in for their unexcused absence from class (walking the halls). After seeing them keep walking around the corridor, I entered a class and began to observe. The students who were walking around did not know what class I had entered because they were on the other floor. It happened that one of the classrooms that they shouted into was the one that I was in.

30. I observed the conversation between the parent and the president of the parent organization that occurred at the public meeting; the conversation between the president of the parent organization and the principal, which also occurred when the president was at the public meeting; the conversation between the president and the supervisor, in which the supervisor was invited to hear the concerns of the local parents at a regularly scheduled monthly meeting; and the conference call involving the president of the parents' association, the supervisor, and the superintendent from the office of the supervisor.

31. See Steven Gregory, *Black Corona: Race and the Politics of Place in the Urban Community* (Princeton: Princeton University Press, 1998), 127–30.

32. See David C. Brotherton, "The Contradictions of Suppression: Notes from a Study of Approaches to Gangs in Three Public High Schools," *Urban Review* 28 (1996): 95–117.

33. See Shirley R. Lal, Dhyan Lal, and Charles M. Achilles, *Handbook on Gangs in Schools: Strategies to Reduce Gang-Related Activities* (Newbury Park, CA: Corwin Press, 1993), 29.

34. Paloma was talking to two of her friends at the Monitor Grocery. I was sitting down with the owner's helper as he put canned food on the shelf.

35. Dawn and three other female teachers were talking as they ate their lunch in the faculty lounge. I was sitting at the table next to them reading a book.

36. Richard and two other male teachers were talking as they ate lunch in the faculty lounge. I was sitting with two other teachers at the next table eating.

37. This is reminiscent of the way Polish workers and managers functioned under communism—"We pretend to work and they pretend to pay us." See Kazimirez M. Slomczynski, introduction to *Social Structure: Changes and Linkages* (Warsaw: Polish Academy of Sciences, 2002), 11–28.

38. See Kozol's *Savage Inequalities,* 23–24, 36–37, 85–88, 99–101, 106–7,158–59, 164–65, which argued that the physical environment was very important in creating a good educational environment.

39. Custodians perform the same functions all through the school districts, but what differs in these poor neighborhoods is that a slip-up by the custodial staff disrupts portions of the school for significant parts of the day. This is because teachers in "better" schools and neighborhoods can move on to teach students without reaction, whereas in poor schools teachers are constantly challenged by a competing culture that does not privilege formal instruction in the school. Thus, when the expected routine is compromised, the students seize the opportunity to do what they want.

40. The three men were talking in the back parking lot at the school. I was in the janitor's office and they were sitting directly in front of me.

41. Albert, Josh, and a friend were talking at a basketball game in the Gardenia Avenue Apartments. I was at the court waiting to play basketball.

42. See Brotherton, "Contradictions of Suppression," 95–117.

43. Both the state's efforts to teach students the "desirable" facts and skills necessary to be socioeconomically mobile and the community's effort to teach the "right" facts and skills necessary to function and contribute to the local subculture were in a condition of uncertainty during these periods.

44. I gathered the data by using a stopwatch and keeping track of the time that randomly selected individuals from each of the five high schools congregated at the store before going home. I then calculated the average (mean) time spent before leaving for home or somewhere else from these individual data.

CONCLUSION

1. Suttles, *Social Order,* 4–6, 23–25.

2. Gans, *Urban Villagers,* 28–32.

3. The important issue of differences among siblings and their divergent socioeconomic values and paths is discussed in Dalton Conley, *The Pecking Order: Which Siblings Succeed and Why* (New York: Pantheon Books, 2004).

4. Often long-term poor neighborhoods are what has been referred to as "areas of first settlement": that is, areas from which people will move once they have secured employment and saved their money and can afford better housing in a another neighborhood. See Oliver Zunz, *The Changing Face of Inequality:*

Urbanization, Industrial Development, and Immigrants in Detroit, 1880–1920 (Chicago: University of Chicago Press, 1982); Conquergood, "Big Red"; Sánchez-Jankowski, "Concentration of African American Poverty"; W. Wilson, *When Work Disappears.*

5. See Albert Hunter, *Symbolic Communities: Persistence and Change in Chicago's Local Communities* (Chicago: University of Chicago Press, 1974), and the recent work of W. Wilson and Taub, *There Goes the Neighborhood.* Although these works do not deal solely with poor neighborhoods, they document the importance of social change when ethnic groups change the present composition of the neighborhood.

6. Ryan first leveled the charge that Lewis's concept of a culture of poverty was essentially "blaming the victim." See Ryan, *Blaming the Victim.*

7. See Lewis, *La Vida* and *Five Families.*

8. For one of the more thoughtful general criticisms of the concept of a "culture of poverty," see Valentine's *Culture and Poverty.* On Daniel Moynihan's report on the black family and the controversy that emerged from it, see Lee Rainwater and William L. Yancy, *The Moynihan Report and the Politics of Controversy* (Cambridge, MA: MIT Press, 1967).

9. There is no question that many of the critiques of Oscar Lewis's work misrepresent the full theoretical explanation involving his "culture of poverty." In *La Vida,* which was his full explication of the theory, Lewis makes the point that it is the structure of capitalist society, particularly in its early phase, that provides the environment for the "culture of poverty" to develop. Thus structure becomes a significant part of the explanatory framework, but often critics of Lewis's conceptual framework do not acknowledge this, apparently because they are so preoccupied with his use of culture. See Lewis, *La Vida,* xliii–xlv.

10. See Lewis, *Five Families,* and Daniel Patrick Moynihan, *Maximum Feasible Misunderstanding: Community Action and the War on Poverty* (Glencoe, IL: Free Press, 1970).

11. See Lewis, *La Vida,* xliii. Moynihan claimed that slavery broke the African Americans' family structure and that the culture that emerged from this situation produced a socially disorganized state for them.

12. See, for instance, Kotlowitz, *There Are No Children Here;* Leon Dash, *Rosa Lee: A Mother and Her Family in Urban America* (New York: Basic Books, 1996); Adrian Nicole LeBlanc, *Random Family: Love, Drugs, Trouble, and Coming of Age in the Bronx* (New York: Scribner, 2003).

13. See Pierre-Joseph Proudhon, "On Poverty," in *Selected Writings of Pierre-Joseph Proudhon,* ed. Stewart Edwards, trans. Elizabeth Fraser (Garden City, NY: Anchor Books, 1969), 260.

14. For studies on working- or lower-class culture, see S. Miller and Riessman, "Working Class Subculture," 86–97; Marc Fried, *The World of the Urban Working Class* (Cambridge, MA: Harvard University Press, 1973); Kornblum, *Blue-Collar Community;* Gans, *Urban Villagers,* 241–82.

15. The work of these scholars is extensive and has been referred to throughout the text. The reader is invited to consult both their works cited in the bibliography and their work more generally.

16. See W. Wilson, *When Work Disappears;* Massey and Denton, *American Apartheid.*

17. See Nathan Glazer, "The South-Bronx Story: An Extreme Case of Neighborhood Decline," *Policy Studies Journal* 16 (1987): 269–76; Jill Jones, *We're Still Here: The Rise, Fall, and Resurrection of the South Bronx* (New York: Atlantic Monthly Press, 1986); Ze'ev Chafets, *Devil's Night: And Other True Tales of Detroit* (New York: Random House, 1990).

18. For Detroit as an example, see Joe T. Darden et al., *Detroit: Race and Uneven Development* (Philadelphia: Temple University Press, 1987), 149–200; for Gary, Indiana, see Edward Greer, *Big Steel: Black Politics and Corporate Power in Gary, Indiana* (New York: Monthly Review Press, 1979), 135–41.

19. One of the best examples is a section of Detroit called Poletown because it was one of the original settlements for Polish immigrants. The area had remained an intact community for decades, only to be condemned by the city to make way for the expansion of a General Motors automobile plant. Ironically, General Motors had offered to take over Chrysler Corporation's abandoned Dodge Main plant only if it could expand, which meant that Poletown had to be razed to make room. Unfortunately, all the houses in the area, as well as the local community Catholic church, were razed to make room for the new plant, even though a plant was never built to the original specifications that had required the area to be totally destroyed. For an account of this process, see Wylie, *Poletown.*

20. See Kevin Fox Gotham, "A City without Slums: Urban Renewal, Public Housing, and Downtown Revitalization in Kansas City, Missouri," *American Journal of Economics and Sociology* 60 (2001): 285–316; Gans, *Urban Villagers,* 323–73.

21. This latter scenario would be similar to a situation in which a renal patient who is on dialysis because both kidneys have failed receives a kidney transplant.

22. J. Jacobs, *Death and Life,* 89–140, makes this argument, but Herbert J. Gans, *People, Place, and Policy: Essays on Poverty, Racism, and Other National Urban Problems* (New York: Columbia University Press, 1991), 17, argues against what he calls Jacob's "physical determinism" and suggests that the larger social system is necessary to evaluate neighborhood vitality. See also Duneier, *Sidewalk,* 287, 313, 232–52, which argues against the "broken windows" thesis and suggests that street life is very socially organized.

23. See W. Wilson, *When Work Disappears,* 3–24.

24. This is my characterization of these researchers' conceptual framework, not theirs. They do not use these terms. It would be fair to say that most would understand neighborhoods as either functional or dysfunctional, but their dysfunctional category includes substantive conditions ("symptoms" in my metaphor) that place these neighborhoods in a decaying ("dying" in my metaphor) social state.

25. A great many researchers have subscribed to some or all of these criteria. A few examples are W. Wilson, *Truly Disadvantaged;* Massey and Denton, *American Apartheid;* Skogan, *Disorder and Decline.*

26. Sampson and Wilson's first articulation of this position can be seen in their jointly authored paper "Toward a Theory of Race," 45, but later Wilson expanded the idea in his *When Work Disappears,* 20–21.

27. Jane Jacobs is a proponent of the idea that poor neighborhoods can be healthy when they are able to govern themselves. See her *Death and Life,* 8–13, 114. In addition, some researchers have attempted to compare African American and Mexican American neighborhoods and have found that although Mexican American communities are poor they are socioeconomically healthy. See W. Wilson, *When Work Disappears,* 3–24; Moore and Pinderhughes, *In the Barrios,* xxxvi–xxxvii; Klinenberg, *Heat Wave,* 78–128.

28. See Whyte's *Street Corner Society,* Gans's *Urban Villagers,* Suttles's *Social Order,* and Small's *Villa Victoria,* all of which found that the conditions used by Sampson, Wilson, and Skogan to determine whether a neighborhood was disorganized were present in the neighborhoods they studied, yet that each of their neighborhoods was structured and organized.

29. See John C. Weicher, "How Poverty Neighborhoods Are Changing," and Christopher Jencks and Susan E. Mayer, "The Social Consequences of Growing Up in a Poor Neighborhood," both in *Inner-City Poverty in the United States,* ed. Laurence E. Lynn Jr. and Michael G.H. McGeary (Washington, DC: National Academy Press, 1990), 68–110 and 111–86 respectively; Greg J. Duncan and Jeanne Brooks-Gunn, eds., *The Consequences of Growing Up Poor* (New York: Russell Sage Foundation, 1997); and Brooks-Gunn, Duncan, and Aber, *Neighborhood Poverty.*

30. See Skogan, *Disorder and Decline;* Sampson and Groves, "Community Structure and Crime," 774–802.

31. See A. O'Connor, *Poverty Knowledge.*

32. See Blank, *It Takes a Nation,* whose argument would be sympathetic to my assertion that any policy intent on effectively dealing with the problem of poverty in the United States will take the commitment of a substantial amount of the nation's resources for a sustained period.

METHODOLOGICAL APPENDIX

1. A description of these techniques may be found in Seymour Sudman, *Applied Sampling* (New York: Academic Press, 1976). Sudman describes them as techniques for survey research use, but they can be used by researchers employing other data-gathering methods as well.

2. See David Halle, ed., *New York and Los Angeles: Politics, Society, and Culture in Comparative View* (Chicago: University of Chicago Press, 2003).

3. For a definition of a tenement, see Riis, *How the Other Half Lives,* 8–11.

4. See Sánchez-Jankowski, *Islands in the Street.*

5. See Daniel Dohan and Martín Sánchez-Jankowski, "Using Computers to Analyze Ethnographic Field Data: Theoretical and Practical Considerations," *Annual Review of Sociology* 24 (1998): 477–98.

Bibliography

Abelmann, Nancy, and John Lie. *Korean Americans and the Los Angeles Riots.* Cambridge, MA: Harvard University Press, 1995.

Abrahams, Roger D. "Playing the Dozens." *Journal of American Folklore* 75 (1962): 209–18.

Adamic, Louis. *Dynamite: The Story of Class Violence in America.* New York: Chelsea House, 1931.

Adamson, Christopher. "Defensive Localism in White and Black: A Comparative History of European-American Youth Gangs." *Ethnic and Racial Studies* 23 (March 2000): 272–98.

Addams, Jane. *Twenty Years at Hull House.* 1910. Reprint, New York: Signet, 1960.

Agee, James, and Walker Evans. *Let Us Now Praise Famous Men.* 1939. Reprint, Boston: Houghton Mifflin, 1988.

Alba, Richard D. *Ethnic Identity: Transformation of White America.* New Haven: Yale University Press, 1990.

Aldrich, Howard E., and Roger Waldinger. *Ethnic Entrepreneurs.* Newbury Park, CA: Sage Publications, 1990.

———. "Ethnicity and Entrepreneurship." *Annual Review of Sociology* 16 (1990): 111–35.

Allport, Gordon W., and Leo Postman. *The Psychology of Rumor.* New York: Russell and Russell, 1965.

Anderson, Elijah. *Code of the Street: Decency, Violence, and the Moral Life of the Inner City.* New York: Norton, 1999.

———. *A Place on the Corner.* Chicago: University of Chicago Press, 1978.

———. *Streetwise: Race, Class, and Changes in an Urban Community.* Chicago: University of Chicago Press, 1990.

Arendt, Hannah. *Eichmann in Jerusalem: A Report on the Banality of Evil.* New York: Viking Press, 1964.

———. *The Human Condition.* Chicago: University of Chicago Press, 1958.

———. *On Violence.* New York: Harcourt, Brace and World, 1969.

Asbury, Herbert. *The Gangs of New York: An Informal History of the Underworld.* Garden City, NY: Garden City Publishing, 1928.

Bahchieva, Raisa, and Amy Hosier. "Determinants of Tenure Duration in Public Housing: The Case of New York City." *Journal of Housing Research* 12, no. 2 (2001): 307–48.

Baldwin, James. *Nobody Knows My Name: More Notes of a Native Son.* New York: Dell, 1961.

Banfield, Edward. *The Moral Basis of a Backward Society.* Glencoe, IL: Free Press, 1958.

———. *The Unheavenly City Revisited.* 1970. Reprint, Boston: Houghton Mifflin, 1974.

Banks, James A. "The Canon Debate, Knowledge Construction, and Multi-Culturalism." *Educational Researcher* 22, no. 5 (1993): 4–14

Banton, Michael. *Racial Theories.* 2nd ed. New York: Cambridge University Press, 1998.

Bauman, John F. *Public Housing, Race, and Renewal: Urban Planning in Philadelphia, 1920–1974.* Philadelphia: Temple University Press, 1987.

Bauman, John F., Norman P. Hummon, and Edward K. Muller. "Public Housing, Isolation, and the Urban Underclass: Philadelphia's Richard Allen Homes, 1941–1965." *Journal of Urban History* 17 (May 1991): 264–92.

Becker, Gary S. *Human Capital: A Theoretical and Empirical Analysis with Special Reference to Education.* 1964. Reprint, Chicago: University of Chicago Press, 1993.

Becker, Howard. *The Outsiders: Studies in the Sociology of Deviance.* Glencoe, IL: Free Press, 1963.

Bellah, Robert, Richard Madsen, Steven M. Tipton, William M. Sullivan, and Ann Swidler. "We Live through Institutions." In *The Good Society,* 5–18. New York: Knopf, 1991.

Berlin, Ira. *Many Thousands Gone: The First Two Centuries of Slavery in North America.* Cambridge, MA: Harvard University Press, 1998.

Bernstein, Basil. "Social Class, Language, and Socialization." In *Power and Ideology in Education,* edited by Jerome Karabel and A.H. Halsey, 473–87. New York: Oxford University Press, 1977.

Bickford, Adam, and Douglas S. Massey. "Segregation in the Second Ghetto: Racial and Ethnic Segregation in American Public Housing, 1977." *Social Forces* 69, no. 4 (1991): 1011–36.

Bing, Léon. *Do or Die.* New York: Harper, 1991.

Blackburn, Simon. *Lust: The Seven Deadly Sins.* New York: Oxford University Press, 2004.

Blank, Rebecca. *It Takes a Nation: A New Agenda to Fight Poverty.* New York: Russell Sage Foundation, 1997.

Bobo, Lawrence D., and Vincent L. Hutchings. "Perceptions of Racial Group Competition: Extending Blumer's Theory of Group Position to a Multiracial Social Context." *American Sociological Review* 61, no. 6 (1996): 951–72.

Bobo, Lawrence D., and Michael P. Massagli. "Stereotyping and Urban Inequality." In *Urban Inequality: Evidence from Four Cities,* edited by Alice O'Connor, Chris Tilly, and Lawrence D. Bobo, 89–162. New York: Russell Sage Foundation, 2001.

Bobo, Lawrence, Melvin L. Oliver, James H. Johnson, and Abel Valenzuela Jr., eds. *Prismatic Metropolis: Inequality in Los Angeles.* New York: Russell Sage Foundation, 2001.

Bourdieu, Pierre. "Cultural Production and Social Reproduction." In *Power and Ideology in Education,* edited by Jerome Karabel and A. H. Halsey, 487–511. New York: Oxford University Press, 1977.

———. *Distinction: A Social Critique of the Judgement of Taste.* Cambridge, MA: Harvard University Press, 1984.

———. *Masculine Domination.* Translated by Richard Nice. Stanford: Stanford University Press, 2000.

Bourgois, Philippe. *In Search of Respect: Selling Crack in El Barrio.* New York: Cambridge University Press, 1995.

Bowles, Samuel, and Herbert Gintis. *Schooling in Capitalist America.* New York: Basic Books, 1976.

Brooks-Gunn, Jeanne, Greg J. Duncan, and J. Lawrence Aber, eds. *Neighborhood Poverty.* New York: Russell Sage Foundation, 1997.

Brotherton, David C. "The Contradictions of Suppression: Notes from a Study of Approaches to Gangs in Three Public High Schools." *Urban Review* 28 (1996): 95–117.

Burawoy, Michael. "The Extended Case Method." *Sociological Theory* 16 (March 1998): 4–33.

Bursik, Robert J., Jr., and Harold G. Grasmick. *Neighborhoods and Crime: The Dimensions of Effective Community Control.* New York: Lexington Books, 1993.

Bushnell, John H. "La Virgen de Guadalupe as Surrogate Mother." *American Anthropologist* 60 (1958): 261–65.

Campbell, Ann. *Girls in the Gang.* 2nd ed. New York: Blackwell, 1991.

Caro Baroja, Julio. "Honor and Shame: A Historical Account of Several Conflicts." In *Honor and Shame: The Values of Mediterranean Society,* edited by J. G. Peristiany, 81–137. London: Weidenfeld and Nicolson, 1965.

Carter, Prudence L. *Keepin' It Real: School Success beyond Black and White.* New York: Oxford University Press, 2005.

Castells, Manuel. *The Rise of the Network Society.* Oxford: Blackwell, 1996.

Chafets, Ze'ev. *Devil's Night: And Other True Tales of Detroit.* New York: Random House, 1990.

Chang, Edward T. "Jewish and Korean Merchants in African American Neighborhoods: A Comparative Perspective." *Amerasia Journal* 19, no. 2 (1993): 5–21.

Chesney-Lind, Meda, Randall G. Shelden, and Karen A. Joe. "Girls, Delinquency, and Gang Membership." In *Gangs in America,* 2nd ed., edited by C. Ronald Huff, 205–21. Newbury Park, CA: Sage Publications, 1996.

Citrin, Jack, Donald Philip Green, Beth Reingold, and Evelyn Walters. "The 'Official English' Movement and the Symbolic Politics of Language in the United States." *Western Political Quarterly* 43 (September 1990): 535–60.

Clark, William A. V. "The Geography of Immigrant Poverty: Selective Evidence of an Immigrant Underclass." In *Strangers at the Gates,* edited by Roger Waldinger, 159–85. Berkeley: University of California Press, 2001.

Cohen, Albert K. *Delinquent Boys: The Culture of the Gang.* Glencoe, IL: Free Press, 1955.

Cohn, Samuel K., Jr. *Death and Property in Siena, 1205–1800: Strategies for the Afterlife.* Baltimore: Johns Hopkins University Press, 1988.

Coleman, James S. "The Emergence of Norms." In *Social Institutions: Their Emergence, Maintenance, and Effects,* edited by Michael Hechter, Karl-Dieter Opps, and Reinhard Wippler, 35–59. New York: Aldine de Gruyter, 1990.

———. *Foundations of Social Theory.* Cambridge, MA: Harvard University Press, 1990.

———. "Social Capital in the Creation of Human Capital." *American Journal of Sociology* 94, suppl. (1988): S95–S120.

Coleman, James S., and Thomas Hoffer. *Public and Private High Schools: The Impact of Communities.* New York: Basic Books, 1987.

Coleman, Richard P., and Lee Rainwater. *Social Standing in America: New Dimensions of Class.* New York: Basic Books, 1978.

Collins, H. Craig. *Street Gangs: Profiles for Police.* New York: City of New York Police Department, 1979.

Conley, Dalton. *Being Black and Living in the Red: Race, Wealth and Social Policy in America.* Berkeley: University of California Press, 1999.

———. *The Pecking Order: Which Siblings Succeed and Why.* New York: Pantheon Books, 2004.

Connell, James P., and Bonnie L. Halpern-Felsher. "How Neighborhoods Affect Educational Outcomes in Middle Childhood and Adolescence: Conceptual Issues and an Empirical Example." In *Neighborhood and Poverty,* edited by Jeanne Brooks-Gunn and Greg J. Duncan, 1:174–199. New York: Russell Sage Foundation, 1997.

Conner, Mark, and Christopher J. Armitage. *The Social Psychology of Food.* Buckingham: Open University Press, 2002.

Conquergood, Dwight. "Life in Big Red: Struggle and Accommodations in a Chicago Polyethnic Tenement." In *Structuring Diversity: Ethnographic Perspectives on the New Immigration,* edited by Louise Lamphere, 95–144. Chicago: University of Chicago Press, 1992.

Coser, Lewis. *The Functions of Social Conflict.* Glencoe, IL: Free Press, 1967.

Cown, Emory L., Ellis L. Gesten, Mary Boike, Pennie Norton, Alice B. Wilson, and Michael A. DeStefano. "Hairdressers as Caregivers: A Descriptive Profile of Interpersonal Help-Giving Involvements." *American Journal of Community Psychology* 7, no. 6 (1978): 633–48.

Crowe, David M. *A History of the Gypsies of Eastern Europe and Russia.* New York: St. Martin's Press, 1995.

Cummings, Scott. *Left Behind in Rosedale: Race Relations and the Collapse of Community Institutions.* Boulder, CO: Westview Press, 1998.

Dahrendorf, Ralf. *Life Chances: Approaches to Social and Political Theory.* Chicago: University of Chicago Press, 1979.

Darden, Joe T., Richard Child Hill, June Thomas, and Richard Thomas. *Detroit: Race and Uneven Development.* Philadelphia: Temple University Press, 1987.

Dash, Leon. *Rosa Lee: A Mother and Her Family in Urban America.* New York: Basic Books, 1996.

Davis, Allison. *Social-Class Influences upon Learning.* Cambridge, MA: Harvard University Press, 1948.

Davis, Mike. *Dead Cities, and Other Tales.* New York: New Press, 2002.

———. *Ecology of Fear: Los Angeles and the Imagination of Disaster.* New York: Metropolitan Books, 1998.

Decker, Scott, and G. David Curry. "Gangs, Gang Homicides, and Gang Loyalty: Organized Crimes or Disorganized Criminals." *Journal of Criminal Justice* 30, no. 4 (2002): 343–52.

Decker, Scott, and B. Van Wincle. *Life in a Gang: Family, Friends and Violence.* New York: Cambridge University Press, 1996.

Denton, Nancy A., and Douglas S. Massey. "Racial Identity among Caribbean Hispanics: The Effect of Double Minority Status on Residential Segregation." *American Sociological Review* 54 (1980): 790–808.

Derné, Steve. "Cultural Conceptions of Human Motivation and Their Significance for Culture Theory." In *The Sociology of Culture,* edited by Diana Crane, 267–87. Cambridge, MA: Blackwell, 1994.

DeSena, Judith. *Protecting One's Turf: Social Strategies for Maintaining Urban Neighborhoods.* Lanham, MD: University Press of America, 1990.

Devine, John. *Maximum Security: The Culture of Violence in Inner-City Schools.* Chicago: University of Chicago Press, 1996.

DiMaggio, Paul. "Culture and Economy." In *The Handbook of Economic Sociology,* edited by Neil Smelser and Richard Swedberg, 41–46. Princeton: Princeton University Press, 1994.

Doeringer, Peter B., and Michael J. Piore. *Internal Labor Markets and Manpower Analysis.* Lexington, MA: D.C. Heath, 1971.

Dohan, Daniel. *The Price of Poverty: Money, Work, and Culture in the Mexican American Barrio.* Berkeley: University of California Press, 2003.

Dohan, Daniel, and Martín Sánchez-Jankowski. "Using Computers to Analyze Ethnographic Field Data: Theoretical and Practical Considerations." *Annual Review of Sociology* 24 (1998): 477–98.

Dollard, John. *Caste and Class in a Southern Town.* Madison: University of Wisconsin Press, 1988.

Douglas, Mary. *How Institutions Think.* Syracuse: Syracuse University Press, 1986.

———. *Natural Symbols.* New York: Pelican Books, 1973.

———. *Purity and Danger: An Analysis of Concepts of Pollution and Taboo.* New York: Praeger, 1966.

———. "Standard Social Uses of Food: Introduction." In *Food in the Social Order: Studies of Food and Festivities in Three American Communities,* edited by Mary Douglas, 1–39. New York: Russell Sage Foundation, 1984.

Drake, St. Clair, and Horace Cayton. *Black Metropolis: A Study of Negro Life in a Northern City.* New York: Harcourt, Brace, 1945.

Du Bois, W.E.B. *The Philadelphia Negro: A Social Study.* 1899. Reprint, Philadelphia: University of Pennsylvania Press, 1996.

Duncan, Greg J., and Jeanne Brooks-Gunn, eds. *The Consequences of Growing Up Poor.* New York: Russell Sage Foundation, 1997.

Duneier, Mitchell. *Sidewalk.* New York: Farrar, Straus and Giroux, 1999.

———. *Slim's Table: Race, Respectability, and Masculinity.* Chicago: University of Chicago Press, 1992.

Durkheim, Emile. *The Division of Labor in Society.* Translated by W. P. Halls. Glencoe, IL: Free Press, 1997.

Eayrs, Michele A. "Time, Trust and Hazard: Hairdressers' Symbolic Roles." *Symbolic Interaction* 16, no. 1 (1993): 19–37.

Edin, Katheryn, and Laura Lein. *Making Ends Meet: How Single Mothers Survive Welfare and Low-Wage Work.* New York: Russell Sage Foundation, 1997.

Eisenstadt, S. N. *Jewish Civilization: The Jewish Historical Experience in Comparative Perspective.* Albany: State University of New York Press, 1992.

Ellison, Ralph. *Invisible Man.* New York: Random House, 1952.

Elster, Jon. *The Cement of Society: A Study of Social Order.* New York: Cambridge University Press, 1989.

Erikson, Erik H. *Childhood and Society.* New York: Norton, 1950.

———. *Identity, Youth, and Crisis.* New York: Norton, 1968.

Fagan, Jeffrey. "The Social Organization of Drug Use and Drug Dealing among Urban Gangs." *Criminology* 27, no. 4 (1989): 633–67.

Fagan, Jeffrey, and Deanna L. Wilkinson. "Guns, Youth Violence, and Social Identity in Inner Cities." *Crime and Justice* 24 (1998): 105–88.

Fantini, Mario, Marilyn Gittell, and Richard Magat. *Community Control and the Urban School.* New York: Praeger, 1970.

Fischer, Claude S. "The Subcultural Theory of Urbanism: A Twentieth-Year Assessment." *American Journal of Sociology* 101 (November 1995): 543–77.

———. *To Dwell among Friends: Personal Networks in Town and City.* Chicago: University of Chicago Press, 1982.

———. "Toward a Sub-cultural Theory of Urbanism." *American Journal of Sociology* 80 (May 1975): 1319–41.

———. *The Urban Experience.* 2nd ed. San Diego: Harcourt Brace Jovanovich, 1984.

Fischer, Claude S., Michael Hout, Martín Sánchez-Jankowski, Samuel R. Lucas, Ann Swidler, and Kim Voss. *Inequality by Design: Cracking the Bell Curve Myth.* Princeton: Princeton University Press, 1996.

Federico, Lisa W. "Hasidic Public School Loses Again before U.S. Supreme Court, but Supporters Persist." *New York Times,* October 13, 1999, 5.

Fligstein, Neil. *Going North: Migration of Blacks and Whites from the South, 1900–1950.* New York: Academic Press, 1981.

Fogel, Robert William. *Without Consent or Contract: The Rise and Fall of American Slavery.* New York: Norton, 1989.

Fogel, Robert William, and Stanley L. Engerman. *Time on the Cross: The Economics of American Negro Slavery.* Boston: Little, Brown, 1974.

Foley, Douglas E. *Learning Capitalist Culture: Deep in the Heart of Tejas.* Philadelphia: University of Pennsylvania Press, 1990.

Fordham, Signithia, and John U. Ogbu. "Black Students' Success: Coping with the Burden of 'Acting White.'" *Urban Review* 18, no. 3 (1986): 176–216.

Foucault, Michel. *Discipline and Punish: The Birth of the Prison.* 1975. Reprint, New York: Vintage, 1979.

Franklin, Clyde W., II. "The Black Male Urban Barbershop as a Sex-Role Socialization Setting." *Sex Roles* 12 (May 1996): 965–79.

Fried, Marc. *The World of the Urban Working Class.* Cambridge, MA: Harvard University Press, 1973.

Gans, Herbert J. *People, Place, and Policy: Essays on Poverty, Racism, and Other National Urban Problems.* New York: Columbia University Press, 1991.

———. "Symbolic Ethnicity: The Future of Ethnic Groups and Culture in America." *Ethnic and Racial Studies* 2 (January 1979): 1–20.

———. "Urbanism and Suburbanism as Ways of Life: A Re-evaluation of Definitions." In *Human Behavior and Social Processes,* edited by Arnold Rose, 625–48. Boston: Houghton Mifflin, 1962.

———. *Urban Villagers: Group and Class in the Life of Italian-Americans.* 1962. Reprint, New York: Free Press, 1981.

Gartner, Lloyd P. *History of the Jews in Modern Times.* New York: Oxford University Press, 2001.

Geertz, Clifford. *The Interpretation of Cultures.* New York: Basic Books, 1973.

———. *Local Knowledge: Further Essays in Interpretive Anthropology.* 3rd ed. New York: Basic Books, 2006.

Gell, Alfred. *The Anthropology of Time: Cultural Constructions of Temporal Maps and Images.* New York: St. Martin's Press, 1992.

Genovese, Eugene D. *Roll, Jordan, Roll: The World the Slaves Made.* New York: Pantheon Books, 1974.

Gilens, Martin. *Why Americans Hate Welfare: Race, Media, and the Politics of Antipoverty Policy.* Chicago: University of Chicago Press, 1999.

Gimlin, Debra. "Pamela's Place: Power and Negotiation in the Hair Salon." *Gender and Society* 10 (October 1996): 505–26.

Ginsberg, Yona. *Jews in a Changing Neighborhood.* New York: Macmillan, 1975.

Giroux, Henry A. *Theory and Resistance in Education: A Pedagogy for the Opposition.* London: Heinemann Educational Books, 1983.

Gitlin, Todd. *The Twilight of Common Dreams: Why America Is Wracked by Culture Wars.* New York: Metropolitan Books, 1995.

Gitlin, Todd, and Nanci Hollander. *Uptown: Poor Whites in Chicago.* New York: Harper and Row, 1970.

Glaser, Barney G., and Anselm L. Strauss. *The Discovery of Grounded Theory: Strategies for Qualitative Research.* Chicago: Aldine, 1967.

Glazer, Nathan. "The South-Bronx Story: An Extreme Case of Neighborhood Decline." *Policy Studies Journal* 16 (1987): 269–76.

Goffman, Erving. *Presentation of Self in Everyday Life.* New York: Anchor Books, 1959.

Goldstein, Ira, and William L. Yancey. "Public Housing Projects, Blacks, and Public Policy: The Historical Ecology of Public Housing in Philadelphia." In *Housing Desegregation and Federal Policy,* edited by John M. Goering, 262–89. Chapel Hill: University of North Carolina Press, 1986.

Gordon, David M., Richard Edwards, and Michael Reich. *Segmented Labor, Divided Labor: Historical Transformations of Labor in the United States.* New York: Cambridge University Press, 1982.

Gordon, Rachel A., Benjamin B. Lahey, Eriko Kawai, Rolf Loeber, Magda Stouthamer-Loeber, and David P. Farrington. "Antisocial Behavior and Youth Gang Membership: Selection and Socialization." *Criminology* 42, no. 1 (2004): 55–88.

Gotham, Kevin Fox. "A City without Slums: Urban Renewal, Public Housing, and Downtown Revitalization in Kansas City, Missouri." *American Journal of Economics and Sociology* 60 (2001): 285–316.

Grasmuck, Sherri, and Patricia R. Pessar. *Between Two Islands: Dominican International Migration.* Berkeley: University of California Press, 1991.

Greeley, Andrew. *The Catholic Imagination.* Berkeley: University of California Press, 2000.

Green, Donald P., Dara Z. Strolovitch, and Janelle S. Wong. "Defended Neighborhoods, Integration, and Racially Motivated Crime." *American Journal of Sociology* 104 (September 1998): 372–403.

Greer, Edward. *Big Steel: Black Politics and Corporate Power in Gary, Indiana.* New York: Monthly Review Press, 1979.

Gregory, Steven. *Black Corona: Race and the Politics of Place in the Urban Community.* Princeton: Princeton University Press, 1998.

Gutierrez, Ramon. *When Jesus Came, the Corn Mothers Went Away: Marriage, Sexuality, and Power in New Mexico, 1500–1846.* Stanford: Stanford University Press, 1991.

Hagan, Jacqueline Maria. "Social Networks, Gender, and Immigrant Incorporation: Resources and Constraints." *American Sociological Review* 63 (February 1998): 55–67.

Hagedorn, John. *People and Folks: Gangs, Crime, and the Underclass in a Rustbelt City.* Chicago: Lakeview Press, 1988.

Halle, David, ed. *New York and Los Angeles: Politics, Society, and Culture in Comparative View.* Chicago: University of Chicago Press, 2003.

Ham, Thomas D. *The Quakers in America.* New York: Columbia University Press, 2003.

Hanna, Judith Lynne. *Disruptive School Behavior: Class, Race, and Culture.* New York: Homes and Meier, 1988.

Hannerz, Ulf. *Soulside: Explorations in Ghetto Culture and Community.* New York: Columbia University Press, 1969.

Harrington, Michael. *The Other America: Poverty in America.* New York: Macmillan, 1962.

Harris, David. "'Property Values Drop When Blacks Move In, Because . . .': Racial and Socioeconomic Determinants of Neighborhood Desirability." *American Sociological Review* 64 (1999): 461–79.

Harris-Lacewell, Melissa. *Barbershops, Bibles, and BET: Everyday Talk and Black Political Thought.* Princeton: Princeton University Press, 2004.

Hart, Daniel, and Robert Atkins. "Civic Competence in Urban Youth." *Applied Developmental Science* 6, no. 4 (2002): 227–36.

Hassard, John, ed. *The Sociology of Time.* New York: St. Martin's Press, 1990.

Hayek, E. A. *Law, Legislation, and Liberty.* 2 vols. Chicago: University of Chicago Press, 1973–76.

———. "Notes on the Evolution of Systems of Rules of Conduct." In *Studies in Philosophy, Politics, and Economics,* 66–81. Chicago: University of Chicago Press, 1967.

Hechter, Michael. "The Emergence of Cooperative Social Institutions." In *Social Institutions: Their Emergence, Maintenance, and Effects,* edited by Michael Hechter, Karl-Dieter Opps, and Reinhard Wippler, 13–33. New York: Aldine de Gruyter, 1990.

———. *Principles of Group Solidarity.* Berkeley: University of California Press, 1987.

Hendrix, Anastasia. "Hill Girls' Gang Preys on Women: Police in S.F. Surprised by the Savagery of Attacks." *San Francisco Chronicle,* September 3, 2003, A11.

Herrnstein, Richard, and Charles Murray. *The Bell Curve: Intelligence and Class Structure in American Life.* New York: Free Press, 1994.

"High Rise Brought Low at Last." *Economist,* July 11, 1998, 31.

Hines, Thomas. "Housing, Baseball, and Creeping Socialism: The Battle of Chavez Ravine, Los Angeles, 1949–1959." *Journal of Urban History* 8 (1982): 123–44.

Hirsch, Arnold. *Making the Second Ghetto: Race and Housing in Chicago, 1940–1960.* New York: Cambridge University Press, 1983.

Hirschi, Travis. *Causes of Delinquency.* Berkeley: University of California Press, 1969.

Hirschman, Albert O. *Exit, Voice, and Loyalty: Responses to Decline in Firms, Organizations, and States.* Cambridge, MA: Harvard University Press, 1970.

Hirschman, Charles, and C. Matthew Snipp. "The State of the American Dream: Race and Ethnic Socioeconomic Inequality in the United States, 1970–1990." In *A Nation Divided: Diversity, Inequality, and Community in American Society,* edited by Phyllis Moen, Donna Dempster-Mcclain, and Henry A. Walker, 89–107. Ithaca: Cornell University Press, 1999.

Hochschild, Jennifer L., and Nathan Scovronick. *The American Dream and the Public Schools.* New York: Oxford University Press, 2003.

Hoffman, Alexander von. "High-Rise Hellholes." *American Prospect,* April 9, 2001, 40–43.

Hondagneu-Sotelo, Pierrette. *Gendered Transitions: Mexican Experiences of Immigration.* Berkeley: University of California Press, 1994.

Horowitz, Ruth. "Community Tolerance of Gang Violence." *Social Problems* 34 (December 1987): 437–49.

———. *Honor and the American Dream: Identity and Culture in a Chicano Community.* New Brunswick: Rutgers University Press, 1983.

———. "Honor, Normative Ambiguity and Gang Violence." *American Sociological Review* 39, no. 2 (1974): 238–51.

Horton, John. *The Politics of Diversity.* Philadelphia: Temple University Press, 1995.

Hostetler, John Andrew. *Amish Society.* 4th ed. Baltimore: Johns Hopkins University Press, 1993.

Hout, Michael. "More Universalism and Less Structural Mobility: The American Occupational Structure in the 1980s." *American Journal of Sociology* 93 (May 1988): 1358–1400.

———. "Occupational Mobility of Black Men: 1962–1972." *American Sociological Review* 49 (June 1984): 308–22.

Howe, Irving. *World of Our Fathers: The Journey of the Eastern European Jews to America and the Life They Found and Made.* New York: Simon and Schuster, 1976.

Huff, C. Ronald, ed. *Gangs in America.* 2nd ed. Newbury Park, CA: Sage Publications, 1996.

Hughes, Everett. *Work, Race, and the Sociological Imagination.* Edited by Lewis A. Coser. Chicago: University of Chicago Press, 1994.

Hull, Cordell. *The Memoirs of Cordell Hull.* Vol. 2. New York: Macmillan, 1948.

Hum, Tarry. "A Protected Niche: Immigrant Ethnic Economies and Labor Market Segmentation." In *Prismatic Metropolis: Inequality in Los Angeles,* edited by Lawrence Bobo, Melvin L. Oliver, James H. Johnson, and Abel Valenzuela Jr., 279–314. New York: Russell Sage Foundation, 2001.

Hunter, Albert. *Symbolic Communities: Persistence and Change in Chicago's Local Communities.* Chicago: University of Chicago Press, 1974.

Ignatiev, Noel. *How the Irish Became White.* New York: Routledge, 1995.

Ihejirika, Maudlyne. "Girl Gang Stalks S. Side School's Halls." *Chicago Sun-Times,* April 30, 2004, 11.

Innai, Francis A. J. *Black Mafia: Ethnic Succession in Organized Crime.* New York: Simon and Schuster, 1974.

Isaacs, Harold. "Basic Group Identity: The Idols of the Tribe." In *Ethnicity: Theory and Experience,* edited by Daniel Patrick Moynihan and Nathan Glazer, 29–52. Cambridge, MA: Harvard University Press, 1975.

———. *Idols of the Tribe: Group Identity and Political Change.* New York: HarperCollins, 1975.

Jackman, Mary R. *The Velvet Glove: Paternalism and Conflict in Gender, Class, and Race Relations.* Berkeley: University of California Press, 1994.

Jackson, Robert K., and Wesley D. McBride. *Understanding Street Gangs.* Costa Mesa, CA: Custom Publishing, 1985.

Jacobs, Bruce A., and Richard Wright. *Street Justice: Retaliation in the Criminal Underworld.* New York: Cambridge University Press, 2006.

Jacobs, Jane. *The Death and Life of Great American Cities.* New York: Vintage Books, 1961.

Jacobson, Matthew Frye. *Whiteness of a Different Color: European Immigrants and the Alchemy of Race.* Cambridge, MA: Harvard University Press, 1998.

Jargowsky, Paul A. *Poverty and Place: Ghettos, Barrios, and the American City.* New York: Russell Sage Foundation, 1997.

Jaros, Dean, Herbert Hirsch, and Frederic J. Fleron Jr. "The Malevolent Leader: Political Socialization in an American Sub-culture." *American Political Science Review* 62 (June 1968): 564–75.

Jencks, Christopher. *The Homeless.* Cambridge, MA: Harvard University Press, 1985.

———. *Rethinking Social Policy: Race, Poverty, and the Underclass.* Cambridge, MA: Harvard University Press, 1992.

Jencks, Christopher, and Susan E. Mayer. "The Social Consequences of Growing Up in a Poor Neighborhood." In *Inner-City Poverty in the United States,* edited by Laurence E. Lynn Jr. and Michael G. H. McGeary, 111–86. Washington, DC: National Academy Press, 1990.

Jepperson, Ronald L. "Institutions, Institutional Effects, and Institutionalism." In *The New Institutionalism in Organizational Analysis,* edited by Walter W. Powell and Paul J. DiMaggio, 143–63. Chicago: University of Chicago Press, 1991.

Johnson, James H., Jr., Walter C. Farrell Jr., and Jennifer A. Stoloff. "African American Males in Decline: A Los Angeles Case Study." In *Prismatic Metropolis: Inequality in Los Angeles,* edited by Lawrence Bobo, Melvin L. Oliver, James H. Johnson, and Abel Valenzuela Jr., 315–37. New York: Russell Sage Foundation, 2001.

Jones, Jill. *We're Still Here: The Rise, Fall, and Resurrection of the South Bronx.* New York: Atlantic Monthly Press, 1986.

Jones, LeRoi. *Home: Social Essays.* New York: William Morrow, 1966.

Joselit, Jenna Weisman. *Our Gang: Jewish Crime and the New York Jewish Community, 1900–1940.* Bloomington: Indiana University Press, 1983.

Kaestle, Carl F. *Pillars of the Republic: Common Schools and the American Society, 1780–1860.* New York: Hill and Wang, 1983.

Kanaiaupuno, Shawn M., and Douglas S. Massey. "Public Housing and the Concentration of Poverty." *Social Science Quarterly* 70 (March 1993): 109–22.

Kasarda, John. "Cities as Places Where People Live and Work: Urban Change and Neighborhood Distress." In *Interwoven Destinies: Cities and the Nation,* edited by Henry G. Cisneros, 81–124. New York: Norton, 1993.

———. "Inner-City Concentrated Poverty and Neighborhood Distress: 1970–1990." *Housing Policy Debate* 4, no. 3 (1993): 253–302.

———. "Structural Factors Affecting the Location and Timing of Urban Underclass Growth." *Urban Geography* 11 (1990): 234–64.

Katz, Daniel, and Robert L. Kahn. *The Social Psychology of Organizations.* 2nd ed. New York: John Wiley and Sons, 1978.

Katz, Jack. *The Seductions of Crime: Moral and Sensual Attractions in Doing Evil.* New York: Basic Books, 1988.

Katz, Michael. *In the Shadow of the Poorhouse: A Social History of Welfare in America.* 1986. Reprint, New York: Basic Books, 1996.

Keiser, R. Lincoln. *The Vice Lords, Warriors of the Streets.* New York: Holt, Reinhart and Winston, 1969.

Kerchoff, Alan C. *Socialization and Social Class.* Englewood Cliffs, NJ: Prentice-Hall, 1972.

Kiev, Ari. *Curanderismo: Mexican-American Folk Psychiatry.* New York: Free Press, 1968.

Kim, Clair Jean. *Bitter Fruit: The Politics of Black-Korean Conflict in New York City.* New Haven: Yale University Press, 2002.

Kim, Illsoo. "The Korean Fruit and Vegetable Business: A Case Study." In *The Apple Sliced: Sociological Studies of New York City*, edited by Vernon Boggs, Gerald Handel, and Sylvia Fava, 107–17. New York: Praeger, 1984.

——. "The Koreans: Small Business in an Urban Frontier." In *New Immigrants in New York City*, edited by Nancy Foner, 219–42. New York: Columbia University Press, 1987.

King, Melvin. *Chain of Change: Struggles for Black Community Development*. Boston: South End Press, 1981.

Klein, Malcolm. *The American Street Gang: Its Nature, Prevalence, and Control*. New York: Oxford University Press, 1995.

Klinenberg, Erik. *Heat Wave: A Social Autopsy of Disaster in Chicago*. Chicago: University of Chicago Press, 2002.

Kluckhohn, Clyde. "Values and Value-Orientations in the Theory of Action: An Exploration in Definition and Classification." In *Toward a General Theory of Action: Theoretical Foundations for the Social Sciences*, edited by Talcott Parsons and Edward Shils, 388–433. New York: Harper and Row, 1951.

Kluckhohn, Florence, and Fred Strodtbeck. *Variations in Value Orientations*. Evanston, IL: Row, Peterson, 1961.

Kluegel, James R., and Eliot R. Smith. *Beliefs about Inequality: Americans' Views of What Is and What Ought to Be*. Hawthorne, NY: Aldine de Gruyter, 1986.

Knight, Jack. *Institutions and Social Conflict*. New York: Cambridge University Press, 1992.

Knox, George. *An Introduction to Gangs*. Berrien-Springs, MN: Van de Vere, 1991.

Kohn, Melvin L. *Class and Conformity: A Study in Values*. Homewood, IL: Dorsey Press, 1969.

Kolchin, Peter. *Unfree Labor: American Slavery and Russian Serfdom*. Cambridge, MA: Harvard University Press, 1987.

Kornblum, William. *Blue-Collar Community*. Chicago: University of Chicago Press, 1974.

Kornhauser, Ruth. *The Social Sources of Delinquent Theory*. Chicago: University of Chicago Press, 1978.

Kotlowitz, Alex. *There Are No Children Here: The Story of Two Boys Growing Up in the Other America*. New York: Anchor Books, 1992.

Kozol, Jonathan. *Savage Inequalities: Children in America's Schools*. New York: Harper Perennial, 1992.

Kwong, Peter. *The New Chinatown*. New York: Hill and Wang, 1997.

Lal, Shirley R., Dhyan Lal, and Charles M. Achilles. *Handbook on Gangs in Schools: Strategies to Reduce Gang-Related Activities*. Newbury Park, CA: Corwin Press, 1993.

Lamont, Michele. *The Dignity of Working Men: Morality and the Boundaries of Race, Class and Immigration*. Cambridge, MA: Harvard University Press, 2000.

Lareau, Annette. *Unequal Childhoods: Class, Race, and Family Life*. Berkeley: University of California Press, 2003.

Leacock, Eleanor Burke, ed. *The Culture of Poverty: A Critique.* New York: Simon and Schuster, 1971.

Leavitt, Jacqueline. "Women under Fire: Public Housing Activism in Los Angeles." *Frontiers* 13, no. 2 (1992): 109–31.

LeBlanc, Adrian Nicole. *Random Family: Love, Drugs, Trouble, and Coming of Age in the Bronx.* New York: Scribner, 2003.

Lee, Jennifer. *Civility in the City: Blacks, Jews, and Koreans in Urban America.* Cambridge, MA: Harvard University Press, 2002.

———. "Retail Niche Domination among African American, Jewish and Korean Entrepreneurs." *American Behavioral Scientist* 42 (1999): 1402–3.

Lemann, Nicholas. *The Big Test: The Secret History of American Meritocracy.* New York: Farrar, Straus, and Giroux, 1999.

———. *The Promised Land: The Great Black Migration and How It Changed America.* New York: Vintage Books, 1992.

Levine, Hillel, and Lawrence Harmon. *The Death of an American Jewish Community: A Tragedy of Good Intentions.* New York: Free Press, 1992.

Lewis, Oscar. *Five Families: Mexican Case Studies in the Culture of Poverty.* New York: Basic Books, 1959.

———. *La Vida: A Puerto Rican Family in the Culture of Poverty—San Juan and New York.* New York: Random House, 1965.

Lieberson, Stanley. *A Matter of Taste: How Names, Fashions, and Culture Change.* New Haven: Yale University Press, 2000.

Liebow, Elliot. *Tally's Corner: A Study of Negro Streetcorner Men.* Boston: Little, Brown, 1967.

Liegeois, Jean-Pierre. *Gypsies: An Illustrated History.* London: Al Saqi Books, 1986.

Lifton, Robert Jay. *Thought Reform and the Psychology of Totalism: A Study of "Brainwashing" in China.* New York: Norton, 1969.

Light, Ivan. *Ethnic Enterprise in America: Business and Welfare among Chinese, Japanese, and Blacks.* Berkeley: University of California Press, 1972.

———. "Numbers Gambling among Blacks: A Financial Institution." *American Sociological Review* 42 (December 1977): 892–904.

Light, Ivan, and Edna Bonacich. *Immigrant Entrepreneurs: Koreans in Los Angeles, 1965–1982.* Berkeley: University of California Press, 1988.

Lin, Nan. *Social Capital: A Theory of Social Structure and Action.* New York: Cambridge University Press, 2001.

Lipset, Seymour Martin. *Political Man: The Social Basis of Politics.* Garden City, NY: Doubleday, 1960.

Logan, John P., and Harvey L. Molotch. *Urban Fortunes: The Political Economy of Place.* Berkeley: University of California Press, 1987.

López, David E. "Language: Diversity and Assimilation." In *Ethnic Los Angeles,* edited by Roger Waldinger and Mehdi Bozorgmehr, 139–64. New York: Russell Sage Foundation, 1996.

López, David E., and Ricardo Stanton-Salazar. "Mexican Americans: A Second Generation at Risk." In *Ethnicities: Children of Immigrants in America,* edited by Rubén G. Rumbaut and Alejandro Portes, 57–90. Berkeley: University of California Press, 2001.

Lorenz, Konrad. *On Aggression.* London: Methuen, 1966.

Loury, Glenn. *The Anatomy of Racial Inequality.* Cambridge, MA: Harvard University Press, 2002.

Lucas, Samuel Roundfield. *Tracking Inequality: Stratification and Mobility in America's High Schools.* New York: Columbia Teacher's College Press, 1999.

Luker, Kristin. *Dubious Conceptions: The Politics of Teenage Pregnancy.* Cambridge, MA: Harvard University Press, 1996.

Lusane, Clarence. *Pipe Dream Blues: Racism and the War on Drugs.* Boston: South End Press, 1991.

MacLeod, Jay. *Ain't No Makin' It: Aspirations and Attainment in a Low-Income Neighborhood.* Boulder, CO: Westview Press, 1995.

Marshall, T.H. *Citizenship and Social Class, and Other Essays.* New York: Cambridge University Press, 1950.

Massey, Douglas, Raphael Alarcón, Jorge Durand, and Humberto González. *Return to Aztlan: The Social Process of International Migration from Western Mexico.* Berkeley: University of California Press, 1987.

Massey, Douglas, and Nancy A. Denton. *American Apartheid: Segregation and the Making of the American Underclass.* Cambridge, MA: Harvard University Press, 1993.

Massey, Douglas, and Mitchell L. Eggers. "The Ecology of Inequality: Minorities and the Concentration of Poverty, 1970–1980." *American Journal of Sociology* 95 (1990): 1153–88.

Matza, David. *Delinquency and Drift.* New York: Wiley, 1964.

———. "Poverty and Disrepute." In *Contemporary Social Problems,* 2nd ed., edited by Robert K. Merton and Robert A. Nisbet, 619–69. New York: Harcourt, Brace and World, 1966.

Maxson, Cheryl, and Malcolm W. Klein. "Street Gang Violence: Twice as Great, or Half as Great?" In *Gangs in America,* edited by C. Ronald Huff, 71–100. Newbury Park, CA: Sage Publications, 1990.

Mayhew, Henry. *London Labor and the London Poor.* 1861–62. Reprint, London: Penguin Books, 1985.

McWhorter, John. *Losing the Race: Self-Sabotage in Black America.* New York: Free Press, 2000.

Mead, Lawrence. *The New Politics of Poverty: The Nonworking Poor in America.* New York: Basic Books, 1992.

Meltzer, Milton. *Brother, Can You Spare a Dime? The Great Depression, 1929–33.* New York: Knopf, 1969.

Merry, Sally Engle. *Urban Danger: Life in a Neighborhood of Strangers.* Philadelphia: Temple University Press, 1981.

Merton, Robert K. *Social Theory and Social Structure.* 1957. Reprint, New York: Free Press, 1968.

Messenger, Paul H. "Public-Housing Perversity: A View from the Trenches." *Public Interest* 108 (Summer 1992): 133–42.

Metcalf, George R. *From Little Rock to Boston: The History of School Desegregation.* Westport, CT: Greenwood Press, 1983.

Miller, S.M., and Frank Riessman. "The Working Class Subculture: A New View." *Social Problems* 9 (1961): 86–97.

Miller, Walter B. "Lower Class Culture as a Generating Milieu of Gang Delinquency." *Journal of Social Issues* 14, no. 3 (1958): 4–19.

———. *Violence by Youth Gangs and Youth Groups as a Crime Problem in Major American Cities.* Washington, DC: Department of Justice, 1975.

Mills, C. Wright, and Hans Gerth. *Character and Social Structure.* New York: Harcourt, Brace, and World, 1953.

Mirandé, Alfredo, and E. Enriquez. *La Chicana.* Chicago: University of Chicago Press, 1979.

Model, Suzanne. "Where New York's West Indians Work." In *Islands in the City: West Indian Migration to New York,* edited by Nancy Foner, 52–80. Berkeley: University of California Press, 2001.

Montgomery, Roger. "Comment on 'Fear and House-as-Haven in the Lower Class.'" *Journal of the American Institute of Planners* 32 (January 1966): 31–37.

Monti, Daniel J. *Gangs: The Origins and Impact of Contemporary Youth Gangs in the United States.* Albany: State University of New York Press, 1993.

———. *Wannabe: Gangs in Suburbs and Schools.* New York: Oxford University Press, 1994.

Moore, Joan. *Going Down to the Barrio: Homeboys and Homegirls in Change.* Philadelphia: Temple University Press, 1991.

———. *Homeboys: Gangs, Drugs, and Prison in the Barrios of Los Angeles.* Philadelphia: Temple University Press, 1978.

Moore, Joan, and Raquel Pinderhughes, eds. *In the Barrios: Latinos and the Underclass Debate.* New York: Russell Sage Foundation, 1993.

Moore, Joan, James Diego Vigil, and J. Levy. "Huisas of the Street: Chicano Gang Members." *Latino Studies Journal* 6, no. 1 (2001): 27–48.

"Motor City Money." *Michigan Daily,* October 15, 1996.

Moynihan, Daniel Patrick. *Maximum Feasible Misunderstanding: Community Action and the War on Poverty.* Glencoe, IL: Free Press, 1970.

Munger, Frank, ed. *Laboring below the Line: The New Ethnography of Poverty, Low-Wage Work, and Survival in the Global Economy.* New York: Russell Sage Foundation, 2002.

Murillo, Nathan. "The Mexican American Family." In *Chicanos: Social and Psychological Perspectives,* edited by N. N. Wagner and M. J. Haug, 97–108. St. Louis, MO: C. V. Mosby, 1971.

Murray, Charles. *Losing Ground: American Social Policy, 1950–1980.* New York: Basic Books, 1984.

Myerson, Martin, and Edward Banfield. *Politics, Planning, and the Public Interest: The Case of Public Housing in Chicago.* Glencoe, IL: Free Press, 1955.

Nayak, Sangeetha, Samuel C. Shiflett, Sussie Eshun, and Fredric M. Levine. "Culture and Gender Effects in Pain Beliefs and the Prediction of Pain Tolerance." *Cross-Cultural Research* 34 (2000): 135–51.

Newman, Catherine. *No Shame in My Game: The Working Poor in the Inner City.* New York: Knopf, 1990.

Noguera, Pedro. *City Schools and the America Dream.* New York: Columbia Teacher's College Press, 2003.

North, Douglass C. *Institutions, Institutional Change, and Economic Perform-ance.* Cambridge: Cambridge University Press, 1990.

Nozick, Robert. *Anarchy, State, and Utopia.* New York: Basic Books, 1974.

O'Connor, Alice. *Poverty Knowledge: Social Science, Social Policy, and the Poor in Twentieth-Century U.S. History.* Princeton: Princeton University Press, 2001.

O'Connor, Carla. "Dreamkeeping in the Inner City: Diminishing the Divide between Aspirations and Expectations." In *Coping with Poverty: The Social Contexts of Neighborhood, Work, and Family in the African-American Community,* edited by Sheldon Danziger and Ann Chih Lin, 105–40. Ann Arbor: University of Michigan Press, 2000.

O'Connor, Michael. "Female Gang Members Rising in Bellevue, Groups Are Told." *Omaha World Herald,* October 25, 1994.

Ogbu, John U. *Black American Students in an Affluent Suburb: A Study of Academic Disengagement.* Mahwah, NJ: Lawrence Erlbaum, 2003.

Oliver, Melvin L., and Thomas M. Shapiro. *Black Wealth/White Wealth: A New Perspective on Racial Inequality.* New York: Routledge, 1995.

Ong, Paul, Kyeyoung Park, and Yasmin Tong. "The Korean-Black Conflict and the State." In *New Asian Immigration in Los Angeles and Global Restructuring,* edited by Paul Ong, Edna Bonacich, and Lucie Cheng, 264–94. Philadelphia: Temple University Press, 1994.

Oppenheim, Felix. "'Power' Revisited." *Journal of Politics* 40 (August 1978): 589–608.

Padilla, Felix. *The Gang as an American Enterprise.* New Brunswick: Rutgers University Press, 1993.

Park, Robert E. "The City as a Social Laboratory." In *Chicago: An Experiment in Social Science Research,* edited by T. V. Smith and Leonard D. White, 1–19. Chicago: University of Chicago Press, 1929.

———. "Human Migration and the Marginal Man." *American Journal of Sociology* 33 (May 1928): 881–93.

Park, Robert E., Ernest W. Burgess, and Roderick D. McKenzie. *The City.* 1925. Reprint, Chicago: University of Chicago Press, 1967.

Parsons, Talcott. *The Social System.* Glencoe, IL: Free Press, 1951.

Parsons, Talcott, Edward Shils, and James Olds. "Values, Motives, and Systems of Action." In *Toward a General Theory of Action,* edited by Talcott Parsons and Edward A. Shils, 47–109. New York: Harper Torchbooks, 1962.

Patillo, Mary. *Black on the Block: The Politics of Race and Class in the City.* Chicago: University of Chicago Press, 2007.

Patillo-McCoy, Mary. *Black Picket Fences: Privilege and Peril in the Black Middle Class.* Chicago: University of Chicago Press, 1999.

Patterson, James T. *America's Struggle against Poverty in the Twentieth Century.* Cambridge, MA: Harvard University Press, 2000.

Patterson, Orlando. "Taking Culture Seriously: A Framework and an Afro-American Illustration." In *Culture Matters: How Values Shape Human Progress,* edited by Lawrence E. Harrison and Samuel P. Huntington, 202–30. New York: Basic Books, 2000.

Peristiany, J. G., ed. *Honor and Shame: The Values of Mediterranean Society*. London: Weidenfeld and Nicolson, 1965.

Perry, Theresa, and Lisa Delpit, eds. *The Real Ebonics Debate: Power, Language, and the Education of African-American Children*. Boston: Beacon Press, 1998.

Phillips, Susan A. "Gallo's Body: Decoration and Damnation in the Life of a Chicano Gang Member." *Ethnography* 2 (September 2001): 357–88.

———. *Wallbangin': Graffiti and Gangs in L.A.* Chicago: University of Chicago Press, 1999.

Pinderhughes, Howard. *Race in the Hood: Conflict and Violence among Urban Youth*. Minneapolis: University of Minnesota Press, 1997.

Pitt-Rivers, Julian. *The Fate of Shechem: or, the Politics of Sex: Essays in the Anthropology of the Mediterranean*. New York: Cambridge University Press, 1977.

Piven, Frances Fox, and Richard Cloward. *Regulating the Poor: The Functions of Public Welfare*. New York: Pantheon Books, 1971.

Plunz, Richard. *A History of Housing in New York City*. New York: Columbia University Press, 1990.

Pope, Hallowell. "Negro-White Differences in Decisions Regarding Illegitimate Children." *Journal of Marriage and the Family* 31 (1969): 756–64.

Poppendieck, Janet. *Sweet Charity? Emergency Food and the End of Entitlement*. New York: Viking Press, 1998.

Portes, Alejandro. "Economic Sociology and the Sociology of Immigration: A Conceptual Overview." In *The Economic Sociology of Immigration: Essays on Networks, Ethnicity, and Entrepreneurship*, edited by Alejandro Portes, 8–23. New York: Russell Sage Foundation, 1995.

Portes, Alejandro, and Rubén G. Rumbaut. *Legacies: The Story of the Immigrant Second Generation*. Berkeley: University of California Press, 2001.

Powell, Walter W., and Paul J. DiMaggio, eds. *The New Institutionalism in Organizational Analysis*. Chicago: University of Chicago Press, 1991.

Pritchett, Wendell. *Brownsville, Brooklyn: Blacks, Jews, and the Changing Face of the Ghetto*. Chicago: University of Chicago Press, 2002.

Proudhon, Pierre-Joseph. "On Poverty." In *Selected Writings of Pierre-Joseph Proudhon*, edited by Stewart Edwards, translated by Elizabeth Fraser, 257–60. Garden City, NY: Anchor Books, 1969.

Rainwater, Lee. *And the Poor Get Children*. Chicago: Quadrangle Books, 1960.

———. *Behind Ghetto Walls: Black Family Life in a Federal Slum*. Chicago: Aldine, 1970.

———. "Lessons of Pruitt-Igoe." *Public Interest* 8 (Summer 1967): 116–26.

Rainwater, Lee, and Timothy Smeedling. *Poor Kids in Rich Countries*. New York: Russell Sage Foundation, 2003.

Rainwater, Lee, and William L. Yancy. *The Moynihan Report and the Politics of Controversy*. Cambridge, MA: MIT Press, 1967.

Raj, Prithvi, Ilona Steigerwald, and Stefan Esser. "Socioeconomic and Cultural Influences on Pain Management in Practice." *Pain Practice* 3 (2003): 80–83.

Rieder, Jonathan. *Canarsie: The Jews and Italians against Liberalism*. Cambridge, MA: Harvard University Press, 1985.

Riis, Jacob. *How the Other Half Lives: Studies among the Tenements*. 1890. Reprint, New York: Dover Publications, 1971.

Rodriguez, Clara E. "Racial Classification among Puerto Rican Men and Women in New York." *Hispanic Journal of Behavioral Sciences* 12 (1990): 366–80.

Rogin, Michael. *Ronald Reagan, the Movie and Other Episodes in Political Demonology*. Berkeley: University of California Press, 1988.

Rollman, Gary. "Culture and Pain." In *Cultural Clinical Psychology: Theory, Research, and Practice*, edited by S. S. Kazarian and David R. Evans, 267–86. New York: Oxford University Press, 1998.

Rosenstone, Steven, and John Mark Hansen. *Mobilization, Participation, and Democracy in America*. New York: Macmillan, 1993.

Rosenzweig, Roy. *Eight Hours for What They Will: Workers and Leisure in an Industrial City, 1870–1920*. New York: Cambridge University Press, 1983.

Rosnow, Ralph L., and Gary Alan Fine. *Rumor and Gossip: The Social Psychology of Hearsay*. New York: Elsevier Scientific Publishing, 1976.

Rumbaut, Rubén G., and Alejandro Portes, eds. *Ethnicities: Children of Immigrants in America*. Berkeley: University of California Press, 2001.

Ryan, William. *Blaming the Victim*. New York: Pantheon Books, 1971.

Saegert, Susan, J. Phillip Thompson, and Mark R. Warren, eds. *Social Capital and Poor Communities*. New York: Russell Sage Foundation, 2001.

Sampson, Robert J. *Juvenile Criminal Behavior and Its Relation to Neighborhood Characteristics*. Washington, DC: Department of Justice, Office of Juvenile Justice and Delinquency Prevention, National Institute for Juvenile Justice and Delinquency Prevention, 1981.

Sampson, Robert J., and W. Byron Groves. "Community Structure and Crime: Testing Social-Disorganization Theory." *American Journal of Sociology* 94 (January 1989): 774–802.

Sampson, Robert J., and Stephen W. Raudenbush. "Systematic Social Observation of Public Spaces: A New Look at Disorder in Urban Neighborhoods." *American Journal of Sociology* 105, no. 3 (1999): 603–51.

Sampson, Robert J., and William Julius Wilson. "Toward a Theory of Race, Crime, and Inequality." In *Crime and Inequality*, edited by John Hagan and Ruth D. Peterson, 37–54. Stanford: Stanford University Press, 1995.

Sánchez-Jankowski, Martín. "The Concentration of African American Poverty and the Dispersal of the Working Class: An Ethnographic Study of Three Inner-City Areas." *International Journal of Urban and Regional Research* 23 (December 1999): 619–37.

———. "Gangs and Social Change." *Theoretical Criminology* 7 (May 2003): 191–216.

———. *Islands in the Street: Gangs and American Urban Society*. Berkeley: University of California Press, 1991.

Sanders, William B. *Gangbangs and Drive-bys: Grounded Culture and Juvenile Gang Violence*. New York: Aldine de Gruyter, 1994.

Saporito, Salvatore, and Sohoni Deenesh. "Coloring Outside the Lines: Racial Segregation in Public Schools and Their Attendance Boundaries." *Sociology of Education* 79 (2006): 81–105.

Schein, Edgar H., Inge Schein, and Curtis H. Barker. *Coercive Persuasion: A Socio-Psychological Analysis of the "Brainwashing" of American Civilian Prisoners by the Chinese Communists.* New York: Norton, 1961.

Scheper-Hughes, Nancy. *Death without Weeping: The Violence of Everyday Life in Brazil.* Berkeley: University of California Press, 1992.

Schmid, Carol. "The English Only Movement: Social Bases of Support and Opposition among Anglos and Latinos." In *Language Loyalties,* edited by James Crawford, 202–9. Chicago: University of Chicago Press, 1992.

Schneider, Eric C. *Vampires, Dragons, and Egyptian Kings: Youth Gangs in Postwar New York.* Princeton: Princeton University Press, 1999.

Schultz, Theodore W. "Investment in Human Capital." *American Economic Review* 51 (March 1961): 1–17.

Schwendinger, Herman, and Julia R. Siegal-Schwendinger. *Adolescent Subculture and Delinquency Subcultures.* New York: Praeger, 1985.

Scott, Allen J. "The Manufacturing Economy: Ethnic and Gender Divisions of Labor." In *Ethnic Los Angeles,* edited by Roger Waldinger and Mehdi Bozorgmehr, 215–44. New York: Russell Sage Foundation, 1996.

Scott, James C. *Moral Economy of the Peasant: Rebellion and Subsistence in Southeast Asia.* New Haven: Yale University Press, 1976.

Sennett, Richard. *The Uses of Disorder: Personal Identity and City Life.* New York: Knopf, 1970.

Sewell, William. "A Theory of Structure: Duality, Agency, and Transformation." *American Journal of Sociology* 98 (1992): 1–29.

Sharff, Jagna Wojcicka. *King Kong on 4th Street: Families and the Violence of Poverty on the Lower East Side.* Boulder, CO: Westview Press, 1998.

Sharkey, Patrick. "Navigating Dangerous Streets: The Sources and Consequences of Street Efficacy." *American Sociological Review* 71 (October 2006): 826–47.

Shepherd, Cynthia. "It's Hard to Exit a Female Gang." *Salt Lake City Desert News,* October 4, 1999, C01.

Simmel, Georg. *Conflict.* Translated by Kurt H. Wolff. Glencoe, IL: Free Press, 1955.

———. "Fashion." In *Georg Simmel: On Individuality and Social Forms,* edited by Donald N. Levine, 294–323. Chicago: University of Chicago Press, 1971.

———. "Group Expansion and the Development of Individuality." In *Georg Simmel: On Individuality and Social Forms,* edited by Donald N. Levine, 251–94. Chicago: University of Chicago Press, 1971.

———. "The Metropolis and Mental Life." In *Georg Simmel: On Individuality and Social Forms,* edited by Donald M. Levine, 324–39. Chicago: University of Chicago Press, 1971.

Simon, Herbert A. "Notes on the Observation and Measurement of Political Power." *Journal of Politics* 15 (November 1953): 500–516.

Sinclair, Upton. *The Jungle.* 1906. Reprint, New York: Bantam Books, 1981.

Singer, Eliot A. "Conversion through Foodways Enculturation: The Meaning of Eating in an American Hindu Sect." In *Ethnic and Regional Foodways in the United States,* edited by Linda Keller Brown and Kay Mussell, 195–214. Knoxville: University of Tennessee Press, 1984.

Skocpol, Theda. *States and Social Revolutions: A Comparative Analysis of France, Russia, and China*. New York: Cambridge University Press, 1979.

Skogan, Wesley G. *Disorder and Decline: Crime and the Spiral of Decay in American Neighborhoods*. Berkeley: University of California Press, 1990.

Skolnick, Jerome. "The Social Structure of Street Drug Dealing." *American Journal of Police* 9 (1990): 1–41.

Slomczynski, Kazimirez M., ed. *Social Structure: Changes and Linkages*. Warsaw: Polish Academy of Sciences, 2002.

Slotkin, Richard. *Gunfighter Nation: The Myth of the Frontier in Twentieth-Century America*. New York: Atheneum, 1992.

Small, Mario Luis. *Villa Victoria: The Transformation of Social Capital in a Boston Barrio*. Chicago: University of Chicago Press, 2005.

Smith, Sandra Susan. *Lone Pursuit: Distrust and Uncooperativeness among Black Poor Jobseekers and Jobholders*. New York: Russell Sage Foundation, 2007.

Snow, David A., and Leon Anderson. *Down on Their Luck: A Study of Homeless Street People*. Berkeley: University of California Press, 1993.

Sonenshein, Raphael J. *Politics in Black and White: Race and Power in Los Angeles*. Princeton: Princeton University Press, 1993.

Sowell, Thomas. *Inside American Education: The Decline, the Deception, the Dogmas*. New York: Free Press, 1993.

Spencer, Margaret Beale, Steven P. Cole, Stephanie M. Jones, and Dena Phillips Swanson. "Neighborhood and Family Influences on Young Urban Adolescents' Behavior Problems: A Multisample, Multisite Analysis." In *Neighborhood and Poverty*, edited by Jeanne Brooks-Gunn and Greg J. Duncan, 1:200–218. New York: Russell Sage Foundation, 1997.

Spergel, Irving A. *The Youth Gang Problem: A Community Approach*. New York: Oxford University Press, 1995.

Squires, Gregory D., Larry Bennett, Kathleen McCourt, and Philip Nyden. *Chicago: Race, Class, and the Response to Urban Decline*. Philadelphia: Temple University Press, 1987.

Stack, Carol. *All Our Kin: Strategies for Survival in a Black Community*. New York: Harper and Row, 1974.

Steele, Shelby. *The Content of Our Character: A New Vision of Race in America*. New York: Harper, 1991.

Stein, R.I., and C.J. Nemeroff. "Moral Overtones of Food: Judgments of Others Based on What They Eat." *Personality and Social Psychology Bulletin* 21 (1995): 480–90.

Stepick, Alex, Carol Dutton Stepick, Emmanuel Eugene, Deborah Teed, and Yves Labissiere. "Shifting Identities and Intergenerational Conflict: Growing Up Haitian in Miami." In *Ethnicities: Children of Immigrants in America*, edited by Rubén Rumbaut and Alejandro Portes, 229–66. Berkeley: University of California Press, 2001.

Stowe, Harriet Beecher. *Uncle Tom's Cabin*. 1852. Reprint, Englewood Cliffs, NJ: Prentice-Hall, 2003.

Sudman, Seymour. *Applied Sampling*. New York: Academic Press, 1976.

Sugrue, Thomas J. *The Origins of the Urban Crisis: Race and Inequality in Postwar Detroit*. Princeton: Princeton University Press, 1996.

———. "The Structure of Urban Poverty: The Reorganization of Space and Work in Three Periods of American History." In *The Underclass Debate: Views from History*, edited by Michael B. Katz, 85–117. Princeton: Princeton University Press, 1993.

Sullivan, Mercer. *"Getting Paid": Youth Crime and Work in the Inner City*. Ithaca: Cornell University Press, 1989.

Susser, Ida. *Norman Street: Poverty and Politics in an Urban Neighborhood*. New York: Oxford University Press, 1982.

Suttles, Gerald D. *The Social Construction of Communities*. Chicago: University of Chicago Press, 1972.

———. *The Social Order of the Slum: Ethnicity and Segmentation*. Chicago: University of Chicago Press, 1968.

Swidler, Ann. "Culture in Action: Symbols and Strategies." *American Sociological Review* 51 (April 1986): 273–86.

———. *Talk of Love: How Culture Matters*. Chicago: University of Chicago Press, 2001.

Synnott, Anthony. "Shame and Glory: A Sociology of Hair." *British Journal of Sociology* 38 (September 1987): 381–413.

Taylor, Carl S. *Dangerous Society*. East Lansing: Michigan State University Press, 1990.

———. *Girls, Gangs, Women and Drugs*. East Lansing: Michigan State University Press, 1993.

Thomas, Piri. *Down These Mean Streets*. New York: Knopf, 1967.

Thomas, Walter Isaac, and Florian Znaniccke. *The Polish Peasant in Europe and America*. New York: Dover Publications, 1958.

Thrasher, Frederic. *The Gang: A Study of 1,313 Gangs in Chicago*. Chicago: University of Chicago Press, 1927.

Tita, George, and Greg Ridgeway. "The Impact of Gang Formation on Local Patterns of Crime." *Journal of Research in Crime and Delinquency* 44, no. 2 (2007): 208–37.

Torney-Purta, Judith. "The School's Role in Developing Civic Engagement: A Study of Adolescents in Twenty-Eight Countries." *Applied Developmental Science* 6, no. 4 (2002): 203–12.

Totten, Mark D. *Guys, Gangs, and Girlfriend Abuse*. Peterborough, Ontario: Broadview Press, 2000.

Vaca, Nicolás C. *The Presumed Alliance: The Unspoken Conflict between Latinos and Blacks and What It Means for America*. New York: HarperCollins, 2004.

Vale, Lawrence J. "Empathological Places: Residents' Ambivalence toward Remaining in Public Housing." *Journal of Planning Education and Research* 16 (1997): 159–75.

———. *From the Puritans to the Projects: Public Housing and Public Neighbors*. Cambridge, MA: Harvard University Press, 2000.

Valentine, Charles A. *Culture and Poverty: A Critique and Counter-Proposals*. Chicago: University of Chicago Press, 1968.

Valenzuela, Abel, Jr. "Day Laborers as Entrepreneurs?" *Journal of Ethnic and Migration Studies* 27, no. 2 (2001): 335–52.

Valenzuela, Abel, Jr., and Elizabeth Gonzalez. "Latino Earnings Inequality: Immigrant and Native-Born Differences." In *Prismatic Metropolis: Inequality in Los Angeles,* edited by Lawrence Bobo, Melvin L. Oliver, James H. Johnson, and Abel Valenzuela Jr., 249–78. New York: Russell Sage Foundation, 2001.

Valenzuela, Abel, Jr., Jennette A. Kawachi, and Michael Marr. "Seeking Work Daily: Supply, Demand, and Spatial Dimensions of Day Labor in Two Global Cities." *International Journal of Contemporary Sociology* 43, no. 2 (2002): 192–219.

Vargas, Zaragosa. *Proletarians of the North: A History of Mexican Industrial Workers in Detroit and the Midwest, 1917–1933.* Berkeley: University of California Press, 1993.

Venkatesh, Sudhir. *American Project: The Rise and Fall of a Modern Ghetto.* Cambridge, MA: Harvard University Press, 2000.

———. "The Gang and the Community." In *Gangs in America,* 2nd ed., edited by C. Ronald Huff, 241–56. Newbury Park, CA: Sage Publications, 1996.

———. "Gender and Outlaw Capitalism: A Historical Account of the Black Sisters United." *Signs: Journal of Women and Culture in Society* 23 (Spring 1998): 683–709.

———. *Off the Books: The Underground Economy of the Urban Poor.* Cambridge, MA: Harvard University Press, 2006.

Verba, Sidney, and Norman H. Nie. *Participation in America: Political Democracy and Social Equality.* New York: Harper and Row, 1972.

Verba, Sidney, Kay Lehman Schlozman, and Henry Brady. *Voice and Equality: Civic Voluntarism in American Politics.* Cambridge, MA: Harvard University Press, 1995.

Vigil, James Diego. *Barrio Gangs: Street Life and Identity in Southern California.* Austin: University of Texas Press, 1988.

———. "The Established Gangs." In *Gangs: The Origins and Impact of Contemporary Youth Gangs in the United States,* edited by Scott Jennings and David J. Monti. Albany: State University of New York Press, 1993.

———. *A Rainbow of Gangs: Street Cultures in the Mega-City.* Austin: University of Texas Press, 2002.

Wacquant, Loïc. *Body and Soul: Notebooks of an Apprentice Boxer.* New York: Oxford University Press, 2004.

———. "In the Zone: The Social Art of the Hustler in the Black American Ghetto." *Theory, Culture and Society* 15, no. 2 (1998): 1–36.

———. "The Rise of Advanced Marginality: Notes on Its Nature and Implications." *Acta Sociologica* 39 (1996): 121–39.

———. "Scrutinizing the Streets: Poverty, Morality, and the Pitfalls of Urban Ethnography." *American Journal of Sociology* 107 (May 2002): 1468–1532.

———. "Three Pernicious Premises in the Study of the American Ghetto." *International Journal of Urban and Regional Research* 21 (June 1997): 341–53.

———. *Urban Outcasts: A Comparative Sociology of Advanced Marginality.* New York: Oxford University Press, 2007.

Waldinger, Roger. *Still the American Dream? Race and Immigrants in New York.* Cambridge, MA: Harvard University Press, 1999.

———. *Still the Promised City? African Americans and New Immigrants in Postindustrial New York.* Cambridge, MA: Harvard University Press, 1996.

———. *Through the Eye of a Needle: Immigrants and Enterprise in New York's Garment Trades.* New York: New York University Press, 1986.

Waldinger, Roger, Howard Aldrich, and Robin Ward. *Ethnic Entrepreneurs: Immigrant Business in Industrial Societies.* Newbury Park, CA: Sage Publications, 1990.

Waldinger, Roger, and Mehdi Bozorgmehr, eds. *Ethnic Los Angeles.* New York: Russell Sage Foundation, 1996.

Waldinger, Roger, and Michael I. Lichter. *How the Other Half Works: Immigration and the Social Organization of Labor.* Berkeley: University of California Press, 2003.

Waters, Mary C. *Black Identities: West Indian Immigrant Dreams and American Realities.* New York: Russell Sage Foundation, 1999.

Weber, Max. *Economy and Society: An Outline of Interpretive Sociology.* Edited by Gunther Roth and Claus Wittich. 1921. Reprint, Berkeley: University of California Press, 1978.

———. *The Methodology of the Social Sciences.* New York: Free Press, 1949.

———. *The Protestant Ethic and the Spirit of Capitalism.* 1938. Reprint, New York: Scribner and Sons, 1958.

Weber, Max, Edward A. Shils, and Henry A. Finch, eds. and trans. *Methodology of the Social Sciences.* New York: Free Press, 1949.

Weicher, John C. "How Poverty Neighborhoods Are Changing." In *Inner-City Poverty in the United States,* edited by Laurence E. Lynn Jr. and Michael G.H. McGeary, 68–110. Washington, D.C: National Academy Press, 1990.

West, Cornel. "Nihilism in Black America." In *Race Matters,* 11–32. Boston: Beacon Press, 1993.

White, Harrison C. *Identity and Control: A Structural Theory of Action.* Princeton: Princeton University Press, 1992.

Whyte, William Foote. *Street Corner Society: The Social Structure of an Italian Slum.* Chicago: University of Chicago Press, 1943.

Williams, Terry, and William Kornblum. *The Uptown Kids: Struggle and Hope in the Projects.* New York: G. P. Putnam and Sons, 1994.

Willis, Paul. *Learning to Labor: How Working Class Kids Get Working Class Jobs.* New York: Columbia University Press, 1977.

Wilson, James Q., and G. Kelling. "Broken Windows." *Atlantic Monthly,* March 1982, 29–38.

Wilson, William Julius. *The Declining Significance of Race: Blacks and Changing American Institutions.* Chicago: University of Chicago Press, 1978.

———. *The Truly Disadvantaged: The Inner City, the Underclass, and Public Policy.* Chicago: University of Chicago Press, 1987.

———. *When Work Disappears: The World of the New Urban Poor.* New York: Knopf, 1996.

Wilson, William Julius, and Richard P. Taub. *There Goes the Neighborhood: Racial, Ethnic, and Class Tensions in Four Chicago Neighborhoods and Their Meaning for America.* New York: Knopf, 2006.

Winnick, Louis. *New People in Old Neighborhoods.* New York: Russell Sage Foundation, 1990.

Wirth, Louis. *The Ghetto.* Chicago: University of Chicago Press, 1956.

———. "Urbanism as a Way of Life." *American Journal of Sociology* 44, no. 1 (1938): 3–24.

Wong, Charles Choy. "Black and Chinese Grocery Stores in Los Angeles' Black Ghetto." *Urban Life* 5 (January 1977): 439–64.

Woodson, Robert L., ed. *Youth Crime and Urban Policy: A View from the Inner City.* Washington, DC: American Enterprise Institute, 1981.

Wrong, Dennis. *The Problem of Order: What Unites and Divides Societies.* New York: Cambridge University Press, 1994.

Wurman, Richard. *NYC Access.* 6th ed. New York: Access Press, 1994.

Wylie, Jeanie. *Poletown: A Community Betrayed.* Urbana: University of Illinois Press, 1989.

Yablonsky, Lewis. *The Violent Gang.* New York: Macmillan, 1962.

Young, Alford A., Jr. *The Minds of Marginalized Black Men: Making Sense of Mobility, Opportunity, and Future Life Chances.* Princeton: Princeton University Press, 2004.

Zelizer, Viviana A. *Pricing the Priceless Child: The Changing Social Value of Children.* New York: Basic Books, 1985.

Zimring, Franklin E., and Gordon Hawkins. *Crime Is Not the Problem: Lethal Violence in America.* New York: Oxford University Press, 1997.

Zippelius, Reinhold. "Exclusion and Shunning as Legal and Social Sanctions." *Ethology and Sociobiology* 7 (1986): 159–66.

Zorbaugh, Harvey Warren. *The Gold Coast and the Slum: A Sociological Study of Chicago's Near North Side.* Chicago: University of Chicago Press, 1929.

Zucker, Lynne. "Institutionalization and Cultural Persistence." In *The New Institutionalism in Organizational Analysis,* edited by Walter W. Powell and Paul J. DiMaggio, 87–88. Chicago: University of Chicago Press, 1991.

Zunz, Oliver. *The Changing Face of Inequality: Urbanization, Industrialization, Development, and Immigrants in Detroit, 1880–1920.* Chicago: University of Chicago Press, 1982.

Index

Text:	10/13 Sabon
Display:	Sabon
Compositor:	BookComp
Indexer:	Thérèse Shere
Illustrator:	Bill Nelson
Printer and binder:	Sheridan Books, Inc.